A Concise Biographical Dictionary of SINGERS

A Concise Biographical Dictionary of SINGERS

From the Beginning of Recorded Sound to the Present

By
K.J. KUTSCH AND LEO RIEMENS

*Translated from the German,
Expanded and Annotated*
By
HARRY EARL JONES

Chilton Book Company
Philadelphia New York London

COPYRIGHT © 1962 AND 1966 BY A. FRANCKE AG VERLAG, BERN
COPYRIGHT © 1969 BY HARRY EARL JONES
FIRST AMERICAN EDITION
ALL RIGHTS RESERVED

*Translated from the German Unvergängliche Stimmen:
Kleines Sängerlexikon by K.J. Kutsch and Leo Riemens.*

PUBLISHED IN PHILADELPHIA BY CHILTON BOOK COMPANY
AND SIMULTANEOUSLY IN ONTARIO, CANADA,
BY THOMAS NELSON & SONS, LTD.
LIBRARY OF CONGRESS CATALOG CARD NUMBER 79-94106
DESIGNED BY WILLIAM E. LICKFIELD
MANUFACTURED IN THE UNITED STATES OF AMERICA

Foreword by the Authors

This book is a collection of the biographies of noted male and female singers. Certainly not all singers are included, for the history of vocal art is as old as that of mankind itself, beginning as it did with the singer Orpheus, to whom Grecian mythology assigned divine ancestry.

The invention of the phonograph record marked a definite break in the history of the art of singing. Today, unfortunately, we can no longer hear how the coloratura voices of Henriette Sontag or Jenny Lind sounded, or what it was like when Wilhelmina Schröder-Devrient displayed her dramatic voice; we can never revive Giovanni Batista Rubini's tenor, the glowing strength of a dramatic tenor like Louis Nourrit, or the voice of a Grisi, a Pasta, or a Viardot-García and can only rely on contemporary written reports of their ability.

But how Francesco Tamagno, Lilli Lehmann, Adelina Patti, or Lillian Nordica sang still can be heard, despite all the technical inadequacy of their records. The scraps of song by Jean de Reszke which Lionel Mapleson recorded during performances at the Metropolitan Opera provide a distant echo of that great singer and personality.

Therefore we have selected only those artists of whom some vocal testimony, however trifling, is preserved, either on records or on their forerunners, cylinders. To this end we have thought it desirable at the close of each biographical sketch to list information about those records by the artist which we think are exceptional. In the case of singers active today, it is especially difficult to make a true judgment about their records, as there are numerous radio and tape recordings which, although presently unavailable, may be issued at any time.

Unfortunately, a few artists have ignored the Age of the Phonograph Record, not trusting their voices to this medium. Of these we mention here only Carl Perron, Marie Wittich, Emmy Krüger, Johannes Messchaert, and William Miller. We regret that, in consideration of our principle of selection, no further consideration of them can be given in this book.

Foreword by the Authors

It would have been desirable to record in full the biographies of all the celebrated male and female singers listed below whose voices are preserved on phonograph records. This is impossible for lack of space. Therefore a selection had to be made. We know that individual viewpoints are brought out in the writing of this book which no editing can entirely obliterate. We also know that one reader will miss one artist or another, and a worthy singer may thus be omitted. We recognize equally that, on account of the difficulty of collecting the material and the very often contradictory dates given by sources, mistakes may have occurred; we shall be grateful for any corrections sent to the publisher.

In this co-operative work it is a pleasure to acknowledge our thanks to Kurt Schnobel (Velbert), Wilhelm Wimmer (Ottobrunn, near Munich), and Jiri Korinek (Brno) for providing information otherwise difficult to obtain. We are especially grateful to Helmut Reinhold (Cologne), Harold Rosenthal (London), Harold G. Byrnes (New York City), Roland Teuchtler (Vienna), Hans Erben (Dresden), Clavi Mathlein (Sinettä, Finland), and Dr. Alfred Frankenstein (Petach-Tikvah, Israel). But all of our work would have been to no purpose if Francke Verlag and its editor in chief, Dr. Helmut Bender, had not so tirelessly set themselves to the task.

KARL JOSEF KUTSCH
Breberen-Brüxgen
LEO RIEMENS
The Hague

Translator's Preface

The number of re-issues of records and re-recordings which continue to appear have encouraged me to believe that the translation of this book would be useful. I have added some information on re-issues and re-recordings in the United States and have silently corrected some misprints and errors of detail from the German-language revised edition (1966). There remain, I am sure, a great many important pieces of information which should be added and some which need to be corrected; I will be grateful to receive such material as may be sent to me in care of the publishers, Chilton Book Company, 401 Walnut Street, Philadelphia, Pennsylvania 19106.

This translation has been made from the second edition of *Unvergängliche Stimmen* (Francke Verlag, Bern, 1966). Karl Josef Kutsch, the senior author, has kindly provided me with corrections, additional details, and more than sixty additional biographies for this translation.

Others who have been helpful, but are not responsible for any imperfections herein, are: Herbert Weinstock, for his many suggestions and even more for his encouragement; Dr. John R. Adams; Dr. Walter J. Ensslin, my colleague and friend at Fresno State College; the staff of the Fresno State College library and that of the De Bellis Collection at the San Francisco State College library; and my wife, Ruby, who not only put up with it all but strongly encouraged me.

HARRY EARL JONES
Fresno, California

February, 1969

Contents

Foreword by the Authors	v
Translator's Preface	vii
Notes for Users of the Dictionary	x
Glossary of Terms Used	xii
Abbreviations of Record Labels	xvi
Principal Operas, Operettas, Composers Referred to in the Text	xvii
Principal "Name" Opera Houses	xxiii
Principal Music Festivals	xxiv
A Concise Biographical Dictionary of Singers	1

Notes for Users of the Dictionary

The biographies of singers in this book contain, in general, the following information:

Name: The name is given as most commonly found; spelling and alphabetizing have been modified in accord with American usage.

Type of voice: As given in the original text, although in the United States the term mezzo-soprano is more commonly used than that of contralto.

Date and place of birth and death: The best available data are used, but singers are often self-indulgent about birth dates and some death dates may not have been widely noticed in the press.

Information on vocal study: Since singers often study with former singers, the continuity of vocal tradition may be traced by the reader.

Information about debut: This is given where available. In accord with the European tradition, the debut listed is often the first performance in an important role rather than the actual first public appearance.

Highlights of the singer's career: These vary in length and detail according to their availability and the importance of the singer.

Post-career occupation: In most cases this is the teaching of singing, but there are some interesting exceptions.

Writing: Memoirs and other books by the singer are given where known. Translations and re-publications of these books are not noted.

Spouses: If well-known in their own right or if connected with music, they are usually mentioned in the text.

Description of the voice: This information will be helpful in placing the singer in the history of vocal art and in giving some idea of his or her special repertory.

Records: The original text identifies the record labels under which a singer's records were first issued, and these names, with the original remarks on record rarity, have been retained. For American readers data on American record labels have been added by the translator. All compositions mentioned in this section are recorded in complete versions unless otherwise noted.

Notes for Users of the Dictionary

Records which were first issued in the United States have an asterisk (*) following the label name; the same symbol is used if the American re-issue of a European recording was sold here under the same label. Recordings issued under a different label from the original are listed as "U.S. re-issue." All re-recordings are listed under the phrase "U.S. re-recording." Mapleson cylinders were only issued in re-recordings. Two Canadian re-recording labels (Rococo and Cantilena) are so widely available in the United States that they are included below.

Since no complete listing of records issued in America is available, it has not been possible in every case to verify that the list of American recordings, re-issues, and re-recordings is complete. About eighty-five per cent of the singers listed, however, have had some commercial sale of their records in the United States and the others may have had their records imported in small quantities under European labels. It is hoped that the label information will give the record collector a clue as to where he should look for recordings of singers in whom he may be interested.

Titles: Titles of works are given in the form most commonly used in the United States (i.e., Mozart's *Le Nozze di Figaro*, Beethoven's *Ninth Symphony* and *Missa Solemnis*). Titles in Slavic languages are given in English (i.e., *The Golden Cockerel* by Rimsky-Korsakov and Smetana's *The Bartered Bride*).

Dates: All information has, so far as possible, been brought up to date as of early winter, 1969. Corrections and additional information should be sent to the translator in care of the publishers.

Glossary of Terms Used

This glossary of terms used is designed to assist the reader, particularly with data on recording terms. Purely musical terms, such as *bel canto*, coloratura, lieder, *régisseur*, et cetera, have not been included in the glossary; for these the reader is referred to any good musical dictionary. Information on musical festivals, individual opera houses, opera companies, et cetera, has also been omitted; additional information on these subjects will be found in published histories of these musical institutions or of music in performance.

Acoustic Recording: The process of recording which utilized a large horn to gather sound waves for transmission to the stylus which cut the record material. It was universally used until about 1925, when it was superseded by the electrical recording (q.v.) process.

Bettini Cylinders: During the 1890's catalogues were issued in Europe and the United States by Lt. Gianni Bettini describing many cylinders by important singers of the day. Bettini, a wealthy musical amateur, had social connections with the singers which he thus turned to account. The cylinders were made in New York and Paris, but so few of them have survived that they are not noted in this book, except one re-recording of the Bettini cylinder by Marcella Sembrich, issued semi-commercially in the United States.

Club Records: Beginning in the early 1930's certain re-issues and re-recordings of vocal records were made in small editions in the United States for collectors. Here called club records, these often featured numbered copies and autographed labels and were responsible for at least part of the interest in collecting and preserving historical records. Although of no great or immediate commercial importance, such organizations as the International Record Collectors' Club (IRCC) and the Historic Record Society (HRS) and others created a small market for such recordings and preserved such treasures as the Mapleson cylinders (q.v.) for a larger audience.

Cylinder Recording: A method of recording and reproducing using the outer surface of a hollow cylinder which was turned by a rotating metal sleeve. It was invented by Thomas A. Edison before 1880, but early cylinders could not be repro-

Glossary of Terms Used

duced in commercial quantities until the late 1890's, by which time the disc record was just coming into use. Before 1900 commercial vocal records of either sort are usually of such poor technical quality as to give little idea of the true quality of a singer's voice. Cylinder records were made commercially chiefly by Columbia, Edison, and Pathé. (*See also* Bettini Cylinders and Mapleson Cylinders.)

Disc Records: The flat circular record developed by Emile Berliner about 1897. Except for early cylinders the disc record became the universal shape of the phonograph record and will probably remain so until it is displaced by tape recordings in the future.

Electric Recording: The process of recording by means of a microphone which changes sound into electrical impulses for recording purposes. Replacing the acoustic recording (q.v.) process about 1925, it has been universally used since then.

Guest Appearances: As used in the text this term refers to a practice common in Europe to distinguish singers who appear briefly or for certain roles only as "guest artists" with a regular opera company. Regular and long-term artists are described as "members" of the company. In England and the United States and at La Scala this distinction is less observed. (*See* the biography of Lilli Lehmann for an example of the control formerly exercised over members of a European opera company.)

"Hill-and-dale" Recording: A recording process invented by Thomas A. Edison. In contrast to lateral-cut (q.v.) recording, in "hill-and-dale" recording the stylus cut the groove in the record vertically and the reproducing process required a special playing mechanism not adaptable to playing lateral-cut records. This process, taken over from cylinder recording, was used on all Edison disc records, on Pathé discs until about 1921, and on Vocalion records briefly about 1916. It may also have been used on other minor labels.

Labels of Records: Well over a hundred labels are mentioned in the text and other labels were used briefly or not at all for the celebrity vocal recordings which the *Dictionary* describes.

American readers interested in the current availability of labels should consult the current issue of *Schwann Long Playing Record Catalog,* issued monthly. For older records, consult dealers in rare and cut-out records.

The following labels are, or have been, used both in Europe and in the United States, with varying degrees of relationship between them: Cetra, Columbia, Decca, Eterna, Heliodor, Philips, Vox, and Westminster.

Lateral-cut Recording: The most common method of recording from about 1900 to the advent of stereophonic recording in the late 1950's. The recording is made by a stylus vibrating laterally in the grooves of the recording master, in contrast to the Edison method of vertical cutting. Also called the "needle-cut" process, lateral-cut recording was invented by Emile Berliner.

Mapleson Cylinders: Thomas A. Edison gave a cylinder recording machine to young Lionel Mapleson, the son of the director of the Metropolitan Opera in the late 1890's, and young Mapleson made recordings of actual stage performances. He first placed his machine in the prompter's box, but the protruding recording horn caused him to be banished to the fly gallery. His collection of cylinders were re-recorded in the 1930's and issued by IRCC in small editions. Of fair to

xiii

Glossary of Terms Used

poor technical quality, the Mapleson cylinder re-recordings are the only existing "vocal documents" for certain historically important singers.

Monophonic Recording: The process of recording all sound through one horn (acoustic) or one microphone (electric) or of combining the sound of several microphones into one sound channel to produce lateral-cut recordings. After the late 1950's this was gradually replaced by stereophonic recording (q.v.).

"Needle-cut" Recording: The same as lateral-cut recording (q.v.).

Opera Houses: Opera was originally supported by royal and aristocratic patrons; therefore such names as the Stockholm Royal Opera, the Vienna Imperial Opera, et cetera, were retained, at least until the end of the aristocratic period.

Since it is common for smaller cities and towns in Europe to maintain a City Theater (*Stadttheater, Teatro Municipale*, et cetera) where opera is given in seasons of varying length, it has seemed sufficient in the translation to omit the names of these theaters and to give merely the name of the city; such houses are frequently described generally in the text as "provincial stages" or "smaller houses."

Conversely, in the case of the great opera houses of the world, such as La Scala in Milan, Covent Garden in London, the Metropolitan Opera in New York, the Teatro Colón in Buenos Aires, et cetera, the name of the city is omitted. In cities with more than one opera house, or where the theater is not associated with opera exclusively, the city is usually added. (A listing of opera houses is given on page xxiii for the reader's convenience.)

Private Recording: Originally the term referred to records made for the artist personally; it now commonly refers to records made for organizations, such as the radio networks or opera houses, and kept as documents of performances. With easy recording on tape, this practice has become much more common. If contractual obligations permit and if there is enough interest, such recordings may be issued commercially. Sometimes the term is used to describe unauthorized recordings (q.v.).

Rarity of Records: Textual remarks on rarity have been translated verbatim for interested American readers. Price is affected by rarity, but condition, desirability, and many other factors also enter in. Persons interested in buying or selling old records should consult dealers in these items.

Re-issue: As used here the term means a record republished from the original master record. The label may be changed, but the actual grooves have not been altered. The quality of the re-issue depends on the quality of the original, the quality of the record material of the re-issue, and the condition of the surface of the re-issue. For example, RCA Victor re-issued certain historic records in the Heritage Series (78 r.p.m.) in the late 1940's; these were pressed from original masters on clear red plastic and probably sounded better than the original records on black shellac.

Re-recording: As used here the term means a process whereby an original record is re-played and the sound undergoes a new, usually electrical, recording process. The new recording may differ in speed, size, label, and other variables, but it is inherently limited by the quality of sound contained on the original recording. Experiments in "enhancing" old vocal records with new accompaniments have been tried, but the best results are obtained by using good re-recording equipment to maximize the total

Glossary of Terms Used

original sound. Records by historically important singers have been frequently re-recorded, as the text shows.

Shellac: Although the earliest cylinders were made of wax and the verb "to wax" was once a fashionable synonym for "to record," old disc records are usually described as being made of shellac. While some shellac was used in the secret compounds of each manufacturer, other substances were also present, until the advent of the all-plastic ("unbreakable") records about 1950. Pre-plastic records were both heavy and brittle, and the latter quality increased greatly with age.

Size of Records: Cylinder records were 2″ or more in diameter and about 4″ long; the early ones played for about 2 minutes and later ones for 4, although some Columbia cylinders have been described which played longer.

Early disc records were 7″ in diameter, but the standard sizes soon came to be 10″ and 12″, playing about 3 and 4½ minutes respectively. Records of 11″, 14″, and 19″ diameters were issued at various times. Radio transcription records were 16″ in diameter, but the advent of long-playing records reduced the need for increased size.

Today most 45 r.p.m. records are 7″ and 33 1/3 r.p.m. are either 10″ or 12″, with the latter size apparently the standard.

Speed of Records: Early disc records varied in speed and in some cases the correct speed or pitch was printed on the label. Edison and Brunswick acoustic records were standardized at 80 revolutions per minute, but otherwise the standard came to be 78 (really 78.26) r.p.m. The long-playing record reduced this to 45 or 33 1/3 r.p.m. about 1948. Earlier experiments, however, had been made to extend the playing time of records both by narrower grooving and by slower speeds. The latter required turntables of a quality not available for home use until much later.

Stereophonic Recording: In contrast to monophonic recording (q.v.) this recording process utilizes two microphones and sound channels to produce a record in which the recording track (in contrast to lateral-cut records) causes the playing needle to produce two slightly different sound tracks as it vibrates both vertically and horizontally. Played through special equipment with the speakers separated by the distance of the original microphone placement, the auditor can hear a slightly different sound track with each ear, and the realism of the recording is thus increased. Common after 1958, this system has been used to "enhance" monophonic recordings with varying results.

Unauthorized Recording: Recordings are sometimes offered for sale which have been made surreptitiously at a performance or from a broadcast. Since these are unauthorized or, more bluntly, pirated recordings, they are usually distributed under transitory labels and may use pseudonyms for the performers. Sometimes called "private recordings," they are for the most part products of the period since 1950, when improvements in microphones and tapes and the wider availability of record-pressing facilities made such practices possible.

Wax Records: Wax was the material used in early cylinder recordings; it quickly deteriorated with heat or repeated playings and was replaced by various proprietary compounds used by each manufacturer. (*See also* Shellac, *above.*)

H.E.J.

Abbreviations of Record Labels

The following are used in the original text:
- APGA: Association phonique des grands artistes
- DGG: Deutsche Grammophon Gesellschaft
- G & T: Gramophone and Typewriter Companies
- HMV: His Master's Voice (used for both British and related continental companies)
- MMS: Musical Masterwork Society

The following are U.S. re-issues or re-recordings labels:
- ASCO: American Stereophonic Corporation
- CRS: Collector's Record Shop
- FRP: Famous Recordings of the Past
- HRS: Historic Record Society
- IRCC: International Record Collectors' Club
- TAP: Top Artist Platters

Principal Operas, Operettas, Composers Referred to in the Text

A

Abduction from the Seraglio, The (see Die Entführung aus dem Serail)
Abisso (Antonio Smareglia)
Abu Hassan (Carl Maria von Weber)
Acis and Galatea (George Frederic Handel)
Adriana Lecouvreur (Francesco Cilea)
Agnes von Hohenstaufen (Gasparo Spontini)
Ägyptische Helena, Die (Richard Strauss)
Aïda (Giuseppe Verdi)
Albert Herring (Benjamin Britten)
Alceste (Christoph Willibald Gluck)
Alcina (George Frideric Handel)
Amantes de Teruel, Los (Tomás Bréton)
Amelia Goes to the Ball (Gian Carlo Menotti)
Amica (Pietro Mascagni)
Amphytrion 38 (Marcel Bertrand)
Andrea Chénier (Umberto Giordano)
Angel of Fire, The (see The Flaming Angel)
Anna Bolena (Gaetano Donizetti)
Antar (Gabriel Dupont)
Anthony and Cleopatra (Samuel Barber)
Antigonae (Carl Orff)
Aphrodite (Camille Erlanger)
Arabella (Richard Strauss)
Ariadne auf Naxos (Richard Strauss)
Ariane et Barbe-Bleue (Paul Dukas)
Arlecchino (Ferruccio Busoni)
Armide (Christoph Willibald Gluck)
Aroldo (Giuseppe Verdi)
Ascanio (Camille Saint-Saëns)
Ascanio in Alba (Wolfgang Amadeus Mozart)
Asrael (Alberto Franchetti)
Assassination in the Cathedral, The (see L'Assasinio nella Cathedrale)
Azora, Daughter of Montezuma (Henry Hadley)

B

Bacchus (Jules Massenet)
Ballad of Baby Doe, The (Douglas Moore)
Ballo in Maschera, Un (Giuseppe Verdi)
Barbares, Les (Camille Saint-Saëns)
Barber of Seville, The (see Il Barbiere di Siviglia)
Barbier von Bagdad, Der (Peter Cornelius)
Barbiere di Siviglia, Il (Giovanni Paisiello)
Barbiere di Siviglia, Il (Gioacchino Rossini)
Bärenhäuter, Der (Siegfried Wagner)
Bartered Bride, The (Bedřich Smetana)
Basoche, La (André Messager)
Bastien und Bastienne (Wolfgang Amadeus Mozart)
Bat, The (see Die Fledermaus)
Battaglia di Legnano, La (Giuseppe Verdi)
Battista, Il (Giocondo Fino)
Beatrice Cenci (Guido Pannain)
Beatrice di Tenda (Vincenzo Bellini)
Beggars' Opera, The (Pepusch and Gay)
Belle Hélène, La (Jacques Offenbach)
Benvenuto Cellini (Hector Berlioz)
Bergwerk von Falun, Das (Rudolf Wagner-Régery)
Bettelstudent, Der (Karl Millöcker)
Billy Budd (Benjamin Britten)
Blaise le Savetier (François André Philidor)
Blossom Time (Heinrich Berté)
Boccaccio (Franz von Suppé)
Bohème, La (Ruggiero Leoncavallo)
Bohème, La (Giacomo Puccini)
Bolivar (Darius Milhaud)
Boris Godounov (Modest Moussorgsky)
Brebis Égarée, La (Darius Milhaud)
Bride of Messina, The (Zdeněk Fibich)
Briséis (Emmanuel Chabrier)

Principal Operas, Operettas, Composers

C

Cabrera, La (Gabriel Dupont)
Cadeaux de Noël, Les (Xavier Leroux)
Cadmus et Hermione (Jean-Baptiste Lully)
Campana Sommersa, La (Ottorino Respighi)
Campanello di Notte, Il (Gaetano Donizetti)
Campiello, Il (Ermanno Wolf-Ferrari)
Cantatrice Vilane, La (Fioravanti)
Cantegril
  (Jean Jules Aimable Roger-Ducasse)
Canterbury Pilgrims, The
  (Reginald de Koven)
Capriccio (Richard Strauss)
Caprices de Marianne, Les (Henri Sauguet)
Cardillac (Paul Hindemith)
Carmélite, La (Reynaldo Hahn)
Carmen (Georges Bizet)
Carmina Burana (Carl Orff)
Casanova
  (Johann Strauss, Jr., arr. Benatsky)
Catulli Carmina (Carl Orff)
Cavalieri di Ekebù, I (Riccardo Zandonai)
Cavalleria Rusticana (Pietro Mascagni)
Cecilia (Licinio Refice)
Cena della Beffe, La (Umberto Giordano)
Cendrillon (Jules Massenet)
Cenerentola (Gioacchino Rossini)
Chalet, Le (Adolphe Adam)
Chemineau, Le (Xavier Leroux)
Chérubin (Jules Massenet)
Christelflein (Hans Pfitzner)
Cid, Le (Jules Massenet)
Cirano di Bergerac (Franco Alfano)
Circé (Paul and Lucien Hillemacher)
Clemenza di Tito, La
  (Wolfgang Amadeus Mozart)
Cloches de Corneville, Les
  (Robert Planquette)
Clown, Le (Isaac de Camondo)
Colloquio de Tajo (de Barfield)
Comme ils s'aiment (André Lavagne)
Comte Ory, Le (Gioacchino Rossini)
Conchita (Riccardo Zandonai)
Condor, O (Carlos Gomes)
Consul, The (Gian Carlo Menotti)
Contes d'Hoffmann, Les (Jacques Offenbach)
Corregidor, Der (Hugo Wolf)
Così fan tutte (Wolfgang Amadeus Mozart)
Credulo, Il (Domenico Cimarosa)
Cristoforo Colombo (Alberto Franchetti)
Cyrano de Bergerac (Walter Damrosch)

D

Dalibor (Bedřich Smetana)
Damnation de Faust, La (Hector Berlioz)
Dantons Tod (Gottfried von Einem)
Daphne (Richard Strauss)
Debora e Jaele (Ildebrando Pizzetti)
Déjanire (Camille Saint-Saëns)
Demon, The (Anton Rubinstein)
Devin du Village, Le
  (Jean-Jacques Rousseau)
Dialogues des Carmélites, Les
  (Francis Poulenc)
Diavolo nel Campanile, Il (Adriano Lualdi)
Dibuk, Il (Lodovico Rocca)
Dido and Aeneas (Henry Purcell)
Dimitrij (Antonín Dvořák)
Dinorah (Giacomo Meyerbeer)
Dolores, La (Tomás Bréton)
Dona Juana la Loca (Emilio Sarrão)
Don Carlos (Giuseppe Verdi)
Don César de Bazan (Jules Massenet)
Don Giovanni (Felice Lattuada)
Don Giovanni (Wolfgang Amadeus Mozart)
Donne Curiose, Le (Ermanno Wolf-Ferrari)
Don Pasquale (Gaetano Donizetti)
Don Quichotte (Jules Massenet)
Dorothy (Alfred Cellier)
Dragons de Villars, Les (Louis Maillart)
Drot og Mark (Peter Arnold Heise)
Dubarry, Die (Karl Millöcker)
Dubarry, La (Carmussi)
Dubrovsky (Eduard Nápravník)
Duke Bluebeard's Castle (Béla Bartók)
Dybbuk, The (Tamkin)

E

Edipo Re (Ruggiero Leoncavallo)
Edmea (Alfredo Catalani)
Elektra (Richard Strauss)
Emperor Jones, The (Louis Gruenberg)
Entführung aus dem Serail, Die
  (Wolfgang Amadeus Mozart)
Ernani (Giuseppe Verdi)
Esclarmonde (Jules Massenet)
Esther de Carpentras (Darius Milhaud)
Eugen Onégin (Peter Ilyich Tchaikovsky)
Euryanthe (Carl Maria von Weber)
Evangelimann, Der (Wilhelm Kienzl)

F

Fair at Sorotchinsk, The
  (Modest Moussorgsky)
Fairy Queen, The (Henry Purcell)
Falstaff (Giuseppe Verdi)
Fanciulla del West, La (Giacomo Puccini)
Farsa Amorosa, La (Riccardo Zandonai)
Faust (Charles Gounod)
Favorita, La (Gaetano Donizetti)
Fedora (Umberto Giordano)
Fedra (Ildebrando Pizzetti)
Ferne Klang, Der (Franz Schreker)
Feuersnot (Richard Strauss)
Fiamma, La (Ottorino Respighi)
Fidelio (Ludwig van Beethoven)
Figlia del Diavolo, La (Virgilio Mortari)
Figlia di Jorio, La (Alberto Franchetti)
Fille de Roland, La (Henri Rabaud)
Fille de Tabarin, La (Gabriel Pierné)
Fille du Régiment, La (Gaetano Donizetti)
Filosofo di Campagna, Il
  (Baldassare Galuppi)
Fils de l'Étoile, Le (Camille Erlanger)
Finta Semplice, La
  (Wolfgang Amadeus Mozart)
Flaming Angel, The (Sergei Prokofiev)
Fledermaus, Die (Johann Strauss, Jr.)
Fliegende Holländer, Der (Richard Wagner)
Fortunio (André Messager)
Forza del Destino, La (Giuseppe Verdi)
Four Saints in Three Acts (Virgil Thomson)

Principal Operas, Operettas, Composers

Fra Diavolo (Daniel François Esprit Auber)
Francesca da Rimini (Eduard Nápravník)
Francesca da Rimini (Riccardo Zandonai)
Frau ohne Schatten, Die (Richard Strauss)
Freischütz, Der (Carl Maria von Weber)
Friedemann Bach (Paul Graener)
Friedenstag (Richard Strauss)
Friederike (Franz Lehár)

G

Geisha, The (Sidney Jones)
Geliebte Stimme, Die (Jaromir Weinberger)
Genesius (Felix Weingartner)
Genoveva (Robert Schumann)
Germania (Alberto Franchetti)
Gesheidene Frau, Die (Leo Fall)
Gezeichneten, Die (Franz Schreker)
Ghisèle (César Franck)
Gianni Schicchi (Giacomo Puccini)
Gioconda, La (Amilcare Ponchielli)
Gioielli della Madonna, I
    (Ermanno Wolf-Ferrari)
Giorno di Regno, Un (Giuseppe Verdi)
Giuditta (Franz Lehár)
Giulietta e Romeo (Riccardo Zandonai)
Giulio Cesare (George Frederic Handel)
Giulio Cesare (Gian Francesco Malipiero)
Gloria (Francesco Cilea)
Gloriana (Benjamin Britten)
Golden Cockerel, The
    (Nikolai Rimsky-Korsakov)
Götterdämmerung (Richard Wagner)
Goyescas (Enrique Granados)
Grisélidis (Jules Massenet)
Guarany, Il (Carlos Gomes)
Guercoeur (Albéric Magnard)
Guglielmo Ratcliff (Pietro Mascagni)
Guillaume Tell (Gioacchino Rossini)

H

Habanera, La (Raoul Laparra)
Hamlet (Amroise Thomas)
Hamlet (Mario Zefred)
Hanneles Himmelfahrt (Paul Graener)
Hänsel und Gretel (Engelbert Humperdinck)
Hans Heiling (Heinrich Marschner)
Hans Sachs (Albert Lortzing)
Harmonie die Welt (Paul Hindemith)
Hélène (Camille Saint Saëns)
Henry VIII (Camille Saint-Saëns)
Hérodiade (Jules Massenet)
Herz, Das (Hans Pfitzner)
Hochzeit des Jobs, Die (Joseph Haas)
Hollandweibchen, Das (Emmerich Kálmán)
Höllische Gold, Das (Julius Bittner)
Hugh the Drover (Ralph Vaughn Williams)
Huguenots, Les (Giacomo Meyerbeer)
Hulla, Le (Marcel Samuel-Rousseau)

I

Idomeneo (Wolfgang Amadeus Mozart)
Il était un petit navire
    (Germaine Tailleferre)
Intermezzo (Richard Strauss)
Intolleranza 60 (Luigi Nono)

Iolanthe (Peter Ilyitch Tchaikovsky)
Iphigénie en Aulide
    (Christoph Willibald Gluck)
Iphigénie en Tauride
    (Christoph Willibald Gluck)
Iris (Pietro Mascagni)
Irische Legende (Werner Egk)
Irrelohe (Franz Schreker)
Isabeau (Pietro Mascagni)
Island God, The (Gian Carlo Menotti)
Ivanhoe (Sir Arthur Sullivan)

J

Jenufa (Leoš Janáček)
Jewels of the Madonna, The
    (see I Gioielli della Madonna)
Jocelyn (Benjamin Godard)
Jongleur de Notre-Dame, Le
    (Jules Massenet)
Jonny Spielt Auf (Ernst Křenek)
Jota, La (Raoul Laparra)
Judith (Sir Eugene Goossens)
Juif Polonais, Le (Camille Erlanger)
Juive, La (Jacques François Halévy)
Julien (Gustave Charpentier)

K

Kaiserin, Die (Leo Fall)
Katya Kabanova (Leoš Janáček)
Khovantchina (Modest Moussorgsky)
King's Henchman, The (Deems Taylor)
Kiss, The (Bedřich Smetana)
Kitty Darling (Rudolf Friml)
Kluge, Die (Carl Orff)
Koanga (Frederick Delius)
Königen von Saba, Die (Carl Goldmark)
König Hirsch (Hans Werner Henze)
Königskinder (Engelbert Humperdinck)
Kreidekreis, Der (Alexander von Zemlinsky)
Kuhreigen, Der (Wilhelm Kienzl)

L

Lachende Erbe, Der (Jaromir Weinberger)
L'Africaine (Giacomo Meyerbeer)
L'Aiglon (Jacques Ibert)
Lakmé (Léo Delibes)
Lalla-Roukh (Félicien David)
L'Amico Fritz (Pietro Mascagni)
L'Amore dei Tre Re (Italo Montemezzi)
L'Ancêtre (Camille Saint-Saëns)
Land des Lächelns, Das (Franz Lehár)
L'Arlesiana (Francesco Cilea)
L'Assasinio nella Cathedrale
    (Ildebrando Pizzetti)
L'Attaque du Moulin (Alfred Bruneau)
Legend of the Invisible City of Kitezh, The
    (Nikolai Rimsky-Korsakov)
L'Elisir d'Amore (Gaetano Donizetti)
L'Enfant et les Sortilèges (Maurice Ravel)
Leone (Marcel Samuel-Rousseau)
Lépreuse, La (Sylvio Lazzari)
L'Heure Espagnole (Maurice Ravel)
Libuše (Bedřich Smetana)
Liden Kirsten
    (Johann Peter Emilius Hartmann)

Principal Operas, Operettas, Composers

Liebe der Danae, Die (Richard Strauss)
Liebesverbot, Das (Richard Wagner)
Life for the Czar, A (Mikhail Glinka)
Lilac Domino, The (Charles Cuvillier)
L'Incoronazione di Poppea
   (Claudio Monteverdi)
Linda di Chamounix (Gaetano Donizetti)
L'Italiana in Algeri (Gioacchino Rossini)
Lituani, I (Amilcare Ponchielli)
Lodoletta (Pietro Mascagni)
Lohengrin (Richard Wagner)
Lombardi, I (Giuseppe Verdi)
L'Oracolo (Franco Leoni)
Loreley (Alfredo Catalani)
Loreley, Die (Max Bruch)
L'Orsèolo (Ildebrando Pizzetti)
Louise (Gustave Charpentier)
Love of Three Oranges, The
   (Sergei Prokofiev)
Lucia di Lammermoor (Gaetano Donizetti)
Lucrezia (Ottorino Respighi)
Lucrezia Borgia (Gaetano Donizetti)
Luisa Miller (Giuseppe Verdi)
Lulu (Alban Berg)
L'Uomo Che Ride (Arrigo Pedrollo)
L'Uragano (Lodovico Rocca)

M

Macbeth (Ernest Bloch)
Macbeth (Giuseppe Verdi)
Macigno, Il (Victor de Sabata)
Madama Butterfly (Giacomo Puccini)
Madame Bovary (Emmanuel de Bondeville)
Madame Roland (Foudrain)
Madame Sans-Gêne (Umberto Giordano)
Maddalena, La (Michetti)
Madeleine (Victor Herbert)
Mademoiselle Modiste (Victor Herbert)
Mage, Le (Jules Massenet)
Magic Flute, The (See Die Zauberflöte)
Mala Pasqua (Stanislaus Gastaldon)
Malbruk (Ruggiero Leoncavallo)
Mamelles de Tirésias, Les (Francis Poulenc)
Manon (Jules Massenet)
Manon Lescaut (Giacomo Puccini)
Manru (Ignace Jan Paderewski)
Man Without a Country, The
   (Walter Damrosch)
Marchand de Venise, Le (Reynaldo Hahn)
Maria di Rohan (Gaetano Donizetti)
Maria Egiziaca (Ottorino Respighi)
Maria Golovine (Gian Carlo Menotti)
Marion (Pierre Wissmer)
Marion Delorme (Amilcare Ponchielli)
Mârouf (Henri Rabaud)
Marriage of Figaro, The
   (See Le Nozze di Figaro)
Martha (Friedrich Flotow)
Martyr of Antioch, The
   (Sir Arthur Sullivan)
Maschere, Le (Pietro Mascagni)
Masked Ball, A (See Un Ballo in Maschera)
Mathis der Maler (Paul Hindemith)
Matrero, El (Felipe Boero)

Matrimonio Segreto, Il (Domenico Cimarosa)
Mavra (Igor Stravinsky)
May Night (Nikolai Rimsky-Korsakov)
Mazeppa (Peter Ilyitch Tchaikovsky)
Medea (Vincenzo Tommasini)
Médecin Magré Lui, Le (Charles Gounod)
Médée (Darius Milhaud)
Mefistofele (Arrigo Boito)
Meistersinger, Die (Richard Wagner)
Merry Mount (Howard Hanson)
Medea (Luigi Cherubini)
Merry Widow, The (Franz Lehár)
Merry Wives of Windsor, The
   (Otto Nicolai)
Mese Mariano (Umberto Giordano)
Messaline (Isidore de Lara)
Midsummer Marriage, A (Michael Tippett)
Midsummer Night's Dream, A
   (Benjamin Britten)
Mignon (Amroise Thomas)
Mireille (Charles Gounod)
Mister Wu (Eugen d'Albert)
Moïse et Pharaon (Gioacchino Rossini)
Mona Lisa (Max von Schillings)
Monna Vanna (Henri Février)
Monsieur Beaucaire (André Messager)
Mori di Valenza, I (Amilcare Ponchielli)
Morte di Frine, Le (Ludovico Rocca)
Mosè (Gioacchino Rossini)
Moses und Aron (Arnold Schoenberg)
Much Ado About Nothing
   (Sir Charles Stanford)

N

Nabucco (Giuseppe Verdi)
Nacht in Venedig, Eine
   (Johann Strauss, Jr.)
Nachtlager von Granada, Das
   (Konradin Kreutzer)
Namiko San (Alberto Franchetti)
Naughty Marietta (Victor Herbert)
Navarraise, La (Jules Massenet)
Nave, La (Italo Montemezzi)
Nero (Anton Rubinstein)
Nerone (Arrigo Boito)
Nerone (Pietro Mascagni)
Noces Corinthiennes, Les (Henri Busser)
Noces de Jeannette, Les (Victor Massé)
Norma (Vincenzo Bellini)
Notturo Romantico
   (Riccardo Pick-Mangiagalli)
Nozze di Figaro, Le
   (Wolfgang Amadeus Mozart)
Nuit de Cléopâtre, Une (Victor Massé)

O

Oberon (Carl Maria von Weber)
Oedipus der Tyrann (Carl Orff)
Oedipus Rex (Igor Stravinsky)
Olympia (Gasparo Spontini)
Orfeo (Claudio Monteverdi)
Orphée et Eurydice
   (Christoph Willibald Gluck)
Otello (Giuseppe Verdi)

Principal Operas, Operettas, Composers

P

Paganini (Franz Lehár)
Pagliacci, I (Ruggiero Leoncavallo)
Palestrina (Hans Pfitzner)
Panurge (Jules Massenet)
Parisina (Pietro Mascagni)
Parsifal (Richard Wagner)
Passion of Jonathan Wade, The (Carlisle Floyd)
Paul et Virginie (Victor Massé)
Pearl Fishers, The (*See* Les Pêcheurs de Perles)
Pêcheurs de Perles, Les (Georges Bizet)
Pêcheurs de Saint-Jean, Les (Charles-Marie Widor)
Peer Gynt (Werner Egk)
Pelléas et Mélisande (Claude Debussy)
Pénélope (Gabriel Fauré)
Penelope (Rolf Liebermann)
Peter Grimes (Benjamin Britten)
Peter Ibbetson (Deems Taylor)
Petronio (Giovanetti)
Philémon et Baucis (Charles Gounod)
Phryné (Camille Saint-Saëns)
Piccolo Marat, Il (Pietro Mascagni)
Pique Dame (*See* The Queen of Spades)
Platée (Jean-Philippe Rameau)
Poliuto (Gaetano Donizetti)
Polyeucte (Charles Gounod)
Porgy and Bess (George Gershwin)
Postillon de Longjumeau, Le (Adolphe Adam)
Poupée de Nuremberg, La (Adolphe Adam)
Preziose Ridicole, Le (Felice Lattuada)
Prince Igor (Alexander Borodin)
Prinz von Hamburg, Der (Paul Graener)
Prophète, Le (Giacomo Meyerbeer)
Prozess, Der (Gottfried von Einem)
Puritani, I (Vincenzo Bellini)

Q

Quattro Rusteghi, I (Ermanno Wolf-Ferrari)
Queen of Spades, The (Peter Ilyitch Tchaikovsky)
Quo Vadis? (Jean Nouguès)

R

Rake's Progress, The (Igor Stravinsky)
Rape of Lucretia, The (Benjamin Britten)
Raquela (Felipe Boero)
Raskolnikov (Heinrich Sutermeister)
Re, Il (Umberto Giordano)
Reine Fiammette, La (Xavier Leroux)
Re Lear (Vito Frazzi)
Rembrandt van Rijn (Paul von Klenau)
Retablo de Maese Pedro, El (Manuel de Falla)
Rheingold, Das (Richard Wagner)
Richard Coeur de Lion (André Ernest Grétry)
Rienzi (Richard Wagner)
Rigoletto (Giuseppe Verdi)
Ring des Nibelungen, Der (*see* Das Rheingold, Die Walküre, Siegfried, and Götterdämmerung)
Risurrezione (Franco Alfano)
Roberta (Jerome Kern)
Robert le Diable (Giacomo Meyerbeer)
Roi de Lahore, Le (Jules Massenet)
Roi d'Ys, Le (Édouard Lalo)
Roi d'Yvetot, Le (Jacques Ibert)
Roi Malgré Lui, Le (Emmanuel Chabrier)
Roland von Berlin, Der (Ruggiero Leoncavallo)
Roméo et Juliette (Charles Gounod)
Rondine, La (Giacomo Puccini)
Rosenkavalier, Der (Richard Strauss)
Rose of Persia, The (Sir Arthur Sullivan)
Rose vom Liebesgarten, Die (Hans Pfitzner)
Rossignol, Le (Igor Stravinsky)
Rusalka (Antonin Dvořák)
Russalka (Alexander Dargomyzhsky)
Ruy Blas (Antonio Carlos Gomez)
Ruy Blas (Filippo Marchetti)

S

Sadko (Nikolai Rimsky-Korsakov)
Saffo (Giovanni Pacini)
Sakuntala (Franco Alfano)
Salammbô (Ernest Reyer)
Salome (Richard Strauss)
Sampiero Corso (Henri Tomasi)
Samson et Dalila (Camille Saint-Saëns)
Sapho (Jules Massenet)
Scala di Seta, La (Gioacchino Rossini)
Schatzgräber, Der (Franz Schreker)
Schmied von Gent, Der (Franz Schreker)
Schule der Frauen, Die (Rolf Liebermann)
Schwanda (Jaromir Weinberger)
Schweigsame Frau, Die (Richard Strauss)
Segreto della Duchesa, Il (Giuseppe Dell'Orefice)
Segreto di Susanna, Il (Ermanno Wolf-Ferrari)
Semiramide (Gioacchino Rossini)
Serse (George Frederic Handel)
Serva Padrona, La (Giovanni Battista Pergolesi)
Shanewis (Charles Wakefield Cadman)
Siberia (Umberto Giordano)
Siegfried (Richard Wagner)
Signa (Sir Frederick Cowan)
Signor Bruschino, Il (Gioacchino Rossini)
Sigurd (Ernest Reyer)
Si j'étais roi (Adolphe Adam)
Silvana (Pietro Mascagni)
Simone Boccanegra (Giuseppe Verdi)
Singende Teufel, Der (Franz Schreker)
Sly (Ermanno Wolf-Ferrari)
Snow Maiden, The (Nikolai Rimsky-Korsakov)
Sonnambula, La (Vincenzo Bellini)
Sophie Arnould (Gabriel Pierné)
Sorcière, La (Camille Erlanger)
Sosarme (George Frideric Handel)
South Pacific (Richard Rodgers)

Principal Operas, Operettas, Composers

Sperduti nel Buio (Stefano Donaudy)
Storm, The (Vitězslav Novák)
Strohwitwe, Die (Leo Blech)
Sturm, Der (Frank Martin)
Suona la Ritrata (Domenico Monleone)
Suor Angelica (Giacomo Puccini)
Susannah (Carlisle Floyd)

T

Tabarro, Il (Giacomo Puccini)
Tale of the Tsar Sultan
  (Nikolai Rimsky-Korsakov)
Tales of Hoffmann
  (see Les Contes d'Hoffmann)
Taming of the Shrew, The
  (Vittorio Giannini)
Taming of the Shrew, The (Hermann Götz)
Tannhäuser (Richard Wagner)
Telephone, The (Gian Carlo Menotti)
Thaïs (Jules Massenet)
Theodora (George Frederic Handel)
Thérèse (Jules Massenet)
Three Musketeers, The
  (Ralph Bernatsky)
Tiefland (Eugen d'Albert)
Tilda, La (Francesco Cilea)
Timbre d'Argent, Le (Camille Saint-Saëns)
Tommaso Chatterton (Ruggiero Leoncavallo)
Tosca (Giacomo Puccini)
Toten Augen, Die (Eugen d'Albert)
Tote Stadt, Die (Erich Korngold)
Traviata, La (Giuseppe Verdi)
Tribut de Zamora, Le (Charles Gounod)
Trionfi
  (see Carmina Burana, Catulli Carmina, and Trionfo di Afrodite)
Trionfo di Afrodite (Carl Orff)
Tristan und Isolde (Richard Wagner)
Tritsh-Tratsch (Nestroy)
Troilus and Cressida (Sir William Walton)
Trovatore, Il (Giuseppe Verdi)
Troyens, Les (Hector Berlioz)
Turandot (Giacomo Puccini)
Turco in Italia, Il (Gioacchino Rossini)
Turn of the Screw, The (Benjamin Britten)
Two Widows, The (Bedřich Smetana)

V

Vanessa (Samuel Barber)
Vedova Scaltra, La (Ermanno Wolf-Ferrari)
Veilchen von Montmartre, Das
  (Emmerich Kálmán)
Verkündigung (Walter Braunfels)
Vespri Siciliani, I (Giuseppe Verdi)
Vestale, La (Saverio Mercadente)
Vestale, La (Gasparo Spontini)
Vicar of Wakefield, The (Liza Lehmann)
Vida Breve, La (Manuel de Falla)
Vigna, La (Guido Guerrini)
Villi, Le (Giacomo Puccini)
Vivandière, La (Benjamin Godard)
Vortice, Il (Renzo Rosselini)

W

Waffenschmied, Der (Albert Lortzing)
Walküre, Die (Richard Wagner)
Wally, La (Alfredo Catalani)
Wanda (Albert Franz Doppler)
War and Peace (Sergei Prokofiev)
Werther (Jules Massenet)
Wiener Blut (Johann Strauss, Jr.)
Wildschütz, Der (Albert Lortzing)
William Tell (see Guillaume Tell)
Wintermärchen, Ein (Carl Goldmark)
Wozzeck (Alban Berg)
Wunder der Heliane, Das (Erich Korngold)
Wuthering Heights (Carlisle Floyd)

X

Xenia (Alexandre Savine)
Xerxes (George Frederic Handel)

Z

Zarewitsch, Der (Franz Lehár)
Zar und Zimmermann (Albert Lortzing)
Zauberflöte, Die
  (Wolfgang Amadeus Mozart)
Zaubergeige, Die (Werner Egk)
Zaza (Ruggiero Leoncavallo)
Zigeunerbaron, Der (Johann Strauss, Jr.)
Zigeunerliebe (Franz Lehár)

Principal "Name" Opera Houses

Bolshoi Theater (Moscow, U.S.S.R.)
Covent Garden (London, England)
Drury Lane Theater (London, England)
Janáček Opera (Brno, Czechoslovakia)
Komische Oper (Berlin, Germany)
Kroll Opera (Berlin, Germany)
La Scala (Milan, Italy)
Manhattan Opera
   (New York City, United States)
Maryinsky Theater
   (St. Petersburg [Leningrad], U.S.S.R.)
Metropolitan Opera
   (New York City, United States)
Opéra (Paris, France)
Opéra-Comique (Paris, France)
Piccolo Scala (Milan, Italy)
Residenztheater (Berlin, Germany)
Teatro Adriano (Rome, Italy)
Teatro Argentina (Rome, Italy)
Teatro Bellini (Naples, Italy)
Teatro Biondo (Palermo, Italy)
Teatro Carcana (Milan, Italy)
Teatro Coliseo (Buenos Aires, Argentina)
Teatro Colón (Buenos Aires, Argentina)
Teatro Costanzi (Rome, Italy)
Teatro Fenice (Venice, Italy)
Teatro Liceo (Barcelona, Spain)
Teatro Lirico (Milan, Italy)
Teatro Manzoni (Milan, Italy)
Teatro Massimo (Palermo, Italy)
Teatro Novedades (Barcelona, Spain)
Teatro Nuovo (Milan, Italy)
Teatro della Pergola (Florence, Italy)
Teatro Politeamo (Buenos Aires, Argentina)
Teatro Puccini (Milan, Italy)
Teatro Quirino (Rome, Italy)
Teatro Real (Madrid, Spain)
Teatro Reale (Rome, Italy)
Teatro Regio (Parma, Italy)
Teatro Regio (Turin, Italy)
Teatro San Carlo (Naples, Italy)
Teatro São Carlos (Lisbon, Portugal)
Teatro Verdi (Bologna)
Teatro Verdi (Florence)
Teatro Verdi (Padua)
Teatro Verdi (Trieste)
Teatro dal Verme (Milan, Italy)
Teatro Vittorio Emmanuele (Turin, Italy)
Theater am Westens (Berlin, Germany)
Theater an der Wien (Vienna, Austria)
Théâtre des Champs-Elysées (Paris, France)
Théâtre de la Haye (The Hague, Holland)
Théâtre Italien (Paris, France)
Théâtre Lyrique (Paris, France)
Théâtre Marigny (Paris, France)
Théâtre de la Monnaie (Brussels, Belgium)
Théâtre Sarah Bernhardt (Paris, France)
Théâtre Trianon-Lyrique (Paris, France)
Ziminia Opera (Moscow, U.S.S.R.)

Principal Music Festivals

Aix-en-Provence Festival
 (Aix-en-Provence, France)
Aldeburgh Festival (Aldeburgh, England)
Arena Festival (Verona, Italy)
Baths of Caracalla Festival (Rome, Italy)
Bayreuth Festival (Bayreuth, Germany)
Birmingham Festival
 (Birmingham, England)
Edinburgh Festival (Edinburgh, Scotland)
Glyndebourne Festival
 (Glyndebourne, England)

Holland Festival (various cities in Holland)
Maggio Musicale Festival (Florence, Italy)
Ravinia Summer Festival
 (Chicago, United States)
Salzburg Festival (Salzburg, Austria)
Spoleto Festival (Spoleto, Italy)
Vancouver Festival (Vancouver, Canada)
Zoppot Festival (Zoppot, Poland)

A

ABARBANELL, LINA, soprano, b. Jan. 3, 1879, Berlin; d. Jan. 6, 1963, New York. She was the daughter of the bandmaster Paul Abarbanell and first appeared as an actress at the Residenztheater in Berlin. Vocal study with Plohn and Steinmann followed. In 1897 she went to Posen, where she appeared as an actress and a singer. From there she returned to Berlin in 1901, but in 1902 moved to the Theater an der Wien in Vienna. She was by this time particularly admired as an operetta diva and had also mastered soubrette opera roles. Following very successful guest appearances in London, she came to the United States in 1904. In 1905 she sang Hänsel in the New York *première* of *Hänsel und Gretel* at the Metropolitan Opera. In the following years she also had great success as an operetta singer in the United States. During her last years she lived in New York.

Records: Six very rare records from operettas for G & T (Vienna, 1903-04).

ABENDROTH, IRENE, soprano, b. July 14, 1872, Lemberg, Austria; d. Sept. 1, 1932, Weidling, near Vienna. She appeared in a concert when she was eight years old; later she studied with Lambertini and Campanini in Milan and with Mme. Wilczek in Vienna. She made her concert debut in Karlsbad (1888) and her operatic debut at the Vienna Imperial Opera as Amina in *La Sonnambula* (1889) and remained there for two years. She then sang at Riga (1891-92), at the Royal Opera in Munich (1892-95), again at Vienna (1895-1900), and at the Royal Opera in Dresden (1900-08), where her career reached its climax. In 1902 she sang the title role there in the first German performance of *Tosca*. Later she appeared as a concert singer and then became a teacher in Vienna. She was married to the Austrian railroad director Joseph Taller, Viscount von Draga. One of the infrequently occurring voices which joins virtuoso coloratura technique and dramatic expressiveness.

Records: Six rare records for G & T (Dresden, 1902). *U.S. re-recording:* IRCC, Belcanto.

ABOTT, BESSIE, soprano, b. 1878, Riverside, N.Y.; d. Feb. 9, 1919, New York City. Originally Bessie Pickens. She appeared at small theaters and in vaudeville houses in New York in 1894 with her twin sister, Jessie Pickens, where the two girls sang duets. She then became an operetta singer in New York, and after 1897, in London. Jean de Reszke heard her there in 1898 and encouraged her to direct her steps toward opera. To this end she studied with Victor Capoul, Bouhy, and Mathilde Marchesi in Paris and made her debut at the Opéra (1901), singing Juliette in *Roméo et Juliette*. For five years she was very successful in Paris and in 1906 was engaged by the Metropolitan Opera in New York, making her debut as Mimi in *La Bohème*. She remained there until 1909, appearing also during this time in Chicago and San Francisco. In 1909 she made guest appearances in Monte Carlo, St. Petersburg, and Lisbon. She then organized her own opera company, which toured the United States (1910). She married the writer Story, whose brother was Emma Eames' first husband, and in 1911 she gave up her career. She had a coloratura voice of outstanding technical excellence.

Records: Edison* cylinders and Victor* discs, the most notable of the latter is the Quartet from *Rigoletto* with Enrico Caruso, Louise Homer, and Antonio Scotti. *U.S. re-recording:* IRCC, Rococo.

ACHSEL, WANDA, soprano, b. Oct. 12, 1891, Berlin. A pupil of Laura Détschys in Berlin, she made her debut in 1910 at the Berlin Summer Opera as Elsa in *Lohengrin*. She sang at Würzburg (1910-12), at the Cologne Opera (1912-23), and at the Vienna State Opera (1923-39) and made guest appearances in Holland, Poland, Yugoslavia, and Czechoslovakia. She sang Rosalinda in *Die Fledermaus* at the 1926 Salzburg Festival. She was married to the tenor Hans Clemens, and now lives and teaches in Vienna.

Records: A few rare electric HMV discs (Vienna, 1930).

ACKTÉ, AINO, soprano, b. Apr. 23, 1876, Helsinki; d. Aug. 8, 1944, Nummela, Finland. A daughter of the soprano Emmy Strömer-Ackté (1850-1924) and sister of the contralto Irma Tervani, she first studied with her mother. She sang in a concert in Helsinki in 1893 when she was only seventeen. Later she studied at the Paris Conservatory under Duvernoy, Girodet, and Paul Vidal and made her debut there at the Opéra as Marguerite in *Faust* (1897); she was thereafter highly successful at that house. Tours as a guest star took her to Stockholm, Dresden, Warsaw, Copenhagen, and to Covent Garden. She sang at the Metropolitan Opera (1903-05) and sang the title role in *Salome* (1910) at Covent Garden in the first performance of the work there. She was soprano soloist in the Verdi *Requiem* at the Birmingham Festival. She married Heikki Renvall, son of the archbishop of Finland, and thereafter made that country her home. She was the director of the Helsinki Opera (1938-39). She wrote *Minnen och fantasier* (Stockholm, 1917), *Muistojeni kirja* (recollections) in Swedish and Finnish (Helsinki, 1925), and *Taiteeni taipaleelta* (memoirs) (Helsinki, 1925). She had a large, dramatic soprano voice which she used brilliantly in the classical and Wagner repertory.

Records: Rare discs for Zonophone (Paris, 1902), G & T (Paris, 1903-05), Fonotipia (Paris, 1905), as well as records for Edison and Pathé. *U.S. re-issue:* Victor, IRCC, HRS. *U.S. re-recording:* IRCC.

ADAM, THEO, bass, b. Aug. 1, 1926, Dresden. He began his career as a choir singer in Dresden's Holy Cross Church. After studies with Rudolf Dittrich in Dresden, he made his debut at the Dresden Opera in 1949. Since 1957 he has been engaged simultaneously at the

Berlin State Opera and the Frankfurt a. M. Opera. He made his first appearance at the Bayreuth Festival in 1952, and has since sung there annually in such parts as King Henry in *Lohengrin*, Titurel in *Parsifal*, Pogner in *Die Meistersinger*, and Fafner and Wotan in the *Ring* cycle; he has become an outstanding Wagner interpreter. Guest appearances have taken him to the Vienna State Opera, the Berlin City Opera, and Paris Opéra. He is also a great oratorio singer.

Records: Eterna, Bertelsmann, HMV, Electrola, and DGG; particularly Bach cantatas on the last two. *U.S. re-issue:* Angel, Vox, Epic (Beethoven's *Ninth Symphony*), Urania.

ADAMS, SUZANNE, soprano, b. Nov. 28, 1872, Cambridge, Mass.; d. Feb. 5, 1953, London. She studied in Paris with Mathilde Marchesi and Bouhy and made her debut (1894) at the Opéra there, against the will of Mme. Marchesi. Her debut role was Juliette in *Roméo et Juliette*. After great successes in Paris, she made brilliant guest appearances at Covent Garden (1898) and sang there regularly until 1906. She sang at the Metropolitan Opera (1898-1903). In 1906 she gave up her career but appeared a few times in 1907 in a London variety hall. She was married to the cellist Leo Stern and later operated an exclusive laundry in the British capital. A technically admirable and thoroughly trained coloratura soprano.

Records: As well as Pathé records, she made five dics for G & T (London, 1902) and eight for American Columbia* (1903). *U.S. re-issue:* Victor. *U.S. re-recording:* Columbia, IRCC, TAP.

ADER, ROSE, soprano, b. Apr. 28, 1890, Oderberg, Germany; d. Mar. 28, 1955, Buenos Aires. She made her debut (1915) at the Hamburg Opera and remained there until 1918. She sang at the Vienna State Opera (1918-19). After 1921 she returned to Hamburg, where she appeared with the most famous artists. Her guest appearances included Amsterdam (1928; 1930), La Scala (1928-29), Berlin and Munich. In 1933 she was forced as a Jew to leave Germany; she made guest appearances then in Vienna and after 1949 taught in Buenos Aires. Her repertory included both coloratura and lyric roles. After her marriage she sang under the name Ader-de Trigona.

Records: Her beautiful voice is preserved on a single Parlophone record of an aria from *La Bohème*.

ADINI, ADA, soprano, b. 1855, Boston; d. 1924, Dieppe, France. Originally Adele Chapman, she studied with Pauline Viardot-Garcia and Giovanni Sbriglia in Paris. She made her debut in Varese (1876) in *Dinorah*. She married the Spanish tenor Antonio Aramburo (1838-1912), and they sang together in the Mapleson company in New York (1879). Guest appearances: Berlin (1882), Prague (1883), and after 1887 the Paris Opéra. In 1893 she sang Brünnhilde at the La Scala *première* of *Die Walküre*, and she scored great success at Covent Garden (1894-97). She sang in *Ghisèlle* at the Opéra (1895), and later guest appearances included Monte Carlo, Madrid, Barcelona, South America, and, in 1897-98, a tour of Germany and Russia. She was especially active at the Opéra (1902-08). Her second marriage was to Paul Milliet, Massenet's librettist. With her flexible and impressive voice, she mastered a wide repertory from coloratura parts to Wagner heroines.

Records: Five very rare records for Fonotipia (Paris, 1905). *U.S. re-issue:* IRCC.

AFFRÉ, AGUSTARELLO, tenor, b. Oct. 23, 1858, St. Chinian, France;

d. Dec. 27, 1931, Cagnes sur Mer, France. After his voice was discovered by Pierre Gailhard, the director of the Paris Opéra, he studied at the Toulouse and Paris Conservatories and made his debut at the Opéra as Edgardo in *Lucia di Lammermoor* with Nellie Melba. For twenty years he was the first tenor of the Opéra, where he had such triumphs that he undertook no extended guest appearances elsewhere. He sang in the world *première* of *Le Mage* there (1891) and Canio in the Paris *première* of *I Pagliacci* (1893). He appeared as guest at Covent Garden as Faust and as Samson in *Samson et Dalila*. When Gailhard left the Opéra, Affré also took his leave of it. He sang at the San Francisco Opera (1911), in New Orleans (1912), Havana (1913), and during World War I he gave concerts for French soldiers. He had a typical French dramatic tenor voice; contemporary critics frequently described him as "the French Tamagno." He often sang Mozart and Wagner roles.

Records: Zonophone (Paris, 1902), G & T, Columbia* (Paris, 1904), Odeon, and Pathé, including a complete recording of *Roméo et Juliette*. *U.S. re-issue:* Victor, IRCC.

AGOSTINELLI, ADELINA, soprano, b. 1882, Bergamo, Italy; d. July 6, 1954, Buenos Aires. She studied with Giuseppe Quirolli in Milan, whom she later married. She made her debut at Pavia (1903) in the title role of *Fedora*. She toured with the Castellano troupe in Greece, Turkey, Russia, Belgium, and Holland (1905-06). She had great successes in Spain and South America and she was admired in 1908 and the following years at the Teatro Coliseo and after 1913 at the Teatro Colón. She sang at the Manhattan Opera (1909-10) and appeared at La Scala with Mattia Battistini in *Simone Boccanegra* (1910). She sang the Marschallin in the first *Der Rosenkavalier* at La Scala (1911). She appeared in 1912 at the Théâtre des Champs-Elysées and at Covent Garden. Later she sang in Italy and South America. She appeared in 1924 as guest in Buenos Aires, where she then lived and where she taught singing.

Records: Edison* cylinders (1910) and discs for Fonografia Nazionale and Pathé.

AGOSTINI, GIUSEPPE, tenor, b. July 21, 1874, Verona, Italy; d. July 26, 1951, Abington, Pa. He made his debut (1895) at Nuovi Ligure in Gomez' *Ruy Blas*. In 1897 he sang Rodolfo in *La Bohème* at Cagliari and he later specialized in this role, which he created in Lisbon, Barcelona, Mexico City, and elsewhere. In 1898 he sang Rodolfo in the American *première* with the Royal Italian Opera Company in Los Angeles and also created the role for New York when he appeared at Wallack's Theater as guest with the same company. He made guest appearances on the leading Italian and South American stages. In 1910 he sang in *Amica* at Teatro Massimo, but his greatest successes were in the United States, where he appeared almost annually with the San Carlo Opera Company. In 1903 he replaced the indisposed Enrico Caruso in two performances at the Metropolitan Opera. He was to be heard with the San Carlo Company until 1921. Although he had not appeared on the stage for years, he substituted with the same company in 1929 in the title role in *Faust* for another singer who was suddenly taken ill. The newspapers reported in sensational style that the singer was a septuagenarian, a considerable exaggeration. At the close of his life he taught in Abington, near Philadelphia.

Records: Arias for Odeon (1905)

and popular songs for American Columbia* (1916).

AHLERSMEYER, MATHIEU, baritone, b. June 29, 1896, Cologne. He studied with Karl Niemann in Cologne, and made his debut (1929) as Wolfram in *Tannhäuser* at München-Gladbach. He sang at the Kroll Opera (1930-31) and was leading baritone at the Hamburg Opera (1931-34). He then came to Dresden, where he sang in the world *première* of *Die schweigsame Frau* (June 24, 1935) and in the first performance of *Die Hochzeit des Jobs* (1944). In 1939, at the Berlin National Opera, he created the title role in *Peer Gynt*. After his Dresden engagement he was jointly under contract with the Berlin and Vienna National Operas, appearing for guest performances. In 1945 he joined the Hamburg Opera, becoming part of the administration of this house. He made guest appearances in Milan, London, Brussels, and Munich. In 1947 he sang at the Salzburg Festival in the world *première* of *Dantons Tod* and in 1953 he sang the title role in *Mathis der Maler* at the Edinburgh Festival. Following 1953 he was a member of the East Berlin National Opera. In 1961 he made his farewell appearance. He had a powerful, heroic baritone voice.

Records: For Urania* and DGG (Götz's *The Taming of the Shrew, Don Giovanni,* and *Macbeth*).

AHLIN, CVETKA, contralto, b. 1927 (?), Ljubljana, Yugoslavia. Her voice was first noticed in a children's choir; later she studied at the Ljubljana Conservatory. She made her debut at the opera house there (1952), followed by further study in Munich. In 1954 she won first prize in an international singing contest conducted by radio stations. In 1955 she signed a contract with the Hamburg Opera, and she has appeared there impressively as Amneris, Azucena, Marina in *Boris Godounov*, Orphée in *Orphée et Eurydice* and in many other roles. She has made guest appearances in Germany and in foreign countries.

Records: DGG*.

AIMARO, LINA, soprano, b. Feb. 6, 1914, Turin. She studied at the Conservatory in Milan and made her debut in Turin (1934) as Lucia di Lammermoor. In the following years she sang in Parma, Palermo, Genoa, Florence, and other Italian cities. In 1938-39 she sang at the Metropolitan Opera, making her debut as Lucia with Beniamino Gigli; she also appeared as guest with the Philadelphia Opera. She was re-engaged at the Metropolitan (1940-41) but was unable to fulfill the engagement due to the outbreak of World War II. She had, however, a successful career during the war years at La Scala and later made guest appearances at the Teatro São Carlos, in Cairo, and in Holland (1940). She sang in 1946 at Covent Garden and in Switzerland and in 1948 made a concert tour of America. Later she became a teacher in Milan. One of the most important Italian coloraturas of her generation, noted especially as Lucia di Lammermoor.

Records: Italian HMV, Columbia* (1938-39) and Westminster (*Don Pasquale*).

ALARIE, PIERETTE, soprano, b. 1922 (?), Montreal. She studied with Elisabeth Schumann in New York, then made her debut (1945) at the Metropolitan Opera as Oscar in *Un Ballo in Maschera*. She was also successful as Olympia in *Les Contes d'Hoffmann* and as Blondchen in *Die Entführung aus dem Serail*. In 1947 she married the Canadian tenor Leopold Simoneau, with whom she was engaged by the Opéra-Comique. She sang thereafter in the most important French and Italian opera houses, including

La Scala, and made guest appearances at the Vienna State Opera. She was widely celebrated as a Mozart singer at the Aix-en-Provence Festivals. In 1954 she made a long concert tour in America with her husband. With her technically outstanding and thoroughly trained coloratura voice, she has attained her best performances in the Italian and French repertories; she is also celebrated as an oratorio singer.

Records: Many discs for Philips, DGG, MMS, including recordings of *Les Pêcheurs des Perles* and *Orphée et Eurydice*. U.S. re-issue: Westminster, Epic.

ALBANESE, LICIA, soprano, b. July 22, 1913, Bari, Italy. She studied first at the Bari Conservatory and then with Giuseppina Baldassare-Tedeschi and made her debut in Bari (1934) (under the name Alicia Albanese) as Mimi in *La Bohème*. By 1935 she was already a much-admired singer at the Arena Festival and later at La Scala, where she was especially popular as a partner to Beniamino Gigli. After a successful career in Italy, she joined the Metropolitan Opera in 1940, making her debut as Butterfly. Here she had her greatest triumph in 1942 as Violetta in *La Traviata*. She was a member of the Metropolitan Opera for twenty years and made very successful guest appearances in both Europe and America. Her lyric soprano voice with its great musicality was especially suited to Puccini and Verdi roles.

Records: HMV (including *La Bohème* with Gigli); RCA Victor (including *La Bohème, La Traviata, Manon Lescaut,* and *Carmen*).

ALBANI, EMMA, soprano, b. Nov. 1, 1847, Chambly, near Montreal; d. Apr. 3, 1930, Kensington, England. Originally Marie Louise Cecilie Emma Lajeunesse. She sang operatic airs at a concert when she was eight years old, accompanying herself at the piano. When she was fourteen, her parents moved to Albany, New York. There she sang solos in St. Joseph's church and was also choir leader and organist. The bishop of the diocese advised her to study singing in Europe and she became a pupil of Gilbert Louis Duprez in Paris and later of Lamperti in Milan. She made her debut in Messina (1870) as Amina in *La Sonnambula*. After guest appearances in Florence and Malta, she had a sensational success in 1872 at Covent Garden as Amina. She sang at the Italian Opera in Paris (1872-73) and was admired at the Imperial Operas in St. Petersburg and Moscow (1874). In October of that year she sang at the Academy of Music in New York. In 1878 she married the impresario Ernest Gye and took up residence in London. She was very successful for many years at Covent Garden, but was especially noted as a concert singer. She created for London both Elisabeth in *Tannhäuser* and Elsa in *Lohengrin*. She was a favorite singer of Queen Victoria. She sang at the Metropolitan Opera (1891-92). In 1896 she retired from the stage and in 1911 from the concert hall. She wrote *Memoirs of Emma Albani: Forty Years of Song* (London, 1911). Her voice was based completely on classical *bel canto* techniques. She joined great musicality and rich expressiveness with an uncommon mastery of technique.

Records: Four especially rare titles for G & T (London, 1904) and a few Pathé discs scarcely give a worthy impression of this singer's voice. U.S. re-issue: IRCC. U.S. re-recording: IRCC, HRS, Belcanto, Rococo.

ALBERS, HENRI, baritone, b. Feb. 1, 1866, Amsterdam, d. Sept. 12, 1925, Paris. Albers was first an actor; his voice was discovered by

De Groot, the director of the Netherlands Opera. After brief study he first appeared in Amsterdam (1889) as Mephistopheles in *Faust*. He came to Antwerp in 1891 but became famous through guest appearances in Le Havre, Bordeaux, Monte Carlo, and London. In 1898 he made an American tour with Jean de Reszke, Nellie Melba, and Emma Calvé. He was a member of the Metropolitan Opera (1898-99) and also appeared in New Orleans, San Francisco, and Mexico City. Engaged by the Opéra-Comique in 1899, he remained a member of that company until his death. After 1901 he appeared regularly at the Brussels Opera. In 1917 he sang at La Scala in the *premiére* there of *Les Cadeaux de Noël*. With his voluminous dark-timbred baritone voice, he was especially effective in the French repertory.

Records: G & T, Odeon, and complete performances of *Rigoletto*, *Roméo et Juliette*, and *Carmen* for Pathé. *U.S. re-recording:* IRCC, HRS.

ALBERTI, WERNER, tenor, b. Jan 21, 1860, Gnesen, Germany; d. Nov. 29, 1934, Berlin. Originally Werner Krzywonos, he worked first in a Berlin bank and then studied singing with Martin Röder. He made his debut as a concert singer in Berlin (1887), followed by a concert tour of Germany. In 1888 he joined the German Theater in Prague, then directed by Angelo Neumann, and made his operatic debut there as Manrico in *Il Trovatore*. While at Prague he appeared (1889) at the Vienna Imperial Opera and later at the Imperial Operas in St. Petersburg and Moscow. He made successful guest appearances in Genoa (1895) and was engaged at the National Opera in Budapest (1899-1902). Later he lived in Berlin and sang often at the Kroll Opera and the Theatre am Westens; at the latter, in 1899, he sang the title role in the first German performance of *Andrea Chénier*. He also pursued a regular concert career; in his later years he taught singing in Berlin. People marveled at the brilliant splendor of his voice, especially in the higher ranges.

Records: Berliner (Berlin, 1901), G & T (Budapest, 1901), Favorite (Berlin, 1907), Beka and Odeon (Berlin, 1905-06); also Edison cylinders.

ALCAÏDE, TOMAZ, tenor, b. Feb. 16, 1901, Estremoz, Portugal; d. Nov. 7, 1967, Lisbon. He originally attended the Military Academy in Lisbon, then studied at the University of Coimbra, and at the same time studied singing with Alberto Sarti and later with Francisco Coutinho and Eugenia Mantelli. After 1925 he became a pupil of Fernando Ferrara in Milan and made his debut there (1925) at the Teatro Carcana as the hero in *Mignon*. An important career in Italy followed; he sang at the Italian Opera in Holland (1928-29) and at the Teatro Reale (1929). In 1930 he came to La Scala and created a sensation in 1931 by his singing of the King's Son in *Königskinder*. He sang Ernesto in *Don Pasquale* at the 1931 Salzburg Festival. In that year he was admired in *La Traviata* with Claudia Muzio. He had great successes in Spain and Portugal in both opera and operetta. He moved to Paris and sang at the Brussels Opera (1937-38), appearing especially in the French repertory. His last stage appearance was in 1948 in São Paulo, Brazil, as Almaviva in *Il Barbiere di Siviglia*, at the close of a long concert tour of Europe and America. From 1949 until his death he held a leading position in the Portuguese radio network in

Lisbon. Beautiful, expressive, lyric tenor voice.
Records: Columbia*. *U.S. re-recording:* Rococo.

D'ALESSIO, AURORA, contralto, b. 1897, Valencia, Spain; d. July, 1965, Florence. She studied in Milan and made her debut in (1918) in Reggio Emilia. In 1921 she sang with outstanding success at the Teatro dal Verme, including a part in the world *première* of *L'Uomo Che Ride*. She then sang in many important Italian theaters, particularly the Teatro Regio in Parma. She appeared in 1926 at the Teatro Colón and in 1927 at Havana, and made other guest appearances in Madrid, Barcelona, Rio de Janeiro, and Montevideo. In 1933-34 she was admired at La Scala as Amneris in *Aida*, and in 1934 she sang Laura in *La Gioconda* at the Arena Festival. She was married to the Italian tenor Roberto d'Alessio. Her records were issued in Europe under the name Aurora Buades-d'Alessio.
Records: Columbia* (*Carmen* and *Falstaff* and duets with Roberto d'Alessio).

ALDA, FRANCES, soprano, b. May 31, 1883, Christchurch, New Zealand; d. May 21, 1952, Venice. She was a pupil of Mathilde Marchesi, and made her debut at the Opéra-Comique (1904) as the heroine in *Manon*. After great success in Italy and France she was invited to the Metropolitan Opera in 1908. Her first great success there was as Gilda in *Rigoletto*. In 1909 she married Giulio Gatti-Casazza (1869-1940), manager of the Metropolitan. She sang there in the world *premières* of *Madeleine* and *Cyrano de Bergerac*. A world-famous artist, she made guest appearances in London, Paris, Milan, Rome, at the Teatro Colón, and at the Chicago Opera. In 1929 she gave up her stage career but thereafter made concert appearances, especially on the American radio. After her husband left the Metropolitan in 1935, they lived in Italy much of the time. With her technically well-grounded, impressive soprano, Alda sang an extensive repertory, starring especially as Mimi (*La Bohème*), Madama Butterfly, Violetta (*La Traviata*), Gilda (*Rigoletto*), and Leonora (*Il Trovatore*). Her memoirs are entitled, *Men, Women and Tenors* (New York, 1937).
Records: Many Victor* discs, including some with Enrico Caruso. *U.S. re-issue:* HRS, IRCC. *U.S. re-recording:* RCA-Victor, Belcanto.

ALDENHOFF, BERND, tenor, b. Duisburg, Germany, June 14, 1908; d. Oct. 8, 1959, Munich. Brought up in an orphanage, he was able to become a member of the chorus of the Cologne Opera. He studied with Professor Lenz in Cologne and was engaged as a soloist there. He came by way of Darmstadt and Erfurt to the Düsseldorf Opera (1938-44) and the Dresden State Opera (1944-52). After World War II he became known as a Wagner singer and was successful as Siegfried at the Bayreuth Festivals (1951; 1952; 1957). After 1952 he was a regular member of the Munich State Opera, and made guest appearances in London, Paris, Zürich, and Milan. He sang at the Metropolitan Opera (1954-55).
Records: Oceanic and Urania* (*Salome*, *Der Freischütz*, and *Die Meistersinger*), *U.S. re-issue:* Vox.

ALFANI-TELLINI, INES (*see* Tellini, Ines Alfani-)

ALPAR, GITTA, soprano, b. March 5, 1903, Budapest, where her father was a cantor in a synagogue. Her voice teacher was Laura Hilgermann in Budapest. She began her stage career at the Budapest Opera (1923) and made guest appearances at the Munich State Opera (1925) and the Vienna State Opera (1927).

In 1927 she came to the Berlin State Opera, where she was successful as the Queen of the Night in *Die Zauberflöte* and Rosina in *Il Barbiere de Siviglia*. In 1930 she had a sensational success at the Metropol Theater in Berlin in *Der Bettelstudent*, whereupon she turned entirely to operetta. She was the reigning diva of the brilliant operetta *premières* in Berlin during the following years. She created (1931), in Berlin, the title role in the *première* of Mackaben's version of *Die Dubarry*. As a Jewess she was forced to leave Germany in 1933. She went first to Vienna and then to the United States (1936), where she appeared as an operetta singer and, just as formerly in Germany, became a beloved film star. She lives in California. She was married first to the Danish dancer Niels Bagge, then to the film star Gustav Frölich, but he later was separated from her.

Records: Homochord, Parlophone, American Columbia*. *U.S. re-issue:* American Decca. *U.S. re-recording:* Scala, Eterna.

ALSEN, ELSA, soprano, b. Apr. 7, 1880, Obra, Germany. Her father was Norwegian and her mother French. At the age of seventeen she went to Breslau, where she began her vocal studies under Jetke Finkenstein. She made her concert debut as a contralto (1900) and her stage debut (1902) in Heidelberg as Azucena in *Il Trovatore*. She sang in Freiburg i. Br. (1903-05) and then in Krefeld, Nuremberg, and Chemnitz. In 1912 she was engaged as a dramatic soprano at the Royal Theater in Braunschweig. Later she sang at the German Opera House in Berlin and as a guest on the leading German stages. She toured North America (1923-24) with the German Opera Company and in the latter year made guest appearances at the Vienna State Opera. From 1925 to 1928 she was an honored member of the Chicago Opera; thereafter she remained in the United States and sang in opera in Philadelphia, San Francisco, and Hollywood. In 1937 she sang Isolde in Detroit. In 1930 she worked in the American film *The Rogue Song*. She lives and teaches in New York. She was especially admired as a Wagner interpreter.

Records: Acoustic operatic discs for Odeon-Parlophone; electric lieder records for American Columbia* (1928). *U.S. re-issue:* Okeh

ALSEN, HERBERT, bass, b. Oct. 12, 1906, Hildesheim, Germany. He first studied the violin, then voice, at the Berlin Music High School, and at the same time studied dramatics at the University of Berlin. He made his debut (1929) in Hagen, Westphalia. He sang in Dessau (1930-31) and in Wiesbaden (1931-34). In 1935 he made guest appearances at the Vienna State Opera as Gurnemanz in *Parsifal* and then became a member of that company (1935-49). After 1936 he made appearances at the Salzburg Festival, and in 1937 at Glyndebourne; he also appeared as a guest at Covent Garden, the Paris Opéra, the Munich State Opera, and in Rome and Monte Carlo. He sang at the Metropolitan Opera (1938-39). He lives in Mörbisch, Austria, where he has founded an opera festival. He had a bass voice of unusual depth and musicality, and he was especially prized in the Wagner repertory.

Records: He made only a few records; he sang small parts in a complete *Salome* for Philips and Rocco in *Fidelio* for Oceanic. *U.S. re-issue:* Vox, Richmond.

ALTEN, BELLA, soprano, b. June 30, 1877, Zaxaczewc, Poland; d. Dec. 31, 1962, London. Trained by Gustav Engel in Berlin and by Aglaia von Orgeni in Dresden, she made her debut (1897) at the Leipzig Opera as Ännchen in *Der Freischütz* and sang there for the next three years. She then appeared at the Braunschweig Royal Theater (1900-03), the Cologne Opera (1903-04), and at the Berlin National Theater, (1904-05). She sang at the Metropolitan Opera (1905-13), making her debut as Gretel in the New York première of *Hänsel und Gretel*, and singing (1905) the role of Adele in the first performance at the Metropolitan Opera of *Die Fledermaus*. Guest tours in both Europe and America brought her great success, and she sang at the Bayreuth Festivals (1908; 1909). She completed her career at the Vienna State Opera (1917-23), and taught singing in Vienna until 1936, when she moved to London. She had a coloratura soprano voice of floating lightness and great virtuosity.

Records: A few rare records of her voice were made for HMV (Hamburg, 1908-09). *U.S. re-issue:* Opera Disc.

ALTGLASS, MAX, tenor, b. Feb. 16, 1890, Warsaw; d. Feb. 13, 1952, New York. He studied in Berlin and made his debut (1913) at the Opera House in Frankfurt a. M. He later sang at the Berlin Imperial Opera and the German Theater in Prague. He was engaged at the Metropolitan Opera in 1924 and sang secondary roles there until 1940. He was an important teacher of singing.

Records: Odeon (acoustic) and small parts on private recordings for the Metropolitan Opera.

ALTHOUSE, PAUL, tenor, b. Dec. 2, 1889, Reading, Pa.; d. Feb. 6, 1954, New York. His teachers in New York were Perley Dunn Aldrich and Percy Rector Stevens, as well as Oscar Saenger. He made his debut at the Metropolitan Opera (1913) as Dmitri in the first American production of *Boris Godounov*, and he remained a member of that company until 1921; there he sang in the first performances of, among others, *Mme. Sans-Gêne* (1915), *The Canterbury Pilgrims* (1917), and *Shanewis* (1918). He appeared as Faust in San Francisco (1925) and sang as guest star in Berlin, Stuttgart, and Stockholm (1929). A visit to the Bayreuth Festival led him to become interested in Wagner roles. He sang Tannhäuser and then Siegmund in 1930 at the Chicago Opera and Tristan at the 1935 Salzburg Festival. From 1934-41 he was again at the Metropolitan Opera, appearing during this time particularly as a Wagner tenor. During these years he also had an important career as an oratorio singer In 1941 he bade farewell to the stage and became one of America's most important voice teachers, numbering among his pupils Richard Tucker, Eleanor Steber, and Irene Dalis.

Records: Edison cylinders* and discs* and Victor* discs, including an electric recording of Schoenberg's *Gurrelieder* under Stokowski (1933); he also made private recordings for the Metropolitan Opera. *U.S. re-recording:* TAP.

ALVA, LUIGI, tenor, b. April 10, 1927, Lima, Peru. He studied with Rosa Mercedes in Lima and made his concert debut there (1949). He made his stage debut there also (1952) as Alfredo in *La Traviata*. He then pursued his vocal studies in Italy and sang there for the first time in 1954 at the Teatro Nuovo. In 1956 he had great success at La Scala and since that time has appeared there frequently. He sang Fenton in *Falstaff* at the Salzburg Festivals (1957-58) and made guest appearances at the Aix-en-Provence Festival (1960). In addition to guest appearances at the Vienna State Opera (1961), he has also appeared very successfully as guest at other major opera houses in Europe and in North and South America. He made his debut at the Metropolitan Opera in the 1963-64 season and has appeared there since. A beautifully trained, clear, lyric tenor voice.

Records: Columbia (*Il Barbiere di Siviglia, Falstaff,* and *Il Matrimonio Segreto*). *U.S. re-issue:* Angel, London, Seraphim, RCA Victor.

ALVAREZ, ALBERT, tenor, b. 1860, Bordeaux; d. Feb. 1, 1933, Nice. Originally Albert Gourron. First the leader of a military band, he began his vocal studies with Martini in Paris (1883), and he made his debut at the Ghent Opera House (1886). He then sang in Lyons and Marseilles before going to the Paris Opéra in 1892. In 1894 he sang the role of Nicias in the world *première* of *Thaïs,* and in 1897 that of Walther in the French *première* of *Die Meistersinger.* He made guest appearances nearly every year at Covent Garden and in 1894 sang in the world *première* of *La Navarraise* there. He sang at the Metropolitan Opera (1899-1903), making his debut as Roméo in *Roméo et Juliette.* After 1903 he returned to the Paris Opéra and later became a teacher in Paris.

Records: Pathé discs and Mapleson cylinders. *U.S. re-recording:* IRCC.

D'ALVAREZ, MARGUERITE, contralto, b. 1886, Liverpool, of Peruvian parents; d. Oct 18, 1953, Alassio, Italy. She studied at the Conservatory in Brussels and made her debut as Dalila in *Samson et Dalila* in Rouen (1904). In 1909 she came to the Manhattan Opera, where she first sang Fidès in *Le Prophète.* She was successful in London (1911) and in 1914 was particularly admired at Covent Garden as Amneris in *Aïda.* She sang with the Boston Opera (1913) and in 1920 sang Dalila at the Chicago Opera. Later she made concert tours, particularly in the United States. She published her memoirs under the title *Forsaken Altars* (London, 1953). She had a dark-timbred contralto voice of exotic tonal color.

Records: Vocalion*, HMV, and Victor*.

AMARA, LUCINE, soprano, b. Mar. 1, 1927, Hartford, Conn. Originally Lucy Armaganian. She is of Armenian extraction. She first studied the violin, then voice with Stella Eisner-Eyn in San Francisco, and sang in the chorus of the San Francisco Opera (1945-46). In 1947 she was auditioned by the Metropolitan Opera, but was not engaged as a soloist. She made her official debut (1947) in the San Francisco Marine Memorial Auditorium. In 1949 she obtained a scholarship at the University of Southern California and in the same year sang in a concert with the San Francisco Symphony Orchestra under Pierre Monteux. In 1950 she made her Metropolitan debut as the Celestial Voice in *Don Carlos.* At first she sang only small roles there, appearing, for example, seventy-seven times in the 1950-51 season. In 1952-53 she had a sensational success as Nedda in *I Pagliacci* and was thereafter granted more important roles. After first appearing there in 1954, she sang the title role in *Ariadne auf Naxos* in 1957 at the Glyndebourne Festival. In 1955 she made guest appearances in Stockholm and in 1960 at the Vienna State Opera as Aïda and Nedda. In 1961 guest appearances at the Stuttgart State Opera closed a concert tour through Germany. In 1962 she was admired at the Metropolitan as Eurydice in *Orphée et Eurydice.*

Records: American Columbia* (*I Pagliacci*) and RCA Victor*. *U.S. re-issue:* Angel, Cambridge, Seraphim.

AMATO, PASQUALE, baritone, b. Mar. 21, 1878, Naples; d. Aug. 13, 1942, New York. He studied singing at the Conservatory of San Pietro a Majella in Naples and made his debut (1900) at the Teatro Bellini there as Lescaut in *Manon Lescaut*. In 1902 he had a great triumph at the Teatro dal Verme and sang at the Genoa Opera; in 1903 he made appearances at Monte Carlo, Nuremburg, Leipzig, and Odessa. The next year the young baritone was well received at the Teatro Costanzi, the Teatro Massimo, and Covent Garden. He reached La Scala in 1907 and sang Golaud in the *première* there of *Pelléas et Mélisande*. From 1908-21 he was an honored member of the Metropolitan Opera (debut as the elder Germont in *La Traviata*), where he was esteemed as a partner to Enrico Caruso. Amato sang the role of Jack Rance there in the world *première* (Dec. 10, 1910) of *La Fanciulla del West*, with Caruso and Emmy Destinn. Other world *premières* in which he sang there were *Cyrano de Bergerac* (1913) and *Mme. Sans-Gêne* (1915). Guest appearances brought him triumphs in both London and Milan, but especially in Buenos Aires, Santiago de Chile, and other South American opera houses. He sang with the Pennsylvania Opera Company (1929), the American San Carlo Company (1932), and also in that year took part in a concert at the Metropolitan Opera. Thereafter he taught singing in New York. The possessor of one of the finest baritone voices of his time, he was deemed outstanding for the beautiful sonority of his voice, for the clarity of his diction, and for his use of shading.

Records: A great many records, both acoustical and electrical, issued by Fonotipia, Victor*, Columbia*, and Homochord. *U.S. re-issue:* Columbia-Fonotipia, Okeh, HRS. *U.S. re-recording:* Belcanto. Eterna, Scala, TAP, RCA Victor, Cantilena.

ANCONA, MARIO, baritone, b. Feb. 28, 1860, Leghorn, Italy; d. Feb. 23, 1931, Florence. After first starting in business, he studied singing with Matteini in Leghorn and with Giuseppe Cima in Milan. In 1890 he made his debut as Scindia in *Le Roi de Lahore* in Trieste and sang a few times at La Scala. On May 21, 1892, he sang the role of Silvio in the world *première* of *I Pagliacci* at the Teatro dal Verme. He appeared as a guest at the Olympic Theater in London (1892) and in 1893 sang the role of Tonio in *I Pagliacci* with great success at Covent Garden in the English *première* with Nellie Melba and Fernando de Lucia. From 1893-97 he sang at the Metropolitan Opera, where in 1893 he again created the role of Tonio. He was greatly admired at Covent Garden and after 1901 he sang there annually. Around the turn of the century he was particularly occupied in singing both in Italy and in South America. He sang at the Manhattan Opera (1906-08) and at the Boston Opera (1913-14), as well as with the Chicago Opera a few times in 1916. He later lived in Florence as a vocal teacher. He had an outstanding voice, especially in the higher register; he made almost the entire Italian repertory his specialty, as well as a few Wagner roles, which he mastered in German.

Records: G & T (London and Milan, 1904), Victor*, Pathé*, and Edison cylinders*. *U.S. re-issue:* RCA Victor, HRS, IRCC. *U.S. re-recording:* Belcanto, Rococo, TAP, CRS, FRP, RCA Victor, Cantilena.

ANDAY, ROSETTE, contralto, b. Dec. 22, 1903, Budapest. After philological studies at the University of

Budapest, followed by violin study under Eugen Hubay, she finally began her singing career. A pupil of Mme. Charles Cahier, Georg Anthes, and Gino Tessari, she made her debut at the Budapest National Opera (1920). Following a guest appearance as Carmen at the Vienna State Opera in 1921, she became a member of that company and remained there until 1961. She had great successes in Vienna and at the Salzburg Festivals, where she sang Orphée, Dorabella in *Così fan tutte*, Fatima in *Oberon*, and Clytemnestra in *Elektra*. In 1947 at Salzburg she appeared in the world *première* of *Dantons Tod*. She also sang as a guest in Milan, London, Munich, Budapest, and Berlin and toured both North and South America and Africa. She made her last stage appearance in 1961 as Clytemnestra at the Vienna State Opera. She had a very impressive contralto voice of an amplitude to master both the opera and concert repertory.

Records Acoustics for Vox (1924); electric for Polydor, HMV, Remington*, and Amadeo (complete *Der Bettelstudent*). She also appeared on Hungarian labels. *U.S. re-issue:* London, Vanguard.

ANDERS, PETER, tenor, b. July 1, 1908, Essen, Germany; d. Sept. 10, 1954, Hamburg. He began as an accountant, but abandoned this career to begin vocal studies under Grenzebach at the Berlin High School of Music; he finally studied with Lula Mysz-Gmeiner, whose daughter he married. He made his debut in Heidelberg (1932), sang in Darmstadt (1933-34), at the Cologne Opera (1935-36), Hannover Opera (1937-38), Munich State Opera (1938-40), and Berlin State Opera (1940-48). After World War II he became one of the best-known German singers, and made very successful guest appearances in Hamburg and Düsseldorf, at the Vienna and Stuttgart State Operas, and at the Berlin City Opera. He sang Tamino in 1943 at the Salzburg Festival and Walther in *Die Meistersinger* at Covent Garden during the Festival of Britain in 1952. He later made guest appearances in Amsterdam, The Hague, and Brussels. He had a radiant, flexible tenor voice, which developed from the lyric repertory to a later mastery of heavier roles, such as Max (*Der Freischütz*), Florestan (*Fidelio*), and Walther (*Die Meistersinger*).

Records: After first singing for Telefunken, he made many records for DGG (including *Martha*). *U.S. re-issue:* Capitol-Telefunken. *U.S. re-recording:* Eterna, Scala, TAP, Fiesta.

ANDERSON, MARIAN, contralto, b. Feb. 17, 1902, Philadelphia. Her voice was first noticed in a church choir, but she had to overcome great difficulties to obtain vocal training. She gave her first concerts in 1928, but it was then very difficult for a Negro to succeed in the United States. A European tour in 1930 brought her great success and thereafter she was honored in both Europe and in America. In 1935 she sang for the first time under Toscanini, who marveled at her voice. In the same year she gave successful concerts in connection with the Salzburg Festival. Concert tours followed in France, England, Germany, Austria, the Scandinavian countries, and Australia. In 1939 she wished to give a recital in Washington's Constitution Hall but was denied its use by the owners, the Daughters of the American Revolution. Miss Anderson then gave an open-air concert at the Lincoln Memorial for 75,000 people; the wife of the President, Mrs. Eleanor Roosevelt, resigned from the D.A.R. Miss Anderson developed a warm friendship with President Roosevelt and his family. In 1938 she was granted an honorary doctorate by Howard University. On Jan. 5, 1955, she sang in one performance of unforgettable splendor as Ulrica in *Un Ballo in Maschera* at the Metropolitan Opera, the first Negro to sing there. She was named in 1957 by the United States government as a delegate to the United Nations. In 1945 she sang for General Eisenhower at a reception following the end of World War II; she also sang at the inaugural balls for Presidents Eisenhower (1957) and Kennedy (1961). She closed her career with a worldwide tour in 1965 and now lives on her estate in Connecticut. She had a masterfully trained contralto voice of velvety timbre and great effectiveness. Above all she was effective as an oratorio and lieder singer in Bach, Handel, Sibelius, Mahler, and Negro spirituals.

Records: Her first records appeared before 1930 on RCA Victor*, then on Arlington* (1930). She made many RCA Victor and HMV discs. *U.S. re-recording:* TAP, Halo.

D'ANDRADE, FRANCISCO, baritone, b. Jan. 11, 1859, Lisbon; d. Feb. 8, 1921, Berlin. He first studied law, but after 1881 studied singing with Ronconi in Milan. In 1882 he made his stage debut in San Remo as Amonasro in *Aida*. In the following years he had great success in Italy, Spain, and Portugal, including appearances at La Scala and the Teatro Costanzi. His guest appearances at Covent Garden began in 1886, where he was always much admired. In 1889 he came to Berlin with an opera troupe of the impresario Gardini, the husband of the soprano Etelka Gerster. He was so successful there that he later made Berlin his residence, traveling from there to his guest appearances in the other music centers of Germany, Holland, Australia, Russia, England, and Scandinavia. He was considered to be unmatched in the role of Don Giovanni, and his fascinating characterization of the Don caused his friend, the painter Max Slevogt, to paint many famous portraits of him in the part. He sang this role at the Salzburg Festival in 1901. He appeared on the stage until 1919, at the last only as Don Giovanni.

Records: In 1906 ten titles were recorded by him for Lyrophone; one of these, the Champagne Aria from *Don Giovanni*, later appeared on Parlophone. *U.S. re-recording:* Rococo, Eterna, TAP.

ANDRESEN, IVAR, bass, b. July 27, 1896, Oslo; d. Nov. 24, 1940, Stockholm. He studied in Stockholm with Gillis W. Bratt and made his debut at the Royal Opera House there (1919) as the Landgrave in *Tannhäuser*. He sang at Stockholm (1919-24) and at the Dresden State Opera (1925-34). He had a very successful career in Germany, especially as a Wagner singer. He sang at the Bayreuth Festivals (1927-36). After 1931 he was under joint contract to the Dresden Opera and to the Berlin City Opera. He was a member of the Berlin State Opera (1934-36). He made guest appearances at Covent Garden, the Teatro Liceo, and in Vienna, Hamburg, and Munich; he was very successful at the Metropolitan Opera in 1930. One of the most beautiful bass voices preserved on records, equally noted as a Wagner singer and for his performance of *buffo* roles.

Records: Acoustic Polyphone records which appeared only in Sweden. Electric records for Odeon, Parlophone, HMV, and Columbia* (including *Tristan und Isolde*, Bayreuth, 1928 and *Tannhäuser*, Bayreuth, 1930). *U.S. re-issue:* Victor, American Decca.

ANGELES, VICTORIA DE LOS, soprano, b. Nov. 1, 1923, Barcelona. Originally Victoria Gómez Cima. She completed the course of study at the Barcelona Conservatory. She made her concert debut there (1944) and her stage debut (1946) at the Teatro Liceo as the Countess in *Le Nozze di Figaro*. In 1947 she won a first prize at an international singing contest in Geneva. In 1948 she sang in *La Vida Breve* on the London radio. She was highly successful in 1949 as Marguerite in *Faust* at the Paris Opéra and was applauded in 1950 at Covent Garden as Mimi in *La Bohème* and in the same year at La Scala in *Ariadne auf Naxos*. After a triumphant South American tour she was engaged at the Metropolitan Opera in 1951, making her debut in *Faust*. Since then she has had a worldwide career with her chief centers of activity at the Metropolitan, La Scala, Covent Garden, and Paris. She has made tours through Australia, New Zealand, the Scandinavian countries, Germany and both North and South America. In 1957 she had a brilliant guest season at the Vienna State Opera and in 1961-62 sang Elisabeth in *Tannhäuser* at the Bayreuth Festivals. Possessing one of the most beautiful soprano voices of her epoch, she is equally noted for the timbre of her voice and for the mature musicality of her conceptions. Her wide-ranging repertory includes roles in operas by Verdi, Puccini, Wagner, Mozart, Massenet, and Bizet, and she has even mastered the technically demanding coloratura-contralto parts in Rossini's operas. She is a superb interpreter of Spanish songs.

Records: A great many records for HMV, Capitol*, and RCA Victor* (including *Faust* [twice], *Carmen*, *Madama Butterfly* [twice], *La Vida Breve* [twice], *La Bohème*, *Il Barbiere di Siviglia*, *Manon*, *I Pagliacci*, *Simon Boccanegra*, *La Traviata*, and *Suor Angelica*). *U.S. re-issue:* Angel. *U.S. re-recording:* Seraphim.

ANGELICI, MARTA, soprano, b. 1916, Cargèse, Corsica. She studied at the National Conservatory in Paris and made her stage debut there (1928) at the Opéra-Comique, singing a small part in *Louise*. Thereafter she had a successful career for over twenty years at that house and at the Paris Opéra. She sang as guest in Monte Carlo, at La Scala, and in Rio de Janeiro. A much-admired concert soprano, especially in the interpretation of baroque music.

Records: Sang before World War II for L'Anthologie Sonore; later made many records for Pathé, Lumen, Columbia* (*Les Pêcheurs des Perles*, *Carmen*), and HMV (*Faust*). *U.S. re-issue:* U.S. Decca, Angel.

ANGELIS, NAZZARENO DE, bass, b. Nov. 17, 1881, Aquila, Italy; d. Dec. 14, 1962, Rome. He studied at the Accademia di Santa Cecilia in Rome and made his debut (1903) in Aquila. He quickly established himself on the larger opera stages of Italy and had great success at La Scala; there on Apr. 10, 1913, in the world *première* of *L'Amore di Tre Rè* he sang the role of King Archibaldo, which became one of his great starring roles. In 1908 he made guest appearances in Holland and sang at the Manhattan Opera (1909-10). He won acclaim at the Arena Festivals (1920; 1925; 1931). He was greatly liked in South America and for many years appeared at the Teatro Colón. He made guest appearances all over Europe, but La Scala remained his real artistic home, so to speak, and he sang there regularly until 1933.

He gave concerts until 1940. After that he taught in Milan and in Rome and passed the last years of his life in his birthplace, Aquila. He had an expressive dark bass voice with which he attained complete mastery of the technique of singing; he sang almost all the important bass roles in the Italian repertory.

Records: He made a great many records, the oldest for Fonotipia (1907-08); later he made both acoustic and electric records for Odeon and Columbia* (including *Mefistofele*). *U.S. re-recording:* Eterna, TAP, Rococo.

D'ANGELO, GIANNA, soprano, b. 1928, Hartford, Conn., to which her Italian parents had emigrated. She studied first with Dolores Wilson in New York and then with Toti dal Monte in Venice and made a highly successful debut (1954) at the Rome Opera. In 1955 she appeared at the Glyndebourne Festival and in 1956 at the Brussels Opera as Gilda in *Rigoletto*. She then sang at many of the large Italian opera houses, including La Scala, and in 1959 at the Baths of Caracalla. She appeared in Paris and London and was successful in the United States; since 1961 she has been heard at the Metropolitan Opera. Her coloratura voice joins both a brilliant technique and a delicate feeling for vocal style.

Records: Arias for Philips, which include selections from the complete operas she has recorded for this company; also the complete opera *Rigoletto* for Philips. She has sung Musetta in a complete *La Bohème* for Decca and Rosina in a complete *Il Barbiere di Siviglia* for DDG*, *U.S. re-issue:* Columbia, Angel, London.

ANGERER, MARGIT, soprano, b. Nov. 6 1903, Budapest. Originally Margit von Rupp. She studied at the Fodor Conservatory and at the Music Academy in Budapest. Soon after her debut in Budapest, she was brought (1926) to the Vienna State Opera, where she sang with great success until 1938. From 1931-35 she was admired as Octavian in *Der Rosenkavalier* at the Salzburg Festivals. In 1933 she also sang Aithra in *Die Ägyptische Helena* there. While at Vienna she undertook many successful guest tours and concert trips. Since 1938 she has lived in London, where she has been particularly active as a concert singer. She has also sung under the name Angerer-Schenker.

Records: Polydor; among the most interesting are her duets with Alfred Piccaver. *U.S. re-recording:* Eterna.

ANITUA, FANNY, contralto, b. Jan. 22, 1887, Durango, Mexico. She studied in Italy, where she made her debut (1909) as Orpheus in Gluck's opera. By 1910 she was already singing at La Scala in Milan. In 1911 she sang small roles at the Teatro Colón but soon became a leading singer. She made guest appearances at the Teatro Massimo (1912) and toured the United States with the Western Metropolitan Opera Company (1913). In 1915 she was again at La Scala. In 1916 at the Teatro Regio in Parma she was the first contralto since Guerrina Fabbri to attempt the part of Rosina in *Il Barbiere di Siviglia*; this was long before Conchita Supervia revived *bel canto* coloratura parts for contraltos. She had great success (1917-19) at both the Teatro Colón and the Rio de Janeiro Opera. Sang in 1921 at the Teatro Costanzi. She was applauded at La Scala (1925-27) in performances directed by Toscanini. She also sang regularly in Mexico City. In 1934 she made a few guest appearances in Turin and sang on the Italian radio; in 1937 she appeared at the Teatro Colón as Dame

Quickly in *Falstaff*. She lives in Mexico City, where she teaches.
Records: Columbia* and Pathé.

ANSELMI, GIUSEPPE, tenor, b. Nov. 12, 1876, Catania, Sicily; d. May 29, 1929, near Rapallo, Italy. First studied violin and appeared as a concert violinist, but later he changed to singing. He made his debut (1896) at the Athens Royal Opera. After a brief career in the larger Italian opera houses, he had a very successful guest season at Covent Garden (1901), followed by guest appearances and concerts in Paris, Vienna, and Berlin. After 1906 he sang almost every season at the Imperial Operas in St. Petersburg and Moscow, where he was especially admired. He had real triumphs in his appearances at the Teatro Real and the Teatro Liceo. Later he appeared regularly in performances at La Scala. He sang at the Teatro Colón (1910-13) and in 1916 made a few appearances again at La Scala. In 1917 he gave up his career and lived on his estate near Rapallo until his death. He was buried in the cathedral at Catania, but, according to his wish, his heart is buried at the Madrid Conservatory. One of the most beautiful tenor voices of his time; he had complete mastery of technique and of the subtle nuances of shading. His best performances were in the classical *bel canto* parts, but he was also a great interpreter of Verdi and Puccini.
Records: Many records for Fonotipia (Milan, 1907-09) and Edison Diamond discs*. *U.S. re-issue:* Columbia, Columbia-Fonotipia, HRS, IRCC. *U.S. re-recording:* Belcanto, Scala, Eterna, TAP.

ANSSEAU, FERNAND, tenor, b. Mar. 6, 1890, Bussu-Bois, near Mons, Belgium. He studied with Demest in Brussels and made his stage debut (1913) at Dijon as Jean in *Hérodiade*. During World War I he objected to entertainments and confined his activity to charity concerts, which made him very popular. In 1918 he again took up his career at the Brussels Opera. He had great success in 1919 at Covent Garden and in 1920 at the Opéra-Comique. He sang at the Paris Opéra (1922), the Chicago Opera (1923-28), and in San Francisco (1925). Guest appearances in Monte Carlo, London, and Paris mark the later stages of his career. He was again at the Brussels Opera (1930-39). He voiced his objections to the occupation of Belgium by the German Army in 1940 by retiring officially. He taught at the Brussels Conservatory (1942-44) and thereafter lived in Brussels in complete retirement. A richly varied, beautiful tenor voice; he showed it to great advantage in the French repertory and, above all, in Puccini roles.
Records: He is heard exclusively on HMV records, both acoustic and electric. *U.S. re-issue:* Victor. *U.S. re-recording:* Scala, TAP, Rococo.

ANTHES, GEORG, tenor, b. Mar. 12, 1863, Bad Homburg, Germany; d. Feb. 23, 1923, Budapest. His father was the conductor of the orchestra in Bad Homburg. He studied first with Julius Stockhausen in Frankfurt a. M. After he had given a few concerts, he resumed his studies with Cesare Galiera in Milan and made his debut (1888) in Freiburg a. Br. as Max in *Der Freischütz*. At the Dresden Royal Opera (1889) his guest appearances were so successful that he was engaged as a successor to Heinrich Gudehus as principal heroic tenor. He remained at Dresden until 1902 and became one of the leading German Wagner tenors. He sang Walther in *Die Meistersinger* at the Bayreuth Festival (1892). In 1902 he went to the Metropolitan Opera for a season and thereby broke his Dresden contract. He sang at the Budapest Opera (1903-13), with guest appearances during this time at Covent Garden. He again appeared at the Metropolitan Opera (1908-09). After 1913 he was a professor at the Budapest Conservatory and after 1920 first *régisseur* of the Budapest Opera.

Records: His voice is preserved only on Mapleson cylinders. *U.S. re-recording:* IRCC.

APPELS, HENDRIK, tenor, b. 1886, Amsterdam; d. Sept. 22, 1947, Berlin. He was brought up in the Municipal Orphanage of Amsterdam, studied dentistry, and practiced as a dentist. He studied singing in Berlin and made his debut there (1925) at the Komische Oper. Also in 1925 he was engaged at the Bavarian State Opera in Munich and remained there until 1928. He made very successful guest appearances, particularly at the Vienna State Opera, in Amsterdam, and in The Hague. He sang in Kiel (1932-35), Dortmund (1935-39), and Neustrelitz (1939-44). He lived thereafter as a teacher in Berlin. He had a heroic tenor voice and was especially noted in Wagner roles.

Records: Acoustic records for Vox and electric records for Tri-Ergon.

ARANGI-LOMBARDI, GIANNINA, contralto-soprano, b. 1890, Marigliano, near Naples; d. July 9, 1951, Milan. She first studied piano at the Conservatory of San Pietro a Majella in Naples and then studied voice there with Beniamino Carelli. She made her debut as a contralto (1920) at the Teatro Costanzi, in the part of Lola in *Cavalleria Rusticana*, and sang for three years as a contralto without special success. After renewed study with Adelina Stehle in Milan, she made her debut as a soprano in 1923 and was quickly successful on the larger Italian stages. After 1926 she sang frequently at La Scala, and appeared as a guest with that company (1929) in Berlin, singing Leonora in *Il Trovatore*. She also sang in Rio de Janeiro, Genoa, Florence, at the Teatro São Carlos, and at the Arena Festival. She made a tour of Australia. At the 1935 Salzburg Festival she sang Donna Anna in *Don Giovanni* under Bruno Walter. Her last stage appearance occurred in 1938. She taught singing thereafter, first in the Conservatory at Ankara, Turkey, and later in Milan. She had a voluminous, dark-timbred soprano voice.

Records: As a contralto, acoustic records on Fonografia Nazionale (in Germany on Artiphon); as a soprano, acoustic and electric records for Columbia* (including *Aida*, 1929; *La Gioconda*, 1930; *Mefistofele*, 1931). *U.S. re-recording:* Eterna.

ARANYI, DESIDER, tenor, b. Aug. 18, 1868, Szathmar-Nemthy, Hungary; d. June 21, 1923, Pesterzsebét, Hungary. He was trained as a singer by Bellovicz in Budapest. He made his debut (1890) in Brünn as Raoul in *Les Huguenots*. He remained at Brünn until 1892, then sang for a season at the Kroll Opera. After further study with Rossi in Milan, he sang at the Budapest National Opera (1893-1900). He made guest appearances at La Scala and in Genoa (1894). Sang at the Theater am Westens (1901-02) and took the role of Don Ottavio in *Don Giovanni* at the Salzburg Festival (1901). He was engaged at the German Opera in Prague (1902-07) and there, on Nov. 15, 1903, he created the role of Pedro in the world *première* of *Tiefland*. After 1907 he returned to the Budapest Opera and later taught singing in that city.

Records: Nine rare records for

G & T (Prague, 1904). *U.S. re-recording:* Rococo.

ARCHIPOVA, IRINA, contralto, b. 1929, Sverdlovsk, Russia. She studied at the Sverdlovsk Conservatory and made her debut there (1953). In 1955 she won an international singing contest in Warsaw. She was called to the Bolshoi Theater in Moscow in 1956. There she was brilliantly successful in such parts as Carmen, Marina in *Boris Godounov,* Amneris, and Princess Eboli in *Don Carlos.* She has had great success in guest appearances in New York, Berlin, Budapest, and Rome in both opera and in recital.
Records: Russian State Record Trust. *U.S. re-issue:* Angel-Melodiya.

ARIË, RAPHAEL, bass, b. Aug. 22, 1922, Sofia. While he was studying the violin, his voice was discovered by the baritone Cristo Brambarov. He made his concert debut in Sofia in Handel's *Messiah* (1939). He sang at the Sofia Opera (1945) and in 1946 won first prize in a singing competition in Geneva. He was under contract at La Scala in 1947 and, being very successful there, he has frequently returned to that house. He has sung at the Arena Festival, the Aix-en-Provence Festival, the Maggio Musicale and has made guest appearances at the leading opera houses in Germany, France, and North America. In 1951 he sang at Venice in the world *première* of *The Rake's Progress;* in 1960 and 1961 he sang the role of the Grand Inquisitor in *Don Carlos* at the Salzburg Festivals. His powerful bass voice is outstanding in the role of Boris Godounov; he is also admired in the Italian and contemporary repertories.
Records: Decca (*La Bohème*) and Columbia (including *Lucia di Lammermoor* with Maria Callas). *U.S. re-issue:* London, Richmond.

ARIMONDI, VITTORIO, bass, b. 1861, Saluzzo, Italy; d. Apr. 15, 1928, Chicago. He made his debut in 1883 at Varese, singing in *Il Guarany.* After ten years of appearances on the smaller Italian stages, he came to La Scala (1893) where he made his debut as Sparafucile in *Rigoletto.* There on Feb. 9, 1893, he sang the role of Pistol in the world *première* of *Falstaff.* He then appeared as guest at Covent Garden, to which he often returned until 1905. He sang at the Metropolitan Opera (1895-96) and followed this with guest appearances in Vienna, St. Petersburg, Moscow, and other opera houses in Russia and Poland. He returned to America to sing at the Manhattan Opera (1906-08) and there created the role of Arkel in the American *première* of *Pelléas et Mélisande.* In 1908 he sang at the Teatro Colón and in 1910 at the Teatro San Carlo, although he had rarely appeared in Italy for many years. He also appeared as a guest in Prague. He was a member of the Chicago Opera (1910-16) and after 1915 taught singing in that city. With his voluminous and extraordinarily well-trained voice he mastered a wide-ranging repertory, in which Verdi roles were most important, but which also included Wagner parts.
Records: A few records for G & T (Vienna, 1904), Nicole (London, 1904), and for American Columbia* (1907). *U.S. re-issue:* IRCC. *U.S. re-recording:* IRCC, Eterna, TAP.

ARKEL, TERESA, soprano, b. 1861, Lemberg, Austria; d. 1929, Milan. She studied at the Conservatory in Lemberg and made her debut there (1884). In the total course of her career she had her greatest successes in Italian opera houses and at the Teatro Real, where she sang in the world *première* of *Dona Juana la Loca.* She made her debut at La

Scala in 1891, singing Venus in *Tannhäuser* with Hariclea Darclée. In 1892 she sang Norma and Desdemona in *Otello* there. After 1896 she appeared principally on Spanish and South American stages, but also made guest appearances in Italy. She later lived in Milan and was an especially sought-after singing teacher there. Her pupils include Claire Dux, Lucette Korsoff, Eugenia Bronskaja, and Irene Eden.

Records: Rare records for G & T (Milan, 1903-05) and Fonotipia (Milan, 1905). *U.S. re-issue:* Victor.

D'ARKOR, ANDRÉ, tenor, b. 1901, Liége, Belgium. He studied in Liége and Brussels, and made his debut in the latter city (1924). He was then engaged by the Théâtre de la Monnaie and for the next twenty-five years was one of the most admired artists there. His guest appearances brought him great success, particularly at the Opéra-Comique. He was also a renowned concert singer. In 1950 he gave up his stage career and became the director of the opera house in Liége. He had one of the most beautiful lyric tenor voices of his time especially in the contemporary French repertory and was greatly admired for the brilliance of his high range.

Records: Many for Columbia*. *U.S. re-recording:* Eterna, Rococo.

ARMANINI, GIUSEPPE, tenor, b. May 14, 1874, Milan; d. May 15, 1915, Milan. He studied with Il Selma and Alberto Selva in Milan. He made his debut (1902) at Monza in *Linda di Chamounix* and then sang with the Castellano company during a European tour. He appeared later on Italian stages, made guest appearances in Lisbon, Moscow, and St. Petersburg, and traveled to South America. About 1910 he began his successful career in Italy under the patronage of Edoardo Garbin. His La Scala debut occurred (1911) in *Il Matrimonio Segreto* and in the same year he sang the role of the King's Son in the *première* there of *Königskinder*. He was also outstanding as Fenton in *Falstaff*. (1912-13). He sang at the Teatro Massimo (1913) and made guest appearances at Covent Garden (1914). He died at the height of his career, one day after his forty-first birthday.

Records: Columbia* and Fonotipia.

ARMSTER, KARL, baritone, b. Dec. 4, 1882, Krefeld, Germany; d. July, 1943, Schloss Hebron-Damnitz. He made his debut in Essen (1906) and sang at the Metropol Theater, Berlin (1907-08), the Komische Oper (1908-11), Elberfeld (1911-12), and at the Hamburg Opera (1912-17). At the Bayreuth Festival (1914) he sang Amfortas in *Parsifal* and Gunther in *Götterdämmerung*. He was a member of the Berlin State Opera (1917-25). In 1922 he married Baroness Ilse von Gamp-Massauen, and lived later at Schloss Hebron-Damnitz in Pomerania. After 1925 he made only occasional guest appearances.

Records: Acoustic records for Odeon (including Biterolf in *Tannhäuser*, 1908), Vox, Homochord, and HMV.

ARNDT-OBER, MARGARETHE (*see* Ober, Margarethe)

ARNOLDSON, SIGRID, soprano, b. Mar. 20, 1861, Stockholm; d. Feb. 2, 1943, Stockholm. Her father, Oskar Arnoldson (1830-81), was a lyric tenor at the Stockholm Opera. She studied in Paris with Maurice Strakosch, Mathilde Marchesi, and Desirée Artôt. She made her stage debut (1885) at the Prague Opera and in 1886 had a sensational success at the Moscow Imperial Opera as Rosina in *Il Barbiere di Siviglia*. In 1887 she sang at the Drury Lane Theater in London, where the critics labelled her as "the new Swed-

ish nightingale," successor to the unforgettable Jenny Lind. She made regular guest appearances at Covent Garden (1888-99) and sang at the Paris Opéra (1891-92) and again in 1902. She was also at the Metropolitan Opera (1893-94). World-wide guest appearances marked her later career. She was engaged at the Dresden Royal Opera (1907-09), and toward the end of her career she had great triumphs in Russia. In 1910 she was made a member of the Swedish Academy. She taught in Vienna (1922-38) and later in Stockholm. With a vocal range of three octaves, she possessed at the time the brilliance and technical command of a coloratura and the highly expressive quality of a lyric soprano, although she even sang such parts as Carmen.
Records: G & T (Berlin, 1906-07), HMV (Berlin, 1908-10), Edison cylinders. *U.S. re-issue:* IRCC. *U.S. re-recordings:* IRCC, Belcanto, TAP, FRP, Rococo.

ARRAL, BLANCHE, soprano, b. 1865, Liége, Belgium; d. 1945, New York. Originally Clara Lardinois. She studied with Mathilde Marchesi in Paris and made her debut there (1880) at the Opéra-Comique. At first she sang small roles, as, for example, a serving girl in the world *première* of *Manon* on Jan. 19, 1884. Later she began a roving career, with guest and concert appearances at the farthest ends of the earth, although she was never engaged by an opera house of the first rank. She undertook an extensive Russian tour, sang in the Balkan countries, in Egypt, in the Far East, and in South America. She signed a three-year contract with the Metropolitan Opera in 1902, but it was broken. She sang in opera in San Francisco in 1908. Later she lived in New York. Her records show a technically well-trained virtuoso coloratura of the most beautiful quality.
Records: Victor* (1909) and Edison cylinders*, all of great rarity. *U.S. re-issue:* IRCC, RCA Victor. *U.S. re-recordings:* IRCC, TAP, Odyssey.

ARTNER, JOSEPHINE VON, soprano, b. Nov. 10, 1867, Prague; d. Sept. 7, 1932, Leipzig. Originally Josephine von Artanyi, she first studied piano at the Conservatory of the City of Vienna, then sang with Johannes Ress there. She made her debut at the Leipzig Opera (1888) and remained there until 1890. She sang very successfully at the Vienna Imperial Opera (1890-93) and at the Hamburg Opera (1893-1908). She made guest appearances in Berlin, Dresden, London, and Vienna, and sang at the Beyreuth Festivals (1896-1906), particularly as the Forest Bird in *Siegfried*. She was also a famous oratorio singer. After 1910 she taught singing in Dresden, later in Leipzig.
Records: One disc for G & T (Bayreuth, 1904).

ARTÔT DE PADILLA, LOLA, soprano, b. Oct. 5, 1880 (?), Sèvres, near Paris; d. Apr. 12, 1933, Berlin. She was the daughter of the famous mezzo-soprano Desirée Artôt (1835-1907) and the Spanish baritone Mariano Padilla y Ramos (1842-1906). She studied with her mother and made her debut at the Opéra-Comique (1904). She was then engaged by the Komische Oper, where she remained until 1908. After a year-long tour of guest appearances in Europe, she became a member of the Berlin Imperial Opera (1909-27). Later she taught singing in Berlin. She had a highly expressive soprano voice with a sovereign mastery of technique and she was especially known as an interpreter of Mozart.
Records: Rather rare records for

HMV, Vox, and Odeon. *U.S. re-issue:* Victor.

AUSTRAL, FLORENCE, soprano, b. Apr. 26, 1894, Richmond, near Melbourne, Australia; d. May 15, 1968, Sydney. Originally Florence Wilson. She studied first at the Melbourne Conservatory, then in New York with Sibella, and finally at the Royal School of Music in London. The conductor Percy Pitt engaged her in 1922 for the British National Opera Company, and with them she made her debut (May, 1922) as Brünnhilde in *Die Walküre.* She then became the principal female Wagner singer at Covent Garden. In 1925 she made a concert tour throughout North America and in the same year married the flutist John Amadio. She made guest appearances in Berlin in 1930 which were highly successful, as were those in Hamburg, Philadelphia, and San Francisco. She made concert tours in England, North America, Holland, South Africa, and Australia. In 1934-35 she made an opera tour through Australia with an English ensemble. The focus of her career, however, remained at Covent Garden, where she appeared until 1940. She then taught singing at the Conservatory at Newcastle, near Sydney, Australia, where she lived, completely paralyzed. One of the most famous Wagner sopranos of her generation.

Records: HMV (acoustic and electric). *U.S. re-issue:* Victor. *U.S. re-recording:* RCA Victor.

AUTORI, FERNANDO, bass, b. 1884, near Palermo; d. Oct. 3, 1937, Florence. He first studied medicine, then wanted to be a painter, but finally began to study singing. He made his debut (1913) in Palermo as the King in *Isabeau,* but his first great success did not come until he sang there in 1916-19. After guest appearances at the Teatro dal Verme, he came to La Scala in 1924, making his debut as Basilio in *Il Barbiere di Siviglia.* He sang there until 1936, especially in *buffo* roles, and was greatly helped by Toscanini. In 1925 he sang in the world *première* of *I Cavalieri di Ekebù.* He appeared each season at Covent Garden (1927-34) and was greatly admired there. He made guest appearances at the Vienna State Opera and at the Salzburg Festivals (1931; 1935-37). In 1933 he sang at the Italian Opera in Holland, with further guest appearances in Copenhagen, Monte Carlo, Berlin, Oslo, The Hague, and Barcelona, and concert tours in Germany, Canada, and Australia. His masterful art of characterization and his lively acting established him in the classic *buffo* parts of the Italian repertory. He was one of the few Italian singers who excelled in the field of German operetta.

Records: A great many records—acoustics for Fonotechnica, Columbia*, and HMV (including *Faust,* 1917); electrics for Fonotipia, Parlophone, HMV, and for Durium (excerpts from *Casanova*).

B

BACCALONI, SALVATORE, bass, b. Apr. 14, 1900, Rome. He sang as a child in the Sistine Chapel Choir and then wanted to become an architect. During these studies he used his free time to study singing with Giuseppe Kaschmann, among others. He made his debut (1922) at the Teatro Adriano as Bartolo in *Il Barbiere di Siviglia*. He soon had a considerable success on the larger Italian stages, especially at La Scala. After 1930 he appeared as guest almost annually in South America, particularly at the Teatro Colón; he was also a frequent and welcome guest at Covent Garden. He sang in the world *premières* of many operas: *La Farsa Amorosa* (Rome, 1933), *La Vigna* (Rome, 1935), and *Il Filosofo di Campagna* (Venice, 1938). From 1936-39 he was admired both at the Glyndebourne and Salzburg Festivals for his Osmin in *Die Entführung aus dem Serail* and for his Bartolo in *Il Barbiere di Siviglia*. He was a member of the Metropolitan Opera (1940-47) and had great triumphs there. After the close of his stage career he was successful in comic film roles. Salvatore Baccaloni was the best Italian *basso-buffo* of his generation, equally celebrated for his talent for masterly vocal characterizations and for the excellent quality of his acting. He was especially admired in the title role in *Falstaff*.

Records: He made many records for Columbia*. These included complete operas (among others, *Don Giovanni* and *La Bohème*) in which he often took smaller roles; his later records were made for RCA Victor. *U.S. re-recordings:* Grand Award, TAP.

BACHMANN, HERMANN, baritone, b. Oct. 7, 1864, Kottbus, Germany; d. July 5, 1937, Berlin. At first a businessman, he made his debut (1890) at Halle, where he stayed until 1894. In 1896 he sang Wotan in the *Ring* cycle at the Bayreuth Festival. He sang at Nuremberg (1894-97) and was a member of the Berlin Imperial Opera (1897-1917). After 1910 he also worked there as a *régisseur*.

Records: G & T (Berlin, 1907) and HMV, for which he sang Escamillo in a complete *Carmen* (1908).

BADA, ANGELO, tenor, b. 1875, Novara, Italy; d. 1941, Novara. He made his debut in 1898 and had his first successes on Italian stages including, among others, La Scala. When Giulio Gatti-Casazza took over the direction of the Metropolitan Opera in 1908, he auditioned Bada among other Italian singers and engaged him for the American house. For thirty years, until 1938, he remained the first *comprimario* tenor there. He sang there in the world *premières* of *La Fanciulla del West* and *Gianni Schicchi* and in many others. He undertook guest performances in the larger Italian theaters and at Covent Garden (1928-29). In 1935 he sang Dr. Caius in *Falstaff* at the Salzburg Festival under Toscanini. He lived at the end of his life in his native city of Novara.

Records: Odeon (Milan, 1905) and Victor*.

BADINI, ERNESTO, baritone, b. 1876; d. July 6, 1937, Milan. At the turn of the century he had great success on the leading Italian stages, especially at La Scala and the Teatro Costanzi. He was much liked in South America, where he regularly appeared as a guest. He later made guest appearances at Covent Garden and sang the title role in the first performance there of *Gianni Schicchi* (1920); he also created the part at the La Scala *première* (1922). World *premières* in which he took part were *Il Piccolo Marat* at the Teatro Costanzi (1921) and *La Cena delle Beffe* at La Scala (1924). He also sang at the Arena Festival.

Records: He left countless records. His wide-ranging repertory, which included both *buffo* and serious parts, is almost all to be heard on records. Most of these appeared on the HMV label, but also on G & T, Columbia*, et cetera. He made records of arias and of complete operas, including *I Pagliacci* (1908), *La Bohème* (1918), and *Don Pasquale* (1933). *U.S. re-issue:* Victor.

BAHR-MILDENBURG, ANNA, soprano, b. Nov. 29, 1872, Vienna; d. Jan. 27, 1947, Vienna. She was the daughter of an Austrian soldier, Major von Bellshau-Mildenburg. Her voice was discovered by the writer Julius Rosen in Görz in 1891, and she studied with Rosa Papier-Paumgartner in Vienna. While still engaged in her vocal studies, she was noticed by the director of the Hamburg Opera, Bernhard Pollini, and was engaged by him; she made her debut in Hamburg (1895) in *Die Walküre*. She was soon noted as a great Wagner interpreter and was engaged for the 1897 Bayreuth Festival, where she sang Kundry in *Parsifal*. She sang at the Vienna Imperial Opera in 1898 under Mahler and experienced great triumphs there. She sang as guest at Covent Garden in 1906 and 1910 and was one of the principal singers at the Bayreuth Festivals (1909-14). In 1909 she married the writer Hermann Bahr. She remained an honored member of the Vienna Imperial Opera until 1917 and appeared there as guest until 1921. In this latter year she became a professor at the Academy of Musical Art in Munich and after 1922 was at the same time a *régisseur* at the Munich State Opera. In both 1923 and 1925 she appeared as an actress at the Salzburg Festivals in Calderón's play *El teatro del mundo*. Her autobiography, *Erinnerungen*, appeared in Vienna in 1921. One of the greatest dramatic sopranos of her time, especially in Wagner roles. She was noted for the beauty of her voice and the outstanding quality of her acting.

Records: One record of her voice exists, the Recitative and Ocean aria from *Oberon*, made for G & T in Vienna in 1905.

BAKER, JANET, soprano, b. Aug. 21, 1933, Yorkshire, England. She was educated in New York and Grimsby, where she sang as an amateur. She studied in London with Helene Isepp and in 1956 won the

London Daily Mail's Kathleen Ferrier Award, which allowed her to continue her studies at the Mozarteum in Salzburg. In 1959 she won the Queen's Prize at the Royal Academy of Music. She was well received in a recital at the Edinburgh Festival of 1960 and in Promenade Concerts in London. In 1961 she sang in Berlin and Copenhagen, singing Bach's *St. John Passion* in the Danish capital. At the 1961 Edinburgh Festival she was the soloist in Mahler's *Second Symphony* under Otto Klemperer. In 1963 she sang the Bach *B Minor Mass* in Zürich and appeared in Oslo. In addition to repeated appearances at the Edinburgh Festivals and in Zürich, she has sung in Stockholm, Brussels, and Barcelona. She married James K. Shelley in 1957.

Records: One record for Saga and many for HMV. *U.S. re-issue:* Angel, Everest, L'Oiseau Lyre.

BAKLANOFF, GEORGES, baritone, b. Dec. 23, 1880, St. Petersburg; d. July 6, 1938, Basel, Switzerland. While he was living in Kiev he lost his parents when he was quite young. He studied law at the Universities of Kiev and St. Petersburg. After 1902 he studied singing with Vittorio Vanza in Milan, but made his debut (1903) at the Kiev Opera, singing the title role in *The Demon*. In 1905 he came to the Moscow Imperial Opera. He had great success there as he did also at the St. Petersburg Imperial Opera. Thereafter he made guest appearances on the principal European stages, La Scala, the Paris Opéra, and the Vienna Imperial Opera, as well as in South America. In 1911 he had sensational successes at the Komische Oper both as Rigoletto and as Scarpia. In 1914 he sang at Monte Carlo in the world *première* of *I Mori di Valenzia*. He was a member of the Boston Opera Company (1911-14) and in the 1920's he had a triumphal career at the Chicago Opera, interspersed with world-wide guest appearances and concert tours. He also sang with the Philadelphia Opera. He had a splendid baritone voice of dominating impressiveness and he was endowed with real acting ability.

Records: HMV, Columbia*, Vox, and Parlophone. *U.S. re-issue:* American Decca. *U.S. re-recordings:* Columbia, Belcanto, TAP.

BALDASSARE-TEDESCHI, GIUSEPPINA, soprano, b. Oct. 28, 1881, Trani, near Bari, Italy. She studied at the Liceo Rossini in Pesaro with Brambilla-Ponchielli and Anna Vestri. She made her debut in Novara (1906) as the heroine in *Iris*. Until 1930 she had a successful career on the larger Italian stages, including La Scala. Her guest appearances included the Teatro Liceo (1908), Teatro São Carlos (1909), and the Budapest Opera (1914). In 1930 she gave up her career to teach singing in Milan. She was a professor at the Accademia di Santa Cecilia in Rome (1936-38) and among her pupils were Licia Albanese, Pia Tassinari, and Stella Roman.

Records: Pathé* and Columbia*, *U.S. re-recordings:* Eterna, Rococo, TAP.

BAMPTON, ROSE, soprano, b. Nov. 28, 1908, Cleveland, Ohio. She grew up in Buffalo, New York, and studied singing at the Curtis Institute of Music in Philadelphia with Queena Mario; she also studied at Drake University in Des Moines, Iowa, where she was graduated. She began her stage career (1929) in New York with a traveling company. After successful appearances at the Worcester Festival in 1929, she sang from 1929-32 as a contralto with the Philadelphia Opera. She made her debut at the Metropolitan

Opera in November, 1932, as Laura in *La Gioconda*. After 1937 she sang soprano parts at the Metropolitan and after 1939 became a Wagner singer. She sang at the New York house until 1950. She made guest appearances at Covent Garden (1937) and sang annually at the Teatro Colón (1942-47). She made long concert tours as well as appearances on the American radio, especially with Toscanini. She is married to the conductor Wilfred Pelletier and lives in New York. The dark-timbred quality of her voice and her dramatic skill were equally admired.

Records: Many RCA Victor* records (including *Fidelio* with Toscanini and Schoenberg's *Gurrelieder* with Stokowski). *U.S. re-recording:* RCA Victor.

BARABAS, SARI, soprano, b. 1918, Budapest. She at first wished to become a dancer, but after a serious accident she turned to vocal study, which she completed under Frau Speckler in Budapest. She made her debut at the National Opera there (1939) as Gilda in *Rigoletto*. At the outbreak of the war she left Hungary and went to Germany, where in 1949 she became a member of the Munich State Opera. She had great success in guest appearances in Vienna and on other important stages. She participated in opera festivals in Munich and Glyndebourne (Adèle in *Le Comte Ory*) and became one of the finest operetta singers of her generation. She visited France, England, Italy, Austria, Switzerland, and the United States many times. She was greatly admired on her concert tours for her style in singing popular songs. She is married to the tenor Franz Klarwein.

Records: DGG, Philips, HMV, (*Le Comte Ory*, Glyndebourne, 1956). *U.S. re-issue:* Epic, Vanguard.

BARACCHI, ARISTIDE, baritone, b. July 31, 1885, Reggio Emilia, Italy; d. September, 1964, Milan. After he had sung on Italian provincial stages, he was engaged by the Metropolitan Opera (1907-09), where he sang, among other roles, Masetto in *Don Giovanni* and Bartolo in *Il Barbiere di Siviglia*. He then returned to Italy and specialized in *comprimario* roles, wherein he mastered an almost unexplored territory. After 1918 he joined the ensemble of La Scala and until 1925 he was frequently heard there, mostly in small parts which he made important by his brilliant interpretations. On Apr. 25, 1926, he sang the part of a Mandarin in the world *première* of *Turandot*; he also sang there in the world *premières* of both the *Nerone* of Boito (1924) and of Mascagni (1935). After 1928 he was an almost annual guest at Covent Garden, where he occasionally undertook such parts as Silvio in *I Pagliacci*. He lived and taught in Milan and ended his days in the Casa di Riposo there.

Records: This artist sang a great many *comprimario* roles in complete operas on records; in 1918-38 alone he sang the role of Schaunard four times in complete recordings of *La Bohème*. His records appeared on HMV, Columbia*, and Odeon-Fonotipia. He made no solo records. *U.S. re-issue:* RCA Victor, Rococo.

BARBATO, ELISABETTA, soprano, b. Sept. 11, 1921, Barleta, Italy. She studied at the Bologna Conservatory and at the Accademia di Santa Cecilia in Rome. She made her debut (1944) as Aïda at the Baths of Caracalla in Rome. After World War II she had sensational success at La Scala, in Rome, Naples, and other centers of Italian musical life. She was very well-liked in South America, especially at the Teatro Colón and in Rio de Janeiro. She sang at the Metropolitan Opera (1951-52). Since 1955 she has appeared chiefly in the Italian provinces and only rarely on the great opera stages there. A musical, well-trained, and expressive voice.

Records: A few Cetra* records. *U.S. re-recording:* Everest-Cetra.

BARBIERI, FEDORA, contralto, b. 1920, Trieste. She studied with Federico Bugamelli and Luigi Toffolo in Trieste, and later with Giulia Tess in Milan. She made her stage debut in Florence (1940) as Fidalma in *Il Matrimonio Segreto*. After early successes in Italy, she made a tour in 1943 through Germany, Belgium, and Holland. In 1943 she married Maestro Barzoletti, the director of the Maggio Musicale Festival and thereupon she gave up her career. In 1945, however, she returned to the operatic stage, singing Azucena in *Il Trovatore* in Florence. She then had brilliant success in all the great Italian opera houses, particularly at La Scala. She made a successful series of guest appearances at the Teatro Colón and later appeared as guest in London, Paris, Vienna, San Francisco, and Chicago. She sang at the Metropolitan Opera (1952-54; 1967-68), and at the Arena Festivals (1955-58). She was one of the best-known contraltos of her time.

Records: HMV (*Un Ballo in Maschera*, 1943), Cetra* (*La Favorita, La Gioconda*), Columbia and RCA Victor* (*Il Trovatore*). *U.S. re-issue:* Angel, Vox.

BARRIENTOS, MARIA, soprano, b. Mar. 20, 1883, Barcelona; d. Aug. 8, 1946, Paris. She was a musical prodigy, beginning her training at the age of six in the Barcelona Conservatory. At twelve she received her diploma in composition, piano, and violin and directed the performance of one of her symphonies. At fourteen she began her vocal studies with Francesco Bonet in Barcelona. She made her debut there at the Teatro Novedades (1898) as Ines in *L'Africaine*. In the same year she came to Milan, where she continued her studies and had a brilliant success at the Teatro Lirico in the title role of *Lakmé*. In 1899 she sang at the Teatro Costanzi and in 1900 made a splendid tour through Germany, with guest appearances in Berlin, Stuttgart, Breslau, and Leipzig. In 1904 she was well applauded at La Scala in the title role of *Dinorah*, and in 1905 as Rosina in *Il Barbiere di Siviglia*. Successful guest appearances followed in South America, Spain, Portugal, and at the Havana Opera. She was a member of the Metropolitan Opera (1915-20); there she was particularly admired opposite Enrico Caruso in *L'Elisir d'Amore*. In the 1920's she appeared frequently in France and at the Monte Carlo Opera, as well as making concert tours. She was a professor at the Buenos Aires Conservatory (1939-45). One of the most beautiful coloratura voices preserved on records, unsurpassed both in her faultless singing techniques and in her great musicality.

Records: Fonotipia (Milan, 1905) as well as Columbia* (including Spanish songs by Manuel de Falla with the composer at the keyboard). *U.S. re-issue:* Columbia-Fonotipia, IRCC. *U.S. re-recording:* IRCC, Scala, TAP.

BARSOWA, VALERIA, soprano, b. June 13, 1892; d. Dec. 15, 1967, Sochi, Russia. She studied under M. B. Vladimirov and U.A. Mazetti at the Moscow Conservatory, and began her career in 1915. She first appeared on the stage of Moscow's Ziminia Opera, and later at other theaters. In 1920 she was engaged by the Bolshoi Opera and was a celebrated artist there for more than thirty years. In addition to her opera performances she was an accomplished concert singer and appeared in foreign countries, including an engagement in Berlin (1929). She was named a People's Artist of the USSR and in 1941 was awarded a Stalin Prize. She was admired in coloratura roles for her virtuoso voice management and in lyric parts for the beauty of her expressiveness.

Records: About 1930 she made records for Odeon and later made many records for the Russian State Record Trust. *U.S. re-issue:* Columbia.

BARTOLOMASI, VALENTINA, soprano, b. 1889; d. 1932, Milan. She began her stage career about 1910. Although she never appeared at La Scala or at the Teatro Costanzi, she was esteemed as one of the finest Italian dramatic sopranos of her generation. She had her greatest successes at the Teatro dal Verme, in Venice, and in Florence. In 1920-21 she was applauded at the Teatro Regio both in Parma and in Bari. She gave up her stage career by 1922. A voluminous and impressive soprano voice.

Records: She appeared on HMV in the title role of a complete *Tosca* recording in 1921. She also sang for Columbia, Fonotechnica, and Pathé. *U.S. re-issue:* Victor.

BARY, ALFRED VON, tenor, b. Jan 18, 1873, La Valetta, Malta; d. Sept. 9, 1926, Munich. He was the son of Erwin von Bary, the African explorer. He first studied medicine and in 1918 passed his state examination and received his medical diploma. He became a neurologist and first assistant in brain pathology to Professor Flechsig at the University of Leipzig. His fine voice was discovered by Arthur Nikisch, and he studied under Richard Müller. He made his debut (1903) at the Dresden Royal Opera as Lohengrin. He made his first appearance at the Bayreuth Festival in the summer of 1904 and until 1914 was a principal singer there. He sang all the larger tenor roles in the Wagner repertory at Bayreuth and was considered one of the greatest Wagner tenors of his generation. He remained in Dresden until 1912 and then sang until 1918 at the Royal Opera in Munich. An eye difficulty, which was rapidly blinding him, caused him to give up his singing career; for a time he resumed his medical calling.

Records: Two very rare Wagner records on G & T (Bayreuth, 1904).

BASIOLA, MARIO, baritone, b. July 12, 1892, near Cremona, Italy; d. Jan. 3, 1965, Annico, Italy. He studied with Antonio Cotogni in Rome and made his stage debut in 1918. He made guest appearances at the Teatro Liceo (1920) and in Florence (1921). He was first baritone of the San Carlo Opera Company (1923-25) and traveled with them throughout the United States. He was a member of the Metropolitan Opera (1925-31), making his debut there as Amonasro in *Aida*. At the Metropolitan he sang all the principal Italian baritone roles, alternating with Titta Ruffo, Giuseppe de Luca, and Giuseppe Danise. From 1924-31 he made annual guest appearances at Ravinia, near Chicago, and in 1926 sang at the Havana Opera. He returned to Italy in 1933 and sang there for fifteen seasons at La Scala, as well as in Rome and at the other large opera houses. He had sensational successes as Iago in *Otello* and as Scarpia in *Tosca* at Covent Garden (1939). He toured Australia with an Italian opera company in 1946. He stayed there as a teacher of singing in Sydney until 1951 and thereafter lived in Milan.

Records: Edison*, Columbia*, and HMV. Sang in complete recordings of *I Pagliacci* and *Madama*

Butterfly with Beniamino Gigli. *U.S. re-issue:* RCA Victor. *U.S. re-recordings:* Angel, FRP, Seraphim.

BASSI, AMADEO, tenor, b. July 29, 1874, Montespertoli, near Florence; d. Jan. 15, 1949, Florence. His singing teacher was Maestro Pavesi in Florence and he made his debut (1897) in Castelfiorentino in Marchetti's *Ruy Blas*. After he had sung in Florence, Venice, Trento, and Genoa, he made guest appearances annually at the Teatro Colón with great success. He was equally successful at La Scala, where he sang in the world *première* of *Gloria* (1907). He came to the Manhattan Opera Company (1906) and later was engaged by the Chicago Opera (1910-12). Guest appearance concerts took him all over the world, but his greatest successes were in Italy and in the United States. He was a member of the Metropolitan Opera (1910-11). He appeared in concerts until 1940, and later taught in Florence. A radiant tenor voice, proven in a repertory which particularly included Italian parts, but also the Wagner heroes.

Records: Rare records for Fonotipia (Milan, 1906) and Pathé*. *U.S. re-issue:* Columbia-Fonotipia. *U.S. re-recordings:* TAP, Eterna, FRP, HRS.

BASTIANINI, ETTORE, baritone, b. Sept. 24, 1922, Siena; d. Jan. 25, 1967, Sirmione, Italy. He made his debut as a bass (1945) at Ravenna as Colline in *La Bohème*. He sang bass parts for several years, but was then changed by his teacher, Rucciana Betarini, and made his debut as a baritone in 1951. He attracted attention when he sang Prince Andrei in the 1953 Maggio Musicale Festival in *War and Peace*. He first sang at La Scala in 1953 and often thereafter. In December of that year he made his debut at the Metropolitan Opera as the elder Germont in *La Traviata*. He was soon one of the best-known Italian baritones and performed on all the great opera stages of the world, especially in New York, Milan, and Vienna. He sang at the Salzburg Festivals (1960; 1961), and made guest tours and concert appearances in Germany, France, Spain, Egypt, and South America. He had a voluminous and impressive baritone voice with which he quickly mastered all the important parts in the Italian repertory.

Records: A great many records for Ricordi and especially for Decca (including many complete operas: *La Favorita, Andrea Chénier, La Gioconda, La Forza del Destino*, and *Il Barbiere di Siviglia*). On DGG* he sang in *Lucia di Lammermoor, Un Ballo in Maschera*, and *Don Carlos. U.S. re-issue:* London, Mercury, Everest-Cetra.

BATHORI, JANE, soprano, b. 1876. She studied at the Paris Conservatory and made her debut there as a concert singer (1898). She married the Belgian tenor Emile Engel. In 1900 she made her stage debut at Nantes and in 1902 she was chosen by Toscanini for La Scala. There she sang Hänsel in the first La Scala performance of *Hänsel und Gretel* with Rosina Storchio. She then sang with her husband at the Brussels Opera but soon devoted herself entirely to concert work. In 1904 she had a sensational success in Paris with Ravel's song cycle *Shéhérazade*. Henceforward she was known as the foremost interpreter of contemporary French songs. Debussy dedicated to her his groups *Promenoir des deux Amants* and *Poèmes de Mallarmé*, which she introduced, along with Ravel's cycle, *Histoires naturelles*. From 1914 to 1918 she directed the Théâtre des Vieux Colombiers in Paris. She promoted the *avant-garde* group

"Les Six," and generally took a leading part in the musical life of the French metropolis. In 1926 she traveled to the Argentine with the music critic Jean Aubry for a recital tour. From that time on she was heard annually in Buenos Aires, where she sang, among others, in Honneger's oratorios *Le Roi David* and *Judith* in their first performances there. In 1933 she returned to the stage a few times and at the Teatro Colón sang the part of Concepcion in *L'Heure Espagnole*. In 1940 she emigrated to Buenos Aires, where she taught during World War II, but she returned to Paris again in 1946. There she occupied herself with teaching and gave lectures on the French radio program "Exposition des mélodies inédites." A highly musical and richly impressive voice.

Records: Columbia* (1929, 1931).

BATTISTINI, MATTIA, baritone, b. Feb. 27, 1856, Rome; d. Nov. 7, 1928, at his estate Colle Baccaro, near Rieti, Italy. He studied with Veneslao Persichini, later with Luigi Mancinelli and Augusto Rotoli in Rome and made his debut at the Teatro Argentina there (1878) as Alfonso in *La Favorita*. He sang at the Teatro Regio in Turin (1880) and at Covent Garden (1883) and in Naples (1886). However, he really became famous through his appearances at La Scala (1888) and from there he went from triumph to triumph on the leading Italian stages, and as a highly honored guest later sang in all the centers of European musical life. He was called "La gloria d'Italia" and "Il ré dei baritoni." Guest appearances brought him great successes in Paris, London, Berlin, Vienna, Lisbon, Madrid, and Barcelona. He was especially beloved in Russia where, from 1892 to 1910, he appeared nearly every year at the Imperial Operas in St. Petersburg and Moscow, in Warsaw, Odessa, and in other cities. Outside Europe he was heard only once, at the beginning of his career, in South America. He declined all invitations to visit the United States. He appeared on the stage for nearly fifty years and his voice retained to the last its original beauty. In 1924 he gave up his stage career and in October, 1927, he gave his last concert in Graz. One of the great vocal personalities of his epoch; his voice combined a complete mastery of singing technique with an uncommonly wide range, so that he could effortlessly reach the high notes of a tenor. His repertory included eighty-two major baritone roles, especially in Italian parts, but also in Wagner.

Records: He made many records, the oldest on G & T (Warsaw, 1903), which are of special interest; he also recorded for G & T in 1907 (Milan). He sang for HMV until 1923. He is said to have made one Swiss record in 1919. *U.S. re-issue:* Victor, Opera Disc, IRCC, HRS. *U.S. re-recordings:* Angel, Belcanto, RCA Victor, Scala, Eterna, TAP, Olympus, Cantilena.

BAUERMEISTER, MATHILDE, soprano-contralto, b. 1849, Hamburg; d. Oct. 15, 1926, on her estate in Kent, England. She came to England as a child and studied at the London Academy of Music. She made her debut about 1886 at Her Majesty's Theater, London. In 1879 she came to the United States for the first time and made altogether sixteen tours with various opera companies, mostly with those of Colonel Mapleson. In 1887 she sang at the Academy of Music with Minnie Hauk in *Manon*. From 1891 to 1906 she was a member of the Metropolitan Opera. She appeared there, as on other stages, in a great variety of small parts, both as a soprano and as a mezzo, and she deserves mention here as the first in a long line of artists who, both on account of their reliability and on account of their meritorious skill in devoting themselves to *comprimario* roles, are indispensable to the management of every opera company. At times she could take over an important part, as when she substituted for Nellie Melba at the last minute in the role of Queen Marguerite in *Les Huguenots*. She developed a warm friendship with Melba, who later arranged that Mathilde Bauermeister appear often at Covent Garden (1905). She sang her farewell to the stage there in a performance of *Faust*.

Records: No disc record of her voice exists, only Mapleson cylinders made at performances at the Metropolitan, among them the Duel Scene from *Faust*. *U.S. re-recording:* IRCC.

BAUGÉ, ANDRÉ, baritone, b. Jan. 4, 1892, Toulouse; d. May 25, 1966, Paris. He was the son of the operetta singer Anna Tariol-Baugé and a singing teacher. He wished originally to be a painter, studied at the École des Beaux-Arts in Paris and exhibited a portrait at the Salon. He received his voice training from his parents. He made his debut in Grénoble (1912) under the name André Grillaud. In 1914 he joined the French Army, was twice wounded, and was made a Chevalier of the Legion of Honor. In 1917 he joined the Paris Opéra-Comique, making his debut as Frédéric in *Lakmé*. He remained there until 1925, meanwhile making guest appearances at all the best-known French theaters. In 1925 at the Théâtre Marigny he sang in *Monsieur Beaucaire* and thereafter appeared a great deal in operetta. In 1929 he became the director of the Théâtre Trianon-Lyrique in Paris and in 1936-37 he sang at the Marseilles Opera. He appeared at the Théâtre Châtelet in Paris in 1938 and at the Théâtre Mogador there in 1940. He scarcely ever appeared abroad and worked in several French films. After 1946 he was a professor at the École Normale de Musique in Paris. He married the soprano Suzanne Laydecker. He had a typical, bright-timbred, French baritone voice.

Records: Many acoustic records for Pathé and HMV, including *Les Cloches de Corneville*. He also made electric records for Pathé. *U.S. re-issue:* Columbia electric.

BAUM, KURT, tenor, b. Mar. 15, 1908, in Bohemia. He studied with Edoardo Garbin in Milan and with Scolari in Rome; he made his debut (1932) at the Zürich Opera in *Der Kreidekreis*. He sang for several years in Zürich and on German stages. He sang at the Chicago Opera (1939-41), making his debut as Radames in *Aïda*, and from 1941-67 was a member of the Metropolitan Opera, being especially successful there as a Wagner tenor. He made guest appearances at La Scala (1947-48) and sang Arnold in *Guillaume Tell* at the Maggio Musicale Festival in 1952. In 1953 he sang at the Arena Festival and made guest appearances at Covent Garden that year during the coronation season.

Records: Remington*, Columbia*, Allegro Royale*. *U.S. re-recording:* TAP.

BAUMER, MARGARETE, soprano, b. May 26, 1898. She made her debut (1920) in Wuppertal, where she sang until 1923. Her later engagements included Düsseldorf (1923-24), Zürich (1924-25), Stuttgart (1925-28), and the Berlin City Opera (1928-31). In 1930 she made a North American tour with the German Opera Company. She sang in Nuremberg (1932-33) and in Mannheim. After 1934 she became principal dramatic soprano at the

Leipzig Opera, where she was much admired. In 1934-37 she was also engaged at both the Munich State Opera and the Breslau Opera. Her career lasted for many years. In 1950 she sang Isolde in *Tristan und Isolde* in Leipzig and appeared as guest there until 1953. Since 1954 she has been a professor at the Leipzig Music High School. Her most famous roles were in the Wagner repertory.

Records: Parlophone, Opera, and Urania* (including a complete *Tristan und Isolde* and *Tannhäuser*). *U.S. re-issue:* American Decca, Vox, Rococo.

BEARDSLEE, BETHANY, soprano, b. Dec. 25, 1927, Lansing, Michigan. She studied at Michigan State University and won a three-year scholarship at the Juilliard School of Music in New York. In 1960 she was singer-in-residence at Princeton University. In 1962 she won the Laurel Leaf Citation for Modern Music of the American Composers' Alliance and she has become internationally famous for singing compositions of Stravinsky, Berg, Babbitt, Schoenberg, Webern, Křenek, and many major American composers in either their world or American first performances. In 1963-64 she received a Ford Foundation grant. She has sung early music with the New York Pro Musica (1958-60), Bach with the Boston Symphony Orchestra, and at Tanglewood Festivals. She has appeared at the Caramoor Festival. She has sung with the Chicago, Minneapolis, Detroit, and St. Louis Symphony Orchestras and with the Buffalo and New York Philharmonic Orchestras.

U.S. records: Dial, American Record Society, Columbia, Epic, and Son-Nova.

BEAUJON, MARISE, soprano, b. Oct. 12, 1890, Lyons. She was discovered by Gaston Beyle, the director of the Lyons Opera, during an amateur singing contest, and she made her debut on that stage (1910) as Micaëla in *Carmen*. For ten years she sang on French provincial stages before she was called to the Paris Opéra in 1920, making her debut there as Mathilde in *Guillaume Tell*. She remained a valued member of the Opéra until 1930, and in 1928 sang the title role in the first performance there of *Turandot*. She made guest appearances in 1926 at Madrid, Barcelona, and Monte Carlo, in 1928 at Brussels and Covent Garden, singing Marguerite in *Faust* at the latter, and in 1929 in Cairo. In 1930 she moved to the Opéra-Comique, first appearing as Tosca. A year later she was forced to give up her stage career for reasons of health. She lives in Paris. She had a full, lyric-dramatic voice.

Records: Acoustic for HMV and electric for Columbia*.

BECHI, GINO, baritone, b. Oct. 16, 1913, Florence. He studied at the Florence Conservatory and made his debut in Rome (1937). During World War II he had a very successful career at La Scala and other well-known Italian theaters. In the post-war period he appeared as a guest in concerts all over the world and at the opera houses in London, Paris, Buenos Aires, Rio de Janeiro, Chicago, and San Francisco. He has also been heard in the Middle East. Increasingly active as a film and recording star, he has been highly successful in these fields.

Records: A great many records for HMV, including some complete operas: *Cavalleria Rusticana* (under the direction of the composer), *Andrea Chénier, Aïda. Un Ballo in Maschera,* and *Il Barbiere di Siviglia.* Some of these were made with Beniamino Gigli as partner. *U.S. re-issue:* Victor. *U.S. re-recordings:* Capitol, Electrola, Seraphim.

BECKMANN, FRIEDEL, contralto, b. 1904 (?). She was engaged at Münster in Westphalia (1927-30), Königsberg (1930-31), Duisburg (1931-34) and the Cologne Opera (1934-38). She had great success after 1938 at the Berlin City Opera, where she sang regularly until 1941 and made guest appearances until 1944. At the same time she was an outstanding oratorio and concert contralto. She was especially admired on the stage as Carmen and as Orphée.

Records: HMV (singing, among others, the contralto part in Bach's *St. Matthew Passion. U.S. re-recording:* Rococo.

BEDDOE, DAN. tenor, b. Mar. 16, 1863, Amerahan, Wales; d. Dec. 26, 1937, New York. At first a miner, he won a gold medal at a singing contest in Wales in 1882. He emigrated to the United States and studied singing, first in Pittsburgh and Cleveland and then in New York. After a concert tour of England which brought him little success, he became a church singer in New York. He made his official debut as an oratorio singer (1903), and the next year Walter Damrosch chose him for a concert performance of *Parsifal.* In 1910 he was admired at the Cincinnati Festival, where he again appeared successfully (1914; 1920; 1925; 1927). In 1925 he sang the tenor part in Mendelssohn's *Elijah* in New York with tremendous success. He was also greatly admired there in Handel's *Messiah* (1925-29) and also in 1934. In 1911 he went to England and sang in *Elijah* at the Crystal Palace during the festivities commemorating the coronation of King George V. He was considered one of the best oratorio singers of his generation. Enrico Caruso attended his concerts in New York and admired his incomparable *messa-di-voce*

technique. He never appeared on the stage.

Records: Five Victor* discs (1911-14), a few Edison* cylinders and discs, and Columbia* discs. He made electrical records for Brunswick* when he was sixty-six years of age. *U.S. re-recording:* Cantilena.

BEETH, LOLA, soprano, b. Nov. 23, 1864, Cracow; d. Mar. 18, 1940, Berlin. She began her vocal studies in Lemberg and then became a student of Louise Dustmann in Vienna; further studies followed with Pauline Viardot-Garcia in Paris, Francesco Lamperti in Milan, and Rosa Deruda in Berlin. She made her debut with sensational success at the Berlin Imperial Opera in 1882 as Elsa in *Lohengrin* and remained a member of this theater until 1888. From 1888-95 she was even more successful at the Vienna Imperial Opera. In 1895 she appeared as guest at the Paris Opéra and during the 1895-96 season was a member of the Metropolitan Opera, where she made her debut as Valentine in *Les Huguenots* with Jean de Reszke. Successful guest appearances followed at Covent Garden, the Imperial Operas in St. Petersburg and Moscow, and at Monte Carlo and Warsaw. From 1898 to 1901 she was again at the Vienna Imperial Opera. Later she lived in Berlin and gave guest performances and concerts. Still later she became a much sought-after teacher.

Records: She had long been thought to have left no records of her voice, but three records for G & T and one for Homophon were found; all are of the greatest rarity.

BEILKE, IRMA, soprano, b. Aug. 24, 1904, Berlin. She was trained by Gertrud Wirtschaft in Berlin and made her stage debut at the Berlin City Opera (1926). She remained at the City Opera until 1928, then sang in Oldenburg (1929-34), at the

Leipzig Opera (1934-35), and from 1936 to the end of her career she was again a member of the Berlin City Opera. Through guest appearances she was connected with the Munich State Opera and the Leipzig Opera. She sang as a member of the Vienna State Opera ensemble (1941-45) and sang Pamina in *Die Zauberflöte* at the Salzburg Festival (1943). Further guest appearances included London, Paris, Brussels, and Milan until 1954. After that year she taught at her own singing studio in Berlin and in 1958 gave up her stage career. She had a beautifully trained soprano voice; starting as a coloratura, she added a long list of lyric roles to her repertory.

Records: HMV (including a complete *Die Zauberflöte* in which she sang both Pamina and the First Boy); her records for Imperial and Urania* included complete recordings of *Fra Diavolo* and *Der Freischütz. U.S. re-issue:* RCA Victor. *U.S. re-recording:* Turnabout.

BEIRER, HANS, tenor, b. June 26, 1911, Wiener Neustadt, Austria. He studied at the Vienna Academy of Music and made his debut (1936) at Linz. He sang in Basel and St. Gallen (1937-39), but his career was then interrupted by World War II. He sang at the Berlin City Opera (1945-48), becoming known as a Wagner singer. After 1958 he was a member of the Hamburg Opera. He made guest appearances in London, Paris, Brussels, at the Vienna State Opera, the Stuttgart State Opera, and at La Scala. He was successful as Parsifal at the Bayreuth Festivals (1958-60), and in the latter year he made guest appearances at the Teatro Colón.

Records: Only one official record by this singer: *Tannhäuser* excerpts on the Opera label.

BELHOMME, HYPOLITE, bass, b. 1854, Paris; d. Jan. 16, 1923, Nice. He studied at the Paris Conservatory and made his debut at the Opéra-Comique there (1879) in *Lalla Rookh*. At this house he sang Crespel in the world *première* of *Les Contes d'Hoffmann* on Feb. 2, 1881. He remained at the Opéra-Comique until 1886, then sang at the Opéra in Lyons (1886-89), and at the Marseilles Opéra (1890-91). In 1891 he returned to the Opéra-Comique and remained there to the end of his career. He sang a small role there on Feb. 2, 1900, in the world *première* of *Louise*. He made regular guest appearances at the Brussels Opera (1902-05) and there he sang the part of Kezal at the first performance at that house of *The Bartered Bride* (1905). He also sang as guest at the opera houses in Monte Carlo and Nice. He gave up his career in 1916. A technically complete and thoroughly prepared bass voice.

Records: G & T (Paris, 1904), Odeon (Paris, 1905), and Pathé*, all in great demand by collectors. *U.S. re-recording:* TAP, FRP, Rococo.

BELLINCIONI, GEMMA, soprano, b. Aug. 19, 1864, Monza, Italy; d. Apr. 23, 1950, Naples. She made her debut in Naples at the age of fifteen in *Il Segreto della Duchessa*. In 1884 she undertook a tour of Spain, in 1885 she sang at the Teatro Costanzi, and in 1886 she made her debut at La Scala. After she had married the famous Italian tenor Robert Stagno (1836-97), they undertook guest appearances in every musical metropolis in the world, appearances which brought them many triumphs and successes. Guest tours and appearances included Vienna, Berlin, Monte Carlo, Budapest, Amsterdam, Warsaw, Dresden, Prague, Paris, Hamburg, Buenos Aires, and Covent Garden (1894). She never appeared in the

United States. In 1906 she sang the title role in the first Italian performance of *Salome*; this remained one of her star parts. Gemma Bellincioni was an especially unforgettable interpreter of soprano parts in the Italian *verismo* operas, which were just then becoming known. She sang in the world *premières* of many of these operas, for example, the role of Santuzza in *Cavalleria Rusticana* on May 17, 1890, at the Teatro Costanzi, on which occasion her husband sang Turiddu. In 1898 at the Teatro Lirico she sang the title role in the world *première* of *Fedora* with Enrico Caruso, and in 1904 she appeared at La Scala in the first performance of *La Cabrera*. After the death of her husband in 1897 she continued her guest tours alone. In 1911 she opened an opera studio in Berlin-Charlottenburg, which she conducted until 1915. She then lived and taught in Rome and (1931-32) in Vienna. In 1933 she became a professor at the Naples Conservatory. She published her memoirs under the title *Io ed il palcosenico* (Milan, 1920).

Records: There are a few rare records by this artist on G & T (Milan, 1903-04) as well as on Pathé, but these scarcely give a true picture of her expressiveness, which was accompanied by a pre-eminent acting talent. There are also unpublished records for Fonotipia. *U.S. re-recording:* IRCC.

BELMAS, XENIA, soprano, b. 1896, Kiev. She studied at the Kiev Conservatory with Päts and made her debut (1917) at the Odessa Opera, where she had her first successes as a Wagner singer and as Tatiana in *Eugen Onégin*. In 1921 she and her husband, the conductor Alexander Kitschin, left Russia and came to Wiesbaden. After further studies in Italy she gave a very successful concert series in Paris and in 1927 made guest appearances at the Opéra, especially as Aïda. In 1928 she gave celebrated concerts in Berlin, where her records were made. In 1929 she traveled with an Italian opera company to Australia and in 1931 gave concerts in Monte Carlo, followed by a tour of guest appearances in the Baltic States. In 1938 she made concert tours with her husband in South Africa and remained in Durban as a teacher. Her delicately beautiful voice was thoroughly expressive of complete musicality.

Records: Polydor and Ultraphon. *U.S. re-issue:* Brunswick. *U.S. re-recording:* American Decca.

BELOV, EUGENII, baritone, b. 1913, Moscow. At first, an engineer, he worked on the building of the Fergansk Canal. During World War II he was a soldier. His voice was discovered at the front when he sang in an amateur concert at a Russian military hospital. Later he studied at the Gnesin Conservatory in Moscow. He made his debut (1947) at the Bolshoi Theater there, where he has had a successful career ever since. He possesses a beautifully trained voice.

Records: Russian State Record Trust (including the title role in a complete *Eugen Onégin*). *U.S. re-issue:* Monitor.

BENDER, PAUL, bass, b. July 28, 1875, Driedorf, Germany; d. Nov. 27, 1947, Munich. He first studied medicine, then voice with Luise Ress and Baptist Hoffmann in Berlin. He made his stage debut (1900) in Breslau, where he remained until 1903. He sang at the Bayreuth Festival (1902). In 1903 he came to the Munich Royal Opera, where he was first bass for thirty years. On June 12, 1917, he appeared there in the world *première* of *Palestrina*. His guest appearances all over the world brought him great success and honor in Vienna, Milan, London, Paris, and Zürich. He sang at the Metropolitan Opera (1922-27). In 1926 he sang Osmin in *Die Entführung aus dem Serail* at the Salzburg Festival. In addition to his widely successful stage career, he was much admired as a concert and lieder singer, being an especially fine interpreter of German ballads. He appeared in concert practically until the time of his death. A large, dark-timbred bass voice of astounding technical competency. On the stage he had mastered the entire range of bass parts from serious to *buffo* roles.

Records: HMV and Ultraphon, all of great beauty. *U.S. re-issue:* Opera Disc. *U.S. re-recordings:* Vox, TAP.

BEN-SEDIRA, LEILA, soprano, b. 1909, Algiers. The daughter of a French officer of Algerian extraction, she first studied piano with Lazare-Lévy in Paris and then singing at the Conservatory. She made her debut (1929) at the Opéra-Comique as Olympia in *Les Contes d'Hoffmann* and had brilliant successes at that house thereafter, including appearances in *Il Barbiere di Siviglia* and in the world première of *Cantegril* (1931) opposite Feodor Chaliapin. She made guest appearances on the more important French stages and at the Cairo Opera. Her most important successes, however, were as a concert singer in France, Belgium, Holland, England, and Italy, where she was prized as an interpreter of both classical and contemporary songs. A technically outstanding coloratura voice.

Records: Odeon-Parlophone records. *U.S. re-issue:* Columbia, RCA Victor, Rococo.

BERBERIAN, CATHY, soprano, b. Attleboro, Mass. She studied at Columbia University and then at the Verdi Conservatory in Milan. In 1950-51 she studied as a Fulbright scholar with Giorgina del Vego in Milan. She appeared in concerts and on radio in Europe. After returning to America in 1953 she sang in the United States and Canada. Music has been written for her by Bussotti, Milhaud, John Cage, and Stravinsky, and she is regarded as one of the foremost interpreters of *avant-garde* music. She sang with the Chicago Symphony Orchestra in 1967, has appeared at festivals in Ravinia and Venice, and has traveled world-wide in recitals. She was formerly married to the composer Luciano Berio and has herself composed songs. She lives in Milan. She has a range of three octaves and great vocal flexibility.

U.S. records: Columbia, Philips, Time, Turnabout, CRI, Angelicum.

BERGANZA, TERESA, contralto-soprano, b. 1934, Madrid. She studied at the Madrid Conservatory and won first prize there in the annual singing competition in 1954. She then made her debut as a concert singer (1955) with concert tours in Spain, Portugal, France, Italy, Austria, and Germany. Her stage debut occurred in 1957 at the Aix-en-Provence Festival as Dorabella in *Così fan tutte*. Since then she has sung every year at Aix and since 1958 in the Glyndebourne Festival. She has appeared at the Metropolitan Opera since 1965-66. Guest appearances at La Scala, the Vienna State Opera, and Covent Garden, as well as at other great opera houses, have brought her many successes. Thanks to the dark-timbred quality of her voice, she can sing the difficult coloratura contralto parts in addition to soprano roles. Her greatest specialities are Mozart and Rossini roles, but she is also celebrated as a singer of oratorio and of Spanish songs.

Records: Her first records were zarzuela airs on London International; since then she has made operatic records for Decca*. U.S. re-issue: London.

BERGÉ, LAURE, soprano, b. 1892 (?); d. May 4, 1961, Brussels. From about 1919-35 this artist was esteemed as the principal dramatic soprano at the Théâtre de la Monnaie. She was frequently a guest at the Paris Opéra, at the Teatro Colón (1919-20), and at opera houses in Italy. Besides roles in the French repertory, she excelled in Wagner parts.
Records: A few records of her voice exist on Tri-Ergon.

BERGER, ERNA, soprano, b. Oct. 19, 1900, Cossbaude, near Dresden. Her parents emigrated after World War I to Paraguay. She took a position as governess in Montevideo and in 1923 returned to Germany. After undergoing great difficulties she was able to obtain vocal training in Dresden. In 1925 she was engaged by Fritz Busch for the Dresden State Opera and made her debut there as one of the Three Boys in Die Zauberflöte. In 1927 she sang the title role there in the world première of Hanneles Himmelfahrt. In 1929 she made a guest appearance at the Berlin City Opera in Christelflein. In 1930 she sang the Shepherd Boy in Tannhäuser at the Bayreuth Festival. After 1934 she was a member of the Berlin State Opera, where she was acclaimed for over twenty years. Guest appearances and concert tours all over the world carried the name of the most famous German coloratura soprano of her generation to fame. She was especially honored at both the Salzburg Festivals and at the Metropolitan Opera (1949-51). In 1949 she traveled to Australia and in 1953 to Japan. She is now a professor at the Music High School in Hamburg. With her coloratura soprano voice of exquisite musical beauty, she has great musical mastery, both in a wide-ranging opera repertory and in lieder.
Records: A great many beautiful records for Columbia*, HMV, and Polydor. About 1930 she sang a role in a complete Tannhäuser recording from Bayreuth for Columbia*. She sang Gilda in Rigoletto for RCA Victor* and DGG. For Urania* she sang in the complete operas Hänsel und Gretel and Martha and an abridged version of Les Contes d'Hoffmann. She also appeared later on a great many LP records, especially for DGG. U.S. re-issues: Angel, Decca, Electrola, Capital-Telefunken. U.S. re-recording: Scala, Telefunken, Turnabout, Rococo.

BERGER, RUDOLF, baritone-tenor, b. Apr. 17, 1874, Brünn, Austria; d. Feb. 27, 1925, New York City. He studied with Alfred Robinson in Brünn and made his debut there (1896) as a baritone. He sang in Olmütz in 1897 and after 1898 at the Berlin Imperial Opera. After 1901 he performed at the Bayreuth Festivals, appearing as Amfortas, Gunther, and Klingsor. He made guest appearances at the Vienna Imperial Opera, Covent Garden, Paris, and Prague. After 1906 he changed to a tenor and was much admired in heroic roles. He was called to the Metropolitan Opera in 1912. In 1913 he married the soprano Marie Rappold. He died at the height of his career.
Records: As both baritone and tenor he recorded for HMV and Odeon. U.S. re-recording: Eterna.

BERGLUND, JOEL, baritone, b. June 4 1903, Torsaker, Sweden. He studied at the Royal Music Conservatory in Stockholm and made his stage debut (1929) at the Opera there as Lothario in Mignon. He remained at the Stockholm Opera until 1949 and meanwhile made successful guest appearances at the Vienna State Opera, the Teatro

Colón, and the Chicago Opera. In 1942 he sang the title role in *Der Fliegende Holländer* at the Bayreuth Festival. He was a member of the Metropolitan Opera (1945-49) and from 1949-59 was artistic director of the Stockholm Opera. His heroic baritone voice was especially admired in Wagner roles.
Records: HMV and Telefunken. U.S. re-issue: RCA Victor.

BERGLUND, RUTH, contralto, b. Apr. 12, 1897, Amal, Sweden. She studied with Grenzebach in Berlin and made her debut at the City Opera there (1926). In 1930 she became a member of the Berlin State Opera, where in 1937 she sang Hendrickje in the world *première* of *Rembrandt van Rijn* opposite Rudolf Bockelmann. As a distinguished Wagner singer she proved herself at the Bayreuth Festivals (1936-39), where she sang such parts as Magdalena in *Die Meistersinger*, Flosshilde, the Second Norn in the *Ring* cycle, and the Heavenly Voice in *Parsifal*.
Records: HMV (where she sang the Three Ladies and the Three Boys in a complete recording of *Die Zauberflöte*). U.S. re-issue: Angel, Turnabout.

BERGONZI, CARLO, tenor, b. 1926, Parma. He studied at the Parma Conservatory and made his stage debut as a baritone (1948) in Lecce in *Il Barbiere di Siviglia*. He then sang baritone roles for three years before turning to tenor parts. He made his stage debut as a tenor in 1951 in Bari in the title role of *Andrea Chénier*. In the same year he sang the tenor parts in a series of Verdi operas produced by the Italian Radio in connection with the fiftieth anniversary of the composer's death. Next came guest appearances in Naples, Brescia, and Rome, concluding with very successful appearances at La Scala. He also sang in Spain, Portugal, England, France, and South America. He came to the Chicago Opera (1955) and to the Metropolitan Opera (1956). He has been applauded there ever since in such roles as Radames in *Aïda* and Manrico in *Il Trovatore*.
Records: Many records for Cetra* (including *I Pagliacci* and *Simon Boccanegra*), Decca (*Aïda* and *Il Trovatore*), and DDG (*Il Trovatore* and *Rigoletto*). U.S. re-issue: London, Angel, RCA Victor, Everest-Cetra.

BERNAC, PIERRE, baritone, b. Jan. 12, 1899, Paris. Originally Pierre Bertin. After appearances in small theaters, he started rather late in life to begin his career as a concert and lieder singer. He made his debut (1933) in Paris, where an encounter with the French composer Francis Poulenc was decisive for him, and a friendship sprang up between the two. In 1934 they gave their first concert together in Salzburg and in 1935 appeared in Paris at the hall of the École Normale. During the next two decades they undertook tours together all over the world. The typically French high baritone voice of Pierre Bernac is heard best not only in the songs of Poulenc, but also in the songs of other French and German composers. He was especially noted for the flexible variety of his expression and for the fine quality of his diction.
Records: Ultraphone, HMV, Pathé. U.S. re-issue: Columbia, RCA Victor, Rococo.

BERRY, WALTER, bass-baritone, b. 1929, Vienna. After planning to become an engineer, he studied voice at the Vienna Music High School with Hermann Gallos. In 1949 he joined the choir of the Vienna Academy and in 1950 was called to the Vienna State Opera. There he had his first great success as Figaro in *Le Nozze di Figaro*. In 1952 he participated in the Salzburg Festival and has returned there every year since. Walter Berry and his wife, the celebrated contralto Christa Ludwig, have had brilliant careers throughout the entire world, with guest appearances and concerts in Milan, London, Chicago, Buenos Aires, San Francisco, Brussels, Munich, and Stuttgart. Since 1961 he has been engaged by the Berlin City Opera.

Records: A great many records for various labels, including among others, Ariola (*Die Fledermaus*), Columbia, Decca, Philips*, Vox*, with complete performances of *Don Giovanni, Le Nozze di Figaro, Die Zauberflöte, Arabella, Der Rosenkavalier, Ariadne auf Naxos,* and *Wozzeck. U.S. re-issue:* Angel, Bach Guild, Desto, DGG, Epic, London, Lyrichord, Haydn Society, Seraphim, Victrola, Richmond, Mercury, Remington, and Vanguard.

BERTANA, LUISA, contralto, b. Jan. 11, 1898, Buenos Aires; d. July 23, 1933. She began her vocal studies at seventeen with Rinaldi in Buenos Aires and made her debut (1921) at the Teatro Colón as Preziosilla in *La Forza del Destino.* She then went to Italy and was promptly engaged by Toscanini for La Scala, making her debut there as Magdalena in *Rigoletto* (1922). She had a highly successful career there from that time on, singing Rubria in Boito's *Nerone* at its world *première* on May 1, 1924, under the baton of Toscanini. Until her death she was a highly honored prima donna at La Scala, Teatro Reale, Teatro San Carlo, and on other Italian stages. She also sang every season at the Teatro Colón. She was on her way to fulfill an engagement there for the 1933 season when she died on shipboard of pneumonia.

Records: Only a few acoustical records for HMV and Fonotipia and some electrics for Odeon. *U.S. re-issue:* Victor.

BERTHON, MIREILLE, soprano, b. Aug. 6, 1889, in the Montmartre quarter of Paris; d. Jan. 16, 1955, Paris. She was trained at the Paris Conservatory under Louise Grandjean, Hettich, and Albert Saléza. After studying Italian repertory with Angelica Pandolfini in Milan, she made her debut (1917) at the Paris Opéra in the title role of *Thaïs.* In 1918 she sang in Rouen, and in 1920 had an enormous success at the Teatro Colón and in Rio de Janeiro and Montevideo. She then returned to France and sang in Monte Carlo and the French provinces until 1922, when she was engaged at the Paris Opéra again, remaining for fifteen years. In 1937 she joined the Opéra-Comique and was highly successful there also. She made guest appearances in Belgium, Spain, Portugal, Egypt, Italy, and North Africa. After World War II she often sang in opera performances on the French radio. She died suddenly during a rehearsal for one of these performances.

Records: All her records, both acoustic and electric, were made for HMV. She sang Marguerite in a complete *Faust* with Marcel Journet and in *La Damnation de Faust. U.S. re-issue:* Victor.

BERTRAM, THEODOR, baritone, b. Feb. 12, 1869, Stuttgart; d. Nov. 24, 1907, Bayreuth. He was the son of the baritone Heinrich Bertram (1825-1905) and the dramatic soprano Marie Bertram (1838-82). He was trained by his father and made his debut in 1889 in Ulm. In 1891 he came to the Hamburg Opera, in 1892 to the Kroll Opera, and from 1883-99 appeared at the Munich Royal Opera. Called to the Metropolitan Opera in 1899, he remained there until 1901 and made guest appearances during this time in Chicago, Philadelphia, and Boston. In

1901 he sang Wotan for the first time at the Bayreuth Festival and was also admired as the Dutchman, Amfortas, and Wolfram. He was engaged at the Vienna Imperial Opera in 1902, but he soon gave up this contract and devoted himself exclusively to guest appearances, especially in Berlin, Hamburg, Munich, Stuttgart, and London. After 1897 he was married to the soprano Fanny Moran-Olden (1855-1905), and after her death he fell more and more under the influence of liquor and died by suicide. He had a marvelously trained voice of inexhaustible volume and expressiveness. He was especially noted in Wagner parts and was an unforgettable Wotan. He was also noted in Mozart roles.

Records: He left an astonishingly large number of records for G & T (Berlin, 1902; Bayreuth, 1904), Lyrophone, Favorite (Berlin, 1905), and Odeon (Berlin, 1905-06). *U.S. re-recording:* Herrold.

BESANZONI, GABRIELLA, contralto, b. Nov. 20, 1890, Rome; d. June 6, 1962, Rome. She studied in Rome under Ibilda Brizzi and made her debut (1913) at the Teatro Costanzi as Ulrica in *Un Ballo in Maschera*. She was highly successful in Italy and Spain and her great success at the Teatro Colón in 1918 caused her to return to South America again and again. She appeared at the Metropolitan Opera (1919-20), singing Isabella in *L'Italiana in Algeri* before the Rossini revival of the 1920's. During a guest appearance as Amneris opposite Enrico Caruso in 1920 at the Havana Opera, a bomb exploded in the auditorium while she was on stage during the second act. In 1921 she was highly successful both at the Chicago Opera and at the Teatro Costanzi. She was also greatly beloved at the Teatro Colón, where she appeared every season. In 1923-24 she appeared at La Scala as Orphée and as Amneris, and again in 1932 as Carmen and Mignon. She also made guest appearances at the Berlin State Opera. In 1939 she sang her farewell performance as Carmen during the Baths of Caracalla Festival. She lived for a time in Rio de Janeiro, but at the last was a teacher in Rome. She succeeded on the stage through the beauty of her expressive contralto voice and the elegance of her acting.

Records: A few acoustic records for Victor* and electric records from *Carmen* for HMV.

BETTENDORF, EMMY, soprano, b. July 16, 1895, Frankfurt a. M.; d. Oct. 20, 1963, Berlin. She studied in Frankfurt and made her debut at the Opera there (1914) in *Das Nachtlager von Granada*. She sang in Frankfurt until 1916, until 1920 in Sweden, and until 1924 at the Berlin State Opera; she then appeared at the Berlin City Opera. She made guest appearances with Bronsgeest's traveling opera company in Holland, Madrid, and Barcelona and on various stages in Germany. After an illness in 1928 she gave up her stage career and devoted herself especially to recordings. In 1930 she appeared in the film *Liebeswalzer*. From about 1930 to 1934 she was a highly popular recording artist in Germany. Thereafter she gave only a few concerts and lived the rest of her life in Berlin.

Records: Numerous records for Vox, Homochord, Polydor, and particularly for Parlophone in a wide-ranging repertory. *U.S. re-issues:* Okeh-Odeon (under the name Emmy Bettendorf-Heckmann), American Decca. *U.S. Re-recordings:* ASCO, Eterna, Rococo.

BETTONI, VINCENZO, bass, b. 1881, Melegnano, Italy; d. Nov. 4, 1954, Melegnano. He made his debut in 1905 and had a successful career in Italy and South America, where after 1910 he sang regularly at the Teatro Colón. In 1914 he sang Gurnemanz in the Spanish *première* of *Parsifal* in Barcelona. In 1925 he began a second career as an excellent *buffo* singer in Rossini's operas with Conchita Supervia. With her he made joint guest appearances in Turin, Barcelona, Paris, London, and South America, but especially at La Scala and on other larger Italian stages. In 1950 he sang at La Scala in *I Quattro Rusteghi*. He died of a heart attack as he was laying a bouquet on his father's grave.

Records: He left an extensive legacy of records, the oldest from about 1910, including duets with Mattia Battistini. He made acoustic records for HMV and Columbia*, electric for Odeon, Columbia* (*Il Barbiere di Siviglia*), and Fonotipia. *U.S. re-issue:* Victor, Opera Disc.

BEUF, AUGUSTO, baritone, b. June 21, 1887, Palermo. After studying the cello, he became a cellist in the orchestra of the Teatro Massimo and traveled with an Italian operetta troupe to Egypt. He made his operatic debut (1908) at Modica, near Ragusa. After later studies with Antonio Cotogni in Rome, he began his real operatic career in 1913 as Alfio in *Cavalleria Rusticana* at the Teatro Biondo. During World War I he served as a soldier in the Italian army. In 1918 he returned to the stage, appearing especially at La Scala. He had his first great success, however, at the Teatro Costanzi, where he had completed his vocal training under Alfredo Martini. In the 1920's he was admired at La Scala, at Rome, and in the other larger Italian houses. Meanwhile, he was singing a great deal in South America. From 1931 to 1934 he was a member of the Chicago Opera. After 1934 he undertook bass roles in Wagner operas. He was especially outstanding at La Scala as Hans Sachs. During the decade 1938-48 he undertook concert tours throughout the world, often with the famous soprano Toti Dal Monte. In 1946 he was the first Italian singer to appear on British television.

Records: Acoustic records for Columbia, electric for HMV; in 1951 at the beginning of the LP era, he sang the bass part in Verdi's *Requiem* for Urania*.

BEYLE, LEON, tenor, b. 1871, Lyons; d. 1922, Lyons. He studied in Lyons and Paris and made his debut at the Paris Opéra (1896). He was then named first tenor at the Opéra-Comique and remained until 1914. He appeared there in several world *premières*: *La Fille de Tabarin* (1901), *La Fille de Roland* (1904), and *La Lépreuse* (1912), among others. Along with a successful career in the French metropolis, he undertook guest appearances in the other large French opera houses. Later he was a teacher, first in Paris and then in Lyons, where his brother, Gaston Beyle, was the director of the opera house.

Records: He made a great many records for Eden, G & T (Paris, 1904-07), HMV, and Pathé*. *U.S. re-issue:* Victor. *U.S. re-recording:* Eterna.

BIASINI, PIERO, baritone, b. 1899. After his debut (1924) he sang at first only on provincial Italian stages. He had great success at the Italian Opera in Holland (1927-30) and reached La Scala in 1932, making his debut there as Paolo in *Simon Boccanegra*. He was very successful thereafter at the great Milan house. In 1937 as a guest at Covent Garden he sang the role of Ford in *Falstaff* and repeated the part at the Salzburg Festivals (1935-38) under Toscanini. He carried on his career in Italy until 1950. He now teaches in Milan.

Records: For HMV he sang Alfio in a complete recording of *Cavalleria Rusticana* and made records for Allegro Royale*. *U.S. re-issue:* RCA Victor.

BINDERNAGEL, GERTRUD, soprano, b. Jan. 11, 1894, Magdeburg, Germany; d. Nov. 3, 1932, Berlin. She studied first at the Magdeburg Conservatory and at the age of seventeen served as an unpaid apprentice at the Municipal Theater there before she undertook further study at the Berlin Music High School (1913-17). She sang at the Breslau Opera (1917-19) and at Regensburg (1919-20). In 1920 she was engaged by the Berlin State Opera, where she remained until 1927. She had great success there, especially in Wagner roles. She made guest appearances in Barcelona, Munich, Hamburg, and Mannheim and after 1927 she appeared chiefly at the Berlin City Opera. In 1930 she appeared as guest at the Vienna State Opera and she sang at the Zoppot Festivals (1926-27; 1931-32). Family difficulties resulted in an attempt on her life by her husband, the banker Wilhelm Hintze, as she was leaving the Berlin City Opera after a performance. She died as a result of the injuries. She had a large dramatic voice of sumptuous volume.

Records: Acoustic records for Vox, Polydor, and Parlophone; electric records for Telefunken. *U.S. re-recording:* Telefunken.

BIRRENKOVEN, WILLI, tenor, b. Oct. 4, 1865, Cologne; d. Mar. 8, 1955, Hanstedt, near Hamburg. He studied at the Cologne Conservatory and made his debut (1888) at the Düsseldorf Opera House. His further engagements included the Cologne Opera (1890-93) and the Hamburg Opera (1893-1912). He was especially known as a Wagner interpreter, and sang both Lohengrin and Parsifal at the Bayreuth Festival of 1894. He made guest appearances in London, at the Vienna Imperial Opera (1904), in Amsterdam, and at the larger German opera houses. He was also successful on a tour of the United States and was both a famous concert and lieder singer. His brother, Franz Birrenkoven, was also a well-known operatic tenor.

Records: A few rare records for G & T (Hamburg, 1904-08). *U.S. re-issue:* Victor.

BISCHOFF, JOHANNES, baritone, b. Mar. 19, 1874, Berlin; d. Oct. 10, 1936, Darmstadt. He first studied law at the University of Berlin, then turned to vocal studies with Mathilde Mallinger, Franz Betz, and H. Weinburg in Berlin. He made his debut (1899) at the Cologne Opera as the Flying Dutchman and remained there until 1904. After guest appearances in the United States (1904-05), he sang at the Hannover Opera until 1908. From 1908-17 he was at the Berlin Imperial Opera. In 1917 he went to Darmstadt, where he worked for a long time as singer and director. He was married to the soprano Sophie Bischoff-David. He died as a result of a traffic accident in Cologne. He had a heroic baritone voice and was noted in Wagner roles.

Records: Some records for HMV (Hannover, 1908), but particularly Edison* cylinders.

BISPHAM, DAVID, baritone, b. Jan. 5, 1857, Philadelphia; d. Oct. 2, 1921, Philadelphia. He studied with Edward Giles in Philadelphia. After his marriage in 1885 he decided to take up singing as a career and he studied further with William Shakespeare in London and Vanuccini and Lamperti in Milan. After he had begun giving concerts in London, he made his stage debut there (1891) in *La Basoche*. In 1892 at Covent Garden he sang Kurwenal in *Tristan und Isolde* and remained there for ten years, becoming famous for his Wagner roles. From 1896 to 1903 he sang at the Metropolitan Opera, making his debut there as Beckmesser in *Die Meistersinger*. In 1903 he began teaching in Philadelphia and became known as one of the outstanding oratorio singers of his time. He managed a chamber opera group in New York (1916-19). Toward the end of his life he gave recitations. His dark-timbred, heroic baritone voice was demonstrated in a many-sided stage and concert repertory.

Records: Columbia*, a few for G & T (London, 1902), Edison, and Pathé*. *U.S. re-issue:* IRCC. *U.S. re-recording:* Pathé Actuelle, TAP, IRCC.

BJONER, INGRID, soprano, b. 1929, Oslo. She worked in an apothecary shop before beginning her vocal studies in 1953 in Wiesbaden. She finished her studies at the Music High School in Frankfurt a. M. and made her debut (1957) at Wuppertal as Donna Anna in *Don Giovanni*. From Wuppertal she went, in 1959, to the German Opera on the Rhine at Düsseldorf-Duisburg. Guest appearance contracts brought her outstanding successes at the Vienna and Hamburg State Operas, as well as in London and San Francisco. Following these guest appearances, she became a member of both the Stockholm and the Oslo Royal Operas. At the Bayreuth Festival she sang Freia and Gutrune in the *Ring* cycle in 1960. In 1961 she was called to the Munich State Opera and in 1962 to the Metropolitan Opera. Famous as a Wagner soprano, she made guest appearances in 1961 in Warsaw and in Vancouver, Canada.

Records: Decca (Gutrune in *Götterdämmerung*), Ariola, Eurodisc, DGG* (in *Die Frau ohne Schatten*). *U.S. re-issue:* London.

BJORLING, JUSSI, tenor, b. Feb. 2, 1911, Stora Tuna, Sweden; d. Sept. 8, 1960, at his country home near Stockholm after a heart attack. He toured the world at the age of six in a vocal quartet, including his father and his brothers, Olle and Gösta. Beginning in 1929 he studied at the Royal Academy of Music in Stockholm as a pupil of John Forsell and made his debut at the Royal Opera House there (1932) as Don Ottavio in *Don Giovanni*, with his teacher in the title role. His first successes came through guest appearances in Copenhagen, Prague, Vienna, and Budapest. He had sensational triumphs at Covent Garden in London, followed by a concert in Carnegie Hall and guest appearances at the Chicago Opera. In 1938 he joined the Metropolitan Opera, making his debut as Rodolfo in *La Bohème*. Thereafter he was greatly honored in many countries for his concerts and guest appearances. From 1938-41 and from 1946 until his death he was engaged at the Metropolitan Opera, singing between seasons in Sweden. In addition to his work in opera, he was a famous concert and lieder singer. Autobiography: *Med bagaget i strupen* (Stockholm, 1945). He had a flexible and radiant tenor voice, whose expressiveness was supported by a mastery of singing technique. In the operatic sphere he was particularly outstanding in the Italian and French repertory.

Records: He made six acoustic records for American Columbia in 1918, two with his brothers and four solos. He left a great many records for HMV and RCA Victor*, including a number of complete operas: *Aida, Madama Butterfly, Rigoletto, La Bohème, Tosca, Cavalleria Rusticana, I Pagliacci,* and *Manon Lescaut*; he also sang the tenor solo in Verdi's *Requiem*. *U.S. re-issue:* Capitol, Angel, Seraphim. *U.S. re-recording:* Rococo.

BJÖRLING, SIGURD, baritone, b. Nov. 2, 1907, Stockholm. He studied at the Royal Academy of Music in Stockholm with John Forsell and Torsten Lennartsson. After further study with the conductor Leo Blech he made his debut (1930) at the Stockholm Royal Opera, of which he remained a member for over thirty years. After World War II he made guest appearances at La Scala, Covent Garden, and in Vienna, Munich, Stuttgart, Paris, Chicago, and San Francisco. In 1951 he sang the part of Wotan in the *Ring* cycle at the Bayreuth Festival, and proved himself an outstanding Wagner singer. He appeared at the Metropolitan Opera (1952-53); since 1946 he has held the title of Singer to the Swedish Court.

Records: HMV and Columbia*; on the latter he sang Wotan in a recording of *Die Walküre*, Act II, made at Bayreuth in 1951.

BLACHUT, BENO, tenor, b. June 14, 1913, near Moravská Ostrava, now in Czechoslovakia. He was first a worker in an ironworks and then studied singing at the Prague Conservatory with Luis Kaderabek (1935-39). He sang at Olomouc (1939-41). After a guest appearance as Jenik in *The Bartered Bride* at the National Theater in Prague in 1942, he was given a contract there and has since become one of the most prominent singers of the company. He has made guest appearances and has given concerts in Austria, Poland, and Hungary. He has a technically outstanding tenor voice, especially noted in the Czech repertory, but also in other roles and in oratorio and lieder.

Records: Many records for Supraphon, including the complete operas *Jenufa, Dalibor, The Kiss*,
and *Rusalka*. *U.S. re-issue:* Artia, Colosseum, Parliament.

BLANC, ERNEST, baritone, b. 1923, Sanary, France. He studied first at the Toulon, and then at the Paris Conservatory and made his debut (1950) at Marseilles. He was engaged by the Paris Opéra in 1954, where he had great success as Rigoletto and as Scarpia, as well as in Wagner roles. His guest appearances took him to Bordeaux, Marseilles, La Scala, Covent Garden, the Théâtre de la Monnaie, and the Vienna State Opera. He sang Telramund at the Bayreuth Festivals (1958-59) and made appearances at the Aix-en-Provence and Edinburgh Festivals. In 1960 he was heard as Don Giovanni at Glyndebourne. He had outstanding successes in 1959 at the San Francisco and Chicago Operas.

Records: HMV-Pathé (including *Faust, Carmen, Iphigénie en Tauride*, and *Les Pêcheurs des Perles*), Decca and London International *(Les Cloches de Corneville)*. *U.S. re-issue:* Angel.

BLANCHART, RAMON, baritone, b. 1865, Barcelona; d. 1934, in San Salvador, Central America. He made his debut under a pseudonym in *Faust* in Barcelona (1885). After two years of further study he appeared in Seville in 1887 and at the Teatro Real in 1888. In 1891 he sang, in Italian, the title role in *Der Fliegende Holländer* at Covent Garden. The next year he made his debut at La Scala as Iago in *Otello*, a part which he alternated with Victor Maurel. He sang again at La Scala a few times in 1903 in *I Lituani*. He made guest appearances in Berlin, Paris, St. Petersburg, Warsaw, and Lisbon and at the Havana Opera for the 1902-03 season. He sang at the Manhattan Opera (1907) and the Boston Opera (1911-14). In 1919-20 he appeared at the Chicago Opera, where he sang *buffo* roles, such as Dulcamara in *L'Elisir d'Amore*. He later lived and taught in Panama.

Records: Fonotipia (Milan, 1905-06), Zonophone (Milan, 1906), and American Columbia* (1910-11). *U.S. re-recording:* Eterna, TAP.

BLAND, ELSA, soprano, b. Apr. 16, 1880, Vienna; d. Sept. 27, 1935, Vienna. A pupil of Marianne Brandt in Vienna, she made her debut (1903) in Olmütz as Fidelio. Engagements: Magdeburg (1904-05), Altenburg (1905-06), guest appearances (1905), at the Vienna Imperial Opera, of which she was a member (1906-08). She then made guest appearances on various other stages, including La Scala (1910-11), and returned to Vienna for the 1912 season. She sang (1913) at the German Opera House in Berlin. Further guest engagements followed, including the Teatro Regio in Parma, and finally she returned to the Vienna State Opera (1920-24). Thereafter she became a teacher in Vienna. She was married to the Austrian cavalry captain Barthelmus.

Records: There are a great many records by this artist on HMV, Pathé, and Odeon, including some interesting duets with Leo Slezak. *U.S. re-recording:* Eterna.

BLANKENHEIM, TONI, baritone, b. 1923, Cologne. He studied at the Music High School in Cologne and made his stage debut (1947) at the Opera in Frankfurt a. M. He stayed in Frankfurt until 1950, and since then has been a member of the Hamburg State Opera. He sang with great success at the Bayreuth Festivals (1954-60), particularly as Beckmesser in *Die Meistersinger*, Donner in *Das Rheingold*, and Klingsor in *Parsifal*. He has also made guest appearances in London and Berlin.

Records: Bastien und Bastienne for DGG. *U.S. re-issue:* American Decca.

BLASS, ROBERT, bass, b. Oct. 27, 1867, New York; d. Dec. 3, 1930, Berlin. Since his family was of German background, he went to Leipzig in 1887 first to study violin and later to study singing with Julius Stockhausen in Frankfurt a. M. He made his debut at Weimar (1892) as the King in *Lohengrin*. In the following eight years he made guest appearances on various German stages and also sang during this time at the Bayreuth Festivals. A guest appearance at Covent Garden in 1899 led to an engagement at the Metropolitan Opera (1900-10), where he made his debut as the Landgraf in *Tannhäuser*. Returning to Germany, he sang at the German Opera in Berlin (1913-19) and then returned to the Metropolitan Opera (1920-22). After 1922 he lived and taught in Berlin.

Records: Rare early records for Victor* (New York, 1903) and also some Edison* cylinders. *U.S. re-recording:* TAP.

BLAUVELT, LILLIAN, soprano, b. Mar. 16, 1873, Brooklyn; d. Aug. 27, 1947, Chicago. She originally wanted to be a violinist and gave concerts in New York at the age of eight. In 1889 she began her vocal studies with Jacques Bouhy in New York and then studied in Paris. She had a very successful concert debut in Brussels in 1893; this led to a contract with the Brussels Opera, where she made her stage debut (1893) as the heroine in *Mireille*. After a tour of Russia she returned to America and dedicated herself especially to concert singing. From 1897 on she had great success in England both on the stage and on the concert platform. In 1898 she sang Verdi's *Requiem* in Rome. In 1902 she sang the Coronation Ode in London at the time of the crowning of King Edward VII. Concert appearances followed in Germany, France, Holland, Belgium, and Switzerland. After 1903 she sang frequently at Covent Garden, making her debut there as Marguerite in *Faust*. In 1905 she traveled in Russia. She created in Zürich the leading role in *Xenia* and married the composer of the opera, Alexander Savine, in 1914. This was followed by concert tours in Europe and America and, in 1920, triumphal tours of Yugoslavia and Czechoslovakia. Until 1920 she appeared regularly in London in concert. Later she lived and taught in Chicago. She was especially famous as a concert artist.

Records: Victor* (Camden, 1903-06) and U.S. Columbia* (1907-09) records.

BLEDSOE, JULES, baritone, b. July 29, 1898, Ward, Texas; d. July 14, 1943, New York. He studied singing in New York, Paris, and Rome. In 1924 he made his debut in the United States. He was the first Negro singer after Roland Hayes to give voice to recitals and his repertory of songs ranged from old Italian arias to modern lieder. Because he was a Negro, at that time he was unable to pursue an operatic career in the United States, but from 1932 on he was successful on European stages in such parts as Amonasro in *Aïda* and Boris Godounov, which he sang, for example, in the Italian Opera in Holland in 1933. Nevertheless, he never attained his much-hoped-for major stage career, and he was finally forced to appear in vaudeville and musical comedy in New York. He created the role of Joe and sang "Old Man River" in the original production of Jerome Kern's *Showboat*. He was also a composer and, in addition to songs, wrote an *African Suite* for violin and orchestra. He had a well-trained, rich voice.

Records: American Decca* recordings of popular songs (ca. 1933).

BOATWRIGHT, McHENRY, bass-baritone, b. Feb. 29, 1928, Tennille, Ga., of a Negro family. As a student he supported himself, his mother, and his sister by playing the piano in restaurants. He graduated from the New England Conservatory of Music in Boston with degrees in both piano and voice. He won the Marian Anderson Award in 1953-54. He made his debut on Feb. 19, 1956, at Jordan Hall in Boston and his New York debut in Town Hall in 1958. In 1957 he won the Young Artists Audition Award of the National Federation of Music Clubs. He also won the Arthur Fiedler Contest over five hundred other contestants. He made debut appearances in London and Milan in 1962. His operatic debut occurred in 1958 at the New England Opera Theater, where he sang Arkel in *Pelléas et Mélisande*. His voice is noted for its volume, its richness of timbre, and for its dramatic expressiveness.

Records: RCA Victor, Columbia.

BOCCOLINI, EBE, soprano, b. 1889, Ancona, Italy. She studied with Ruzzo in Bologna and made her debut (1910) in Cento as Charlotte in *Werther*. She sang at the Italian Opera in Holland (1911-12). In 1914 she sang Felice at the Teatro Lirico in the Italian *première* of *I Quattro Rusteghi*. She sang with great success at the Teatro San Carlo (1914-15). In 1921 she undertook long guest tours through Chile, Peru, and Cuba with Bernardo de Muro and other artists. She appeared at the Teatro Liceo in 1925 and in various Italian opera

Bockelmann · Böhme

houses during the 1930's. She was married to the actor Ermete Zacconi.
Records: HMV. *U.S. re-issue:* Victor.

BOCKELMANN, RUDOLF, baritone, b. Apr. 2, 1892, near Celle, Germany; d. Oct. 9, 1958, Dresden. He first studied languages at the University of Leipzig and then voice with Oscar Lassner and Walter Soomer. He made his debut at Celle (1920). He then sang at the Leipzig Opera (1921-26) and at the Hamburg State Opera (1926-32). In 1928 he appeared for the first time at Bayreuth and returned there until 1942; he was an incomparable Wotan, but was also successful in other roles. From 1932 to 1944 he was one of the most prominent members of the Berlin State Opera. He sang in the world *premières* there of *Der Prinz von Homburg* (1935) and *Rembrandt van Rijn* (1937). His guest appearances also brought him great success in many countries: from 1929 to 1938 he sang each year at Covent Garden; he sang at the Chicago Opera (1930-31) and also at La Scala, the Paris Opéra, and in Rome, Brussels, Amsterdam, Vienna, and Munich. He lived and taught singing in Hamburg (1946-54) and in 1955 became professor at the Music High School in Dresden. He was married to the opera singer Maria Weigand. He had a full heroic baritone voice and he developed its greatest intensity in Wagner parts.
Records: HMV, Telefunken, and Columbia* (including a *Tristan und Isolde* performance, Bayreuth, 1928). *U.S. re-issue:* RCA Victor. *U.S. re-recording:* Telefunken.

BOERNER, CHARLOTTE, soprano, b. June 22, 1900, Leipzig. She completed her first musical studies with Max Wünsche in Leipzig, but she also had vocal training under her mother, the concert soprano Hildegard Boerner. From 1921-23 she was busy as an operetta singer in Berlin. She made her operatic debut (1923) at the Dresden State Opera and was engaged as a lyric soprano at the Berlin State Opera (1923-28). In 1928 she came to the United States where she undertook a long series of concert tours and guest appearances. She sang with the Philadelphia Opera (1931-33) and appeared frequently with the San Francisco Opera, where her appearances included Eudoxia in *La Juive* (1936) and Musetta in *La Bohème* (1937). She was also very successful in South America. In 1931-32 she made a concert tour of Holland.
Records: Vox and Polydor; private recordings in America. *U.S. re-issue:* American Decca.

BÖHME, KURT, bass, b. May 5, 1908, Dresden. He completed his vocal studies at the Dresden Conservatory. After his debut in Bautzen, he was engaged at the Dresden State Opera (1930-49). Since 1950 he has been a member of the Munich State Opera and since 1955 concurrently a member of the Vienna State Opera. He has been highly successful at the Salzburg Festivals, especially as Baron Ochs in *Der Rosenkavalier*, but he has also appeared there in the first performances of such modern operas as *Penelope* (1954) and *Irische Legende* (1955). In 1952 he sang Pogner in *Die Meistersinger* at Bayreuth. He has made guest appearances at La Scala and in London, Lisbon, and Budapest. He made his Metropolitan Opera debut in 1954 as Pogner and has toured South Africa. He is especially noted in *buffo* parts in his voice range, but is also famous in Wagner roles.
Records: His first recordings appeared after World War II, particularly for DGG* (including a complete *Der Rosenkavalier*).

These were soon followed by LP discs for Decca, Urania* (*The Bartered Bride, Der Rosenkavalier, Lohengrin*), Columbia (*Der Waffenschmied*), Ariola, HMV, Philips (including *Don Giovanni, Die Zauberflöte*, and *Die Frau ohne Schatten*). *U.S. re-issue:* Vox, London, Turnabout.

BOHNEN, MICHAEL, bass-baritone, b. May 2, 1887, Cologne; d. Apr. 26, 1965, Berlin. He studied singing at the Cologne Conservatory with Schulz-Dornburg and made his debut (1910) at the Düsseldorf Opera House; he was then engaged at Wiesbaden (1911-14). In 1914 he stepped in for Paul Knüpfer, who was ill, at the Berlin Imperial Opera as Gurnemanz in *Parsifal* and had a sensational success. He also made guest appearances in 1914 at Covent Garden and at the Bayreuth Festival. At the outbreak of World War I he became a soldier, but was called to the Berlin Imperial Opera, where he remained until 1918 and where he later made frequent guest appearances. In 1922 he was engaged by the Metropolitan Opera, where he remained with great success until 1933. He then returned to Germany and was engaged at the German Opera House in Berlin (1935-45), as well as performing in films. He made guest appearances and concertized in all the great musical centers of the world. He was the director of the Berlin City Opera (1945-47) and on this stage made his farewell appearance (1951) as Hans Sachs in *Die Meistersinger*. For a short time he was married to the soprano Mary Lewis and later to the dancer La Jana. He has a powerful voice of great compass and exciting impressiveness, with which he mastered a wide range of both bass and baritone roles; he was also a skillful actor.

Records: A great many records for Brunswick*, Pathé, HMV, Polydor, Odeon, Ultraphon, including a complete performance of *Abu Hassan* for Urania* (1941). *U.S. re-issue:* Okeh, Telefunken, Vox, American Decca. *U.S. re-recording:* ASCO, Eterna, Rococo.

BOKOR, MARGIT, soprano, b. 1905, Budapest; d. Nov. 9, 1949, New York. She studied singing in both Budapest and Vienna. She made her debut at the Budapest National Opera (1928) and sang in guest appearances in Berlin as Leonora in *Il Trovatore* in 1930. She was a member of the Dresden State Opera (1931-35). There, on July 1, 1933, she sang Zdenka in the world *première* of *Arabella*. After 1934 she was associated with the Salzburg Festivals, especially as Octavian in *Der Rosenkavalier*. She sang at the Vienna State Opera (1935-38) and made guest appearances during these years in Italy and Amsterdam. In 1939 she came to the United States, where she sang in the Chicago and Philadelphia companies; she made one appearance at the Metropolitan Opera House with the Philadelphia ensemble. In 1947 she joined the N.Y. City Opera.

Records: Only one official record of her voice exists, a duet from *Arabella* with Viorica Ursuleac on Polydor. *U.S. re-issue:* Brunswick. *U.S. re-recording:* Belcanto.

BONCI, ALESSANDRO, tenor, b. Feb. 2, 1870, Cesena, Italy; d. Aug. 10, 1940, Viserba, near Rimini, Italy. At first he was a shoemaker's apprentice, but after the discovery of his voice he studied singing at the Pesaro Conservatory under Felice Coen, followed by further training with Enrico Delle Sedie in Paris. In 1892 he became a soloist in the choir of the Pilgrimage Church at Loreto and in 1896 made his stage debut at Parma as Fenton in *Falstaff*. A guest performance in Leghorn in 1897 led to his appearance

Bonelli · Boninsegna

at La Scala as Arturo in *I Puritani*. Guest appearances followed in St. Petersburg, Vienna, Berlin, Lisbon, and Madrid. He made his first appearance at Covent Garden in 1900 and appeared there frequently in the following years. Engaged by the Manhattan Opera in 1906, he sang Arturo in the first performance at the newly opened Manhattan Opera House. He was a member of the Metropolitan Opera (1907-10), making his debut as the Duke in *Rigoletto*. After 1909 he had great successes in South America. He made a long American tour (1910-11) and sang in Madrid and Barcelona (1913-14). He was a member of the Chicago Opera (1914; 1919-21). During World War I he served as a volunteer in the Italian Air Force. In 1918 he took up his career again at the Teatro Colón. He sang at the Teatro Costanzi (1922-23). From 1923 on he taught singing in New York, but in 1945 he returned to Italy and lived in Milan in complete retirement. He had one of the most beautiful tenor voices preserved on records; he was unexcelled in his mastery of technique and in the refined use of his voice.

Records: Edison*, both cylinders and discs, and also for Columbia* and Fonotipia. *U.S. re-issue:* Okeh. *U.S. re-recording:* Belcanto, Eterna, FRP, Rococo, Scala, TAP, Odyssey.

BONELLI, RICHARD, baritone, b. Feb. 6, 1894, Port Byron, N.Y. Originally Richard Bunn. After studying at Syracuse University, he began his voice training. He made his debut at the Brooklyn Academy of Music (1915) as Valentin in *Faust*. After World War I he studied further with Jean de Reszke in Paris, and then made guest appearances at Monte Carlo, La Scala, and in the Paris opera houses. He had outstanding successes at the Chicago Opera (1925-31) and was a member of the Metropolitan Opera (1932-45). He lives and teaches in New York. He was especially famous as an interpreter of Italian roles, but also sang Wolfram in *Tannhäuser*.

Records: Vocalion*, Brunswick*, Allegro Royale*. *U.S. re-recording:* TAP.

BONINI, FRANCESCO MARIA, baritone, b. 1865, Naples; d. Jan. 11, 1930, Milan. He studied at the Conservatory of San Pietro a Majella in Naples with Beniamino Carelli, and made his debut (1896) in Foggia. He sang at the Theater Royal in Malta (1897-98); guest appearances at the Cairo Opera and on Italian stages followed. He sang at the Odessa Opera (1900-02), and at the Teatro Colón (1901). In 1903 he came to Milan and sang at both the Teatro Lirico and La Scala. He was highly successful from 1904-08 and again in 1918 at the Teatro San Carlo. He was engaged at the Teatro São Carlos (1905-07) and (1913) at the Teatro Real. He appeared a few times again at La Scala in 1912 and 1918 at the Teatro Costanzi. In 1927 he gave up his career and thereafter taught.

Records: Fonotipia (Milan, 1905-06). *U.S. re-recording:* Belcanto.

BONINSEGNA, CELESTINA, soprano, b. Feb. 26, 1877, Reggio Emilia, Italy; d. Feb. 14, 1947, Milan. At the age of fifteen she sang Norina in *Don Pasquale* in an opera performance in Reggio Emilia. She then studied at the Liceo Rossini in Pesaro with Virginia Boccabadati. In 1899 she made her stage debut in *Die Königin von Saba* at Piacenza. She also sang at the Teatro dal Verme, the Teatro Costanzi, and in Cremona and Genoa. She made guest appearances (1901-02) in South America, at Covent Garden (1904-05), and in the same years sang Aïda at La Scala. She made her Metropolitan Opera debut in the 1906-07 season as Aïda opposite Enrico Caruso. These appearances were followed by guest performances in Spain and South America. She was a member of the Boston Opera (1909-10) and in 1913 made guest appearances in Russia. In 1920 she sang at the Havana Opera. In 1923 she gave up her career and later lived at the Casa di riposo in Milan. The records of this artist preserve one of the most beautiful soprano voices of her epoch, both in the thorough musical training and in the variety of nuances which her voice shows. It can be said truthfully that she was more famous for her records than for her career itself.

Records: G & T (Milan, 1904-07), HMV, Columbia*, Edison*, and Pathé*. *U.S. re-issue:* Victor, Opera Disc, HRS, IRCC. *U.S. re-recording:* Columbia, CRS, Eterna, FRP, IRCC, Scala, TAP.

BORG, KIM, bass-baritone, b. Aug. 7, 1919, Helsinki. He first studied chemistry and then became a certified engineer; later he took up singing at the Sibelius Academy in Helsinki under Heikki Teittinen. He later studied under Magnus Andersen in Copenhagen and with Adelaide von Skilondz in Stockholm. He made his debut (1947) in concert and his stage debut (1951) at Aarhus. Since 1952 he has had contracts for guest appearances with the Helsinki and Copenhagen Operas. Concert tours followed in Germany, Austria, Holland, the United States, Canada, and Israel. He has had successful guest seasons in Vienna, Munich, and Berlin and has sung at the opera festivals in Glyndebourne, Edinburgh, and Salzburg. He was called to the Metropolitan Opera in 1959 and made his debut as Almaviva in *Le Nozze di Figaro*. He lives in Glostrup, Denmark. His dark-timbred powerful bass voice has been proved in a many-sided stage repertory as well as in those of oratorio and song. He eventually became a baritone.

Records: HMV (*Boris Godounov*), but especially for DGG* (*Die Schöpfung*, the Verdi and Mozart *Requiems*, *Die Zauberflöte*, *Madama Butterfly*, and *Tosca*). *U.S. re-issue:* Capitol, Columbia, Angel, Heliodor, Artia, Epic, Decca.

BORGATTI, GIUSEPPE, tenor, b. Mar. 19, 1871, Cento, near Bologna; d. Oct. 18, 1950, Milan. His voice was discovered while he was working as a mason. He made his debut (1893) at Castelfranco Veneto. He sang for the first time at La Scala in 1896 and on March 28th of that year created the title role there in the world *première* of *Andrea Chénier*. Thereafter he was a ranking tenor at that house. In 1900 he sang Cavaradossi in La Scala's first performance of *Tosca* and in 1906 Herod in La Scala's first *Salome*. He became the most famous Italian Wagner tenor of his time and was invited to sing at the Bayreuth Festivals. He was especially beloved in South America, particularly at the Teatro Colón. In 1913 he suddenly became blind on the stage at La Scala during a rehearsal of *Tristan*. Thereafter he sang only in the concert hall and became a teacher.

Records: Fonotipia (Milan, 1905) and Pathé, the latter very rare; in 1928 an electric recording of his voice was made. *U.S. re-issue:* HRS. *U.S. re-recording:* HRS.

BORGIOLI, ARMANDO, baritone, b. 1898 (?), Florence; d. Jan. 20, 1945, near Bologna. He began his stage career in 1923 and appeared in 1926 in Catania and at the Verona Festival. He was called to La Scala in 1927, making his debut as

Alfio in *Cavalleria Rusticana*. Until 1944 he was to be heard there as well as at the other leading Italian theaters. He made guest appearances at Covent Garden (1928; 1933; 1938) and was a member of the Metropolitan Opera (1932-36). He had great successes in South America, especially in Buenos Aires and Rio de Janeiro. During World War II he sang in Italy and made guest appearances in Germany and Holland. On Jan. 20, 1945, as he was traveling from Milan to Bologna for an appearance there, he was killed during an air raid. With his splendid and impressive baritone voice, he was successful in the Italian repertory.

Records: He sang Amonasro in a complete *Aïda* for Columbia* and Scarpia in a complete *Tosca* for HMV. *U.S. re-issue:* RCA Victor.

BORGIOLI, DINO, tenor, b. Feb. 15, 1891, Florence; d. Sept. 13, 1960, London. After originally studying law he began his vocal studies and made his debut (1918) at the Teatro dal Verme. He soon came to La Scala, where he was assisted by Toscanini. Guest appearances took him to Covent Garden, the Teatro Colón, to Paris, Brussels, and Berlin. In 1931 he sang Almaviva in *Il Barbiere di Siviglia* at the Salzburg Festival and in 1935-36 Fenton in *Falstaff* there. He was a member of the Metropolitan Opera (1934-35). After 1939 he lived in London with his wife, the Australian soprano Patricia Moore. In 1939 he bade farewell to the stage and founded and managed an opera company, the New London Opera Company; at the same time he taught singing in London. He had a beautiful lyric tenor voice.

Records: Columbia*, among others, in complete recordings of *Rigoletto* and *Il Barbiere di Siviglia*. *U.S. re-recording:* FRP.

BORI, LUCREZIA, soprano, b. Dec. 24, 1887, Valencia, Spain; d. May 14, 1960, New York. She studied piano and theory at the Valencia Conservatory. Her vocal talent was discovered during a visit to Italy in 1908. In the same year she made her debut at the Teatro Adriano as Micaëla in *Carmen*. She was so successful in this appearance that she was engaged the following season at La Scala. In 1911 she sang Octavian there in the Milan *première* of *Der Rosenkavalier*. After 1910 she appeared frequently at the Teatro Colón. She was also highly successful in Paris and London. In 1912 she was called to the Metropolitan Opera and first appeared there in the title role of *Manon Lescaut*, opposite Enrico Caruso. After outstanding successes she retired from the stage on account of illness (1915-19). From 1921-36 she was again one of the great prima donnas of the Metropolitan Opera. Her guest appearances and concert tours all over the world took an especially brilliant turn. After her retirement from the stage in 1936, she was the first woman to serve on the Metropolitan's board of directors. She had a marvelously trained lyric soprano voice of extraordinarily rich shading, admired especially in the Italian and French repertories.

Records: Edison* cylinders and discs, and many records for Victor*. *U.S. re-issue:* Opera disc. *U.S. re-recording:* ASCO, Eterna, RCA Victor, Rococo, Scala, IRCC, Odyssey.

BORKH, INGE, soprano, b. May 26, 1917, Mannheim, Germany. The daughter of a Swedish diplomat, she studied at the Reinhardt-Seminar at the Vienna Burgtheater to become an actress and appeared as such in 1937 at Linz and after 1938 in Basel. She then took up vocal studies with Muratti in Milan and made her debut (1940) in Lucerne as Agathe in *Der Freischütz*. She sang during World War II in Lucerne, Basel, and Zürich and in 1950 began a long extended series of guest appearances, first in Munich and Berlin. In 1952 she sang Sieglinde in *Die Walküre* at Bayreuth. She made brilliant guest appearances at the State Opera Houses in Vienna, Hamburg, and Stuttgart, in Barcelona, Lisbon, and Naples. She was praised for her Eglantine in *Euryanthe* at the 1954 Maggio Musicale Festival. At the 1954 Salzburg Festival she sang Cathleen in the first performance of *Irische Legende*. In 1955 she sang as guest at the San Francisco Opera. She was honored at La Scala, Covent Garden, and in Berlin as an interpreter of such dramatic soprano roles as Salome and Elektra. In 1957 she made her Metropolitan Opera debut in *Salome*. She is married to the baritone Alexander Welitsch.

Records: Her first records appeared in Switzerland on the Imperial label and included selections from operettas. She sang for Decca (*Turandot*), RCA Victor, and DGG* (including *Antigonae, Elektra*, and *Die Frau ohne Schatten*). *U.S. re-issue:* London.

BORONAT, OLIMPIA, soprano, b. 1867, Genoa; d. 1934, Warsaw. Her father was an Italian officer and her mother was Spanish; she studied at the Milan Conservatory under Leoni. Her debut (1886) at Naples was followed by a tour of Mexico and South America. She then appeared at the larger Italian theaters, including La Scala. In 1891 she made guest appearances at the Imperial Opera in St. Petersburg, where she was extraordinarily successful. In 1903 she married the Polish Count Rzewuski, to whom she had been introduced at a soiree given by the Grand Duke Nicholas.

She lived in retirement for a time on her enormous estates in Poland, but in 1905 she resumed her career. Once again she had brilliant successes in St. Petersburg, Moscow, Kiev, and Warsaw. In 1914 she opened a vocal studio in Warsaw and in 1922 she made her final appearance at a charity concert. One of the most beautiful coloratura voices on records because of her complete mastery of technique and her sensitivity to style.

Records: A few records for G & T (St. Petersburg, 1904) and for HMV (Milan, 1908). *U.S. re-issue:* Victor, IRCC. *U.S. re-recording:* Angel, Belcanto, Eterna, Rococo, Scala, TAP.

BORTHAYRE, JEAN, baritone, b. 1907 (?), Mauleon in the Basque Pyrenees, France. His voice was discovered while he was performing compulsory military service. Thereafter he studied at the National Conservatory in Paris and made his debut (1937) at the Algiers Opera. In 1939 he was recalled to the army upon the outbreak of war. In 1943 he began his career again in Toulouse. After 1945 he sang in Bordeaux, Lyons, Marseilles, and Strasbourg and made guest appearances at the opera houses in Ghent and Antwerp. In 1951 he came to the two great Paris houses, the Opéra and the Opéra-Comique. Since then he has been valued as one of the oustanding French representatives of his voice range. A highly impressive baritone voice.

Records: A great many records for Pathè (*Faust*), HMV (Massenet's *Manon*), Decca (*Lakmé*), and Nixa (*Un Ballo in Maschera*). *U.S. re-issue:* Capitol, London, Period, Everest-Cetra.

BOSETTI, HERMINE, soprano, b. Sept. 28, 1875, Vienna; d. May 1, 1936, Hohenrain, Bavaria. Originally Hermine von Flick. She stud-

Bötel · Boué

ied with Aurelie Jäger-Wilczek in Vienna and made her debut in Wiesbaden (1898) as Ännchen in *Der Freischütz*. She remained there until 1900, then sang at the Vienna Imperial Opera (1900-01). From 1901 until her retirement from the stage in 1924 she was a member of the Munich Royal Opera, where she was greatly beloved. Her debut role in Munich was Marie in *La Fille du Régiment*. Guest appearances brought her great success in Holland and Belgium as well as at Covent Garden and in Russia. In St. Petersburg she sang opposite Mattia Battistini. From 1924 to 1930 she taught at Hoch's Conservatory in Frankfurt a. M. and later in Munich. She had a brilliantly managed, virtuoso coloratura voice.

Records: G & T (Munich, 1906), later for Odeon and Polydor. *U.S. re-issue:* Opera Disc.

BÖTEL, HEINRICH, tenor, b. Mar. 6, 1854, Hamburg; d. Jan. 6, 1938, Hamburg. At first a driver in his father's transport business, his voice was discovered by Bernhard Pollini, the director of the Hamburg opera houses, who had him study with the conductor Zumpe and with Franz Krükl in Hamburg. He made his debut in 1883 at the Hamburg Opera as Manrico in *Il Trovatore*. He remained in Hamburg for his entire career but made guest appearances in Berlin, Vienna, Cologne, Stuttgart, and Breslau. His outstanding role was Chapdelou in *Le Postillon de Longjumeau*, in which audiences were astonished at his skill with the whip; however, he also sang a wide repertory of other roles. His son, Bernhard Bötel (b. 1883), also had a very successful career as a tenor.

Records: Six rare records for HMV (Hamburg, 1908), including the Postilion's Song from *Le Postillon de Longjumeau*.

BOTTA, LUCA, tenor, b. Apr. 16, 1882, Amalfi, Italy; d. Sept. 29, 1917, New York. A student of Guglielmo Vergine in Naples, he made his debut there (1911) as Turiddu in *Cavalleria Rusticana* and then sang guest appearances in Turin, Mantua, Verona, Milan, and Malta. In 1913 he came to the United States and sang first with the Western Metropolitan Opera Company in California. During a temporary appearance of this troupe in New York he was heard by the famous soprano Frances Alda, who arranged an engagement for him with the New York Metropolitan Opera in 1914. As his debut role there he sang Rodolfo in *La Bohème* with great success. In the following years he went from one success to another at that house and came to be looked upon as a probable successor to Enrico Caruso. He appeared as guest at the Teatro Colón in 1914. He died of a brain tumor. A masterful tenor voice of great brilliance.

Records: A few records for HMV. *U.S. re-issue:* Victor.

BOUÉ, GÉORI, soprano, b. Oct .16, 1918, Toulouse. She studied at the Conservatory at Toulouse and made her debut at that opera house (1935). After completing her studies in Paris with Reynaldo Hahn and Henri Busser, she sang in operetta theaters in the French capital and in 1938 came to the Opéra-Comique, making her debut as Mireille. She had important successes at both major Paris opera theaters and after World War II made guest appearances in Brussels and Nice, at the Teatro Liceo, the Mexico City Opera, and in Germany and Italy. In France she was scarcely surpassed in her generation as a lyric soprano. She married the baritone Roger Bourdin.

Records: Odeon, Urania* (*Thaïs*), HMV (*Faust*, under Beecham), and Columbia (*Les*

Contes d'Hoffmann). *U.S. re-issue:* RCA Victor.

BOURDIN, ROGER, baritone, b. June 14, 1900, Paris. He studied at the National Conservatory in Paris and made his debut (1922) at the Opéra-Comique, of which he thereafter remained a member, making guest appearances at the Paris Opéra, in Nice, Monte Carlo, Marseilles, and Brussels. In 1930 he sang Pelléas at Covent Garden and also made guest appearances in Italy. He sang in many first performances at the Opéra-Comique: *Sophie Arnould* (1927), *Le Roi d'Yvetot* (1930), *Amphytrion 38* (1944), *Bolivar* (1950), and *Madame Bovary* (1951). He married the soprano Géori Boué.

Records: Odeon and Urania* (*Thaïs* and *Werther*) as well as Decca (*Manon*). *U.S. re-issue:* London, American Decca, RCA Victor.

BOURGIGNON, JANE, contralto, b. 1894, Bordeaux. After studying at the Paris Conservatory she made her debut (1918) at the Opéra-Comique. She remained a highly esteemed artist at that house for over twenty years. In 1925-28 and again in 1936 she made successful guest appearances at Covent Garden, first in Italian parts, later as the Mother in *Louise*. In 1928 she sang Carmen in Amsterdam under Pierre Monteux. During World War II she retired from the stage and thereafter taught in Paris.

Records: Only two Columbia records exist of her beautifully trained contralto voice.

BOUVIER, HÉLÈNE, contralto, b. June 20, 1905, Paris. After studying at the National Conservatory in Paris, she made her debut at Nantes (1930) in the title role of *Orphée et Eurydice*. In 1939 she came to the Paris Opéra and the Opéra-Comique. Thereafter she had a distinguished career in the French metropolis. She was internationally famous as Dalila in *Samson et Dalila* and as Geneviève in *Pelléas et Mélisande*. She made guest appearances in Holland and Belgium as well as in Monte Carlo. In 1947 she sang as a guest at the Teatro Colón; in 1952 she sang Jocaste in *Oedipus Rex* at the Holland Festival. She was the most famous French contralto of her time.

Records: Pathé, among others, in complete recordings of *Samson et Dalila* and in Berlioz' *L'Enfance du Christ*; for Decca in Stravinsky's *Oedipus Rex* and *Pelléas et Mélisande*. *U.S. re-issue:* Box, Epic, Columbia.

BOVY, VINA, soprano, b. May 22, 1900, Ghent. She studied at the Conservatory in Ghent, where she also made her debut (1917) in *Hänsel und Gretel*. She sang at the Théâtre de la Monnaie (1920-23) and then had outstanding successes on Italian stages. She completed a guest season at the Teatro Colón in 1927 and later appeared in Barcelona, Madrid, Monte Carlo, Venice, Milan, and Rome, and especially in Brussels and Paris. She was engaged at the Metropolitan Opera (1936-39). From 1947-56 she was director of the Ghent Opera. She had an especially well-trained coloratura voice, at home in both the French and Italian repertory.

Records: HMV and Columbia*, including for the latter a complete recording of *Les Contes d'Hoffmann*. *U.S. re-recording:* Rococo.

BRANDT, MARIANNE, contralto, b. Sept. 12, 1842, Vienna; d. July 9, 1921, Vienna. Originally Marie Bischof. She attended the Vienna Municipal Conservatory (1862-66) as a pupil of Zeller and Frau Marschner. She made her debut (1867) at Olmütz as Rachel in *La Juive*. After a guest appearance at Graz, she created a sensation among audiences at the Berlin Imperial Opera as Fidès in *Le Prophète* in 1868, and she was first contralto there from 1868-86. She then resumed her studies, this time with Mme. Viardot-Garcia in Baden-Baden (1869-70). After 1872 she often appeared as a guest at Covent Garden, and also at the Vienna Imperial Opera (1873-83). She was especially prized as a gifted Wagner singer. In 1876 she sang the part of Waltraute in Bayreuth at the world *première* of *Götterdämmerung*. Wagner assigned her the role of Kundry at the world *première* of *Parsifal* at Bayreuth in 1882, in which she alternated with Amelia Materna and Therese Malten. She had great success at the Metropolitan Opera (1884-88). After 1890 she lived as a singing teacher in Vienna and occasionally appeared in concert. She had a large dramatic voice of such great range that she could also sing dramatic soprano parts.

Records: In 1905 her voice was recorded on three Pathé cylinders as a vocal document. *U.S. re-recording:* IRCC, TAP.

BRANDT-FORSTER, ELLEN, soprano, b. Oct. 11, 1866, Vienna; d. 1921, Vienna. She began her vocal studies when she was fourteen years old with Louise Dustmann and Emilie Dorr in Vienna, and made her debut (1885) at Danzig as Marguerite in *Faust*. She was connected with the Bayreuth Festival in 1886. In 1887 she was called to the Vienna Imperial Opera, where she remained until the end of her career. On Feb. 16, 1892, she sang the part of Sophie in the first performance there of *Werther*. She was also very successful as a concert and lieder singer, and often appeared in Vienna at court concerts. She ended her stage career in 1909.

Records: Her voice is preserved on a few rare G & T records (Vienna, 1902).

BRANNIGAN, OWEN, bass, b. 1917, in Northumberland, England. He studied until 1942 at the Guildhall School of Music in London and sang first with the Sadler's Wells Opera Company and then with great success at Covent Garden. He participated in the world *premières* of several of Benjamin Britten's operas—Swallow in *Peter Grimes* at Sadler's Wells (June 7, 1945), in *The Rape of Lucretia* at Glyndebourne (1946), and in *Albert Herring* again at Glyndebourne (1947), as well as in *A Midsummer Night's Dream* at the Aldeburgh Festival in 1960. He is also famous as an oratorio singer.

Records: Decca in *Peter Grimes*, *Albert Herring*, *The Messiah*; and HMV. *U.S. re-issue:* Angel, London, Richmond, Westminster, L'Oiseau Lyre.

BRANZELL, KARIN, contralto, b. Sept. 24, 1891, Stockholm. Originally an organist in Stockholm, she studied singing with Thekla Hafer there, with Ludwig Mantler and Louis Bachner in Berlin, and finally with Enrico Rosati in New York. She made her stage debut (1912) at the Stockholm Royal Opera, where she remained until 1918. She was a member of the Berlin State Opera (1918-33) and was admired there in a variety of roles. In 1924 she came to the Metropolitan Opera for the first time and also gave her farewell performance there in 1944. She had a brilliant guest season at the Teatro Colón (1926). In 1930-31 she sang Fricka and Waltraute at the Bayreuth Festivals. She made guest appearances in Paris, Vienna, Milan, London, Brussels, Chicago, and San Francisco and was also very successful on the concert stage. After 1946 she taught at the Juilliard School of Music in New York. She had a wide-ranging velvety voice of great flexibility.

Records: Acoustic records for

Homochord, Brunswick*, and Homophon; electric records for Parlophone, HMV, Brunswick*, Odeon, Urania, and Remington*.
U.S. re-issue: American Decca.
U.S. re-recording: Eterna, FRP, Rococo, TAP.

BRASLAU, SOPHIE, contralto, b. Aug. 16, 1892, New York; d. Dec. 22, 1935, New York. She was the daughter of the Russian scholar Abel Braslau. After first studying piano, she studied singing with Buzzi-Peccia, Sibella, Herbert Witherspoon, Marafioti, and finally with Marcella Sembrich. She made her debut at the Metropolitan Opera (1914), singing the Voice from on High in *Parsifal*. From 1914 to 1920 she was very successful at the Metropolitan, where she sang, among other roles, in the world *premières* of *Mme. Sans-Gêne* (1915) and *Shanewis* (1918). In 1918 she sang at Ravinia, near Chicago. After 1920 she had a great career as a concert artist. In 1930-31 she appeared a few times at the Philadelphia Opera as Carmen and as Marina in *Boris Godounov*. She had a heavy, dark-timbred voice of great impressiveness.
Records: Victor* and American Columbia*.

BRAUN, CARL, bass, b. June 2, 1886, Meisenheim, Germany; d. Apr. 24, 1960, Hamburg. He studied with Hermann Gausche in Kreuznach and in 1904 came as a pupil to the Berlin Imperial Opera. There he studied further with Eugen Robert Weiss. He sang at the Wiesbaden Royal Opera (1906-11) and at the Vienna Imperial Opera (1911-12). He was engaged at the Berlin City Opera (1912-1914). He was especially noted as a Wagner singer and took part in the Bayreuth Festivals (1906-31). He was a member of the Metropolitan Opera (1912-17) and was engaged at the Berlin State Opera (1920-27). In 1922 and 1923 he had great success on South American tours and later on tours of North America in 1928 and 1931. In 1933 he was engaged as a singer and *régisseur* at the German Opera in Berlin and in 1935-36 at both the Berlin Volksoper and the Danzig Municipal Theater. After 1937 he lived and acted as a concert agent, first in Oberhausen and after 1949 in Hamburg.
Records: Odeon, Vox, and Columbia*.

BRAUN, HANS, baritone, b. May 14, 1917, Vienna. As a child he belonged to the Wiener Sängerknaben and studied voice with Hermann Gallos and Hans Duhan there. He made his debut in Königsberg (1938) as Count Almaviva in *Le Nozze di Figaro*. Contracts followed with Bremerhaven, Saarbrücken, and the German Opera in Berlin. In 1945 he was called to the Vienna State Opera, to which he has since belonged. He made guest appearances at Covent Garden, La Scala, the Teatro San Carlo, the Maggio Musicale Festival, and in Berlin, Munich, and Hamburg. At the Salzburg Festival of 1950 he stirred up great interest by his singing of the role of Olivier in *Capriccio*. In 1953 he sang the Herald in *Lohengrin* at the Bayreuth Festival. He was married for a time to the contralto Dagmar Hermann (b. 1921).
Records: He sang for many labels and in complete operas, including DGG* (Carl Orff's *Carmina Burana*), Cetra* (*Elektra*), Decca (*Salome*, *Lohengrin*), Philips, Vanguard-Amadeo, MMS, and Bertelsmann. *U.S. re-issue:* London, Bach Guild, Everest, Haydn, Remington, Vox, Richmond.

BRAUN, HELENA, soprano, b. 1903, Düsseldorf. She studied in Düsseldorf and Cologne and made her debut (1929) at Coblenz. In

1931 she went to Bielefeld, in 1933 to Wuppertal, and in 1934 to Wiesbaden, where she remained until 1940. After 1940 she was a member of the Munich State Opera. She was also engaged at the Vienna State Opera (1941-49). In 1942 she sang the Countess in *Le Nozze di Figaro* at the Salzburg Festival. Guest appearances took her to the State Operas in Berlin, Hamburg, and Stuttgart, as well as to La Scala and Covent Garden. She was married to her heroic baritone Ferdinand Frantz and accompanied him to New York; she made guest appearances at the Metropolitan Opera while he was under contract there. She was especially prized in dramatic, particularly Wagner, parts. After the early death of her husband, she bade farewell to the stage in a performance at Munich in which she sang Ortrud in *Lohengrin*. She lives in Hohenpeissenberg in Upper Bavaria.

Records: A few records by this artist appeared on DGG, including a complete *Lohengrin*, in which she sang Ortrud. *U.S. re-issue:* American Decca.

BREITENFELD, RICHARD, baritone, b. Dec. 13, 1869, Reichenburg, Bohemia; d. 1943 (?), Theresienstadt. A pupil of Johannes Ress in Vienna, he made his debut (1897) at the Cologne Opera as Count de Luna in *Il Trovatore*. He remained in Cologne until 1902 and then went to the opera house in Frankfurt a. M., where he remained for nearly thirty years. He sang at the Bayreuth Festivals and made guest appearances on the more important German stages and at the Wagner Society in Amsterdam. Since he was Jewish, he was placed in the Theresienstadt ghetto during World War II; he probably died there in 1943. He was especially known as a Wagner singer.

Records: HMV and Odeon.

BRÉJEAN-SILVER, GEORGETTE, soprano, b. Sept. 22, 1870, Paris. Originally Georgette-Amélie Sisout. She studied at the National Conservatory in Paris and made her debut (1890) at the Bordeaux Opera. In 1894 she came to the Opéra-Comique (under the name Mme. Bréjean-Gravières), where as her first part she sang Manon in Massenet's opera. This was her particular starring role and Massenet composed for her, for a Brussels production, as an addition to the famous Gavotte, a bravura aria, the so-called Fabliau. In 1899 she sang the role of the Fairy in the world *première* of *Cendrillon* at the Opéra-Comique. A starring career in Paris and guest appearances in Brussels, Nice, and Monte Carlo sum up her career. She later lived and taught in Paris. Her second marriage was to the composer Charles Silver. She had a brilliantly managed coloratura voice of soaring lightness in tone production.

Records: Fonotipia and Odeon De Luxe (Paris, 1905-06). *U.S. re-recording:* Rococo.

BRESSLER-GIANOLI, CLOTILDE, contralto, b. June 3, 1874, Geneva; d. May 12, 1912, Geneva. Her first vocal studies were at the Geneva Conservatory, then in Milan with Sangiovanni, Giacosa, and Ronconi. She made her debut in Geneva (1891) as Dalila in *Samson et Dalila*. In 1893 she made guest appearances at La Scala, then in Brussels, Lyons, Bordeaux, and at the Opéra-Comique. After a tour through the United States with the San Carlo Opera Company, she sang with the Manhattan Opera in New York (1907-10), her roles including that of the Mother in the first American production of *Louise*. Later she appeared in Philadelphia and Chicago. Her particular starring part was Carmen.

Records: Only a single Odeon

record of her voice exists. *U.S. re-recording:* IRCC, FRP, TAP.

BREUER, HANS, tenor, b. Apr. 27, 1868, Cologne; d. Oct. 11, 1929, Vienna. On the advice of Wüllner he studied with Benno Stolzenberg in Cologne; advanced study followed at the Bayreuth school with Julius Kniese and Cosima Wagner. He made his debut at the Bayreuth Festival (1894), singing small roles in *Lohengrin* and *Parsifal*. In 1896 he sang with sensational success at Bayreuth the role of Mime in the *Ring* cycle; he continued in this part each season until 1914. He also sang David in *Die Meistersinger* there (1898-1904). He was engaged at Breslau (1896-97), and made a guest tour of the United States in 1897. He was a member of the Metropolitan Opera (1898-1900) and was a frequent guest at Covent Garden. He became an honored member of the Vienna Imperial Opera (1900-09). At the 1910 Salzburg Festival he sang Monostatos in *Die Zauberflöte* and in 1922 and 1925 also sang Basilio in *Le Nozze di Figaro*, as well as Monostatos. He was an operatic coach at the Salzburg Festivals and elsewhere. He was one of the greatest *buffo*-tenors of his time; unmatched as Mime, he was also respected as a Mozart singer.

Records: Quite rare records—one for G & T (Bayreuth, 1904), and one for HMV on which he sang patriotic German songs with Georg Maikl, Carl Ritmann, and Lorenz Corvinus.

BRÉVAL, LUCIENNE, soprano, b. Dec. 5, 1859, Berlin; d. Aug. 15, 1935, Neuilly-sur-Seine, near Paris. Originally Bertha Schilling. She came of a Swiss family. She first studied piano at the Geneva and Lausanne Conservatories, then singing at the Paris Conservatory with Victor Warot. She made her stage debut (1892) at the Paris Opéra as Selika in *L'Africaine*. She was one of the great prima donnas of the French metropolis and appeared on the stage of the Opéra for over twenty-five years. She sang there in many world *premières*, notably in *Grisélidis* (1901) and *Monna Vanna* (1909). In 1913 she sang at Monte Carlo in the world *première* of *Pénélope*. She was engaged at the Metropolitan Opera (1900-02) and there she also demonstrated her ability as a Wagner soprano. She made guest appearances in Italy, England, France, Holland, and Belgium. At the last she was a teacher in Paris.

Records: Mapleson cylinders. *U.S. re-recording:* IRCC.

BRIESEMEISTER, OTTO, tenor, b. May 18, 1866, Arnswalde, Prussia; d. June 16, 1910, Berlin. After studying medicine at the Universities of Würzburg and Leipzig, he became a military physician. He studied singing with Wiedemann in Leipzig. At first he was a concert singer, but made his stage debut in Dessau (1893) as Manrico in *Il Trovatore*. He was engaged at Breslau (1894-95). In 1899 he sang Loge in the *Ring* cycle at the Bayreuth Festival; he delighted audiences in this part at Bayreuth until the summer of 1909, and he remains unmatched in that role. He made guest appearances in Berlin, Munich, and the other large German opera houses. He later lived in Berlin and during his singing career carried on a practice as a throat specialist.

Records: Rare records, mostly from his Wagner repertory, for Odeon and Anker.

BRODERSEN, FRIEDERICH, baritone, b. Dec. 1, 1873, Bad Boll, Germany; d. Mar. 19, 1926, Krefeld, Germany. After study and practice as an architect, he studied singing with Heinrich Bertram in Stuttgart. He made his debut (1900) at Nuremburg. In 1903 he came to the Munich Royal Opera and remained a member of that organization until his death. He was greatly beloved in the Bavarian capital and appeared there in many world *premières*—for example, in *Le Donne Curiose* (1903), in *Il Segreto di Susanna* (1909), and in *Palestrina* (1917). Later he had great success as a concert singer, particularly as an interpreter of lieder; in these he was frequently accompanied at the piano by his daughter, the pianist Linde Brodersen.

Records: Parlophone, Beka, Homochord, Pathé*.

BROHLY, SUZANNE, contralto, b. 1882. She studied at the Paris Conservatory and made her debut at the Opéra-Comique there, remaining an honored member of that organization until 1930. There she sang the role of Sélysette in the world *première* (1907) of *Ariane et Barbe-Bleue*; she sang Lehl in a memorable production of *The Snow Maiden* (1908). Her particular starring role, however, was Carmen. She did not appear outside of France.

Records: Many records were made for HMV (Paris, after 1908). *U.S. re-issue:* Victor. *U.S. re-recording:* Eterna, Scala.

BRONSGEEST, CORNELIS, baritone, b. July 24, 1878, Leyden, Holland; d. Sept. 22, 1957, Berlin. He was taught by Schulz-Dornburg in Berlin and by Julius Stockhausen in Frankfurt a. M. He made his debut (1900) at Magdeburg, where he sang until 1903. After singing at the Hamburg Opera (1903-06), he appeared as guest at the Berlin Imperial Opera (1906) in the role of Amonasro in *Aida* and was immediately offered a contract. Just before World War I he made a starring guest tour of Holland, Belgium, and France. He sang Papageno in *Die Zauberflöte* in the Drury Lane Theater under Sir Thomas Beecham in 1914. He toured the United States (1919-20). He was attracted to radio and was director (1923-24) of the "Radio Opera Stage" of the Berlin Radio. He founded the Berlin Radio Orchestra and its Choir. With a traveling company he appeared throughout Holland and until 1935 occasionally made guest appearances at the Berlin State Opera. In 1933 he was forced to give up his position with the Berlin Radio for political reasons. After World War II he arranged for the first opera performances in the ruins of Berlin. He had a warm and flexible baritone voice, which he used to brilliant advantage in a many-sided repertory.

Records: Edison cylinders*, Tri-Ergon, Ultraphon, HMV, and Parlophone; the oldest, however, are on Odeon (Berlin, 1906-07).

BRONSKAJA, EUGENIA, soprano, b. Feb. 2, 1884, St. Petersburg. Her first training was under her mother, a well-known singer under the name Mme. de Hacké; she then studied with Teresa Arkel in Milan and made her debut (1902) in the opera house in Tiflis. She sang at the Kiev Opera (1903-04) and after 1905 had great success at the Moscow Imperial Opera. She made guest appearances in Italy at Trieste, Florence, Bologna, Venice, and the Teatro Costanzi in 1907. She sang (1909-11) in the United States, where she appeared with the Boston, Chicago, and Philadelphia companies. In 1911 she returned to Russia and became one of the great prima donnas of the St. Petersburg Opera. In 1923 she retired from the Leningrad Opera and from then until 1950 was a professor at the Municipal Conservatory in Leningrad. A virtuoso, but still uncommonly warm and expressive, coloratura voice.

Records: She sang in the United States for Columbia* and in Russia for HMV. *U.S. re-recording:* Columbia, TAP.

BROTHIER, YVONNE, soprano, b. June 6, 1880, St. Julien l'Ars, France; d. Jan. 22, 1967, Paris. After 1910 she studied at the National Conservatory in Paris, where she won many prizes for her singing. She made some appearances in 1914 in Brussels, but she began her true stage career in 1916, when she made her debut as Lakmé at the Opéra-Comique. For twenty years she was one of the most prominent singers there. She was especially liked as Cherubino in *Le Nozze di Figaro*, as Virginie in *Paul et Virginie*, and in the *première* (1923) of *La Hulla*. After 1931 she sang at the Paris Opéra, but she rarely appeared in foreign countries. She made guest appearances in 1927 and 1928 in Amsterdam as Micaëla in *Carmen* and as Mélisande. In 1939 she gave up her career and thereafter taught in Paris. She had a charming and brilliantly handled coloratura voice somewhat like that of Erna Berger.

Records: Acoustic and electric records, all appearing on the HMV label, including *Les Cloches de Corneville*, Micaëla in *Carmen*, and scenes from *Pelléas et Mélisande* with Charles Panzéra. *U.S. re-issue:* RCA Victor. *U.S. re-recording:* Rococo.

BROUWENSTEIN, GRÉ, soprano, b. Aug. 26, 1915, Den Helder, Holland. She studied at the Music Lyceum in Amsterdam with Jaap Stroomenbergh and then with Boris Pelsky and Ruth Horna. She made her debut there (1940) as one of the Three Ladies in *Die Zauberflöte*. She was a concert singer during World War II. In 1946 she came to the Netherlands Opera, of which she is still a member, and her first great success there was as Tosca in 1946. She became internationally known through her guest appearances; since 1953 she has been a regular guest at Covent Garden, making her debut there as Aïda. Since 1956 she has sung at the Vienna State Opera. She sang at the San Francisco and Chicago opera houses (1959-60) and in the latter year at the Teatro Colón—all with great success. She has been admired at the Bayreuth Festivals since 1954 as Elsa in *Lohengrin*.

Records: Philips (including *Tiefland*), HMV (Beethoven's *Ninth Symphony*) and Decca (Sieglinde in *Die Walküre*). *U.S. re-issue:* RCA Victor.

BROWNLEE, JOHN, baritone, b. Jan. 7, 1900, Geelong, Australia; d. Jan. 12, 1969, New York City. He served in the Navy in World War I and then studied at Geelong College to become a bookkeeper. His voice was discovered by Nellie Melba and he then went to Paris to study with Dinh Gilly. He made his debut in 1926 in *Lakmé* at the Théâtre Trianon-Lyrique and sang with Melba in the same year in her farewell performance at Covent Garden. He sang at the Paris Opéra (1927-36), making his debut as Athanaël in *Thaïs*. During these years he made guest appearances in London, Antwerp, Brussels, Buenos Aires, and Rio de Janeiro. After 1935 he had great successes at the Glyndebourne Festivals, especially as Don Giovanni. He was engaged by the Metropolitan Opera (1937-53), first appearing as Rigoletto. In 1953 he gave up his stage career and became the director of the Manhattan Institute of Music. He was president (1953-55) of the American Guild of Musical Artists. He was especially appreciated as a Mozart singer.

Records: HMV with Melba, 1926; complete operas for HMV at Glyndebourne (*Le Nozze di Figaro, Don Giovanni, Così fan tutte)*; for Columbia* a complete *Hänsel und Gretel*; opera arias for Allegro Royale*. *U.S. re-issue:* RCA Victor. *U.S. re-recording:* Vox.

BRUNA-RASA, LINA, soprano, b. Sept. 24, 1907, Milan. She studied in Milan and made her debut in 1927. Also in the same year she opened the season at La Scala as Elena in *Mefistofele* under Toscanini. Again in December of that year she sang in the first La Scala performance of *Sly*. She had a starring career at La Scala and in other large houses in Italy and South America. Her voice was particularly admired by Mascagni, and Santuzza in his *Cavalleria Rusticana* was her particular starring role. In 1934 she made a German tour and in 1935 took part in the *première* of Mascagni's *Nerone* at La Scala. In 1938 she made guest appearances in Holland, Belgium, and France. After the death of her mother in 1935 the symptoms of schizophrenic mental illness became more marked in the singer and in 1937 she attempted, during a performance, to throw herself into the orchestra. In 1940 she was institutionalized. However, she mastered her former repertory again and managed to give occasional concerts. One such concert took place in Milan in 1947 with Toscanini present.

Records: Columbia (complete recording of *Andrea Chénier*) and HMV (*Cavalleria Rusticana*, under the direction of the composer). *U.S. re-issue:* Seraphim.

BRUNSKILL, MURIEL, contralto, b. Dec. 18, 1899, Kendal, England. A pupil of Blanche Marchesi in London, she made her concert debut there (1920) and her stage debut (1922) with the British National Opera Company, with which she remained until 1927. In 1925 she married the conductor Robert Ainsworth (d. 1947). She was considered the outstanding oratorio contralto of her generation. In 1930 she toured Canada and in 1931 the United States. In the latter year she sang in Amsterdam in *The Dream of Gerontius*. In 1933 the Italian contralto Nini Giani having become ill while under contract to Covent Garden, Miss Brunskill took over the part of Amneris in *Aida* there, but, in spite of a brilliant success, she was not engaged by that house. In 1934-36 she sang in Australia and in both 1937 and 1946 gave concerts in Holland. Later she lived in London, where in 1952 she appeared a few times in the American musical *Roberta*. She had an expressive contralto voice of unusual size and her diction showed fine style.

Records: Columbia*.

BRUSCANTINI, SESTO, bass, b. Dec. 10, 1919, Porto Civitanova/Macerata, Italy. At first he studied law, then turned to singing and studied with Luigi Ricci in Rome. He was a prize winner in a singing contest on the Italian radio in 1947 and made his debut (1949) at La Scala as Geronimo in *Il Matrimonio Segreto*. This was followed by appearances on the larger Italian stages and on the radio. He had great success at various Glyndebourne Festivals: Alphonso in *Così fan tutte* (1951), Guglielmo in the same opera (1952), Dandini in *La Cenerentola* (1953), and Figaro in *Il Barbiere di Siviglia* (1954). In 1952 he was greatly admired in the title role in *Don Pasquale* at the Salzburg Festival. He has made very successful guest appearances at the Vienna State Opera, and in Brussels, Monaco, and Zürich. Since 1953 he has been married to the soprano Sena Jurinac. His bass voice, noted for its outstanding technical qualities, is best heard in Mozart operas and in Italian *bel canto* roles.

Records: Cetra* (*La Fille du Régiment*), HMV (*Le Nozze di Figaro* and *La Cenerentola*), Columbia (*Così fan tutte*). U.S. re-issue: London, Angel, Mercury, Everest-Cetra.

BRYHN-LANGAARD, BORGHILD, soprano, b. July 23, 1883, Kongsvinger, Norway; d. Nov. 20, 1939, Oslo. She sang first at Oslo and made guest appearances (1907-08) at Covent Garden as Santuzza in *Cavalleria Rusticana*. In 1911 she appeared at the Vienna Imperial Opera as Santuzza and as Aïda. She made guest appearances also in Milan and Budapest as well as in Copenhagen (1914) as Tosca and as Elsa in *Lohengrin*. In 1919 in Chicago she sang Amelia in *Un Ballo in Maschera* opposite Alessandro Bonci. She appeared first under the name Borghild Bryhn, later as Borghild Langaard, and during the 1920's, when she appeared on Scandinavian stages, as Borghild Lindvig; her guest appearances in Milan were as Borghild Brunelli.

Records: HMV and Pathé*.

BUADES-D'ALESSIO, AURORA (see d'Alessio, Aurora).

BUERS, WILHELM, baritone, b. May 1, 1878, Krefeld, Germany; d. Apr. 20, 1926, Hamburg. He studied at the Conservatory in Cologne and made his debut (1905) at the Komische Oper, where he remained until 1907. He sang at the Vienna Volksoper (1909-10) and at the Leipzig Opera House (1911-13). In 1912 he went to the Metropolitan Opera, but in 1913 he was engaged by the Hamburg Opera, where he remained until his death. During the 1920's he often made guest appearances in Munich, at the Vienna State Opera (1921), and at Covent Garden, where (1924) he sang the Wanderer in *Siegfried*. He sang Wotan at the Zoppot Festival in 1924. He was unfortunately killed in a street-car accident in Hamburg. He had a warm-timbred and pleasingly expressive voice.

Records: Edison* cylinders.

BUFF-GIESSEN, HANS, tenor, b. Feb. 13, 1862, Giessen, Germany; d. 1907, Dresden. He came from an old Hessian family and his great-aunt, Lotte Buff, had been the inspiration for Charlotte in Goethe's *Werther*. As his father was a justice in the Imperial Law Courts in Leipzig, he first studied law at the Universities of Giessen and Leipzig, but in the years 1884-87 he undertook the study of singing with Scharfe in Dresden and came to the Dresden Royal Opera in 1887 as an unpaid apprentice. He sang at Weimar (1888-94) and Wiesbaden (1894-98). He was engaged at the Vienna Imperial Opera in 1898, but moved to the Dresden Royal Opera in 1899, where he appeared until his tragic death by suicide. His guest appearances brought him great success, at the Copenhagen Opera among others. He had a magnificent tenor voice, especially in the highest-ranging parts, and he was particularly notable in the French and Italian repertory.

Records: Six extremely rare titles for G & T (Dresden, 1905-07).

BUGG, MADELEINE, soprano, b. 1894 (?), Rheims; d. 1936, Paris. She was a pupil of Guillamat at the Paris Conservatory and by 1914 was already under contract to the Paris Opéra, where she made her debut as Thaïs. She sang for six years at that house and on other French stages. In 1920 she made guest appearances in Barcelona and Lisbon and sang in 1921 at the Teatro Costanzi as Eva in *Die Meistersinger* and as Lauretta in *Gianni Schicchi*. In 1924 she visited the Teatro Colón. In December, 1924, she appeared at La Scala as Eva under Toscanini. She made guest appearances in Parma, Genoa, Marseilles, Toulouse, and Bordeaux, but after about 1927 she was heard of no more. In June, 1936, a pathologist in Paris was sent a female cadaver from a charity hospital for dissection; to his horror the pathologist recognized the formerly famous singer, who had been taken to the hospital under an assumed name.

Records: Four double-sided acoustic records of her voice were issued in Italy by Columbia; all are exceedingly rare.

BUMBRY, GRACE, contralto-soprano, b. Jan. 4, 1937, St. Louis, Mo. She studied at Boston University, at Northwestern University, and at the Music Academy of the West in Santa Barbara. Helped by Lotte Lehmann, she studied art songs under Pierre Bernac in Paris. She made her stage debut (1958) at Basel. A guest appearance in 1960 at the Paris Opéra as Amneris in *Aida* caused a sensation. In 1961 she appeared in Brussels as Carmen and also sang in London and Vienna. She was the first Negro artist to participate (1961-63) in the Bayreuth Festivals, where as a dramatic soprano she sang Venus in *Tannhäuser*. She was admired at the Salzburg Festival in 1964 as Lady Macbeth in *Macbeth*. Her full and expressive voice is also admired in songs and lieder.

Records: Israel in Egypt for Westminster*; *The Messiah* for Decca; also DGG* and American Columbia*. *U.S. re-issue:* London, Philips.

BUNLET, MARCELLE, soprano, b. Oct. 9, 1900, Strasbourg. She made her concert debut (1926) at the Straram Concerts in Paris so successfully that she was engaged by the Opéra, where she first appeared as Brünnhilde in *Götterdämmerung* in 1928. She then sang a great many dramatic soprano parts at the Théâtre de la Monnaie. She was very successful as a concert singer in Antwerp, Rome, Athens, Genoa, and South America. Toscanini chose her for the role of Kundry in *Parsifal* at the 1931 Bayreuth Festival; but, in spite of great success there, she was assigned only two small parts in the 1933 Festival. In 1934 she traveled to the Teatro Colón, and in 1935 sang the title role at the French *première* of *Arabella* at Monte Carlo. She later gave excellent concerts in Strasbourg. Her career lasted until 1950. After Germaine Lubin, she was the most famous French Wagner soprano of her time.

Records: Only two records of her voice exist—one each for HMV and Polydor.

BURG, ROBERT, baritone, b. Mar. 29, 1890, Prague; d. Feb. 9, 1946, Dresden. Originally Robert Bartl. After first studying mathematics, he studied singing with Hans Pokorny in Prague and made his debut there at the German Theater in 1915. After singing in Augsburg (1915-16), he joined the Dresden Royal Opera, to which he belonged until 1944. Together with such artists as Tino Pattiera and Meta Seinemeyer he was principally responsible for the Verdi Renaissance in Germany in the 1920's. In 1926 he sang the title role in the world *première* of *Cardillac* at Dresden. He made guest appearances in Munich, Berlin, Vienna, Amsterdam, Zürich, and Budapest. From 1933-42 he participated in the Bayreuth Festivals, especially as Alberich in the *Ring* cycle. He died in Dresden of a heart attack during a concert.

Records: Parlophone. *U.S. re-issue:* American Decca.

BURGSTALLER, ALOYS, tenor, b. Sept. 27, 1871, Holzkirchen, Germany; d. Apr. 19, 1945, Gmünd, Germany. He studied watchmaking before his voice was discovered by Hermann Levi and Cosima Wagner; he then studied singing with Bellwidt in Frankfurt a. M., but particularly at the Bayreuth School with Julius Kniese. In 1894 he made his debut at the Bayreuth Festival in small roles and in 1897 had a great success there as Siegfried. Thereafter he was one of the chief strengths of the Bayreuth Festival ensembles. He took no long-term engagements in Germany, but made only guest appearances. In 1897 he sang as guest at Covent Garden and in Amsterdam, Paris, and Brussels. He was a member of the Metropolitan Opera (1903-09). There, on Dec. 24, 1903, he sang, in spite of the prohibition of Bayreuth, the title role in the first production of *Parsifal*. His differences with Bayreuth first came to light in 1908, after which he sang Siegfried at the Festival only a few times. His voice was worn out early through the constant singing of Wagner parts. He later taught in Munich.

Records: Very rare Edison* and Columbia cylinders; also Mapleson cylinders. *U.S. re-recording:* IRCC.

BURRIAN, KARL, tenor, b. Jan. 12, 1870, Rousinov, Rumania; d. Sept. 25, 1924, Senomaty, near Prague. He studied with Franz Piwoda in Prague and Felix von Kraus in Munich, making his stage debut in 1891 at Brünn as Manrico in *Il Trovatore*. He sang in Reval (1892-94), Aachen (1894-95), at the Cologne Opera (1895-96), the Hannover Opera (1897-98), and the Hamburg Opera (1898-1902). In 1902 he was called to the Dresden Opera to replace Georg Anthes; there he was especially honored as a Wagner interpreter. On Dec. 9, 1905, he sang Herod at Dresden in the world *première* of *Salome*. He appeared at the Metropolitan Opera (1906-13) and sang Parsifal at the 1908 Bayreuth Festival. Later he made guest appearances at the Vienna Imperial Opera, in Prague, and in Budapest; nevertheless, his voice faded early. At the end of his life he lived in Prague. He possessed one of the most renowned tenor voices of his time, filled with a passionately dramatic quality and deep musicality; he was unmatched as Tristan.

Records: His oldest records were made for G & T (Dresden, 1906); later he sang for HMV and Pathé* and made one record for Parlophone. *U.S. re-issue:* Victor, Opera Disc.

BURZIO, EUGENIA, soprano, b. June 20, 1872, Turin; d. May 18, 1922, Milan. She studied with Aversa and Benvenuti in Milan and made her stage debut (1903) at the Teatro Vittorio Emmanuele. She appeared in 1904 in Parma and Palermo. In 1906 she sang Caterina in *La Risurrezione* as her debut role at La Scala and in 1907 she had a sensational success there in the title role of *Loreley*. Thenceforward she was known as one of the most famous female interpreters of *verismo* Italian opera. After 1909 she was frequently a guest at the Teatro Colón. In 1911 she sang at La Scala in *Saffo* and *Armide* and in 1912 in *Norma*. Her last few appearances were at the Teatro Lirico in 1919 in *Marion Delorme*; at this time she was already suffering from heart disease. She had a luxuriantly dramatic soprano voice, filled with the ability to project passion.

Records: Columbia*, Pathé*, Fonografia Nazionale. *U.S. re-issue:* HRS. *U.S. re-recording:* IRCC, HRS, FRP, Belcanto, TAP.

BUTT, CLARA, contralto, b. Feb. 1, 1873, Southwick, Sussex, England; d. Jan. 23, 1936, on her estate near Oxford. She passed her early days in Bristol and in 1889 won a singing contest and a scholarship to the Royal College of Music in London. There she first appeared in 1892 in a school performance of *Orphée et Eurydice*. In 1893 she sang the same role at the Lyceum Theater in London, and then renewed her studies with Bouhy in Paris and with Etelka Gerster in Berlin. In 1895 she began her official career, which brought her the highest triumphs in the concert hall. In contrast she sang only occasionally on the stage; in 1920 she appeared at Covent Garden in *Orphée et Eurydice*. In 1899 and 1913 she made brilliant concert tours in North America, the latter as part of a world tour. In 1914 and 1922 she appeared in the Sunday Night Concerts at the Metropolitan Opera in New York. She was one of the most renowned English female singers of her generation and in 1920 was made a Dame of the British Empire. She was married to the baritone Kennerley Rumford (1870-1957). The dark full quality of her deep contralto voice found its most comfortable expression in oratorio and song literature.

Records: HMV, later Columbia*. *U.S. re-issue:* Victor. *U.S. re-recording:* FRP, TAP, Belcanto.

BUTTER, CAREL (*see* Hulst, Carel van)

C

CABALLÉ, MONTSERRAT, soprano, b. 1932 (?), Barcelona. Her family was a musical one and she studied at the Conservatory in Barcelona. She was engaged at the Municipal Theater in Basel (1957-60) and sang in Bremen (1960-62). She sang as a free-lance in 1962-63 and made a concert tour of Mexico. In 1963 she made her Barcelona debut. On Apr. 20, 1965, she substituted for Marilyn Horne in New York in a concert performance of *Lucrezia Borgia* and had an outstanding success. Since 1966 she has been a member of the Metropolitan Opera, and in 1967 she sang Violetta in *La Traviata* in the first performance of the season. She is married to the tenor Bernadé Marté. She is especially noted for her singing of soprano roles in early nineteenth-century *bel canto* operas.

Records: Zarzuela arias for Verganza and Spanish songs for Odeon. For RCA Victor* she has recorded *Lucrezia Borgia, La Traviata*, arias, and lieder, among others. *U.S. re-issue:* RCA Victor.

CABANEL, PAUL, baritone, b. June 29, 1891, Paris. He studied at the National Conservatory in Paris and made his debut there (1912). He was highly successful at both the Opéra and the Opéra-Comique. Guest appearances took him to the Teatro Colón, the Teatro Liceo, to Amsterdam, and especially to the Brussels Opera. There he sang Boris in *Boris Godounov* in 1954. He is presently a professor at the Conservatory in Paris. A voluminous and dark-timbred voice.

Records: Pathé (*Samson et Dalila*) and HMV (*La Damnation de Faust*). *U.S. re-issue:* Pathé-Marconi, Columbia.

CAHIER, MME. CHARLES, contralto, b. Jan. 6, 1870, Nashville, Tenn.; d. Apr. 15, 1951, Manhattan Beach, Calif. Originally Sarah Jane Walker. She was the daughter of a general in the American army. She studied first with Ernestinoff in Indianapolis, then with Jean de Reszke in Paris and with Amalie Joachim in Berlin. She made her debut (1904) in Nice. After she married the English nobleman Sir Charles Cahier, she appeared under the name Mme. Charles Cahier. After guest appearances in France and Germany she was engaged (1906) for the Vienna Imperial Opera by Gustav Mahler and remained there until 1912. She was especially liked as Carmen. She also performed the music of Mahler and sang the contralto solo in the world *première* in Vienna of Mahler's *Das*

Lied von der Erde (1908). After 1912 she sang in concerts and made guest appearances all over the world. She sang at the Metropolitan Opera (1911-13). She lived for the most part in her palace at Helgerum, near Skaftet, Sweden. Later she became a much-sought-after teacher, first in Nöresund, Sweden, then in Salzburg, and finally in New York. She had a broad, impressive voice, notable in both the opera and concert repertory.

Records: One G & T, one Ultraphon, one Swedish Odeon, three HMV. *U.S. re-issue:* IRCC.

CALLAS, MARIA, soprano, b. Dec. 4, 1923, New York. Originally Maria Kalogeropoulos. She was the daughter of an immigrant Greek apothecary. At the age of thirteen she was taken to Greece and studied singing at the Athens Conservatory as a pupil of Elvira de Hidalgo. She made her debut (1945) at the Athens Royal Opera as Martha in *Tiefland*. After her Tosca had created great excitement in Athens, she returned to the United States but could find no engagement here. In the summer of 1947 she sang the title role in *La Gioconda* at the Arena Festival and had a sweeping success. There she met the Italian industrialist Giovanni Battista Meneghini, whom she married in 1949, but from whom she separated in 1959. After Verona she had triumphs on all the larger Italian stages. It appeared that Maria Callas would turn next to dramatic, even Wagner, roles, but she surprised the specialists in such matters by singing one of the most difficult of coloratura parts—that of Elvira in *I Puritani* at the Teatro Fenice (1948). She substituted in this role for Margherita Carosio, who was ill. Since then she has become the classic type of dramatic coloratura soprano. In 1950 she began a magnificent career at La Scala, sang at the Maggio Musicale Festival, at Covent Garden, the Paris Opéra, in Mexico City, Rio de Janeiro, Chicago, San Francisco, Dallas, Berlin, and Vienna. In 1956 she first appeared at the Metropolitan Opera in *Norma* and was successful there for three seasons. Maria Callas has often been brushed by scandal, but has remained the unique prima donna *assoluta* of her times. Her voice unites in the highest degree the most brilliant coloratura technique with physical strength and glowingly dramatic diction; in addition, she carries the public away by her acting. She acquired special merit in restoring to favor the many forgotten *bel canto* operas of Bellini, Rossini, Donizetti, and Cherubini, as she in general expanded her repertory into an almost limitless area of artistic possibility.

Records: She made a very large number of records, first for Cetra (*La Traviata* and *La Gioconda*) and then for Columbia (including *I Puritani, Lucia di Lammermoor, Tosca, Norma, Cavalleria Rusticana, I Pagliacci, La Forza del Destino, Il Turco in Italia, Madama Butterfly, Aida, Rigoletto, La Bohème, La Sonnambula, Un Ballo in Maschera, Il Trovatore, Il Barbiere di Siviglia, Turandot, Carmen,* and *Manon Lescaut*). *U.S. re-issue:* Angel, Mercury (Cherubini's *Medea*), Everest-Cetra.

CALVE, EMMA, soprano, b. Aug. 15, 1858, Décazeville, France; d. Jan. 6, 1942, Millau. Her vocal talents were evident while she was still attending a convent school in Montpellier, where she was reared. She studied singing with Jules Puget in Paris and made her debut as Marguerite in *Faust* at the Brussels Opera (1882). She then continued her studies with Rosine Laborde and Mathilde Marchesi in Paris and appeared at the Opéra-

Campagnola · Campora

Comique in 1886. She made guest appearances in the same year at La Scala, followed by others at all the important opera houses in France and Italy. She appeared in many world *premières,* including *L'Amico Fritz* at the Teatro Costanzi (1891) with Fernando de Lucia, *La Navarraise* at Covent Garden (1894), *Sapho* at the Opéra-Comique (1897) and *La Carmélite* at the same house (1902). In 1891 at the Comique she sang the role of Carmen for the first time, a part in which she became immortal and in which she had great triumphs throughout the world. She sang this part in Moscow, St. Petersburg, London, Madrid, Milan, Vienna, and Berlin. She was a much-feted member of the Metropolitan Opera (1893-1904), making her debut there as Santuzza. She sang at the Manhattan Opera (1907-09) and in 1915-16 made a brilliant North American tour. Even in the 1920's she occasionally appeared as Carmen. She gave her last concert in 1938. She wrote her autobiography under the title *Sous tous les ciels j'ai chanté.* She had a wide-ranging, passionately dramatic voice and showed great intensity in her acting.

Records: Fragments on Mapleson cylinders; records for G & T (London, 1902), HMV, Victor* (New York, 1907-16) and Pathé*. *U.S. re-issue:* Victor, IRCC. *U.S. re-recording:* RCA Victor, TAP, FRP, Belcanto, Rococo, Scala, CRS, HRS, IRCC, Cantilena.

CAMPAGNOLA, LÉON, tenor, b. Feb. 8, 1875, Marseilles; d. Jan. 11, 1955, Paris. He studied in Marseilles and in Paris and made his debut in 1909. For more than ten years he sang in the French provinces and in Brussels, where he was especially well-liked. He was engaged by the Opéra-Comique in 1913 and thereafter had great success in the French metropolis. He made guest appearances at the Chicago Opera (1913) and was also very successful at La Scala and at Covent Garden. He sang for the last time in 1919 at the Brussels Opera. He then occupied himself as a singing teacher and as a painter in Paris. One of the best French tenors of his generation, he was especially excellent in the operas of Puccini, Bizet, and Gounod.

Records: HMV and Pathé. *U.S. re-issue:* Victor. *U.S. re-recording:* Eterna, Scala.

CAMPANARI, GIUSEPPE, baritone, b. Nov. 17, 1855, Venice; d. May 31, 1927, Milan. He studied singing but lost his voice on account of a premature debut at the Teatro dal Verme. He then became a cellist in the orchestra of La Scala. In 1884 he came to America and joined the Boston Symphony Orchestra. In 1893 he determined to try a singing career again and sang Tonio in *I Pagliacci* with a traveling opera company which toured the United States under the direction of Gustav Hinrichs. He was engaged by the Metropolitan Opera in 1894 and remained there until 1912. There he sang, among other roles, the title role in *Falstaff* in its American *première* (1895). After his retirement from the stage he became a teacher of singing, first in New York and then in Milan. His daughter was the well-known soprano Marina Campanari. He was equally outstanding in both serious and *buffo* roles in the Italian repertory.

Records Columbia*, Victor*, Edison* cylinders. *U.S. re-issue:* IRCC. *U.S. re-recording:* Columbia, TAP, FRP, IRCC.

CAMPORA, GIUSEPPE, tenor, b. Sept. 9, 1912, Tortona, Italy. He studied with Magenta in Genoa, then with Schiavone in Milan. He made a surprising debut when he substituted for an indisposed colleague as Rodolfo in La Bohème at Bari (1949). After engagements in the Italian provinces he was selected (1951) by Tullio Serafin for La Scala. Henceforth he had an international starring career. In 1952 he appeared as guest at the Teatro Colón and the Rio de Janeiro Opera. In 1954 he made his debut at the Metropolitan Opera as Rodolfo. He has appeared at the Arena Festivals and at the Maggio Musicale Festivals. His best parts are the lyric roles in Italian opera.

Records: Urania* (*La Gioconda*), Decca (*Madama Butterfly* and *Tosca*, as partner to Renata Tebaldi), HMV (*Simon Boccanegra* with Tebaldi). U.S. re-issue: London, Richmond, Cetra, Angel, Capitol.

CANIGLIA, MARIA, soprano, b. May 11, 1906, Naples. She studied at the Conservatory di San Pietro a Majella in Naples with P.A. Roche and made her debut Jan. 1, 1930, in Turin as Chrysothemis in *Elektra*. During that same year she was called to La Scala, where she made her debut as Rosaura in *Le Maschere* and remained as principal prima donna until 1948. She sang there in the world *première* of *Lucrezia* in 1937. Guest appearances took her to all the music centers of the world. In 1935 she was admired at the Salzburg Festival as Alice Ford in *Falstaff*. After 1937 she was a regular guest at the Teatro Colón. She also made guest appearances at Covent Garden (1937 and 1939) and at the Vienna State Opera, in Prague, at the Maggio Musicale Festivals, at the Arena Festivals, and at all the larger Italian houses. She sang at the Metropolitan Opera in 1938 and 1939. In 1951 she sang at the Arena Festival and in 1955 appeared in Brussels as a guest in *Tosca*. She lives in Milan. Her soprano voice showed masterly musical training, which she demonstrated dramatically in the Italian repertory.

Records: She sang first for Columbia, later for HMV, on which she appeared in many complete operas, mostly with Beniamino Gigli (*Aïda, Tosca, Andrea Chénier, Un Ballo in Maschera*, and Verdi's *Requiem*. She also sang for Cetra* (*Fedora, La Forza del Destino, Don Carlos*, and Zandonai's *Francesca da Rimini*). U.S. re-issue: RCA Victor, Angel, Pathé-Marconi, Seraphim.

CANNE MEYER, CORA, contralto, b. Aug. 11, 1929, Amsterdam. She studied singing at the Amsterdam Conservatory and made her debut there with the Netherlands Opera (1951). She attracted attention as Cherubino in *Le Nozze di Figaro* at the Glyndebourne Festival in 1957. In 1959 she sang in Haydn's *Il Mondo nella Luna* at the Salzburg Festival. She was engaged concurrently at Zürich and the Netherlands Opera (1960-62). She has made guest appearances on French stages, in Brussels and Lisbon, and has sung almost every year at the Holland Festival. Her complete mastery of singing technique allows her to overcome the greatest difficulties.

Records: HMV (*Le Comte Ory* at Glyndebourne); Philips (*Les Noces* by Stravinsky), and MMS. U.S. re-issue: Lyrichord.

CANTELO, APRIL, soprano. She studied piano and voice with Hans Oppenheimer at Cambridge, and later with Imogen Holst and Julien Kimball in London. She also studied at what later became the National Opera School there with Joan Cross and Kurt Joos. She first sang in small groups and then joined the chorus at the Glyndebourne Festival. Next came small parts at Covent Garden and singing with the Deller Consort. Her roles with the English Opera Group included Helena in the *première* of *A Midsummer Night's Dream* at the 1960 Aldeburgh Festival, a role in the 1963 *première* of Britten's *Our Man in Havana* and in his *British Eccentrics* at the 1964 Aldeburgh Festival. She has also sung in Vienna and Munich, appears regularly in broadcasts, and sings in operas, oratorios, and in lieder concerts.

U.S. records: L'Oiseau Lyre, London (*Albert Herring*), Angel, Somerset, Bach Guild.

CAPECCHI, RENATO, baritone, b. Nov. 6, 1923, Cairo, of Italian parents. He studied the violin and served in the army during World War II. After the end of the war he studied singing and made his debut (1948) in a concert on the Italian Radio. His stage debut occurred (1949) at Reggio Emilia as Amonasro in *Aïda*. In 1950 he appeared at La Scala and in 1952 came to the Metropolitan Opera, making his debut there as the elder Germont in *La Traviata*. In addition to great successes at the Aix-en-Provence Festival as Don Giovanni, at Verona as Bartolo in *Il Barbiere di Siviglia* (1955), and at the Maggio Musicale Festival, he has sung at the Vienna State Opera, in Chicago, San Francisco, South America, and on the most important Italian stages.

Records: A great many records for Decca (*L'Elisir d'Amore* and *La Forza del Destino*), Philips (*Rigoletto*, *Don Pasquale*, *Gianni Schicchi*), Cetra (*Un Giorno di Regno*), Columbia (*Norma*), DGG* (*Le Nozze di Figaro* and *Il Barbiere di Siviglia*). *U.S. re-issue:* London, Epic, RCA Victor, Mercury, Angel, Vox, Everest-Cetra.

CAPOUL, VICTOR, tenor, b. Feb. 2, 1839, Toulouse; d. Feb. 13, 1924, Pujaudran-du-Gers, France. He began his studies at the Paris Conservatory in 1859 with Revial and Mocker and made his debut (1861) at the Opéra-Comique in *Le Chalet*. He sang there until 1870, then (1871-75) at the Italian Opera in London, and (1875-79) at Covent Garden. He made his American debut (1888) at the New York Academy of Music in *Mignon*. In 1888 he sang at the Opéra-Comique in the first performance there of *Jocelyn*. He was at the Metropolitan Opera (1883-4; 1891-96). From 1892-97 he lived in New York as a singing teacher, and then became a *régisseur* at the Paris Opéra. He finally lost his entire fortune through speculation, retaining only a small peasant hut in southern France to which he retired. There he burned all mementos of his career, such as records, photographs, programs, et cetera.

Records: Some exceedingly rare records made in Paris in 1905 for Fonotipia.

CAPSIR, MERCEDES, soprano, b. July 20, 1895, Barcelona, in the house where eleven years earlier Maria Barrientos had been born. She studied in Barcelona with Bidai Neunei and made her debut (1914) at the Teatro Liceo as Gilda. After her first successes in Madrid and Barcelona she visited the Teatro Colón in 1916 and 1920. In 1922 she came to Italy, where she first sang at the Teatro dal Verme. In 1924 she sang Gilda at La Scala under Toscanini. From that time on she had great success on the leading Italian opera stages. She sang with the Italian Opera in Holland (1923-24) and later made guest appearances and gave concerts in Paris, Ostend, Monte Carlo, Spain, and South America. Her special triumphs were as Rosina in *Il Barbiere di Siviglia* at Covent Garden (1926), in the world *première* of *Il Re* at La Scala (1929), and as Elvira in *I Puritani* at the first Maggio Musicale Festival (1933). She never came to the United States. From 1940-50 she sang at the Teatro Liceo, especially in lyric parts such as Butterfly and as Elsa in *Lohengrin*. A composer herself, she wrote, among other works, a set of coloratura variations on a theme by Mozart, which she frequently sang in *Il Barbiere di Siviglia*. On the whole she had one of the largest coloratura voices on records; she was noted for the crystal clarity of her tone production and for her technical mastery of bravura singing.

Records: Her first records appeared about 1914. She made acoustics for Odeon and HMV and electrics for Columbia* (including *Rigoletto*, *Il Barbiere di Siviglia*, *Lucia di Lammermoor*, and *Don Pasquale*). U.S. re-recording: Eterna.

CAPUANA, MARIA, contralto, b. 1891, near Pesaro, Italy; d. Feb. 22, 1955, Cagliari, Sardinia. She was the older sister of the conductor Franco Capuana, and she studied singing and piano at the Conservatory of San Pietro a Majella in Naples. She made her debut in 1918 at the Teatro San Carlo there as Urbain in *Les Huguenots*. In 1920 she had a huge success at the Teatro Regio in Turin as Brangaene in *Tristan und Isolde* and Wagner roles became her specialty. In 1922 she made her first appearance at La Scala, singing Ortrud in *Lohengrin*; in 1923 she was also successful there as Herodias in *Salome*. Among her other successes at La Scala were Fricka in *Die Walküre* in 1925-27 and as Rubria in *Nerone*, by Boito. She sang at the Teatro Colón in 1925 and later appeared as guest in Barcelona, Lisbon, Cairo, South Africa, at the Arena Festival and on other important Italian stages. Her dark-timbred voice made her especially important in Wagnerian roles.

Records: Acoustic records for the Fonotechnica label, electric for Columbia*, including a complete *Aïda* (1929).

CARBONE, MARIA, soprano, b. June 12, 1912 Naples. She studied at the Conservatory of San Pietro a Majella in Naples and made her debut at the Teatro San Carlo there (1932) as Marguerita in *Mefistofele*. In 1933 she sang the title role in *Lodoletta* at the Rome Opera, and in that summer made a concert tour through Holland. She had a long and highly successful career on the largest Italian stages. In 1936 she made her debut at La Scala as Giorgetta in *Il Tabarro*; in 1948 she was very successful there as Salome, a role which she first sang at Turin and which she repeated on many other Italian stages.

Records: In 1933, a year after her debut, she sang in two complete operas for HMV (Desdemona in *Otello* and Micaëla in *Carmen*). These are her only records. U.S. re-issue: RCA Victor.

CARELLI, EMMA, soprano, b. May 12, 1877, Naples; d. Aug. 17, 1928, Rome, as a result of an auto accident in Montefiascone. She was a pupil of her father, Beniamino Carelli, at the Conservatory of San Pietro a Majella in Naples and she made her debut (1895) at Altamura in *La Vestale*, by Mercadente, during the festivities celebrating the centenary of the composer's birth. She then appeared at the Teatro dal Verme and the Teatro Lirico and in Mantua, Bologna, and Naples. In 1899 she came to La Scala, making her debut there as Desdemona in *Otello* opposite Francesco Tamagno. Thereafter she often sang at La Scala as well as at the Teatro Costanzi and in Madrid, Barcelona, Bucharest, Buenos

Aires, Rio de Janeiro, St. Petersburg, Marseilles, and Monte Carlo. In 1910 she and her husband, the journalist Walter Mocchi, took over the direction of the Teatro Costanzi. In 1912 she sang the title role there in *Elektra* at its *première* in Rome. She then gave up her active stage career. In 1926 she relinquished the direction of the Costanzi. She was a dramatic soprano and was noted as a Wagner singer.
Records: Pathé*, Fonotipia, and G & T. *U.S. re-recording:* Eterna, TAP, Rococo, HRS.

CARENA, MARIA, soprano, b. 1894, Turin. She studied with Virginia Ferni-Germano in Turin and made her debut there (1917) as Leonora in *Il Trovatore*. She next sang at the Teatro Costanzi, the Teatro San Carlo, and the Teatro Lirico. She appeared as guest (1919) at the Teatro Coliseo and in 1920-21 at the Teatro Real, singing there as elsewhere opposite Giacomo Lauri-Volpi. In 1920 she sang at the Teatro Costanzi in the world *première* of *L'Uomo Che Ride* and in January, 1922, made her La Scala debut in *Suor Angelica*. She remained an esteemed prima donna at La Scala until 1932. There in 1924 she alternated with Rosa Raisa in the role of Asteria in the first production of Boito's posthumous opera, *Nerone*. In 1932 she was very successful at the Teatro Costanzi as Giulia in Spontini's *La Vestale*, which became one of her starring roles. She appeared regularly at the Teatro Regio in Turin and the Teatro San Carlo and even sang after 1940 in Rome.
Records: Acoustic records for Fonotipia, including a duet with Luisa Bertana; electric records, including a complete *Il Trovatore* with Aureliano Pertile and Apollo Granforte, in addition to Fonotipia Records. *U.S. re-issue:* RCA Victor.

CARON, ROSE, soprano, b. Nov. 17, 1857, Monnerville, France; d. Apr. 9, 1930, Paris. She began her vocal studies in 1878 at the Paris Conservatory with Tharset, and studied thereafter with Marie Sasse. She made a highly successful debut (1884) at the Brussels Opera as Brunehild in the world *première* of *Sigurd*. In 1885 she came to the Paris Opéra, where she went from triumph to triumph, particularly as a Wagner singer. For Paris she created Desdemona in *Otello* (1888), Elsa in *Lohengrin* (1891), and Sieglinde in *Die Walküre* (1892). In Brussels, where she was often a guest, she sang (1890) in the world *première* of *Salammbô*. In 1902 she became a professor at the Paris Conservatory, where she taught for twenty-five years. Her soprano voice was large, full of dramatic fire, and noted for the flexibility with which she handled it.
Records: Very rare records; four for Zonophone (Paris, 1903) and three for Fonotipia (Paris, 1904) *U.S. re-issue:* HRS, IRCC. *U.S. re-recording:* HRS, IRCC, FRP.

CAROSIO, MARGHERITA, soprano, b. June 4, 1908, Genoa. Her father, the composer Natale Carosio, undertook her voice training. She sang in the concert hall when she was only sixteen. In 1926 she made her stage debut in Nuovi Ligure as Lucia di Lammermoor. By 1928 she was appearing as guest at Covent Garden. In 1932 she came to La Scala, where she appeared regularly thereafter. In 1935 she sang there in the world *première* of Mascagni's *Nerone*. She had an important career all over the world, with guest appearances in Antwerp, Nice, Monte Carlo, and at the Teatro Colón, the Teatro Liceo, and the Vienna and Berlin State Operas. In 1939 she sang Rosina in *Il Barbiere di Siviglia* and in 1951 Carolina in *Il Matrimonio Segreto* at the Salzburg Festivals. In 1936 she appeared at La Scala in the world *première* of *Il Campiello*. She sang also in the world *première* of *Beatrice Cenci* at the Teatro San Carlo in 1924. She made a concert tour through Germany (1948) and toured England and South Africa (1951). She had a virtuoso coloratura voice and was particularly outstanding in the Italian repertory.

Records: Parlophone, Homochord, and HMV (*L'Elisir d'Amore* and *Amelia Goes to the Ball*). *U.S. re-issue:* Angel, RCA Victor.

CARRACCIOLO, JUANITA, soprano, b. 1890, Palermo; d. July 6, 1924, Milan. She made her debut (1908) at Genoa in *Le Maschere*. Then for twelve years she sang in various Italian opera houses, until in 1920 she had a sensational success as the title heroine in *Manon Lescaut* at the Teatro Costanzi. Also in 1920 she sang as guest at the Teatro Colón and at the Madrid Opera. In 1922 she came to La Scala, making her debut there as Eva in *Die Meistersinger* under Toscanini. In the following season she had great starring triumphs at La Scala, but she became very ill in the fall of 1923.

Records: HMV, Columbia, Fonografia Nazionale, and Pathé. *U.S. re-recording:* TAP, Scala, Angel.

CARRÉ, MARGUERITE, soprano, b. 1881, Bordeaux; d. 1947, Paris. Originally Marguerite Giraud. She studied at the Conservatory in Bordeaux and then at the Conservatory in Paris. She made her debut at the Opéra-Comique (1902). In the same year she married Albert Carré, the director of the Opéra-Comique, who placed her in leading parts. She participated there in a number of world *premières*, including *La Reine Fiammette* (1903) and *La Fille de Roland* (1904). She sang the title role in the first French performance of *Madama Butterfly* (1907) and appeared (1908) in the memorable French production of *The Snow Maiden*. In 1909 she sang Pamina in an important production of *Die Zauberflöte*. Although the critics frequently gave her small praise, she remained one of the great prima donnas at the Opéra-Comique until the 1920's. She almost never appeared outside the French metropolis. She finally became a singing teacher in Paris.

Records: One record for G & T (Paris, 1904) and also some records for Pathé. *U.S. re-issue:* IRCC.

CARTERI, ROSANNA, soprano, b. Dec. 14, 1930, Verona, Italy. Her musical talent showed itself early. By the age of twelve she had already given a sensational concert. In 1953 she made her stage debut at the Rome Opera as Elsa in *Lohengrin*. This was followed by a guest tour in Spain, then by engagements at all the larger Italian theaters. She was particularly successful at La Scala. She became one of the best-known Italian concert sopranos of her generation, and sang frequently in the concert performances of the Academia di Santa Cecilia in Rome under Franco Molinari-Prandelli. She also sang in Naples in an important production of Donizetti's *Requiem*. Guest tours brought her great success in Spain, England, France, and in both North and South America.

Records: RCA Victor* (*La Traviata*), Cetra* (*Falstaff, Guillaume Tell, Suor Angelica, La Bohème*), and Columbia (*La Serva Padrona*). *U.S. re-issue:* Angel, DGG, Seraphim.

CARUSO, ENRICO, tenor, b. Feb. 25, 1873, Naples; d. Aug. 2, 1921, near Naples. Since he came of a poor family, rich only in children, he was able only with great difficulty to afford the study of singing, which he finally completed with

Guglielmo Vergine in Naples. He made his debut in November, 1894, with a touring company at the Teatro Nuovo in Naples and then sang without particular success on provincial Italian stages and at Monte Carlo. His great triumph came on Nov. 17, 1898, when he sang the part of Loris at La Scala in the world *première* of *Fedora*. Then came an almost fairy-tale rise to world fame. After great triumphs at La Scala and on other important Italian stages, he came (1902) to Covent Garden. A tour of the United States (1903) confirmed him as the first tenor of his time. Engaged by the Metropolitan Opera in 1903, he first appeared before the New York public as the Duke in *Rigoletto*. Thenceforward until the end of his career the Metropolitan Opera remained the center of his artistic focus, although he undertook annual guest appearances at all the principal opera houses of the world. He appeared in a number of *première* performances— *L'Arlesiana* (1897) at the Teatro Lirico and *Adriana Lecouvreur* at the same theater (1902); in 1903 he sang in *Germania* at the Teatro dal Verme and on Dec. 10, 1910, in *La Fanciulla del West* at the Metropolitan Opera. After a career laden with honors and successes, he fell ill of a lung infection in the winter of 1920 in New York. He sought to regain his health in the neighborhood of his native Naples, and there in 1921 he died. From his union with the little-known singer Ada Giacchetti there were two sons; later, in America, he married Dorothy Benjamin. They had a daughter, Gloria. Dorothy later wrote a moving biography of her husband, *Enrico Caruso, His Life and Death* (New York, 1945). Caruso was, beyond doubt, the best-known singing personality of his time, even of the last century. His voice was originally a lyric tenor, but capable of the most dramatic climaxes. His phenomenal tone production, the smoothness of his registers, the nobility of his acting and singing style are even today to be marveled at on his more than two hundred records. One can say that not only did he become famous through the phonograph, but that also through him the phonograph— then a relatively new musical phenomenon itself—also became famous.

Records: His first records appeared on Zonophone (Milan, 1902) and they are particularly sought-after by collectors. He also sang for G & T, but by far the largest number of his later records appeared first in the United States on Victor*; he also made Pathé and other cylinders. *U.S. re-issue:* Opera Disc, IRCC, RCA Victor. *U.S. re-recording:* RCA Victor, Angel, TAP, Scala, Belcanto, Eterna, Rococo, ASCO, FRP, Olympus, Audio-Rarities, IRCC, Emerson, Cantilena.

CASAZZA, ELVIRA, contralto, b. Nov. 15, 1887, Ferrara, Italy; d. Jan. 1965, Milan. She was a distant relative of Giulio Gatti-Casazza, the well-known manager of the Metropolitan Opera. After studying in Ferrara and Milan, she made her debut (1911) with the Lombardi Opera Company in the United States, after which she never sang here again. In 1916 she sang at the Teatro Colón and in 1917 for the first time at La Scala, appearing as Amneris in *Aïda*. In 1920 she appeared as guest at the Teatro Real and in 1921 was applauded at La Scala as Dame Quickly in *Falstaff*, a role which she made her starring part. For the following twenty years she had a successful career at La Scala, where she appeared in the world *premières* of *Deborah e Jaele* (1922) and *I Cavalieri di Ekebù*

(1925). In 1929 she appeared with the La Scala ensemble in Berlin, and was very successful in Spain and South America. She sang her last role, the Witch in *Hänsel und Gretel*, at La Scala in 1942. She lived and taught in Milan. She was praised for the musical and dramatic art of her characterizations as well as for the beauty of her voice.

Records: A few records for Fonografia Nazionale and HMV, the latter including duets with Beniamino Gigli. *U.S. re-issue:* Victor. *U.S. re-recording:* Scala, Rococo.

CASE, ANNA, soprano, b. Oct. 29, 1889, Clinton, New Jersey. Her teacher was Mme. Ohrstrom-Renard in New York. She made her debut (1909) with the Metropolitan Opera ensemble at the New Theater in New York in a small role in *Werther*. At the Metropolitan Opera itself she took small roles until 1913, when she sang the role of the child, Feodor, in the first American production of *Boris Godounov*. In the same year she was greatly admired as Sophie in *Der Rosenkavalier* at its American première. She remained a member of the Metropolitan Opera until 1915 and sang there again in the 1916-17 and 1919-20 seasons, but then only in the concert performances regularly given at that time in the opera house. After 1920 she became exclusively a concert soprano, and as such she toured America and Europe, making a tour through Holland in 1925. In 1929 she married the multimillionaire telegraph king Clarence Mackay (the father of Mrs. Irving Berlin) and withdrew from musical life.

Records: Edison* and Columbia* records and one Victor* record. *U.S. re-recording:* FRP.

CASEI, NEDDA, contralto, b. 1935 (?), Baltimore, Md. Her mother was a singer and her father a member of John Philip Sousa's band. She studied piano at the Juilliard School of Music in New York and, at the same time, acting. She finally studied singing with Vittorio Peccinini in Milan and first appeared in 1959 at the Empire State Festival (N.Y.) in *Oedipus Rex* under the composer's direction. Since 1964 she has had a successful career at the Metropolitan Opera, where she made her debut as Magdalena in *Rigoletto*. She has made guest appearances and given concerts in European music centers.

Records: On Cetra a complete *La Bohème* by Leoncavallo and on MMS Beethoven's *Missa Solemnis*, Bach's *Magnificat*, and *Il Trovatore*. *U.S. re-issue:* Vanguard-Everyman.

CASTAGNA, BRUNA, contralto, b. Oct. 15, 1908, Bari, Italy. She first studied piano and then voice in Milan, where she was a pupil of Tina Scognamiglio. She made her debut (1925) at Mantua in *Boris Godounov*. Tullio Serafin negotiated engagements for her in South America, where she sang (1927-30), particularly at the Teatro Colón. In 1931 she was, through the offices of Toscanini, called to La Scala in Milan, and she had a huge success there in 1933 as Isabella in *L'Italiana in Algeri*. Then followed guest appearances in Barcelona, Chicago, St. Louis, and San Francisco, as well as tours in Australia, Egypt, Rumania, and Spain. She was a member of the Metropolitan Opera, where she first appeared as Azucena in *Il Trovatore* (1936-45). Above all, she was particularly admired as Carmen. She now teaches singing in Milan.

Records: American Columbia* and RCA Victor.

CAVALIERI, LINA, soprano, b. Dec. 25, 1874, Rome; d. Feb. 8, 1944, near Florence. She appeared first at small theaters and on variety stages in Rome and became an internationally known revue star at the Folies Bergère in Paris and at the Empire Theater in London. In 1900 she married, in Russia, Prince Bariatonsky and then decided to become an opera star. After brief study with Maddelena Mariani-Masi, she made her debut in December, 1900, at the Teatro São Carlos as Mimi in *La Bohème*. In 1901 she made brilliant guest appearances in St. Petersburg; she also had great successes in Monte Carlo and Warsaw, where she returned almost annually. In Monte Carlo she sang Ensoleidad at the world *première* of *Chérubin* (1905). In the same year she was admired in Paris opposite Enrico Caruso and Titta Ruffo. Later (1905) she was called to the Metropolitan Opera; there she sang in the first American performances of *Fedora* and *Manon Lescaut* with Caruso. In 1907 she was married to the American millionaire Winthrop Chandler, but she left him within a week. The scandal that ensued made her further appearances at the Metropolitan Opera impossible. She then made guest appearances at Covent Garden and in 1909 appeared a few times at the Manhattan Opera House in New York. In 1913 she married the French tenor Lucien Muratore, and although they were both engaged at the Chicago Opera, she never sang there. Lina Cavalieri, who was known as "the most beautiful woman of her time," made several American silent films. In 1919 she was separated from Muratore, and in 1922 she contracted again to sing at the Chicago Opera, but still never appeared there. In the same year she settled down in Paris, where she operated a beauty salon. With her fourth husband, Paolo D'Arvanni, she lived later in the Villa Cappucina near Florence, which she owned. They were both killed there in an air raid in 1944. The dramatic life of the singer was filmed in 1957 under the title "La donna più bella della mondo," with Gina Lollobrigida in the title role.

Records: A few records for American Columbia*, Victor*, and Pathé. (She is not to be confused with the soprano Elda Cavalieri, who made a few records for Victor* about 1910.) *U.S. re-recording:* Scala, TAP.

CAVELTI, ELSA, contralto-soprano, b. May 4, 1915, Rorschach, Switzerland. She studied both piano and singing in Zürich and Frankfurt a. M. and later in Vienna. She made her debut (1936) at Katowice, Poland, and came by way of the Düsseldorf Opera to the Dresden State Opera in 1939. During World War II she remained in her Swiss homeland and was chosen as first dramatic contralto at Zürich. Since 1946 she has often been a guest at La Scala as well as at the Vienna State Opera. Guest appearances and concerts have brought her great success in Paris, London, New York, Chicago, Buenos Aires, and San Francisco. Lately she has been heard on the stage in dramatic soprano parts. She is especially admired as a concert and oratorio singer, particularly as a Bach interpreter. She lives in Basel. *Records:* Decca and MMS. *U.S. re-issue:* Vox.

CEBOTARI, MARIA, soprano, b. Feb. 10, 1910, Kischinev, Rumania; d. June 9, 1949, Vienna, after a long illness. She joined the Moscow Art Theater, a traveling company of Russian emigrants who were appearing in her homeland, and later married the director, Count Alexander Wirubov. In 1929 she came to Paris to become a singer. After studying briefly with Daniel in Berlin, she was chosen by Fritz Busch to join the Dresden State Opera in 1931, where she had a successful career until 1943. In 1935 she sang Aminta in the world *première* of *Die Schweigsame Frau* there. Guest appearances brought her great success in Berlin, Vienna, Munich, Zurich, Bucharest, Milan, and Rome. She was also one of the best-loved film singers of her generation. At the Salzburg Festivals she was particularly admired as a Mozart singer. In 1938 she was divorced from Count Wirubov and married the film actor Gustav Diessl. In 1943 she was invited to the Vienna State Opera, where she sang with great success in the years following World War II. In 1947 she sang in the world *première* of *Dantons Tod* at the Salzburg Festival. She had a light but impressive voice which she showed to advantage in a broad stage and concert repertory; she was particularly noted as an interpreter of Richard Strauss' music.

Records: Parlophon, HMV, Polydor, Urania*, and DGG. *U.S. re-issue:* American Decca. *U.S. re-recording:* Scala, TAP, Electrola.

CEHANOVSKY, GEORGE, baritone, b. 1895 (?), St. Petersburg. During World War I he served in the Russian navy and was severely wounded in the naval battle of Gotland. After the war his voice was trained by his mother, who was a singer. He made his debut in Leningrad (1921) as Valentin in *Faust*. In 1923 he emigrated to the United States, where he sang first with the De Feo Opera Company and (1924-25) as leading baritone with the San Carlo Opera Company. In 1926 he came to the Metropolitan Opera, first appearing as a Mandarin in the Metropolitan *première* of *Turandot*. He remained a member of the company for over thirty-six years, the longest career any singer has ever had at the Metropolitan Opera. In general he sang *comprimario* roles, but was often given leading parts. His particular starring role was Schaunard in *La Bohème*. Altogether, he sang seventy-eight roles at the Metropolitan. From 1927-31 he sang at Ravinia, near Chicago, and after 1936 was a regular guest at the San Francisco Opera. He married the soprano Elisabeth Rethberg in 1957.

Records: His first records appeared very late; these were six complete operas for Columbia* and RCA Victor* in which he took smaller roles, including *La Bohème* and *La Traviata* under Toscanini.

CERNAY, GERMAINE, contralto, b. 1900, Le Havre; d. 1943, Paris. Originally Germaine Pointu. She made her debut (1927) at the Opéra-Comique, where she began with small parts and was promoted to such roles as Charlotte in *Werther*, Carmen, Mignon, and Geneviève in *Pelléas et Mélisande*. She had great success at the Théâtre de la Monnaie and on French provincial stages; she also became known as one of the best French concert contraltos of her generation, being particularly admired as an interpreter of Bach's music. She was considering retiring to a convent when she died suddenly.

Records: Many records for Odeon, Columbia*, and HMV (*Pelléas et Mélisande*). *U.S. re-issue:* American Decca.

CERQUETTI, ANITA, soprano, b. Apr. 13, 1931, Macerata, Italy. She studied at the Morlacci Musical Lyceum in Perugia. She made her debut in 1951 as Aïda and sang the same part in 1953 at the Arena Festival. She made guest appearances on the larger stages of Italy, in France, Switzerland, and was engaged by the Chicago Opera (1955-56). This young singer became world-famous when, in January, 1958, she replaced Maria Callas in *Norma* at the first performance of the season at the Rome Opera; Callas had already caused great talk by breaking her agreement to appear in this opening performance. Since that time Cerquetti, who possesses a large dramatic soprano voice, has appeared at all the principal opera houses of the world as a guest, although she has been inactive recently.

Records: Decca (including *La Gioconda*). *U.S. re-issue:* London.

ČERVENÁ, SONJA, contralto, b. Sept. 9, 1925, Prague. She first devoted herself to light music and sang in an operetta theater in Prague. She then studied with Robert Rozner and Lydia Wegner-Salmova in Prague and made her operatic debut (1945) at the Janáček Opera in Brno, where she remained until 1957 and where she had her first success as Octavian in *Der Rosenkavalier*. In 1957 she made guest appearances at the National Theater in Prague and since 1958 she also has been a member of the Berlin State Opera. She has appeared as guest at the State Operas in Dresden, Vienna, and Hamburg, and at the Berlin City Opera. In London she sang the contralto part in a performance of Beethoven's *Missa Solemnis* and in 1960 she appeared at the Bayreuth Festival.

Records Supraphon, Eterna (in the title role in *Carmen*).

CESBRON-VISEUR, SUZANNE, soprano, b. 1878; d. December, 1967, Paris. She studied at the National Conservatory in Paris and made her debut at the Opéra-Comique there (1900). For twenty-five years she was a highly valued artist of this theater. She appeared as a guest repeatedly in Nice and Bordeaux, but, except for a guest appearance in Holland in 1918, she did not sing abroad. After the end of her career as a singer, she was a famous teacher at the Paris Conservatory.

Records: Acoustic records appeared on HMV after 1918; her electric records were made for Odeon. *U.S. re-issue:* Decca.

CHALIA, ROSALIA, soprano, b. 1866, Havana; d. 1961, Havana. She came of a noble Cuban family and at first sang only at charity concerts. In 1896 she appeared for an indisposed singer with a traveling Italian company then touring Cuba, and she was sensationally successful as Santuzza in *Cavalleria Rusticana*. Against the will of her family she then took up a stage career which brought her great success, particularly in Latin America. She sang Santuzza at the Metropolitan Opera (1898-99) and later traveled with the San Carlo Opera Company in the United States. After the end of her career she lived in great poverty in New York. Finally the Cuban government granted her an honorary pension and brought her back to her homeland. This singer is more famous for her records than for her personal career.

Records: Many of her records first appeared on the "Eldridge R. Johnson Improved Record"* label (1900-01) and then later on Victor*. She also sang for Zonophone* (1901), Columbia*, and HMV. *U.S. re-recording:* TAP.

CHALIAPIN, FEODOR, bass, b. Feb. 11, 1873, Ometave, near Kazan, Russia; d. Apr. 12, 1938, Paris. After a youth of deprivation and unhappiness, he worked at various jobs and finally, in Ufa, joined a traveling operetta company which was touring southern Russia. In 1892 his voice was discovered by Ursatov in Tiflis and he taught the young man. In 1893 he made his debut in Tiflis as Mephistopheles in *Faust*. In 1894, he came to St. Petersburg, but his great success came only after 1896, when he appeared in Moscow at S.J. Marmontov's private opera. He was also highly successful after 1899 at the Moscow Imperial Opera. In 1901 he appeared at La Scala in the title role in *Mefistofele* and enjoyed great success. In 1906 he was paid the honors due a great artist for his appearances in Paris. He became world-famous for his incomparable acting in the title role of *Boris Godounov*. He sang this part in Paris in 1908, in 1909 at La Scala, and in 1913 at Covent Garden; he was the first singer to perform this outstanding masterpiece on the stages of western Europe. In spite of this he was not particularly successful in his appearances at the Metropolitan Opera in 1907. In 1910 he sang the title role in *Don Quichotte* in its world *première* at the Monte Carlo Opera, where he was a frequent guest. In St. Petersburg he created the role of Dositheus in the world *première* of *Khovantchina*. At the outbreak of World War I he returned to Russia. Although he was named an "Artist of the People" by the Russian government, he left his native Russia permanently in 1920. From 1921 to 1928 he sang—now with continuous success—at the Metropolitan Opera, and from 1922-24 at the Chicago Opera. World-wide tours and guest appearances marked his career and caused him to be esteemed, next to Enrico Caruso, as the greatest artist of his time. After 1927 he lived in Paris; he sang his farewell performance at Monte Carlo in 1937. His memoirs, *Pages from My Life* (1926) and *Man and Mask* (1932) were published in New York. He was especially noted as an outstanding actor. He was a typical Russian bass in the elementary strength of his expressiveness and the tonal volume of his voice. On the stage he was characterized by a self-willed, but always artistic, performance and by eminent acting skill.

Records: His first records appeared in Moscow in 1901 on G & T; later he made a great many for HMV, even electric records appearing on this label. *U.S. re-issue:* Opera Disc, Victor. *U.S. re-recording:* RCA Victor, Angel, Scala, TAP, Harvest, Design, Electrola.

CHALMERS, THOMAS, baritone, b. Oct. 20, 1884, New York; d. Jan. 12, 1966, Greenwich, Conn. He sang originally in a New York church choir, then studied singing with Lombardi in Florence. He made his debut (1911) in Fossombrone as Marcello in *La Bohème*. He then sang in the United States with the Savage Opera Company, the Aborn Opera Company, the Century Opera Company, and the Rabinoff-Boston Company. In 1917 he joined the Metropolitan Opera, making his debut as Valentin in *Faust*. He was very successful there until 1922, when a throat operation put an end to his singing career. Thereafter he became an actor.

Records: Zonophone*, Edison* cylinders and discs, and one Columbia* disc of arias from the Italian and French repertories for which he was so highly esteemed.

CHAMLEE, MARIO, tenor, b. May 29, 1892, Los Angeles; d. Nov. 13, 1966, Hollywood, Calif. Originally Archer Cholmondeley. He was a pupil of Achille Albertti in Los Angeles and made his debut there in 1916 as Edgardo in *Lucia di Lammermoor*. He served in the United States army (1916-19) and after his release sang with the Scotti Opera Company. In 1920 he came to the Metropolitan Opera, making his debut as Cavaradossi in *Tosca*, and he remained there until 1928. During this time he also sang at the San Francisco Opera and at Ravinia. He appeared in Europe (1928-36), particularly at the Opera-Comique, where he was especially liked as Marouf in the opera of the same name. He also appeared in Brussels, Liège, Lille, Bordeaux, Nice, and at both the Vienna Volksoper and the German Theater in Prague. From 1936-39 he was again a member of the Metropolitan. He married the soprano Ruth Miller.

Records: Brunswick*. *U.S. re-recording:* IRCC, TAP.

CHAVANNE, IRENE VON, contralto, b. Apr. 18, 1868, Graz, Austria; d. Dec. 26, 1938, Dresden. She began her study of singing with Johannes Ress in Vienna, then became a pupil of Desirée Artôt de Padilla in Paris and Souvestre in Dresden. She made her debut (1885) at the Dresden Royal Opera and remained there during her entire· career. She sang the role of Herodias there on Dec. 9, 1905, in the world *première* of *Salome*. In 1915 she gave up her career and was then made an honorary member of the Dresden Opera.

Records: Two excessively rare records for HMV, both ensemble numbers (Dresden, 1908).

CHENAL, MARTHE, soprano, b. Aug. 24, 1881, St. Maurice, near Paris; d. Jan. 29, 1947, Paris. She began her studies in 1901 at the Paris Conservatory, but she was discouraged by the officials and all the teachers there. After a year she was prevailed upon to take an engagement at the Moulin Rouge. She was not disheartened, however, but studied under Martini and in 1905 won first prize at the Paris Conservatory. She made her debut in the same year at the Paris Opéra as Brunehild in *Sigurd*. In 1908 she came to the Opéra-Comique, where she first appeared in *Aphrodite*. She had great success at Monte Carlo (1908-10) and also at the two great Paris houses. She also sang at the Manhattan Opera House. In 1923 she sang in *Le Roi d'Ys* at the Opéra-Comique on the occasion of the Lalo Centenary. Her vocal qualities were admired as much as her acting ability and the grace of her elegant bearing. Her dramatic ability in the world *première* of *La Sorcière* at the Opéra-Comique in 1912 caused the critics to compare her with the great Sarah Bernhardt.

Records: Pathé*.

CHRIST, RUDOLF, tenor, b. 1916, Vienna. He began as a chorister at the Vienna Volksoper, then studied for three years with Adolf Vogel in Vienna and made his debut in 1941 at Innsbruck. He sang in Zürich as lyric tenor and operetta singer (1946-49) and came to the Vienna Volksoper in 1949. Since 1956 he has also been engaged at the German-Opera-on-the-Rhine at Düsseldorf-Duisburg. He has made guest appearances at the leading opera houses in Belgium, Italy, and Switzerland and since 1955 has appeared many times at the Salzburg Festivals.

Records: Decca (*Der Barbier von Bagdad* and *Die Kluge*), Philips, Columbia (*Die Fledermaus*), HMV, Vanguard-Amadeo (*Der Zigeunerbaron*), and MMS. *U.S. re-issue:* Epic, Westminster, Angel, Vanguard, Richmond.

CHRISTOFF, BORIS, bass, b. May 18, 1918, Plovdiv, Bulgaria. He first studied law, but his singing ability was discovered in a men's chorus. With the help of a stipend from King Boris of Bulgaria he became a pupil of Riccardo Stracciari in Milan and also studied in Salzburg After the dislocations of the war he began his career as a concert singer in Italy. In 1946 he made his stage debut as Colline in *La Bohème* at the Teatro Adriano. In the same year he sang Pimen in *Boris Godounov* at La Scala, and in 1947, again at La Scala, the title role in the same opera, a part which has since become one of his greatest roles. Since 1949 he has been successful at the Metropolitan Opera and has made guest and concert tours to all the music centers of the world. He has sung at the Arena and Edinburgh Festivals. In 1960 and 1961 he was honored for his performances as King Philip in *Don Carlos* at the Salzburg Festivals. He is held to be one of the best bass singers of his time. The powerful voice and the intensity of his musical and dramatic skill in shaping his roles makes him one of the outstanding interpreters of the Russian as well as the French and Italian repertories. He is also a great lieder singer.

Records: HMV (Mephistopheles in two complete versions of *Faust*, *Boris Godounov*, in several parts including the title role, *A Life for the Czar*, *Aïda*, *Don Carlos*, and *Simon Boccanegra*; he has also sung the songs of Moussorgsky, Glinka, and Tchaikovsky); for DGG* a complete version of *Boris Godounov*. *U.S. re-issue:* RCA Victor, Capitol, Angel, Seraphim.

CICCOLINI, GUIDO, tenor, b. 1885, Rome. He studied with Antonio Cotogni in Rome and made his debut in Bologna (1907) as Alfredo in *La Traviata*. In 1909 he traveled through Belgium and Holland with the opera troupe of Mme. de Restier. Guest appearances followed in England, Ireland, and France. He was particularly successful in Russia. In 1911 he made a tour of Australia in an opera company collected by Nellie Melba. In 1914 he sang in the Italian *première* of *I Quattro Rusteghi* at the Teatro Lirico. After 1914 he was a guest for several seasons at the Boston Opera, in 1915 at the Havana Opera, and 1918-19 at the Chicago Opera. In 1926 he sang at the memorial service for his friend Rudolph Valentino, the film star. After 1930 he gave up his career.

Records: He recorded for HMV in Europe; in the United States exclusively for Edison*, making both cylinders and discs. *U.S. re-issue:* Victor, Opera Disc.

CIGADA, FRANCESCO, baritone, b. Oct. 3, 1878, Bergamo, Italy; d. Aug. 6, 1966, Bergamo. He studied with Vincenzo Sabatini in Milan and made his debut in Trieste in 1900. In 1903 he sang in Rio de Janeiro, in 1904 at the Teatro dal Verme, and after 1906 at the Teatro Costanzi with great success. In 1914 he made guest appearances at Covent Garden, where he sang, among other operas, in the *première* of Zandonai's *Francesca da Rimini*. In 1914 he sang at the Théâtre des Champs-Elysées with the ensemble of the Boston Opera Company. He never appeared in North America. Later he appeared as guest in Madrid, Barcelona, Rio de Janeiro, Santiago de Chile, and Havana; he was unusually successful in 1920 at the Teatro Colón. He appeared on the stage for the last time in Bergamo in 1924. After he lost his only daughter when she was twenty-one years of age, he gave up his career and lived in retirement in his villa at Bergamo.

Records Many G & T records, which were all made in 1905-08, at the beginning of his career, before his voice had reached its full development. *U.S. re-issue:* Victor.

CIGNA, GINA, soprano, b. Feb. 6, 1900, near Paris. Her family was of Italian extraction. She first studied piano and theory at the National Conservatory in Paris. In 1923 she married the singer Maurice Sens and began her vocal studies with Lucette Korsoff. Under the name Ginette Sens she made her debut (1927) at La Scala as Freia in *Das Rheingold*, but without particular success. After further study she returned to La Scala in 1929, now under the name of Gina Cigna, and was sensationally successful. Thereafter she appeared there and at other large Italian theaters regularly, being helped particularly by Toscanini. From 1929-37 she sang almost every year at the Arena Festival and made guest appearances at Covent Garden, the Paris Opéra, the Teatro Colón, and in Berlin, Vienna, Amsterdam, and Brussels. She was equally successful at the Metropolitan Opera (1937-39). Thereafter she sang especially at La Scala and the Rome Opera. After an accident in 1947 she was forced to give up her career. She then taught singing, first in Toronto, later in Milan. She had a large dramatic voice of inexhaustible volume and exciting intensity of expression.

Records: Columbia*, Telefunken*, Cetra* (*Norma* and *Turandot*). U.S. re-issue: American Decca. U.S. re-recording: Scala, Rococo.

CILLA, LUIGI, tenor, b. 1885 (?), Rimini, Italy. After he had first sung larger roles in the provincial Italian theaters, he specialized in the smaller parts for tenor and was one of the most-sought-after interpreters of these roles. From 1910-40 he appeared at all the leading Italian opera houses, including La Scala and the Teatro Costanzi. In 1910 he made guest appearances at the Boston Opera, and from 1925-34 sang at Covent Garden, where he was much admired. One of those singers who in smaller roles—if this classification is particularly apt—become better known than the average singer of leading parts.

Records: American Columbia*, Edison cylinders (1912); about 1928 he made solo records for Imperial and one record for HMV, the Drinking Scene from *Otello* with Giovanni Inghilleri.

CINISELLI, FERDINANDO, tenor, b. Mar. 14, 1893, Mortara, near Milan; d. Jan. 30, 1954, Mortara. He made his debut at Novara (1919). In 1920 he sang in Palermo, Madrid, Barcelona, and Bologna and in the same year appeared very successfully at the Teatro Colón. In 1923 he was engaged at La Scala and first appeared as Fenton in *Falstaff*. He had great success in the two following seasons there, his career being assisted greatly by Toscanini. These were followed by guest appearances at the Teatro Costanzi, in Naples, and in Paris, and a tour with the troupe of Max Sauter through Germany and Switzerland. At the beginning of the 1930's he gave up his career and retired to his birthplace. A clear lyric tenor voice, wonderfully trained.

Records: Acoustic for Pathé, Columbia, and HMV; electric for Fonotipia-Odeon. U.S. re-issue: Victor.

CISNEROS, ELEONORA DE, contralto, b. Nov. 1, 1878, New York; d. Feb. 3, 1934, New York. Originally Eleanor Broadfoot. She studied with Mme. Murio-Celli in New York. During her studies she was discovered by Jean de Reszke, who brought her to the attention of the Metropolitan Opera; she made her debut there (1900) as Rossweisse in *Die Walküre*. In 1901 she married the Cuban count Francesco de Cisneros, and from that time on she appeared under that name. In 1901 she went to Europe for further study with Jean de Reszke and Victor Maurel in Paris and with Trabadello and Lombardi in Milan. In 1902 she appeared in Turin and had a starring career for the next twelve years at the largest Italian theaters. She sang at La Scala in 1906 in the world *première* of *La Figlia di Jorio*, and in 1908 in the first performance there of *Elektra* and *Queen of Spades*. She was a guest in Lisbon, Paris, Vienna, Madrid, Barcelona, Antwerp, St. Petersburg, and regularly in London (1903-08). From 1906-11 she was the principal contralto at the Manhattan Opera; she then sang with the Philadelphia-Chicago Company and until 1916 with the Chicago Opera. In 1914 she sang Brangäne in *Tristan und Isolde* at the Théâtre des Champs-Elysées. In 1915 she toured Cuba, Australia, and New Zealand. In 1925 she appeared occasionally at La Scala as Herodias in *Salome* and she lived until 1929 in Paris. Thereafter she became a singing teacher in New York. She had a large-dimensioned contralto voice of great expressiveness.

Records: G & T, Nicole (London, 1904), Columbia (Milan, 1904), Pathé*, American Columbia*, (about 1915), and Edison* Amberola cylinders and discs. *U.S. re-recording:* IRCC, TAP.

CLAIRBERT, CLAIRE, soprano, b. 1895 (?), Brussels. She left her homeland in 1914 with her parents upon the invasion of Belgium and worked during World War I in the Belgian War Ministry in Le Havre. She then studied singing in Brussels and made her debut at the Opera there in 1922 as Musetta in *La Bohème*. For thirty years she was the chief prima donna of the Brussels Opera and enjoyed great popularity. Her guest appearances were made especially in Paris, but also in Monte Carlo and Bucharest. In 1931 she sang in San Francisco and Los Angeles, including appearances opposite Beniamino Gigli. She remained active in Brussels until 1953, when she became a singing teacher. The most famous coloratura of the French repertory of her generation. Her voice was equally impressive for its technical brilliance and for its over-all musicality.

Records: Polydor.

CLAIRE, MARION, soprano, b. Feb. 25, 1904, Chicago. Her father was a judge and her mother a well-known pianist. She began the study of the violin at the age of six and in 1914 gave a violin concert with the Chicago Symphony Orchestra. Until 1925 she appeared as a concert violinist, but also studied singing. After studies with Ettore Titta, the brother of Titta Ruffo, and Mario Malatesta in Milan, she made her debut in Venice (1926) as Mimi in *La Bohème*. After her first successes in Italy, she sang at the Berlin State Opera (1927-31). In 1931 she made a successful American debut at the Chicago Opera as Elsa in *Lohengrin*. In 1929 she married the conductor Henry Weber. She sang again with great success in Chicago in 1934 and 1937. She then turned to operettas and musicals and became a widely known radio singer. After 1940 she also appeared in American films.

Records: Unfortunately, she made only three records of operetta numbers for Victor.*

CLAUSSEN, JULIA, contralto, b. June 11, 1879, Stockholm; d. May 1, 1941, Stockholm. She studied at the Royal Conservatory in Stockholm (1898-1902) and made her debut at the Royal Opera there (1902); she remained a member of the company until 1912. She devoted the period 1903-05 to further study in Berlin and had great success in guest appearances there and in Vienna, London, Paris, Brussels, and Amsterdam. She sang at the Chicago Opera (1913-17) and was called then to the Metropolitan Opera, where she enjoyed success until 1932. During these years she expanded her activities with further guest appearances and concerts. After the close of her career she lived in Stockholm and taught singing there. A contralto voice of the highest musical rank in both opera and concert repertory.

Records: Only a few records of her voice exist, some on Swedish HMV, others on American Columbia*.

CLEMENS, HANS, tenor, b. 1890, Bichern, Germany; d. Aug. 25, 1958, Montrose, Colorado. He began his stage career in 1912 at the Cologne Opera. He later married the soprano Wanda Achsel, from whom, however, he was later separated. He made successful guest appearances in 1924-29 and in 1935 at Covent Garden. In 1930 he was a member of the Metropolitan Opera, making his debut as the Steersman in *Der Fliegende Holländer*. Until 1938 he was an important singer at the Metropolitan, singing *buffo* roles, particularly David in *Die Meistersinger* and Mime in the *Ring* cycle; he also sang lyric parts in his voice range.

Records: A few rare titles for Parlophone, as well as private recordings for the Metropolitan.

CLÉMENT, EDMOND, tenor, b. Mar. 28, 1867, Paris; d. Feb. 24, 1928, Nice. He studied at the National Conservatory in Paris and made his debut in November, 1889, at the Opéra-Comique as Vincent in *Mireille*. He soon became the most famous French lyric tenor of his time and, after his successes in Paris, he appeared as guest in Brussels, at Covent Garden, and at the Teatro Real. At the Opéra-Comique he sang in the world *premières* of *La Vivandière* (1895) and *La Fille de Tabarin* (1901). In 1909 he was invited to the Metropolitan Opera, appearing first in the title role of *Werther* with Geraldine Farrar and Alma Gluck. He remained only one season at the Metropolitan, but sang with the Boston Opera Company (1911-13). In France his career lasted a long time; he appeared in the concert hall there in 1927. During this same time he was teaching in Paris. The fine shading of his voice and its brilliant luster were greatly admired, especially in lyric parts in the French operatic repertory.

Records: Odeon De Luxe (Paris, 1905), Pathé*, and Victor*. *U.S. re-issue:* IRCC. *U.S. re-recording:* IRCC, Rococo, Scala, RCA Victor, TAP, HRS.

CLEWING, CARL, tenor, b. Apr. 22, 1884, Schwerin, Germany; d. May 15, 1954, Badenweiler, Germany. He was at first an actor and appeared in Bromberg and Strasbourg as well as at Berlin theaters and (1911-17) at the Royal Dramatic Theater in Berlin. After 1917 he studied singing with Francisco d'Andrade, Wilhelm Grüning, Ernst Grenzebach, and Wilhelm Flam in Berlin. He became known as a singer through his recitals, at which he accompanied himself on the lute. After having made guest appearances since 1920 as an opera singer, he was engaged as a heroic tenor at the Berlin State Opera (1922). In 1924-25 he sang Walther in *Die Meistersinger* at the Bayreuth Festivals, but was unsuccessful there. In 1925 he sang the title role in the world *première* of *Paganini* in Vienna. By 1926 he had already given up his career as a singer and become a teacher of musicology in Berlin and after 1929 was a professor at the Vienna Academy of Music. He was the artistic director of the Telefunken recording firm (1932-45). He became best known as a musical scholar and editor of folk songs: *Carl Clewing's Liederbuch*, "Music and Hunting" in *Denkmaler Deutscher Jagdkultur*, and *Sammlung Alter Volkslieder*. The proper domain of this artist was doubtless that of song—and especially that of folk singing—whereas he lacked the real basis for a stage career.

Records: Vox, in songs with lute accompaniment.

COATES, JOHN, tenor, b. June 29, 1865, Girlington, England; d. Aug. 16, 1941, Northwood, England. As a child he sang in a boys' choir and later became a bookkeeper and foreign representative for a commercial firm. In 1893 he decided to become a singer and for five years sang as a baritone with the D'Oyly Carte Opera Company, with whom he came to America in 1895. However, since he still wanted to become a tenor opera singer, he sang for another year in small theaters to pay for voice lessons. He made his operatic debut at Covent Garden (1901) in *Much Ado About Nothing*. He then went on to become the greatest English oratorio tenor of his generation, being particularly admired in the works of Elgar. In 1904 he made an extensive tour of Germany, during which he appeared at the Cologne Opera as Faust, Romeo, and Lohengrin. In 1905 he sang again at Covent Garden and in 1907-08 with the Moody-Manners Opera Company. In 1910-11 he sang under Sir Thomas Beecham in heroic Wagner roles, particularly Tristan and Siegfried, but after 1914 he specialized in lieder. In 1925 he made an extensive North American tour. Near his seventy-first birthday he gave lieder recitals on the radio from London, in which he accompanied himself on the piano.

Records: G & T (London, 1907), HMV, and Pathé*. *U.S. re-issue* Columbia.

COBELLI, GIUSEPPINA, soprano, b. Aug. 1, 1898, Maderno on Lake Garda, Italy; d. Sept. 2, 1948, Barbarano di Salò, Italy. She studied in Milan and made her debut in Piacenza (1924) in the title role of *La Gioconda*. She sang with brilliant success in 1924-25 with the Italian Opera in Holland. At this time she was engaged by La Scala, where (1925) she made her debut as Sieglinde in *Die Walküre*. She remained for more than fifteen years one of the major prima donnas at La Scala, and made guest appearances in 1927 and 1931 at the Teatro Colón and later in Belgium and Holland. In 1937 she appeared at the Festival in the Boboli Gardens in Florence in *L'Incoronazione di Poppea*. She was greatly admired at La Scala until 1947. Becoming deaf, she was forced to end her career prematurely. She had a sumptuous and well-trained dramatic soprano voice.

Records: Unfortunately, she made only two acoustic records for HMV.

COERTSE, MIMI, soprano, b. June 12, 1932, Durban, South Africa. She studied in Johannesburg and after 1954 with Josef Witt in Vienna. In 1955 she made her debut as a Flower Maiden in *Parsifal* during a guest performance of the Vienna State Opera in Naples. A year later she had her first great success at Basel as the Queen of the Night in *Die Zauberflöte*. She sang the same part also in 1956 at the Teatro San Carlo. Since 1957 she has been a member of the Vienna State Opera. She has made guest appearances at Covent Garden and in Rome, Brussels, Cologne, Frankfurt a. M., and Munich. She made a South African tour in 1956. She is married to the South African musicologist David Engela. Her coloratura voice is outstanding for its technical training.

Records: Decca (as Fiakermilli in a recording of *Arabella*), Vox, and Bertelsmann. *U.S. re-issue:* Bach Guild, Westminster, RCA Victor, Turnabout.

COLOMBO, SCIPIO, baritone, b. May 25, 1913, Vicenza. He made his debut in 1937. After World War II he became well known through his appearances at important Italian theaters, including La Scala. There (1947) he sang in the first performance at that house of *The Love of Three Oranges* and (1957) at the world *première* of *Les Dialogues des Carmélites*. He made guest appearances at Covent Garden and the Vienna State

Opera and is greatly admired in Holland. In 1959 he sang *Il Campanello* at the Bregenz Festival.

Records: Westminster (*Tosca* and *Don Pasquale*); Cetra* (*Luisa Miller* and *Fedora*); MMS (*Don Giovanni* and *Aïda*). *U.S. re-issue:* Perfect.

COLZANI, ANSELMO, baritone, b. Mar. 28, 1918, Budrio, near Bologna. He studied with Corrado Zambelli in Bologna and made his debut there (1947) as the Herald in *Lohengrin*. After his first successes in Italy he reached La Scala in 1954, having appeared many times after 1952 at the Arena Festivals. In 1956 he sang at the San Francisco Opera and in 1960 in Chicago. In the latter year he was engaged by the Metropolitan Opera, making his debut in the title role of *Simone Boccanegra* with brilliant success. Since then he had been admired there as well as in all the opera houses of world rank. The powerful sonority of his voice is even more famous than his acting talent.

Records: Urania* (*La Gioconda* and *La Forza del Destino*).

CONCATO, AUGUSTA, soprano, b. 1895; d. June, 1964, Carate Brianza, Italy. This singer had a successful career on the leading Italian stages in the 1920's. In 1921 she was engaged by Arturo Toscanini for La Scala, where she was admired as Giorgetta in *Il Tabarro*. In 1923 she sang there in the *première* of *Sakuntala*. In 1924 she made a tour of Australia with a company which Nellie Melba had collected; with this troupe she sang Aïda and Butterfly. She later made guest appearances at Monte Carlo, Cairo, Barcelona, Rio de Janeiro, and Montevideo. For some time she was married to the tenor Nino Piccaluga.

Records: Columbia and HMV. *U.S. re-issue:* American Decca.

CONLEY, EUGENE, tenor, b. Mar. 12, 1908, Lynn, Mass. He studied with Harriet E. Barrows and Ettore Verna. He created a sensation at the outset of his career in America, singing in concerts with the NBC orchestra as well as in a performance of Brahms' *Liebeslieder Waltzes* under Toscanini. In 1948 he went to Europe and was highly successful in guest appearances at the Opéra-Comique, at Covent Garden, and in Stockholm, Florence, Turin, and Genoa. He appeared at the Arena Festival and in 1949 sang Arturo in *I Puritani* at La Scala. In 1950 he was engaged by the Metropolitan Opera, making his debut there in the title role of *Faust*. He was married to the concert contralto Winifred Heidt in 1948. He has a beautiful and technically well-trained voice and specializes in classical *bel canto* parts.

Records Columbia* (including *Faust* and *The Rake's Progress*), Decca, and HMV (*Missa Solemnis* under Toscanini). *U.S. re-issue:* RCA Victor, Request.

CONSTANTINO, FLORENCIO, tenor, b. 1869, Bilbao, Spain; d. Nov. 19, 1920, Mexico City. He was at first a machinist and then a ship's engineer before studying singing. He made his debut (1892) at the Montevideo Opera in *La Dolores*. After huge successes on South American stages, he was equally successful on a European tour (1903-04), particularly in Spain and Germany. In 1906 he appeared at the New Orleans Opera and in 1908 at the Manhattan Opera in New York. In 1909 he sang Enzo in *La Gioconda* with Lillian Nordica and Louise Homer at the gala opening of the newly built Boston Opera House. In 1910-11 he sang at the Metropolitan Opera and from 1909-12 he was admired at the Teatro Colón; in the latter year he toured Argentina with an opera company. In 1915 he appeared for the last time on the stage in Los Angeles. Thereafter he lived in Mexico City, where he was reduced to complete poverty. He died in a charity hospital there, after he had been found lying unconscious in the street. He had a bright and glowing tenor voice.

Records: G & T (Berlin, 1905), Excelsior Reale, Odeon (Paris, 1906), Favorite (Paris, 1906), Victor* (1907-08), Columbia*, Edison* cylinder, and Pathé*. *U.S. re-recording:* TAP, Columbia, Odyssey, Cantilena.

CORDES, MARCEL, baritone, b. Mar. 11, 1920, Stelzenberg, Germany. Originally Kurt Schumacher. He studied singing at the Kaiserslautern Conservatory (1936-38), and at the Mannheim Music High School (1938-40). He made his debut (1941) at Eger, Czechoslovakia. He then became a soldier and was not able to resume his career until 1948. He sang in Kaiserslautern (1948-50), Mannheim (1950-51), Karlsruhe (1951-54), and since 1954 has been engaged by the Munich State Opera. Guest appearances have brought him great success at La Scala, the Brussels Opera, and the State Operas in Hamburg, Vienna, and Stuttgart. He also sings regularly at the German-Opera-on-the-Rhine at Düsseldorf-Duisburg. He has a strong and impressive baritone voice with which he has mastered a wide-ranging opera and concert repertory.

Records: Electrola (*The Bartered Bride*), Columbia (*Die Kluge* and *Carmina Burana*), and DGG (*Die Zaubergeige*). *U.S. re-issue:* Angel, Bruno.

CORELLI, FRANCO, tenor, b. 1925 (?), Ancona, Italy. He turned down a civil service career after vocal studies at the Conservatories of Pesaro and Milan. In 1950 he won a singing contest in Florence and made his debut after further study (1952). For three years he sang on provincial stages and on the radio in Italy, then (1954) he came to La Scala. He quickly attained stardom on the more important stages in Italy and at the Maggio Musicale and Arena Festivals. His guest appearances include the Vienna State Opera, Covent Garden, the Paris Opéra, and the Chicago and San Francisco Operas. In 1960 he made a very successful debut at the Metropolitan Opera as Manrico in *Il Trovatore*. He sang the same role at the Salzburg Festival in 1962. He is married to the soprano Loretta di Lelio. A fresh and radiant tenor voice of great brilliance filled with musicality and artistic expressiveness.

Records: His first records appeared on the Cetra* label (*Aida* and *Tosca*), he then made many records for Columbia (including *Norma* with Maria Callas and *I Pagliacci*). *U.S. re-issue:* Angel, RCA Victor, London.

CORENA, FERNANDO, bass, b. Dec. 22, 1916, Geneva. His father was Turkish and his mother Italian. He began the study of Catholic theology at the University of Fribourg, but, encouraged by the conductor Vittorio Gui, he took up singing. He studied with Enrico Romani in Milan and made his debut in Trieste (1947) as Varlaam in *Boris Godounov*. He had great successes in Italy, where he appeared at La Scala, other important opera houses, and the Maggio Musicale Festival. In 1953 he was greatly admired at the Edinburgh Festival as the title hero in *Falstaff*. In 1953 he came to the Metropolitan Opera, where he has since remained with great success. He has made guest appearances in London, Paris, Vienna, Buenos Aires, Chicago, San Francisco, Mexico City, and Holland. In 1965 he sang Osmin in *Die Entführung aus dem Serail* at the Salzburg Festival. Among his other famous roles are Leporello in *Don Giovanni* and the Sacristan in *Tosca*. A full-sounding, but extraordinarily flexible, bass voice. He is known as one of the most famous *buffos* in the Italian repertory of the past.

Records: A great many records, especially for Decca (*Le Nozze di Figaro, Don Giovanni, L'Elisir d'Amore, La Bohème, Madama Butterfly, Il Barbiere di Siviglia, Aïda, La Forza del Destino, Rigoletto, Otello, Andrea Chénier, Tosca, Manon Lescaut*), RCA Victor* (*Don Giovanni*), Urania* (*Don Pasquale*), and Cetra* (*Gianni Schicchi* and *I Quattro Rusteghi*). *U.S. re-issue:* London, Richmond, Vox.

CORNELIUS, PETER, tenor, b. Jan. 21, 1865, Labjergaard, Denmark; d. Dec. 25, 1934, Copenhagen. Originally Cornelius Peterson. He worked as a waiter in a restaurant in Copenhagen and was discovered there by the tenor Nyrop, who then became his teacher. He made his debut at the Copenhagen Royal Opera (1892) as a baritone, singing Escamillo in *Carmen*. Further study in Berlin with Hermann Spiro and Julius Lieban followed. After 1899 he sang tenor parts, but retained much of his baritone repertory. After 1902 he was greatly admired as a Wagner tenor and sang Siegmund at the Bayreuth Festival in 1906. From 1907-14 he was an annual guest at Covent Garden and also sang at the Paris Opéra, the Royal Opera in Stockholm, and in Oslo and Karlsruhe. In 1922 he gave his farewell stage performance at the Copenhagen Opera, to which he had belonged for thirty years. He then became a teacher in the Danish capital.

Records: A great many records for G & T, HMV, and Pathé; also Edison and Pathé cylinders. *U.S. re-recording:* Belcanto.

CORNUBERT, PIERRE, tenor, b. 1863; d.?. He made his debut (1888) at the Opéra-Comique and on May 14, 1889, created there the role of the Byzantine Herald in the world *première* of *Esclarmonde*. After first singing small roles he became the best-known French tenor of his generation and sang at all the most important French opera houses. He sang at the Havana Opera (1899-1900) and from there he was engaged by the Metropolitan Opera as a substitute for the tenor Albert Saléza, who had become ill. He made his New York debut (February, 1900) as Vasco di Gama in *L'Africaine*. In 1904 he sang as guest at Covent Garden. In 1911 he became a professor at the Paris Conservatory. His wife, Suzanne Cornubert was also an opera singer. His was an aristocratic voice which he used intelligently.

Records: A few Edison cylinders and discs for Odeon-Fonotipia (Paris, 1905), all of the greatest rarity. *U.S. re-recording:* IRCC.

CORRADETTI, FERRUCCIO, baritone, b. Feb. 22, 1866, San Severino, Italy; d. August, 1939, New York. At first a journalist, he studied singing with Giuseppe Faini. After 1892 he had great successes at all the large Italian opera houses. In 1898 he sang with the Italian Opera in Holland and then made guest appearances in London, Paris, Buenos Aires, Rio de Janeiro, Madrid, and Barcelona. In 1910 he sang the title role in *Malbruk* in Paris. In 1914 he went to the United States, but made only guest appearances and turned more and more to teaching. He was married to the soprano Bice Adami, and their daughter, Iris Adami-Corradetti, was also a well-known singer.

Records: He left a great many

records of his voice; the oldest are on Berliner (Milan, 1899-1901), but he also sang for G & T, Fonotipia, Odeon, and Columbia*. Some of his titles were re-pressed on Victor* under the name Carlo Feretti. *U.S. re-issue:* HRS, IRCC, Okeh. *U.S. re-recording:* Belcanto, Eterna, TAP, Rococo.

CORTIS, ANTONIO, tenor, b. Aug. 12, 1891, Valencia, Spain; d. Apr. 2, 1952, Valencia. He studied at the Valencia Conservatory, not just singing, but also composition and conducting, and made his debut in 1915. After his first success on Spanish and Italian stages, he came to the Chicago Opera in 1924, where he made his debut as Radames in *Aida*. In Chicago he had a sensational success in *La Cena della Beffe* and he remained there until 1932. Thereafter he appeared principally at Covent Garden, but also sang at La Scala and on other large Italian stages. He appeared on the stage until 1948, and lived later in his native Spain, where he became a composer. He had a glowing tenor voice of brilliant quality in the upper ranges; he was particularly famous as an interpreter of Puccini.
Records: Parlophone, Victor*, HMV. *U.S. re-recording:* TAP, Eterna, Scala, Rococo.

CORTIS, MARCELLO, baritone, b. Nov. 23, 1915, Prague; d. May 23, 1962, Vienna. He studied piano and musical theory at the Prague Conservatory; then studied singing with Giovanni Binetti in Milan. He made his debut there (1940) and soon had important successes at Italian theaters, particularly at La Scala. In the years after the war he repeated these successes in guest appearances in Paris, London, Brussels, and Amsterdam, but especially in Vienna. He sang at the Glyndebourne and Aix-en-Provence Festivals. After 1950 he worked simultaneously as a singer and as a *régis-seur*, and his stage management of Mozart operas at the Aix-en-Provence Festivals was particularly noteworthy. He is especially remembered for his performances of Mozart.
Records: Columbia (*L'Italiana in Algeri* and *Mireille*), DGG* (*La Serva Padrona*), as well as on a few less important labels. *U.S. re-issue:* Angel, Vox.

COSSOTTO, FIORENZA, contralto, b. 1935, Crescentino, near Turin. She studied at the Turin Conservatory. After she had won a singing contest, she enrolled in 1955 at La Scala as a student. There she sang small roles at first, but was given increasingly important parts, and in the winter of 1961 had great success as Leonora in *La Favorita*, alternating in the part with Giulietta Simionato. She appeared as guest at the Vienna State Opera in 1958 as Maddelena in *Rigoletto* and in 1962 as Amneris in *Aida*. She has also had great success at the Arena and Baths of Caracalla Festivals, as well as in the great opera houses in Germany, Austria, England, France, and South America. She is married to the bass Ivo Vinco. She has an expressive and warm-timbred contralto voice, and she sings almost all the important contralto parts in the Italian literature.
Records: Decca (small part in a complete *Andrea Chénier*), Columbia (a small role in *La Sonnambula*); DDG* (principal roles in *Don Carlos* and *Il Trovatore*), and for Harmonia Mundi*. *U.S. re-issue:* Angel, London, Everest-Cetra.

COTOGNI, ANTONIO, baritone, b. Aug. 1, 1831, Rome; d. Oct. 15, 1918, Rome. He attended singing school of the Hospice of San Michele in Rome until he was twelve years old, then worked in his father's majolica factory. He resumed his study of singing at the

Couzinou · Craft

Capella di Santa Maria Maggiore and finally became a pupil of Faldi in Rome. In 1849 young Antonio Cotogni took part in the defense of the Roman Republic. He made his debut in Rome as Belcore in *L'Elisir d'Amore* at the Teatro Metastasio in 1852. At first he sang in small theaters, but was very successful in Rome, Nice, and Turin; he appeared at La Scala in the 1860-61 season. From that time he chronicled great triumphs in guest appearances in St. Petersburg, Madrid, Barcelona, London, Paris, Lisbon, and on all the large Italian stages. Verdi, who was especially fond of his voice, was once moved to tears by his singing. He taught singing at the St. Petersburg Conservatory (1894-98) and after 1899 at the Accademia di Santa Cecilia in Rome. Becoming one of the most famous teachers of his time, he counted among his pupils Mattia Battistini, Jean de Reszke, Giacomo Lauri-Volpi, and Beniamino Gigli.

Records: Antonio Cotogni was the oldest singer whose voice is preserved on records. In 1908, when he was past seventy-seven, he sang, with the tenor Francesco Marconi, the duet "I Mulatieri," by Masini, for G & T. This is his only record. *U.S. re-recording:* TAP, Rococo.

COUZINOU, ROBERT, baritone, b. 1888; d. 1958, Paris. He made his debut (1912) at the Opéra-Comique. He was a member of the Metropolitan Opera (1918-20), making his debut there on the evening of Armistice Day, Nov. 11, 1918, as the High Priest in *Samson et Dalila*, with Enrico Caruso and Louise Homer in the cast. Later he sang more important parts there, such as Athanaël in *Thaïs* and Escamillo in *Carmen* opposite Geraldine Farrar, as well as Valentin in *Faust*. In the 1920's he was a frequent guest at Covent Garden, where he sang in the first performance there of *Iris* with Margaret Sheridan. His most important successes, however, were at the Opéra-Comique. He spent his last years as a teacher in Paris.

Records: Acoustic records for Odeon (1912) and electric for Polydor (1930). *U.S. re-recording:* FRP.

CRABBÉ, ARMAND, baritone, b. Apr. 23, 1883, Brussels; d. July 24, 1947, Brussels, after a heart attack. A pupil of Demest in Brussels, he made his debut at the Opera in Brussels (1904) in the first performance there of *Le Jongleur de Notre Dame*. After guest appearances in Paris he came to the Manhattan Opera in 1907 and appeared as guest in Chicago and Philadelphia. In 1914 he first sang at La Scala, appearing in the title role of *Rigoletto*. He was frequently heard there until 1929. From 1916-26 he was an annual guest at the Teatro Colón, where he was particularly beloved. In 1926 he was applauded at the Opéra-Comique for his performance in the title role of *Marouf*. In 1929 he sang at La Scala in the world *première* of *Il Re*. He made regular guest appearances at Covent Garden until 1937, but toward the end of his career he appeared principally at Brussels and Antwerp. He gave concerts even after World War II, when he was teaching singing in Brussels. He had an exceptionally well-schooled voice of great expressiveness and classic beauty, particularly in the higher register.

Records: Canadian Victor, HMV, and Fonotipia. *U.S. re-issue:* Victor and American Decca.

CRAFT, MARCELLA, soprano, b. Aug. 11, 1880, Indianapolis, Ind.; d. Dec. 12, 1959, Riverside, Calif. She first studied with Charles R. Adams and later in Milan and Munich. She made her debut in the Italian provinces and was engaged in 1905 at

Elberfeld. She sang in Mainz (1905-07), Kiel (1907-09), and at the Munich Royal Opera (1909-14). She had great success at the latter house in 1910 as the title figure in *Salome* under the direction of the composer. She made guest appearances in Berlin, Schwerin, and Hannover. In 1914 she went to Paris for further study just as World War I broke out. She then returned to America, where she appeared almost exclusively on the concert platform. She was engaged by the San Carlo Opera Company (1917-18). After 1930 she lived and taught singing in California.

Records: Although it was thought for many years that she had made no records, a single Edison* disc of her voice has been found.

CRASS, FRANZ, bass-baritone, b. Feb. 9, 1928, in the Odenwald, Germany. At first he was an actor with a traveling company, and then he studied singing at the Cologne Music High School with Klemens Glettenberg. He made his debut (1954) at Krefeld. In 1956 he was engaged by the Hannover Opera, where he still sings. His guest appearances elsewhere made him well known; he has a guest-appearance contract with the Cologne Opera and has also appeared at the Vienna State Opera, the Berlin City Opera, and the German-Opera-on-the-Rhine at Düsseldorf-Duisberg. He is well known at the Bayreuth Festivals as a Wagner interpreter; there he sang King Heinrich in *Lohengrin* (1959) and the Flying Dutchman (1960-61). He also sang the Commandant in *Don Giovanni* at La Scala in 1960. He appeared at the Salzburg Festival in 1963.

Records: Philips (the title role in a complete recording of *Der Fliegende Holländer* in a Bayreuth production), DGG*, Opera, and Electrola. *U.S. re-issue:* Angel, Philips, Archive of Recorded Sound.

CRESPIN, REGINE, soprano, b. 1927, Marseilles. After she had first studied pharmacy, she studied singing in Paris with Suzanne Cesbron-Viseur and Georges Jouatte and made her debut (1950) in Mulhouse. In 1951 she came to the Opéra-Comique, making her debut there as Tosca. In the same year she was applauded at the Opéra as Elsa in *Lohengrin*. She became the most famous Wagner dramatic soprano in France. Although permanently engaged at the Opéra, she has had frequent opportunities for guest appearances; these include La Scala, Covent Garden, the Berlin City Opera, and trips to South America. She sang Kundry in *Parsifal* at Bayreuth Festivals (1958-61) and the Marschallin in *Der Rosenkavalier* at the Glyndebourne Festival (1959). She first appeared at the Metropolitan Opera in 1962, singing the Marschallin. A dark-timbred large soprano voice of deeply expressive quality.

Records: HMV (including *Les Dialogues des Carmélites*). *U.S. re-issue:* Angel, London, Pathé-Marconi, DGG.

CRIMI, GIULIO, tenor, b. May 10, 1885, Paternò, Sicily; d. Oct. 29, 1939, Rome. He made his debut (1910) in Rome in *La Wally*. After initial successes in Italy, he created a sensation when he appeared in 1914 at the Théâtre des Champs-Elysées. He sang in the same year at Covent Garden and in 1916 was very successful at the Teatro Colón. He was engaged at Chicago (1916-18) and at the Metropolitan Opera (1918-22). At the latter he appeared in the world *premières* of *Il Tabarro* and *Gianni Schicchi* in 1918. He returned to the Chicago Opera (1922-24) and during the summer months sang at the Teatro Colón. In 1924 he returned to Italy and was applauded at the Teatro Costanzi as Vasco di Gama in *L'Africaine*. In 1926 he gave up his singing career and then taught voice in Rome, where his pupils included Tito Gobbi.

Records: A few rare Vocalion* records (New York, 1920).

CROIZA, CLAIRE, contralto, b. Sept. 14, 1882, Paris; d. May 15, 1948, Paris. Originally Claire Conoly. She studied at the Paris Conservatory and made her debut at the Brussels Opera (1905) as Geneviève in *Pelléas et Mélisande*. She remained in Brussels until 1914. She sang as guest at Monte Carlo in 1908 and in 1910 appeared with the ensemble of the Brussels company as Carmen in a guest performance at Cologne. In 1914 she came to the Opéra-Comique, but from then on she became more and more attracted to concert singing and especially to art songs. She became one of the best-known lieder singers of her epoch, noted both for her feeling for style and for her ability to express nuances through shading. She made many wide-ranging concert tours, which limited her to rare stage appearances. Later she held a professorship in the Paris Conservatory.

Records: Columbia*.

CROOKS, RICHARD, tenor, b. June 26, 1900, Trenton, N.J. He created a stir as a boy soprano in a church choir. After serving during World War I in the American Air Corps, he studied with Frank La Forge in New York and then became a soloist in a Presbyterian church there. He had his first big success in 1923 when he gave nine concerts with the New York Symphony Orchestra under Walter Damrosch. In 1926 he made a long concert tour in Europe. His stage debut occurred in 1927 when he sang Cavaradossi in *Tosca* at the Hamburg State Opera. This success was followed by guest appearances in Berlin, Holland, Belgium, England, and Sweden, after which he joined the Philadelphia Opera. He had a triumphal career at the Metropolitan Opera (1933-46), following his debut there as Des Grieux in *Manon*. Concert tours took him all over the world, including Africa and Australia. In 1946 he gave up his stage career. He had a beautifully trained, impressive tenor voice, best heard in lyric roles.

Records: Victor* and HMV. *U.S. re-recording:* TAP, IRCC, Camden.

CROSS, JOAN, soprano, b. Sept. 7, 1900, London. She first studied violin at the Trinity College of Music in London, then studied singing with Peter Dawson. After spending two years in the chorus at the Old Vic in London, she was put forward in 1924 in her first solo part, that of Cherubino in *Le Nozze di Figaro*. From 1931 on she was the first soprano of the Sadler's Wells Opera in London. She first appeared at Covent Garden in 1931, but was particularly admired in 1934 as Desdemona in *Otello*, under Beecham, and as Micaëla in *Carmen* in 1935. In 1941 she became the director of the Sadler's Wells Company and, in spite of great difficulties caused by wartime conditions, was highly successful. On June 7, 1945, she sang Ellen Orford at the world *première* of *Peter Grimes* there. Thereafter she was closely identified with the work of the composer, Britten, and sang in the world *premières* of his other operas: *The Rape of Lucretia* (Glyndebourne, 1946), *Albert Herring* (Glyndebourne, 1947), *Gloriana* (Covent Garden, 1953), and *The Turn of the Screw* (Venice, 1954). In 1955 she gave her farewell stage performance, choosing Covent Garden for the occasion. Thereafter she busied herself as *régisseur* at

Covent Garden, Sadler's Wells, the Edinburgh Festival, and at Amsterdam. Since 1948 she has conducted an opera studio in London.

Records: Columbia, HMV (including *The Rape of Lucretia*), and Decca (including *The Turn of the Screw*). *U.S. re-issue:* RCA Victor, London.

CROSSLEY, ADA, contralto, b. 1874, Tarraville, Australia; d. Oct. 17, 1929, London. She studied in Melbourne and made her debut there as a concert singer (1892). In 1894 she came to London for further training and became a pupil of Sir Charles Santley; later she studied with Mathilde Marchesi in Paris. In 1895 she gave her first concert in London and thereafter had great success in the concert hall. In 1897 she sang at the English court for Queen Victoria and in 1903 she made a long American tour. In Amsterdam she sang under Willem Mengelberg, and in 1912 gave a concert in London under the direction of Henry J. Wood for the benefit of the victims of the "S.S. Titanic" disaster. Later she expanded her teaching activities in the English metropolis. She never appeared on the stage. She had a dark-timbred and melodic contralto voice.

Records: Victor* (1903) and Pathé*. *U.S. re-recording:* IRCC.

CUÉNOD, HUGUES, tenor, b. June 26, 1902, Vevey, France. He studied singing at the Institut Ribaupierre in Lausanne, at the Geneva and Basel Conservatories, and finally in Vienna with Singer-Beirian. He began his career in Paris in 1928 and also sang in the same year in New York. He appeared in Geneva (1930-33) and Paris (1934-37), both in the concert hall and on the stage. In 1937-39 he undertook a long North American tour with the composer Nadia Boulanger. He was a professor at the Geneva Conservatory (1940-46) and thereafter increased his concert activity in the music centers of both North America and Europe, sang at concerts in connection with the larger international music festivals, and also appeared as an opera singer in various productions. He participated in the world *première* of *The Rake's Progress* in Venice in 1951. He was highly prized as an interpreter of Bach's music.

Records: Nixa (*St. Matthew Passion*), Decca (*L'Enfant et les Sortilèges, Ariadne auf Naxos,* and *Oedipus Rex*), HMV (*Le Nozze di Figaro*). *U.S. re-issue:* Vanguard, London, Westminster, Bach Guild, Decca, Lyrichord, Angel, Cambridge, Columbia, Vox, Richmond, Period, Technichord, Music Guild, Turnabout.

CULP, JULIA, contralto, b. Oct. 6, 1880, Groningen, Holland. She originally studied violin, but at the age of fourteen came to the Amsterdam Conservatory, where she was a singing pupil of Cornélie van Zanten. She completed her vocal studies with Etelka Gerster in Berlin and made her debut (1901) in a concert in Magdeburg in which Ferruccio Busoni took part. She then gave song recitals in Berlin and undertook a tour through Holland. She was soon judged one of the greatest interpreters of lieder of her generation. From 1906-13 she was accompanied at the piano on all her tours by the well-known pianist Eric J. Wolff. In 1913 she came to the United States and from her first concert in New York experienced success of the highest order. Her first marriage was to one of the personal attachés of Kaiser Wilhelm II, Mertens; in 1919 she married the Viennese industrialist, Baron von Ginskey. Thereafter she lived in her castle in Maffersdorf, near Reichenberg in Bohemia, and appeared in the concert hall only rarely. She never sang in opera. In 1938 she returned to her Dutch homeland, where, during the German occupation of 1940-44, she had to remain concealed because she was a Jew. She lives in Amsterdam. She was one of the most noted lieder singers of the century, equally finished in the art of phrasing and in the subtlety of her interpretation of the text.

Records: Anker, Odeon, HMV, and Victor*. *U.S. re-issue:* Opera Disc, IRCC. *U.S. re-recording:* IRCC, Rococo.

CUNITZ, MAUD, soprano, b. 1911, London, the daughter of German parents. At the age of three she was taken to Nuremburg and there studied singing and dancing and joined the Nuremburg Opera chorus in 1931. She made her debut as a soloist (1934) at Gotha-Sondershausen. Various engagements followed at Coburg (1936-38), Lübeck (1939-40), Magdeburg (1940-41), and at the State Opera in Stuttgart (1941-44). In 1945 she made a successful guest appearance as Elisabeth in *Tannhäuser* at the Vienna State Opera, and she remained a member of that company until 1950. During this time she was very successful at the Salzburg Festivals as Donna Elvira in *Don Giovanni* and as Octavian in *Der Rosenkavalier*. After 1950 she sang at the Munich State Opera. Guest appearances took her to the Opéra in Paris, to Nice, Brussels, and Rome. In 1951 she sang at the Maggio Musicale Festival in *Genoveva*; in 1953 she appeared at Covent Garden in the title role of *Arabella* and as the Countess in *Capriccio*.

Records: Telefunken, Decca (*Der Freischütz*), HMV (*Lohengrin*), and DGG (*I Vespri Siciliani*). *U.S. re-issue:* American Decca.

CURTIN, PHYLLIS, soprano, b. Dec. 3, 1927, Clarksburg, W. Va. She graduated form Wellesley College and made her debut with the New England Opera Theater. She became a leading soprano at the New York City Opera and created there the title role in *Susannah* and a leading role in *The Passion of Jonathan Wade*; in 1958 she also sang a leading role in *Wuthering Heights* at Santa Fe. She sang in the New York *premières* of *Troilus and Cressida* and Giannini's *The Taming of the Shrew*, as well as in the first American performances of *Peter Grimes*, *Les Mamelles de Tirésias*, and *Der Prozess*, creating in this last work the three leading female roles. She sang Fiordiligi on the NBC television production of *Così fan tutte* and made her Metropolitan Opera debut in this role in 1961. She sang Mélisande in a concert performance of Debussy's opera with the New York Philharmonic and has appeared with other orchestras and in recitals. She has sung regularly at the Aspen Festivals.

Records: Columbia and Allegro Royale, Westminster, RCA Victor, Odyssey, Vanguard, Cambridge, Louisville, Cook, and Desto (in American songs).

CVEJIČ, BISERKA (*see* Tzveych, Biserka).

CZERWENKA, OSCAR, bass, b. 1925, Linz, Austria. He studied with Otto Iro in Vienna and made his debut (1947) in Graz, where he remained for three years. In 1951 he was engaged by the Vienna State Opera, of which he has been a member ever since. He has appeared as guest at La Scala, Covent Garden, the Zürich Opera, the State Operas in Munich and Stuttgart, and has also sung at the Salzburg, Edinburgh, and Holland Festivals. In 1958 he came to the Metropolitan Opera, where he had brilliant success as Baron Ochs in

Der Rosenkavalier. He is particularly admired as an interpreter of rich *buffo* roles.

Records: Columbia (*Der Barbier von Bagdad*), MMS (the Commandant in *Don Giovanni*), Philips (*Tiefland* and *Salome*), and Decca (*Die Frau ohne Schatten*). U.S. re-issue: Remington, London, Electrola.

D

DADDI, FRANCESCO, tenor, b. 1864, Naples; d. 1945, Chicago. He made his debut (1891) in Milan. On May 7, 1892, at the Teatro dal Verme he sang Beppe in the world *première* of *I Pagliacci*. During the next fifteen years he had great success as a *buffo* tenor on various Italian stages, including La Scala. In 1907 he was engaged by the Manhattan Opera Company and remained there until 1910. He next sang at Chicago (1911-20), and was extremely successful at Ravinia, near Chicago, where he appeared until the late 1920's in such *buffo* parts as Dulcamara in *L'Elisir d'Amore* and Bartolo in *Il Barbiere di Siviglia*. After 1920 he directed a singing school in Chicago. In 1938 he sang a few times at the Chicago Opera in the small bass role of Bricoleur in *Louise*. One of the best-known *buffo* singers of his time, he was outstanding on the stage for his sparkling acting talent.

Records: Edison* cylinders, Columbia*, Zonophone*, G & T, and Victor*. He recorded the Serenade of Harlequin from *I Pagliacci* twice, a selection which he sang at the world *première* of the work.

DALBERG, FREDERICK, bass, b. Jan. 7, 1908, Newcastle-on-Tyne, England. Originally Frederick Dalrymple. He was taken as a child to South Africa and there began the vocal studies which he completed in Dresden and Leipzig. He made his debut (1931) in Leipzig and sang in Germany under the name Frederick Dalberg. He stayed for many years at Leipzig, then sang at the Berlin State Opera, making guest appearances in Vienna, Munich, and Dresden. He was considered an oustanding Wagner singer and appeared at the Bayreuth Festivals (1942-43; 1951). From 1948-51 he was first bass at the Munich State Opera. In 1951 he went to London, where he had a notable career at Covent Garden. He sang in the first performance at Covent Garden of *Wozzeck* and in 1953 in the world *première* of *Gloriana*. Since 1959 he has sung at the National Theater in Mannheim.

Records: Columbia* (Pogner in *Die Meistersinger*).

DALIS, IRENE, contralto, b. 1929, San Jose, Calif. She studied in New York with Edyth Walker and Paul Althouse and finally in Italy, but made her debut in 1953 in Oldenburg. She was first contralto of the Berlin City Opera (1955-60). In 1957 she was called to the Metropolitan Opera, where she has had great success. Since 1958 she has been a regular guest at Covent Garden. She was highly applauded at the Chicago Opera in 1958 and she sang Kundry in *Parsifal* at the Bayreuth Festivals (1961-63). She is also a very successful concert contralto.

Records: Telefunken. *U.S. reissue:* Philips.

DALLA RIZZA, GILDA, soprano, b. Oct. 2, 1892, Verona, Italy. She made her stage debut at eighteen in *Werther* in Bologna. After her first successes on Italian stages, she appeared as guest at the Teatro Colón in 1915. She was very much admired there and sang during eight seasons before 1930 at that house. She sang in 1917 in the world *première* of *La Rondine* at Monte Carlo; in 1918 she sang Lauretta in the Italian *première* of *Gianni Schicchi* at the Teatro Costanzi. She also appeared there in the world *premières* of *Il Piccolo Marat* in 1921 and *Giulietta e Romeo* in 1922. In the 1920's she was one of the chief prima donnas at La Scala, being particularly admired there for her Violetta in *La Traviata*. Guest appearances took her to France and England and (1930-31) to the Italian Opera in Holland. Her career lasted a long time; in 1933 she sang at La Scala in the first performance there of *La Vida Breve* and in 1936 she sang in Genoa in the first Italian performance of *Arabella*. She lives and teaches in Venice and was married to the singer Agostino Capuzzo (d. 1963). Her voice was admired equally for its volume of tone and for her expressively dramatic way of handling it.

Records: Acoustic for Columbia*, electric for Odeon and Fonotipia. *U.S. re-recording:* Eterna.

DAL MONTE, TOTI, soprano, b. June 22, 1898, Venice. Originally Antonietta Meneghelli. She at first wanted to become a pianist, but had to give this up after an injury to her hand. She then studied singing with Barbara Marchisio and made her stage debut (1916) at La Scala. She sang Biancofiore in the first performance there of Zandonai's *Francesca da Rimini*. In the years following she appeared at various Italian opera houses and also gave concerts. In 1922 she was engaged for La Scala by Toscanini and had a sensational success there as Gilda in *Rigoletto*. From that time on she went from triumph to triumph all over the world. She sang at the Metropolitan Opera (1924-25), first appearing as Lucia di Lammermoor, and at the Chicago Opera (1925-28). She made guest appearances in Paris, London, Buenos Aires, Rio de Janeiro, Madrid, Barcelona, Vienna, and Berlin. During a tour of Australia in 1929 she married the tenor Enzo di Muro Lomanto, but she was separated from him in 1932. After World War II this famous soprano rarely appeared on stage, but she did sing in 1949 at the Arena Festival. She gave occasional concerts and became a much-sought-after teacher. The floating lightness of her tone production and the exactitude and brilliance of her intonation in the most difficult coloratura passages made Toti dal Monte one of the most noted coloraturas of the century.

Records: Victor* and HMV (including *Madama Butterfly*, 1929). *U.S. re-recording:* Angel, Cantophone.

DALMORÈS, CHARLES, tenor, b. Dec. 21, 1871, Nancy, France; d. Dec. 6, 1939, Los Angeles. He completed studies as a horn player at the Conservatories in Nancy and Paris. For two years he played this instrument in the Cologne Orchestra, and for another two years in the Lamoureux Orchestra in Paris. He studied singing with Dauphin

Danco · Darclée

there and made his debut in Rouen in 1899. In 1900 he came to the Brussels Opera and sang there with great success until 1906. After 1904 he appeared annually at Covent Garden and in 1905 sang there in the world première of *L'Oracolo*. He was admired at the Manhattan Opera (1906-10). During this time he was also studying the Wagner repertory with Franz Emmerich in Stuttgart and he made guest appearances (1907-08) at the opera houses in Cologne, Berlin, Vienna, and Hamburg. In 1908 he sang Lohengrin at the Bayreuth Festival. He belonged to the joint Philadelphia-Chicago company (1910-12) and sang as first tenor at the Chicago Opera (1913-18). After the close of his stage career he taught first in Paris, then in New York, and finally in Los Angeles. He had a powerful tenor voice and was famous both as a Wagner tenor and as an interpreter of the French and Italian repertories.

Records: Victor* and Pathé*. *U.S. re-recording:* TAP, Scala, Belcanto, Rococo.

DANCO, SUZANNE, soprano, b. Jan. 22, 1911, Brussels. She studied at the Brussels Conservatory. After she had won a singing contest in Vienna, she completed her studies with Fernando Carpi in Prague. She gave her first concert in Italy in 1940. In 1941 she made her stage debut in Genoa as Fiordiligi in *Cosi fan tutte*. She then sang in other Italian opera houses, particularly at La Scala and the Rome Opera. She became known as a great Mozart singer through her appearances at the Festivals in Edinburgh, Glyndebourne, and Aix-en-Provence. She made successful guest appearances at the Vienna State Opera, Covent Garden, and on the most important American opera stages. She was highly regarded for her concert tours all over the world. She had a musically distinguished and well-trained soprano voice, excellently managed, not only in opera, but also in the song literature.

Records: Supraphon, Philips, and Decca (including *Pelléas et Mélisande*, *Le Nozze di Figaro*, *Don Giovanni*, and *L'Heure Espagnole*). *U.S. re-issue:* London, Vox, RCA Victor, Epic, Richmond.

DANISE, GIUSEPPE, baritone, b. Jan. 11, 1883, Naples; d. Jan. 4, 1963, New York. He studied singing with Colonnesi and Petillo in Naples and made his debut there (1906) at the Teatro Bellini. After singing for some time in small Italian opera houses, he had his first great success in 1913 at the Teatro Massimo. In the same year he sang in the Verdi Commemorative Festival in Parma. After 1915 he appeared almost annually as a guest at the Teatro Colón. He was highly successful at La Scala (1915-17). He was invited to join the Metropolitan Opera in 1920 and remained a member of that company until 1932. He appeared each year (1922-31) at Ravinia, near Chicago. After 1932 he was again highly successful at La Scala and was especially admired in 1933 as Telramund in *Lohengrin* in Turin under Max von Schillings. After World War II he again returned to the United States. In 1947 he married the Brazilian soprano Bidu Sayao and lived for a time in Brazil, later in New York. He was admired for his warm-timbred voice and for both his dramatic expressiveness and the complete musicality of his diction.

Records: Brunswick* and HMV (including *Rigoletto*, 1925).

DARCLÉE, HARICLEA, soprano, b. 1860, Bucharest; d. Jan. 12, 1939, Bucharest. Originally Hariclea Hartulari. She studied in several places, including Paris, and made her debut at the Opéra there (1888) as Marguerite in *Faust*. In 1891 she sang for the first time at La Scala, where she appeared in *Le Cid*, *Cavalleria Rusticana*, and in the world *première* of *Condor*. In 1892 she created the title role at La Scala in the world *première* of *La Wally*; in 1898 she also created the title role in *Iris*. She then had great successes on all the most important Italian stages, including Milan and Rome, in other roles. On Jan. 14, 1900, at the Teatro Costanzi she sang the title role in the world *première* of *Tosca*, and created the part again in the first performance of the work at La Scala. She was a guest almost every year at the Imperial Opera Houses in St. Petersburg and Moscow. She was also greatly beloved in Spain and in 1896 had great success at the Teatro Real in *I Lombardi*. In 1897 and in 1903 she sang at the Teatro Colón; in the latter year she sang Eva in the first performance there of *Die Meistersinger*. Highly successful extensive tours of South America were followed by another appearance at the Teatro Colón in 1909. In 1911 she sang the Marschallin in the Italian *première* of *Der Rosenkavalier* at the Teatro Costanzi. She was one of the few singers who, true to the nineteenth-century tradition, mastered the entire range of soprano parts from coloratura to Wagner roles.

Records: She made six extremely rare titles for Fonotipia (Milan, 1904) including two arias each from *Tosca* and *Iris*.

DAVID, LÉON, tenor, b. Dec. 18, 1867, Les Sables d'Olonne, France; d. Oct. 27, 1962, Les Sables d'Olonne. He studied at the Paris Conservatory and made his debut (1892) at the Opéra-Comique in *Les Troyens*. In the following years he sang a great deal at Monte Carlo as well as in the French provinces, but in 1897 he returned to the Opéra-Comique and remained for many years one of the most prominent singers at that house. He made frequent guest appearances in Brussels, Nice, Marseilles, and Geneva. After the end of his career he lived and taught singing in Paris. The last years of his life were spent on his estate on the Atlantic coast. He had a clear lyric tenor voice with exquisite tonal production and fine gradations of shading.

Records: Fonotipia (Paris, 1905) and Odeon (Brussels, 1908-09), all very rare.

DAVIDOV, ALEXANDER, tenor, b. Sept. 4, 1872, in the Russian district of Poltava; d. June 28, 1944, Moscow. Originally Alexander Levinson. He made his stage debut (1893), at the Tiflis Opera. He came in 1896 from the Odessa Opera to Marmontov's private opera in Moscow, where he created the title role in *Sadko* on Dec. 12, 1897. In 1900 he was engaged by the Imperial Opera in St. Petersburg. He appeared with great success in guest performances in Paris and remained a member of the St. Petersburg Opera until 1917, but on account of increasing deafness he was rarely able to perform after 1912. He was later made a Meritorious Artist of the USSR. He had a beautifully trained voice and was particularly admired in the heroic repertory.

Records: His first records for G & T appeared in 1900, including duets with Maria Michailova; his later records were made for Zonophone, Favorite, and HMV (three titles for the latter). *U.S. re-issue:* Victor. *U.S. re-recording:* TAP.

DAVIDOVA, VERA, contralto, b. Sept. 3, 1906, Nishnii Novgorod, Russia. She studied piano and sang in a school chorus in Nicholaievsk on the Amur River in Siberia, where she passed her youth. She then studied with E.V. Gebos-Sobeleva in Leningrad and made her stage debut at the Opera there in 1929, singing Urbain in *Les Huguenots*; she had already appeared there in school productions of the Conservatory. She sang with the Leningrad Opera until 1932 and thereafter was an esteemed member of the Bolshoi Theater. She won the Stalin Prize in 1946 and 1950 and was a deputy in the Supreme Soviet of the USSR. She had a large-dimensioned contralto voice and was esteemed in a wide-ranging concert and opera repertory.

Records: Russian State Record Trust. (She is not to be confused with the contralto Maria Davidova, who recorded for HMV.) *U.S. re-issue:* Colosseum.

DAVIES, BEN, tenor, b. Jan. 6, 1858, Pontardwe, Wales; d. Mar. 28, 1943, Bath. After he had won a singing contest in Swansea, he became a pupil of Alberto Randegger in London. In 1881 he made his debut with the Carl Rosa Opera Company, remaining with them until 1887. He married the prima donna of that troupe, the soprano Clara Perry. In 1887 he turned to musicals and operettas and sang in the first production of *Dorothy*. In 1891 he appeared at Covent Garden in the world *première* of *Ivanhoe*, and in 1893 sang in *Signa* there. He then left the stage and turned entirely to concert singing. In 1893 he undertook his first North Amrican tour. In 1896 he sang in the first performance of Liza Lehmann's song cycle, *In a Persian Garden*, with Emma Albani and David Bispham. In 1898 he was greatly admired at the Cincinnati Festival and during the 1890's he gave a great many concerts in Germany. The career of this singer lasted a long time; he sang in England until 1925, particularly in oratorio, and in 1934 he made his last phonograph records. He had an outstandingly beautiful tenor voice, particularly noted for his rich shading and his good diction.

Records: Acoustics for G & T, Pathé*, and HMV; electric records for Columbia in 1934. *U.S. re-issue:* Victor.

DAVIS, ELLABELLE, soprano, b. Mar. 17, 1907, New Rochelle, N.Y.; d. Nov. 11, 1960, New Rochelle. Her voice was discovered in a church choir and she studied with William Patterson in New York. She made her debut in 1942 and was in demand thereafter as a concert soprano. Later she was the first female Negro singer to have a highly successful stage career. She sang Aïda with great success in Mexico City in 1946 and in the same year she undertook an extensive European tour, during which she demonstrated her mastery of the art of song. She mastered to perfection both German and French art songs as well as Negro spirituals. Her greatest triumph came when she sang Aïda at La Scala in 1949, although she had brought this role to life a number of other times at other important opera houses.

Records: Decca and Philips; unpublished records for Columbia. *U.S. re-issue:* London.

DAVRATH, NETANIA, soprano, b. Israel. She studied singing in Israel and with Jennie Tourel in the United States. She has sung leading roles with the Israel Opera Company and has appeared with the London Philharmonic and the Utah Symphony Orchestras, among others. She made her New York debut in Town Hall in 1962.

Records: Bach Guild, Vanguard, Columbia.

DAVY, GLORIA, soprano, b. Mar. 29, 1931, New Rochelle, N.Y. She completed work at the Juilliard School of Music in New York and

Dawison · Debicka

in 1953 won the Marian Anderson Prize. In 1954 this young Negro soprano created great excitement during a world tour with the American company presenting *Porgy and Bess*. After further study in Milan she appeared at the Metropolitan Opera in *Aïda* in 1956. Then came concert tours and guest appearances in European musical centers, with particular success at the Vienna State Opera and in London, Paris, Zürich, and Brussels. She created the *Nightpieces and Arias* by Hans-Werner Henze at the Music Festival of 1957 in Donaueschingen, and in 1958 gave brilliantly successful concerts in connection with the World Exposition in Brussels. She has also appeared in opera at the Festivals in Salzburg, Edinburgh, and Lucerne. She lives in Zürich and is occupied with extended concert and guest performance activities, including highly successful appearances at the Berlin City Opera. She is admired as much for her musical qualities as for her stylistic rapport with her material.

Records: DGG and London. *U.S. re-issue:* Columbia.

DAWISON, MAX, bass-baritone, b. Feb. 17, 1869, Schwedt a.d. Oder, Germany; d. Apr. 22, 1953, Hamburg. He studied at the Kullak Conservatory in Berlin with Adolf Zebrian and then with Benno Stolzenberg in Cologne, as well as with Mariano Padilla and Desirée Artôt de Padilla in Paris. He made his debut (1889) at the Düsseldorf Opera as the Herald in *Lohengrin*. He sang at the German Theater in Prague (1890-1900) and at the Hamburg Opera (1900-26). He made guest appearances in Copenhagen and Amsterdam and he was admired at the Bayreuth Festivals as Alberich in the *Ring* cycle (1906-09), Telramund (1908), and Klingsor (1909). He was esteemed a first-rate Wagner interpreter, but was an equally great oratorio singer. After 1926 he taught singing in Hamburg.

Records: A few titles for G & T (Bayreuth, 1904; Hamburg, 1904) and Odeon (Frankfurt a. M., 1906).

DAWSON, PETER, bass-baritone, b. 1882, Adelaide, Australia; d. Sept. 26, 1961, Sydney. In his youth he was a professional boxer, but in 1902 he came to England to study singing and became a pupil of Sir Charles Santley. His first records had appeared by 1904. He appeared only rarely on the stage; for example, in 1907 and 1909 he sang small parts in *Die Meistersinger* at Covent Garden. The real domain of this artist was concert singing and recordings. Altogether he made over three thousand records, mostly songs, but also arias from oratorios and operas. His career lasted an uncommonly long time. In 1955 he sang on the British radio and his last records were made after his seventieth birthday.

Records: A great many titles for G & T, Zonophone, HMV, and Edison cylinders; he also made electric records. *U.S. re-issue:* Victor.

DEBICKA, HEDWIG VON, soprano, b. 1890, Warsaw. She studied at the Warsaw Conservatory, then with the conductor and teacher Pietro Stermich de Valcrociata, whom she married in 1916. She made her debut (1910) at the German Opera in Prague. From there she moved in 1914 to the Vienna Imperial Opera, but in 1915 she shifted to the Vienna Volksoper, where she remained until 1924. She was a member of the Berlin State Opera (1924-29) and continued to appear there as a guest until 1936. She sang as guest at the Vienna State Opera (1920-23) and later sang in Amsterdam, Budapest, Basel, Paris, Barcelona, Copenhagen, Stockholm, Lvov, Posnan, and

Warsaw. After World War II she lived and taught in Rome. In 1950 she became a professor at the Academy of Music in Vienna. This artist was famous both as a coloratura and as a lyric soprano.

Records: Polydor. *U.S. re-issue:* Brunswick. *U.S. re-recording:* Eterna, Rococo.

DE LA TOUR, GEORGES IMBART (*see* Imbart de la Tour, Georges)

DEL CAMPO, SOFIA, soprano, b. 1884, Chile; d. June 24, 1964, Santiago de Chile. She first studied singing in Chile, then in Italy. This singer only very rarely—and then only in South America—appeared on the stage. In other respects she limited her career to concert activity, partly in South America, partly in Europe, where she appeared more as a society woman than as a professional singer. She was the mother of the popular singer and film star Rosita Serrano. She had a virtuosic, well-trained voice.

Records: Victor* *U.S. re-recording:* Belcanto.

DELLA CASA, LISA, soprano, b. Feb. 2, 1919, Burgdorf, Switzerland. She studied singing with Margarethe Haeser in Zürich and made her debut there as Mimi in *La Bohème*. She became internationally known, however, when she sang Zdenka in *Arabella* at the Salzburg Festival in 1947. In the same year she joined the Vienna State Opera, where she had great success. In 1949 she appeared to brilliant applause in Salzburg as the Countess in *Capriccio*. In 1953 again in Salzburg, where she appeared almost every year, she created the three women's roles in the world *première* of *Der Prozess*. In 1952 she sang Eva in *Die Meistersinger* at the Bayreuth Festival. After 1953 she was frequently heard at Covent Garden and she was admired at La Scala as much as in Paris, Chicago, Buenos Aires, and Rome. Since 1953 she has been a member of the Metropolitan Opera. She sang the Marschallin in *Der Rosenkavalier* in 1960 at the opening performance in the new Salzburg Festival Theater. Guest appearances and concerts have taken her to all the music centers of the world. She lives in her castle, Gottlieben, in Switzerland on the shores of Lake Constance. She has a soprano voice which joins bright timbre, perfection of the art of phrasing, and a deeply artistic ability to shape a role; she is particularly famous as an interpreter of Mozart and Richard Strauss.

Records: Many records for Decca (including *Le Nozze di Figaro, Don Giovanni, Cosi fan tutte,* and *Arabella*), HMV, and RCA Victor*. *U.S. re-issue:* Columbia, London, Haydn, Electrola, DGG, Turnabout.

DELLER, ALFRED, countertenor, b. May 30, 1912, Margate, England. He first sang in a church choir in his native village, then in the choir of Canterbury Cathedral (1940-47). Since 1947 he has been soloist and choir director of St. Paul's Cathedral in London. He has become well known through the creation of a vocal ensemble, the Deller Consort, with which he undertook the presentation of old English music. He trained himself to become a countertenor, that is, a singer who uses his tenor voice in the alto range. Through artistic tours which he has undertaken, either with the Deller Consort or alone, he has brought new life to this aspect of vocal performance, which was thought to have fallen completely into oblivion.

Records: Primarily Vanguard* and HMV, but also L'Oiseau Lyre* (*Sosarme*) and Decca. *U.S. re-issue:* Bach Guild, Angel, London.

DELMAS, JEAN-FRANÇOIS, bass-baritone, b. Apr. 14, 1861, Lyons; d. Sept. 29, 1933, St. Alban de Monthel, France. He studied at the National Conservatory in Paris with Bussine and made his stage debut in 1886 at the Opéra, to which he belonged until 1927. There he sang in a notable number of first performances: Wotan in the first presentation of *Die Walküre* at the Opéra (1892); Hagen in the Paris *première* of *Götterdämmerung* (1908); in the first French performance of the complete *Ring* cycle (1911); and in the *première* of *Parsifal* (1914). He was esteemed an outstanding Wagner singer, but was also admired in the French and Italian repertory. At the Opéra on Mar. 16, 1894, he sang Athanaël in the world *première* of *Thaïs* and in 1909 he sang Marco in the world *première* of *Monna Vanna*. Except for a few guest performances, this famous singer spent his entire artistic career at the Paris Opéra. A voluminous bass voice, whose wide range permitted him to undertake heroic baritone parts also.

Records: The oldest for Zonophone (Paris, 1902) and G & T (Paris, 1902-03), but also for Fonotipia, Odeon De Luxe, and Pathé*. *U.S. re-issue:* Victor. *U.S. re-recording:* HRS, Eterna, TAP, Rococo.

DELMAS, SOLANGE, soprano, b. 1907(?). She studied at the National Conservatory in Paris and made her debut at the Opéra (1930), where she had a starring career for over twenty years. In 1938 she first sang at the Opéra-Comique, appearing as Micaëla in *Carmen*. In 1947 she was greatly admired at the Opéra in *Lucia de Lammermoor* with Giacomo Lauri-Volpi, and in 1948 she made a guest appearance at Covent Garden as Gilda in *Rigoletto*. In 1950 she gave up her career and became president of the Nice Conservatory. A brilliant coloratura voice.

Records: Odeon.

DEL MONACO, MARIO, tenor, b. May 27, 1915, Florence. He passed his youth in Pesaro and entered the Conservatory there, where he devoted himself to painting and sculpture. At the age of twenty he won a prize in a singing contest arranged by the conductor Tullio Serafin in Rome. At the beginning of World War II he joined the army, but obtained a leave for his debut (1941) at the Teatro Puccini. During the war he was able to appear only rarely, but his career developed all the more rapidly after the war's end. In 1946 he created a sensation as Radames in *Aida* at the Arena Festival and in the same year he sang the title role in *Andrea Chénier* at Trieste. A highly successful tour with the ensemble of the Teatro San Carlo made him internationally known in 1948. He then sang at La Scala, and in London, Paris, and Vienna. In the summer of 1950 he was applauded at the Teatro Colón and in November of that year at the San Francisco Opera. Since 1951 he has been a member of the Metropolitan Opera. Guest appearances and concert tours have brought him great success all over the world. In 1960 he toured the Soviet Union and in 1961-62 Germany. He is one of the greatest heroic tenors Italy has produced in the twentieth century, with a voice filled with elemental power of expression and glowing brightness in the high register. He is particularly famous as a Verdi and Puccini interpreter.

Records: HMV and Decca (*Aida*, *Il Trovatore*, *Rigoletto*, *Otello*, *La Bohème*, *Manon Lescaut*, *La Gioconda*, *Turandot*, *Andre Chénier*, *I Pagliacci*, *La Forza del Destino*, *Cavalleria Rusticana*, and *Adriana Lecouvreur*). *U.S. re-issue:* London, Richmond.

DELNA, MARIE, contralto, b. 1875, Meudon, France; d. June 24, 1932, Paris. Originally Marie Ledan. Her voice was discovered when she was fifteen, while she was singing in the kitchen of an inn which belonged to her father. She studied singing with Rosine Laborde in Paris and she made her debut at seventeen at the Paris Opéra as Dido in *Les Troyens* in 1892. In 1893 she sang Charlotte in the first Paris performance of *Werther* and in the same year at the Opéra-Comique she sang Dame Quickly in the first performance in Paris of *Falstaff* in the presence of the composer. She also sang there in the world *première* of the opera *L'Attaque du Moulin* in 1893. In 1894 she married and planned to give up her career, but in 1895 she sang again at the Opéra-Comique in the world *première* of *La Vivandière*. Guest appearances followed in Bordeaux, Marseilles, Brussels, and Monte Carlo. In 1907 she was greatly admired for her singing of the title role in *Orphée et Eurydice* at La Scala under the direction of Toscanini. She was notably successful at Covent Garden, but not at the Metropolitan Opera, where she came for a season in 1910. In 1912, at the Opéra-Comique, she sang in the world *première* of *La Lépreuse*. She appeared during the Verdi Commemorative Festival at the Teatro Regio in Parma in 1913. Toward the end of her career she appeared principally at the Brussels Opera and on French provincial stages. In 1930 she sang on the French radio. She died in a poorhouse, after she had lost all her possessions. She had a wonderfully trained and darkly glowing contralto voice, of which the wide tonal range was as famous as the expressiveness of her art.

Records: Rare records for Pathé*, Edison* discs and cylinders (1910). *U.S. re-recording:* IRCC, FRP, TAP, Odyssey.

DEMOUGEOT, MARCELLE, soprano, b. 1876, Dijon, France; d. 1931, Paris. Originally Jeanne Marguerite Marcelle Decorne. She studied in Dijon with Charles Laurent and at the Paris Conservatory with Hettich. She made her debut at the Paris Opéra (1902) as Donna Elvira in *Don Giovanni*. In 1904 she sang there in the world *première* of *Les Fils de l'Etoile*, in 1911 at Monte Carlo she created the title role in *Déjanire*, and in 1911 she sang Fricka in the first performance at the Opéra of *Das Rheingold*. In 1914 she was applauded there as Kundry in the first *Parsifal*. She was considered the most famous French Wagner soprano of her generation and was highly successful in guest appearances in Monte Carlo, Nice, and Bordeaux. In 1930 she sang Brünnhilde in Strasbourg in a production of the *Ring* cycle.

Records: A great many records for G & T (Paris, 1904-06), Zonophone (Paris, 1905), Favorite (Paris, 1906), Odeon, and HMV.

DEMUTH, LEOPOLD, baritone, b. Nov. 2, 1861, Brünn, Austria; d. Mar. 4, 1910, Czernowitz, Rumania, from a heart attack suffered during a concert. Originally Leopold Pokorny. His voice having been discovered during his compulsory military service, he studied with Joseph Gänsbacher in Vienna and made his debut in 1889 at Halle as the title hero in *Hans Heiling*. He sang at the Opera in Leipzig (1891-95), at the Hamburg Opera (1895-97), and was engaged at the Vienna Imperial Opera (1897); where his career reached its climax. In 1908 he sang there in the world *première* of *Ein Wintermärchen*. He made guest appearances at German and Austrian opera houses as well as at Covent Garden. In 1899 he sang Hans Sachs in *Die Meistersinger* and Gunther in *Götterdämmerung* at the Bayreuth Festival. One of the most beautiful baritone voices of his time; he was outstanding in both the Wagner and Mozart repertory for his controlled

diction and for his feeling for style.
Records: There are a great many fine records of his voice, the oldest having appeared on G & T in 1902, and later ones for HMV. *U.S. re-issue:* Victor, Opera Disc. *U.S. re-recording:* TAP, FRP, HRS.

DENERA, ERNA, soprano, b. Sept. 4, 1881, Pila Castle, near Posen, Germany; d. Mar. 3, 1938, Berlin. She originally studied piano and music theory with Spangenberg in Wiesbaden, with Kufferath in Bonn, and then becaue a pupil of Max Reger. In 1904 she decided to study singing, which she did with Franz Dulong in Berlin and Heinrich Feinhaus in Milan. She made her debut (1906) at Kassel as Senta in *Der Fliegende Holländer.* She was engaged at Wiesbaden (1907-08). In 1908 she was called to the Berlin Imperial Opera, where she was very successful. She made guest appearances in Madrid, Barcelona, Budapest, Bucharest, Brussels, and Antwerp. Engaged for the 1916-17 season at the Metropolitan Opera, she was prevented from fulfilling the contract by the entrance of the United States into World War I. In 1921-22 she made guest appearances at various Italian opera houses. She remained active at the Berlin Opera until 1921. She then lived and taught in Berlin. She had an outstanding and well-trained expressive voice and was highly successful in a wide-ranging repertory.
Records: HMV, Pathe*, and Parlophone. *U.S. re-issue:* Opera Disc.

DENS, MICHEL, baritone, b. June 22, 1914, Roubaix, France. Originally Maurice Marcel. His father, a journalist, supported his studies at the Roubaix Conservatory. He made his debut (1938) at Lille and sang later in Bordeaux, Grenoble, Toulouse, and Marseilles. After World War II he had a successful period (1946-48) at the Paris Opéra and the Opéra-Comique, and he appeared later at both houses as a guest. Since then he has made guest appearances at the other large opera houses in France, and in Belgium, North Africa, Canada, and Switzerland. He has been named Chevalier of the Legion of Honor. He has a beautifully trained and expressive baritone voice.
Records: Michel Dens was the first singer to make a record of operatic music which sold over a million copies. His records appeared on the labels of Columbia (*Carmen, Les Pêcheurs des Perles, Mireille*), HMV (*Manon* with Victoria de Los Angeles) and Pathé (*Il Barbiere di Siviglia*). *U.S. re-issue:* Angel, Capitol, Pathé-Marconi.

DERMOTA, ANTON, tenor, b. June 4, 1910, Kropa, Slovenia, Austria. He first studied composition and organ at the Conservatory of Ljubljana, then studied singing with Elisabeth Rado in Vienna. In 1936 he made his debut as Don Ottavio in *Don Giovanni* at the Vienna State Opera, of which he has been a member throughout his entire career. He had his first great success in 1937 as Lenski in *Eugen Onégin.* In 1938 he was admired as Don Ottavio at the Salzburg Festival, to which he has returned almost annually. After World War II he became internationally known through his guest appearances at Covent Garden, La Scala, and in Rome, Naples, Paris, and at the Metropolitan Opera. He was especially admired as a Mozart singer, but also as a fine interpreter of lieder. He made a great number of concert tours, including one through Australia in 1954. In his song recitals he was usually accompanied by his wife, the pianist Hilde Berger-Weyerwald. An expressive tenor voice, completely stamped by Viennese musical culture.
Records: A great many records

for Telefunken*, for Decca (*Don Giovanni, Arabella, Die Meistersinger, Così fan tutte, Die Zauberflöte*, and others), and Vanguard (*The Creation*). U.S. re-issue: Bach Guild, Westminster, London, Richmond, Vox, DGG, Angel, Nonesuch.

DERSHINSKAYA, XENIA, soprano, b. Jan. 25, 1889, Kiev; d. June 9, 1961, Moscow. She studied first with Flora Paskovskaya in Kiev; then, helped by Rachmaninoff, with E.I. Teryan-Karganova in St. Petersburg. She made her debut (1913) at the Serievskii Theater in Moscow in *Mazeppa*. She was engaged at the Bolshoi Theater in 1915 and she remained there, one of Russia's most honored singers, until 1948. In 1926 she made a guest appearance in Paris in *The Tale of the Invisible City of Kitezh*. She was invested with the Order of Lenin and won the Stalin Prize. After 1947 she was a professor at the Conservatory in Moscow. She had a strong dramatic soprano voice in which the clarity of intonation was particularly admired.

Records: Russian State Record Trust. U.S. re-issue: Colosseum.

DESCHAMPS-JEHIN, BLANCHE, contralto, b. Aug. 18, 1857, Lyons; d. June, 1923, Paris. She studied at the Conservatories of Lyons and Paris and made her debut at the Brussels Opera (1879) as the title heroine in *Mignon*. In 1881 she sang there in the world première of *Hérodiade*. She then came to the Opéra-Comique, where she appeared in more first performances: *Une Nuit de Cléopâtre* (1885), *Le Médecin Malgré Lui* (1886), and *Le Roi d'Ys* (May 7, 1888). In 1892 she sang Dalila at the Paris Opéra in the first French production of *Samson et Dalila*. In 1900 she created the role of the Mother in *Louise* at the Opéra-Comique. In 1889 she was married to the conductor Léon Jehin (1853-1928) who was very active at the Monte Carlo Opera, and she frequently appeared there as guest. In October, 1902, she sang her last stage role in a performance at the Opéra-Comique, but she later appeared in the concert hall. She had a very expressive voice of great tonal range.

Records: Rare records for Odeon (Paris, 1908-09) and a few Pathé cylinders. U.S. re-recording: IRCC.

DESSOIR, SUSANNE, soprano, b. July 23, 1869, Grünberg, Germany; d. June 24, 1953, Königstein, Germany. Originally Susanne Triepel. She studied with Amalie Joachim, Blanche Corelli, and Etelka Gerster in Berlin. She became a very famous concert soprano, particularly admired as an interpreter of lieder. In 1899 she married the philosopher-aesthetician-psychologist Max Dessoir (1867-1947), who published important essays on musical aesthetics in his periodical "Zeitschrift für Aesthetik und allgemeine Kuntswissenschaft." She had a starring career until 1912 as a concert singer in Germany, Austria, and Holland; she later became a teacher in Berlin. She published, with B. Hinze-Reinhold, the so-called *Dessoir Album*, a collection of folk songs and children's songs, which also included lieder from the time of Schubert (Berlin, 1912).

Records: Interesting lieder records on Odeon (Berlin, 1906) and HMV.

DESTINN, EMMY, soprano, b. Feb. 26, 1878, Prague; d. Jan. 28, 1930, České Budějovice, Czechoslovakia. Originally Emmy Kittl. She wished first to become a violinist and gave concerts when she was only eight years old. At fourteen she began her study of singing with Frau Marie Loewe-Destinn in Prague. Out of gratitude to her teacher, she took the professional name Emmy Destinn. She made her debut at the

Kroll Opera as Santuzza in *Cavalleria Rusticana* in 1898. The success of her debut performance was so great that she was awarded a five-year contract by the Berlin Imperial Opera. There, in 1904, she sang in the world *première* of *Der Roland von Berlin*. In 1901 she was admired at the Bayreuth Festival as Senta in *Der Fliegende Holländer*. After highly successful guest appearances in Vienna, London, Prague, and Paris, she was engaged by the Metropolitan Opera in 1908; there she sang Minnie in the world *première* of *La Fanciulla del West* on Dec. 10, 1910. During World War I she left the United States (1916) and returned to her homeland. As an enthusiastic patriot she worked so hard for the independence of Czechoslovakia that she was temporarily jailed by the Austrian authorities. In 1919 she returned to the Metropolitan Opera for two seasons. In 1926 she gave up her stage career. She lived thereafter at her palace in Stráz in Bohemia and only rarely gave concerts. A soprano voice of mellow beauty, an extraordinary range, and great expressiveness; she mastered a repertory of over eighty major roles.

Records: A great many records for Columbia*, Odeon, HMV, and Edison*. For G & T she sang, among other releases, in *Faust* and *Carmen* (Berlin, 1908). *U.S. reissue:* Victor, Opera Disc, Okeh, HRS, IRCC. *U.S. re-recording:* RCA Victor, Columbia, ASCO, Belcanto, Design, Scala, TAP, Cantilena, Rococo.

DEVRIÈS, DAVID, tenor, b. 1881, Bagnères-de-Luchon, France; d. 1936, Paris. He was the uncle of the famous Dutch soprano Rosa Devriès-van Os and the nephew of the opera singers Hermann and Maurice Devriès; he made his debut (1903) at the Opéra-Comique, where he had a long and highly successful career. He sang there opposite Mary Garden in the world *première* of *Aphrodite* (1906) and also in the first performance of *Circe* (1907). He appeared at the Manhattan Opera in New York (1910-11), but almost his entire career was spent in France. He was a noted concert singer. One of the most beautiful lyric tenor voices of his generation; particularly outstanding in the French repertory.

Records: Pathé* and Victor* (1910), but mostly for Odeon.

DICKIE, MURRAY, tenor, b. Apr. 3, 1924, Glasgow. He studied in London, where his teachers included Dino Borgioli and Guido Farinelli. He made his debut (1947) at the Cambridge Theater, London, where he sang until 1949. He appeared at Covent Garden (1949-51) and was then engaged by the Vienna State Opera, of which he is still a member. There he has established himself as a *buffo*-tenor. He sang in 1956 in the world *première* of *Der Sturm*. He has appeared at the Glyndebourne Festivals since 1951, at Salzburg since 1955, especially as Pedrillo in *Die Entführung aus dem Serail*. He has sung at the Metropolitan since 1962-63, making his debut in that season as Don Ottavio in *Don Giovanni*. He has made guest appearances at La Scala, the Teatro Liceo, in Paris and Munich. He is an esteemed oratorio singer and performer of lieder. He is married to the soprano Maureen Springer-Dickie.

Records: Philips, Vox*, HMV, Decca (*Arlecchino, Die Frau ohne Schatten,* and *Salome*), and DGG (*Fidelio*). *U.S. re-issue:* Westminster, Angel, Epic, Electrola, Turnabout, Columbia, Richmond.

DIDUR, ADAMO, bass, b. Dec. 24, 1874, Wola Sekowa, Poland; d. Jan. 7, 1946, Katowice, Poland. He studied at the Conservatory in Lemberg and in Milan; he made his debut (1894) at the Rio de Janeiro Opera. The young singer was greatly helped in his career by the celebrated baritone Mattia Battistini. In 1896 he came to La Scala, where he had great successes in the following years. He sang at the Warsaw Opera (1899-1903) and later made frequent guest appearances there. His guest appearances at other great European houses led him to be engaged (1907) at the Manhattan Opera. In 1908 he was engaged at the Metropolitan Opera, of which he remained a member until 1933. In 1910 he sang in the world *premières* there of both *La Fanciulla del West* and *Königskinder* and in 1913 sang the title role in *Boris Godounov* under Toscanini at its first North American production. In 1930 he returned to Poland, where he was chiefly occupied as a teacher, but at the same time he was the director of the Municipal Theater of Cracow. In 1939 he was made professor at the Conservatory of Lvov, but was unable to accept the honor on account of the outbreak of the war. In 1945 he was appointed professor at the Katowice Conservatory, but died a short time later. The tonal volume of his voice was as much the object of admiration as his dramatic expressiveness. He was particularly famous as Mephistopheles in *Faust* and as Boris.

Records: G & T (Milan, 1903-04), Fonotipia, Pathé*, and electric Brunswick*. *U.S. re-issue:* Columbia. *U.S. re-recording:* Pathé-Perfect, IRCC, TAP, FRP, Eterna, ASCO.

DIEMAN, URSULA VAN, soprano, b. 1897, Schwerin, Germany. She studied with Selma Nicklas-Kempner, Lola Beeth, and Louis Bachner in Berlin and made her debut (1918) in a song recital in Schwerin. Until 1933 she had a celebrated career as a concert and oratorio singer. In Frankfurt she was applauded in recitals with the celebrated pianist Edwin Fischer as her accompanist. She appeared only incidentally on the stage; for example, in 1929 in a Berlin production by Max Reinhardt of *La Belle Hélène*. After 1945 she gave a few concerts and since 1946 has lived and taught singing in Stuttgart. A well-trained and expressive soprano voice.

Records: A few records for Electrola. *U.S. re-issue:* American Decca, RCA Victor.

DIETRICH, MARIE, soprano, b. Jan. 27, 1867, Weinsberg, Germany; d. Dec. 14, 1940, Berlin. She was trained by Frau Bader at the Stuttgart Conservatory and also studied with Ferdinand Jäger in Stuttgart and with Pauline Viardot-Garcia in Paris. At first she sang only in concert, but was engaged by the Stuttgart Royal Opera and made her debut there in 1888. She remained there until 1891 and during this time sang at the Bayreuth Festivals. She made guest appearances at the Vienna Imperial Opera in 1891. In the same year she was invited to the Berlin Imperial Opera, to which she belonged until 1915. She married the Berlin Imperial Opera tenor Robert Philipp. After her retirement from the stage she was a concert soprano and teacher in Berlin. A technically admirable and well-trained coloratura voice.

Records: G & T, Odeon, Anker, Edison* cylinder, and Zonophone*.

DIPPEL, ANDREAS, tenor, b. Nov. 30, 1866, Kassel, Germany; d. May 12, 1935, Hollywood. He first studied with Nina Zottmayr in Kassel, then with Julius Hey in Berlin, Alberto Leoni in Milan, and Johannes Ress in Vienna. He made his debut (1887) at Bremen as Lionel in *Martha*. He remained at Bremen until

1892 and sang at the Bayreuth Festival in 1889. He was engaged at Breslau (1892-93) and in 1893 was called to the Vienna Imperial Opera. In 1897 he had great success at Covent Garden in a presentation of the *Ring* cycle, and he returned there until 1900. In 1898 he was engaged at the Metropolitan Opera, where he was equally successful; he participated in the management of the Metropolitan Opera (1908-10). He then became the director of the Philadelphia-Chicago Opera Company (1910-13). Later he organized his own opera company, with which he made tours throughout North America. At the end of his life he was a teacher in Hollywood. A large tenor voice of great expressiveness; he reached his peak in the Wagner repertory.

Records: Mapleson cylinders, Edison* cylinders, and unpublished Victor records. *U.S. re-recording:* IRCC.

DIRKENS, ANNIE, soprano, b. Sept. 25, 1869, Berlin; d. Nov. 11, 1942, Vienna. She studied at the Stern Conservatory in Berlin, then with Nina Falkenberg in Dresden, making her debut (1890) at the Viktoria Theater, Berlin. She later sang there at the Adolf-Ernst Theater and was engaged at the Leipzig Municipal Theater as a soubrette (1893-96). In the latter year she went to Vienna, where she made her debut at the Theater an der Wien in her starring role, Adele in *Der Fledermaus*. Thereafter she became the principal operetta diva of the Austrian metropolis. In Vienna, after 1899, she sang at the Theater in der Josephsstadt. Also very successful in guest appearances, she was greatly admired when she sang with the Coburg theater ensemble in London in 1894. During World War I the singer worked as a volunteer nurse in an Austrian military hospital on the eastern front and was wounded there. Later she managed a tobacco shop under the Vienna Burgtheater. As an operetta singer Annie Dirkens was as famous in her generation as Fritzi Massary was in hers. She had a fiery but technically well-trained voice.

Records: Rare records for Berliner (1899) and G & T (Berlin, 1903).

DOBBS, MATTAWILDA, soprano, b. July 11, 1925, Tennessee. Her ancestors were partly of Negro and partly of American Indian stock. She began her studies with Lotte Lehmann in New York, and then became a pupil of Pierre Bernac in Paris. In 1948 she began her career as a concert singer, and particularly as a lieder singer. In 1951 she won first prize in an international singing contest in Geneva and her stage debut followed in 1952. She had great success in guest appearances on the most important opera stages all over the world. She sang at La Scala, at the Metropolitan Opera, in Paris and London, and at the Edinburgh, Glyndebourne, and Holland Festivals. Concert tours have taken her through Belgium, Holland, Sweden, Denmark, North America, and Australia. A coloratura voice of brilliant technique and impressively musical diction.

Records: On Nixa (*Les Pêcheurs des Perles*), DGG, Columbia, and MMS (including *Don Giovanni* and *Les Contes d'Hoffmann*). *U.S. re-issue:* Perfect Harmony, Epic, Angel, Polymusic, Everest-Cetra.

DOLCI, ALESSANDRO, tenor, b. 1888, Bergamo, Italy; d. Sept. 17, 1954, Bergamo. He studied singing with V. Baccanelli in Bergamo and with D. Lari in Milan and made his debut about 1910. In 1916 he appeared at La Scala as Rhadames in *Aïda*. He sang again at La Scala in 1918 as Elisero in *Mose in Egitto*. He was engaged at the Chicago

Opera (1918-19) and often made guest appearances there later. He appeared at the Lexington Theater in New York (1919-20), and sang in *Norma, La Traviata,* and *Loreley.* He made successful appearances at La Scala as Herod in *Salome* and in *Debora e Jaele* under Toscanini (1923-25). At the Teatro Regio in Turin in 1925 he sang Bacchus in the first Italian performance of *Ariadne auf Naxos.* In the following years he appeared on all the leading Italian stages and in the 1932-33 season he was again admired at La Scala as Aegisthus in *Elektra.* Later he became a teacher in Bergamo. His classical diction was admired as much as the brilliance of his heroic tenor voice.

Records: After the world *première* of *Parisina,* there appeared twelve Fonotipia records (1913) from this opera in which Dolci took the leading role. These discs, among the rarest discs in the world, are his only records.

DOLUKHANOVA, ZARA, contralto, b. 1918, Moscow. She entered the Gnesin Music School in Moscow when she was only sixteen and remained there until 1938. In that year she made her debut at the opera house in Erivan, Armenia. After guest appearances in various Russian cities, she was engaged by the Bolshoi Theater in 1944 and has been one of the most prominent singers there. In 1949 she won first prize at a singing contest sponsored by the World Youth Congress in Budapest. In 1950 she was greatly admired for her singing of the vocal music of Bach at the Commemoration of the 200th Anniversary of his Death in Leipzig. Concert tours have taken her throughout Europe, to the two Americas, and to Cuba. In 1966 she won the Lenin Prize. The many-sided expressiveness of Dolukhanova, the most important Russian singer of her time, reaches from the coloratura-contralto parts of the *bel canto* masters and the classic operatic repertory to art songs.

Records: Russian State Record Trust. *U.S. re-issue:* Monitor, Artia.

DOMGRAF-FASSBAENDER, WILLI, baritone, b. Feb. 19, 1897, Aachen, Germany. He first studied piano and musicology with Felix Knubben in Aachen, then singing with Jacques Stückgold and Paul Bruns in Berlin and with Giuseppe Borgatti in Milan. He made his stage debut (1922) at Aachen. He then sang at the German Opera in Berlin (1923-25), was first lyric baritone at the Düsseldorf Opera (1925-27) and appeared at the Stuttgart State Opera (1927-30). He was called to the Berlin State Opera in 1930 and appeared there with great success until 1946. Guest appearances took him to Austria, Italy, France, and England particularly. From 1934-39, he was especially admired for his singing of Mozart at the Glyndebourne Festival; he also appeared in the Salzburg Festivals during that time. After 1946 he was chief producer at the Nuremberg Municipal Theater, and he occasionally appeared on the stage there. The fine musicality of his voice handling as well as the clarity of his diction were always greatly admired.

Records: Polydor, HMV, (including *Le Nozze di Figaro* and *Così fan tutte* from Glyndebourne), Artiphon, and Parlophone. *U.S. re-issue:* American Odeon, RCA Victor, Brunswick. *U.S. re-recording:* Electrola, Eterna, Turnabout.

DOMINGUEZ, ORALIA, contralto, b. 1928, San Luis Potosí, Mexico. She studied at the Mexican National Conservatory and, during her first year of study, sang the solo part in *La Demoiselle Élue.* She

made her stage debut (1953) at the Mexico City Opera. In that year she also went to Europe and gave her first concert in London's Wigmore Hall. After concert tours through France, Spain, Germany, and Holland, she appeared as guest at La Scala. Other guest appearances have included the Teatro San Carlo, the Brussels Opera, the Vienna State Opera, and the Paris Opéra. In 1955 she sang at Covent Garden in the world *première* of *A Midsummer Marriage.* She sang at the Glyndebourne Festival in 1957. A technically well-trained and voluptuous voice of exotic timbre.
Records Columbia and DGG*. *U.S. re-issue:* Angel, London.

DONALDA, PAULINE, soprano, b. 1882, Montreal. Her family was of Russian-Polish extraction and she studied with Clara Lichtenstein in Montreal and with Edmond Duvernoy in Paris. She made her debut (1904) at the Nice Opera as the title heroine in *Manon.* In 1905-06 she was very successful at the Brussels Opera. She married the French baritone Paul Seveilhac in 1906. She sang a great deal at Covent Garden, where in 1905 she created the role of Ah-Joe in the world *première* of *L'Oracolo.* She made guest appearances at the Opéra-Comique, the Teatro Colón, and La Scala with great success and undertook concert tours in Germany, Holland, and Russia. She appeared a few times at Covent Garden (1919-20), which ended her stage career. After an extended concert tour in 1921-22, she lived and taught singing in Paris (1932-37), and later in Montreal, where she was also an operatic coach.
Records: Relatively rare records for G & T (London, 1907-08), one record of the Card Scene from *Carmen* for Emerson*. *U.S. re-issue:* Victor, IRCC, Rococo.

DÖNCH, KARL, bass-baritone, b. Aug. 1, 1915, Hagen, Germany. He studied at the Conservatory in Dresden and made his debut at Görlitz in 1936. Engagements followed in Liberec, Bonn, and Salzburg. In 1947 he was engaged at the Vienna State Opera. Since then he has often been engaged at the Salzburg Festivals, where in 1951 he was greatly admired as the Doctor in *Wozzeck.* He also sang the role of Leiokritos there in 1954 in the world *première* of *Penelope.* At the Vienna State Opera he sang in the world *première* of *Der Sturm* in 1956. He is linked by guest contracts both to the Berlin City Opera and to the German-Opera-on-the-Rhine at Düsseldorf-Duisburg. He has sung in guest performances at La Scala and at the Teatro Colón (1952-53). He made his Metropolitan Opera debut as Beckmesser in 1959-60 and sang there again in 1966-67.
Records: Decca (Beckmesser in *Die Meistersinger, Ariadne auf Naxos* and *Der Freischütz*), Columbia (*Die Fledermaus, Wiener Blut,* and *Eine Nacht in Venedig*). *U.S. re-issue:* Angel, London.

DOSIA, ELEN, soprano, b. 1915 (?), Athens. She came as a child to France and was reared in Paris and Neuilly. She first studied dancing with Loie Fuller, but began her vocal studies at sixteen and came to the National Conservatory in Paris at eighteen. She made her debut at the Opéra-Comique (1935) as Tosca. Her most successful roles at that house were Mélisande, Mimi in *La Bohème,* and Manon in Massenet's opera. At the Paris Opéra she was particularly admired as Thaïs and as Marguerite in *Faust.* She married the tenor André Burdino, and they were both engaged by the Chicago Opera (1937-39). She made guest appearances in Brussels, Prague, Zürich, Belgrade, Athens, and Istanbul; in 1939 she sang Mé-

lisande at Scheveningen. During World War II she appeared at both the great Paris opera houses. She was a member of the Metropolitan Opera (1947-49), making her debut there as Tosca; and she was especially admired there as Mélisande. She retired from the stage in 1952. She had a beautiful lyric soprano voice.
Records: Two records for HMV.

DUA, OCTAVE, tenor, b. Feb. 28, 1882, Ghent; d. Mar. 8, 1952, Brussels. Originally Leo Van der Haegen. He made his debut at the Brussels Opera (1904) as Wenzel in *The Bartered Bride.* After originally singing lyric parts, he specialized in *buffo* roles during his ten years at Brussels. He made guest appearances under Sir Thomas Beecham in London (1914-15), he had great success at the Chicago Opera House (1915-19), and was engaged as tenor-*buffo* in the ensemble at the Metropolitan Opera (1919-21). He returned to Chicago (1921-22) and there, on Dec. 30, 1921, he created the part of Truffaldino in the world *première* of *The Love of Three Oranges.* In 1920 he underwent a nasal operation in New York, as a result of which he lost an eye. Therefrom there developed a sensational suit for damages by the singer against the surgeon. He had his greatest successes at Covent Garden, where he appeared every season until 1931. In 1931-32 he made a few appearances again at Chicago and in 1937 he sang at Covent Garden for the coronation season. After 1926 he was also occupied as a stage manager, first at the Brussels Opera, later in Ghent.
Records: A few HMV records, none of them solos.

DUCHÊNE, MARIA, contralto, b. 1880. She made her debut (1904) at the Opéra-Comique, where she sang small parts in the following years. She appeared there in 1906 in the world *première* of *Aphrodite.* She then married the famous bass Léon Rothier and, although later separated from him, she also became a member of the company when he was called to the Metropolitan Opera in 1911. She made her debut there as La Cieca in *La Gioconda.* She remained at the Metropolitan until 1916 and appeared there in the first American production of *Boris Godounov* (1913) and *L'Amore dei Tre Re.* Later she returned to France, but rarely appeared in productions there.
Records: Victor[*], including scenes with Emmy Destinn, Enrico Caruso and Léon Rothier, and two Edison[*] discs. Many years after she had ceased appearing on the stage she sang again in an HMV recording of a scene from *Samson et Dalila* with tenor César Vezzani; her voice still retained its original beauty. *U.S. re-recording:* Rococo.

DUFRANNE, HECTOR, baritone, b. 1870, Belgium; d. May 3, 1951, Paris. He studied in Brussels and made his debut at the Théâtre de la Monnaie there in 1896. In 1899 he came to the Opéra-Comique and was a member of that organization for many years. There he sang in several world *premières:* in 1901 in *Grisélidis;* on Apr. 30, 1902, in *Pelléas et Mélisande,* he created the role of Golaud, thereafter one of his starring parts; in *La Fille de Roland* in 1904; in *Le Chemineau* in 1907; in *Habanera* in 1908. At Monte Carlo he sang in the world *première* of *Thérèse* (1907). He was engaged at the Manhattan Opera (1908-10) and sang with the Philadelphia-Chicago Opera Company (1910-12). From 1913-22 he was an admired member of the Chicago Opera Company, where in 1921 he sang in the world *première* of *The Love of Three Oranges.*

After 1923 he was again applauded in Paris, where he sang in the first performance of *El Retablo de Maese Pedro* at the private theater of the Princess de Polignac. His career lasted a long time; he appeared in 1939 as Golaud in *Pelléas et Mélisande* at Vichy. His very expressive and full baritone voice was used to master a great many of the difficulties of operatic literature.

Records: G & T (Paris, about 1904), Zonophone, HMV, American Columbia*, both acoustic and electric for European Columbia* (*Pelléas et Mélisande* and *L'Heure Espagnole*). U.S. re-issue: Victor.

DUHAN, HANS, baritone, b. Jan. 27, 1890, Vienna. He studied at the Vienna Music Academy and made his debut (1910) at Troppau, where he remained until 1913. He sang at Teplitz-Schönau (1913-14) and was called in 1914 to the Vienna Imperial Opera, where he stayed until the end of his stage career in 1940. In Vienna he was a singer of enormous popularity, and was also greatly in demand at the Salzburg Festivals, where he created a sensation, not only in Mozart roles, but in others as well. He made guest appearances in Amsterdam in 1922. After 1932 he became professor of opera at the Vienna Music Academy; he also worked as *régisseur*, conductor, and writer of vocal music. He had a warm-timbred and flexible voice. In addition to his wide-ranging operatic repertory, he was admired as a concert and lieder singer.

Records: Odeon and HMV discs, the latter including complete performances of the Schubert cycles *Die schöne Müllerin* and *Winterreise*. U.S. re-issue: Victor.

DUNCAN, ROBERT TODD, baritone, b. 1904, Danville, Ky. He came of a Negro family and was carefully educated. He received his B.A. at Butler University and his master's degree at Columbia University. In 1934 he made his stage debut in *Cavalleria Rusticana*. In the following year, when George Gershwin was looking for a singer for the role of Porgy in *Porgy and Bess*, he chose Duncan, who created the part at the first performance of the work in Boston on Sept. 30, 1935. Thereafter he sang this role in theaters all over the world. In 1938 he came to London for a long series of guest appearances, but returned to America upon the outbreak of World War II. There he also appeared as an actor. After the war he undertook starring tours in America, Europe, Australia, and New Zealand. He was especially admired in concert for his singing of Negro spirituals, but also was highly thought of as an interpreter of German lieder from Schubert to Hugo Wolf.

Records: Allegro Royale*, American Decca*.

DURIGO, ILONA, contralto, b. May 13, 1881, Budapest; d. Dec. 25, 1943, Budapest. She began her study of singing with Frau Maleczky in Budapest and in 1902 came to the Conservatory of the City of Vienna, where Philipp Forstén was her teacher. She made her debut in the concert hall there in 1906. In 1908 she studied from time to time with Bellwidt and Etelka Gerster in Berlin. She was soon the most respected concert contralto of her time. She sang in the music centers of Germany, Austria, Belgium, and Switzerland. She was particularly beloved in Holland, where she appeared every season with the Amsterdam Concertgebouw Orchestra. She was especially effective in the contralto solo parts of Mahler's *Das Lied von der Erde* and the *St. Matthew Passion* of Bach. Her only appearance on the operatic stage was on Oct. 5, 1912, when she sang the

Dux · Dworsky

Orphée in *Orphée et Eurydice* at the 150th anniversary of the opera house in Frankfurt a. M. In 1921 she was made professor at the Zürich Conservatory, but she continued her concert work. In 1937 she was made professor at the Budapest Conservatory. She had a sensuous dark-timbred voice and her style was as much admired as her classical singing technique. She was treasured both as an oratorio and as a lieder singer, particularly in the songs of Othmar Schoeck.
Records: Acoustics for Pathé, electrics for Columbia* and Philips, including the *St. Matthew Passion* under Mengelberg.

DUX, CLAIRE, soprano, b. Aug. 8, 1885, Witkowicz, Poland; d. Oct. 8, 1967, Chicago. The daughter of German parents, at the age of twelve she sang the role of Gretel in a school production of *Hänsel und Gretel.* She then studied singing with Maria Schwadtke and Adolf Deppe in Berlin and finally with Teresa Arkel in Milan. She made her debut (1906) at the Cologne Opera as Pamina in *Die Zauberflöte.* She remained at the Cologne Opera until 1911 and had already become internationally known through guest appearances—for example, in 1909 at the Berlin Imperial Opera as Mimi in *La Bohème* with Enrico Caruso. In 1911 she was engaged at the Berlin Imperial Opera and made starring guest appearances at Covent Garden (1911, 1913-14). After seven years in Berlin she turned to concert appearances (1918-21), although she sang as guest at the Stockholm Royal Opera. In 1920 she was applauded at the Metropol Theater in Berlin in the operetta *Das Hollandweibchen.* In 1921 she came to the United States. After her first great successes here as a concert singer, she appeared at the Chicago Opera (1921), at Ravinia (1922), and toured America (1922-23) with the German Opera Company. She was again an honored member of the Chicago Opera (1923-26) with a few guest appearances in Berlin in 1925. She was first married to the writer Imperatori, then to the film actor Hans Albers, and after 1926 to Charles H. Swift, the packaged-food magnate. After her third marriage she gave only occasional concerts. The soprano voice of Claire Dux was outstanding for the lightness of its timbre, the charm and grace of her diction, and the ease of her tonal production. Her most important parts were lyric roles.
Records: Pathé*, Odeon, Polydor, Brunswick*, and Victor*. *U.S. re-issue:* Opera Disc. *U.S. re-recording:* Rococo.

DVOŘAKOVÁ, LUDMILLA, soprano, b. July 11, 1923, Kolin, Czechoslovakia. She studied at the Prague Conservatory with J. Vavrdova and made her debut (1949) in Ostrava, singing the title role in *Katya Kabanova.* In 1952 she came to the Smetana Theater in Prague and was a member of the Prague National Theater (1954-57). She also appeared in Bratislava (1954-59). She caused great excitement at the Dvořák Memorial Festival (1954). She was engaged by the National Opera in East Berlin (1962), and guest appearances in Russia, France, and Belgium followed. At the Bayreuth Festival (1965) she sang Venus in *Tannhäuser* and Gutrune in *Götterdämmerung.* She made her Metropolitan Opera debut (1966) as Leonora in *Fidelio* and sang this role with great success in Munich. She is married to the conductor Rudolf Vasata.
Records: Supraphon.*

DWORSKY, JARO, tenor, b. Jan 24, 1891, Königsberg, Germany. His father, Jaroslav Dworsky (d. 1935),

Dworsky

sang for many years at the Königsberg Opera. From him the son had his first voice training; he later studied with Ernst Grenzebach and Oscar Daniel in Berlin. He made his debut (1921) at the Königsberg Opera and from there he went, in 1924, to the Berlin State Opera; to this latter he returned (1927-30) after being engaged (1926-27) at the Dresden Opera. He made guest appearances in Austria, Holland, and Spain. Until 1944, from his base in Berlin, he made an extraordinary number of guest appearances. He lives and teaches singing in Berlin. His best parts were in lyric tenor roles.

Records: HMV. *U.S. re-recording:* Rococo.

E

EAMES, EMMA, soprano, b. Aug. 13, 1865, Shanghai, of American parents; d. June 13, 1952, New York. Her father was a lawyer in China, but she was brought up by her mother in Bath, Maine. Her first singing lessons were given her by her mother; she then studied with Clara Mungen in Boston and finally became a pupil of Mathilde Marchesi in Paris. She made her debut there (1889) at the Opéra as Juliette in *Roméo et Juliette* opposite Jean de Reszke. She remained for two years at the Opéra, where she sang in the world *premières* of *Ascanio* and *Zaïre*, both in 1890. In 1891 she made her debut at Covent Garden with such success that she regularly appeared there as a guest until the end of her career. Also in 1891 she was engaged by the Metropolitan Opera, again making her first appearance as Juliette. For eighteen years she was one of the great prima donnas at the New York house. She sang as guest at the Teatro Real (1892-93) and sang at the Queen's Jubilee Festival in London (1897), where she appeared as Elisabeth in *Tannhäuser*. After 1891 she was married to the painter Julian Story; when they separated in 1907, the trial was a sensation of the day. In 1909 she gave what she thought would be her last performance on the stage, singing Tosca at the Metropolitan Opera, but she appeared a few times in the 1911-12 season of the Boston Opera. In 1911 she married the baritone Emilio de Gogorza, but was later separated from him. She then lived in New York as a singing teacher. In 1927 her memoirs appeared in New York under the title *Some Memories and Reflections*. One of the loveliest voices of her time in which wideness of range, absolute technical mastery, and dramatic skill were most fortunately combined.

Records: Victor* (1905-11); she may also be heard on Mapleson cylinders. *U.S. re-issue:* IRCC, HRS. *U.S. re-recording:* IRCC, HRS, Belcanto, Rococo, Cantilena.

EASTON, FLORENCE, soprano, b. Oct. 24, 1884, Middleborough-on-Tees, England; d. Aug. 13, 1955, New York. Although she was reared in Canada, she returned to England in 1898 and studied at the Royal College of Music in London and in Paris. She made her debut (1903) in London with the Moody-Manners Opera Company as the Shepherd Boy in *Tannhäuser*. She then toured the United States with the Savage Grand Opera Company.

In 1906 she married the tenor Francis Maclennan, and in 1907 they were both engaged by the Berlin Imperial Opera. She had great success in Berlin (1907-13), at the Hamburg Opera (1913-15), and at the Chicago Opera (1915-16). In 1917 she was engaged by the Metropolitan Opera, where her career reached its highest point. In 1918 she sang Lauretta in the world première there of *Gianni Schicchi*; in 1926 she sang in the world première of *The King's Henchman*. She sang at the Metropolitan until 1929, when she returned to England; there she was highly successful at Covent Garden and in concert appearances. She made an unusual number of guest and concert appearances, including a few performances at the Metropolitan Opera again in 1936, this time as Brünnhilde in *Die Walküre*. Later she lived in Montreal and finally in New York. The quality of her voice and the skill of her expressiveness enabled her to master a wide-ranging repertory.

Records: A few for Vocalion* (1926) and Edison*; a great many for Brunswick* (1920-30); HMV (the final scene of *Siegfried*). Private records have been issued by IRCC*. *U.S. re-issue:* RCA-Victor. *U.S. re-recording:* Rococo, FRP, TAP, IRCC.

EBERS, CLARA, soprano, b. Dec. 26, 1902, Karlsruhe, Germany. She studied with Eduard Erhard in Karlsruhe and began her career in 1924 as an unpaid assistant at the Landestheater there. She then sang at München-Gladbach (1925-26), at the Opera in Düsseldorf (1926-28), and at the Opera in Frankfurt a. M. (1928-34). In 1934 she was engaged as first soprano at the Hamburg Opera, where she remained for twenty-five years. She had great success in guest appearances at the State Operas in Berlin and Munich, at La Scala, and in Amsterdam and Brussels. She appeared at the Edinburgh Festivals and was sought after as a concert singer. Her rich and well-trained voice brought her on the stage in a wide repertory of important roles.

Records: She made a few records for DGG and Eterna.

EDDY, NELSON, baritone, b. June 29, 1901, Providence, R.I.; d. Mar. 6, 1967, Miami Beach, Fla. Before dedicating himself to singing he traveled a great deal and worked at many jobs, including a stint as a reporter in Philadelphia. In 1922 he appeared in Gilbert and Sullivan operettas, then changed to operatic singing and took an engagement with the Philadelphia Opera Company, including a New York appearance as the Drum Major in *Wozzeck* (1931). Through his appearances on radio he became one of the best-loved American singers. In 1933 he signed a film contract with Metro-Goldwyn-Mayer and thereafter he appeared in numerous musical films in the 1930's, often with Jeanette MacDonald. As a film star he attained an immense popularity. Later he returned to the stage and the concert hall. After 1939 he lived in California and Florida. He had a well-trained and warm-timbred baritone voice, outstanding in opera and song literature.

Records: RCA Victor* and Columbia*. *U.S. re-issue:* Camden, Harmony, Everest.

EDELMANN, OTTO, bass-baritone, b. Feb. 2, 1917, Brunn-am-Gebirge, near Vienna. He studied at the Vienna Academy of Music with Lierhammer and made his debut (1937) in Gera. He was engaged in Nuremberg (1937-40). He was a soldier in World War II and was imprisoned in Russia. In 1947 he came to the Vienna State Opera, of which he is still a member. Since

1947 he has appeared almost every year at the Salzburg Festivals. In 1951 he sang Hans Sachs in *Die Meistersinger* at the Bayreuth Festival and the same part in 1952 at the Edinburgh Festival. In 1954 he made his debut, again as Hans Sachs, at the Metropolitan Opera. His later guest appearances included La Scala, Berlin, Munich, and Hamburg. Since 1955 he has also been a member of the Munich State Opera. He was much applauded as Baron Ochs in *Der Rosenkavalier* in the opening production of the new Festival House in Salzburg in 1960. He has a strong dark voice, equally proven in Wagner parts and in *buffo* roles, such as Ochs, Leporello, and Kezal in *The Bartered Bride*.

Records: Philips, Decca (*Arabella*); Columbia (Sachs in *Die Meistersinger*, Bayreuth 1951, and *Der Rosenkavalier*). *U.S. re-issue:* Angel, Vanguard, London, Electrola, Epic.

EDEN, IRENE, soprano, b. 1893, Munich. Originally Irene Edenhofer. She studied singing with Frau Flam-Plomiensky in Berlin and with Teresa Arkel in Milan. She made her debut (1915) in Zürich. She sang at the National Theater in Mannheim (1916-23) and through her guest appearances elsewhere created sensational interest. She sang in 1920 at the Vienna State Opera and (1923-24) at the Munich State Opera. She appeared at the Berlin State Opera (1924-29) and sang with the ensemble of this company in Holland in 1925. Until 1943 she worked at the Bayreuth Festivals as vocal adviser and as assistant *régisseur*. At the same time she was a popular teacher in Berlin. Bravura technique and unusual lightness and brilliance of tone were joined in her coloratura voice.

Records: Rare acoustic records for Polydor.

EDVINA, MARIE-LOUISE, soprano, b. 1880 (?), Vancouver, Canada; d. Nov. 13, 1948, Nice. Originally Marie Louise Martin. In 1901 she married Cecil Edwards and sang for a few years with a traveling company. She then studied with Jean de Reszke in Paris (1904-08) and made her official debut (1908) at Covent Garden as Marguerite in *Faust*. She sang there regularly until 1920 and was greatly admired. She appeared in the first performance at Covent Garden of *La Dubarry* (1913), *I Gioielli della Madonna* (1912), and *Francesca da Rimini* by Zandonai (1914). In 1912 she joined the Boston Opera Company, where she was particularly admired as Louise and as Mélisande. In 1914 she sang Fiora in *L'Amore dei Tre Re* with the Boston ensemble at the Théâtre des Champs-Elysées. She was engaged by the Chicago Opera (1915-17) and in 1915 she appeared once at the Metropolitan Opera as Tosca with Enrico Caruso and Antonio Scotti. In 1920 she sang a few times at Covent Garden and then turned to operetta. In 1926 she appeared at the Strand Theater, London, in the musical comedy *Hearts and Diamonds*. Her second marriage was to Stuart Worthley. Later she managed an antique shop on the French Riviera.

Records: Three records for HMV (1919). *U.S. re-issue:* Rococo.

EGENER, MINNIE, soprano contralto, b. 1881; d. 1938, New Orleans. She made her debut (1904) at the Metropolitan Opera as a Flower Maiden in *Parsifal*. After one season there she went to Italy (1906), where she sang at various theaters in the years following. In 1910 she sang Alisa in *Lucia di Lammermoor* with Luisa Tetrazzini at Parma; she also appeared in small roles at Covent Garden and at the

Manhattan Opera. She sang with the Philadelphia-Chicago Company (1910-14). In 1914 she returned to the Metropolitan, where she busied herself in *comprimario* roles. In December, 1932, she sang Flora in *La Traviata* there as her farewell to the stage. Thereafter she taught, first in New York and later in New Orleans. She was married to the conductor Louis Hasselmans.

Records: A few Victor* records, among others in the Sextette from *Lucia di Lammermoor* with Enrico Caruso and Amelita Galli-Curci. *U.S. re-recording:* RCA Victor.

EGENIEFF, FRANZ, baritone, b. May 31, 1874, Niederwalluf, Germany. He was the son of Prince Emil zu Sayn-Wittgenstein-Berleburg by a morganatic marriage with Baroness von Kleydorff, whose maiden name was Stefanska. The singer's original name was Franz, Baron von Kleydorff. Until 1900 he was a German army officer. He then studied singing with Lilli Lehmann and Alfredo Cairati in Berlin and with Victor Maurel in Paris. Under the name Franz Egenieff he began his career with the Savage Opera Company in the United States. In 1907 he was engaged by the Komische Opera, where he was very successful until 1910; then he became a member of the Berlin Imperial Opera (1910-11). After 1911 he lived in his palace at Oberwerda, near Gelnhausen, and from there made guest appearances and sang in concerts. In 1927 he sang Klingsor in *Parsifal* at the Bayreuth Festival. In 1929-32 he toured the United States with the German Opera Company which Johanna Gadski had collected.

Records: Pathé, DGG (Musica, Polydor), Odeon, and Edison* Amberola cylinders.

EIBENSCHÜTZ, RIZA, soprano-contralto, b. Feb. 17, 1870, Budapest; d. 1946, Perchtoldsdorf, near Vienna. She studied with Joseph Gänsbacher and Marianne Brandt in Berlin and made her debut (1895) at the Leipzig Opera House as Selika in *L'Africaine*. She sang in Strasbourg (1895-97), made an American tour with the Damrosch Opera Company (1897-99), returned to the Leipzig Opera (1899-1902), and after 1902 sang at the Dresden Royal Opera. There she sang the part of the Duenna in the world *première* of *Der Rosenkavalier* on Jan. 26, 1911. She was married to the conductor Oskar Malata, and after the close of her career she taught in Vienna. Her wide tonal range gave her the mastery of both soprano and contralto parts.

Records: HMV (Dresden, 1908) and Odeon.

EIPPERLE, TRUDE, soprano, b. 1910, Stuttgart. She studied singing a the Music High School in Stuttgart and was engaged as an unpaid a. sistant at the opera house there. She began her real stage career in 1930 at Wiesbaden. She then sang in Braunschweig and Nuremberg and in 1938 moved to the Munich State Opera, where she remained until 1944. She was first soprano at the Cologne Opera (1944-51) and since 1951 she has been a member of the Stuttgart Opera. At the 1942 Salzburg Festival she sang Zdenka in *Arabella*; at Bayreuth in 1952 she appeared as Eva in *Die Meistersinger*. Her other guest appearances included Vienna, London, Paris, Milan, Barcelona, Lisbon, and Brussels. In 1948 at the Cologne Opera she sang in the world *première* of *Verkündigung*.

Records: DGG (*Tannhäuser*), Opera, and MMS* (*The Creation*, by Haydn). *U.S. re-issue:* Haydn Society.

EISINGER, IRENE, soprano, b. Dec. 8, 1903, Kosel, Silesia, Austria. She studied with Paula Mark-Neusser in Vienna and made her debut (1926) at Basel. She was engaged at the Kroll Opera (1928-31). She made very successful guest appearances at the Vienna State Opera (1930-31) and was admired as a Mozart interpreter at the Salzburg Festivals (1930-33). In 1932 she was engaged at the Berlin State Opera, but in 1933 she was forced to leave Germany because she was Jewish. She sang at the German Theater in Prague (1933-37) and made guest appearances in Brussels and Amsterdam. In 1937 she was very successful both at Covent Garden and as Despina in Così fan tutte at the Glyndebourne Festival. Since 1938 she has lived in England, where in the postwar years she appeared in radio concerts. She also appeared in German films in the early 1930's. She had a brilliantly managed coloratura voice and found her best roles in soubrette parts.

Records: Ultraphon, HMV (the Glyndebourne complete *Così fan tutte*), and Orchestrola. *U.S. re-recording:* Telefunken, Eterna, Electrola, Turnabout.

EKEBLAD, MARIE, soprano, b. 1875 (?), Stockholm. She studied with Frau von Milde in Hannover and with E. Fessler in Berlin and made her debut in Würzburg (1901), singing Elsa in *Lohengrin*. She sang at Halle (1902-05) and at the Berlin Imperial Opera (1905-11). She appeared as a guest in Stockholm in 1906. Nothing is known of her later career. She was especially admired as a lieder singer. Her voice is distinguished by rich shading and expressivity.

Records: A few rare records for Anker.

ELIAS, ROSALIND, contralto, b. March 13, 1929, Lowell, Mass. Her family was of Lebanese extraction. She studied for four years at the New England Conservatory of Music in Boston and finally in Italy. She made her debut (1945) at the Metropolitan Opera as one of the Valkyries in *Die Walküre*. After she had sung other small parts at the Metropolitan, she was successful as Olga in *Eugen Onegin* and as Marina in *Boris Godounov*. In 1958 she created the role of Erika in the world *première* of *Vanessa* and sang the role at the Salzburg Festival that same year. She has made guest appearances at the Chicago and San Francisco Operas and has undertaken concert tours in Europe and the United States.

Records: RCA Victor* *(La Gioconda, La Forza del Destino, Der Fliegende Holländer,* and *Falstaff)* and American Columbia*. *U.S. re-issue:* Victrola.

ELIZZA, ELISE, soprano, b. Jan 6, 1870, Vienna; d. June 3, 1926, Vienna. Originally Elisabeth Letztergroschen. She studied with Adolf Limley in Vienna, whom she later married. She began her career in 1892 at the Carltheater in Vienna as an operetta soubrette, first appearing as Margit in *Der Lachende Erbe*. In 1894 she sang in Olmütz. After further study with Amelia Materna, she was engaged in 1895 by the Vienna Imperial Opera, where she made her debut as Ines in *L'Africaine*. She remained a member of that company until 1919 and then taught singing in Vienna. Aside from her great successes on the stage, she was a highly esteemed concert singer. She possessed one of the loveliest soprano voices of her time. She joined classical style, complete mastery of technique, and deep musicality in her repertory, which ranged from coloratura roles to Wagner parts.

Records: Many records for G & T (Vienna, 1903-07), Columbia, Odeon (Vienna, 1905), Favorite, HMV, and Pathé. *U.S. re-issue:*

Victor. *U.S. re-recording:* Eterna, TAP.

ELMO, CLOË, contralto, b. Apr. 9, 1909, Lecce, Italy; d. May 25, 1962, Ankara, Turkey. She studied at the Accademia di Santa Cecilia in Rome with Edvige Ghibaudo and began her stage career in 1935 in Cagliari, Sardinia; she soon had major successes in Italy and sang at La Scala, the Rome Opera, and on other important opera stages. At the Maggio Musicale Festival in 1939 she sang in the first performance of *Il Re Lear*. After World War II she made successful guest appearances in France, England, Austria, Holland, Belgium, Germany, Switzerland, and South America. She sang at the Metropolitan Opera (1947-48), where she was admired as Azucena in *Il Trovatore*. Later she sang chiefly in Italy. After 1954 she taught at the Conservatory in Ankara. A well-trained and expressive voice.

Records: HMV, RCA Victor* (*Falstaff* under Toscanini), and Cetra*. *U.S. re-issue:* Angel.

ELWES, GERVASE, tenor, b. Nov. 15, 1888, Billing Hall, Northampton, England; d. Jan. 12, 1921, Boston, as a result of a fall under a moving train in the Boston station. He belonged to the landed gentry of England and was at one time in the diplomatic service, having been employed in various embassies abroad (1891-95). He began his study of singing with Demest in Brussels and continued with Henry Russell in London and with Bouhy in Paris. In 1903 he made his debut at the Westmoreland Festival in Humperdinck's concert work *Wallfahrt nach Kevalaer*. He gave his first London concert in October, 1903. In 1904 he sang the solo in Elgar's *The Dream of Gerontius* for the first time and thenceforth was considered unsurpassed in this part. He made a German tour with the pianist Fanny Davies (1907), gave concerts in Brussels (1908), and (1909) was greatly admired for his song recitals in Boston and New York and as the Evangelist in the *St. Matthew Passion*. He sang the same part in Amsterdam in 1914 under Willem Mengelberg. During World War I he appeared in England and gave concerts for Allied soldiers in France. Later he undertook a very extensive North American tour (1920-21). He had a dark-timbred expressive tenor voice, his feeling for style was admired as much in oratorio singing as in art songs.

Records: HMV, Columbia*.

ENDERLEIN, ERIK, tenor, b. Feb. 18, 1887, Dresden. He was engaged as first lyric tenor at the Dresden Royal Opera (1912-17). In 1918 he came to Schwerin, where he changed to heroic roles. He sang at the Hamburg State Opera (1919-26) then came to the City Opera in Berlin, but remained associated with Hamburg through a contract for guest appearances. In 1925 he sang Walther in *Die Meistersinger* at the Bayreuth Festival and in 1927-28 sang Parsifal and Siegfried in *Götterdämmerung* at the Zoppot Festival. Other guest appearances included the Vienna State Opera (1926, 1928-29) and the Teatro Real (1926). After the close of his career he taught singing in Berlin.

Records: His records, made for the most part under the name Emil Enderlein, were for Pathé and Polyphon.

ENDERT-BÖHM, ELISABETH VAN, soprano, b. Dec. 31, 1876, Neuss, Germany; d. Feb. 27, 1956, New York City. She studied singing with Richard Müller in Dresden and first sang in concerts and oratorios. She made her stage debut at the Dresden Royal Opera in 1908 and sang there until 1911. She sang at the Berlin Imperial Opera (1911-13) and the German Opera House in Berlin-Charlottenburg (1913-21), and then returned to the Berlin State Opera (1921-23). Guest appearances and concerts took her to England, Belgium, Holland, and Switzerland and she made several tours of the United States. Her second marriage was to Leo Curth, the director of the Electrola Phonograph Record Corporation. After the close of her singing career, she lived and taught in Berlin for sometime. In 1935 she settled in the United States.

Records: Mostly for HMV, but she also recorded for Parlophone, Polydor, and Anker. *U.S. re-issue:* Opera Disc.

ENDRÈZE, ARTHUR, baritone, b. Nov. 28, 1893, Chicago, Ill. Originally Arthur Krackman. He came to France in 1918 as a pupil at the American Conservatory at Fontainebleau, later studied with Jean de Reszke in Paris, and made his stage debut in 1921. He came to the Paris Opéra in 1925 and was very successful there. In 1931 he sang there in the world *première* of *Guercoeur*. He often appeared in operatic productions in Cannes under the direction of Reynaldo Hahn. He made guest appearances in opera in Brussels, Nice, and Monte Carlo and was a much-admired concert singer. After the close of his public career, he became a professor at the Conservatory in Kansas City in 1948. Later he returned to France, where he lived and taught in Paris. His dark-timbred and warm baritone voice was particularly admired in lyric roles.

Records: Odeon and Pathé, *U.S. re-issue:* American Decca.

ENGEL, WERNER, baritone, b. 1884, Berlin. He studied at the Eichelberg Conservatory in Berlin with Paul Bulss and Mathilde Mallinger and made his debut in 1906 at the Theater am Westens in Berlin. He sang at Lübeck in 1907 and later at Posen and Mulhouse. He appeared in Zürich in 1911 and took the part of Amfortas in *Parsifal* at the Bayreuth Festivals (1911-12). During World War I he sang at Dessau. After two seasons at the Vienna State Opera (1912-21), he then appeared at the Berlin City Opera. Guest appearances took him to London, Stockholm, Copenhagen, and Bucharest. In 1922 he sang the Wanderer in *Siegfried* at the Zoppot Festival. He then lived as a teacher in Berlin.

Records: Parlophone. *U.S. re-issue:* Okeh-Odeon.

ENGELEN-SEWING, CATO, soprano, b. Jan. 27, 1868, Amsterdam; d. Dec. 17, 1961, Amsterdam. She studied at the Amsterdam Conservatory with Mme. Collin-Tobisch and with Johannes Messchaert, then with Knudson in Berlin. She made her debut (1890) at the Netherlands Opera as Maritana in *Don César de Bazan*. She remained as the principal prima donna of this house until 1898. She then sang at the Royal Theater in Hannover (1898-1901). In the latter year she became celebrated for her performance at the Theater am Westens in Berlin as the Queen of the Night in *Die Zauberflöte*. In 1901 she returned to the Netherlands Opera and thereby broke a five-year contract with Hannover. She appeared at the Antwerp Opera (1903-04), and thereafter, until 1915, sang with various Dutch opera associations. She was married to the opera director Henry Engelen. From 1915-39 she lived and taught singing in Antwerp, but she returned to Holland in 1939. At the age of seventy-four she gave occasional concerts in Amsterdam. Her supremely well-managed voice, originally a coloratura soprano, was used to master a wide-ranging repertory, even including Wagner heroines.

Records: A great many records for G & T, Zonophone (Holland, about 1901), Pathé (including duets with Jacques Urlus), Anker, Favorite, and Lyrophone.

ENGELL, BIRGIT, soprano, b. 1886, Copenhagen. She studied with Etelka Gerster in Berlin. After originally appearing as a concert singer, she made her stage debut (1909) at Wiesbaden, remaining there until 1912, when she went to the Berlin Imperial Opera. In 1919 she gave up the stage and had a highly successful second career as a concert singer, particularly as an interpreter of lieder. Her concert activity took her all over Germany and to Holland, England, Denmark, and Switzerland. She continued this career until World War II, when she occupied herself with teaching in Copenhagen. She was married to the singing teacher Hans Erwin Hey. A beautifully trained and impressive voice.

Records: HMV, but only in duets and ensembles.

ENGEN, KIETH, bass, b. April 5, 1925, Irazee, Minn. He studied first in the United States and then at the Vienna Music Academy. At first active as a concert bass, he made his stage debut (1954) at Graz. Since 1955 he has been first bass at the Bavarian State Opera in Munich. Since 1958 he has sung at the Bayreuth Festivals and has made highly successful guest appearances and given concerts in all the music centers of Germany and Europe. A voluminous and well-managed bass voice of great expressiveness, celebrated in opera, in oratorio, especially Bach and Handel, and in lieder singing.

Records: DDG* (*St. Matthew Passion* and *Fidelio*), HMV (*The Merry Wives of Windsor*), Telefunken, and Eurodisc.

ERB, KARL, tenor, b. July 13, 1877, Ravensburg, Germany; d. July 13, 1958, Ravensburg. He was a municipal employee in Ravensburg when his voice was discovered by the director of the Stuttgart Royal Opera. He sang in Lübeck (1908-10) but later returned to Stuttgart (1910-12). Called to the Munich Royal Opera in 1912, he had great success there. On June 12, 1917, he sang the title role in the world *première* of *Palestrina*, and this became one of his starring roles. He married the soprano Maria Ivogün in 1920, but they were separated in 1931. He remained a member of the Munich State Opera until 1925 and appeared there as a guest until 1930. After a very severe accident in 1930, he devoted himself entirely to concert work. In this he became the unforgettable interpreter of the Evangelist roles in the *Passions* of Bach and he sang them in all the music centers of the world. He was also one of the most famous interpreters of lieder of his time. He retained his beautiful voice for a long time and was able to appear in the concert hall until the end of his seventieth year. His highly expressive, clear tenor possessed an uncommon splendor. His ability to enter fully into the spirit of what he sang was repeatedly the subject of admiring comment.

Records: Acoustic records for Odeon and electric records for HMV. He sang in a complete performance of *Der Corregidor* for Urania* in 1944. *U.S. re-issue:* Okeh-Odeon, RCA Victor, Columbia. *U.S. re-recording:* FRP, Electrola, Scala, Seraphim.

ERICSDOTTER, SIW, soprano, b. 1926 (?). She first studied art at the Art Academy in Stockholm, but after the discovery of her voice she became a pupil of Nanny Larsén-Todsen. In 1948 she took part in an international singing contest in Scheveningen. She made her debut at the Royal Opera in Stockholm and remained a member of this institution until 1954, when she was engaged by the Hamburg State Opera. In 1959 she appeared at the Berlin City Opera in *Der Fliegende Holländer*, and has maintained a guest-appearance contract with that institution since that time. She has also made guest appearances in the Vienna and Stuttgart State Opera Houses, in Stockholm, Paris, and in theaters in Italy. She is particularly admired as a Wagner singer.

Records: Electrola (Herodias in *Salome*). *U.S. re-issue:* Vox.

ERNSTER, DEZSÖ, bass, b. Nov. 23, 1898, Pécs, Hungary. He studied singing in Budapest and Vienna and made his debut (1926) at the Düsseldorf Opera. In 1929 he came to the Berlin State Opera, where he initially sang small roles. In 1931 he sang Titurel in *Parsifal* and the Steersman in *Tristan und Isolde* at the Bayreuth Festival. He was a guest at both the Vienna State Opera and the Brussels Opera and made a successful tour in Egypt (1933). He became principal bass at the City Theater in Graz (1935-36) and then came to the United States (1936) with the Salzburg Opera Guild, a chamber group. He remained here and in 1938 was engaged by the Chicago Opera. In 1940 he came to the Metropolitan Opera, to which he belonged for almost twenty years. He was a guest at Covent Garden in 1949; he also appeared as guest at Geneva and, after 1955, frequently at the Vienna State Opera. Since 1958 he has belonged to the ensemble of the German-Opera-on-the-Rhine at Düsseldorf-Duisburg. He had a large, dark-timbred bass voice.

Records: About 1930 he sang small roles for Polydor in so-called "Operas-in-Brief." After more than twenty-five years had passed without any records, he sang the role of Alfonso in a complete *Così fan tutte* for Philips in 1956, then sang in *The Seasons* for Vox*, and in 1962 sang Rocco in *Fidelio* for Westminster. *U.S. re-issue:* Philips World Series.

ERSCHOV, IVAN, tenor, b. Nov. 8, 1867, Novotscherkask, Russia; d. Nov. 21, 1943, Leningrad. After his debut (1894) at the Kharkov Opera, he came, in 1895, to the Imperial Opera in St. Petersburg. He sang there until 1925 and was much admired, not only as a Wagner tenor, but also as Otello and in other heroic tenor parts. He taught at the Conservatory of St. Petersburg (1916-43). As well as having a highly successful stage career, he was admired as a concert and lieder singer. He had a well-managed, large heroic tenor voice.

Records: Very rare records for G & T (St. Petersburg, 1903) and Columbia* (St. Petersburg, 1905).

ESCALAÏS, LÉON, tenor, b. 1859, Cuxac d'Aude, near Toulouse; d. November, 1941, Paris. He studied at the Conservatories in Toulouse and Paris, then made his debut at the Paris Opéra (1883) as Arnold in *Guillaume Tell*. The critics designated him admiringly as the successor to the heroic tenor Villaret. In 1890 he appeared at the Opéra in the *première* of *Zaïre*. After 1885 he appeared regularly at the Théâtre de la Monnaie. In 1892 he fell out with the directorate of the Opéra and then undertook guest appearances and tours which led him to all the music centers of Europe and America. During this time he was frequently a guest at La Scala and in the United States he sang at the opera house in New Orleans. After 1896 he began to teach singing. In 1908 his differences with the Opéra were overcome and thereafter he again had great triumphs there. He was married to the soprano Marie Lureau.

A typically French heroic tenor, with a brilliant, radiant high voice and a moving intensity of expressiveness.
Records: His records, much sought after by connoisseurs, were made exclusively for Fonotipia (Milan and Paris, 1905-06). *U.S. re-recording:* TAP, HRS, Scala, FRP, Eterna, Belcanto, Rococo.

EVANS, GERAINT, baritone, b. Feb. 16, 1922, Pontypridd, Wales. After he had first prepared for a business career, he studied singing in Cardiff. This was interrupted, however, by military service in World War II. In 1945 he was a program arranger and singer for the English military radio in Hamburg. He continued his studies with Theo Hermann in Hamburg, Fernando Carpi in Geneva, and Walter Hyde in London and made his debut (1948) at Covent Garden as the Night Watchman in *Die Meistersinger.* In 1949 he had great success there in the title role of *Le Nozze di Figaro.* He also sang in several world *premières* at Covent Garden: Mr. Flint in *Billy Budd* (1951), Montjoy in *Gloriana* (1953), and Antenor in *Troilus and Cressida* (1954). Since 1950 he has appeared at the Glyndebourne Festivals, where he is particularly admired as a Mozart singer. He also sings these roles at Covent Garden. In 1960 he sang as guest at La Scala in *Il Barbiere di Siviglia.* He appeared at the Vienna State Opera (1960-62) and in 1960 sang the title role in *Wozzeck* in San Francisco. His Figaro in the Mozart opera was highly successful at the 1963 Salzburg Festival. Since making his debut in the title role of *Falstaff* in 1963, he has sung annually at the Metropolitan Opera. He has a well-trained and expressive baritone voice.
Records: HMV (*Arlecchino* at Glyndebourne), Parlophone, and RCA Victor (*Falstaff*). *U.S. re-issue:* Angel, London.

EWEYK, ARTHUR VAN, baritone, b. May 27, 1866, Milwaukee, Wisc.; d. (?). His father, Henry van Eweyk, was a Dutch painter and his mother was German. He studied singing in 1890-92 with Felix Schmidt in Berlin and made his debut there (1891) with the Berlin Philharmonic Orchestra, singing in the *Frithjof Saga* of Max Bruch. He subsequently had a brilliant career as a concert and oratorio singer. He was especially admired as an interpreter of Bach and Handel as well as a lieder singer. Concert tours took him to Holland, Belgium, Russia, Italy, Norway, and Switzerland. He made several successful concert tours of the United States. After 1923 he lived in Villa Park, Illinois. He never sang on the stage.
Records: Seven Victor* records (1910) preserve the voice of this artist, whom the critics always compared to Johannes Messchaert. *U.S. re-issue:* Opera Disc.

EXNER, INGEBORG, soprano, b. 1925, Berlin. She studied both piano and singing at the Conservatory of the city of Berlin. Further vocal instruction from Frieda Leider and Ivo Götte there was followed by her debut (1949) as Pamina in *Die Zauberflöte* in the opening performance at the new Municipal Theater in Dessau. In 1951 she went from Dessau to Karlsruhe; she sang at Bielefeld (1953-55) and at the Berlin City Opera (1955-59). Since 1959 she has been first soprano at the Cologne Opera and has made guest appearances at the Vienna State Opera, in Hamburg, Munich, and Berlin. She has a warm-timbred, flexible soprano voice.
Records: Opera, Electrola.

F

FABBRI, GUERRINA, contralto, b. 1886, Ferrara; d. Feb. 21, 1946, Turin. She made her debut in Viadana (1885) and quickly became known in Italy. She appeared as guest in Madrid (1886), at the Drury Lane Theater (1887), and returned to London as guest every year until 1892. She gave concerts in New York's Steinway Hall (1888) and then collected her own opera troupe, with which she appeared in Chicago and New York (1889). She made her debut at La Scala in 1908. In the same year she had brilliant successes at the Teatro Colón. In 1910 she appeared, but only in concert, at the Metropolitan Opera. In 1914 she sang the role of Margarita in *I Quattro Rusteghi* at La Scala; this became one of her starring roles and she sang it at La Scala until 1926. After leaving the stage, she lived and taught in Turin. Guerrina Fabbri was one of the last coloratura-contraltos, a voice type which, although common in the nineteenth century, disappeared until the emergence of Conchita Supervia. The technical qualities and the beauty of her dark-timbred voice were greatly admired.

Records: Very rare records for G & T and Zonophone* (Milan, 1903-04). *U.S. re-issue:* IRCC. *U.S. re-recording:* TAP, Belcanto, Rococo.

FARNETI, MARIA, soprano, b. 1878; d. Oct. 17, 1955, Milan. After her debut in 1898 she became especially well-known as an interpreter of the soprano roles in the *verismo* operas. Mascagni particularly admired her after hearing her in 1899 at the Teatro Costanzi in the title role of his *Iris*. When he undertook a tour of North America in 1902, she was part of the company he assembled. She also appeared at La Scala and had great triumphs in South America, especially at the Teatro Colón. In 1911 she sang the title role in *Isabeau* at the world *première* in the Teatro Coliseo. In the same year she married a lawyer, Riboldi, and retired from the stage.

Records: Acoustics for Fonotipia (1910), Edison* cylinders and discs; electric records for Columbia*, made in 1930, showed that her voice retained all its former beauty.

FARRAR, GERALDINE, soprano, b. Feb. 28, 1882, Melrose, Mass.; d. Mar. 11, 1967, Ridgefield, Conn. She began studying singing with Emma Thursby in New York at the age of fifteen. In 1899 she went to Paris to study with Trabadello, then moved to Berlin and finished her studies with Lilli Lehmann. She made her stage debut at the Berlin Imperial Opera (1901) as Marguerite in *Faust*. The young American singer was a much-admired member of the Imperial Opera until 1906, and she was befriended by the German crown prince and his family. During this time she made guest appearances in Monte Carlo, Paris, London, Stockholm, and Brussels. In Monte Carlo in 1905 she sang in the world *première* of *Amica* and in 1906 in the world *première* there of *L'Ancêtre*. In 1906 she was engaged by the Metropolitan Opera, her debut role being Juliette in *Roméo et Juliette*. She was for many years the prima donna *assoluta* of the Metropolitan, where she was much admired as a partner to Enrico Caruso. She appeared there in several world *première* performances: The Goose Maid in *Königskinder* (1910), the title heroine in *Mme. Sans-Gêne* (1915), and the title role in *Suor Angelica* (1918). She was one of the first opera stars to appear in silent films. In 1922 she retired from the Metropolitan Opera and thereafter appeared only occasionally in the concert hall and on opera tours. She then lived in Ridgefield, Connecticut. Her autobiographical books, *Geraldine Farrar by Herself* and *Such Sweet Compulsion*, appeared in New York in 1916 and 1938, respectively. After 1916 she was married for a short time to the actor Lou Tellegen. Possessing one of the best soprano voices of her time, she was noted for her wide range and for her expressive art. Best known as a Puccini interpreter, she also was famous for her Carmen and many other roles.

Records: G & T (Berlin, 1904-06) and Victor*. She also made electric recordings. *U.S. re-issue: IRCC. U.S. re-recording:* RCA Victor, Belcanto, Camden, Rococo, IRCC.

FARRELL, EILEEN, soprano, b. 1921 (?). Her family, which was of Irish extraction, traveled in vaudeville. She made her debut in a concert on the Columbia radio network in 1942. In the next five years she sang on the radio in her own program, "Eileen Farrell Presents." She first appeared on the concert stage in 1947 and had a brilliant success. In 1950 she sang at Carnegie Hall in New York, taking the part of Marie in a famous concert performance of *Wozzeck*, and in 1955 at Town Hall she sang the title role in a concert performance of Cherubini's *Medea*. She first appeared on the stage at the San Francisco Opera in 1956 as Leonora in *Il Trovatore*. A year later she sang the title role in *La Gioconda* at the Chicago Opera. After 1960 she was a member of the Metropolitan Opera for a few years; she also made guest appearances at the Rome Opera. She had a starring career as a concert soprano, but later turned to popular music. This artist possessed a large voice of almost inexhaustible volume and her dramatic art compelled admiration.

Records: RCA Victor* and Columbia*. *U.S. re-issue:* American Decca, Angel, MGM, London.

FAVERO, MAFALDA, soprano, b. Jan. 6, 1905, Portomaggiore, near Ferrara. She studied in Bologna with Alessandro Vezzani and made her stage debut (1927) at the Bologna Opera as Elsa in *Lohengrin*. On New Year's Eve, 1929, she sang for the first time at La Scala, appearing as Eva in *Die Meistersinger* under Toscanini; in 1929 she sang there in the world *première* of *Le Preziose Ridicole* and had many triumphs there until 1946. She made successful guest appearances at Covent Garden in 1937 and came to the Metropolitan Opera for one season in 1938. She also sang often in the larger South American opera houses and in San Francisco. After

1946 she appeared only once in concert. Her voice was remarkable through her mastery of singing technique and through the beauty of its lyric expressiveness.

Records: Columbia* (*Mefistofele*), HMV, Colosseum (*Adriana Lecouvreur*). *U.S. re-issue:* RCA Victor. *U.S. re-recording:* Angel.

FAY, MAUDE, soprano, b. Apr. 18, 1878, San Francisco; d. Oct. 7, 1964, San Francisco. She studied with Aglaia von Orgeni in Dresden and made her debut (1906) at the Munich Royal Opera as Marguerite in *Faust*. She remained in Munich until 1914 and became known especially as a Wagner soprano. During this time she sang at Covent Garden, in Brussels, and in Amsterdam (1913). She sang at the Metropolitan Opera (1915-17). After she married an American officer, she gave only rare concerts and made few stage appearances. She had a beautiful soprano voice, noted particularly in Wagner parts.

Records: Only a single HMV record of her voice exists (Munich, 1907).

FEDERICI, FRANCESCO, baritone, b. 1873, Ferrara; d. Jan. 28, 1934, The Hague. He made his debut in 1898 and then sang in the Italian provinces. He had an outstanding success at Palermo (1911), made guest appearances in Helsinki with Elvira de Hidalgo (1911), and in the same year sang in Havana. He was engaged by the Chicago Opera (1913-16). Guest appearances and concert tours took him to South Africa and to Indonesia. In the 1920's he gave up his lyric baritone career, changed to *buffo* parts, and had great success in such roles in Italy. He was engaged by the Italian Opera in the Netherlands in 1933, but he suddenly died there of pneumonia. He had a beautiful lyric voice.

Records: HMV (Milan, 1908-12). *U.S. re-issue:* Victor.

FEHENBERGER, LORENZ, tenor, b. Aug. 24, 1912, Oberweidach, Bavaria. He was a member of the choir of the Pilgrimage Church in Altötting, studied with Elisabeth Wolff in Munich, and made his debut in Graz (1939). He sang at the Dresden State Opera (1941-45) and in 1946 came to the Bavarian State Opera in Munich. Guest tours took him to all the important theaters in Italy, Austria, Belgium, Holland, Switzerland, Scandinavia, and South America. He also sang at the Salzburg and Munich Festivals. He was very successful as a concert and oratorio singer.

Records: DDG* (a complete *Lohengrin*) and Remington*. *U.S. re-issue:* Urania, MGM, Lyrichord.

FEINHALS, FRITZ, baritone, b. Dec. 11, 1869, Cologne; d. Aug. 30, 1940, Munich. He first studied engineering at the Polytechnicum in Berlin-Charlottenburg, then singing with Alberto Giovanni in Milan and with Alberto Selva in Padua. He made his debut (1895) in Essen as Silvio in *I Pagliacci* and sang there until 1897. After singing in Mainz (1897-98), he came to the Munich Royal Opera, where he remained until the end of his career in 1927. Guest appearances took him to the Paris Opéra, Covent Garden, the Vienna Imperial Opera, and to the operas of Zürich, Brussels, and Budapest. He traveled many times to the United States, where he was engaged by the Metropolitan Opera (1908-09). He was especially admired as a Wagner singer. In 1917 he sang in the world *première* of *Palestrina* in Munich.

Records: Odeon, HMV, and Edison* cylinders. *U.S. re-issue* Victor, Opera Disc.

FELBERMAYER, ANNY, soprano, b. 1924, Vienna. She studied at the Vienna Academy of Music with Josef Witt and Elisabeth Rado, and won the Cebotari Prize in Vienna as well as singing contests in Ge-

Féraldy · Ferrari-Fontana

neva and Verviers. In 1951 she was engaged by the Vienna State Opera, of which she has since been a member. She has appeared at the Salzburg Festivals annually since 1952. Her guest appearances include La Scala and the Brussels Opera, among others. She has a well-trained lyric soprano voice, which is admired on the stage in a great many roles and also in the concert hall and in oratorio.

Records: Decca (Barbarina in *Le Nozze di Figaro*, small parts in *Der Rosenkavalier*, *Die Frau ohne Schatten*, and *Der Freischütz*), Columbia (Zdenka in *Arabella*, Barbarina in *Le Nozze di Figaro*, and *Hänsel und Gretel*), oratorio and lieder records for Amadeo-Vanguard. *U.S. re-issue:* Bach Guild, Vanguard, Vox, Lyrichord, Angel, Electrola, RCA Victor, and Everyman.

FÉRALDY, GERMAINE, soprano, b. 1894, Toulouse, d. June 19, 1946, Toulouse. She studied at the Conservatory in Toulouse and at the National Conservatory in Paris. After she had first sung in French provincial theaters, she came to the Opéra-Comique in 1924. She remained there until 1942 and had great success both in coloratura parts and in lyric roles, such as Manon, Marguerite, and Violetta. She made guest appearances at the opera houses in Nice, Monte Carlo, Brussels, and London and was very successful as a concert singer. After her retirement from the stage, she held a professorship at the Toulouse Conservatory.

Records: Columbia* (*Manon* and *Werther*). *U.S. re-issue:* Pathé. *U.S. re-recording:* Vox, Pathé-Marconi.

FERNANDI, EUGENIO, tenor, b. 1928 (?), Turin. He studied in Turin with Aureliano Pertile, then at the Opera School at La Scala. After great successes at the leading Italian opera houses, including La Scala, he was engaged (1958) by the Metropolitan Opera. After 1959 he also had great success at the Vienna State Opera in such parts as Cavaradossi in *Tosca*, Alfredo in *La Traviata*, and the title role in *Don Carlos*. He sang this last at the Salzburg Festivals (1958-60).

Records: Columbia (including *Turandot* with Maria Callas). *U.S. re-issue:* Angel, Capitol.

FERRANI, CESIRA, soprano, b. May 8, 1863, Turin, d. May 4, 1943, Pollone, Italy. She studied with Antonietta Fricci in Turin and made her debut there in (1887) as Gilda in *Rigoletto*. She then sang in Venice, Catania, and again in Turin and appeared as a guest in French opera houses. On Feb. 1, 1893, she sang the title role in *Manon Lescaut* in its world *première* at the Teatro Regio in Turin. At the same theater, on Feb. 1, 1896, she created the role of Mimi in *La Bohème*. She was a guest at the Teatro Colón in 1893 and came to La Scala in 1894, remaining there for the next fifteen years. She sang the role of Mélisande in 1908 at the first performance there of *Pelléas et Mélisande*. She made successful tours in Spain and Russia and appeared as guest at the Cairo Opera (1898). In 1909 she left the stage and taught in Turin.

Records: A few rare records for G & T (Milan, 1903). *U.S. re-issue:* Victor. *U.S. re-recording:* FRP, IRCC.

FERRARI-FONTANA, EDOARDO, tenor, b. July 8, 1878, Rome; d. July 4, 1936, Toronto, Canada. He studied medicine at first, then about 1902 entered the diplomatic service and was a secretary at the consulate in Montevideo. He was a self-taught singer and sang first in amateur concerts. In 1908 he returned to Italy and began as an operetta tenor. In 1910 he made a sensational debut as Tristan at the Teatro Regio in Turin, when he substituted for Giuseppe Borgatti, who was ill; he soon became the principal Italian Wagner tenor. He made guest appearances at the Teatro Colón in 1911-12. He married the contralto Marguerite Matzenauer, but was separated from her after a few years. He sang the role of Avito at La Scala in 1913 in the world *première* of *L'Amore dei Tre Re* and also created this part at the first performances in Monte Carlo, Paris, and Buenos Aires. He sang at the Boston Opera (1913-14), came to the Metropolitan Opera for two seasons (1914-15) and then sang at the Chicago Opera (1915-16). He had further successes at the Teatro Colón in 1920 as Tristan and as Siegmund in *Die Walküre*. After 1926 he taught in Toronto.

Records: American Columbia* and Edison*. *U.S. re-recording:* Columbia, TAP.

FERRARIS, INES-MARIA, soprano, b. 1886 (?). She made her stage debut in Bologna in 1908 as Philine in *Mignon*. She came to La Scala in 1911, making her debut as Carolina in *Il Matrimonio Segreto;* she sang Sophie in the first performance there of *Der Rosenkavalier* in the same year and appeared in the same part in Rome in 1914. She had enormous success in South America, especially at the Teatro Colón. In 1917 she sang Lisette in the world *première* of *La Rondine* at Monte Carlo. She had her greatest triumphs, however, at La Scala, where for two decades she was counted among the prima donnas of the institution. In the 1920's she appeared there with Conchita Supervia in *Hänsel und Gretel*. In 1934 she gave up her stage career and lived and taught in Milan. She had a virtuoso coloratura voice; on the stage she was effective because of both her acting skill and the grace of her presence.·

Records: Columbia* (Gilda in an acoustic recording of *Rigoletto*), Pathé*, Odeon-Fonotipia, including duets with Conchita Supervia, and Parlophone. *U.S. re-issue:* American Decca.

FERRIER, KATHLEEN, contralto, b. Apr. 22, 1912, Higher Walton, England; d. Oct. 8, 1953, London. She passed her youth in Blackburn and originally wanted to become a pianist, but the necessity of earning her living caused her to become a telephone operator for some years. Her voice was discovered during World War II, when she sang folk songs for British soldiers. The conductor, Sir Malcolm Sargent, urged her even at the age of thirty to take up singing. She studied first with Hutchinson in Blackburn and then with Roy Henderson in London. She made her debut (1942) in Newcastle, singing the contralto solo in Bach's *St. Matthew Passion*, and after 1944 she was highly successful as an oratorio singer in England. She made her stage debut (1946) at the Glyndebourne Festival, where she sang the title role in the world *première* of *The Rape of Lucretia*. In 1947, at Glyndebourne, she amazed the spectators with her gripping acting in *Orphée et Eurydice*. These two roles remained her only stage parts, although she had now become world-famous. She sang—particularly in the concert hall— in Vienna, Milan, at the Salzburg Festivals, in Amsterdam, Brussels, New York, San Francisco, Stockholm, and Oslo, and she was esteemed as the greatest contralto of her time. The career of this artist was interrupted early by an incurable illness. In February, 1953, by superhuman effort she sang the role of Orphée a few times at Covent Garden. Her warm, velvety contralto voice had a fascinating quality which made each of her interpretations an unforgettable experience. She was an unequaled performer in Bach and Handel as well as in art songs.

Records: Columbia* (including *St. Matthew Passion* and excerpts from *Orphée et Eurydice*) and Decca (Mahler's *Das Lied von der Erde*). *U.S. re-issue:* London, Richmond, Seraphim, Keynote, Rococo.

FEUGE, ELISABETH, soprano, b. 1902, Dessau, Germany; d. July 4, 1942, Munich, by suicide. She was the daughter of a famous pair of singers, her father, Oscar Feuge (1861-1913), sang tenor roles for many years at Dessau; her mother, Emilie Feuge-Gleiss (1863-1923), was coloratura soprano at the same theater and also sang elsewhere, including the Bayreuth Festivals. The daughter was trained by her mother and made her debut in Dessau in 1922. In 1923 she came to the Munich State Opera, where she remained until her death. She completed her training in Munich with Hans Bussmeyer and appeared as guest in Dresden and Stuttgart, but especially at the Vienna State Opera. At the Salzburg Festivals she sang the role of Donna Anna in *Don Giovanni*. In 1931 she appeared at Munich in the world *première* of *Die Geliebte Stimme* and she was also assistant *régisseur* at Munich. She made guest appearances in 1932 in Amsterdam and The Hague. With a rich soprano voice of the greatest stylistic flexibility, she was particularly admired in Wagner and Strauss roles.

Records: A single Parlophone.

FEUGE-GLEISS, EMILIE, soprano, b. 1863, in the Rhenish Palatinate; d. 1923, Dessau, Germany. She studied with Adolf Schimon in Munich and in Leipsic. She began her career (1890) at the Berlin Imperial Opera, where she remained until 1892. Then she sang at Schwerin in 1893-94 and thereafter until 1922 at Dessau, where she was greatly admired. She participated in the Bayreuth Festivals (1897-1906), especially as the Forest Bird in *Siegfried*. She also sang under the name Emmy Feuge-Gleiss, and was married to the lyric tenor Oscar Feuge, who also appeared at Dessau. Their daughter, Elisabeth Feuge, was also a well-known soprano.

Records: A few extremely rare G & T records.

FIDESSER, HANS, tenor, b. 1889. He began his career as a baritone (1922) at Plauen and sang at the National Theater, Mannheim (1924-26). After his voice had changed to tenor, he was engaged at Elberfeld and, after 1928, at the City Opera in Berlin; he also sang frequently at the Berlin State Opera. He was regularly engaged as guest at the Vienna State Opera (1929-31) and sang Tamino in *Die Zauberflöte* at the Salzburg Festivals. In 1934 he made guest appearances in Amsterdam as Belmonte in *Die Entführung aus dem Serail*. He later made guest appearances in Paris and Stockholm and sang in German films. His lyric voice was especially prized in the Mozart repertory, and he was also an important operetta singer.

Records: Very few records for Parlophone.

FIGNER, NICHOLAI, tenor, b. 1856, St. Petersburg; d. Dec. 13, 1919, Kiev. He studied at the Conservatory in St. Petersburg and in Italy and made his debut (1882) at the Teatro San Carlo. He had great success on Italian stages, including La Scala. There he sang in 1887 in the world *première* of *Edmea*; at this performance the conducting was entrusted to a young man, then entirely unknown, Arturo Toscanini. After guest appearances in Madrid and Bucharest he was engaged in 1887 by the Imperial Opera in St. Petersburg. There he went from one triumph to another, as did his wife, the Italian soprano Medea Mei-Figner. These singing artists had a notable influence on the musical life of their time. Their friend, the composer Tchaikovsky, completed his opera *The Queen of Spades* on the Figners' estate near Tula. In the world *première* of the opera, Dec. 19, 1890, in St. Petersburg, Figner sang Hermann and his wife sang Lisa. Later world *premières* in St. Petersburg in which these artists took part included *Iolanthe* (1891), *Dubrovsky* (1895), and *Francesca da Rimini* by Nápravník (1902). Nicholai Figner remained a member of the Imperial Opera until 1903 and gave concerts and made guest appearances afterwards. During the 1917 Revolution this once-idolized artist lost all his possessions.

Records: A few extremely rare records for G & T, the oldest from 1901. *U.S. re-recording:* TAP.

FILIPPESCHI, MARIO, tenor, b. June 6, 1907, Pisa. He was originally a police official. After studying singing, he made his debut (1937) and had his first great success with the Italian Opera in Holland (1938-40). During World War II he sang a great deal in Germany with Italian opera troupes. After 1946 he had a highly successful career at La Scala as well as at the Rome Opera, the Teatro San Carlo, and in Florence, where he appeared in 1952 in *Armide*. Guest appearances took him to the Teatro Colón, the Mexico City Opera, and to the operatic stages of Spain and Portugal. His strong and brilliant voice was heard in many roles, especially in the heroic parts in Italian opera.

Records: Solo records for HMV; a complete *Guillaume Tell* for Cetra*; *Norma* with Maria Callas for Columbia; the title role in *Don Carlos* for HMV; *Moïse et Pharaon* for Philips*. *U.S. re-issue* Angel, Capitol. *U.S. re-recording:* TAP, Everest-Cetra.

FINESCHI, ONELIA, soprano, b. Apr. 5, 1924 (?), Florence. She made her stage debut in Florence (1943) as Desdemona in *Otello*. In 1943 she also made a tour with an opera company through Holland and Germany. She later had outstanding successes at La Scala, the Rome Opera, and the Teatro Fenice. In 1946 she sang Mimi in *La Bohème* at Covent Garden and in 1948 sang Leila in *Les Pêcheurs des Perles* at La Scala. She appeared in the Arena Festival as early as 1946. In the 1950's she suffered from a vocal affliction, but after a long rest she was able to resume her career at the Rome Opera. She is married to the tenor Francesco Albanese. Her particular starring roles were Violetta and Butterfly.

Records Certa*. *U.S. re-recording:* Everest-Cetra.

FINZI-MAGRINI, GIUSEPPINA, soprano, b. May 5, 1878, Turin; d. Nov. 30, 1944, Turin. She made her debut in 1900 and had a highly successful career in Italy, singing at both La Scala and the Teatro Costanzi. She made guest appearances in Belgium in 1910 and later in France. During World War I she lived and taught in Turin. During World War II she was forced as a Jew to go into hiding and died in great poverty. She had a technically well-managed and completely trained, brilliant coloratura soprano voice and she was especially prized in the classic *bel canto* parts.

Records G & T (Milan, 1904), Fonotipia (Milan, 1905), Columbia*, Pathé, for HMV she recorded one duet with Titta Ruffo. *U.S. re-issue:* Victor.

Fischer · Fischer-Dieskau

FISCHER, LORE, contralto, b. May 27, 1911, Stuttgart. She studied voice and violin at the Music High School in Stuttgart; she then went to the Music High School in Cologne as a pupil of Maria Philippi. She gave her first concerts in 1934 and rapidly became known as a soloist in oratorio and as an interpreter of songs in the music centers of both Germany and foreign countries. In 1942 she married the violist Rudolf Nel. With her husband and the composer Hermann Reutter she founded the Lore Fischer Trio, which specialized in performances of baroque music. She lives in Munich-Gräfeling.
Records Polydor and Philips. *U.S. re-issue:* DGG, L'Oiseau Lyre.

FISCHER, RES, contralto, b. Nov. 8, 1896, Berlin. She studied at the Conservatories in Berlin, Prague, and Stuttgart and then became a pupil of Lilli Lehmann in Berlin. She made her debut in Basel (1927) and remained there until 1935. She sang at the Frankfurt a. M. Opera (1935-41) and after 1941 was a member of the Stuttgart State Opera. She appeared at the Salzburg Festival in 1942. After World War II she developed a great international career, with guest appearances at the State Operas in Vienna, Munich, and Hamburg, as well as at La Scala, the Paris Opéra, the operas in Brussels and Amsterdam, and particularly at the Teatro Colón. Her career lasted a long time; she was greatly admired at the Bayretuh Festivals in 1959-61 as Mary in *Der Fliegende Holländer*.
Records: DGG (including the Witch in *Hänsel und Gretel*) and Philips (including *Der Fliegende Holländer* from Bayreuth).

FISCHER-DIESKAU, DIETRICH, baritone, b. May 28, 1925, Berlin. He began his study of singing at sixteen with Georg A. Walter in Berlin. In 1943 he became a soldier and was an English prisoner of war in Italy until 1945. After his release he studied again in Berlin with Hermann Weissenborn. He first appeared as the soloist in the *Deutsches Requiem* of Brahms in Freiburg a. Br. in 1948 and made his stage debut in the same year at the City Opera, Berlin; he has since remained a member of that organization. He sang next at the State Operas in Munich and Vienna; he appeared in London in 1951 under Sir Thomas Beecham and in 1952 under Wilhelm Furtwängler. In 1952 he appeared again at the Vienna State Opera and the Salzburg Festival. He has had triumphal successes at the Festivals at Salzburg, Glyndebourne, Edinburgh, Lucerne, and, since 1954, at Bayreuth. His guest appearances have brough him great success in all the other centers of musical life in both Europe and America. He was especially successful at Covent Garden in 1965 as Mandryka in *Arabella*. He is world famous as a song interpreter and is generally conceded to be one of the most renowned lieder singers of his time. In this realm he is admired equally for the clarity of his diction, his great musicality, and his ability to enter into the spirit of the music he interprets. After the death of his first wife, the cellist Irmgard Popper, he married the film star Ruth Leuwerik in 1965, from whom he later separated. He has a warm and expressive baritone voice and is admired in an enormous repertory both on the stage and in the concert hall.
Records: Many records by this artist have appeared on both HMV and DGG*, particularly of lieder. His operatic recordings include *Orphée et Eurydice, Don Giovanni, Le Nozze di Figaro, Fidelio, Elktra, Capriccio, Rigoletto, Der Fliegende Holländer,* and *Die Zauberflöte*

(two versions). *U.S. re-issue:* Angel, Electrola, London, Seraphim, American Columbia, Heliodor, American Decca, RCA Victor.

FISHER, SYLVIA, soprano, b. 1911, Melbourne. She studied piano and voice at the Albert Street Conservatory in Melbourne, then studied with Adolf Spirakovsky. She made her operatic debut in Melbourne in 1932 as Hermione in *Cadmus et Hermione*. In the following years she often appeared on the Australian radio and also in opera and concert. In 1947 she went to London, where she made her debut at Covent Garden as Leonora in *Fidelio*; in 1948 she sang Elisabeth in *Tannhäuser* and the Marschallin in *Der Rosenkavalier* there. After renewing her studies with Frida Leider in Berlin, she came to be greatly admired in Wagner roles. She was a guest at the Rome Opera in 1952 and was greatly applauded in London as Brünnhilde in the *Ring* cycle in 1957.

Records: The first records of this artist appeared late in her career, when she sang for Decca in a complete performance of *Albert Herring*. *U.S. re-issue:* London, Vanguard-Everyman.

FITZIU, ANNA, soprano, b. 1888, Virginia; d. Apr. 20, 1967, Hollywood. Originally Anna Fitzhugh. She studied with William Thorner in Paris. After she had appeared in musical comedies in Chicago, she went to Italy and made her operatic debut in Milan in (1910) as Elsa in *Lohengrin*. Guest appearances followed in Rome, Naples, Palermo, Florence, and at the Teatro Colón and the Mexico City Opera. In 1915 she joined the Metropolitan Opera where, on Jan. 28, 1916, she sang Rosario in the world *première* of *Goyescas*. This was the only role she interpreted at the Metropolitan; however, she did sing there in the Sunday Night Concerts. She sang at the Chicago Opera (1917-19) and made a tour through the United States with the San Carlo Opera Company in 1921, returning to Chicago Opera again in 1922. She remained at Chicago until 1925, sang as guest at the Havana Opera in 1924 as Desdemona and Tosca, and sang again with the San Carlo Company occasionally in 1926. She then became a singing teacher in Chicago.

Records: American Pathé*, *U.S. re-recording:* Pathé Actuelle, IRCC.

FLAGSTAD, KIRSTEN, soprano, b. July 12, 1895, Hamar, Norway; d. Dec. 8, 1962, Oslo. She studied with Ellen Schytte-Jacobsen in Oslo and made her debut there (1913) as Nuri in *Tiefland*. After further study with Albert Westwang in Oslo and Gillis Bratt in Stockholm, she returned to Oslo in 1917 as a soubrette at the Mayol Theater and specialized in operetta. In 1921 she undertook a tour of France, but had no special success there. She was engaged at the City Theater in Göteborg (1928-32). In 1933 she appeared at the Bayreuth Festival and in 1934 had her first great success there as Sieglinde in *Die Walküre* and as Gutrune in *Götterdämmerung*. Thereupon she was engaged by the Metropolitan Opera, where she made a sensational debut in 1935 as Sieglinde, suddenly becoming one of the outstanding Wagner sopranos of her time. At the Metropolitan she went from triumph to triumph until 1941. In 1936 she made guest appearances at Covent Garden and the Vienna State Opera. She was greatly admired in San Francisco, Chicago, Zürich, and Teatro Colón. She lived in retirement in her native Norway (1941-45), but after the war she and her husband, Henry Johansen, were blamed, entirely without reason, for having collaborated with the German occupation authorities. She undertook a tour of the United States (1947-48) and she sang especially at Covent Garden (1948-51). She was greatly admired as Leonora in *Fidelio* at the Salzburg Festivals (1949-50). In 1951 she appeared at the Mermaid Theater in London as Dido in *Dido and Aeneas* and in 1952 she was applauded at the Metropolitan in *Alceste*. She made her farewell stage appearances in 1955. She was the director of the opera houses in Oslo (1958-60). She had one of the most beautiful dramatic soprano voices of the twentieth century, in which were joined a dark quality of voice with highly artistic expressiveness and unfailingly accurate technique.

Records: Acoustic records for Odeon; electrics for HMV, including a complete *Tristan und Isolde* under Furtwängler and *Dido and Aeneas*. She also sang for RCA Victor* and Decca (including *Das Rheingold, Die Walküre, Götterdämmerung,* and *Alceste*.) U.S. re-issue: RCA Victor, London, Angel, Electrola. U.S. re-recording: Harvest, Camden, RCA Victor, Seraphim, London.

FLEISCHER, EDYTHA, soprano, b. Apr. 5, 1898, Falkenstein, Germany. She studied in Berlin with Lilli Lehmann and made her debut in 1919 at the German Opera House there. She sang Susanna in *Le Nozze di Figaro* and Zerlina in *Don Giovanni* at the Salzburg Festival in 1922 and made a North American tour with the German Opera Company (1922-24). She then remained in the United States and joined the William Wade Hinshaw Opera Company. In 1926 she joined the Metropolitan Opera in the role of First Lady in *Die Zauberflöte* as her debut role. She remained at the Metropolitan for ten years and was very successful there in coloratura roles. She was very highly regarded as a concert soprano in the United States, Germany, and Denmark. She sang under contract at the Teatro Colón (1946-49). After that she became a singing teacher at the Conservatory of the city of Vienna.

Records: A few records for Polyphone and Victor*.

FLEISCHER-EDEL, KATHARINA, soprano, b. Sept. 27, 1873, Mulheim, Germany; d. July 18, 1928, Dresden. She studied at the Dresden Conservatory with August Iffert and made her debut (1893) at a concert of the Dresden Liedertafel; she made her stage debut (1894) at the Dresden Royal Opera as a Bridesmaid in *Der Freischütz*. After three years at Dresden she was offered a contract in 1899 by Pollini, the director of the Hamburg Opera. She remained there for more than twenty highly successful years, being especially admired in Wagner roles. Her guest appearances included the Vienna Imperial Opera (1901), Berlin and Covent Garden later, and a season at the Metropolitan Opera (1906-07). She sang at various Bayreuth Festivals: Elisabeth in *Tannhäuser* (1904), Gutrune in *Götterdämmerung* (1904), Brangäne in *Tristan und Isolde* and Sieglinde in *Die Walküre* (1906), Sieglinde again and Elsa in *Lohengrin* (1908). She later lived and taught in Dresden.

Records: A few rare records for Odeon (Hamburg, 1906-09).

FLESCH, ELLA, soprano, b. June 16, 1900, Budapest; d. June 6, 1957, New York. She was a niece of the violinist Karl Flesch and studied in Budapest and Vienna, making her debut (1922) at the Vienna State Opera as Aïda. She remained in Vienna until 1925, when she went to the Munich State Opera, where she stayed until 1934. At this house she was greatly admired as Tosca, Salome, Venus in *Tannhäuser*, Octavian in *Der Rosenkavalier*, and in many other parts. In 1934 she had to leave Germany because she was Jewish; she sang at the German Theater in Prague (1934-36) and was engaged at the Vienna State Opera (1936-38). In 1938 she emigrated to the United States and was a member of the Metropolitan Opera (1943-47). Later she lived and taught in New York.

Records: Her voice is preserved in only one short passage from the Finale of Act II of *Die Walküre* in a complete recording of the opera for HMV; in this scene she substituted for Martha Fuchs as Brünnhilde. *U.S. re-issue:* Electrola.

FLETA, MIGUEL, tenor, b. Dec. 28, 1893, Albalata del Cinca, near Huesca, Spain; d. May 31, 1938, La Coruña, Spain. He studied at the Conservatories in Barcelona and Madrid, then worked temporarily as a miner in Belgium, and made his debut (1919) at the Trieste Opera in *Francesca da Rimini* by Zandonai. He married the soprano Luisa Perrick, but later he was separated from her. He had great success on the Italian operatic stage, where the critics compared his voice to that of Enrico Caruso. In 1922 he sang in the world *première* of *Giulietta e Romeo* at the Teatro Costanzi. He was a member of the Metropolitan Opera (1923-25), singing Cavaradossi in *Tosca* at his debut, and he made regular guest appearances at the Teatro Colón (1922-27). He was greatly admired at La Scala, Covent Garden, the Paris Opéra, and in Vienna, Madrid, Barcelona, Rome, and Budapest. On Apr. 25, 1926, at La Scala he sang the role of Prince Kalaf in the world *première* of *Turandot*. He was re-engaged for the 1926-27 season at the Metropolitan Opera, but he did not appear there, ostensibly because he was required to undergo compulsory military training in Spain. From this grew a legal action between the singer and the directorate of the Metropolitan, which was settled against him in 1931. After 1928 he sang exclusively in Spain, where he enjoyed enormous popularity. During the Spanish Civil War he sided with General Franco and was condemned to death *in absentia* by his opponents. He died in 1938 after an operation. Possessing a superbly trained bright lyric tenor voice with great powers of expression, he was particularly admired in lyric roles.

Records: Victor* and HMV. *U.S. re-issue:* HRS. *U.S. re-recording:* Scala, Eterna, ASCO, TAP.

FOERSTER-LAUTERER, BERTHA, soprano, b. Jan. 11, 1869, Prague; d. Apr. 9, 1936, Prague. She was a student of Antonia Plodková and of Tauwitz in Prague and made her debut at the National Theater there (1888) as Agathe in *Der Freischütz*. In 1890 she married the composer Joseph Bohuslav Foerster (1859-1951). In 1892 she made guest appearances with the ensemble of the Prague Opera in Vienna, in connection with the world exposition there. She was greatly admired there as Xenia in *Demitrij*. She remained at Prague until 1893 and from then until 1901 was very successful at the Hamburg Opera. In 1901 she was engaged by the Vienna Imperial Opera. She sang there under Mahler, among others, and made guest appearances in Berlin and Munich. In 1914 she gave up her career and lived and taught thereafter in Prague. She was admired for the beauty of her voice and for the warmth and maturity of her expressiveness.

Records: She made eight rare records for G & T (Vienna, 1903). *U.S. re-recording:* Rococo.

FOHSTRöM, ALMA, soprano, b.

Jan. 2, 1856, Helsinki; d. Feb. 20, 1936, Helsinki. She came of a very musical family; her brother, Karl Ossian Fohström, was a famous cellist and conductor, and her sister, Elin Fohström, was a well-known soprano under the professional name Elina Vandár. She studied with H. Nissen-Saloman in St. Petersburg, Francesco Lamperti in Milan, and Desirée Artôt in Paris. In 1878 she made her debut in Helsinki as Marguerite in *Faust*. Although she undertook very successful guest tours in Europe and America, she had her greatest triumphs in the years 1890-1900 at the Imperial Opera Houses in St. Petersburg and Moscow. She lived in St. Petersburg (1889-1917). In 1909 she appeared publicly for the last time in a performance in Helsinki and thereafter she taught at the St. Petersburg Conservatory. After the 1917 Revolution, she left Russia and taught at the Conservatory in Helsinki, and for a few years in the 1920's she taught at Hoch's Conservatory in Berlin. A coloratura voice of the highest technical finish.

Records: After it had long been thought that she had made no records, a single Pathé disc was found.

FORMICHI, CESARE, baritone, b. Apr. 15, 1883, Rome; d. July 21, 1949, Rome. He originally studied law and was graduated from the University of Rome as a Doctor of Jurisprudence. For a time he practiced law in Rome, but then studied singing with Vincenzo Lombardi, Di Pietro and Luigi Rasi in Rome. After a few trials at small theaters, he made his official debut (1911) at the Teatro Lirico. His career developed quickly and by 1914 he was one of the best-known Italian baritones. He made a tour of Russia in 1914 and also sang at the Teatro Colón, including the role of Klingsor in the first performance there of *Parsifal*. He appeared on the most important Spanish stages, particularly Madrid and Barcelona (1918-22), and in the latter year first sang at the Paris Opéra, where he appeared annually thereafter. He also sang in Monte Carlo, Vienna, and Prague. He was the much-admired first baritone of the Chicago Opera (1922-32) and appeared at Covent Garden (1924; 1931; 1933). He returned to the Teatro Colón (1925-26) and in 1934 he was honored at the Copenhagen Opera. In 1934 he sang Iago in *Otello* several times at the Teatro San Carlo and then gave up his career. Thereafter he became an impresario. A baritone voice of extraordinary volume and a particularly dramatic expressiveness.

Records: Columbia* (1911-33; including a complete *Rigoletto* in 1924). U.S. re-recording TAP, FRP, Eterna.

FORNIA, RITA, soprano-contralto, b. 1878, San Francisco; d. Oct. 27, 1922, Paris. Originally Regina Newman. She studied with Emil Fischer and Sofia Scalchi in New York and with Selma Nicklass-Kempner in Berlin. She made her debut at the Hamburg Opera (1901) as Eudoxia in *La Juive*. Further study in Paris with Jean de Reszke followed in 1902. She sang Siebel in *Faust* at the Academy of Music in Brooklyn in 1903 and made an American tour with the Savage Opera Company (1904-06). In 1907 she was engaged by the Metropolitan Opera, making her debut as the Geisha in *Iris*. She sang a great many small roles there, both in the contralto and soprano range. She once stepped into the role of Rosina in *Il Barbiere di Siviglia* without a rehearsal, replacing the indisposed Marcella Sembrich; on another occasion she replaced Emma Eames in *Il Trovatore*. In 1915 she sang in the world *première* of *Mme. Sans-Gêne* and on Dec. 14, 1918, in the world *première* of *Suor Angelica*. She died while on a visit to her sister in Paris.

Records: She sang exclusively for Victor*, except for a single duet record (with May Peterson) for Vocalion*, which was released shortly before her death.

FORRESTER, MAUREEN, contralto, b. July 25, 1930, Montreal, Canada. She studied with Bernard Diamant in Toronto. After she had appeared on the Canadian radio, she made her concert debut in Montreal (1953). In 1956 she had brilliant success at Town Hall in New York, singing in Mahler's *Resurrection Symphony* under the direction of Bruno Walter. She then appeared in concerts with the leading American orchestras, including the Boston, Philadelphia, and San Francisco Symphonies. Her concert tours took her to Germany, Holland, France, Spain, Belgium, and Scandinavia with great success. She has rarely appeared on the stage.

Records: RCA Victor* and DGG. *U.S. re-issue:* Columbia, Westminster, Bach Guild, Vanguard.

FÖRSELL, JOHN, baritone, b. Nov. 6, 1868, Stockholm; d. May 30, 1941, Stockholm. At first he was an officer in the Swedish army, but while he was still a lieutenant he began studying singing at the Royal Academy of Music in Stockholm with Julius Günther. After further study with Willman and Signe Hebe, he made his debut (1896) there as Figaro in *Il Barbiere di Siviglia*. In 1901 he left the army; he sang as guest at the Copenhagen Opera in 1902 and he appeared there regularly (1903-06). He caused a great sensation at Covent Garden as Don Giovanni in 1909 and he sang at the Metropolitan Opera (1909-10). During his entire career he remained a member of the Stockholm Opera, but was extremely active in guest appearances at the same time. He sang in Berlin, Vienna, Amsterdam, Helsinki, Salzburg, and London. In 1909 he was named Singer to the Swedish Court. He was director of the Stockholm Opera (1932-39) and he appeared occasionally as a singer. (He sang Don Giovanni in Copenhagen in 1938.) At the last of his life he was a singing teacher in Stockholm. With a warm and expressive baritone voice, he mastered a repertory of over ninety roles, but his particular starring part was Don Giovanni.

Records: Berliner (Stockholm, 1901-02), G & T, Lyrophone, HMV, and Pathé. *U.S. re-issue:* Victor.

FORST, GRETE, soprano, b. Dec. 16, 1880, Vienna. She studied with Hermine Granichstätten in Vienna. In 1898 she first sang publicly in a school concert in Vienna and made her stage debut (1900) at Cologne as Lucia di Lammermoor. She remained there two years and was then called to the Vienna Imperial Opera, where she also first appeared as Lucia. She enjoyed great success in Vienna and in 1908 sang in the world *première* there of *Ein Wintermärchen*. She remained at Vienna until 1911, but later made concert and guest appearances. She then taught singing in Vienna. As a concert soprano she sang among others, at the Music Festivals of the Lower Rhine. The artistic quality of her coloratura soprano was proved by her technical brilliance and by the soaring lightness of her tone production.

Records: G & T (Vienna, after 1905) and Pathé. *U.S. re-issue:* Opera Disc. *U.S. re-recording:* TAP, Scala, Belcanto, HRS.

FÖRSTEL, GERTRUDE, soprano, b. Dec. 21, 1880, Leipzig; d. June 7, 1950, Bad Godesburg, Germany.

Her father was a member of the Leipzig Gewandhaus Orchestra and she studied piano at the Leipzig Conservatory, making her debut as a pianist (1897). Her voice was discovered by Angelo Neumann, who sent her to Berlin to study with Selma Nicklass-Kempner at his expense. She completed her training with Aglaia von Orgeni in Dresden and made her operatic debut at the German theater in Prague (1900) as Amina in *La Sonnambula*. She remained in Prague until 1906 and then was an honored member of the Vienna Imperial Opera until 1912. In 1911 she sang Sophie in the first Vienna performance of *Der Rosenkavalier*. She appeared at the Bayreuth Festivals (1904-12). In 1910 she sang Pamina in *Die Zauberflöte* at the Salzburg Festival. After 1912 she was generally known as a concert soprano, and she sang in 1920 at the Gustav Mahler Festival in Amsterdam and in 1927 at both the Beethoven Centenary in Vienna and the Bonn Beethoven Festival. Toward the end of her career she taught singing at the Cologne Music High School. In addition to the brilliant technical qualities of her voice, she was admired on both the stage and the concert platform for the delicate nuances of her expression.

Records: G & T (Prague, 1904-06, and Bayreuth 1904), Pathé, and Polydor. *U.S. re-recording:* Rococo.

FORT, LUIGI, tenor, b. Nov. 2, 1907, Turin. He made his debut in 1930 and in the same year gave a few highly successful concerts in Holland. In 1931 he sang Nadir in *Les Pêcheurs des Perles* at the Italian Opera in Holland with overwhelming success. Until 1937 he appeared every year in Holland, where his great popularity continued. In 1935 he sang *L'Orsèolo* at the Maggio Musicale Festival. He came to La Scala in 1936 and sang there in the world *première* of *Il Campiello*. He was a guest at Covent Garden in 1937 and in 1938 at both Antwerp and Glyndebourne Festival. During World War II he scarcely sang at all, being occupied with Italian Resistance. After the end of the war, he was unable to recapture his former success. In 1947 he traveled a few times to Holland, but in 1950 he gave up his career. He had a clear lyric tenor voice of fascinating beauty.

Records: Columbia*.

FORTI, HELENA, soprano, b. Apr. 25, 1884, Berlin; d. May 11, 1942, Vienna. She studied with Karl Schiedemantel in Dresden and with Theodore Emmerich in Berlin. Her debut took place (1906) at Dessau, where she sang Valentine in *Les Huguenots*. She remained at Dessau until 1907; she then sang in Brünn (1908-09), at the German Theater in Prague (1910-11) and at the Dresden Royal Opera (1911-24). In 1914 she was applauded as Sieglinde in *Die Walküre* at the Bayreuth Festival, and was thenceforth deemed a great Wagner soprano. In 1916 in Dresden she sang the role of Myrtocle at the world *première* of *Die Toten Augen*. She made successful guest appearances in Berlin, Vienna, Cologne, Brussels, Amsterdam, and Bucharest. After 1917 she married the *régisseur* and intendant of the Dresden Opera, Walter Bruno Iltz.

Records: Rare Odeon records.

FRANCELL, FERNAND, tenor, b. 1880, Paris; d. February, 1966, Paris. He studied at the National Conservatory in Paris and made his debut at the Opéra-Comique as Vincent in *Mireille* (1906). In 1908 he was highly successful at the Théâtre Gaîté Lyrique in Paris as Wilhelm Meister in *Mignon*, opposite Jean Marié de l'Isle. He had a long starring career at the Opéra-

Comique, where he sang in many world *premières* and first performances. In 1913 he sang Paco there in the Paris *première* of *La Vida Breve.* He scarcely ever appeared outside France. After the end of his active stage career he was for many years professor at the Conservatory in Paris. He had a beautiful and impressive lyric tenor voice.
Records: Odeon.

FRANCESCHI, ENRICO DE, baritone, b. Sept. 3, 1885, Turin; d. Jan. 8, 1945, Turin. After beginning his career in Italy, he appeared in 1917 at the Teatro Colón, where he sang only small parts. He then appeared at the Opera in Rio de Janeiro and in other South American theaters until, in 1919, he became first baritone at the Teatro Colón. After his successes in South America he returned to Italy. In 1923 he sang with great success in *Lucia de Lammermoor* at La Scala with Toti dal Monte and Aureliano Pertile. He was admired at the Teatro Costanzi in 1923-24. In the latter year he sang the part of Mephistopheles in *La Damnation de Faust* at the Arena Festival. He appeared frequently in Palermo (1924-29) and in Parma (1927). He made many guest appearances in Germany and in Switzerland with Max Sauter's Opera Association. He was very much liked in Vienna, where he often appeared in concert. He sang again at La Scala (1937-38) and was an annual guest at the Italian Opera in Holland. (1938-40). During the war he sang on smaller Italian stages. He committed suicide in the last months of World War II. He had a wonderfully trained baritone voice.
Records: Acoustics for Columbia, Fonografia Nazionale, Parlophone (Berlin, 1924) and Edison cylinders; he made a number of electric recordings for Fonotipia and for HMV a complete recording of *Orfeo* (1939). *U.S. re-recording:* Scala, Rococo.

FRANCI, BENVENUTO, baritone, b. July 1, 1892, Pienza, near Siena. He studied at the Accademia di Santa Cecilia in Rome and made his debut at the Teatro Costanzi (1917) as Giannetto in *Lodoletta.* He also sang there in 1921 in the world *première* of *Il Piccolo Marat.* After his first successes in other Italian theaters, he came to La Scala in 1923, making his debut as Amonasro in *Aida* under Toscanini. For more than twenty years he remained one of the most prominent artists at La Scala, singing there in several world *premières: La Cene delle Beffe* (1924) and *I Cavalieri di Ekebù* (1925), among others. In the latter year he was admired at Covent Garden as Scarpia in *Tosca* with Maria Jeritza. After 1926 he sang almost annually at the Teatro Colón in Buenos Aires, but he was never heard in the United States. In 1940 he sang Barak in the first La Scala performance of *Die Frau ohne Schatten.* In 1944 he was brilliantly successful at the Teatro San Carlo and in 1946 made a few guest appearances in London. After a serious accident in Trieste in 1955, he retired from musical life. One of the most beautiful Italian baritone voices of his time; he mastered both Italian roles and Wagner parts, notably that of Hans Sachs.
Records: First for Phonotype (Naples, 1920), then HMV and Columbia* (including *Carmen*). *U.S. re-issue:* Victor.

FRANCILLO-KAUFMANN, HEDWIG, soprano, b. Sept. 30, 1878, Vienna; d. April 1948, Rio de Janeiro. She studied with Franzi Müller and Emilie Dorr in Vienna, then with Aglaia von Orgeni in Dresden and Rosario in Milan. After making her debut (1898) in Stettin, she sang at Wiesbaden (1899-1902), at the Munich Royal

Opera (1902-03), at the Berlin Imperial Opera (1903-05). She was very successful at the Komische Oper (1905-07) and was re-engaged at the Imperial Opera (1907-08). In 1908 she came to the Vienna Imperial Opera, where she sang with great success until 1912, and from 1912-17 she was heard at the Hamburg Opera. After 1917 she undertook guest and concert tours to many cities, including Vienna, Berlin, Brussels, Paris, London, and Munich, as well as to South America. In 1927 she gave up her career and lived as a teacher, first in Berlin and then in Vienna. After World War II, since she was married to a Brazilian, she emigrated to South America. She possessed a trained and beautiful coloratura voice, and she was unexcelled in her mastery of the highest vocal ranges.

Records: Her first records (under the name Hedi Kaufmann) appeared on Berliner Records (1900-01); later she made records for G & T, Parlophone, Artiphone, and Pathé*. *U.S. re-recording:* Rococo.

FRANCL, RUDOLF, tenor, b. Apr. 20, 1920, Ljubljana, Yugoslavia. He studied at the Ljubljana Conservatory with Julius Betetto and made his debut at the Opera there (1948). In 1952 he came to the Belgrade National Opera and in 1958 became a member of the German Opera-on-the-Rhine at Düsseldorf-Duisburg. As guest he sang Pinkerton in *Madama Butterfly* at the Munich State Opera in 1961 and Tamino in *Die Zauberflöte* at the Netherlands Opera in Amsterdam in 1962.

Records: DGG* (including the Italian Singer in *Der Rosenkavalier*).

FRANZ, FERDINAND, baritone, b. Feb. 8, 1906, Kassel, Germany; d. May 25, 1959, Munich. His voice was discovered in a church choir. Without further training he began his career as a bass in 1930. As such he sang at Chemnitz (1932-37) and at the Hamburg Opera (1937-43). In 1943 he was called to the Munich State Opera, where he changed to heroic baritone roles and where his wife, the dramatic soprano Helena Braun, also sang. Regular guest appearances brought him great success at the Vienna State Opera and the Dresden State Opera. In 1940-41 he sang at the Zoppot Festivals. After World War II he appeared as guest at La Scala, Covent Garden, the Teatro San Carlo, and on other famous stages; he was a member of the Metropolitan Opera (1952-53) and also sang at the Salzburg Festivals. He remained a member of the Munich institution until his death, which was caused by a heart attack at the high point of his career. He was one of the best-known singers of his time in the heroic baritone repertory, and he was famous both as a Wagner singer and in concert.

Records: Urania* (including *Die Meistersinger*), DGG* (including *Lohengrin* and *Elektra*), and HMV (*Die Walküre*). *U.S. re-issue:* Electrola, Angel, Vox, Remington, Seraphim.

FRANZ, PAUL, tenor, b. Nov. 30, 1876, Paris; d. April, 1950, Paris. Originally François Gauthier. At first he worked on railroads, but after he had won a singing contest for amateurs in 1907 he was engaged by the Paris Opéra. His career then developed quickly and he sang Samson in the first performance in England of *Samson et Dalila* at Covent Garden (1909). In Paris he was especially famous as a Wagner tenor and in 1914 he sang the title role in the first Paris performance of *Parsifal*. The center of his artistic life remained the Paris Opéra, where he appeared for many years, although he made guest appearances on other important French stages and in Brussels. After the end of his singing career he taught in Paris. With his large-dimensioned tenor voice of great dramatic intensity, he remains unmatched in France as a Wagner singer.

Records: HMV, Columbia, and Pathé. *U.S. re-recording:* FRP, TAP, Eterna.

FREMSTAD, OLIVE, soprano, b. Mar. 14, 1871, Stockholm; d. Apr. 21, 1951, Irvington-on-Hudson, near New York City. Originally Olivia Rundquist. She came as a child of ten to the United States, and early appeared in public as a pianist; later she studied singing. In 1893 she went to Europe and studied with Lilli Lehmann in Berlin. Lehmann increased her vocal range so that she could sing soprano parts. She made her debut (1894) at Cologne as Azucena in *Il Trovatore*, and she remained there for six years. She sang in the Bayreuth Festival of 1896 and in 1897 at Covent Garden, appearing as Venus in *Tannhäuser*. She was engaged at the Munich Royal Opera (1900-03) and was then called to the Metropolitan Opera, where she made her debut as Sieglinde in *Die Walküre*. She was brilliantly successful in 1906 as Carmen at the Metropolitan and in 1907 she created the role of Salome at the American *première* of the opera of the same name. She made guest appearances at the Paris Opéra in *Armide* under Toscanini in 1910 and also sang at the Chicago and Boston Opera Houses. She remained at the Metropolitan until 1914 and later gave concerts. In 1920 she gave her farewell concert in New York and later became a teacher there. She had a sumptuous soprano voice, at its best in the Wagner repertory.

Records: She made relatively few records for American Columbia*. *U.S. re-issue:* IRCC, CRS. *U.S. re-recording:* IRCC, TAP, Rococo, FRP, Columbia, Audio Rarities.

FRENI, MIRELLA, soprano, b. Feb. 27, 1935, Modena, Italy. She made her debut (1955) in Modena as Micaëla in *Carmen*. After her marriage and the birth of a child, she again took up her career in 1957. Further study with Campogalliani followed, and in 1958 she won the first prize in the Concorso Viotti in Vercelli. She then had great successes in all the most important stages both in Italy and abroad. In 1959 she appeared at the Holland Festival and in 1960 at the Glyndebourne Festival as Zerlina in *Don Giovanni*. In 1961 at Covent Garden she sang both Zerlina in *Don Giovanni* and Nanetta in *Falstaff*. In 1962 she opened the season at the Piccolo Scala in *Serse*. Since 1963 she has been highly successful at La Scala in a great many roles. She later made guest appearances at the Wiesbaden Festival, at the Vienna State Opera, and in other centers of international musical life. In 1965 she came to the Metropolitan Opera. She appeared as Mimi in a notable film of *La Bohème*. She has a beautifully expressive voice, at home in both lyric and coloratura roles.

Records: Ariola, RCA Victor* (*Carmen* and *Falstaff*), Decca, and Columbia (*La Bohème*). *U.S. re-issue:* London, Angel.

FRIANT, CHARLES, tenor, b. 1890, Paris; d. Apr. 22, 1947, Paris. At first an actor and dancer, he studied singing and made his debut as an opera singer in 1914. He came to the Paris Opéra-Comique in 1916 and was highly successful there until 1939. In this long period of time he was applauded as Don José in *Carmen*, Des Grieux in *Manon*, Werther, Cavaradossi in *Tosca*, and in many other roles. In 1923 he sang at the Opéra-Comique in the world *première* of *La Hulla*. He made guest appearances at the opera houses in Brussels, Nice, Monte Carlo, and in the French provinces.

Records: His first records appeared for Pathé, then for HMV; electric records for Odeon, *U.S. re-issue:* American Decca. *U.S. re-recording:* Eterna.

FRICK, GOTTLOB, bass, b. July 28, 1908, Ölbrönn, Germany. The youngest of thirteen children, he grew up in a Swabian forester's home. He began his career as a singer in the chorus at the Stuttgart State Opera, but studied singing during this time. His debut as a soloist occurred (1934) in Coburg. He then sang in Freiburg im Br. and Königsberg, and in 1938 came to the Dresden State Opera. After World War II he began an international starring career. He was frequently engaged at the opera houses in Vienna, Hamburg, and Munich and after 1951 sang at the Bayreuth Festivals, where he was esteemed one of the most important Wagner singers in his voice range. After successful guest appearances at La Scala, Covent Garden, the Paris Opéra, in Brussels and Amsterdam, and at the Salzburg Festivals, he became a member of the Metropolitan Opera in 1950 and had great success in the United States. He has a large, deep bass voice, great dramatic expressiveness, and a fine feeling for style. He is particularly famous as a Wagner singer, but is also well-known in *buffo* roles.

Records: There are a great many records of his voice on HMV, Urania*, Columbia, and DGG* (including *Fidelio, Die Entführung aus dem Serail, Lohengrin, Die Meistersinger, Die Walküre, Die Kluge,* and *The Bartered Bride*). *U.S. re-issue:* Angel, Electrola, Bruno, London, Seraphim.

FRIEDRICH, ELISABETH, soprano, b. 1893, Karlsruhe, Germany. She studied with Mary Esselsgroth-von Ernst in Karlsruhe and made her debut there (1917), remaining until 1923. She sang at the Frankfurt a. M. Opera (1923-30), and at the Berlin City Opera (1930-44) with great success. There, in 1932, she sang the role of Astarte in the world *première* of *Der Schmied von Gent.* She made guest appearances at the Vienna State Opera in 1928 and 1931. She was esteemed both as a Wagner interpreter and as a lyric-dramatic soprano.

Records: Parlophone (duets with Carl Hartmann and Friedel Schuster) and Electrola. *U.S. re-issue:* American Decca, Capitol-Telefunken.

FRIEDRICHS, FRITZ, baritone, b. Jan. 13, 1849, Braunschweig, Germany; d. May 15, 1918, Königslutter, Germany. Originally Fritz Christofes. He worked first as a carpenter, but after 1869 became a chorister and performer in small acting roles in Braunschweig and later in Potsdam, Stettin, Elbing, St. Gallen, and Düsseldorf. In 1883 he came to the Municipal Theater in Nuremberg and there, in 1884, without any special training, began his career as an opera singer. He continued in Nuremberg until 1886 and in Bremen until 1890. In 1888 he sang Beckmesser at the Bayreuth Festival and had an overwhelming success. From 1890-93 a nervous difficulty limited him to a few isolated appearances in concert. In 1896 he was admired at Bayreuth as Alberich in the *Ring* cycle and in 1902 as Klingsor in *Parsifal.* After 1896 he was engaged again at Bremen, but made a large number of guest appearances elsewhere. During the 1899-1900 season he sang at the Metropolitan Opera and also appeared in Berlin, Vienna, London, and Hamburg. The last sixteen years of his life were passed in mental darkness.

Records: Two records of popular songs on the obscure Globus label; they are of the greatest rarity.

FRIJSCH, POVLA, soprano, b. Aug. 3, 1881, Aarhus, Denmark; d. July 10, 1960, Blue Hills, Maine. Originally Paula Frisch. The daughter of a physician, she first studied piano and music theory at the Copenhagen Conservatory; then she studied singing with Jean Périer and Sarah de Lalande in Paris. She gave her first concert in Paris in 1907. In 1910 she sang there under Gustav Mahler and also in 1911 in the Liszt Centenary. She made a tour of Holland (1912-13). She was often accompanied in her song recitals by the famous pianist Alfred Cortot. She appeared in Copenhagen in 1913, and in 1915 sang in concerts in New York before beginning an American concert tour. During World War I she sang for French soldiers. She rarely appeared on the operatic stage, but in 1919 she sang Ingeborg in *Drog og Marsk* at the Copenhagen Opera, and later in Paris she sang in *L'Incoronazione di Poppea* at the Théâtre des Arts. Triumphal concert tours all over the world marked the later career of this artist. She lived in Copenhagen (1928-30) and then in Paris. In 1940 she came to New York, where she taught at the Juilliard School of Music. Povla Frijsch belongs with the greatest song interpreters of the twentieth century. She was unequalled in the art of expression and in the delicate feeling she had for style. She was particularly famous as an interpreter of French songs.

Records: HMV and RCA Victor*.

FRIND, ANNIE, soprano, b. Feb. 2, 1900, Nixdorf, Bohemia. After 1914 she studied with Frau Köhler-Riese in Dresden. She sang in concerts in the Dresden Kreuzkirche in 1916 and followed this with study until 1922 with Grete Merrem-Nikisch there. She made her debut (1922) at the Berlin Volksoper and was then soubrette as the Munich State Opera (1925-27). Later she sang particularly at the Dresden State Opera and the German Opera House in Berlin. She made guest appearances in Paris, The Hague, Amsterdam, Prague, Riga, Copenhagen, and London. In 1928 she had a brilliant success at the Metropol Theater in Berlin in the *première* of *Casanova*. Thereafter she was a much-esteemed operetta diva in Berlin, but she also appeared regularly at the German Opera House there until 1932. During World War II she sang for soldiers at the front and worked as a volunteer nurse. After she had married a Czech in 1945, she emigrated to the United States, where she lived and taught in New Orleans.

Records: HMV and many operetta selections for Odeon. *U.S. re-issue:* Capitol-Telefunken. *U.S. re-recording:* ASCO, Rococo.

FUCHS, EUGEN, baritone, b. 1895, Nuremberg. He studied at the Conservatory in Nuremberg, made his debut there (1914), and remained there until 1920. After engagements in Saarbrücken and Wroclaw, he sang at Freiburg i. Br. (1927-30). In 1930 he was called to the Berlin State Opera, of which he was a member for thirty years. He made guest appearances at Covent Garden and in Rome, Paris, and Amsterdam. He sang at the Bayreuth Festivals (1933-34) and again in 1943 when he appeared as Beckmesser; he also sang Hans Foltz in *Die Meistersinger* there (1956-61).

Records: Relatively few records, mostly for Columbia* and DGG (*Martha*). *U.S. re-issue:* Urania, RCA Victor, Capitol-Telefunken. *U.S. re-recording:* Rococo.

FUCHS, MARTHA, soprano, b. Jan. 1, 1898, Stuttgart. She began her studies at the Stuttgart Conservatory and completed them in Munich and Milan. Her career began in 1923 as a concert contralto. After five years as a concert singer, she made her stage debut, still as a contralto, at Aachen. After 1930 she sang at the Dresden State Opera, where her voice changed to a dramatic soprano. There in 1935 she sang in the world *première* of *Die Schweigsame Frau*. After 1935 she was under a simultaneous contract with the Berlin State Opera and the Dresden house. She sang Annina in *Der Rosenkavalier* at the Salzburg Festival in 1930, but by then she had become known as one of the most famous Wagner sopranos of her generation. She was a center of attraction at the Bayreuth Festivals (1933-43), singing Isolde and Kundry, and particularly Brünnhilde to great applause. In 1933 and in 1935-37 she appeared in Wagner operas in Amsterdam. In 1936 she appeared as guest with the ensemble of the Dresden State Opera at Covent Garden, singing Donna Anna in *Don Giovanni*, the Marschallin in *Der Rosenkavalier*, and Ariadne in *Ariadne auf Naxos*. In 1938 she sang Isolde at the Théatre des Champs-Elysées. After 1945 she lived in Stuttgart, where she occasionally gave concerts and made guest appearances. She had a large, dark-timbred soprano voice, and her intensity of expression in Wagner roles produced an unforgettable effect.

Records: Telefunken (duets from *Arabella*), HMV (*Die Walküre* and songs for the Hugo Wolf Society), Urania (*Der Corregidor*), and DGG. U.S. re-issue Electrola, RCA Victor, Seraphim.

FÜGEL, ALFONS, tenor, b. Aug. 10, 1912, Bonlanden, near Biberach, Germany; d. November, 1960, Bonlanden. He was originally a tilesetter. After his naturally beautiful voice had been discovered, he sang for the intendant of the Munich State Opera, Clemens Krauss, and began a brief study of singing. He made his debut in Ulm (1938) and from there he went in 1940 to the Munich State Opera, where he was very successful. On Oct. 28, 1942, he sang the part of the Italian singer in the world *première* of *Capriccio*. He remained at Munich until 1945, but because of the circumstances of the times he was unable to win an international career. After World War II he made guest appearances in Stuttgart and Ulm and also appeared as a concert singer. His impressive lyric tenor voice was admired in both the Italian repertory and in songs.

Records: A few records for DGG.

FUGÈRE, LUCIEN, bass, b. July 22, 1848, Paris; d. Jan. 15, 1935, Paris. At the age of fourteen he was apprenticed to a sculptor. Since he could not enter the National Conservatory, he studied in evening classes with Ragueneau and Edouard Batiste. He made his first public appearance (1871) at the café-concert Ba-ta-clan in Paris. In 1874 he came to the Bouffes Parisiens, an operetta theater. In 1877 he was called to the Opéra-Comique, where he made his debut as Jean in *Les Noces de Jeannette*. For a generation he was the best-loved artist at the Comique. There he appeared in many world *premières*: *Le Roi Malgré Lui* (1887), *Las Basoche* (1890), *Phryné* (1893), *La Vivandière* (1895), *Cendrillon* (1899), *La Fille de Tabarin* (1901), and *Fortunio* (1907). On Feb. 2, 1901, he sang the role of the Father in the world *première* of *Louise*. This much-admired artist made only very rare guest appearances—for example, at Covent Garden (1897) and in Nice and Marseilles (1906-10). During World War I he gave many concerts for French soldiers. His career was one of the longest that any musician—particularly any singer—ever had. In 1927 he celebrated the fiftieth anniversary of his stage debut and in 1932 he was still appearing at the Opéra-Comique. He was noted for the subtlety of his expressiveness and the sovereign mastery of his singing technique as well as for his skill in acting.

Records: A few rare records for Zonophone appeared in 1902, but no others were issued until Columbia released some electric records in 1928. *U.S. re-recording:* TAP, FRP, IRCC.

FUSATI, NICOLA, tenor, b. 1885 (?), Rome. Originally Nicola Fusacchia. He studied medicine at the University of Rome and passed his state examination, but in 1907 he made his debut as a singer. In 1908 he was admired in Palermo and in 1915 at the Teatro Costanzi as the title hero in *Ernani*. He was also applauded in the same role at La Scala in 1917. He sang at all the important Italian theaters. In 1925 he appeared at the Arena Festival in *Mosè in Egitto* and in 1929 he made a guest appearance at Covent Garden as Pollione in *Norma* with Rosa Ponselle. After his retirement from the stage he lived in Rome. He had a powerful and impressive heroic tenor voice.

Records: He made acoustic records for Fonotipia and Edison Bell, and electric records for HMV (including the title role in *Otello*, 1932). *U.S. re-issue:* RCA Victor. *U.S. re-recording:* Camden.

G

GADSKI, JOHANNA, soprano, b. June 15, 1872, Anklam, Pomerania, Germany; d. Feb. 22, 1932, Berlin, after an auto accident. She was a pupil of Frau Schröder-Chaloupka in Stettin and made her debut at the age of seventeen at the Kroll Opera as Agatha in *Der Freischütz* (1889). Further engagements followed: Stettin (1889-90), Mainz (1890-91), again in Stettin (1891-92), at the Kroll Opera (1892-93), and in Bremen (1893-95). After a concert tour through Holland (1895-97), she visited the United States with the Damrosch Opera Company. She was admired at the Bayreuth Festival (1899) as Eva in *Die Meistersinger*. She sang regularly at Covent Garden (1899-1901). In 1900 she came to the Metropolitan Opera, making her debut as Senta in *Der Fliegende Holländer*. Here she went from triumph to triumph and was a celebrated prima donna until 1917. In 1905 and 1906 she was one of the chief attractions at the Munich Opera Festival and at the Salzburg Mozart Festivals she sang Donna Elvira in *Don Giovanni* (1906) and Pamina in *Die Zauberflöte* (1910). In 1917 she had to leave the United States on the outbreak of war with Germany, where her husband, Hans Tauscher, was a member of the German military. She then lived in Berlin and gave concerts and made guest appearances. In 1928 she assembled the German Opera Company, with which she made a two-year tour through the United States. With a wonderfully trained soprano voice she was valued for her sweepingly dramatic ability, particularly in Wagner roles.

Records: Her records all appeared after 1903 for Victor*. She also is heard on a few Mapleson cylinders. *U.S. re-issue* IRCC, HRS, Opera Disc, RCA Victor. *U.S. re-recording:* RCA Victor, Belcanto, IRCC, Cantilena, Rococo.

GAILHARD, PIERRE, bass, b. Aug. 1, 1848, Toulouse; d. Oct. 12, 1918, Paris. After his study at the Conservatory of Paris he made his debut (1867) at the Opéra-Comique, but transferred to the Paris Opéra in 1872 and his career was mainly centered there. During the forty-five years of his career he sang at both great opera houses of the French metropolis in seventeen world *premières*. In 1884 he was chosen for the directorate of the Opéra, where he served first with Ritt, then with E. Bertram (1893-99), and thereafter alone. He also appeared as a singer during this time until he gave up his career in 1907.

Records: Four excessively rare records of his voice appeared on Fonotipia (Paris, 1905) under the name Pedro Gailhard. *U.S. re-recording:* TAP.

GALEFFI, CARLO, baritone, b. June 4, 1882, Rome; d. Sept. 22, 1961, Rome. A pupil of Antonio Cotogni in Rome, he made his debut there (1907) as Amonasro in *Aïda* at the Teatro Quirino. In 1910 he came to the Metropolitan Opera, where he first appeared as the elder Germont in *La Traviata* with Nellie Melba. In 1913 he enjoyed a major success at La Scala in the title role of *Nabucco*. In the same year he sang there in the world *première* of *L'Amore dei Tre Re*, and the following year he sang Amfortas in the La Scala *première* of *Parsifal*. He was admired at the Chicago Opera (1914 and 1920). During the 1920's he became one of the most prominent artists at La Scala, being often chosen by Toscanini for various productions. There in 1924 he sang the role of Fanuel in the world *premiére* of Boito's *Nerone*. After 1922 he appeared regularly at the Teatro Colón and other guest appearances took him to Covent Garden, the Paris Opéra, Brussels, Amsterdam, and Vienna. In 1954 at the Teatro Colón he sang the title role in *Gianni Schicchi*. He then lived as a teacher in Argentina and finally in Rome. He had a baritone voice of rare volume and flexibility.

Records: He sang for HMV, including *Nerone* (1924); other acoustic records included Columbia discs and Edison* cylinders. He made electric records for Columbia* (including *La Traviata, I Pagliacci, Andrea Chénier,* and *Martha*). *U.S. re-issue:* Victor. *U.S. re-recording:* FRP.

GALL, YVONNE, soprano, b. Mar. 6, 1885, Paris. She studied at the National Conservatory in Paris and made her debut (1908) at the Paris Opéra, singing one of the Rhine Maidens in the *première* there of *Götterdämmerung*. She was soon one of the great prima donnas of Paris, singing at both the Opéra and the Opéra-Comique. At the latter she created the role of Daphne in the world *première* of *Les Noces Corinthiennes* (1922). She sang at the Chicago Opera (1918-20) and at the nearby Ravinia summer opera (1927-29). She made guest appearances on all the largest stages in Italy, England, Belgium, and Germany with huge success; she also made concert tours of Europe and North America. After her career ended, she held a professorship at the Conservatory in Paris. She had a brilliant soprano voice, filled with shadings of expression; she was outstanding in the French repertory.

Records: Pathé* (including *Roméo et Juliette*) and Columbia*. *U.S. re-recording:* Pathé Actuelle.

GALLI-CURCI, AMELITA, soprano, b. Nov. 18, 1882, Milan; d. Nov. 26, 1963, La Jolla, Calif. She originally studied piano at the Milan Conservatory with Vicenzo Appiani. She began teaching the piano, but after the discovery of her voice, she made her debut, without special study of singing. She first appeared as Gilda in *Rigoletto* at the Teatro Costanzi in 1909. By 1910 she was already singing at La Scala in Milan. This was followed by guest appearances at the leading Italian theaters and by a tour of South America. In November, 1916, the young singer, then entirely unknown made a sensational success in her American debut at the Chicago Opera, again as Gilda. She became world-famous overnight. She sang in Chicago (1916-18) and at the Metropolitan Opera (1921-31), making her debut at the latter in the title role in *Dinorah*. She was soon held to be the greatest coloratura soprano of her time, and at the Metropolitan and in her concerts and guest appearances she went from one triumph to another. She gave up her career in 1936 after a larynx operation. She was married first to the painter Marchese Curci and then to the pianist Homer Samuels (d. 1956). After 1940 she lived in Rancho Santa Fe in California. Amelita Galli-Curci was the first among the coloraturas, not only of her generation, but of the entire century. The floating lightness and the effortless brilliance of her singing have been unmatched since her retirement.

Records: Victor* and HMV, *U.S. re-issue:* HRS. *U.S. re-recording:* RCA Victor, Camden, Belcanto.

GALLOS, HERMANN, tenor, b. Jan. 21, 1886, Vienna; d. Feb. 20, 1957, Vienna. At first he studied law at the University of Vienna, but then took up singing at the Conservatory of the city of Vienna with Philipp Forstén. He entered the Singing Society of the Vienna Academy and his voice was discovered while he was on a tour of the United States with this organization. He made his debut (1915) at the Vienna Imperial Opera, where he spent his entire long career. He became first *buffo* tenor there and obtained an almost unbelievable degree of admiration from the opera-going public of the Austrian metropolis. In 1922 he sang Pedrillo in *Die Entführung aus dem Serail* at the Salzburg Festival, and he appeared there almost every year thereafter, as Valzacchi in *Der Rosenkavalier*, Jaquino in *Fidelio*, Monostatos in *Die Zauberflöte*, and in other parts. He was also a very famous concert and oratorio singer, and as such had brilliant success in the concerts he gave at the Salzburg Festivals. He appeared at the Vienna State Opera almost until the time of his death. After 1937 he was also active as a professor at the Vienna Academy of Music.

Records: Polydor (Valzacchi in an abbreviated version of *Der Rosenkavalier*, 1934), Christschall, Decca (a small role in *Die Meistersinger* about 1952), *U.S. re-issue:* Richmond. *U.S. re-recording:* Angel.

GALVANY, MARIA, soprano, b. 1878, Granada, Spain; d. Nov. 2, 1949, Rio de Janeiro. She made her debut at the age of eighteen and became well known first in Spain and then about the turn of the century in Italy. She sang at various theaters, including La Scala, and undertook highly successful guest tours, particularly in Spain, Portugal, and South America. At times she traveled with her own opera troupe, as in 1905 when she toured Holland, Belgium, and France. The end of her brilliant career was, however, unfortunate. After World War I she was heard no more; she lived in great poverty in South America and died suddenly in a charity hospital in the Brazilian metropolis. Her coloratura soprano was characterized by a phenomenal mastery of singing technique and by the uncommonly brilliant quality of her delivery in the most difficult coloratura passages.

Records: G & T (Milan, about 1903), HMV, Pathé*, and Edison* cylinders. *U.S. re-issue:* Victor, HRS, IRCC, Opera Disc. *U.S. re-recording:* HRS, TAP, Scala, Eterna, Rococo, Belcanto, Audio Rarities.

GARBIN, EDOARDO, tenor, b. 1865, Padua; d. Apr. 12, 1943, Brescia. He studied in Milan with Alberto Selva and Vittorio Orefice, and made his debut (1891) in Vicenza as Alvaro in *La Forza del Destino*. He then appeared as guest artist at the Teatro dal Verme, the Teatro San Carlo, the Genoa Opera, before coming to La Scala. There, on Feb. 6, 1893, he created the role of Fenton in the world *première* of *Falstaff*, while his wife, the soprano Adelina Stehle, created the role of Nanetta. In 1900 he again sang at La Scala, this time creating the role of Dufresne in the world *première* of *Zaza*. Although he sang principally at La Scala and at the Teatro Costanzi, he also appeared as guest at the Vienna and Berlin Imperial Operas, at the Teatro São Carlos, the Teatro Liceo, Covent Garden, the Opéra-Comique, and the opera houses in Odessa and Warsaw. In 1898 he and his wife sang together at the Teatro Massimo in a brilliant production of *La Bohème*, a production which determined the success of the opera. At the end of his life he taught in Milan. With a highly expressive lyric tenor voice he was greatly admired in a wide-ranging repertory.

Records: G & T (Milan, 1903) and Fonotipia. *U.S. re-issue:* Columbia, Victor. *U.S. re-recording:* TAP, Scala, Rococo.

GARDEN, MARY, soprano, b. Feb. 20, 1874, Aberdeen, Scotland; d. Jan. 3, 1967, Aberdeen. She came from a Scottish family which emigrated to the United States. She studied singing in Paris with Trabadello and Lucien Fugère and made her debut at the Opéra-Comique (1900), taking over for a colleague who had become ill during a performance in the title role in *Louise*; this part thereupon became, and remained, one of her chief starring roles. Her triumphant debut was a musical sensation and she remained at the Opéra-Comique until 1906. She sang there in several world *première* performances: *La Fille de Tabarin* (1901), *Chérubin* (1905), and *Aphrodite* (1906). On Apr. 30, 1902, she created the role of Mélisande in the world *première* of *Pelléas et Mélisande*, a role which proved to be an additional starring part during her later career. After extremely successful guest appearances in London, she sang at the Manhattan Opera House (1907-10). She was particularly successful there as Salome. In 1910 she went to the Chicago Opera, where she remained for twenty years as the true prima donna of the house. She was the "directa" there (1922-23). She was largely responsible for making the American Middle West acquainted with the vast and unknown repertory of French operatic literature. In 1930 she returned to the Opéra-Comique for four seasons, making occasional appearances. Her final role there was Katiushka in *Risurrezione* in 1934. She later made wide-ranging lecture tours in the United States and in England. After 1939 she lived in Aberdeen. She published her memoirs under the title *Mary Garden's Story* (New York, 1951). She had a sumptuous and well-trained soprano voice, filled with excitingly dramatic qualities, which made her one of the greatest actresses who ever appeared on the operatic stage.

Records: Relatively few records for G & T (Paris, 1904, including Debussy songs with the composer at the piano), Columbia*, Pathé*, and Edison* cylinders. There are also electric records made for Victor*. *U.S. re-issue:* IRCC. *U.S. re-recording:* IRCC, TAP, FRP, Design, Scala, Columbia, RCA Victor, Odyssey.

GARMO, HARRY DE, baritone, b. Apr. 19, 1887, Detroit, Mich.; d. Apr. 21, 1919, Wiesbaden, Germany. The son of a Spaniard and an Englishwoman, he went to Germany to study medicine. After the discovery of his voice he made his debut (1910) at the Hamburg Opera and remained there until 1912. He sang in Lübeck (1912-14) and thereafter at the Royal Theater in Wiesbaden. In 1914 he married the soprano Tilly Jonas (see following biography). He was engaged at the Metropolitan Opera for the 1917-18 season, but the outbreak of the war hindered his leaving Germany for New York. In 1919 he was again engaged by the Metropolitan, but he died a few days before his departure. He had a baritone voice of full dramatic expressiveness and great flexibility.

Records: HMV, Odeon, and Parlophone. *U.S. re-issue:* Opera Disc.

GARMO, TILLY DE, soprano, b. Apr. 3, 1888 (?), Dresden. Originally Mathilde Jonas. She studied at the Stern Conservatory in Berlin and then with Curt Hoche in Wiesbaden. In 1914 she married the American baritone Harry de Garmo, who had been engaged at Wiesbaden, where she made her debut (1914). She sang in Elberfeld (1921-23) and at the German Theater in Prague (1923-26). In 1924 she married the conductor Fritz Zweig. She was a much-esteemed member of the Berlin State Opera (1926-33). In 1933 she left Germany for Paris and sang and taught there. In 1940 she fled to North America; she lives and teaches in Hollywood. A virtuoso coloratura voice of great beauty.

Records: Relatively few electric records for HMV and Polydor. *U.S. re-issue:* RCA Victor.

GARRIS, JOHN, tenor, b. 1911, Frankfurt a. M.; d. Apr. 21, 1949, Atlanta, Ga. Originally Hans Gareis. He was the son of the baritone Joseph Gareis, who sang for many years at the Opera in Frankfurt.

John Garris studied at the Music High School in Frankfurt, then was active as a conductor and piano accompanist. In 1939 he came to New York, where he first worked as a *répiteteur* at the Metropolitan Opera. After his beautiful voice had been discovered, he made his debut at the Metropolitan (1942). He remained a member of that company until his tragic death. He sang *buffo* tenor roles especially, but also appeared in lyric parts. In April, 1949, the Metropolitan Opera made its usual spring tour. In Atlanta Garris disappeared shortly before the departure of the train on which the company was traveling. He was later found murdered in another quarter of the city. The mystery of his murder has never been solved.

Records: His only official recordings are *La Traviata* under Toscanini, in which he sings the role of Gaston and a part in the *Romeo et Juliette Symphony* of Berlioz, both for RCA Victor*. He also sang in a recording of the Quintet from *Die Meistersinger* for Columbia*. A great many unpublished recordings of broadcasts from the Metropolitan also exist.

GARRISON, MABEL, soprano, b. Apr. 24, 1886, Baltimore, Md.; d. Aug. 15, 1963, Northampton, Mass. She studied with Odenthal in Baltimore and at the Peabody Conservatory there with Heimendahl. In 1908 she married the professor of harmony George Siemonn, and then studied further with Oscar Saenger and Herbert Witherspoon in New York. She made her debut (1912) with the Aborn Opera Company as Philine in *Mignon*. She was engaged at the Metropolitan Opera (1913-20) and was successful there. In 1921 she made guest appearances at the Berlin State Opera, in Hamburg, and at the Cologne Opera. In the same year she

made a world tour, singing in concert. She was a member of the Chicago Opera (1925-26). She was a teacher at Smith College in Northampton after 1933. She had an admirably trained coloratura voice, as she demonstrated in both opera and in concert.
Records: Victor*.

GARRISON, MAX, baritone, b. Apr. 18, 1867, New York; d. July 14, 1927, Berlin. He studied violin and became the first violinist of the Metropolitan Opera orchestra in New York. He then went to Germany in 1890 to study singing and completed his studies at the Dresden Conservatory. He sang at Elberfeld (1893-97), at the Breslau Opera (1897), at the Vienna Imperial Opera (1897-98), and at Königsberg (1898-99). He sang at Graz (1899-1900) and at the Theater an der Wien (1900-02). He toured Russia with an Austrian operetta company (1901-02) and later became a concert singer in Berlin. He was the director of the Lortzing Theater, once a much-loved operetta theater in Berlin.
Records: Odeon (Berlin, 1905), Favorite (Berlin, 1906), and Edison* cylinders.

GATTI, GABRIELLA, soprano, b. July 5, 1916, Rome. At first she studied piano but then changed to singing at the Accademia di Santa Cecilia in Rome. In 1934 she won first prize in a singing contest there. In December, 1934, she made her debut in a concert performance of *Orfeo.* In 1937 she was admired at the Rome Opera and in 1937 and 1938 at the Arena Festivals as Elena in *Mefistofele* and as Elisabeth in *Tannhäuser.* In 1939-40 she was highly applauded at the Maggio Musicale Festival, both as Semiramide in Rossini's opera of the same name and as Iphigénie in *Iphigénie en Tauride.* In 1940 she made her debut at La Scala as Rezia in *Oberon,* and she had great successes at that house. She also gave brilliant concerts in London. Later she worked as a teacher at the Accademia di Santa Cecilia in Rome. Her soprano voice was outstanding, both for the coloration of its timbre and for the delicacy of her feeling for style.
Records: Cetra* (including *Le Nozze di Figaro* and Verdi's *Nabucco*) and HMV. *U.S. re-recording:* Seraphim.

GAUTHIER, EVA, soprano, b. Sept. 20, 1885, Ottawa, Canada; d. Dec. 26, 1958, New York. As a young girl she sang contralto parts in a church choir in Ottawa. In 1901 she created a sensation in a recital she gave in Ottawa and was sent to Europe for further study. She studied with Dubulle and Bouhy in Paris, with William Shakespeare in London, and with Anna Schoen-Rene in Berlin. In 1905 she had great success in a Paris concert. After renewed study with Giuseppe Oxilia in Milan she made her stage debut (1910) at the Teatro Regio in Parma, now as a soprano, in the role of Micaëla in *Carmen.* In 1911 she married a Dutch citizen, with whom she went to Batavia in Java. In 1916 she was separated from him and returned to the United States. She then gave highly successful concerts here, in which she interpreted exclusively works by contemporary masters, mostly songs. She was particularly friendly with the composers Schoenberg, Satie, Ravel, Honneger, and Poulenc and was considered a fine interpreter of their songs. Her career lasted until the outbreak of World War II.
Records: Victor*, Columbia* (issued under the name S. Gauthier), and Musicraft*. *U.S. re-issue:* IRCC. *U.S. re-recording:* Town Hall.

GAY, MARIA, contralto, b. June 13, 1879, Barcelona; d. July 29, 1943, New York. She originally wanted to be a sculptress, but at the same time she taught herself singing. She appeared for the first time (1902) in Brussels in a concert where she sang with the pianist Raoul Pugno and the violinist Eugène Ysaye. She made her debut in the same year at the Brussels Opera as Carmen. Further study with Ada Adini in Paris followed and she had great success on the stage in France and Italy. After 1906 she was often a guest at Covent Garden. She sang at the Metropolitan Opera (1908-09), making her debut as Carmen opposite Enrico Caruso. She appeared with the Boston Opera Company (1910-12). In 1913 she married the tenor Giovanni Zenatello. In 1913 she sang at the Arena Festival as Amneris in *Aida* and in 1914 in her special starring role, Carmen. In the years following she appeared as a guest at the largest theaters in Spain, Italy, and South America and for several seasons she was a member of the Chicago Opera. After the close of her career she lived and taught in New York.

Records: G & T (HMV), Columbia*, Favorite, and electric records for Victor.* *U.S. reissue:* Victor. *U.S. re-recording:* Scala, FRP, Columbia, TAP.

GEDDA, NICOLAI, tenor, b. July 11, 1925, Stockholm. His father was a bass in the Don Cossack Choir and his mother was Swedish. He passed his early days in Leipzig, where his father was cantor for the Russian Orthodox congregation. In 1934 he returned to Sweden. By chance his voice was discovered and he studied with Carl Martin Öhmann in Stockholm. In 1951 he made his debut at the Royal Opera there as Chapdelou in *Le Postillon de Longjumeau*. In 1953 he spent a guest season at La Scala singing Don Ottavio in *Don Giovanni* and in *Trionfi*. Guest appearances followed in Turin and Rome; in 1954 at the Paris Opéra he sang Huon in *Oberon*, and in that year he also appeared at Covent Garden. In 1957 he sang at the Salzburg Festival, where he was greatly admired as Belmonte in *Die Entführung aus dem Serail*. He was then heard regularly at La Scala and the Vienna State Opera. In 1957 he was engaged by the Metropolitan Opera, first appearing in *Faust*. Since then he has been highly successful there, as well as in San Francisco and Chicago. He made a long concert tour of the United States in 1961. With an expressive and musically polished lyric tenor voice, he has been particularly successful in Mozart roles and in the Italian repertory.

Records: Columbia* and RCA-Victor* (including *Faust*, *Mireille*, *Boris Godounov*, *Der Barbier von Bagdad*, *Madama Butterfly*, *Der Rosenkavalier*, *Capriccio*, *A Life for the Czar*, *Il Turco in Italia*, and *Carmen* with Maria Callas). *U.S. re-issue:* Angel, Capitol, Vox, Electrola, Seraphim.

GEISLER, WALTER, tenor, b. 1918 (?), Oppeln, Silesia, Germany. He began his stage career (1939) in Griefswald and sang then at Göttingen, Wiesbaden, and the Hannover Opera. After World War II he was engaged at the Berlin City Opera until 1948, during which time he appeared at the Komische Oper there. He was first heroic tenor at the Hamburg Opera (1948-56) and since then has sung at the Berlin City Opera again. He made very successful guest appearances at the Vienna State Opera, especially in Wagner parts. In 1957 he sang Walther in *Die Meistersinger* at the Beyreuth Festival and in 1960 sang Florestan in *Fidelio* in Amsterdam.

Records: Opera.

GEISSE-WINKEL, NICOLA, baritone, b. Feb. 27, 1872, Bad Ems, Germany; d. Aug. 11, 1932, Wiesbaden, Germany. After first studying at the Universities of Marburg and Strasbourg, he began the study of singing. He made his debut (1905) at Wiesbaden and remained there until 1928. He first sang at the Bayreuth Festival in 1908 and in 1912 had great success there as the Herald in *Lohengrin*. His guest appearances were made at the Vienna and Munich Royal Operas, in Budapest, Amsterdam, and The Hague, as well as on the most important Swiss stages. He committed suicide. He had a heroic baritone voice, outstanding in Wagner roles.

Records: HMV, Anker, Favorite, and Pathe*.

GENCER, LEYLA, soprano, b. 1927, Ankara, Turkey. She studied at the Ankara Conservatory with Elvira de Hidalgo and made her debut in Italy (1952). Since then she has had a highly successful career there, and has sung at La Scala, where in 1957 she appeared in the world *première* of *Les Dialogues des Carmélites*. She appeared frequently in San Francisco after 1956. In 1959 she sang at the Maggio Musicale Festival and at the Spoleto Festival appeared in *The Flaming Angel*. She made guest appearances at the Vienna State Opera in 1961 and also in that year sang Amelia in *Simon Boccanegra* at the Salzburg Festival. In 1965 she sang the title role in *Norma* at the Arena Festival. She is a dramatic soprano who has also mastered the art of coloratura singing.

Records: A few for Cetra.

GENTILE, MARIA, soprano, b. Nov. 17, 1902, Catania, Sicily. She made her debut in 1924. In 1925 she sang at the Italian Opera in Holland and also sang concurrently on the most important Italian stages as well as at the Arena Festival. She was greatly beloved in Latin America, where she appeared at the Havana, Mexico City, and Rio de Janeiro Opera Houses and at the Teatro Colón almost every year. In the 1930's she appeared as guest in the greatest German opera houses. She was married to the conductor Rotondo. After her retirement from the stage, she lived and taught singing in Catania. Her virtuoso coloratura voice had a sweet expressiveness.

Records: Columbia* and Polydor.

GENTNER-FISCHER, ELSE, soprano, b. Sept. 5, 1883, Frankfurt a. M.; d. Apr. 26, 1943, Prien-am-Chiemsee, Germany. She studied in Frankfurt and made her debut there (1905) at the opera house. She then married the tenor Karl Gentner (1876-1922), who was also engaged there. She remained in Frankfurt for her whole career. After having sung small roles at the beginning, she became one of the most famous German dramatic sopranos. She traveled with the German Opera Company in the United States (1923-24). She sang Isolde and Brünnhilde at the Teatro Colón in 1926. She regularly appeared as guest at the Berlin State Opera, the Teatro Liceo, and the Teatro Real. In 1934 she joined the ensemble of the Frankfurt Opera for guest appearances in Holland and was applauded for her Marschallin in *Der Rosenkavalier*. Her second marriage was to the baritone Benno Ziegler, who fled to England in 1934 because he was Jewish. She joined him there and gave up her career. After World War II she lived in retirement in Oberbayern.

Records: Polydor and HMV.

GERHARDT, ELENA, mezzo-soprano, b. Nov. 11, 1883, Leipzig; d. Jan. 11, 1961, London. At the age of sixteen she entered the Leipzig

Conservatory, where Marie Hedmont was her teacher. She was discovered and helped by Arthur Nikisch, and, with him as her accompanist, she gave her first lieder recital in Leipzig in 1903. She sang at the Leipzig Opera (1903-04), but then gave up her stage career to devote herself entirely to lieder singing. She had an enormous success in London in 1906, and in 1912, accompanied by Nikisch, she undertook her first American tour. She traveled in England, Spain, Russia, Holland, and Belgium—all with triumphal success. When her husband, Fritz Kohl, lost his position with the German radio in 1933, she emigrated to England. She settled down in London, resumed her concert activity, and also began teaching. She made phonograph records until 1953. She published her memoirs under the title *Recital* (London, 1953). One of the greatest lieder singers of the twentieth century, unforgettable in the delicacy of her interpretation of texts and spirituality of her singing.

Records: G & T (including those accompanied by Nikisch), HMV, Vocalion*, and American Columbia*. *U.S. re-issue:* IRCC. *U.S. re-recording:* Angel, Rococo.

GERHART, MARIA, soprano, b. 1896, Vienna. She studied at the Conservatory of the city of Vienna with Irene Schlemmer-Ambros. After making her debut (1918) at the Vienna Volksoper, she sang at the Berlin State Opera (1918-19), at the German Theater in Prague (1919-21), and at the Opera in Frankfurt a. M. (1921-22). In 1922 she was called to the Vienna State Opera, where she had brilliant success until 1948. She was admired in the Salzburg Festivals after 1922 in such roles as Konstanze in *Die Entführung aus dem Serail* (1922), Zerbinetta in *Ariadne auf Naxos* (1926), and Fiordiligi in *Così fan tutte* (1928). Her particular starring role remained, however, the Queen of the Night in *Die Zauberflöte*. She made guest appearances in London, Berlin, Paris, Brussels, Milan, and Munich. Since 1947 she has been a professor at the Vienna Academy of Music. One of the coloratura sopranos of importance in her time because of the brilliance of her technique and the spontaneity of her vocal production.

Records: Relatively rare Odeon records.

GERLACH-RUSNAK, RUDOLF, tenor, b. July 24, 1895, Dubloutz, near Czernowicz, Rumania; d, Jan. 23, 1960, Munich. Originally Orest Rusnak. He was of Ukrainian extraction and fought in World War I as an officer in the Austro-Hungarian army. He then studied singing with Egon Fuchs in Prague and made his debut (1923) at Olomouc as Rodolfo in *La Bohème*. He sang at Königsberg (1924-26) and Stettin (1926-27). After further study with Jacques Stückgold in Berlin and with Lari in Milan, he sang in Chemnitz (1928-30) and Graz (1930-31). In 1931 he was engaged by the Munich State Opera and appeared there under the name Rudolf Gerlach-Rusnak. He remained a member of the Munich company until 1937 and later was a guest there as well as at the Vienna State Opera in 1938. In 1944 he was called to duty in an armaments plant, but in 1945 was sent back to the Munich Opera. After a heart attack in 1946, from which he did not entirely recover, he undertook a tour of the United States and Canada (1956-57). He was noted for the dramatic management and the brilliance of tone of his voice.

Records Electrola; his latest records, of Ukrainian folk songs, were made in the United States in 1957.

GERVILLE-RÉACHE, JEANNE, contralto, b. Mar. 26, 1882, Orthez, France; d. Jan. 15, 1915, New York. Her father was the governor of Martinique and Guadaloupe and she came to Paris when she was fifteen to study singing with Rosine Laborde. Through the intercession of Emma Calvé, she was able to finish her studies with Pauline Viardot-Garcia. In 1899 she had a successful debut at the Opéra-Comique in the title role of *Orphée et Eurydice* and on Apr. 30, 1902, she created the role of Geneviève in *Pelléas et Mélisande* there. In 1903 she made guest appearances at the Brussels Opera and in 1905 at Covent Garden. In 1907 she came to the Manhattan Opera. Thereafter she was uncommonly successful in the United States. She also sang in Boston, Philadelphia, Chicago, and Montreal. In 1910 she married the director of the Pasteur Institute in New York, Georges Ribier Rambaud. She had a sumptuous, warm-timbred contralto voice of great dramatic quality.

Records: Rare records for Victor* (1908-11) and one for American Columbia* (1912). *U.S. re-issue:* IRCC, HRS. *U.S. re-recording:* TAP, Scala, Rococo, FRP.

GHIAUROV, NICOLAI, bass, b. 1929, Velimgrad, Bulgaria. The son of a sacristan, he sang as a child in a church choir, but his voice was really discovered during his military service. He began studying in Sofia and completed his training at the Moscow Conservatory (1950-55). He made his debut in Sofia (1955) as Basilio in *Il Barbiere di Siviglia*. In the same year he won first prize at an international singing contest in Paris. Thereupon his starring career began. In 1957 he sang Ramfis in *Aïda* at the Vienna State Opera and also had great success at the Bolshoi Opera. He was greatly admired in 1959 at La Scala, where he has since added other laurels. In 1961 he sang at the Arena Festival and toured Germany with the ensemble of the Sofia Opera. His special successes have been at the Vienna State Opera, the Metropolitan Opera, in Brussels, Liège, and other music centers. He has a large bass voice of the highest powers of expressiveness.

Records: Decca, Columbia (Verdi *Requiem*), Supraphon, Balkanton. *U.S. re-issue:* London, Angel.

GHIRARDINI, EMILIO, baritone, b. 1885 (?); d. July 17, 1965, Ferrara, Italy. He began his studies in 1908 with Lelio Casini and followed his teacher to Argentina, where he made his debut (1910) as Rigoletto at the Teatro Politeamo. Guest appearances followed in Rio de Janeiro, São Paulo, and Santiago de Chile; in 1916 he sang at the Havana Opera. He then returned to Italy and served as a volunteer in the Italian army during World War I. After 1919 he had a successful career in the Italian opera houses, particularly at the Teatro Massimo and the Teatro Costanzi. In 1922 he sang in the Italian Opera in Holland. He first appeared at La Scala in 1930 and in 1934 he made guest appearances at Covent Garden and in Barcelona and Paris. After 1937 he sang at the Rome Opera. Later he taught in Rome.

Records: Electric records for Columbia* (about 1930).

GIANI, NINI, contralto, b. 1907. She began her career in the smaller Italian opera houses about 1930 and sang with the Italian Opera in Holland (1932-33). She appeared as guest at Covent Garden, singing Princess Eboli in *Don Carlos* and Amneris in *Aïda* in 1933. She had many successes at La Scala (1933-45), including among other roles one in the first La Scala production of *Sadko* in 1938. She sang at the Arena Festivals (1932; 1933; 1936) and made very successful appearances in South America, particularly at the Teatro Colón and in Rio de Janeiro. In the last years of her career she sang dramatic soprano parts, such as Santuzza in *Cavalleria Rusticana*. After her marriage to a physician in 1945 she gave up the stage. Her voice was darkly gleaming and passionate.

Records: A few Telefunken records.

GIANNINI, DUSOLINA, soprano, b. Dec. 19, 1902, Philadelphia. She was the daughter of the Italian tenor Ferruccio Giannini (1868-1948) and the pianist Antonietta Briglia-Giannini; her brother Vittorio is a well-known composer. After her first studies with her parents she became a pupil of Marcella Sembrich in Philadelphia. In 1923 she gave her first concert in Carnegie Hall in New York, followed by concerts in London (1924) and in Berlin (1925). In the latter year she made her stage debut at the Hamburg State Opera as Aïda. In 1926-27 she made a series of guest appearances which took her to the State Operas in Berlin, Vienna, and Hamburg. She sang regularly at the latter after 1930. In 1928 she had great success at Covent Garden. At the Salzburg Festivals she sang Donna Anna in *Don Giovanni* (1934-35) and Alice Ford in *Falstaff* under Toscanini (1936). Later guest appearances brought her to the stages in Zürich, Monte Carlo, Oslo, Brussels, Amsterdam, San Francisco, and Mexico City. In 1936 she joined the Metropolitan Opera, making her debut as Aïda; she remained there until 1941. In 1947 she undertook a European tour and appeared as guest at the Berlin State Opera (1949) and at the Vienna State Opera as Carmen (1950). Since 1962 she has conducted an opera studio in Zürich. The fine sound and great volume of her soprano voice were fortunately joined; she was famous as an oratorio and lieder singer.

Records: Victor* and HMV, including a complete *Aïda*. *U.S. re-issue:* Angel.

GIBIN, JOÃO, tenor, b. 1929, Peru. After beginning his study of singing in his native land, he made his first appearance in Lima as a baritone. In 1954 he won the Mario Lanza Prize of the Coca-Cola Corporation and therewith a stipend for further study in Italy. At the La Scala School in Milan he became a tenor. After first successes on the stage in Italy he was offered guest appearances at the Netherlands Opera in Amsterdam in 1958; there he sang Calaf in *Turandot* and *Andrea Chénier*. Since 1958 he has repeatedly appeared at the Vienna State Opera. He was greatly admired also in 1958 when he appeared at Covent Garden in *Lucia di Lammermoor* opposite Joan Sutherland. Since 1960 he has had great success at La Scala. He has also sung under the name Giovanni Gibin. He is particularly famous in the heroic roles in the Italian repertory.

Records: Columbia (including *La Fanciulla del West* with Birgit Nilsson). *U.S. re-issue:* Angel.

GIEBEL, AGNES, soprano, b. Aug. 10, 1921, Heerlen, Holland. She studied at the Folkwang Schools in Essen with Hilde Wesselmann and began her career in 1947 as a concert soprano. She became well known when, in 1950, she sang the soprano solo parts in Bach cantatas which were broadcast weekly by RIAS in Berlin. Since then she has been prized as one of the most famous German concert singers of her generation, particularly as a great interpreter of Bach. She has appeared at many international music festivals and very successfully in all the music centers of Germany, Austria, France, Italy, Belgium, Holland, and Switzerland. She has also made successful American tours. She has never appeared on the stage, however, but has sung operatic roles for radio broadcasts and on records. Her vocal security and clarity and her delicate stylistic sensitivity make each of her vocal interpretations outstanding.

Records: HMV (Bach's *Christmas Oratorio*), L'Oiseau Lyre* (*St. Matthew Passion*), DGG* (*St. John Passion*), and MMS. *U.S. re-issue:* Electrola, Lyrichord, Cantata, Westminster, Harmony, Angel, Turnabout, Nonesuch, Telefunken, Philips, London, Everest-Cetra.

GIGLI, BENIAMINO, tenor, b. Mar. 20, 1890, Recanati, Italy; d. Nov. 30, 1957, Rome. He first worked in a pharmacy, but studied singing in his free time with Lazzarini in Recanati. In 1911 he won a scholarship to the Accademia di Santa Cecilia in Rome and became a pupil of Antonio Cotogni and Enrico Rosati. He made his debut (1914) at Rovigo as Enzo in in *La Gioconda*. In the first years he sang in provincial Italian theaters, but in 1917 he appeared at the Teatro Costanzi, in Madrid, and in Barcelona. On Apr. 17, 1917, he sang opposite Rosina Storchio at the Teatro Costanzi in the world *première* of *Lodoletta*. After guest appearances in Paris and Berlin, Toscanini brought him to La Scala in 1920; there he had a sensational debut as Faust in *Mefistofele*. A world-wide starring career both on the opera stage and in the concert hall followed. After the death of Enrico Caruso he was generally held to be the most famous tenor of his generation. In 1921 he came to the Metropolitan Opera, making his debut there as Andrea Chénier. He belonged to this company until 1931 and again in 1938 and 1939. There was scarcely an opera stage of world rank which was not the scene of his triumphs. In the 1930's he began a film career unequalled among singers. After World War II he often sang, in person and on records, with his daughter, the soprano Rina Gigli (b. Jan. 30, 1916). He gave his last concert in 1955 and lived thereafter on his estate near Recanati. He published his autobiography, *Confidenze* (Rome, 1943). Scarcely any singer except Caruso had a more lasting world fame. The splendor of his voice, the colorful shading of his singing, the minute voice control, especially in *mezza di voce* singing, remain vividly alive on his many phonograph records.

Records: HMV and Victor* (including *La Bohème*, *I Pagliacci*, *Tosca*, *Aïda*, *Andrea Chénier*, *Un Ballo in Maschera*, *Madama Butterfly*, and the Verdi *Requiem*). *U.S. re-issue:* Victor, RCA Victor. *U.S. re-recording:* Victor, Scala, Electrola, Eterna, Pathé-Marconi, Angel, Rococo, TAP, Seraphim.

GILIBERT, CHARLES, baritone, b. Nov. 29, 1866; d. Oct. 10, 1910, New York. He was a student at the National Conservatory in Paris and made his debut there at the Opéra-Comique (1888). In 1889 he came to the Brussels Opera, where he was greatly beloved. He sang annually at Covent Garden (1894-1909) and he was equally admired there. In 1900 he was engaged by the Metropolitan Opera, to which he belonged until 1903. From 1903-06 he again enjoyed great success at the Brussels Opera. He was offered a contract by the Manhattan Opera in 1906 and was so successful that he was re-engaged by the Metropolitan for the 1910-11 season, but he died suddenly a few days before the opening performance. He was married to the Belgian soprano Gabrielle Lejeune, who also made records under the name Mme. Charles Gilibert.

Records: Mapleson and Edison* cylinders and a few rare discs for Victor* and Columbia*. *U.S. re-recording:* Columbia, IRCC, Scala, FRP, Belcanto, RCA Victor, Cantilena, Rococo.

GILLY, DINH, baritone, b. 1877, Algiers; d. May 19, 1940, London. He was the son of a French officer stationed in Algiers and he studied first at the conservatory in Toulouse, then with Antonio Cotogni in Rome, and finally at the Paris Conservatory. He made his debut (1899) at the Paris Opéra as a Priest in *Sigurd*. In the following years he sang at both great opera houses in Paris and in South America, particularly at Teatro Colón—all with great success. Further guest appearances followed in Spain and Germany and at the Monte Carlo Opera. He sang at the Metropolitan Opera (1909-14), making his debut there as Albert in *Werther*. There he sang in the world *première* of *La Fanciulla del West* (1910). In 1911 he came to Covent Garden, remaining as first baritone until 1924, although he was detained in Austria in World War I. He sang his last role at Covent Garden in 1924, appearing as the elder Germont in *La Traviata*. In 1925 he sang occasionally on the British radio; he then lived and taught in London. He had an expressive and fine-sounding baritone voice.

Records: Beka, Odeon, HMV, Victor*, and Edison* cylinders; unpublished Edison discs. *U.S. re-recording:* Belcanto, IRCC, Cantilena, Rococo.

GINSTER, RIA, soprano, b. Apr. 15, 1898, Frankfurt a. M. She studied at Hoch's Conservatory in Frankfurt, then at the Music High School in Berlin with Louis Bechner. In 1923 she gave her first lieder recitals and soon became internationally famous as a lieder singer. Although her repertory included operatic roles, she hardly ever appeared on the stage. She sang in Germany, Austria, Belgium, Holland, England, France, and Switzerland and was highly successful on her tours of the United States and Canada. At the same time she carried on teaching activities in Philadelphia. After 1938 she was professor at the Zürich Music High School and since 1949 she has offered master courses during the Salzburg Festivals. Her beautiful soprano voice was much admired for her management of shading and for the delicacy of her feeling for style. She is a famous and first-rank interpreter of lieder.

Records: Homochord and HMV. *U.S. re-issue:* Victor, American Decca, Rococo.

GIORGINI, ARISTODEMO, tenor, b. 1879, Naples; d. Jan. 19, 1937, Naples. He studied at the Accademia di Santa Cecilia in Rome and, after making his debut without success (1903), he renewed his studies under Massimo Perilli in Naples. His first records appeared in 1904. In 1905 he made a second debut, this time at La Scala as Ernesto in *Don Pasquale*. He then had a famous career at both La Scala and at the other large Italian theaters. In 1910 at La Scala he was highly successful in *La Sonnambula* opposite Rosina Storchio. He made guest appearances at Covent Garden, the Teatro Liceo, the Teatro Real, the Teatro São Carlos, the Warsaw Opera, and in Russia. He was engaged at the Chicago Opera (1912-14). He sang Faust in *Mefistofele* at the Teatro dal Verme in 1920. He made a concert tour through Belgium and Holland in 1923 and appeared on the stage until 1930. Thereafter he lived and taught in Naples. A beautiful lyric tenor voice, particularly at home in the Italian repertory.

Records: Edison* cylinders; discs for Pathé*, G & T, and HMV (including *La Bohème*, 1928). *U.S. re-issue:* Victor, IRCC. *U.S. re-recording:* TAP, ASCO, Eterna, FRP.

GIRALDONI, EUGENIO, baritone, b. Apr. 20, 1871, Marseilles; d. June 24, 1924, Helsinki. He was the son of the famous baritone Leone Giraldoni (1825-1879), one of the most famous Verdi interpreters of his time, and the soprano Cardina Ferni. He made his debut (1891) at the Teatro Liceo as Escamillo in *Carmen* and then had a successful career at La Scala, the Teatro Costanzi, and other important Italian theaters. At the Teatro Costanzi on Jan. 14, 1900, he created the role of Scarpia in the world *première* of *Tosca*. A few months later he sang the same part in the first performance at La Scala. He was a member of the Metropolitan Opera (1904-05), making his debut as Barnaba in *La Gioconda*. He sang in Buenos Aires (1909), Geneva (1909-10), Cairo (1910), and Paris (1913). He was a frequent guest in Italy, Russia, and South America. He had a wide-ranging baritone voice of particular power and expressiveness.

Records: G & T (Milan, 1903), Fonotipia, Odeon. *U.S. re-issue:* Victor, Columbia, HRS. *U.S. re-recording:* TAP, Eterna.

GIRARDI, ALEXANDER, tenor, b. Dec. 5, 1850, Graz, Austria; d. Apr. 20, 1918, Vienna. At first a locksmith, he was a self-taught singer and first appeared on the stage (1869) in Rohitsch-Sauerbrunn in Nestroy's farce *Tritsch-Tratsch*. He appeared next at Krems, Karlsbad, Bad Ischl, and Salzburg in the same season, and in 1871 came to Vienna. There he first appeared in comic roles at the Strampfer Theater. After his voice had been admired in the interpolated songs he sang, he came (1874) to the Theater an der Wien, where he became the unsurpassed master of comic roles in the classic Viennese operettas. Scarcely any of the operettas of Joseph Strauss, Millöcker, Zeller, or Eysler was first produced without his having a part in it. He enjoyed unimaginable popularity in Vienna. In 1898 he changed from the Theater an der Wien to the Deutsches Volkstheater, but he returned to the former house in 1902. He was famous both for his skill with topical songs and with Viennese songs, which he sang in an inimitable way. For a whole generation he incorporated in his own person the comfortable and jolly Viennese style of life.

Records: Four rare records for G & T (Vienna, 1903) and a few for Zonophone.

GIRAUD, FIORELLO, tenor, b. 1868, Parma; d. Mar. 20, 1928, Parma. His father, Lodovico Giraud (1846-1882), was a famous tenor. He made his debut (1891) at Vercelli in the title role of *Lohengrin*. On May 21, 1892, at the Teatro dal Verme he sang Canio in the world *première* of *I Pagliacci*. Guest appearances on various provincial Italian stages followed; he sang at the Teatro Liceo (1896), in Santiago de Chile (1898), and at the Teatro São Carlos. He had a very successful career at the most important Italian opera houses. He was esteemed both as a singer in *verismo* operas and in Wagner parts. In 1906 at the Trieste Opera he sang in the world *première* of *Medea* by Tommasini; in 1907 at the Teatro Massimo he appeared in the world *première* of *Sperduti nel Buio*. In 1907 he sang Siegfried in

Götterdämmerung at La Scala under Toscanini and in 1908 he sang Pelléas there in the Italian *première* of *Pelléas et Mélisande*.

Records: There are only seven very rare records of his voice, made for G & T (Milan, 1904). *U.S. re-issue:* Victor.

GIRAUDEAU, JEAN, tenor, b. July 1, 1916, Toulon, France. His voice studies were interrupted by World War II. He made his debut at the Opéra-Comique (1947) as Nadir in *Les Pêcheurs des Perles*. Since then he has had a starring career at both the Opéra-Comique and the Paris Opéra. At the former he has sung in several world *premières: Blaise le Savetier* (1949), *Il Était Un Petit Navire* (1951), and *Marion* (1951). His guest appearances have included Monte Carlo, Nice, Marseilles, and Brussels. In 1952 he sang Aeneas in a production of *Les Troyens* on the BBC. He has had great success in international music festival presentations, particularly at Aix-en-Provence. One of the most important French lyric tenors of this generation.

Records: Urania* (including *Thaïs*), Pathé, and Decca. *U.S. reissue:* Vox, Westminster, Pathé-Marconi, DGG.

GITOWSKY, MICHAEL, bass, b. Dec. 28, 1887, Poltava, Russia. He completed the military cadet school in Orel, the military academy in Moscow, and became a Russian officer. In 1914 he was captured and placed in an Austrian prisoner-of-war camp; after 1917 he was interned in Norway. He studied singing there with Piero Coppola in Oslo, and after 1919 continued with August Iffert in Dresden, with Lapierre and Waldemar Bernhardt in Paris, and with Vittorio Vanza in Milan. He made his debut as a concert bass in Germany (1923) and sang at the Hamburg State Opera (1924-25); the next year he was engaged by the North German radio. In 1926-27 he appeared at the New Theater in Leipzig. In 1926 he went to Paris, where he had great success at the Opéra Russe. In 1936 he returned to Germany and sang, now under the name Michael von Roggen, at the Berlin State Opera (1937-43). He also appeared in the Bayreuth Festivals (1937-39) as Titurel and Fafner. He appeared in guest performances and concerts until 1946 and lives in Berlin. He had a true Russian bass voice, that is to say, a large and deep one.

Records: Homochord (about 1929) as Michael Gitowsky.

GIUDICE, MARIA, contralto-soprano, b. 1870, Lisbon; d. (?). Originally Maria Júdice da Costa. She studied with Melchior Olivier in Lisbon and made her debut there as a contralto (1890). She sang in Havana (1891-92) and Buenos Aires (1893), where she appeared as Dame Quickly in the South American *première* of *Falstaff*. In 1897 she was called to La Scala, making her debut as Princess Eboli in *Don Carlos*. Guest appearances followed at the Teatro Costanzi and again in Argentina in 1898. After 1900 she began to add dramatic soprano roles to her repertory. She married the baritone Guglielmo Caruson, from whom she was later separated. In 1907 she traveled through Chile and also appeared at Parma as Brünnhilde in *Die Walküre*. She sang again at Havana (1907-08) and in 1909 at the Teatro Real. Later she was a teacher of singing in Milan and in 1935 she joined the Casa di Riposo, founded by Verdi. She was related to the Italian family of singers named Lo Giudice, from which came the singers Silvio Costa Lo Giudice, Franco Lo Giudice, and Pietro Lo Giudice.

Records: Fonotipia (1907-08), all as a soprano.

Gläser · Gluck

GLÄSER, JOHN, tenor, b. June 12, 1888, Berlin; d. April, 1968, Frankfurt a. M. He studied in Berlin, made his debut in Ulm (1911), and came in 1912 to the Breslau Opera, where he remained for five years. In 1917 he was engaged by the Frankfurt a. M. Opera and remained there until the end of his career. In 1926 he sang there the role of Elis in the world *première* of *Der Schatzgräber*. His guest appearances include Berlin, Munich, Hamburg, and Vienna. He was greatly admired as Bacchus in *Ariadne auf Naxos* at the 1926 Salzburg Festival. In 1942 he sang his farewell performance at the Frankfurt Opera, appearing as Canio in *I Pagliacci*, on the occasion of his twenty-fifth anniversary at that house. Thereafter he lived and taught in Frankfurt. After 1951 he was the president of the German Association of Stage Employees. He was married to the singer Agnes Werninghaus. A beautifully trained heroic tenor voice.
Records: Polydor and Parlophone.

GLAZ, HERTHA, contralto, b. Sept. 16, 1908, Vienna. Originally Hertha Glatz. She made her debut (1931) at the Breslau Opera House, but in 1933 she was forced to leave Germany because she was Jewish. She then undertook concert tours through Austria and Scandinavia and sang at the German Theater in Prague (1935-36). In 1935 she sang at the Glyndebourne Festival and in 1936 made an American tour with the Salzburg Opera Guild. She remained here and developed a wide-ranging concert activity. She sang at the Chicago Opera (1940-42) and at the Metropolitan Opera (1942-56). She was particularly admired as a lieder singer. Since 1956 she has taught at the Manhattan Conservatory.
Records: RCA Victor*, Columbia*, and MGM*.

GLESS, JULIUS, bass, b. Mar. 24, 1886, Oltingen, in Alsace. He studied at the Conservatory in Strasbourg and made his debut there (1910), remaining until 1914. He was engaged at the Cologne Opera (1914-20), and during this time he made guest appearances at the Vienna Imperial Opera (1916) and in Amsterdam (1918 and 1919). He was a much-admired member of the Bavarian State Opera in Munich (1920-29). In 1928 he became a singer and the chief stage manager for the Bavarian Landesbühne, a traveling group, with which he appeared as a guest in Holland in 1932. He then became a singer and stage manager in Schwerin. He was a professor at the Cologne Music High School (1938-45). He had a large and expressive bass voice.
Records: Vox.

GLUCK, ALMA, soprano, b. May 11, 1884, Bucharest; d. Oct. 27, 1938, New York. Originally Reba Fiersohn. She came to the United States as a child and studied after 1906 with Alberto Buzzia-Peccia in New York. She made her debut (1909) at the New Theater, which led to her being engaged by the Metropolitan Opera in the same year. Her debut at the Metropolitan was as Sophie in *Werther*. She had a highly successful career at the Metropolitan until 1918. In 1913 she went to Europe for further study and became a pupil of Marcella Sembrich in Berlin. After World War I she appeared only occasionally and then in concert; even at the Metropolitan she confined her appearances to the Sunday Night Concerts. Her second marriage was to the violinist Efrem Zimbalist. After the close of her career she lived and taught in New York. Her lyric soprano voice was admired as much for the clarity of her intonation as for the noble musicality of her vocal management. She was also a famous concert singer.

Records: Victor*. U.S. *re-issue:* HRS. *U.S. re-recording:* RCA Victor, Belcanto, Rococo.

GMIRYA, BORIS, baritone, b. 1903, Lebedin, Russia. The son of a mason, he first worked as a longshoreman, then as a stoker and seaman in the Russian Black Sea fleet. He studied singing at the Kharkov Conservatory with P.V. Golubev and made his debut there (1936). In 1939 he was engaged by the Kiev Opera, where he appeared thereafter. He became famous through his concerts and guest appearances in the various centers of Russian musical life. He was awarded the Stalin Prize in 1952 and has been named a People's Artist of the USSR. A warm and expressive baritone voice of great sincerity and conviction in both the operatic and song repertories.

Records: Russian State Record Trust and Supraphon. *U.S. re-issue:* Bruno, Monitor.

GOBBI, TITO, baritone, b. Oct. 24, 1915, Bassano del Grappa, near Venice. He first studied law at the University of Padua, then singing with Giulio Crimi in Rome. He took first prize in an international singing contest in Vienna in 1938. In 1939 he made his debut as the elder Germont in *La Traviata* at the Teatro Costanzi. He first sang at La Scala in 1942 and has appeared there regularly ever since. After the end of World War II he developed into a great international star. His guest appearances included Covent Garden, the Paris Opéra, the State Operas in both Vienna and Munich, Barcelona, Lisbon, Chicago, San Francisco, the Teatro Colón, and the Opera in Rio de Janeiro. He has made concert tours in South America, Scandinavia, England, Egypt, and Israel. He was greatly admired at the Salzburg Festivals as Don Giovanni (1950) and Falstaff (1957). He has had great starring successes as well at the Arena Festival in Verona and at the Maggio Musicale Festival in Florence. A member of the Metropolitan Opera since 1956, he made his debut there as Scarpia in *Tosca*. He resides in Rome, which has become the center of his world-wide concert and operatic activity. The best-known Italian baritone of his generation. The power of his voice and the overmastering intensity of his expression have marked each of his interpretations.

Records: A great many records of HMV, DGG* (*La Bohème*), and Columbia (*Lucia di Lammermoor, I Pagliacci, Madama Butterfly, Il Barbiere di Siviglia, Aïda, Un Ballo in Maschera, Rigoletto, Falstaff,* et cetera). *U.S. re-issue:* Angel, Capitol, RCA Victor, Seraphim, London.

GOETZE, MARIE, contralto, b. Nov. 2, 1865, Berlin; d. Feb. 18, 1922, Berlin. She studied at the Stern Conservatory in Berlin with Jenny Meyer, then became a pupil of Désirée Artôt de Padilla. She made her debut (1884) at the Kroll Opera as Azucena in *Il Trovatore*. In the same year she was engaged by the Berlin Imperial Opera, where she remained until 1886. She sang at the Hamburg Opera (1886-90), in New York (1890-91), and in 1891 had brilliant successes in guest appearances at the Vienna Imperial Opera as Fidès in *Le Prophète* and as Amneris in *Aïda*. In 1892 she returned to the Berlin Imperial Opera, where she was highly successful until 1920. She created there the role of Magdalena

in the world *première* of *Der Evangelimann* in 1895; in 1906 she sang Herodias in the first Berlin performance of *Salome*. With her expressive and flexible contralto voice she mastered a wide-ranging concert and stage repertory.
Records: G & T (the oldest from Berlin, 1901), Odeon, Beka, and HMV. *U.S. re-issue:* Okeh-Odeon, IRCC.

GOGORZA, EMILIO DE, baritone, b. May 29, 1874, Brooklyn; d. May 10, 1949, New York. The son of Spanish parents, he was taken to Spain as a child, and was educated and began his vocal studies there. Returning to the United States, he studied with Moderati and Agramonte in New York and made his debut (1897) in a concert with the famous Marcella Sembrich. He soon became known in America as a concert singer, particularly through the medium of his many phonograph records. For years he was the artistic director of the Victor Company, one of the largest producers of records in the world. He never appeared on the stage, because he was afflicted with extreme shortsightedness. For a few years he was married to the famous soprano Emma Eames. He retired in the 1930's and then lived and taught in New York. He counted among his pupils the baritone John Brownlee. This artist possessed one of the most beautiful baritone voices of his time, outstanding for its dark tonal color and for his skill in using it in musical declamation.
Records: Emilio de Gogorza is included among the singers who have left behind the largest number of phonograph records, and these appeared under various professional names. He first made records for Berliner* (1898) as E. Francisco. As Carlos Francisco he sang for Zonophone* (1900-01), Climax* (ca. 1901), Eldridge R. Johnson Records* and Victor* (1903-05). Under the name Edward Franklin he sang for Zonophone* and Climax*. As M. Fernand he sang for Eldridge R. Johnson Records* and Victor*; as Herbert Goddard he sang for these same two labels. Under his real name he sang for Victor* only. He also made Edison* cylinders and discs. *U.S. re-recording:* IRCC, HRS, TAP, Cantilena, Rococo.

GOLTZ, CHRISTEL, soprano, b. July 8, 1912, Dortmund, Germany. She studied ballet and singing with Ornelli-Leeb in Munich and with the pupil of Hindemith, Theodor Schenk, whom she later married. In 1935 she was engaged as a dancer and chorus singer in Fürth. She then came to Plauen, where the director of the Dresden State Opera, Karl Böhm, discovered her. She began her career as a soloist on that stage (1941) as Rezia in *Oberon*. She stayed eight years in Dresden and in 1947 came to the Berlin State Opera, later to the Berlin City Opera as a dramatic soprano. Finally, in 1951, she came to the Vienna State Opera, where she has since been counted as one of the most prominent artists. She has made very successful guest appearances at La Scala, the Rome Opera, Covent Garden, and in Paris and Brussels. In 1954 she came to the Metropolitan Opera, making her debut as the title heroine in *Salome*. She has appeared almost annually at the Salzburg Festivals; there she sang in 1954 the title part in the world *première* of *Penelope*. She has a large soprano voice, whose expressiveness in the dramatic soprano repertory produces first-rate performances.
Records: DGG, Urania (*Salome*), Decca (*Salome* and *Die Frau ohne Schatten*). *U.S. re-issue:* Columbia, London, Richmond, Vox, American Decca.

Gordon · Goritz

GORDON, CYRENA VAN, contralto, b. Sept. 4, 1893, Camden, Ohio; d. Apr. 4, 1964, New York City. Originally Cyrena Pocock. She studied at the Conservatory in Cincinnati with Louise Dotti. She first sang in public in 1912 and in the same year was engaged by the Chicago Opera Company, where she remained until 1932. She made her debut as Amneris in *Aïda*. In 1921 she sang Brünnhilde in *Die Walküre* at Chicago, and this remained her only dramatic soprano role. In 1933 she came to the Metropolitan Opera, again making her debut as Amneris; but she remained there for only one season. She later lived in New York and was active as a concert singer and teacher; in 1948 she gave a concert there in Town Hall. A darktimbred and expressive contralto voice.
Records: Edison* discs (1919), acoustics and electrics for Columbia*.

GORDON, JEANNE, contralto, b. 1893, Wallaceburg, Canada; d. Feb. 22, 1952, Macon, Mo. She studied in Toronto and married an American from Detroit. When he entered the navy in 1917, she accompanied him to New York and sang there in cinemas, particularly at the Rialto Theater. Her beautiful voice was so astonishing that the band director, Creatore, had her sing Azucena in *Il Trovatore* in Brooklyn. This led, in turn, to the offer of a contract with the Metropolitan Opera, where (1919) she made her debut as Azucena. She was highly successful there for the next ten years. In 1920 she sang with the Scotti Opera Company. In 1928 she made a guest appearance at the Monte Carlo Opera as both Princess Eboli in *Don Carlos* and as Dalila. Thereafter nothing was heard from her. After her death it was learned that, since 1929, she had suffered from a mental illness in a sanatorium in Macon. She had a dark-timbred contralto voice of great volume.
Records: American Columbia* and one for Victor*. *U.S. re-recording:* ASCO, Rococo.

GORIN, IGOR, baritone, b. Oct. 26, 1908, Gradizhak, Russian Ukraine. After his family moved to Vienna he studied medicine there and sang in a medical school choral group. He then studied at the Vienna Conservatory of Music (1925-30) and, after making his debut at the Vienna Volksoper, sang at the Vienna and Czech State Operas, among others. In 1933 he came to the United States, where he sang in radio recitals before making his concert debut at the Hollywood Bowl. He first appeared in the United States as Charles Gorin. He then sang with leading American symphony orchestras and in various opera houses. After 1948 he sang annually the role of Brigham Young in *All Faces West*, the Mormon pageant, at Ogden, Utah. He appeared as the elder Germont in *La Traviata* and as Rigoletto on NBC television. In 1959 he toured Australia and New Zealand. He has composed songs and has appeared in motion pictures. He became an American citizen in 1939.
Records: Golden Crest, RCA Victor.

GORITZ, OTTO, baritone, b. June 8, 1873, Berlin; d. Apr. 16, 1929, Berlin. He passed his youth in Bremen, where he was trained musically by his mother. He made his debut in Neustrelitz (1895) as Matteo in *Fra Diavolo*. He stayed there for three years, then sang at the Breslau Opera (1898-1900) and at the Hamburg Opera (1900-03). In 1903 he accepted an invitation to the Metropolitan Opera. He was highly successful there, particularly as a Wagner interpreter. In 1905 he sang in the American *premières* there of *Die Fledermaus* and *Hänsel und Gretel*. He also created the role of the Spielmann there in the world première of *Königskinder* on Dec. 28, 1910, and in 1911 sang the first Baron Ochs in *Der Rosenkavalier* in America. He remained at the Metropolitan until 1917 and later made guest appearances, particularly in Hamburg and Berlin.

Records: Odeon, Victor* and American Columbia* records, and on both cylinders and discs for Edison* and Pathé* *U.S. re-issue:* IRCC. *U.S. re-recording:* Pathé Actuelle, Cantilena.

GORR, RITA, contralto, b. Feb. 18, 1926, Ghent. She began her studies in 1943 at the Brussels Conservatory and made her debut (1949) at the Ghent Opera. At the beginning she sang chiefly in the opera houses in Ghent, Brussels, and Antwerp. In 1952 she won first prize in an international singing contest in Lausanne, and in the same year she came to the Paris Opéra, where she was highly successful. After guest appearances in Turin and Rome, she sang in 1958 at the Bayreuth Festival, especially the role of Ortrud in *Lohengrin*. At La Scala she appeared as guest in the role of Santuzza in *Cavalleria Rusticana* (1958) and as Kundry in *Parsifal* (1960). She was also greatly admired in guest appearances at the Vienna State Opera. She joined the Metropolitan Opera in 1962 and also in that year sang as guest at the Chicago Opera. She has a wide-ranging and full voice; her expressive skill has been proved in both Wagner roles and other parts.

Records: Philips (*Pelléas et Mélisande*), HMV (*Les Dialogues des Carmélites* and *Iphigénie en Tauride*), Columbia (*Le Roi d'Ys*), and RCA Victor* (*Aida*). *U.S. re-issue:* Angel, Epic, Pathé-Marconi.

GOTTLIEB, HENRIETTE, soprano, b. 1884, Berlin; d. 1943, Berlin. She made her debut (1909) in Plauen and came to the Berlin City Opera in 1913, remaining there until 1934. She was a particularly noted Wagner interpreter. She sang in the Bayreuth Festivals (1927-30) and was a guest in Amsterdam in 1928. She had one of her greatest successes in 1930 at the Théâtre des Champs-Elysées, singing Brünnhilde in the *Ring* cycle under Hoesslin. Since she was Jewish, she could not appear in Germany after 1934, although she was still living in Berlin in 1940. She was later seized there and put into a concentration camp. She had a big dramatic soprano voice.

Records: Ensemble scenes on acoustic HMV and electric records for Pathé of the 1930 Paris Wagner Festival, also electric records for HMV and Polydor, including highlights from *Lohengrin*. *U.S. re-issue:* RCA Victor.

GRAARUD, GUNNAR, tenor, b. June 1, 1886, Holmestrand, near Oslo; d. Dec. 6, 1960, Stuttgart. He had originally planned to be an engineer and came for these studies to the Technical High School in Karlsruhe, but he then studied singing with Husler and K. von Zawilowski in Berlin. He made his debut (1919) in Kaiserslautern and sang at Mannheim (1920-22), the Berlin Volksoper (1922-25), and the Hamburg State Opera (1926-28). He sang in the Bayreuth Festivals after 1927, his roles being those of Tristan, Siegmund, Siegfried and Parsifal. He was a member of the Vienna State Opera (1928-37). His guest appearances took him to Covent Garden, the Paris Opéra, La Scala, and the Stockholm, Copenhagen, and Amsterdam Operas. At the Salzburg Festivals he sang Aegisthus in *Elektra* and the title role in *Der Corregidor*. His expressive art and the dramatic management of his voice allowed him to give his best performance in Wagner parts.

Records: Polydor, Odeon, and Columbia* (including *Tristan und Isolde,* Bayreuth, 1928).

GRANDA, ALESSANDRO, tenor, b. Nov. 26, 1898, Peru; d. Sept. 9, 1962, Lima. He was partly of Negro and partly of Indian extraction. The Peruvian government sent him to Milan, where he studied with Alfredo Cecchi. He made his debut (1927) in Como in *Iris.* After a tour of Germany he sang in 1928 in Venice and Genoa, where he was highly successful as Cavaradossi in *Tosca.* In 1928 he came to La Scala, first singing Cavaradossi and later the Duke in *Rigoletto* under Toscanini. After singing on all the important Italian stages, he appeared in 1934 at the Hippodrome in New York in a troupe led by Pasquale Amato. In 1936 he made guest appearances at the Italian Opera in Holland and later made long tours in South and Central America. From 1945-50 he was first tenor for the San Carlo Opera Company in the United States.

Records: Columbia* (*Tosca, La Gioconda, Madama Butterfly*).

GRANDI, MARGHERITA, soprano, b. Oct. 10, 1899, Tasmania. Her family was of Italian and Irish extraction. She studied with Giannina Russ in Milan and made her debut there (1932) at the Teatro Carcano as Aïda. In 1934 she sang Elena in *Mefistofele* at La Scala. Thereafter she had a celebrated career on all the leading Italian stages. In 1938 she made guest appearances in Holland and was acclaimed at the Glyndebourne Festival as Lady Macbeth in Verdi's opera. Later she appeared as guest in Brussels, Egypt, and South America. During World War II she sang in Italy. In 1945 she took up residence in England, where she was highly successful at Covent Garden. She appeared at the Edinburgh Festival as Amelia in *Un Ballo in Maschera* and as Lady Macbeth. She had a large dramatic soprano voice, which found its best expression in the Italian repertory.

Records: Toward the end of her career a few records appeared on HMV. *U.S. re-issue:* London.

GRANFELT, HANNA, soprano, b. June 2, 1884, Sakkola, Finland; d. Nov. 3, 1952, Helsinki. She studied in Helsinki and Paris, but began her stage career (1909) at the Mannheim Court Theater, to which she belonged until 1915. Since she had had great successes in guest appearances in Berlin (1910-12), she became a member of the Berlin Imperial Opera (1915-22). In 1914 she sang as a guest in London. After 1922 she had great successes in guest appearances all over Europe, and she also toured the United States. She was especially prized as a Wagner interpreter, but was also greatly admired as an oratorio and lieder artist. She also sang under the names Hanna von Granfelt and Lillian von Granfelt.

Records: Polydor.

GRANFORTE, APOLLO, baritone, b. July 20, 1886, Legnano, near Verona. He emigrated to Argentina at the age of eighteen and worked there with his brother as a shoemaker. He studied singing with Guido Capocci and Nicola Guerrera in Buenos Aires and made his debut (1913) at the opera in Rosario, Argentina, as the elder Germont in *La Traviata.* When Italy entered World War I, he returned home and served in the Italian army. In 1916 he sang in Malta and Zürich and in 1917 he appeared at the Teatro Costanzi. In 1918 he had a starring success at the Teatro dal Verme. He made his debut at

La Scala in 1921 and frequently sang there subsequently. He sang as guest in Paris in 1922 and traveled to Australia in 1934 with a troupe which Nellie Melba had gathered together. He made a South American tour (1924-25) and in the latter year made guest appearances in England. In 1928 and again in 1932 he toured Australia. He sang at the Teatro Colón in 1929 in the world *première* of *El Matrero*. In 1935 he sang the part of Mencrate in the world *première* of Mascagni's *Nerone* at La Scala; he then continued his career at the largest Italian opera houses. After World War II he was given a professorship at the Conservatory in Ankara and was briefly the director of the National Opera in Prague. He lives and teaches in Milan. He had a baritone voice of luxuriant sound and great expressiveness, with which he mastered all the important roles in the Italian repertory.

Records: Fonografia Nazionale and HMV (*Tosca, Otello, Il Trovatore*). *U.S. re-issue:* RCA Victor. *U.S. re-recording:* TAP, Eterna, Camden, IRCC, Rococo.

GRAVEURE, LOUIS, baritone-tenor, b. Mar. 18, 1888, London; d. November, 1965, San Francisco. Although this artist always denied it, it appears certain that he was the same as the tenor Wilfrid Douthitt (Graveure was his mother's maiden name), who in 1914 created without particular success the tenor role in *The Lilac Domino* in New York. In 1916 he married the prima donna of that production, the soprano Eleanor Painter (d. 1935). Originally he had studied architecture at the South Kensington Art School and had passed some time in South Africa and Canada. In 1915 he appeared as baritone soloist under the name Louis Graveure in a production of Mendelssohn's *Elijah* in Portland, Maine. He claimed that he was a Belgian. His success there was very great and he undertook a triumphal tour of the United States. At one of his concerts there was a scandal when a woman in the audience arose and denounced him as a German spy. For twelve years he remained one of the best-liked concert singers in America. In 1920 he gave his first lieder recital in Berlin with sensational success. He then busied himself with lieder singing and at the same time held a position as a singing teacher at the University of Michigan. In 1928 he returned to Europe. By this time his voice had changed to that of a tenor and his appearance had changed; he seemed to be definitely much younger than formerly. In 1929 he made his stage debut at the Berlin-Charlottenburg Opera House. He had a brilliant career as an opera and operetta tenor, but particularly as a singer in films in Germany. At this time he was married to the film actress Camilla Horn. Shortly before the outbreak of World War II he returned to America, where he worked as a singer and also as a voice teacher. He lived first in Los Angeles, then in Texas, and finally in San Francisco.

Records: As a baritone he sang for Columbia*; as a tenor for Columbia*, Polydor, and Ultraphon. *U.S. re-recording:* Telefunken.

GRAVINA, GIOVANNI, bass, b. 1872; d. November, 1912, Boston. He began his career in Italy before the turn of the century. In 1902 he sang for the first time at La Scala, appearing in a production of *Il Trovatore* with Rosa Caligari, Julian Biel, and Antonio Magini-Coletti. In the same year he also sang in Milan in the world *première* of *Germania*; others in the cast were Enrico Caruso, Amelia Pinto, and Mario Sammarco. He was highly successful in the following years in Italy and South America, but particularly in Russia, where he sang almost every year with Mattia Battistini. He was engaged by the Metropolitan Opera (1907-08) but sang only once there as Sparafucile in *Rigoletto*. In 1912 he came to the Boston Opera. After a brilliant success in *Aïda* with Carmen Melis, he died suddenly at the high point of his career. He possessed one of the finest bass voices of his epoch.

Records: A very few rare G & T records. *U.S. re-recording:* TAP, HRS.

GREEF-ANDRIESSEN, PELAGIE, soprano, b. June 20, 1860, Vienna; d. 1937, Frankfurt a. M. She had her first vocal training under her mother, Marie Andriessen von Lingke, who was a professor of singing at the Vienna Conservatory. At first she was an operetta singer at the Carltheater in Vienna, then at the Theater am Gartnerplatz in Munich, and in Nuremberg, Cologne, and Dresden. She decided to become an opera singer and came to the Berlin Imperial Opera, but she was dismissed as having no talent. She toured with the Wagner Traveling Opera under Angelo Neumann (1882-83) and came to the Leipzig Opera in 1884, making her debut there as Aïda. After study with Dreyschock in Leipzig, she became one of the best-known dramatic sopranos in Germany. She stayed at Leipzig until 1890, making guest appearances during this time at the Imperial Operas in Berlin and Vienna and at Covent Garden. At the Mozart Centenary Festival in Salzburg in 1891 she sang the Countess in *Le Nozze di Figaro* and in 1896 she was admired at the Bayreuth Festival for an unforgettable Brangäne in *Tristan und Isolde*. She was engaged at the Cologne Opera (1892-93) and at the Opera in Frankfurt a. M. (1893-97). Her first marriage was to Lieutenant von Sthamer, her second to the architect Walter Ende, and her third to the bass Paul Greef. A full dramatic soprano voice, especially noted in Wagner roles.

Records: Berliner (Frankfurt, 1900-01), and G & T (Frankfurt also, 1904 and 1907), all of the greatest rarity.

GREENE, HARRY PLUNKET, baritone, b. June 24, 1865, near Dublin; d. Aug. 19, 1936, London. He studied with Hromoda in Stuttgart, Vannuccini in Florence, and Blume in London and made his debut (1888); he sang originally in the bass range. He appeared in 1890 at Covent Garden as the Commandant in *Don Giovanni*, but then changed to baritone and finally confined himself to concert and song recital appearances. In 1892 he sang in the first performance of Parry's oratorio *Job*. In 1899 he married the daughter of this composer. He undertook his first American tour, which was highly successful, in 1893. He lost his voice early and had difficulty with intonation, but his interpretations were so fascinating that the public overlooked his faults. He was a teacher at the Royal College of Music in London and was highly influential in all aspects of English musical life. He wrote *Interpretation in Song* (London, 1912).

Records: G & T (London, 1904-05), mostly English folk songs, but one song by Schubert. In January, 1934, four new records appeared on Columbia; then almost seventy years old, he delivered the songs in the grand manner.

GREINDL, JOSEF, bass, b. Dec. 23, 1912, Munich. He studied (1932-36) with Paul Bender and Anna Bahr-Mildenburg at the Music Academy in Munich and made his debut as

Hunding in *Die Walküre* (1936) in Krefeld. He sang at the Düsseldorf Opera (1936-42) and in the latter year Heinz Tietjen brought him to the Berlin State Opera, where he stayed until 1948. He first appeared at the Bayreuth Festivals in 1943 as Pogner in *Die Meistersinger*. In 1948 he came to the Berlin City Opera and was at the same time a member of the Vienna State Opera. After World War II he had a great international career. After 1952 he sang almost every year at Bayreuth and was esteemed at the Salzburg and Edinburgh Festivals. Guest appearances in London, Paris, at La Scala, and at the Teatro Colón brought him great success. In 1952 he joined the Metropolitan Opera. He was thought to be one of the great Wagner singers of his time. After 1961 he was professor at the Music High School in Saarbrücken. He had a powerful and expressive voice and was esteemed not only in both serious and *buffo* roles on the stage but also as a many-sided concert bass.

Records: DGG* (including *Die Zauberflöte, Die Entführung aus dem Serail, Der Fliegende Holländer, The Seasons*), Urania (*Martha*), Philips (*Der Fliegende Holländer* at Bayreuth). *U.S. re-issue:* Columbia, Electrola, London, Angel, Bruno, Remington, Turnabout, American Decca.

GRESSE, ANDRÉ, bass b. Mar. 23, 1868, Lyons; d. 1937, Paris. He was the son of the bass André Gresse, who sang at the Paris Opéra and who created for that house the roles of Lodovico in *Otello*, Pogner in *Die Meistersinger*, and Hunding in *Die Walküre*. The son studied at the Paris Conservatory with Taskin, Léon Melchissèdec, and Duvernoy and made his debut (1896) at the Opéra-Comique as the Commandant in *Don Giovanni* with Victor Maurel. When his father gave up his stage career at the Paris Opéra in 1900, the son became his successor. His debut role there was St. Bris in *Les Huguenots*. In 1910 at the Monte Carlo Opera he created the role of Sancho Panza in the world *première* of *Don Quicchote*. His other creations, those at the Opéra-Comique, were a role in the world *première* of *Sapho* (1897) and *Le Juif Polonais* (1900); while at the Opéra he sang in *Bacchus* (1909). After his retirement from the stage he was a professor at the Paris Conservatory.

Records: Many records for G & T, HMV, Lyrophone, Zonophone, and Pathé* (a complete *Faust*, among others). *U.S. re-issue:* Victor.

GREY, MADELEINE, soprano, b. June 11, 1897, Villaines-la-Juhel, France. At the National Conservatory in Paris she first studied piano with Alfred Cortot and then singing with Hettich. She gave her first concerts in Paris (1921) and had an immediate success. She dedicated herself to the interpretation of contemporary French works and was the first person to sing the *Chansons Hébraïques* of Ravel (1922) and the *Chansons d'Auvergne*, collected and harmonized by Canteloube (1923). Long concert tours brought her great success all over the world, especially in Italy and the United States. Her presentations of French art songs were esteemed as models of their kind.

Records: Polydor. *U.S. re-issue:* Brunswick, American Columbia, Vox. *U.S. re-recording:* Electrola, Angel.

GRIEBEL, AUGUST, bass, b. July 2, 1900, Bochum, Germany. He studied at Hochs' Conservatory in Frankfurt a. M., making his debut (1922) at Heidelberg. He came in 1924 to Krefeld, sang at Aachen (1925-28), Breslau (1928-30), and

Frankfurt (1930-34). He then spent twenty-five years at the Cologne Opera. His guest appearances in Holland in 1938 as Baron Ochs in *Der Rosenkavalier*, at the Paris Opéra in 1942, at the Berlin City Opera, and the Vienna State Opera were all highly successful, as were his appearances in Munich, Hamburg, Brussels, and at the Teatro Liceo. He sang particularly *buffo* parts, but was also admired as a Wagner singer.

Records: One record for Columbia*; for MMS he sang Osmin in *Die Entführung aus dem Serail*.

GROBE, DONALD, b. Dec. 16, 1929, Ottawa, Ill. After originally studying engineering, he studied singing at Millikan University, the Chicago Musical College, and the Mannes College in New York. He was a concert and operetta singer in New York (1953-56). In 1956 he went to Europe and sang first at Krefeld and at München-Gladbach, then at Hannover (1957-60). Since 1960 he has appeared at the Berlin City Opera. His guest appearances at the Cologne Opera, the Salzburg and Schwetzingen Festivals, as well as in Vienna, have brought him additional laurels. He has an impressive lyric tenor voice.

Records: Telefunken, DGG*, Decca (*Fidelio*). *U.S. re-issue:* Audio Spectrum.

GRÖBKE, ADOLF, tenor, b. May 26, 1872, Hildesheim, Germany; d. Sept. 16, 1949, Epfach, Germany. At first a railway employee, he then studied at the Conservatory in Sondershausen with Schröder and made his debut there (1895). He sang at Essen (1896-99) and Cologne (1899-1905). In 1907 he sang Walther in *Die Meistersinger* as a guest in Amsterdam. Other engagements followed in Frankfurt a. M., in Hannover, and at the Vienna Imperial Opera (1910-14). Later he appeared in Schwerin and Halberstadt. In 1935 he was the leader of a singing class at the German Opera House in Berlin-Charlottenburg. The beautiful voice of this artist was distinguished by the stylistic security of his diction and the masterly art of his phrasing.

Records: G & T (Cologne, 1904), Zonophone, and Odeon, all rare.

GROB-PRANDL, GERTRUDE, soprano, b. 1917, Vienna. She studied at the Vienna Music Academy with Singer and made her debut (1939) at the Vienna Volksoper, where she stayed for six years. She was engaged at Zürich (1945-47). In 1947 she was called to the Vienna State Opera, where she has since appeared with great success. Guest appearances by this artist include La Scala, the Rome Opera, the Teatro San Carlo, Covent Garden, the Teatro Colón, and the Teatro Liceo. Since 1954 she has been first dramatic soprano at the Berlin State Opera, but has retained a guest contract with the Vienna house. In 1954 she sang at the Arena Festival. Her large dramatic soprano voice is particularly admired in Wagner parts.

Records: Nixa (Donna Anna in *Don Giovanni*) and Remington* (the title role in *Turandot*). *U.S. re-issue:* Haydn Society (*Idomeneo*).

GROENEN, JOSEPH, baritone, b. May 5, 1885, Waalwijk, Holland; d. Mar. 29, 1959, Hamburg. He studied singing in Amsterdam, Milan, and Stuttgart. After making his debut in Mainz (1913), he sang at the Hamburg Opera (1914-15), the Vienna Imperial Opera (1915-16), and the Berlin Imperial Opera (1916-17). From 1917 to the end of his career he was again at the Hamburg Opera, where he was greatly admired. He appeared regularly at the Vienna State Opera (1923-26). He was valued as an outstanding interpreter of heroic baritone roles.

He lived after his retirement in Hamburg.
Records: Polydor.

GROH, HERBERT ERNST, tenor, b. 1906, Lucerne. After studies in Zürich and Milan, he made his debut in Darmstadt (1927). In the following three years he sang successively in Frankfurt and Cologne, but then shifted to operetta and especially to radio and recording work. In 1930 he was engaged as first soloist for the Hamburg radio; in 1933 he came to the German radio in Berlin and then became a much-sought-after guest on all radio networks. He also engaged in a wide range of concert activities. In 1946 he undertook, together with the operetta composer Robert Stolz, a brilliant tour throughout Europe. His career lasted for many years. He had a tenor voice of lyric expressiveness and brilliant luster in the upper register.
Records: Many records for Parlophone, Opera, and Urania*. *U.S. re-issue:* American Decca, MGM. *U.S. re-recording:* Eterna, Scala, Rococo.

GROSAVESCU, TRAJAN, tenor, b. 1894, Klausenburg, Rumania; d. Feb. 15, 1927, Vienna. He studied in Bucharest and Milan and began his career at the Bucharest Opera. In 1924 he came to the Vienna Volksoper and in 1925 to the Vienna State Opera. At the same time he made regular guest appearances at the Berlin City Opera. The very promising career of this artist ended tragically; after an opera performance in Vienna his wife shot him in a fit of groundless jealousy. He had a bright voice of great sympathetic qualities, and was at home above all in the Italian repertory.
Records: Rare Odeon records.

GROSSMANN, WALTER, baritone, b. Jan. 7, 1900, Dresden. He was a pupil of Waldemar Staegemann in Dresden. He made his debut (1922) in Kiel, where he remained for three years. He sang heroic baritone parts in Altenburg (1925-27) and Chemnitz (1928-30). He came to the Berlin State Opera in 1930 and remained there until World War II. He sang at the Zoppot Festivals in 1931 and 1937 and was applauded at the Salzburg Festival in 1938 as Hans Sachs in *Die Meistersinger*. He was a member of the Vienna State Opera ensemble during the 1934-35 season. He made successful guest appearances at the Teatro Colón and on other South American stages.
Records: HMV and Columbia*, all ensemble recordings. *U.S. re-issue:* RCA Victor, Rococo.

GRÜMMER, ELISABETH, soprano, b. Mar. 31, 1911, Niederjentz, Lorraine, Germany. She spent her youth in Meiningen and attended the acting school there. She was discovered relatively late as a singer by Herbert von Karajan and made her debut in Aachen (1941). In 1942 she came to the City Theater in Duisburg and in 1946 she was engaged by the Berlin City Opera, of which she has since remained a member. She soon became internationally known, and guest appearances followed at La Scala, the Rome Opera, Covent Garden, the Brussels Opera, the State Operas in Vienna, Munich, and Hamburg, the Paris Opéra, and the Teatro Colón. She sang Eva in *Die Meistersinger* at the Bayreuth Festival in 1958 and also appeared at the Festivals in Salzburg and Glyndebourne; at the latter she was particularly noted in Mozart roles. She is also a famous concert soprano, particularly in the *St. Matthew Passion*. A fully trained and beautiful soprano voice of rare lightness of timbre and fine shading of expression; she is particularly at home in the lyric repertory.

Grüning · Gueden

Records: HMV (*Der Freischütz, Die Meistersinger,* and *Tannhäuser*), Urania (*The Queen of Spades*), and Columbia (*Hänsel und Gretel*). U.S. *re-issue:* Angel Electrola, Turnabout, Seraphim.

GRÜNING, WILHELM, tenor, b. Nov. 2, 1858, Berlin; d. Dec. 2, 1942, Berlin. He studied in Berlin with Julius Stern and Jenny Meyer and made his debut (1881) in Danzig. By way of Chemnitz and Magdeburg he came to the Düsseldorf Opera (1883-85). He sang at the German Opera in Rotterdam (1885-87), the Hannover Opera (1888-95), at Hamburg (1895-98), and in 1898 answered a call to the Berlin Imperial Opera, where he stayed until 1911 and where, in 1895, he sang the role of Matthias in the world *première* of *Der Evangelimann*. He was particularly admired as a Wagner singer and appeared at the Bayreuth Festivals (1891-98) as Parsifal and Tannhäuser, as well as in *Siegfried* and *Die Meistersinger*. In 1904 he sang at the Berlin Imperial Opera in the unlucky world *première* of *Der Roland von Berlin*. He made guest appearances at Covent Garden and Amsterdam and in 1895-96 was engaged in the United States by the Damrosch Opera Company. After 1911 he made only occasional guest appearances and taught in Berlin. A large heroic tenor voice.

Records: Odeon (Berlin, 1905), G & T (Berlin, 1905-07), Columbia (Berlin, 1906), and HMV.

GUARRERA, FRANK, baritone, b. 1925, Philadelphia. Of Sicilian immigrant parents, he studied with Richard Bonelli and in 1949 won the Metropolitan Opera Auditions of the Air contest. He made his debut (1949) at the Metropolitan as Escamillo in *Carmen*. Through the good offices of Arturo Toscanini he was able shortly thereafter to appear at La Scala. He later appeared as guest in London, Paris, Chicago, and Los Angeles. In 1952 he was chosen by Toscanini to sing Ford in the conductor's NBC radio production of *Falstaff*.

Records: Philips (*Faust* and *Cavalleria Rusticana*) and RCA Victor* (Ford in *Falstaff* under Toscanini). U.S. *reissue:* Columbia*.

GUEDEN, HILDE, soprano, b. Sept. 15, 1917, Vienna. She studied singing, piano, and dance at the Vienna Music Academy. She made her debut (1938) in Zürich as Cherubino in *Le Nozze di Figaro*. In 1942 she came to the Munich State Opera as the successor to Adele Kern, and remained there until 1947. In 1942 she also made guest appearances in Rome and Florence under Tullio Serafin; she had a sensational success at the Salzburg Festival in 1946 as Zerlina in *Don Giovanni*. She was called to the Vienna State Opera in 1947 and has been a greatly admired singer at that house ever since. She has had a brilliant international career, with guest appearances at La Scala, Covent Garden, in Paris, at the Salzburg, Edinburgh, Glyndebourne, Venice and Maggio Musicale Festivals. After 1952 she was a member of the Metropolitan Opera, where she had an overwhelming success as Rosalinda in *Die Fledermaus*. At the 1954 Salzburg Festival she sang the technically difficult role of Zerbinetta in *Ariadne auf Naxos*. In 1960 she sang the role of Sophie in *Der Rosenkavalier* at the opening performance of the new Festival Theater there. She has also had brilliant successes in the concert hall. She has a sumptuously trained, technically perfect soprano voice and her expressiveness is much admired.

Records: A great many records for Columbia*, Philips, DGG, Decca (including *Rigoletto, L'Elisir d'Amore, La Bohème, Le Nozze di*

Figaro, Arabella, Die Meistersinger, Don Giovanni, Die Fledermaus, The Merry Widow, Giuditta and *The Rake's Progress. U.S. re-issue:* Richmond, London, Angel, Mercury, Remington, Seraphim.

GUERRINI, ADRIANA, soprano, b. 1917, Florence. She studied at the Conservatory in Florence and in 1943 won a singing contest on the Italian radio network. She then received an offer to sing Stefana in *Siberia* on the Italian radio under the direction of the composer and she was also engaged for a series of radio opera performances. Until the end of World War II she also sang in various Italian theaters. In 1945-47 she sang with brilliant success at the Teatro San Carlo. She appeared at the Verona and Florence Festivals, as a guest at La Scala, the Paris Opéra, the Teatro Liceo, the Teatro São Carlos, the Vienna State Opera, and the Zürich Opera. She had a lyric-dramatic voice of great expressive power.

Records: Columbia* (*La Traviata*), Urania* (*La Forza del Destino*) and Cetra* (*Tosca*).

GUGLIELMETTI, ANNA-MARIA, soprano, b. 1895(?). This artist had, during the 1920's, a short but successful career on Italian stages, including, among others, Naples, Turin, Verona, Bari, and Ravenna. She also appeared as guest during this time in Barcelona, Cairo, Budapest, Ostend, and in Switzerland. In 1926 she undertook, with other artists, a tour of England. In 1927 she appeared without success at Covent Garden as Marguerite in *Les Huguenots*. She traveled in Central Europe with the opera troupe of Max Sauter. After the sudden loss of her voice, she studied for a time with Giuseppina Finzi-Magrini in Turin. She then married and settled in Geneva, where she appeared as a guest in lyric roles in the opera house there around 1930. Since then she became a teacher in Geneva. She had a virtuoso coloratura soprano voice of outstanding brilliance.

Records: Her records, made for Columbia* from about 1925-30, are much sought after by collectors.

GUICHANDUT, CARLOS MARIA, baritone-tenor, b. Nov. 4, 1919, Buenos Aires. After studying philosophy, he studied singing with A. Benta in Buenos Aires and made his debut there (1945) in *Rigoletto*. He sang as a baritone at the Teatro Colón, La Scala, and elsewhere. In 1952 he broke off his career and studied with the singer Fidelia Campigna, whom he later married. In 1953 he made his debut, then as a tenor, as Bari in *Die Walküre*. In the same year he also had great success at the Maggio Musicale Festival in Cherubini's *Medea*, opposite Maria Callas. In 1954 he sang Bacchus in *Ariadne auf Naxos* at the Glyndebourne Festival. In 1955 he was admired at the Arena Festival as Otello and as Don José in *Carmen*. He has appeared as guest from time to time at the Teatro Colón, the Vienna State Opera, Covent Garden, the Paris Opéra, the Teatro Liceo, and in Palermo, Naples, and Mexico City. His particular starring part is the title role in *Otello*.

Records: As a baritone for Cetra*; as a tenor also for Cetra*, including the title role in *Otello*.

GUILLEAUME, MARGOT, soprano, b. Jan. 12, 1910, Hamburg. She studied singing in her native city and made her debut at the State Opera there (1933). After engagements at various German opera houses, she sang until 1944 at the Hannover Opera. During World War II she was under contract to the Northwest German Radio in Hamburg and also became a fine concert soprano. She made guest appearances in opera only occasionally thereafter, mostly in Mozart and Verdi roles. In the concert hall she was most admired for her singing of baroque music and of older oratorios. Since 1950 she has also taught at the Music High School in Hamburg.

Records: Telefunken, but particularly DGG* (*Orfeo*) and exceptional performances in the Archive Series. *U.S. re-issue:* Lyrichord, Vox, Period, American Decca, Everest-Cetra.

GULBRANSON, ELLEN, soprano, b. Mar. 8, 1863, Stockholm: d. Dec. 3, 1946, Oslo. Originally Ellen Norgren. She had her singing training at the Royal Conservatory in Stockholm with Günther, then in Paris as a pupil of Mathilde Marchesi and Ellena Kenneth. Her debut as a concert singer occurred in Stockholm (1886) and her stage debut (1889) at the Royal Opera there as Aïda. She became internationally known as a Wagner singer. By 1892 she was already singled out for the Bayreuth Festival, but she was not able to appear there until 1896; thereafter she was intimately connected with succeeding festivals. She was particularly admired as Brünnhilde in the *Ring* cycle and as Kundry in *Parsifal*. She was to be heard regularly at Bayreuth until 1914. After 1890 she was married to the Norwegian Major Gulbranson and lived at Haug Manor, near Oslo. From there she undertook guest appearances which took her to Covent Garden, the Imperial Operas in Berlin and Vienna, to Budapest, St. Petersburg, Brussels, and Copenhagen with enormous success; Bayreuth, however, remained the artistic center of her career. A dark-timbred high dramatic soprano, which found its best expression in the Wagner repertory.

Records: One record for G & T (Bayreuth, 1904) and some for Pathé; all extremely rare. *U.S. re-recording:* IRCC, Pathé.

GÜNTER, HORST, baritone, b. May 23, 1917, Leipzig. He studied singing at the Leipzig Conservatory and made his debut (1941) at Schwerin, remaining there until 1944. After World War II he was first able to resume his career in 1948 at Göttingen. He sang at Wiesbaden (1948-50) and thereafter at the Hamburg State Opera. After 1955 he was also engaged by the Munich State Opera. This artist has made guest appearances at the State Operas in Vienna, Berlin, and Stuttgart, at Covent Garden, and at the Edinburgh Festival. In 1954 he sang in the first performance of *Moses und Aron* on the Hamburg radio. He has had great success as a concert and oratorio singer and has taught at the Conservatory of Detmold.

Records: DGG* (*Hänsel und Gretel* and *Zar und Zimmermann*) and HMV (*Lohengrin*). *U.S. re-issue:* Columbia, L'Oiseau Lyre, Turnabout, Philips.

GÜNTHER, CARL, tenor, b. Nov. 22, 1885, Ottenson, near Buxtehude, Germany; d. Sept. 9, 1958, Hamburg. His father was a cigar maker and he himself was a coppersmith at the Blohm and Voss shipyard in Hamburg. His voice was discovered at a song recital which he gave (1911) in Altona as an amateur. He made his debut (1912) at the Hamburg Opera as Florestan in *Fidelio* and remained a member of this opera company until the end of his career. His guest appearances were specially notable at the Berlin City Opera (1924) and at the Vienna State Opera (1927), as well as at The Hague in *Der Freischütz*. He sang until the outbreak of World War II; he then taught singing in Hamburg.

Records: Acoustics for Vox and Polydor. *U.S. re-recording:* Rococo.

GÜNTHER, MIZZI, soprano, b. Feb. 8, 1879, Warnsdorf, Bohemia; d. Mar. 18, 1961, Vienna. She was prepared for a stage career by, among others, A. Fischer, whom she married. She made her debut (1897) in Hermannstadt, where she remained for two years; she then sang in Teplitz and Karlsbad. In 1901 she was engaged by the Carltheater in Vienna, where she made her debut in *The Geisha*. She became the great operetta diva of the Austrian capital and had great triumphs as the idolized star of the Carltheater, the Theater an der Wien, and the Vienna Volksoper. In 1903 she traveled through Russia with the ensemble of the Carltheater. She enjoyed her greatest triumph, however, on Dec. 30, 1905, when she sang the title role in the world *première* of *The Merry Widow* at the Theater an der Wien. She sang this role, there and in London and Paris, more than a thousand times. She also had great success as an actress. She was later married to the actor Fred Hennings and was honorary president of the Vienna Lehár Association. She had a flexible and impressive soprano voice, which found its true expression in soubrette parts.

Records: Two very rare selections from *The Merry Widow* appeared on G & T (Vienna, 1906).

GURA, HERMANN, baritone, b. Apr. 5, 1870, Breslau, Germany; d. Sept. 13, 1944, Bad Weissee, Germany. Son of the Wagner singer Eugen Gura (1843-1906), he studied with his father and also at the Munich Academy of Music with Hasselbeck and Zenger. He made his debut (1890) at the Royal Theater in Weimar as the Flying Dutchman. Later engagements: Riga (1890-91), the Kroll Opera (1891-92), Aachen (1892-93), Zürich (1893-94), Basel (1894-95), the Munich Royal Opera (1895-96), and as singer and *régisseur* at Schwerin (1896-1908); with the ensemble of this house he made guest appearances in 1898 at the Berlin Imperial Opera. In 1908 he founded his own opera theater, the New Royal Opera, in Berlin, which he directed until 1910. He was briefly the director of the Berlin Komische Oper in 1911. He made guest appearances at Covent Garden and lived until 1921 as a teacher in Berlin. Hhe then became *régisseur* of the Helsinki Opera (1921-26). He again resumed his teaching activity in Berlin, where he founded an opera association, the German Gastspieloper, in 1928. As his third wife he married the dramatic soprano Annie Gura-Himmel (b. 1884). His daughter, Anita Gura (b. 1911), was also a well-known soprano. He had a well-trained flexible voice, outstanding in both opera and song.

Records: G & T (Schwerin, 1905) and HMV.

GUSALEWICZ, GENIA, contralto-soprano, b. 1902, Prague. She was the daughter of the tenor Eugen Gusalewicz and the soprano Alice Gusalewicz, both of whom made interesting records for Zonophone. She was a pupil of her mother, who had been engaged at the Cologne Opera not long after her daughter was born. In 1923 she made her debut as Mignon at the Berlin State Opera, to which she belonged until 1929; there she sang mostly small mezzo-soprano roles. In 1929 she made guest appearances at the Vienna State Opera and in 1930 was engaged by the Opera in Chemnitz, where she sang dramatic soprano parts. Later she turned to operetta and had great success in these parts, particularly in Munich. After World War II she settled in Cologne as a teacher.

Records: Acoustic records for Vox as a soprano, electric records for HMV and Polydor, all ensemble scenes. U.S. re-issue: Victor.

GUTHEIL-SCHODER, MARIE, soprano, b. Feb. 16, 1874, Weimar, Germany; d. Oct 1, 1935, Ilmenau, Germany. She completed the Archducal Music School in Weimar and became a pupil of Virginia Naumann-Gungl there; she made her debut in Weimar (1891) as the First Lady in Die Zauberflöte. In the first years she sang only small roles, but in 1895 she had great success as Carmen. In 1899 she made guest appearances in Leipzig, Berlin, and Vienna. She came to the Vienna Imperial Opera in 1900 and became one of the best-loved singers there. She sang at that house in many important premières, including the title role in Elektra (1909) and Octavian in Der Rosenkavalier (1911). She appeared as Susanna in Le Nozze di Figaro at the Salzburg Festival (1906). She favored contemporary music and in 1914 sang works by Arnold Schoenberg at the Association for Private Musical Performances. She was admired as a highly successful artist in Vienna until 1926, and occupied herself as opera régisseur at both the Vienna Opera and the Salzburg Festivals. Her first marriage was to the conductor Gustav Gutheil (1868-1914), and her second to the photographer Franz Setzer. She had a well-trained and musical soprano voice of great expressive quality, with which she was able to master all the riches of operatic literature. She was also famous as a concert soprano.

Records: Five very rare records for G & T (Vienna, 1902).

GUTHRIE, FRANK, bass, b. 1924, Idaho. He studied first in Los Angeles, but became a soldier in World War II. In 1950 he had his first engagements with small opera troupes in the United States. In 1953 he went to Europe to complete his vocal training and studied with Elisabeth Rado in Vienna. There he sang in concert performances of Oedipus Rex under Von Karajan in 1953. He sang at the Vienna State Opera (1954-58) and since then at the Opera in Frankfurt a. M. He has made guest appearances in Rome, Trieste, and Munich. In 1956 he sang Sarastro in Die Zauberflöte at the Glyndebourne Festival and in 1959 the same role at the Aix-en-Provence Festival. He is a famous oratorio soloist.

Records: Amadeo-Vanguard (The Creation), HMV and Vox. U.S. re-issue: Bach Guild, Westminister, SPA, Vanguard.

GUTSTEIN, ERNST, baritone, b. May 15, 1924, Vienna. He studied at the Vierna Music Academy with Fuhsperg, Josef Witt, and Hans Duhan and made his debut (1948) in Innsbruck as Fernando in Fidelio. He remained there until 1952, sang in Heidelberg (1953-54), Kassel (1954-58), at the German-Opera-on-the-Rhine at Düsseldorf-Duisberg (1958-59), at Frankfurt (1959-62), and since 1962 at Cologne and Frankfurt. He appeared in the Salzburg Festival in 1959. He has made guest appearances at Zürich, Wiesbaden, Hamburg, and many other famous German opera houses. He has sung abroad in Florence, Rome, Brussels, and Holland. In 1959 he appeared in Haydn's Il Mondo nella Luna at Salzburg. He is particularly esteemed as a Verdi and Wagner interpreter.

Records: Ariola (Jochanaan in Salome, Rigoletto, Herr Fluth in The Merry Wives of Windsor). U.S. re-issue: Angel, Vox.

H

HABICH, EDUARD, baritone, b. Sept. 3, 1880, Kassel, Germany; d. Mar. 15, 1960, Berlin. He attended the Raff Conservatory in Frankfurt a. M. as a pupil of Max Fleisch and made his debut (1904) in Coblenz. He then sang in Posen and Halle, at the Düsseldorf Opera, and after 1910 at the Berlin Imperial Opera. He was admired there for more than twenty-five years. His special role was Alberich in the *Ring* cycle, which he sang at Bayreuth (1911-31). In 1912 he appeared at Bayreuth as Klingsor in *Parsifal* and in 1927 as Kurwenal in *Tristan und Isolde*. After 1923 he sang almost every year as a guest at Covent Garden, in Amsterdam (1928), at the Chicago Opera (1930-32), and at the Metropolitan Opera (1935-37). He was especially admired in New York as Alberich and as Telramund in *Lohengrin*. After the close of his long career he lived and taught in Berlin.

Records: HMV and Odeon in the acoustic period; electrics for HMV. *U.S. re-issue:* Opera Disc; RCA Victor, American Decca. *U.S. re-recording:* TAP.

HACKETT, CHARLES, tenor, b. Nov. 21, 1889, Worcester, Mass.; d. Jan. 1, 1942, New York. His voice was discovered by Lillian Nordica, who took him with her on a concert tour. He then studied with Hubbard in Boston, with Lombardi in Milan, and made his debut (1915) under the name Carlos Hackett in Pavia as Faust in *Mefistofele*. After his debut he appeared at various Italian theaters, including La Scala. In 1917-18 he had great success at the Teatro Colón and in 1919 was invited to the Metropolitan Opera, making his debut there as Almaviva in *Il Barbiere di Siviglia*. He remained at the Metropolitan until 1922, and then had a highly successful career at La Scala, Monte Carlo, and Paris. He was engaged at the Chicago Opera (1923-31) and sang as guest at Covent Garden (1926). He was well-liked at the Ravinia Summer Opera, near Chicago where he appeared frequently. He was again at the Metropolitan Opera (1934-40) and thereafter was a teacher at the Juilliard School of Music. One of the most beautiful lyric tenor voices of his generation. He was particularly outstanding in *bel canto* roles and Mozart parts.

Records: Edison* cylinders and discs were made while he was still a student; he made Columbia* discs later. *U.S. re-recording:* TAP.

HADRABOVÁ, EVA, soprano, b.

Oct. 12, 1902, Lunza, near Raknovic, Czechoslovakia. She studied at the Conservatory in Prague as well as with Steiner and Lunzer in Vienna. She made her debut (1922) as Micaëla in *Carmen* at Moravská Ostrava. After singing at Olomouc (1923-26) and Bratislava (1926-27), she was engaged by the Vienna State Opera (1928-36). During this time she also had great success at the Salzburg Festivals as Dorabella in *Così fan tutte* and as Octavian in *Der Rosenkavalier*. She sang at the Prague Opera (1936-37), at Graz (1938-39), and Nuremberg (1939-42). In 1934 she traveled through the United States; she made guest appearances also at Covent Garden, in Cracow and Antwerp, and in 1938 a few times at the Vienna State Opera. She lives in the Heitzing district of Vienna. She had a strongly expressive voice and was most successful in dramatic roles.

Records: Two Ultraphon discs in duets with Wilhelm Rode.

HADWIGER, ALOYS, tenor, b. Aug. 11, 1879, Olmütz, Austria; d. Mar. 23, 1948, Graz, Austria. His voice was discovered by Cosima Wagner and he studied under Julius Kniese at the Bayreuth School. He made his debut at the Bayreuth Festival (1904) as Froh in *Das Rheingold*; in 1906 and 1908 he was applauded there as Parsifal. He sang at Bremen (1910-18), Graz (1918-20), Freiburg im Br. (1921-26), and after 1927 at Kaiserslautern. In 1910 he appeared briefly and unsuccessfully at the Dresden Opera. After the end of his singing career he directed the Mecklenburger Theater in Schwerin (1933-34). A heroic tenor voice, noted in Wagner roles.

Records: HMV.

HAEFLIGER, ERNST, tenor, b. July 6, 1919, Davos, Switzerland. He attended the teachers' course in Wettingen and took his diploma as a school music teacher but studied singing at the same time. After completing his vocal training with Julius Patzak in Vienna, he made his debut (1942) as a concert singer. In 1943 he was engaged in Zürich, where he stayed until 1952. Also in 1943 he created a sensation when he sang the Evangelist in Bach's *St. Matthew Passion* in various Swiss cities. During his stay in Zürich he gave many successful concerts in Switzerland, Germany, Austria, Italy, France, Belgium, and Holland. He was hired as first lyric tenor by the Berlin City Opera in 1952. At the same time he strengthened his international career as both a concert and operatic tenor. He has made highly successful tours in the United States. With a great musical imagination and a fine feeling for style, he excelled in a wide repertory, but his most famous performances have been in oratorio and in song recitals.

Records: Philips (*Oedipus Rex*), but particularly for DGG* (*Die Entführung aus dem Serail, Don Giovanni, Fidelio,* and *Die Zauberflöte*). U.S. re-issue: Angel, Columbia, Epic, London, Swiss Record Library, Heliodor.

HAFGREN, LILY, soprano, b. Oct. 7, 1884, Stockholm; d. Feb. 27, 1965. Berlin. Her father, Erik Hafgren, was a theater manager; her mother, Maria Malmgren, a concert singer. She began her studies at the Raff Conservatory in Frankfurt a. M. and then became a pupil of Max Fleisch in Stuttgart. After completing her studies in Milan, she made her debut at the Bayreuth Festival (1908) as Freia in *Das Rheingold*. She sang at Mannheim (1908-12) and at the Berlin Imperial Opera (1912-20). She then made guest appearances on many famous stages including La Scala, the Paris Opéra, the Teatro Costanzi, the Stockholm Royal Opera, and in Madrid, Bu-

charest, Warsaw, and Prague. She was highly successful at the Bayreuth Festivals, singing Elsa in *Lohengrin* (1909), Eva in *Die Meistersinger* (1911-12; 1924). She sang at the Dresden State Opera (1933-34) and then lived in Berlin. Her first marriage was to the intendant Waag; her second to the merchant Dinkela. A beautifully managed and uncommonly melodious soprano voice, prized mostly in Strauss and Wagner operas; she was esteemed as a great actress.
Records: Odeon and Polydor.

HALLER, VALENTIN, tenor, b. May 1, 1901, Munich; d. Mar. 24, 1944, Munich. He began his career in Gera in 1924, sang in Plauen (1924-26), Augsburg (1926-28), Mannheim (1928-29), Braunschweig (1929-32), Leipzig (1932-33), and finally was engaged at the Berlin City Opera (1933). In 1934-35 he was simultaneously engaged at Kassel. In Berlin he caused great excitement by his singing of heroic parts, such as Manrico in *Il Trovatore*, for the brilliance of his voice in the higher ranges. He died as a consequence of a spinal injury.
Records: A few Parlophone records.

HALLSTEIN, INGEBORG, soprano, b. 1931, Munich. She took her first voice lessons from her mother, who was a singer; she then studied at the Music High School in Munich and made her stage debut in Passau (1956). After engagements in Basel and at the Theater am Gärtnerplaz in Munich, she was chosen for the Munich State Opera in 1959. Since then she has had an international starring career, with guest appearances at the Salzburg Festivals, at Covent Garden, and in South American opera houses. In 1962 she sang at the opening performance in the newly remodeled Theater an der Wien under Von Karajan. She has had great success as an operetta singer on German television. She has a beautiful and technically brilliant coloratura voice, complemented by an outstanding acting talent.
Records: DGG (Marzelline in *Fidelio*) and Eurodisc-Ariola. *U.S. re-issue:* Angel.

HALMOS, JÁNOS, tenor, b. Dec. 27, 1887; d. Oct. 7, 1961, Budapest. At first a choir singer in Arad, he later studied singing in Budapest, but was really self-taught. He was engaged at the Budapest National Opera in 1928 and remained there as first tenor until 1950, appearing as a guest even later. He was very successful in guest appearances at La Scala and in Breslau and Florence. One of the most beautiful voices of his epoch, outstanding in heroic parts.
Records: HMV.

HAMMES, KARL, baritone, b. Mar. 25, 1896, Zell-am-Mosel, Germany; d. Sept. 10, 1939, near Warsaw. After he had served in the air force in World War I, he took up singing and made his operatic debut (1925) in Cologne; from there he went in 1927 to the Kroll Opera for two years. In 1927 he sang Amfortas in *Parsifal* and Gunther in *Götterdämmerung* at the Bayreuth Festival. He was a highly successful member of the Vienna State Opera (1929-35). He sang almost every year in the Salzburg Festivals, particularly in the title roles in *Don Giovanni* and *Le Nozze di Figaro*. His guest appearances included Brussels, Amsterdam, London, Munich, and Hamburg. At the beginning of World War II he volunteered for the Luftwaffe and shortly thereafter was fatally wounded in an air battle over Warsaw.
Records: HMV. *U.S. re-recording:* Belcanto.

HAMMOND, JOAN, soprano, b. May 24, 1912, Christchurch, New

Zealand. She studied piano and violin at the Conservatory in Sydney, Australia, and for a few years was a violinist in an Australian orchestra. In 1931 she gave her first vocal concert in Sydney. In the following years she undertook tours through Australia with English opera troupes, and at the same time worked as a sports writer for a newspaper. In 1936 she came to England for three years of study, which she completed with Dino Borgioli in London, in Italy, and in Austria. She gave her first concert in Europe at Aeolian Hall in London (1938). She sang at the Vienna State Opera (1946-48) and during that time made successful guest appearances at Covent Garden, the Paris Opéra, the Brussels Opera, and many other famous theaters. She also gave very successful concerts and made guest appearances in North America. She gave up her career in 1965.

Records: HMV (*Dido and Aeneas*) and Columbia.

HANN, GEORG, bass, b. Jan. 30, 1897, Vienna; d. Dec. 9, 1950, Munich. He volunteered for the Austrian army in World War I and rose to the rank of lieutenant before his discharge in 1918. He then tried his hand at various occupations before beginning to study singing at the Vienna Academy of Music with Theodor Lierhammer. He was engaged in 1927 by the Bavarian State Opera in Munich and remained a member of this organization until his death. He was highly successful as a singer in Munich and had many opportunities for guest appearances in Vienna, Brussels, Berlin, Paris, London, and at La Scala. He also sang at the Salzburg Festivals: Pizarro in *Fidelio* (1931), Sarastro in *Die Zauberflöte*, Faninal in *Der Rosenkavalier* (1946), Leporello in *Don Giovanni* (1947), and Waldner in *Arabella* (1947). He had great success as a concert singer. His sumptuous and thoroughly trained bass voice was one of the best of his generation.

Records: His first records appeared relatively late in World War II. He sang particularly for DGG (*Cavalleria Rusticana, I Pagliacci,* and *Rigoletto*), Vox (*Der Fliegende Holländer* and *Der Rosenkavalier*), Urania* (*Der Corregidor*), and MMS* (*The Creation*). *U.S. re-issue:* Haydn Society.

HANSEN, POUL, tenor-baritone, b. Apr. 3, 1886, Copenhagen; d. Dec. 11, 1967, Helsinki. He was originally a copper engraver, then studied singing with Albert Hoeberg and Hermann Spiro in Copenhagen, and made his debut at the Opera there (1908) as Sverkel in *Lida Kirsten*. He remained at the Copenhagen Opera until 1913, then sang at the Berlin-Charlottenburg Opera (1913-14). In Berlin he studied further with Lilli Lehmann, Louise Reuss-Belce, and Richard Loewe. In 1919 he changed to a baritone, but sang tenor parts until 1921, these last mostly *buffo* roles. This artist was greatly admired in Berlin and in 1918-22 he appeared in a number of silent films, including *Der Müde Tod* with Lil Dagover and *Herrin der Welt* with Mia May and Michael Bohnen. He directed the theater in Gera (1925-30), where he also appeared as a singer. Thereafter he lived and taught in Copenhagen, then in Helsinki. Through his change of voice he mastered a stage repertory in both ranges of over one hundred and fifty roles.

Records: As a tenor for HMV and Polydor; as a baritone for Parlophone.

HARRELL, MACK, baritone, b. Oct. 8, 1909, Celeste, Tex.; d. Jan. 28, 1960, New York. He first studied violin, then singing, at the Juilliard School of Music in New York and made his debut there in a song recital (1934). At first he appeared only as a concert singer. In 1937 he had great success in a European concert tour, particularly in Holland and Belgium. In 1939 he was engaged at the Metropolitan Opera, where his debut role was Biterolf in *Tannhäuser*; he remained there until 1954. Although he sang as guest at the larger American opera houses, he was heard in Europe only in concert. He sang Nick in the Metropolitan *première* of *The Rake's Progress*. In 1949 he made a tour through Germany, Holland, and England. In 1952 he appeared at the Edinburgh Festival and was active as a teacher at the Juilliard School (1945-56).

Records: RCA Victor*, Remington*, and American Columbia* (for the latter he sang the title role in *Wozzeck*, among others).

HARROLD, ORVILLE, tenor, b. 1878, Muncie, Ind.; d. Oct. 23, 1933, Darien, Conn. He sang as a boy in a vocal quartet and was encouraged by Ernestine Schumann-Heink to take up a singing career. However, at first he sang only in cabarets and in small vaudeville theaters. Oscar Hammerstein arranged to have him study singing with Oscar Saenger in New York. In 1910 he made his debut at Hammerstein's Manhattan Opera House as Canio in *I Pagliacci*. In 1911-12 he again returned to the operetta stage, but resumed his studies in Paris and made guest appearances in London. He was highly successful at the Chicago Opera (1912-13; 1916-19; 1922), but in between he appeared in operettas and musical comedies. He was a member of the Metropolitan Opera (1919-24), making his debut there as Leopold in *La Juive* with Enrico Caruso and Rosa Ponselle. In 1920 he made an American tour with the Scotti Opera Company. After 1924 he chose to sing only in operettas.

He had a well-trained lyric tenor voice.

Records: Edison*, American Columbia*, and Victor*. *U.S. re-recording:* TAP.

HARSHAW, MARGARET, contralto-soprano, b. May 12, 1912, Philadelphia. She studied at the Curtis Institute of Music in Philadelphia and sang first as a contralto with various opera associations there. In 1934 she appeared at Atlantic City, New Jersey, with the Steel Pier Opera Company. In 1942 she was engaged at the Metropolitan Opera, where she first sang the Second Norn in *Götterdämmerung*. She was highly successful there, particularly as a Wagner singer. In the 1950-51 season she stepped in for an indisposed colleague in the role of Senta in *Der Fliegende Holländer*. She then added the most important dramatic soprano roles to her repertory and was esteemed as a worthy successor to Helen Traubel. In 1953 she appeared at Covent Garden as Brünnhilde in the *Ring* cycle. In 1954 she sang Donna Anna in *Don Giovanni* at the Glyndebourne Festival.

Records: As a contralto for RCA Victor (duet from *Norma* with Zinka Milanov and duets with Eleanor Steber); as a soprano for American Columbia* (Philips) (including *Cavalleria Rusticana* with Richard Tucker).

HARTMANN, CARL, tenor, b. May 2, 1895, Solingen, Germany. He first worked in a razor-blade factory in Solingen and in 1921 began his study of singing with Senff in Dusseldorf. He made his debut as *Tannhäuser* (1928) in El berfeld. In 1930 he created great excitement in America as a member of the German Opera Company led by Johanna Gadski. After 1930 he sang frequently at the Zoppot Festival. In 1931 he was engaged by the City Opera in Berlin and became one of the most famous Wagner tenors of his time. He appeared as guest at the Vienna State Opera, in Italy, France, and Switzerland. In 1937 he came to the Metropolitan Opera, making his debut as Siegfried; he remained there until 1940 and was highly successful in Wagner roles. In 1938 he sang Tristan at the Bayreuth Festival. After World War II he chose to appear no more. He lives in Pasing, a suburb of Munich.

Records: He left only a few records; the earliest were popular songs for Homochord, then two operatic records for the same label; finally he made Parlophone records (including the Bridal Chamber Scene from *Lohengrin*). U.S. reissue: American Decca.

HAYDTER, ALEXANDER, bass-baritone, b. 1872, Vienna; d. Feb. 13, 1919, Vienna. He was at first a worker in fancy leather goods, then began to study singing with Joseph Gänsbacher and Geiringer in Vienna. He made his debut (1896) as St. Bris in *Les Huguenots* at Zürich. Further vocal study with Adolf Uttner in Zürich followed and he sang at the German Theater in Prague (1898-1905). In 1905 he was engaged at the Vienna Imperial Opera and remained there until his death. At the Salzburg Festival of 1906, organized by Lilli Lehmann, he sang Bartolo in *Le Nozze di Figaro* and in 1910 the Speaker in *Die Zauberflöte*. He was married to the contralto Hermine Kittel. His was a dark-timbered voice and he was much admired in a wide-ranging repertory.

Records: G & T (Prague, 1904), Favorite (Vienna, 1905-06), and Odeon (Vienna, 1906-07).

HAYES, ROLAND, tenor, b. June 3, 1887, Curryville, Ga. His parents were originally Negro slaves; after their freedom was obtained, they worked on a farm. After the death of his father he came to Chattanooga in 1900. Here he had his first vocal study with Calhoun. In 1905 he obtained a scholarship to Fisk University, but had to give it up. He found work in Boston and studied singing with Arthur Hubbard there. As a Negro he had great difficulty in establishing his career. He gave his first concert without particular success in 1915. In 1917 he appeared in Boston Symphony Hall in a program which included Schubert lieder and arias by Mozart and Tchaikovsky; this concert and extended concert tours through the United States. brought him his first success. In 1920 he went to London, where he won great acclaim and where he studied again, this time lieder singing, with Sir George Henschel. He quickly became world-famous. He sang in Paris, Vienna, Budapest, Prague, Leipzig, Munich, The Hague, Amsterdam, Madrid, and Copenhagen. In 1924 he undertook an American tour of more than eighty concerts which was a great triumph. He toured Italy (1927) and Russia (1928). In Vienna he resumed his studies with Theodor Lierhammer. Since 1926 he has lived on his estate near Brookline, Mass. The brilliant career of this singer lasted a long time; in 1954 he again undertook a European tour and earned great admiration in England, Holland, and Denmark. He wrote an autobiography, *Angel Mo' and Her Son, Roland Hayes* (New York, 1942). He was greatly admired for the beauty of his interpretation of song texts and for the proper shadings and style of his enunciation. He was an unsurpassed interpreter of Negro spirituals and at the same time one of the greatest lieder singers of the twentieth century, as well as the first Negro singer to obtain a really worldwide reputation.

Records: Vocalion*, American Columbia*, and Vanguard* labels; he also sang for a few other minor labels. *U.S. re-recording:* Veritas.

HEIDERSBACH, KÄTHE, soprano, b. Oct. 30, 1897, Breslau, Germany. She first studied piano at the Breslau Conservatory, but after 1918 concentrated on the study of singing with Juan Luria, Fred Husler, and Lola Beeth in Berlin. She made her debut (1922) at Detmold; she was engaged at the Breslau Opera House (1924-27) and at the Berlin State Opera (1927-44). She sang at the Zoppot Festivals in 1930 and 1935. In 1928 she married the Swedish opera singer Nils Källe. She made guest appearances in Zürich, Vienna, Hamburg, and Munich and was highly successful at the Bayreuth Festivals, where she first sang in 1928; her roles there included Eva in *Die Meistersinger* (1933-34), Elsa in *Lohengrin* (1937), Freia in *Das Rheingold* (1933-42) and the Forest Bird in *Siegfried* (1934-40). In 1938 she appeared as guest in Amsterdam as Gutrune in *Götterdämmerung*. Since 1945 she has lived as a concert soprano and teacher in Stockholm.

Records: A few records for Odeon and HMV. *U.S. re-issue:* American Decca. *U.S. re-recording:* Eterna, Seraphim.

HEILBRONNER, ROSE, soprano, b. 1884, Paris, where her family had come from Alsace. She studied with Mme. Martini and Rosa Bauer in Paris and made her debut in 1907 at the Opéra-Comique as Diane in *Iphigènie en Aulide*. She remained a member of the Opéra-Comique until 1912 and appeared with the ensemble of this house during their guest season in Buenos Aires in 1911. After 1912 she sang at the most important French theaters, particularly at Nice and Monte Carlo. Upon the outbreak of World War I she gave up her career to become a nurse. Nevertheless, she sang in 1917 in Bordeaux, Marseilles, Geneva, and Nantes and in 1918 in Algiers and Tunis. She sang at the Brussels Opera (1919-22) and until about 1930 had a very successful career in France, especially as a concert singer and in song recitals. She had a warm and excellently trained voice.

Records: Odeon and HMV discs as well as Edison* cylinders. *U.S. re-issue:* Victor.

HEIM, MELITTA, soprano, b. Jan. 7, 1888, Vienna; d. January, 1950, London. She studied with Johannes Ress in Vienna and made her stage debut (1909) in Graz. She came to the Frankfurt Opera House in 1911 as first coloratura soprano and remained there until 1916. She made many guest appearances at the Vienna Imperial Opera and also at the Drury Lane Theater in London, where she appeared in 1912 and 1914 as the Queen of the Night in *Die Zauberflöte*. She had great success at the Vienna State Opera (1917-22). On account of a nervous disability she had to give up her stage career in 1922. She appeared only occasionally thereafter in the concert hall. Because she was Jewish, she had to flee to England, together with her mother, in 1938. In London she suffered such poverty that she had to earn her living as a scrubwoman for a time.

Records: Odeon discs as well as Edison* cylinders.

HEINRICH, JULIA, b. 1880 (?), Alabama; d. Oct. 18, 1919, Louisiana. The daughter of the German baritone Max Heinrich (1853-1916), she studied first with her father, then worked as a music teacher in a college. She sang with her father in Montreal in 1899 and then went to Europe and sang in Elberfeld (1910-13). She appeared with the ensemble of the Elberfeld house as a guest in Amsterdam, singing Sieglinde in *Die Walküre* (1913). She was a member of the Hamburg Opera (1913-15) and then was called to the Metropolitan Opera, where she made her debut as Gutrune in *Götterdämmerung*; however, she was given no other important roles there. She undertook concert tours in 1916 and appeared as an oratorio singer. In 1919, in a small Louisiana town, she made so-called "direct comparison tests," in which she sang and her Edison discs were played at the same time. She was killed by a locomotive at the railroad station there, while the pianist Lucille Colette, standing next to her, was uninjured.

Records: Only a few rare records by this artist exist on the Edison* label; these appeared under the name Julia Henry. *U.S. re-recording:* Odyssey.

HELDY, FANNY, soprano, b. 1888, Liège, Belgium. She studied at the Liège Conservatory and made her debut (1913) at the Brussels Opera. She sang there for two seasons, then at Vichy and Aix-les-Bains and in 1917 was engaged by the Opéra-Comique, making her debut as Violetta in *La Traviata*. She remained for more than twenty years the admired prima donna of this house and of the Paris Opéra. At the latter she sang in several world *premières*, including *Antar* (1921) and *Le Marchand de Venise* (1935). At Monte Carlo she appeared in the world *première* of *L'Aiglon* (1937). In 1923 she was admired at La Scala in *Louise* under Toscanini; she also appeared as a guest at Covent Garden (1927-28) and at the Teatro Colón (1927). She made regular guest appearances at the Teatro Liceo and also at the opera houses in Brussels, Nice, Monte Carlo, and Marseilles. In 1939 she retired to live in her chateau in the Loire valley. Her interpretations were marked by beauty of tone, lyric expressiveness, and absolute mastery of singing technique.

Records: Pathé (including *Manon*, 1923); then electric records for HMV.

HELGERS, OTTO, bass, b. Dec. 4, 1882, Frankfurt a. M. First a pupil of Eugen Hildach in Frankfurt, he made his debut (1909) as a pupil of the Opera House School in Hannover and remained there until 1911. He sang at Aachen (1911-13) and at the Royal Opera in Stuttgart (1913-20). After 1920 he was a member of the Berlin State Opera, where he remained for over twenty years. He was a regular guest at Covent Garden (1925-33), singing particularly Wagner roles there; he was also greatly admired at the Zoppot Festivals. He had a large bass voice, particularly outstanding in Wagner parts, but he was also famous as a concert singer.

Records: Acoustics for Polydor, electrics for Polydor and HMV. *U.S. re-issue:* RCA Victor. *U.S. re-recording:* Angel, Rococo, Veritas.

HELLETSGRUBER, LUISE, soprano, b. 1898 (?), Vienna; d. Jan. 1, 1967, in an auto accident near Vienna. She began her stage career at the Vienna State Opera in 1922 and remained there throughout her entire career. She was particularly admired as a Mozart singer, and as such she sang in the Salzburg Festivals (1928-37), especially as Cherubino and Donna Anna. After 1934 she also belonged to the ensemble of the Glyndebourne Festival, where her Mozart interpretations delighted the public. She remained at the Vienna State Opera until 1942. In 1943 she was engaged for a season at the Neues Lustspielhaus in Berlin.

Records: Parlophone and HMV, including complete operas from Glyndebourne, *Le Nozze di Figaro*, *Don Giovanni*, and *Così fan tutte*. *U.S. re-issue:* American Decca, RCA Victor. *U.S. re-recording:* Electrola, Vox.

HELM, ANNY, soprano, b. 1903, Vienna. She was trained by Marie Gutheil-Schoder and Gertrude

Förstel in Vienna, then by Ernst Grenzebach in Berlin, and made her debut (1924) at Magdeburg, where she remained until 1927. She was a member of the Berlin City Opera (1927-33) and guest appearances took her to the Vienna State Opera, to Munich, Hamburg, Dresden, Paris, Milan, Rome, and Brussels. She sang at the Bayreuth Festivals (1927-31) and was particularly admired there as Brangäne in *Tristan und Isolde*. In 1933 she went to Italy, where she married and where she had great success under the name Anny Helm-Sbisà. She sang as guest at La Scala and elsewhere, including the 1934 Arena Festival. In 1941 she withdrew from the stage and now lives in Trieste.

Records: HMV and Columbia*, (including *Tristan und Isolde*, Bayreuth, 1928).

HEMPEL, FRIEDA, soprano, b. June 26, 1885, Leipzig; d. Oct. 7, 1955, Berlin. She studied at the Stern Conservatory in Berlin with Selma Nicklass-Kempner and made her debut (1905) in Breslau; she then sang in Schwerin (1905-07). As early as 1905 she appeared in the Bayreuth Festival. In 1907 she was engaged by the Berlin Imperial Opera, where she had great success After 1907 she made brilliant guest appearances at Covent Garden. In 1912 she went to the Metropolitan Opera, where she remained until 1920. There she sang the Marschallin in the first New York performance of *Der Rosenkavalier* in 1913; in 1916 she was highly admired there in *L'Elisir d'Amore* opposite Enrico Caruso. Guest appearances in Berlin, Hamburg, London, and Paris brought her the greatest success. In 1920-21 she sang at the Chicago Opera. Thereafter she dedicated herself entirely to concert work and became famous for her "Jenny Lind" concerts, in which she sang in the costume and with the repertory of the unforgettable Swedish singer; she made these appearances in all the important centers of American musical life as well as in England, France, Belgium, and Holland. Her memoirs were published under the title *Mein Leben dem Gesang* (Berlin, 1955). Her coloratura soprano was admired for its virtuoso management, for the clarity of tonal production, and for the musical maturity of her conceptions.

Records: She made a great many records for Odeon, HMV, Victor*, Polydor, and both Edison* discs and cylinders. *U.S. re-issue:* IRCC, HRS, Okeh, Opera Disc. *U.S. re-recordings:* Scala, Eterna, FRP, Rococo, RCA Victor, Belcanto, Odyssey.

HENDERSON, ROY, baritone, b. July 4, 1889, Edinburgh. He made his concert debut in London (1925) in Delius' *A Mass of Life*, after his studies at the Royal Academy of Music there and after winning several prizes. In 1928 he had his first great success at Covent Garden, where he often appeared thereafter. At the first Glyndebourne Festival in 1934 he sang Count Almaviva in *Le Nozze di Figaro* and appeared there annually until 1940. In 1933 he sang in the International Festival for Contemporary Music in Amsterdam. After 1940 he became a professor at the Academy of Music in London; among his pupils was the great contralto Kathleen Ferrier. After World War II he was one of the founders of the Edinburgh Festival, where he sang in productions in 1947-48. Since 1951 he has been occupied solely as a teacher. On the stage he was admired especially as a Mozart singer; in the concert hall as an interpreter of modern English music.

Records: HMV (*Le Nozze di Figaro* and Masetto in *Don Giovanni*, both Glyndebourne, 1935) and U.S. Columbia* (*Les Noces* conducted by Stravinsky). *U.S. re-issue:* RCA Victor. *U.S. re-recording:* Vox-Turnabout.

HENKE, WALDEMAR, tenor, b. Mar. 24, 1876, Königsberg, Germany; d. 1945 (?). He was first an actor and began this career in Posen in 1896. Two years later he decided to become an opera singer and was engaged in Posen (1898-1901) and Wiesbaden (1901-11). In 1911 he came to the Berlin Imperial Opera, where he was an admired *buffo* tenor for over twenty years. He sang Valzacchi there in the first performance of *Der Rosenkavalier* in 1911 and in 1925 he sang in the world *première* of *Wozzeck*. In these two decades he made guest appearances mostly with the Berlin ensemble in Holland, England, Spain, and Switzerland. After the end of his career he was active as a *régisseur*. In 1944 he left Berlin and returned to his birthplace, Königsberg; he probably perished in flight from this beleaguered city in the winter of 1945. He was one of the most famous *buffo* tenors of his time.

Records: Acoustics for HMV, Beka, Pathé*, and Odeon; electrics for Polydor, including many operatic highlights. *U.S. re-issue:* Brunswick. *U.S. re-recording:* Eterna.

HENSCHEL, SIR GEORGE, baritone, b. Feb. 18, 1850, Breslau, Germany; d. Sept. 10, 1934, on his estate, Aviemore, in Scotland. He studied at the Leipzig Conservatory (1867-70) and in Berlin became a pupil of the composer Friederich Kiel. He quickly became famous as a conductor and concert singer. Johannes Brahms greatly admired his voice and often appeared as his accompanist. He was the conductor of the newly founded Boston Symphony Orchestra (1881-84) and then settled down in London and directed the London Symphony Orchestra until 1886, while he was also active as a concert and lieder singer. At these recitals he nearly always accompanied himself at the piano. In 1886 he became a teacher at the Royal College of Music and in 1890 he became an English citizen. He was the director of the Scottish Symphony Orchestra in Glasgow (1893-95). In 1914 he was knighted by King George V. Sir George Henschel was also a successful composer: he wrote three operas, *Friederich der Schöne, A Sea Change,* and *Nubia,* as well as incidental music for Shakespeare's *Hamlet,* an eight-part Mass, a Stabat Mater, a string quartet, sacred choral songs, and lieder. He published several interesting books, including *Personal Recollections of J. Brahms* (Boston, 1907) and *Musings and Memories of a Musician* (London, 1918). His daughter published his biography under the title *When Soft Voices Die* (London, 1944). He retained his beautiful voice for an unusually long time; in 1928 he allowed records to be issued, which are of great documentary worth. He never appeared on the stage, but once in London he sang Hans Sachs in a concert performance of *Die Meistersinger*.

Records: Acoustics for HMV; electrics for Columbia* (1928); he conducted Beethoven's *First Symphony* for Columbia.

HENSEL, HEINRICH, tenor, b. Oct. 29, 1874, Neustadt an der Haardt, Germany; d. Feb. 23, 1935, Hamburg. His voice was discovered by the conductor Felix Mottl, and he studied with Gustav Walker in Vienna, as well as with Eduard Bellwidt in Frankfurt. He made his debut (1897) in Freiburg im Br. and from there he came to the Opera in Frankfurt, where he remained until 1906. He sang at Wiesbaden (1906-11). In the latter year his Parsifal and his Loge in the *Ring* cycle were greatly admired at the Bayreuth Festival. He sang at the Metropolitan Opera (1911-12) and at the Chicago Opera (1912). He was the admired first heroic and Wagner tenor at the Hamburg Opera (1912-29). In 1914 he sang Parsifal in the first local performances of the work at both Covent Garden and the Brussels Opera; other guest appearances included Copenhagen, Berlin, Vienna, Munich, Paris, and Amsterdam. At the end of his life he became a teacher in Hamburg. He was married to the dramatic soprano Elsa Hensel-Schweitzer (b. 1878, Frankfurt a. M.), who sang in Dessau (1898-1901) and after that at the Frankfurt Opera; they were separated in 1910.

Records: G & T (Frankfurt 1903-06), HMV, Pathé*, Parlophone, and Edison* discs. (The voice of Elsa Hensel-Schweitzer is preserved on a few very rare records for Berliner [Frankfurt, 1901] and on G & T.) *U.S. re-recording* (of Heinrich Hensel): IRCC, Pathé.

HERLEA, NICOLAE, baritone, b. 1927, Bucharest. He studied at the Bucharest Conservatory with Aurelius Costescu-Duca and made his debut at the National Opera there (1950) as Silvio in *I Pagliacci*; he has remained there as first baritone. In 1951 he won prizes in international singing contests in Geneva, Prague, and Brussels and has added great success in guest appearances at La Scala and the Prague National Opera; he has appeared repeatedly at both the Bolshoi Theater and the State Opera in East Berlin. In 1961 he was admired at Covent Garden in London and as a guest with the Bucharest Opera in its performances in Brussels. He has sung at the Metropolitan Opera since 1964. In 1965 he sang at the Salzburg Festival. He has been successful on the stage in the Italian repertory particularly and in various roles in the concert hall. He is also an active music critic.

Records: Supraphon, Electrochord (a Rumanian label), and SSP.

HEROLD, VILHELM, tenor, b. Mar. 19, 1865, Hasle, Denmark; d. Dec. 15, 1937, Copenhagen. He started his studies in Copenhagen and completed them with Devellier in Paris. He made his stage debut at the Copenhagen Royal Opera (1893) as Faust. During the same year he gave concerts at the World's Fair in Chicago. He was engaged at the Stockholm Royal Opera (1901-03; 1907-09) and made guest appearances in Oslo, Prague, Berlin, Dresden, Hamburg, and Stuttgart. In 1904 he sang Lohengrin at Covent Garden with Emmy Destinn; in 1907 he sang Walther in *Die Meistersinger* there. In 1915 he ended his career at the Copenhagen Opera, where he had sung for over twenty years. He was director of the Copenhagen Opera (1922-24) and later became a teacher in Copenhagen. A brilliant tenor, he was particularly esteemed in Wagner parts, but was also admired in the Italian repertory.

Records: G & T, HMV, and Pathé.

HERRMANN, JOSEF, baritone, b. Apr. 20, 1903, Darmstadt, Germany; d. Nov. 19, 1955, Hildesheim, Germany. He studied at the Darmstadt Conservatory and made his debut (1925) in Kaiserslautern. He then sang successively in Stettin, Königsberg, and Nuremberg, as well as at the Zoppot Festivals (1939-41). In 1939 he was called to the Dresden State Opera as a heroic baritone and remained there until 1945. He was a member of the City Opera in Berlin (1944-55), but during this time also held a guest contract with Dresden. Guest appearances at La Scala, the Paris Opéra, and the

Teatro Colón permitted him to become one of the best-known Wagner singers of his time. He was admired for his several appearances at the Salzburg Festivals in the title role of *Wozzeck*. In 1955 he was engaged by the State Opera in East Berlin.
Records: HMV, Urania* (*Der Corregidor*) and DGG. *U.S. re-recording:* Rococo.

HERRMANN, THEO, bass, b. Jan. 26, 1902, Vienna. He made his debut as Mephistopheles in *Faust* (1922) at the Zagreb Opera and sang at the German Theater in Prague (1922-27) and at Darmstadt (1927-34). In 1934 he was called to the Hamburg State Opera as principal bass and remained there for a starring career during the next thirty years. In 1936 he appeared with the ensemble of the Dresden Opera in a guest season at Covent Garden. He was a guest at the Vienna State Opera in 1937 and 1938; in 1948 he appeared at the Cambridge Theater in London. In 1952 he sang Rocco in *Fidelio*, Baron Ochs in *Der Rosenkavalier*, and Riedinger in *Mathis der Maler* at the Edinburgh Festival. His later guest appearances include La Scala, the Teatro Liceo, the Salzburg and Maggio Musical Festivals, and the Marseilles Opera.
Records: Strangely enough there exists only a single Columbia record of Schubert lieder to show the beautiful voice of this artist, who mastered a many-sided repertory. He is not to be confused with the *buffo* tenor Theo Herrmann, who was engaged in the 1930's at Düsseldorf and who left no recordings.

HERWIG, KÄTHE, soprano, b. Dec. 9, 1891, Berlin; d. Oct. 28, 1953, Berlin. She studied with Ernst Grenzebach in Berlin and made her debut (1914) at the German Opera House there as the Shepherd Boy in *Tannhäuser*. She then became first coloratura at the Cologne Opera House (1919-34), where she was greatly beloved. She was also a successful concert singer. After the close of her career she lived and taught in Berlin.
Records: A great many acoustics for Polydor.

HERZOG, EMILIE, soprano, b. 1859, Ermatingen, Switzerland; d. June 19, 1923, Aarburg, Switzerland. She studied at the Zürich Music School with Karl Gloggner and in Munich with Adolf Schimon. She made her debut (1880) at the Munich Royal Opera as the Page in *Les Huguenots* and remained in Munich for nine years. In 1887 she married the Swiss writer on music, Heinrich Welti. After 1883 she sang several times at the Bayreuth Festivals. She was called to the Berlin Imperial Opera in 1889 and her career reached its highest point there. She was particularly admired as a Mozart interpreter. Guest appearances took her to the opera houses of London, Paris, Vienna, and Brussels; in 1896 she appeared as guest at the Imperial Opera in Moscow. She was a member of the Metropolitan Opera (1899-1900). After 1903 she taught at the Music High School in Berlin and sang until 1910 at the Opera there. She was a teacher at the Zürich Conservatory (1910-22). A virtuoso, but at the same time an expressive, coloratura voice.
Records: Rare G & T and Columbia* records. *U.S. re-recording:* Rococo.

HESCH, WILHELM, bass, b. July 3, 1860, Elbeteinitz, Bohemia; d. Jan. 4, 1908, Vienna. Originally Vilhelm Heš. While quite young he joined a traveling Bohemian theatrical troupe; he was then engaged by the director of the Prague National Opera and in 1880 made his debut there as Plunkett in *Martha*. He first excited great comment when he appeared with the Prague ensemble at the World Exposition in Vienna in 1892 as Kezal in *The Bartered Bride*. In 1893 he made an equally successful guest appearance at the Hamburg Opera. In 1895 he sang as guest at the Vienna Imperial Opera as Leporello in *Don Giovanni* and was then offered a contract there. Until his death he remained one of the best-loved members of the Vienna Opera. His Leporello was greatly admired at the 1901 Salzburg Festival. Possessing one of the most attractive bass voices of his time, he was outstanding for his deep and musical voice and for the skill in his management of it.

Records: A great many records, mostly for G & T (the oldest from 1902), one for Columbia*, more for Odeon and HMV. *U.S. re-issue:* IRCC. *U.S. re-recording:* TAP, Eterna.

HEYNIS, AAFJE, contralto, b. May 2, 1924, Krommenie, Holland. She studied with Aaaltje Noordewier-Reddingius in Hilversum after 1946 and later with Laurens Bogtman. After she has first appeared in church concerts, she sang the *Alto Rhapsody* of Brahms with the Amsterdam Concertgebouw Orchestra in 1958. Since then she has had great success as a concert and oratorio singer in Holland, Germany, Belgium, France, and Switzerland. She has not appeared on the stage. The luxuriant contralto voice of this singer is outstanding for the animated and stylistically controlled quality of her delivery.

Records: Philips*. *U.S. re-issue:* Epic, Mercury.

HIDALGO, ELVIRA DE, soprano, b. 1892, Aragon, Spain. She was a prodigy and appeared in public as a pianst at the age of twelve; she then studied singing in Barcelona and with Raoul Vidal in Milan. She made her debut (1908) at the age of sixteen at the Teatro San Carlo as Rosina in *Il Barbiere di Siviglia*. Her career developed quickly. In 1909 she appeared as guest at the Théâtre Sarah Bernhardt, in Cairo, and in Monte Carlo. She was engaged at the Metropolitan Opera (1910-11; 1924-26). She appeared at La Scala in 1916, at the Teatro Costanzi in 1919, and at the Teatro Colón in 1922. In 1924 she was greatly admired at Covent Garden as Gilda in *Rigoletto* and there followed a tour with the famous Russian bass Feodor Chaliapin. She married the director of the Casino in Ostend and appeared frequently in concert thereafter. After 1932 she lived and taught singing on the Grecian island of Corfu, then became a professor at the Conservatory in Athens, where she was the teacher of Maria Callas. In 1946 she became a professor at the Conservatory in Ankara. She now lives in Milan. People marveled both at the dark richness of her coloratura voice and at the technical skill of her vocal ornaments.

Records: Fonotipia and Columbia*, all rare. *U.S. re-recording:* TAP, Scala, FRP.

HIEDLER, IDA, soprano, b. Aug. 24, 1867, Vienna; d. Aug. 8, 1932, Berlin. She studied with Johannes Ress in Vienna. The intendant of the Berlin Imperial Opera, Count Hochberg, engaged her directly from the Conservatory and she made her debut (1887) as Marguerite in *Faust*. She remained an admired member of this company until 1908, sometimes appearing in dramatic and Wagner roles. In 1896 she was highly successful in a guest appearance in Moscow on the occasion of the Czar's coronation. After her retirement from the stage, she was a professor at the Berlin Music

High School (1910-26). She was also highly esteemed as a concert singer.

Records: Two extremely rare records for Columbia* (Berlin, 1904).

HILGERMANN, LAURA, contralto-soprano, b. Oct. 13, 1867, Vienna; d. 1937, Vienna. Her voice was discovered by an operetta singer and she was trained by Karl Maria Wolf and S. Rosenberg in Vienna. In 1885 she made her debut as Azucena in *Il Trovatore* at the German Theater in Prague. She remained there until 1889 and then sang at the Budapest National Opera (1890-1900). In 1900 she was engaged by Gustav Mahler for the Vienna Imperial Opera, and she remained a member of this organization until 1920. In Vienna she earned great admiration for her repertory, which included both contralto and soprano parts. In 1900 she sang Dorabella there in a memorable new production of *Cosi fan tutte*. After her retirement she was a much-sought-after singing teacher.

Records: G & T (Vienna, 1902), Odeon (Vienna, 1905-06), Zonophone (Vienna, 1907-08), and HMV (Vienna, 1908), all very rare.

HILLEBRECHT, HILDEGARD, soprano, b. Nov. 26, 1927, Hannover, Germany. She first studied medicine, then took up singing and made her debut (1951) at Freiburg im Br. as Leonora in *Il Trovatore*. Subsequent engagements included Zürich (1952-54), the German-Opera-on-the-Rhine at Düsseldorf-Duisberg (1954-59), and the Cologne Opera (1959-61). Since 1961 she has had brilliant success at the Munich State Opera and has made regular guest appearances at the State Operas in Vienna and Hamburg and at the Berlin City Opera. She has also been admired at the Salzburg and Munich Festivals, at the Holland Festival, and in Rio de Janeiro, Tunis, Paris, and Rome. She has a well-trained large voice and is especially admired in the operas of Verdi, Puccini, Mozart, Wagner, and Strauss.

Records: Electrola* and a recording of highlights from *Tannhäuser* for Opera. *U.S. re-issue:* Turnabout.

HINCKLEY, ALLEN, bass, b. Oct. 11, 1877, Gloucester, Mass.; d. Jan. 28, 1954, Yonkers, N.Y. He prepared himself to become a minister at Amherst College and the University of Pennsylvania, but was persuaded by the conductor Walter Damrosch to take up singing. He studied with Oscar Saenger in New York, then in Germany, and made his debut at the Hamburg Opera (1903), remaining there until 1908. His Wagner roles were greatly admired at the Bayreuth Festivals (1906-08), where he sang Hagen and Hunding in the *Ring* cycle and King Henry in *Lohengrin*. He was a member of the Metropolitan Opera (1908-14) and concurrently gave concerts and made guest appearances in the United States. He led the vocal classes at the Kansas City Conservatory (1917-23) and thereafter became a teacher and choir director in New York. He had a powerful and dark bass voice which reached its peak in Wagner roles.

Records: Rare records for HMV, the oldest from Hamburg in 1908.

HINES, JEROME, bass-baritone, b. 1918, Hollywood, Calif. He first studied mathematics and chemistry at the University of California at Los Angeles, then studied singing with Gennaro Cuni and made his debut at the San Francisco Opera (1941) as Biterolf in *Tannhäuser*. He sang opera in New Orleans and performed with various American orchestras. He was engaged by the Metropolitan Opera in 1946 and is still a member. Guest appearances brought him great success at the Opera Houses in Rio de Janeiro, São Paulo, Mexico City, and the Teatro Colón. In 1953 he sang Nick Shadow in *The Rake's Progress* at the Edinburgh Festival. In 1954 he was much admired as Don Giovanni in Munich and later made brilliant guest appearances at the Paris Opéra, the Vienna State Opera, the Rome Opera, the Maggio Musicale Festival, and in 1959 at La Scala. He has appeared at the Bayreuth Festivals since 1958; his most important success there was as Wotan (1960-61). He is also a composer. He has a splendidly trained voice of inexhaustible volume and a special intensity of dramatic expressiveness; he is equally admirable in Wagner roles and in all other areas of opera and oratorio. His autobiography, *This is My Story. This is My Song* was published in 1968.

Records: RCA Victor* (*Macbeth*) and Decca (*La Favorita*, among others). *U.S. re-issue:* London, Columbia, Word, Angel.

HIRZEL, MAX, tenor, b. Oct. 18, 1888, Zürich; d. May 12, 1957, Zürich. At first he was an engineer who practiced this profession in Zwickau and Augsburg. After studying singing in Dresden, he sang in Zürich (1917-22). In 1923 he came to the Dresden State Opera, where he was first lyric tenor and a much admired member of the company. Guest appearances took him to Covent Garden, among other places, where he sang Lohengrin and Tamino in *Die Zauberflöte*, the latter being one of his particular starring roles. He sang as guest at the Vienna State Opera (1935-36). In 1936 he had to leave Dresden because he had become known publicly as an opponent of National Socialism. He returned to Switzerland and sang there for several years in Zürich, Basel, and Bern. He had a well-trained and expressive voice.

Records: Swiss Gramophone Association and Parlophone. *U.S. re-issue:* American Odeon, American Decca.

HISLOP, JOSEPH, tenor, b. Apr. 5, 1884, Edinburgh, Scotland. At first he was a press photographer. His voice was discovered during a sojourn in Stockholm; he studied there with Gillis Bratt. He made his debut at the Royal Opera in Stockholm (1915) as Faust in Gounod's opera of that name. After remaining at the Stockholm Opera until 1919, he came to Covent Garden, where he was also highly successful. In 1923 he sang with the British National Opera Company and appeared as guest at La Scala as Edgardo in *Lucia di Lammermoor*. In 1920-21 he appeared in America with the Scotti Opera Company and later at the Chicago Opera. He sang as guest in 1925 at the Teatro Colón and in 1926 at the Opéra-Comique, and appeared frequently at the opera houses in Brussels, Liège, and Ghent. In 1927 he was admired at Covent Garden in *Faust* with Feodor Chaliapin. He became a regular guest at the Opera in Stockholm, where he had taken up residence. Later he settled down in Gothenburg as a teacher and became director of the Municipal Theater and the Conservatory there. After 1948 he became singing master at Covent Garden and at Sadler's Wells in London; since 1951 he has been a teacher at the Guildhall School of Music in London.

Records: Many recordings for HMV and a few for Pathé.

HOEKMAN, GUUS, bass, b. 1908 (?), Hilversum, Holland. Before World War II he became an officer in the Dutch navy, and during the war years he studied singing with Aaltje Noordewier-Reddingius in Hilversum. At the beginning of his career he sang particularly in the concert hall and the radio. In 1952 he made his stage debut at the Antwerp Opera, but his first big success was at the Netherlands Opera in Amsterdam. He sang at Düsseldorf-Duisberg (1961-62) and has made guest appearances at the Salzburg and the Glyndebourne Festivals, where in 1963-64 he sang Arkel in *Pelléas et Mélisande*, and in Boston as Osmin in *Die Entführung aus dem Serail*. He lives in Zandvoort.

Records: MMS (Sarastro in *Die Zauberflöte*) and Decca (*Pelléas et Mélisande*). *U.S. re-issue:* London. *U.S. re-recording:* Cantilena, Rococo.

HÖFFGEN, MARIA, contralto, b. Apr. 26, 1921. She studied at the Berlin High School for Music and with Weissenborn there, making her debut as a concert contralto in Berlin in 1952 (?). In 1953 she had great success as soloist in the *St. Matthew Passion* in Vienna under Von Karajan. Since then she has had a starring career as an oratorio and lieder singer. She has performed in concerts all over Europe and has had outstanding success at the great international music festivals. She has sung only a single role on the stage, that of Erda in the *Ring* cycle. In this part she appeared as guest at Covent Garden in 1959, at the Vienna State Opera, the Teatro Colón, and since 1960 at Bayreuth.

Records: DGG*, Columbia, HMV (mostly in oratorios and other sacred works). *U.S. re-issue:* Electrola, Angel, Turnabout, London, Philips, Nonesuch, Vox.

HOFFMANN, BAPTIST, baritone, b. July 9, 1864, Garitz, near Kissingen, Germany; d. July 5, 1937, Garitz, Germany. He studied with Julius Stockhausen in Frankfurt a. M. and with Frau Weinlich-Tripka in Munich. He made his debut (1888) at Graz as the Hunter in *Das Nachtlager von Granada*. He then sang at the Cologne Opera (1888-94), the Hamburg Opera (1894-97), and the Berlin Imperial Opera (1897-1919). There he appeared in the world *première* of *Der Roland von Berlin* in 1904 and sang Jochanaan in the Berlin *première* of *Salome* in 1906. In the course of his career he made guest appearances in Munich, Dresden, Hamburg, London, and Brussels. After he had left the stage he was active as a teacher in Berlin. His large-dimensioned baritone voice had great dramatic expressiveness; he found his most celebrated roles in the Wagner repertory.

Records: Berliner (Berlin, 1901), G & T (Berlin, 1901-07), Odeon (Berlin, 1905), HMV, Pathé*, and Parlophone. *U.S. re-recording:* Pathé Actuelle.

HOFFMANN, GRACE, contralto, b. Nov. 14, 1925, Cleveland, Ohio. She studied literature and musicology, then began her vocal studies with Friedrich Schorr and Giuseppe Gentile. She concluded her studies with Mario Basiola in Rome. After she had won a singing contest in Lausanne in 1951, she made her stage debut in Zürich (1952) as Azucena in *Il Trovatore*. She came to the Stuttgart State Opera in 1955 and has remained there ever since. She has been very successful in guest appearances at La Scala and Covent Garden, as well as in Vienna, Munich, San Francisco, and at the New York City Center Opera. She has appeared since 1957 at the Bayreuth Festivals, where she is particularly admired as Brangäne in *Tristan und Isolde*. Since 1958 she has also sung successfully at the Metropolitan Opera, her debut role there being Brangäne, and at the

Teatro Colón. The wide range of her voice is happily supplemented by her skill in delivery. She has appeared on the stage and in the concert hall in a great variety of roles. She is not to be confused with the coloratura soprano Grace Hoffman, who made acoustical records for American Pathé.

Records: DGG, Decca, Columbia, Opera (including *Salome* and *Der Barbier von Bagdad*). *U.S. re-issue:* Vox, London, Nonesuch, Angel, Fiesta.

HOFFMANN, LUDWIG, bass, b. Jan. 14, 1885, Frankfurt a. M.; d. Jan. 2, 1964, London. He studied with Ricutini in Frankfurt, then in Milan, and made his debut (1918) at Bamberg. His later engagements included Dessau (1919-20), Bremen (1920-25), Wiesbaden (1925-28), the Berlin City Opera (1928-32), and, after 1935, the Vienna State Opera. He first sang at the Bayreuth Festivals in 1928 and he appeared there in various Wagner roles until 1942; he also sang at the Zoppot Festivals (1930-34). His very successful appearances at the Salzburg Festivals included Osmin in *Die Entführung aus dem Serail*, the title role in *Le Nozze di Figaro*, and King Mark in *Tristan und Isolde* in 1935 under Toscanini. He sang as guest at first-rank opera houses all over the world: La Scala, Covent Garden, the Metropolitan Opera (1932-38), and all the largest German houses. He belonged to the Vienna State Opera until 1942, but made occasional guest appearances there until 1954 and was especially successful there after World War II. With his wide-ranging dark bass voice full of dramatic weight, he was particularly admired in Wagner roles.

Records: Parlophone, Polydor, and Pathé. *U.S. re-issue:* American Decca, RCA Victor. *U.S. re-recording:* Eterna.

HOLLWEG, ILSE, soprano, b. Feb. 23, 1922, Solingen, Germany. She studied at the Cologne Music High School with Gertrude Förstel and made her stage debut (1943) at Saarbrücken. From there she went to the Düsseldorf Opera in 1946 as first coloratura soprano. After singing briefly in Berlin and Hamburg (1951-52), she came to the Vienna State Opera in 1952. Since 1955 she has had a concurrent contract at Düsseldorf-Duisberg. She was admired as Konstanze in *Die Entführung aus dem Serial* at the Glyndebourne Festival in 1950 and since then has appeared there repeatedly and at the Edinburgh Festivals. She was a sensational success at Glyndebourne in 1955 as Zerbinetta in *Ariadne auf Naxos*. Since 1954 she has also sung at the Bayreuth Festivals and was very successful at the Salzburg Festival in 1955 as Konstanze. She has made guest appearances at the principal German theaters, at La Scala, Covent Garden, and many other noted operatic stages. Contemporary music is one of her specialties.

Records: Decca, Columbia (*Die Entführung aus dem Serail*), HMV, and Philips*. *U.S. re-issue:* Angel, Seraphim.

HOLM, RENATE, soprano, b. Aug. 10, 1931, Vienna. She first worked as an assistant to a dentist, then studied singing with Föhr-Waldeck and Maria Ivogün in Vienna. Since 1953 she has had a very successful career as a film singer and a singer of popular songs. In 1957 she appeared in operetta at the Theater an der Wien in Vienna, and a little later as Gretchen in *Der Wildschütz* at the Vienna Volksoper. She then was greatly admired at the Vienna State Opera. In 1961 she sang Blondchen in *Die Entführung aus dem Serail* at the Salzburg Festival. She has been admired both for her performances in soubrette

roles and for her unusual stage presentations.
Records: Particularly for Ariola-Bertelsmann (*Die Fledermaus*). *U.S. re-issue:* MGM.

HOLM, RICHARD, tenor, b. Aug. 3, 1912, Stuttgart. He studied at the Stuttgart Music High School and with Rudolf Ritter. He lived in Stuttgart, until 1937, as a concert singer and appeared on the Stuttgart radio; in that year he made his stage debut in Nuremberg and came by way of the Hamburg State Opera to the Bavarian State Opera in Munich (1952). There, as well as by guest appearances at leading theaters all over the world, he acquired fame as a Mozart interpreter. His guest appearances included La Scala, Covent Garden, the Vienna State Opera, as well as performances in the United States and at the Salzburg and Glyndebourne Festivals. He is also well known as a concert singer.
Records: DGG* (including *The Creation*, *Catulli Carmina*, *Die Meistersinger*, Mozart's *Requiem*, *Der Freischütz*, and *Bastien und Bastienne*). *U.S. re-issue:* Heliodor, American Decca.

HOMER, LOUISE, contralto, b. Apr. 28, 1871, Pittsburgh; d. May 6, 1947, Winter Park, Fla. Originally Louise Beatty. She studied in Philadelphia, Boston, and Paris, and made her debut (1898) at Vichy as Leonora in *La Favorita*. She sang for a time at Covent Garden and at the Théâtre de la Monnaie. In 1900 she returned to the United States and first sang in San Francisco as Amneris in *Aïda*. In the same year she joined the Metropolitan Opera, making her debut there also as Amneris. She sang at the Metropolitan for many years (1900-19; 1927-30). She sang the role of the Witch in the world *première* there of *Königskinder* (1910). She was a member of the Chicago Opera (1920-25) and appeared in opera in Los Angeles and San Francisco (1926). Guest appearances brought her great success all over the world, since she was considered one of the finest contraltos of her time. In 1909 she appeared in Paris in the title role of *Orphée et Eurydice*. In 1930 she retired from active musical life. She had married the composer Sidney Homer (1864-1953), and he wrote their memoirs under the title *My Wife and I* (New York, 1939). She was an aunt of Samuel Barber, the American composer. She had a contralto voice of great power and beauty. Although at first she confined herself to the French and Italian opera repertory, she later became a noted Wagner singer; she was also highly successful in the concert hall.
Records: Victor* (including some with Enrico Caruso); she is also to be heard on re-recordings of Mapleson cylinders. *U.S. re-issue:* HRS, IRCC. *U.S. re-recording:* IRCC, RCA Victor, Rococo, Belcanto, Cantilena.

HÖNGEN, ELIZABETH, contralto, b. Dec. 7, 1906, Gevelsberg, Germany. She appeared in public as a violinist at the age of fifteen, then studied German philology at the university and musicology at the Music High School in Berlin; her vocal studies were with Weissenborn. She made her debut (1933) in Wuppertal. From there she went to Düsseldorf in 1935, remaining until 1940. After singing at the Dresden State Opera (1940-43), she was engaged by the Vienna State Opera, where she remained for the next twenty years. She was admired in her appearances at La Scala, Covent Garden, the Teatro Colón, and the Paris Opéra; other cities where she was heard were Amsterdam, Zürich, Berlin, and Munich. She sang at the Metropolitan Opera (1951-52) and had great success at the opera festivals in Salzburg, Edinburgh, Bayreuth, and Florence. In 1957 she was given a professorship at the Vienna Academy of Music and gave up her starring career. With a wide-ranging and well-trained voice, her dramatic expressiveness, and her feeling for style, she was an admirable singer.

Records: HMV, Philips, DGG* (*Elektra*), Urania (*Macbeth*), and Decca (*Die Frau ohne Schatten*). *U.S. re-issue:* Angel, Everest, Electrola, Bach Guild, Haydn Society, American Decca, London, Vanguard, Vox.

HOOSE, ELLISON VAN, tenor, b. Aug. 18, 1868, Murfreesboro, Tenn.; d. Mar. 24, 1936, Houston, Tex. He began his voice study with his mother, then with Perry Averill and Isadora Luckstone in New York City, later with Jean de Reszke in Paris, Fidèle König in London, and Antonio Cotogni in Rome. After he had first appeared as a soloist in New York churches, he made his debut (1897) with the Damrosch-Ellis Opera Company in Philadelphia as Tannhäuser; he remained there for two years and sang with them in a guest appearance at the Metropolitan Opera. He then went to England, where he studied further with Sir Henry Wood and worked as a concert and oratorio tenor. In 1903 he sang the solo in the first New York performance of Elgar's *The Dream of Gerontius*. In 1903-05 he accompanied Nellie Melba, as in 1906-07 he accompanied Marcella Sembrich, on concert tours through the United States. In 1908 he went to Germany, where he appeared as a concert singer, including performances with the Leipzig Gewandhaus Orchestra under Artur Nikisch. He was engaged at the Mainz Opera (1909-10). He sang at the Chicago Opera (1911-12), but had his most important successes in the concert hall. Later he taught in New York City.

Records: Victor* (1906-08), one Columbia* record of lieder, all rare. *U.S. re-issue:* IRCC. *U.S. re-recording:* Cantilena.

HOPF, HANS, tenor, b. Aug. 2, 1916, Nuremberg. He studied with Paul Bender in Munich and made his debut (1936) at the Bavarian Landestheater there. He sang as a lyric tenor in Augsburg (1939-42). In 1942 he was engaged by the Dresden State Opera and he then specialized in heroic tenor parts. He was a member of the Berlin State Opera (1946-49) and thereafter a member of the Munich State Opera; but he also had a concurrent guest contract with the Vienna State Opera. After 1951 he sang almost every year at the Bayreuth Festivals and after 1952 at the Metropolitan Opera, where he made his debut as Walther in *Die Meistersinger*. Guest appearances at La Scala, the Paris Opéra, Covent Garden, and the Teatro Colón brought him great fame, particularly as a Wagner singer. He sang Max in *Der Freischütz* at the Salzburg Festival in 1954.

Records: Decca (*Der Freischütz* and *Die Frau ohne Schatten*), Columbia (*Die Meistersinger*), DGG (*Don Giovanni*), HMV (*Tannhäuser*), and Philips (*Tiefland*). *U.S. re-issue:* Angel, Epic, Electrola, London, Urania, Vox.

HOPPE, HEINZ, tenor, b. Jan. 26, 1924, Saerbeck, Germany. He was held in a Russian prisoner-of-war camp during World War II until 1949. He then studied singing at the Detmold Conservatory and made his debut (1953) at Münster as the title hero in *Xerxes*. He sang at Bremen (1955-57) and since then has been first lyric tenor at the Hamburg State Opera. He has been a regular guest at the Opera House in Frankfurt and has had great success at the Edinburgh Festival and on other stages of the first rank. He is married to the pianist Carla Hoppe-Linzen. He has a beautiful and well-trained voice and is admired not only in opera but in operetta and song as well.

Records: Telefunken*, DGG, Electrola. *U.S. re-issue:* Angel, Remington, Vox.

HORNE, MARILYN, contralto, b. 1929 (?). She made her debut in Los Angeles in a small part in *The Bartered Bride.* Thereafter she was occupied particularly as a concert singer and in 1954 she sang for the film star Dorothy Dandridge in the film *Carmen Jones.* In 1956 she went to Europe, where she was engaged at Gelsenkirchen (1956-59). During this time she also appeared as guest in Vienna, in Venice, and on German stages. In 1960 she returned to the United States and sang in a production of *Wozzeck* in San Francisco (1960) and appeared at the Chicago Opera. In 1964 she had great success at Covent Garden and at the Edinburgh Festival. In the concert hall she appeared frequently with Joan Sutherland. She is married to the conductor Henry Lewis. She has a well-trained, technically excellent voice.

Records: Decca and RCA Victor* (*Norma* with Joan Sutherland). *U.S. re-issue:* Columbia, Capitol, London.

HOTTER, HANS, baritone, b. Jan. 19, 1909, Offenbach a. M., Germany. He studied at the Munich Music High School (1928-30), where his voice was chiefly trained by Matthaüs Roemer. He made his debut (1930) at Troppau and sang in the German Theater in Prague (1932-34) and at the Hamburg State Opera (1934-37). In 1937 he was chosen for the Munich State Opera; there he appeared in the world *premières* of two operas by Richard Strauss: as the Commandant in *Friedenstag* in 1938 and as Oliver in *Capriccio* in 1942. He has been a guest at the State Operas in Vienna, Hamburg, and Stuttgart. Other guest appearances took him to leading opera stages all over the world, including La Scala, Covent Garden, the Teatro Colón, the Paris Opéra, and the Chicago Opera. He had great success at the Metropolitan Opera (1950-54). After 1952 he was admired as a great Wagner singer at the Bayreuth Festivals, particularly as Wotan and as the Flying Dutchman; he has also appeared at the Salzburg and Edinburgh Festivals and had a highly successful career as a concert singer. A powerful dark voice, particularly outstanding in Wagner roles but also in lieder.

Records: DGG*, HMV, Columbia (*Capriccio*), Decca (*Siegfried*) and Vox (*Der Fliegende Holländer*). *U.S. re-issue:* Angel, London, Electrola, Philips, RCA Victor, Seraphim, Urania.

HOWARD, KATHLEEN, contralto, b. July 17, 1880, Niagara Falls, Canada; d. Aug. 15, 1956, Los Angeles. Her studies took her to Buffalo, New York City, Paris, and Berlin and she made her debut in Metz (1907) as Azucena in *Il Trovatore.* She sang at Darmstadt (1909-12) and then studied with Jean de Reszke in Paris. She returned to the United States and sang with the Century Opera Company (1914-15) and in 1916 came to the Metropolitan Opera, where she appeared with brilliant success until 1928. She participated there, on Dec. 14, 1918, in the world *première* of Puccini's *Gianni Schicchi.* After her retirement she was occupied with films and as a journalist. She published her memoirs under the title *Confessions of an Opera Singer* (New York, 1918). She had a distinguished, beautiful dark contralto voice; her particular starring role was that of Orphée in Gluck's opera, but she also sang dramatic parts in the French and Italian repertory.

Records: Hill-and-dale records for Pathé* and Edison*. *U.S. re-recording:* IRCC.

HUBERDEAU, GUSTAVE, bass-baritone, b. 1874, Paris; d. 1945, Paris. He studied at the Paris Conservatory and made his debut at the Opéra-Comique (1898). At first he sang only small roles in several world *premières* of operas there: *Louise* (1900), *Le Juif Polonais* (1900), *Grisélidis* (1901), *La Fille de Roland* (1904). Later the most important parts for his voice range were offered to him. He was highly successful at the Manhattan Opera House (1908-11) and in 1910 he sang Orestes there in the first American production of *Elektra*. He appeared with the Chicago-Philadelphia Opera (1911-12) and at the Chicago Opera (1913-20). He made guest appearances at Covent Garden (1914, 1919, 1920). In the 1920's he also appeared as guest at Nice, Monte Carlo, Vichy, and Brussels, as well as in Paris and Amsterdam. He appeared in several films.

Records: Edison* cylinders, Odeon and American Pathé* discs; one electric record for HMV.

HUBERTY, ALBERT, bass, b. 1881, Seraing-sur-Meuse, Belgium; d. March, 1955, Knokke-le-Zoute, Belgium. He studied at the Brussels Conservatory with Demest and in 1903 came to the Flemish Opera in Antwerp as *comprimario*; he sang similar roles at the Théâtre de la Haye (1903-1906) and, after further study with Hypolite Belhomme in Paris, became the principal bass at the Rouen Opera (1908). After guest appearances in Nantes and Algiers, he sang at Covent Garden (1908-09), the New Orleans Opera (1909-11), Montreal (1911-13), and Liège (1913-14). In 1915 he came to the Paris Opéra-Comique and in 1916 made his debut at the Opéra, where he stayed until the end of his career in 1939. He made regular guest appearances at the Brussels Opera and other guest appearances at Vichy, Antwerp, Ostend, and at the Teatro Colón (1921). Later he became a professor at the Conservatory in Brussels.

Records: Acoustic and electric records for Pathé.

HUDEMANN, HANS-OLAF, bass, b. Aug. 25, 1915, Leipzig. His father, Ernst Hudemann, was a well-known concert baritone. At the age of ten he was a member of the St. Thomas Church choir in Leipzig. Beginning in 1934 he studied musicology at the Universities of Freiburg and Kiel, where he was graduated. At the same time he studied singing, and after World War II the cantor of St. Thomas Church asked him to come to Leipzig. He undertook long concert tours with the St. Thomas choir and was very successful at the Leipzig Bach Festival, as well as in concerts in Belgium, Holland, France, and Switzerland. He was chiefly famous for his art in Bach's vocal works, but he also dedicated himself to contemporary music. Since 1961 he has been a teacher at the Music High School in Heidelberg.

Records: DGG*, particularly baroque music in the Archive Series (*St. John Passion*), and Cantate*.

HUEHN, JULIUS, baritone, b. Jan. 12, 1904, Revere, Mass. He completed his vocal studies in New York and made his debut (1933) at the Philadelphia Opera as Kurwenal in *Tristan und Isolde*. In 1934 he came to the Metropolitan Opera where he remained until 1942. Here he was particularly noted for Wagner roles, but also for his portrayal

Huguet · Hüni-Mihaczek

of the title hero in *Gianni Schicchi*, Orestes in *Elektra*, and Jochaanan in *Salome*. In 1942 he volunteered for the U.S. air force and served in Europe as a bombardier. After the war he was again engaged at the Metropolitan Opera (1946-47).

Records: No commercial records of his heroic baritone voice exist, but there are private recordings at the Metropolitan Opera, including a complete *Elektra* in which he sings Orestes.

HUGUET, JOSEPHINA, soprano, b. Sept. 22, 1871, Barcelona; d. 1951, Barcelona. After her first successes in Spanish theaters, she came (1895) to Italy, where she was successful at the most important houses, including La Scala and the Teatro Costanzi. In 1898 she made a long American tour and later had guest appearances in London, Paris, Madrid, Barcelona, Monte Carlo, and Lisbon. After the end of her active singing career she lived and taught in Barcelona. She had a technically outstanding and thoroughly trained soprano voice, which shone brilliantly both in coloratura parts and in the lyric repertory.

Records: Her first records for G & T appeared by 1903; later records were made for HMV (including *I Pagliacci* under the direction of the composer, 1908). *U.S. reissue:* Victor, IRCC. *U.S. re-recording:* IRCC, TAP, Rococo.

HULST, CAREL VAN, baritone, b. Dec. 20, 1881, Amsterdam; d. Apr. 30, 1937, San Francisco. Originally Carel Butter. He sang under his own name in Holland, while he made his international reputation under the family name of his mother. He studied with various teachers in Amsterdam and Berlin, including Cornélie van Zanten and made his debut (1906) at the Berlin Imperial Opera as Silvio in *I Pagliacci*. After a successful guest series he was engaged at the Vienna State Opera in 1911, but remained there only for a month. In 1914 he made a guest appearance at Covent Garden as Amfortas and Telramund, and in the same year he sang in Russia. During World War I he sang in Holland and then was a member of the Chicago Opera (1917-19). In 1919 he again appeared at Covent Garden, this time as Rigoletto. He taught in San Francisco at the end of his life.

Records: Odeon (including Silvio in *I Pagliacci*, 1910), Edison* Amberola cylinders. Under the name Carel Butter he made records for Anker and Columbia which appeared only in Holland. *U.S. reissue:* Pathé.

HÜNI-MIHACZEK, FELICIE, soprano, b. Apr. 4, 1896, Fünfkirchen, Hungary. She studied at the Music Academy in Vienna with Rosa Papier-Paumgartner and made her debut (1919) at the Vienna State Opera, where she remained until 1925. She was then invited to the Munich State Opera, where she was the prima donna for the next twenty years. She was very successful at the Salzburg Festivals, singing Fiordiligi in *Così fan tutte* in 1922 and later appearing as a concert soloist. Although she was originally a coloratura soprano, in Munich she undertook lyric and even dramatic soprano parts. She made regular guest appearances at the Vienna State Opera, whose ensemble she rejoined (1942-45). She was married to the Swiss industrialist Alfred Hüni. In 1945 she retired from the stage and thereafter appeared only occasionally in concerts and occupied herself with teaching. A nobly trained voice in which the mastery of technique and the fullness and brilliance of tone production were luckily complemented by the quality of her expressive art.

Hüsch · Hybbinette

Records: Polydor. *U.S. re-recording:* Eterna, Rococo.

HÜSCH, GERHARD, baritone, b. Feb. 21, 1901, Hannover, Germany. He began his career as an actor at the theater in Hannover, but gave this up for voice training by Hans Emge there. In 1923 he made his operatic debut in Osnabrück and engagements followed at the Bremen and Cologne Operas. He was invited to join the Berlin State Opera in 1930 and he stayed there until 1944. He made guest appearances at many important theaters, including La Scala, Covent Garden, and the State Opera Houses in Vienna, Hamburg, Dresden, and Munich. He also appeared at the Bayreuth Festival. He was particularly famous as an interpreter of lieder and gave his first recital in Berlin in 1932; soon thereafter he was esteemed one of the greatest lieder singers of his time. Concert tours took him as far as Japan. In 1938 he was made professor at the Munich Academy of Musical Art. He held master courses for the interpretation of lieder in Switzerland, England, and Finland. The warm and personal timbre of his baritone voice was particularly impressive in the high art of his interpretation of lieder.

Records: Odeon and HMV (including lieder cycles and *Die Zauberflöte*). *U.S. re-issue:* American Decca, RCA Victor. *U.S. re-recording:* Angel, Electrola, Rococo.

HUSSA, MARIA, soprano, b. Dec. 7, 1894, Vienna. She studied there with Elise Elizza and Greve, whom she later married. She made her debut (1917) at the Vienna Volksoper. Her later engagements included the Vienna State Opera (1918-19), Graz (1919-21), the German Theater in Prague (1922-23), and the Berlin State Opera (1923-24). After 1924 she sang for several summers at the Zoppot Festivals. She appeared at the Hamburg State Opera (1926-36), where in 1927 she sang in the world *premières* of the two operas *Das Wunder der Heliane* and *La Campana Sommersa*. In 1933 she sang for one season in Düsseldorf. She then emigrated to the United States, where she joined the Chicago Opera (1934). In 1940 she appeared as a guest at the Metropolitan Opera as the Marschallin in *Der Rosenkavalier*. She maintains a vocal studio in Chicago.

Records: Homochord and HMV.

HUTT, ROBERT, tenor, b. Aug. 8, 1878, Karlsruhe, Germany; d. Feb. 25, 1942, Berlin. At first he was an engineer, but the conductor Felix Mottl urged him to study singing, which he did with Wilhelm Guggenbühler in Karlsruhe and at the Bayreuth School with Julius Kniese. He made his debut (1903) at Karlsruhe. By way of the Düsseldorf Opera he came (1910) to the Opera at Frankfurt a. M. and from there, in 1917, he went to the Berlin Imperial Opera, where he stayed until 1927. In 1913 he sang Walther in *Die Meistersinger* at the Drury Lane Theater under Sir Thomas Beecham. In 1914 he sang the same part and also Parsifal at Covent Garden. In 1923 he made a tour of the United States with the German Opera Company. He was especially prized as a Wagner singer.

Records: Odeon, Polydor, and HMV (including *Die Meistersinger*, 1928). *U.S. re-issue:* Opera Disc, Victor. *U.S. re-recording:* TAP, Rococo.

HYBBINETTE, SAMUEL, tenor, b. 1876, Osteråkers, near Stockholm; d. Feb. 12, 1939 Stockholm. He dedicated himself to medicine at Stockholm University and became one of the most celebrated Swedish surgeons of his time. After 1926 he directed the Seraphiner Hospital in

Stockholm; after 1933 he was a member of the Caroline Medical Institute there, and after 1936 a professor. He was also physician to the Swedish king. In addition to this successful activity as a medical man, he had a second career as a concert singer. He was a pupil of Gillis Bratt in Stockholm and about 1900 he won a singing contest in Uppsala. Later he gave frequent concerts in the capital, in 1916 he undertook a Scandinavian tour, and in 1919 he sang in Denmark. He appeared only once on the operatic stage at a charity affair in Stockholm in 1921. Unquestionably, he possessed the most beautiful tenor voice in Scandinavia in his time; it was remarkable both for the fine shadings of his expression and for its deep musicality.

Records: G & T (Stockholm, 1906), but especially for HMV.

HYDE, WALTER, tenor, b. Feb. 6, 1875, Birmingham, England; d. November, 1951, London. He studied at the Royal College of Music with Gustave García, Sir Charles Stanford, and Sir Walter Parratt and began his career in 1905. In 1906 he sang in the world *première* of *The Vicar of Wakefield* in London. He came to Covent Garden in 1908, making his debut as Pinkerton in *Madama Butterfly* opposite Emmy Destinn. He appeared there both in the Italian and German repertories until World War I. In 1910 he made a guest appearance at the Metropolitan Opera as Siegmund in a performance of *Die Walküre*; he also sang as guest at the Budapest Opera. He had great success in 1911 singing in opera at the Drury Lane Theater under Sir Thomas Beecham. In the 1920's he sang especially with the British National Opera Company. After the close of his career he became a professor at the Royal College of Music in London.

Records: Odeon, HMV, and a few for Pathé; also Edison cylinders.

I

ILITSCH, DANIZA, soprano, b. 1914, Belgrade; d. Jan. 17, 1965, Vienna. She studied at the Stankovič Conservatory in Belgrade, then in Berlin, and made her debut (1936) at the Berlin State Opera as Nedda in *I Pagliacci*. She was highly successful at the Vienna State Opera (1938-47) and during this time made guest appearances in Germany, Austria, and Italy. In 1947 she came for several seasons to the Metropolitan Opera. She sang Chrysothemis in *Elektra* at the Maggio Musicale Festival in 1951. Other guest appearances included Prague and Milan and later all the most important opera houses in South America. After 1959 she lived in retirement in Vienna. Her expressive soprano voice was particularly admired in the dramatic roles in the Italian repertory.

Records: Supraphon, Telefunken, Cetra* (*Elektra*), and Remington*. *U.S. re-recording:* Telefunken.

ILOSVAY, MARIA VON, contralto, b. 1913, Budapest. She studied at the Conservatory in Budapest and at the Vienna Music High School. In 1937 she won first prize in an international singing contest in Vienna and toured the United States (1937-39) with the Salzburg Opera Guild under the name Esther von Ilosvay; she was the subject of admiring comment on this tour for her performance as Dorabella in *Così fan tutte*. In 1940 she was called to the Hamburg State Opera, of which she has since been a member. Guest appearances after World War II took her to the State Operas in Vienna, Munich, and Stuttgart, as well as to Covent Garden and La Scala. After 1951 she sang at the Bayreuth Festivals, particularly as Erda in the *Ring* cycle; and she also appeared at the music festivals in Salzburg, Edinburgh, and Holland. She was engaged by the Metropolitan Opera (1956-57). The darkly glowing quality and the expressive richness of her contralto voice were admired in a wide-ranging repertory both on the opera stage and in the concert hall.

Records: Columbia (*Hänsel und Gretel*), Philips, and Opera. *U.S. re-issue:* Angel.

IMBART DE LA TOUR, GEORGES, tenor, b. May 20, 1865, Paris; d. 1911, Paris. He completed the military course at St. Cyr, but had to give up an officer's career on account of ill health. He then studied singing at the Paris Conservatory with Bax and made his debut in Geneva (1890) as Raoul in *Les Huguenots*. He came to the Opéra-Comique in 1893 and in 1895

to the Marseilles Opera. In 1897 he moved to the Théâtre de la Monnaie, where he had a brilliant career for many years. He was occasionally a guest at the Opéra-Comique in 1898. At Covent Garden in 1900 he sang the roles of Radames in *Aïda* Don José in *Carmen*, Faust, and Tannhäuser. He also appeared at the Metropolitan Opera during the 1900-01 season, making his debut as Radames in *Aïda*.
Records: Rare cylinders and discs for Pathé.

L'INCOGNITA, soprano. Zonophone* discs under this name appeared in England about 1912. The artist who sang on them appeared at the recording studio masked. Strange rumors about the identity of the singer grew up after the appearance of her records. People conjectured that behind the pseudonym was Luisa Tetrazzini, who had just had great triumphs in England, or Alice Verlet or Yvonne de Tréville. Actually, they were made by the Australian music-hall singer Violet Mount, who was at that time appearing at the Alhambra Music Hall. She had already made popular records for Zonophone (1910) under her own name, and the leader of the orchestra for the Zonophone Company, George Byng, had the idea of having her make records of operatic arias while wearing a mask, accompanied by the Australian flautist John Amadio. The records, which appeared under the name L'Incognita and sold in large numbers, presented a lovely coloratura soprano, who possessed a thoroughly trained and virtuoso voice, which would not have been suspected of a music-hall singer. She never appeared on the operatic stage and later retired in Australia.

INFANTINO, LUIGI, tenor, b. 1921, Racalmuto, Sicily. He made his debut (1943) in Parma as Rodolfo in *La Bohème*. In 1945 he was highly successful at the Teatro San Carlo and made guest appearances with the ensemble of this theater in London in 1946. A very important career in Italy followed. In 1948 he sang Nadir in *Les Pêcheurs de Perles* at La Scala and in the same year appeared at the Arena Festival. In 1949 he made a guest appearance with the New York City Opera Company as Don Ramiro in *La Cenerentola*. Concert tours in Italy and Australia added to his reputation and in 1961 he appeared in the world *première* of *Hamlet* at the Rome Opera.
Records: Columbia* and Cetra* (*Il Barbiere di Siviglia*).

INGHILLERI, GIOVANNI, baritone, b. Mar. 9, 1894, Porto Empedocle, Sicily; d. Dec. 10, 1959, Milan. He first became a pianist and was employed as a *répétiteur* at various Italian opera houses. His debut as a singer followed (1921). After his first success at the Teatro Costanzi, he appeared on other important Italian stages, including La Scala. He was an annual guest at Covent Garden, where he was greatly liked (1928-35). He was engaged at the Chicago Opera (1929-30) and also had great successes on the French and Spanish opera stages. In 1936 he sang in the world *première* of *Giulio Cesare* by Malipiero at the Genoa Opera. After World War II he centered his career on La Scala and other important Italian theaters and appeared at the Arena and Maggio Musicale Festivals. In 1956 he became a professor at the Pesaro Conservatory. One of the best baritone voices of his generation in Italy.
Records: HMV (*Aïda*) and Odeon. After World War II he made two records for HMV and also sang for Decca (*Madama Butterfly* and *La Bohème*). U.S. re-

issue: RCA Victor, Richmond, American Decca.

IRACEMA - BRÜGELMANN, HEDY, soprano, b. Aug. 16, 1881, Porto Alegre, Brazil; d. Apr. 9, 1941, Karlsruhe, Germany. She came of a German family and studied at the Cologne Conservatory. On the advice of Max von Schillings she took up operatic singing after she had first been active in concert. She made her debut at the Stuttgart Royal Opera (1910) as Elisabeth in *Tannhäuser,* and had great success there until 1917. She sang the title role in *Mona Lisa* there in its world *première* on Sept. 26, 1915, and she appeared as guest in the same role in Amsterdam in 1916. She was a member of the Vienna Imperial Opera (1917-20), but had to give up her career on account of ill health. She lived later as a teacher in Karlsruhe. A splendid dramatic voice, especially admired in Wagner parts.

Records: Odeon.

ISALBERTI, SILVANO, tenor, b. 1875; d. July 11, 1940, Brussels. He made his debut in Italy about 1903 and was engaged by the Italian Opera in Holland in 1904, where he immediately had a sensational success. Until 1908 he sang with this ensemble and was greatly admired in *verismo* roles for his voice range. He undertook a long guest-appearance tour in Germany (1907-08) with great success. In 1910 he sang at La Scala opposite Ester Mazzoleni in a production of Cherubini's *Medea.* He later appeared in Holland and Belgium with small opera troupes and finally was reduced to singing in music halls and cinemas. At the end of his life he became a teacher in Brussels.

Records: G & T (Milan, 1904) and Lyrophone (Holland, 1908). *U.S. re-issue:* Victor.

IVOGÜN, MARIA, soprano, b. Nov. 18, 1891, Budapest. She cut her original name of Ilse von Günther to Ivogün. Her father was an officer in the Austro-Hungarian army and her mother was an operetta singer. She studied singing with Irene Schlemmer-Ambros in Vienna and, through the good offices of Bruno Walter, was offered a contract at the Munich Royal Opera, where she made her debut (1913) as Mimi in *La Bohème.* She was a greatly admired prima donna at Munich (1913-25); there in 1917 she sang in the world *première* of *Palestrina.* In 1916 she appeared as guest at the Berlin Imperial Opera and in the same year sang Zerbinetta in the revised version of *Ariadne auf Naxos* at the Vienna Imperial Opera. She was married from 1921-32 to the tenor Karl Erb and after 1933 to the pianist and accompanist Michael Raucheisen. After 1925 she joined the ensemble of the Berlin City Opera. She appeared with great success at Covent Garden, La Scala, the Vienna State Opera, and the Chicago Opera. In 1922 she undertook a brilliant concert tour of the United States and in 1926 she appeared with the ensemble of the Chicago Opera as Rosina in *Il Barbiere di Siviglia* at the Metropolitan Opera. She was also greatly admired at the Salzburg Festivals. In 1932 she gave up her career and in 1948 became a professor at the Vienna Academy of Music and in 1950 at the Berlin Music High School. She had one of the most beautiful coloratura voices of the twentieth century, and was as consummately successful in the exactitude and brilliancy of her coloratura as in the refinement of her sense of style.

Records: Acoustics for Odeon and Polydor; electrics for HMV and Brunswick*. *U.S. re-issue:* Odeon-Okeh. *U.S. re-recording:* TAP, Scala, Eterna, RCA Victor, Rococo.

J

JACOBY, JOSEPHINE, contralto, b. 1875, New York; d. Nov. 13, 1948, New York. She studied in New York and first sang publicly at Temple Emanu-El. She then worked as a concert contralto and appeared with the Boston Symphony Orchestra under Goricke and with the New York Philharmonic under Seidl, as well as at the Cincinnati Festival in 1899. In 1903 she appeared at the Metropolitan Opera, making her debut as Maddalena in *Rigoletto*; she sang there with great success until 1908. In that year she gave up her stage career and appeared only occasionally on the concert platform and in operetta productions in New York. Later she became a singing teacher there.

Records: Four Edison* cylinders and rare records for Victor* (including a duet from *Madama Butterfly* with Geraldine Farrar and the Quartet from *Rigoletto* with Luisa Tetrazzini, Enrico Caruso, and Pasquale Amato). *U.S. re-recording:* RCA Victor.

JADLOWKER, HERMANN, tenor, b. July 5, 1877, Riga, Latvia; d. May 13, 1953, Tel Aviv. He studied at the Conservatory of the City of Vienna with Joseph Gänsbacher and made his debut at the Cologne Opera (1899). In 1900 he sang at Stettin, then at Riga, and in 1906 at Karlsruhe. In 1909 he joined the Berlin Imperial Opera. He sang at the Metropolitan Opera (1910-12), making his debut as the King's Son in the world *première* of *Königskinder* opposite Geraldine Farrar. On Oct. 25, 1912, he sang Bacchus in the world *première* of *Ariadne auf Naxos* at the Dresden Royal Opera. Guest appearances at all the leading opera houses in the world brought him brilliant success—at Covent Garden, the two great Paris houses, and particularly at the State Operas in Vienna, Berlin, and Munich. In 1929 he accepted the appointment as chief cantor at the Riga synagogue and at the same time taught at the Conservatory there. Later he lived in Vienna and in 1938 settled down as a singing teacher in Tel Aviv. He was admired equally for the fineness of his conception of roles and the complete mastery of voice technique, as well as for the exemplary skill in his art of phrasing.

Records: Odeon, HMV, and Victor* (one duet with Geraldine Farrar); electric records for Polydor. *U.S. re-issue:* Victor, Opera Disc, Okeh, HRS. *U.S. re-recording:* TAP, Scala, FRP, Rococo, Eterna, HRS.

JAGEL, FREDERICK, tenor, b. June 10, 1897, Brooklyn. He began his study of singing with William

Brady in New York and completed it in Milan; he made his debut (1924) at the Opera in Leghorn under the name Frederico Jeghelli as Rodolfo in *La Bohème*. He made guest appearances on various Italian stages and sang during one season with the Italian Opera in Holland. In 1927 he went to the Metropolitan Opera, where he appeared for more than twenty-five years under his own name. He was particularly admired as an interpreter of the Italian repertory. After 1931 he was a regular guest at the San Francisco Opera and he sang in 1928 and 1939-41 at the Teatro Colón. In 1948 he sang the title role in the American *première* of *Peter Grimes*. He lives and teaches in New York.

Records: Victor*, Allegro Royale*, Columbia*, Philips (*Wozzeck*); many American record-club recordings. *U.S. re-issue:* Golden Crest. *U.S. re-recording:* TAP, Ultraphonic, Rococo.

JANOWITZ, GUNDULA, soprano, b. Aug. 2, 1937, Berlin. She studied at the Steiermark Conservatory in Graz, Austria with Hubert Thöny and, through Herbert von Karajan, she was immediately engaged for the Vienna State Opera in 1959, making her debut as Barberina in *Le Nozze di Figaro*. There she experienced a quick rise in rank and was equally successful in the concert hall. After 1960 she appeared at the Bayreuth Festivals. She has made guest appearances in Hamburg, Graz, Munich, and, in 1964, at the Edinburgh Festival. She made her Metropolitan Opera debut as Sieglinde in *Die Walküre* in 1967.

Records: DGG* (Beethoven's *Ninth Symphony*) and Columbia (*Die Zauberflöte*). *U.S. re-issue:* Angel.

JANSEN, JACQUES, baritone, b. 1910, Paris. He studied with Louis Jouvet and Charles Panzéra in Paris and began his career during World War II on the Rennes radio. In 1941 he made his stage debut at the Opéra-Comique as Pelléas in Debussy's opera, a part which remained his particular starring role. He sang regularly at both the Paris Opéra and the Opéra-Comique and made guest appearances at Covent Garden, the Vienna State Opera, the Teatro Colón, and the opera houses in Brussels and Rome. In 1948 he was greatly admired as Pelléas at the Holland Festival, and he sang this part with great success at the Metropolitan Opera. He was highly regarded for his singing of the role of Cithéron in *Platée* at the Aix-en-Provence Festival in 1956. He was considered to be the best French lieder singer of his generation and the real successor to the unforgettable Charles Panzéra.

Records: HMV (including two recordings of *Pelléas et Mélisande*) and Decca. *U.S. re-issue:* Angel, London.

JANSSEN, HERBERT, baritone, b. Sept. 22, 1895, Cologne; d. June 3, 1965, New York. He first studied law at the University of Berlin, then took up singing with Oscar Daniel there. Through Max von Schillings he was immediately engaged at the Berlin State Opera, where he made his debut (1922) in *Der Schatzgräber*. After 1925 he appeared for several summers at the Zoppot Festivals. After great success in Berlin he appeared as guest at Covent Garden in 1926 and returned there almost every season until 1939. In 1929 he made a series of guest appearances at The Hague and also appeared successfully at the Paris Opéra, the Teatro Liceo, and at the opera houses in Vienna, Munich, and Dresden. In 1928 he appeared at the Metropol Theater in Berlin, opposite Göta Ljungberg, in the musical *The Three Muske-*

teers. In 1930 he sang Wolfram in *Tannhäuser* under Toscanini at the Bayreuth Festival. Until he left Germany in 1937 for political reasons, he was admired annually in his Wagner appearances at Bayreuth. In that year he emigrated to the United States and sang with the Philadelphia Opera Company in 1939. From 1939-52 he was a greatly honored member of the Metropolitan Opera. After 1940 he sang regularly during the summer seasons at the Teatro Colón. In 1946 he became an American citizen, and at the end of his life he lived and taught in New York. The baritone voice of this artist was characterized by a special warmth and a large tone. He was esteemed not only for his successful stage appearances, particularly in Wagner roles, but also as one of the greatest interpreters of lieder of his generation.

Records: Odeon, Ultraphon, HMV, Columbia* (*Tannhäuser* from Bayreuth, 1930), and RCA Victor* (*Fidelio* under Toscanini). *U.S. re-recording:* ASCO, Eterna, Telefunken, Rococo.

JEPSON, HELEN, soprano, b. Nov. 28, 1906, Titusville, Pa. At the age of thirteen she sang in an amateur operetta association. In order to finance her vocal studies she worked in the record department of a large department store. She studied at the Curtis Institute of Music in Philadelphia with Queena Mario and during this time also sang small roles at the Philadelphia Opera (1928-30). She then sang at the Montreal Opera, but was at the same time active as a radio singer and as a vocalist with Paul Whiteman's band. In 1935 she was engaged by the Metropolitan Opera, where she remained until 1943; she was admired there in a large number of roles in the French and Italian repertory. In 1936 she studied again, this time with Mary Garden in Paris. She sang at the Chicago Opera (1936-40). She married the flutist George Possel, and after 1943 taught voice.

Records: RCA Victor*.

JERGER, ALFRED, bass-baritone, b. June 9, 1889, Brünn, Austria. He studied musicology and conducting at the Vienna Academy of Music with Fuchs, Graedner, and Gutheil, and after 1913 was engaged as an operetta conductor; he was active at Passau until 1915 and thereafter at Zürich. In the latter city his beautiful voice was discovered and in 1917 he made his debut there as Lothario in *Mignon*. In 1919 he was engaged for the Munich State Opera by Richard Strauss and he remained there until 1921. In that year he moved to the Vienna State Opera, where he remained for more than thirty years. He had great success at the Salzburg Festivals, particularly as a Mozart interpreter and he made guest appearances on all the leading stages in Italy, France, Belgium, and Holland and appeared in both North and South America. On July 1, 1933, he created the role of Mandryka in the world *première* of *Arabella* at the Dresden Opera. He also worked as an opera *régisseur* and made new editions of *Don Pasquale* and *The Two Widows*, as well as of *Die Fledermaus*. After World War II he temporarily undertook the direction of the Vienna State Opera, where on May 1, 1945, he re-opened the house with a performance of *Le Nozze di Figaro*. His career lasted a long time; as late as 1959 he sang a small role in *Die Zauberflöte* at the Salzburg Festival. After 1947 he was a professor at the Vienna Academy of Music. A bass-baritone voice of rich tonal quality and great expressiveness.

Records: Polydor, Parlophone,

HMV. *U.S. re-issue:* Brunswick. *U.S. re-recording:* Belcanto, Electrola, Vanguard.

JERITZA, MARIA, soprano, b. Oct. 6, 1887, Brünn, Austria. Originally Maria Jedlitzka. She studied at the Brünn Conservatory and then became a chorus singer at the Municipal Theater there. In 1910 she appeared as an operetta singer at the Munich Artists' Theater. The director of the Vienna Volksoper, Rainer Simons, heard her and engaged her for his theater. At the latter she sang the role of Blanchefleur in the world *première* of *Der Kuhreigen* in 1911. In 1912, at the instigation of the Kaiser Franz Josef, who had heard her sing in Bad Gastein, she was called to the Vienna Imperial Opera. She was soon the real prima donna at this house, and she experienced great triumphs there. In 1912 she sang as guest the title role in *Ariadne auf Naxos* when the work had its *première* at the Stuttgart Royal Opera. On Oct. 10, 1919, she sang the Empress in *Die Frau ohne Schatten* at its world *première* at the Vienna State Opera. In 1918 she created for Vienna, as in 1924 she created for New York, the title role in *Jenufa*. Guest appearances brought her success after success in the great opera houses of France, England, Sweden, Denmark, Russia, and Hungary. In the period 1921-32 she was a greatly admired member of the Metropolitan Opera, making her debut there in the New York *première* of *Die Tote Stadt*. She also sang there the title role in the first American production of *Turandot* in 1926. She remained a member of the Vienna State Opera until 1935; during the 1930's she appeared successfully in motion pictures. In 1919 she married Baron von Popper, but they were later separated. After World War II she concerned herself with the restoration of the war-damaged Vienna State Opera House and made several charity appearances on behalf of this object on the stages of New York and Vienna; she was ecstatically received and admired in these appearances. Her memoirs appeared under the title *Sunlight and Song* (New York, 1924). Maria Jeritza was one of the greatest singing personalities of her time. Along with the brilliance of her voice, she was admired for the passionately dramatic quality of her acting and her magnificent stage presence.

Records: Pathé, Odeon, and Victor*. *U.S. re-issue:* Odeon-Okeh, IRCC. *U.S. re-recording:* TAP, FRP, Belcanto, Camden, Rococo.

JESSNER, IRENE, soprano, b. 1909, Vienna. Her father was a well-known physician in Vienna and her mother was the sister of the novelist Jakob Wassermann. She studied at the Vienna Academy of Music and made her debut in Teplitz (1930) as Elsa in *Lohengrin*. In 1931 she came to the German Theater in Prague. After very successful guest appearances in Brno and Munich, she was engaged in 1936 by the Metropolitan Opera, making her debut there as Hänsel in *Hänsel und Gretel*. She was a highly popular singer there until 1952; she once stepped in for Lotte Lehman, who was ill, on less than twenty-four hours' notice. She made guest appearances in San Francisco, Chicago, and at the Teatro Colón. She now teaches singing in New York. She mastered a many-sided repertory, specializing in youthful dramatic parts. She was also a very important interpreter of Richard Strauss' music.

Records: RCA Victor*, Columbia* (Sieglinde in a recording of Act III of *Die Walküre*).

JOACHIM, IRENE, soprano, b. 1913, Paris. Her great-uncle was the famous violinist Joseph Joachim (1831-1907). After her studies at the Paris Conservatory she appeared as a concert soprano and then made her stage debut (1938) at the Opéra-Comique as Mélisande in Debussy's opera. This remained her specialty role and she performed it in Paris, London, Brussels, Monte Carlo, and Marseilles, as well as in a guest appearance in 1948 at the Holland Festival. In 1944 she sang the part of Leda in the world *première* of *Amphytrion 38*. Since her stage repertory was small, she was held in higher esteem as one of the outstanding French song interpreters of her generation.

Records: Boîte à Musique, HMV (*Pelléas et Mélisande*, 1942), and Chant du Monde. *U.S. re-issue:* Monitor.

JOBIN, RAOUL, tenor, b. Apr. 8, 1906, Quebec, Canada. He studied at the Paris Conservatory and sang first on French provincial stages. In 1937 he became a member of the Opéra-Comique and had great success there as well as at the Paris Opéra. He sang at the Metropolitan Opera (1940-50), making his debut as Des Grieux to the Manon of Grace Moore. He sang Luca there in the world *première* of *The Island God* in 1942. He also appeared as guest in Chicago, San Francisco, Rio de Janeiro, and at the Teatro Colón. In 1950 he returned to Europe and thereafter had great success at both the Opéra-Comique and the Paris Opéra, where he then sang heroic tenor roles. He was particularly admired as an interpreter of the French repertory.

Records: Decca (including *Roméo et Juliette* and *Alceste*) and Columbia* (Don José in *Carmen*). *U.S. re-issue:* London.

JOESTEN, AGA, soprano, b. 1912 (?), Remagen, Germany. She studied with Otto Watrin in Cologne and began her career as an apprentice at the Opera there in 1934. She was engaged as a dramatic soprano at Remscheid (1935), Wuppertal (1936-38), Essen (1938-40), the Hamburg State Opera (1940-43), and the Frankfurt Opera (1943-45), where she was highly successful. She made guest appearances, gave concerts in German music centers, and often sang on the Frankfurt radio. After she gave up her career, she opened a flower shop in Frankfurt. A large-dimensioned and expressive dramatic soprano voice.

Records: DGG (Venus in *Tannhäuser*).

JOHNSON, EDWARD, tenor, b. Aug. 22, 1878, Guelph, near Toronto, Canada; d. Apr. 20, 1959, Guelph. He studied with Frau von Feilitsch in New York, then with Vincenzo Lombardi in Florence, and made his debut under the name Eduardo di Giovanni in 1912 at the Teatro Verdi in Padua as the title hero in *Andrea Chénier*. He had great success in Italy, where from 1913 on he appeared at La Scala. He was a guest at the Teatro Colón in 1916 and at the Teatro Real in 1917. In 1918 he sang in the first performance in Rome of *Gianni Schicchi* at the Teatro Costanzi. He sang with great success at the Chicago Opera (1919-22) and with equally great success at the Metropolitan Opera (1922-35). He appeared in several world *premières*: at La Scala in *La Nave* (1918); at the Metropolitan Opera in *The King's Henchman* (1927), *Peter Ibbetson* (1931), and *Merry Mount* (1934). In 1935 he was named director of the Metropolitan and until 1950 he managed this tradition-rich house. He lived after his retirement in his native town in Canada.

Records: Columbia* and Victor*. *U.S. re-recording:* TAP, RCA Victor, Rococo.

JÖKEN, KARL, tenor, b. Nov. 3, 1893, Krefeld, Germany. He originally studied chemistry, and then served in World War I. He made his debut, without special study of singing at Krefeld (1918) as Manrico in *Il Trovatore*. His later engagements included Freiburg im Br. (1920-23) and after 1923 at the Berlin State Opera. There he was highly successful and in 1924 appeared in the Berlin première of *Jenufa*. He remained a member of the Berlin State Opera until 1934, when he turned entirely to operetta, in which he had already had great success in 1930 at the Berlin Metropol Theater in a revival of *Der Bettelstudent* and in the première of *Das Veilchen von Montmartre*. In 1930 he sang in *Der Fledermaus* under Bruno Walter in Amsterdam and in the same production when it was taken to Covent Garden in London. In 1931-32 he was active at the Teatro Colón, singing *buffo* roles particularly. The career of this singer lasted a long time; in 1956 he was singing in an operetta theater in Hamburg. He was greatly admired in both lyric and *buffo* roles, particularly in operetta.

Records: Polydor, HMV, Tri-Ergon, Brilliant-Special, and Orchestrola (duets with Irene Eisinger). *U.S. re-issue:* Brunswick.

JOKL, FRITZI, soprano, b. Mar. 23, 1895, Vienna. She studied with Frau Rosental-Ranner in Vienna and made her debut (1917) at the Frankfurt a. M. Opera, staying there until 1922. She sang in Darmstadt (1922-23), at the Berlin Volksoper (1923-25), and Cologne Opera (1925-26). In 1926 she came to the Munich State Opera as first coloratura soprano, and was particularly admired there in Mozart roles. In 1928 she sang Despina in *Così fan tutte* at the Salzburg Festival. She made guest appearances at the Vienna State Opera (1930) and at Amsterdam (1932) as Konstanze in *Die Entführung aus dem Serail*. In 1933 she was forced to leave Germany, because she was Jewish. She first went to Austria and then (1938) to the United States, where she appeared only rarely.

Records: Parlophone. *U.S. re-recording:* Eterna.

JÖRN, KARL, tenor, b. Jan. 5, 1873, Riga, Latvia; d. Dec. 19, 1947, Denver, Colo. He studied with Schütte-Harmsen, Jacobs, and Frau Ress in Berlin and made his debut (1896) at Freiburg im Br. as Lionel in *Martha*. Later engagements were at Zürich (1898-99) and Hamburg Opera (1899-1902). He was a renowned member of the Berlin Imperial Opera (1902-08) and a regular guest at Covent Garden (1905-08). In 1908 he joined the Metropolitan Opera and remained there until 1914. In the latter year he sang the title role in the first performance of *Parsifal* given at the German Opera House in Berlin. Although it was hoped that he would remain in Berlin—and even Kaiser Wilhelm II intervened in the matter—he returned to the United States. In 1916 he became an American citizen, but gave up his singing career and lost his entire fortune through speculation. He then lived almost entirely forgotten as a singing teacher in Denver. When Johanna Gadski undertook an American tour with the German Opera Company in 1928, she invited him to take part in it. As a consequence he again had a brilliant success as a singer, particularly as Tristan. He opened a voice studio in New York in 1932, but later returned to Denver. He was married to the soprano Else Jörn (b. 1884, Berlin). A strongly impressive and brilliantly managed tenor voice; at the outset of his career he was particularly noted for lyric roles, but later was admired for his singing of heroic, especially Wagner, parts.

Records: A great many records for G & T (Berlin, 1903-07) and Columbia*. He sang for HMV

(*Faust* and *Carmen*, both Berlin, 1908); later he made Edison* cylinders and discs. *U.S. re-issue:* Opera Disc, IRCC. *U.S. re-recording:* Cantilena.

JOUATTE, GEORGES, tenor, b. June 17, 1892, Paris. In order to finance his vocal studies at the Paris Conservatory, he appeared as a dancer at the Casino de Paris. He studied later in Germany and first appeared as a concert singer. In 1923 he appeared in the silent film *Land Ohne Frauen* with Birgitte Helm and Conrad Veidt. In 1932 he sang at the Théâtre Mogador in Paris and in 1934 he came to the Opéra, where he made his debut in the title role of *Faust*. He had great success there until 1946, particularly as a Mozart singer and in lyric roles in the French repertory. He made guest appearances at Covent Garden, Salzburg, and various Italian theaters. His farewell appearance was as Tamino in *Die Zauberflöte* at the Paris Opéra in 1946. Since then he has been a professor at the National Conservatory.

Records: Odeon. *U.S. re-issue:* Columbia.

JOURNET, MARCEL, bass, b. July 25, 1867, Grasse, near Nice; d. Sept. 9, 1933, Vittel, France. He studied at the National Conservatory in Paris with Obin and Seghettini and made his debut (1893) at Montpellier. He had his first success singing at the Brussels Opera in 1894. He sang next at the Paris Opéra. After guest appearances at Covent Garden, he was engaged by the Metropolitan Opera in 1900 and was highly successful there until 1908. He then returned to France and went from triumph to triumph for the next twenty-five years at both of the great Paris houses, in Brussels and Monte Carlo, but especially at La Scala. There he sang the part of Simon Mago in the world *première* of Boito's *Nerone* when it was given under Toscanini on May 1, 1924. In 1931 he sang Hans Sachs in *Die Meistersinger* at the Arena Festival. His career lasted a long time, so that he appeared on the stage practically up to the time of his death. He was a great actor and one of the best-known bass singers of his time. He mastered a repertory of over sixty roles in the French repertory, along with the entire Wagner literature and twenty-seven Italian roles. His starring part was Mephistopheles in *Faust*.

Records: Victor*, some with Enrico Caruso; later he recorded for Columbia*, Pathé (including *Roméo et Juliette*), and HMV (including *Faust* about 1932). His voice is also preserved on Mapleson cylinders. *U.S. re-issue:* HRS, IRCC. *U.S. re-recording:* IRCC, TAP, FRP, Scala, Eterna, ASCO, RCA Victor, Rococo, Cantilena.

JUCH, EMMA, soprano, b. July 4, 1863, Vienna; d. Mar. 6, 1939, New York. Her father was an Austrian who became an American citizen. She studied with Mme. Murio-Celli in Detroit and made her debut (1881) with Mapleson's company at Her Majesty's Theater, London, as Philine in *Mignon*. In the same year she sang at the Academy of Music in New York. She was engaged (1881-86) by the American Opera Company, led by Mapleson. Her attempt to sign a contract with the Metropolitan Opera miscarried on account of the terms of her agreement with the American Opera Company. She traveled throughout the United States and Mexico with her own company (1888-91). Later she was active as a concert singer, making her final appearance in the New York Festival of 1894. In 1905 she married the lawyer Francis A. Wellman, but was separated from him in 1911.

Records: In 1904, after she had given up her singing career for a decade, she allowed Victor* to publish three interesting records of her voice; all of these are among the great recorded rarities. *U.S. re-issue:* IRCC.

JUNGKURTH, HEDWIG, soprano, b. June 22, 1900, Darmstadt, Germany. She made her debut (1921) at the Stuttgart State Opera, where she sang soubrette parts until 1925. She then sang at the Berlin State Opera (1925-30). She undertook a long American tour with the German Opera Company in 1931; in this undertaking she had great success as Nuri in *Tiefland* with Johanna Gadski. In the 1930's she often appeared as a concert soprano on the German radio. During World War II she gave concerts for German soldiers and appeared in the concert hall. She made a guest tour in Holland (1941-42).

Records: Acoustics for Polydor; electrics for Polydor (opera highlights) and HMV. *U.S. re-recording:* Eterna.

JURINAC, SENA, soprano, b. Oct. 24, 1921, Travnik, Yugoslavia. Originally Srebrenka Jurinac. She was the daughter of a Yugoslavian physician and his Viennese wife. She studied at the Music Academy in Zagreb and with Milka Kostrencic. She made her debut at the Zagreb Opera (1942) as Mimi in *La Bohème*. In 1944 she signed a contract with the Vienna State Opera, but was unable to make her debut there until 1945, when she appeared as Cherubino in *Le Nozze di Figaro* in the first performance given after the end of the war. She soon scored magnificent successes both in Vienna and in guest appearances in the centers of international musical life. She sang at the Festivals in Salzburg, Edinburgh, Glyndebourne, and Florence, as well as at the Holland Festival; she also appeared at La Scala, Covent Garden, the Teatro Colón, and the Metropolitan Opera, where she was idolized. In 1953 she married the baritone Sesto Bruscantini. She was admired principally as a Mozart singer and as Octavian in *Der Rosenkavalier*, but also in a great many other roles. She sang Octavian at Salzburg in 1960 at the opening performance in the new Festival House. She was also a greatly admired concert soprano. She had a magnificently trained and admirable soprano voice, and was noted for her art of phrasing and for the noble simplicity of her bearing.

Records: HMV, Vox, Westminster, Philips, RCA Victor*, Decca (including *Fidelio, Le Nozze di Figaro, Don Giovanni, Die Zauberflöte, Idomeneo, Der Rosenkavalier, Ariadne auf Naxos*). *U.S. re-issue:* Westminster, Electrola, DGG, Epic, Angel, London, Seraphim.

JURJEWSKAYA, ZINAIDA, soprano, b. 1896 (?), Russia; d. Aug. 3, 1925, Andermatt, Switzerland. After the October Revolution of 1917 she left Russia with her family, studied in Berlin, and made her debut there (1922) at the Berlin State Opera in *The Golden Cockerel*. She was highly successful at the State Opera and sang the title role in *Jenufa* at its *première* there in 1924. In 1925 she appeared as guest with the ensemble of the Berlin State Opera in Amsterdam, singing Sophie in *Der Rosenkavalier*. During a vacation in Switzerland she took poison during a fit of melancholy and threw herself into a glacial stream. The voice of this artist was equally outstanding for her complete mastery of vocal technique and for the spiritual quality of her expressiveness.

Records: In spite of the brevity of her career, she made records for Parlophone (*Jenufa*), Polydor, and Homochord.

JUYOL, SUZANNE, soprano, b. Jan. 1, 1920, Paris. She studied at the National Conservatory in Paris and made her debut there at the Opéra-Comique (1942); on this occasion she sang Carmen with great success. After 1945 she was also a member of the Paris Opéra. She began to concentrate on Wagner roles and in 1948 she sang Isolde in *Tristan und Isolde* at the Opéra. In 1950 she sang Kundry in *Parsifal* as a guest at the Monte Carlo Opera, and in 1951 she appeared as Isolde and as Brünnhilde in the *Ring* cycle at the Berlin City Opera. She later made concert and guest appearances in Spain, Belgium, and Switzerland. One of the best-known French dramatic sopranos of her time.

Records: HMV, Decca (*Carmen*), and Urania* (*Werther*). *U.S. re-issue:* London.

K

KAART, HANS, tenor, b. May 10, 1920, The Hague; d. June 18, 1965, Lugano, Switzerland, after an ear operation. Orginally Johannes Jansen. He came from an old theatrical family and was at first an actor. After World War II he discovered his voice and studied with Johanna Seghers-de Beijl in The Hague, with Fred Husler in Detmold, and in Italy. He made his debut (1956) in Karlsruhe and in 1957 sang Canio in *I Pagliacci* in Amsterdam. He had great success at Covent Garden from 1958 on, particularly as Kalaf in *Turandot*, as Canio, Radames in *Aïda*, and Don José in *Carmen*. After 1960 he was engaged at the German-Opera-on-the-Rhine at Düsseldorf-Duisburg, where he was equally successful. In 1962 he sang Samson in *Samson et Dalila* at the Chicago Opera. He was married to the Scottish mezzo-soprano Caroline Raitt.
Records: HMV (including duets with his wife).

KALENBURG, JOSEF, tenor, b. Jan. 7, 1886, Cologne; d. Nov. 8, 1962, Vienna. He intended to become an electrical engineer, but at the age of twenty began to study singing at the Cologne Conservatory and made his debut (1911) at the opera house there as Turiddu in *Cavalleria Rusticana*. He sang at Krefeld (1912-16), Barmen (1919-21), the Düsseldorf Opera (1921-25), and the Cologne Opera (1925-27). A guest appearance at the Vienna State Opera as Parsifal in 1927 led to a contract there and he remained at Vienna until 1942. He had great successes at the Salzburg Festivals, where he appeared regularly (1928-36), including Tristan, which he sang under Toscanini in 1935. Guest appearances brought him additional applause on the leading stages in Germany, France, Italy, and England. He continued singing for a long time and appeared on the stage until he was sixty-three years old. At the end of his life he lived in Vienna. His was a skillfully handled and expressive tenor voice; he had a repertory of 120 parts.
Records: Polydor, Vox, HMV, and Kristall.

KALTER, SABINE, contralto, b. Mar. 28, 1889, Jaroslav, Russia; d. Sept. 1, 1957, London. Originally Sabine Aufrichtig. After study at the Vienna Academy of Music, she made her debut (1913) at the Vienna Volksoper. In 1915 she joined the Hamburg Opera as first contralto and remained there until 1933. In 1933, because she was Jewish, she was required to leave Germany and went to England. There she had great success at Covent Garden, particularly as Brangäne in *Tristan und Isolde* in 1936 opposite Kirsten Flagstad. In 1939 she gave up her stage career and continued as a concert contralto and singing teacher in London. In 1950 she sang again in Hamburg in a radio concert.

Records: Odeon. *U.S. re-recording:* Eterna.

KAMANN, KARL, baritone, b. 1899, Cologne; d. Apr. 10, 1959, Vienna. He studied with Max Büttner in Munich and in Milan and made his debut (1922) in Karlsruhe. Later engagements included Freiburg i. Br. (1923-25), Nuremberg (1925-27), the Brunschweig State Theater (1927-31), and Chemnitz (1931-37). In 1937 he was engaged by the Vienna State Opera and remained there until his death. He was especially esteemed in Wagner roles. He sang Hans Sachs in *Die Meistersinger* at the 1938 Salzburg Festival and appeared as guest at Covent Garden in 1938, singing Wotan in *Die Walküre* with Frida Leider. His other guest appearances were in Paris, Rome, Florence, Naples, and Trieste.

Records: No commercial recordings of his heroic baritone voice exist; there is, however, a private recording of his Covent Garden performance and a private recording of marching songs made in Vienna in 1946.

KANDL, EDUARD, bass, b. Jan. 2, 1876; d. Jan. 17, 1967, Herrsching, Germany. He began his stage career in 1904 in Nuremberg; he was (1905-06), Kiel (1906-12), and finally at the German Opera House in Berlin (1912-44). He attained an international reputation as a *buffo* bass and was particularly admired in *buffo* roles in the works of Lortzing. He made guest appearances at the Vienna State Opera (1931; 1939), The Hague (1929), and Amsterdam, where he appeared as Beckmesser in *Die Meistersinger* (1941). He lived later in Herrsching on the Ammersee.

Records: Vox and Polydor. *U.S. re-issue:* Brunswick.

KAPPEL, GERTRUD, soprano, b. Sept. 1, 1884, Halle, Germany. She studied at the Conservatory in Leipzig; during her studies her voice changed from contralto to soprano. She made her debut (1903) at the Hannover Opera as Leonore in *Fidelio* and remained there until 1924. Her voice soon became a dramatic soprano and she earned great renown as a Wagner singer. She was a member of the Vienna State Opera (1924-29) and was greatly admired there. She was engaged at the Munich State Opera (1929-32). Guest appearances brought her additional fame, particularly in Wagner parts; she appeared at Covent Garden, in Berlin, Hamburg, and Amsterdam. She was a member of the Metropolitan Opera (1927-36). She had a sumptuously textured voice, and her dramatic ability was very impressive, particulary in such parts as Brünnhilde and Isolde.

Records: Favorite (Hannover, 1908) and Polydor.

KASCHMANN, GIUSEPPE, baritone, b. July 14, 1850, Lussimpiccolo, Italy; d. Feb. 7, 1925, Rome. At first he studied law at the University of Padua; then he turned to singing, studying with Alberto Giovanni in Milan. He made his debut (1876) in Turin as Alfonso in *La Favorita*. He had great success in Spain and Portugal, particularly at the Teatro Real and at the Teatro São Carlos (1879-82). While in Italy he was also admired at La Scala, the Teatro Costanzi, and on other important stages. In 1883 he came to the Metropolitan Opera, where he was best liked as Enrico in *Lucia di Lammermoor*. His other guest appearances were made at Covent Garden, St. Petersburg, Moscow, Monte Carlo, Cairo, at the Teatro Colón, and in Rio de Janeiro. At the Bayreuth Festivals of 1892-94 he sang Wolfram in *Tannhäuser* and Amfortas in *Parsifal*. In 1922 he closed his stage career with a farewell performance at the Teatro Quirino. After that he became a singing teacher in Rome. He had a baritone voice of great tonal beauty. On the stage he was most liked in classic and Wagner parts; in the concert hall in the oratorios of Perosi.

Records: A few rare records for G & T (Milan, 1903) and unpublished titles for Edison Diamond Disc. *U.S. re-recording:* IRCC, TAP, HRS, Belcanto.

KASCHOWSKA, FELICIE, soprano, b. May 12, 1872, Warsaw; d. 1951, Cracow, Poland. Her voice was discovered when she was fifteen years old by the famous tenor Tamburlik. She then studied with Troschei in Warsaw, at the Vienna Conservatory with Joseph Gänsbacher, and in Paris with Jean de Reszke. She gave her first concert in Warsaw at the age of sixteen and only a little later made her stage debut at the Opera there as Alice in *Robert le Diable*. In 1888 she was engaged by the Metropolitan Opera and she remained there for two years, being particularly successful as a Wagner soprano. She also made guest appearances in St. Louis, Boston, and Buffalo and sang with the great American symphony orchestras. In 1893 she was engaged at the National Opera in Budapest, and sang later in the opera houses in Brussels, Düsseldorf, and Leipzig. After 1897 she appeared at the Darmstadt Royal Theater, then in Karlsruhe, and for the 1908-09 season returned to the Metropolitan Opera. After the end of her stage career she taught for a long time in Vienna and was much-sought-after in this capacity. At the end of her life she lived in Poland. She had a large dramatic voice, especially admired in Wagner roles.

Records: Her records are rare: there is one solo record for Anker (1912) and a few may be found on Pathé; in 1921 she made two duets for Polydor with Frieda Hempel. *U.S. re-issue:* IRCC. *U.S. re-recording:* IRCC.

KASE, ALFRED, baritone b. Oct. 28, 1877, Stettin, Germany; d. Jan. 11, 1945, Leipzig. He studied at the Munich Academy of Musical Art with Emanuel Kroupa and made his debut (1902) at Kassel, where he stayed until 1907. He had great successes at the Leipzig Opera (1907-20) and was often a guest there later. He sang at the Cologne Festivals (1908-13) and in 1910 at the Berlin Imperial Opera in *L'Elisir d'Amore* with Enrico Caruso and Frieda Hempel. He sang a guest season at the Vienna Imperial Opera in 1911. He finally lived and taught in Leipzig.

Records: Odeon and Pathé as well as minor labels.

KATULSKAYA, ELENA, soprano, b. 1888; d. Nov. 22, 1966, Moscow. She studied at the St. Petersburg Conservatory with I.P. Prianishnikov and after 1907 with Natalia Iretzkaya. Her debut occurred (1909) at the Maryinsky Theater, where she sang until 1913. She was a highly honored singer at the Bolshoi Theater (1913-45), and after 1945 she was active there as vocal adviser; after 1948 she became a professor at the Moscow Conservatory. In 1950 she was awarded the Stalin Prize. She had a coloratura soprano voice of great tonal range and was also successful in the lyric repertory.

Records: Russian State Record Trust.

KEMP, BARBARA, soprano, b. Dec. 12, 1881, Kochem, Germany; d. Apr. 17, 1959, Berlin. She studied at the Strasbourg Conservatory (1902-05) but had also become an apprentice at the Strasbourg Opera by 1903. She sang in Rostock (1906-08) and at Breslau (1909-13). In Breslau she married the physician Dr. Mickley, but was later separated from him. In 1913 she signed a contract with the Berlin Imperial Opera, where she had a triumphal career. At the Bayreuth Festivals she sang Senta in *Der Fliegende Holländer* in 1914 and Kundry in *Parsifal* (1924-27). After World War I she had brilliant successes in guest appearances; she appeared regularly at the Vienna State Opera (1922-27) and she sang at the Metropolitan Opera (1922-24), making her debut as Mona Lisa in the opera of the same name. She sang later in The Hague, Amsterdam, Budapest, Prague, Munich, Dresden and Hamburg. In 1923 she married her second husband, the conductor-composer Max von Schillings, who as general intendant directed the Berlin State Opera (1919-25). She gave up her career in 1922 and lived thereafter as a singing teacher in Berlin. Possessed of a highly musical and dramatic voice, she was outstanding in Wagner and also many other parts.

Records: Polydor and Odeon; electrics for Parlophone and HMV. *U.S. re-issue:* Odeon-Okeh, IRCC, Victor. *U.S. re-recording:* Eterna, Rococo.

KERN, ADELE, soprano, b. Nov. 25, 1901, Munich. She studied in Munich and made her debut (1924) at the State Opera there as Olympia in *Les Contes d'Hoffmann*. She was engaged at Munich until 1926; she sang at the Frankfurt Opera (1926-27). After a South American tour in 1927 she returned to Munich in 1928. She became widely known, particularly for her appearances at the Salzburg Festivals, in such parts as Susanna in *Le Nozze di Figaro*, Zerlina in *Don Giovanni*, Despina in *Così fan tutte*, and Sophie in *Der Rosenkavalier*. Guest appearances took her to Covent Garden, La Scala, the Rome Opera, and the State Opera Houses in Berlin and Vienna. She was very successful on a tour of Egypt. She was a member of the Berlin State Opera (1935-37), but in 1938 she returned to Munich, where she was particularly beloved. She gave up her career in 1947. She had a coloratura soprano of silvery-bright sound quality and gave uncommonly brilliant performances.

Records: Parlophone, Polydor, and Vox (*Der Rosenkavalier*, 1940). *U.S. re-issue:* Brunswick, American Decca. *U.S. re-recording:* Eterna, Vox.

KESTEREN, JOHN VAN, tenor, b. May 4, 1921, The Hague. He studied at the Conservatory in The Hague with Lothar Wallerstein, among others, and made his debut (1947) in Scheveningen as the Italian Singer in *Der Rosenkavalier*. He then sang in Holland with operetta companies, on the radio, and at the Utrecht Opera. After further study with Vera Schwarz in Salzburg, he came to the Komische Oper in East Berlin. He was engaged at the Berlin City Opera (1953) and since 1958 he has been principal lyric tenor at the Theater an Gärtnerplatz in Munich. A successful concert tenor, he also sang at the 1965 Salzburg Festival. A clear, lyric tenor voice.

Records: MMS (*Die Entführung aus dem Serail*), Heliodor, Ariola (*Le Postillon de Longjumeau*). *U.S. re-issue:* Westminster, DGG, Telefunken.

KIEPURA, JAN, tenor, b. May 16,

1902, Sosnowiece, Poland; d. Aug. 15, 1966, Harrison, New York. He first studied political economy, then singing in Warsaw with Tadeusz Leliva, and made his debut (1924) in Lvov in *Faust*. After he had sung at the opera houses in Warsaw and Posnań, he appeared with brilliant success as guest at the Vienna State Opera and remained there until 1928. Guest appearances followed at La Scala, the Opéra-Comique, the Berlin State Opera, the Teatro Colón, and the Chicago Opera. In the 1930's he was more and more attracted to musical films, first in Germany, then in Hollywood. He often appeared in films with his wife, the soprano Marta Eggerth (b. 1912), whom he married in 1936. He sang at the Metropolitan Opera (1938-42), making his debut as Rodolfo in *La Bohème*. He appeared frequently at other American opera houses, in operettas, and in films; he once appeared for over a year on Broadway in a production of *The Merry Widow*.

Records: Odeon, Parlophone, and Columbia*. *U.S. re-issue:* American Decca. *U.S. re-recording:* Electrola, TAP, Continental.

KINDERMANN, LYDIA, contralto, b. 1891, West Prussia; d. January, 1954, Warsaw. She began her career in the 1920's at the Stuttgart State Opera, and then appeared at the Berlin State Opera with great success (1928-33). She was also famous as a concert contralto and often sang in Holland with the Amsterdam Concertgebouw Orchestra under Willem Mengelberg. Since she was Jewish, she left Germany in 1933 and was engaged at the German Theater in Prague (1934-38). In 1938 she emigrated to South America. There she had a highly successful career at the Teatro Colón, remaining until 1948. Thereafter she lived and taught in Poland.

Records: Three records of ensemble scenes for HMV. *U.S. re-issue:* RCA Victor.

KING JAMES A., tenor, b. May 22, 1925, Dodge City, Kansas. After his service in the U.S. Naval Reserve (1943-45), he studied music at Louisiana State University, receiving his degree there in 1950 and his master's degree at the University of Kansas City in 1952. He has been a member of the German Opera in Berlin since 1962. At the re-opening of the Munich State Opera he sang the part of the Kaiser in *Die Frau ohne Schatten*. His guest appearances have taken him particularly to the State Operas in Vienna and Munich, but he has also sung at Covent Garden and at the Bayreuth and Salzburg Festivals. He made his Metropolitan Opera debut in 1966, but he lives in Munich.

Records: Decca (*Salome*, *Die Frau ohne Schatten*), HMV and DGG*. *U.S. re-issue:* London.

KINGSTON, MORGAN, tenor, b. 1881, Wednesbury, England; d. Aug. 4, 1936, London. He was first a miner; his voice was discovered by accident. He made his debut as a concert singer (1909) in Queen's Hall, London, and shortly thereafter made his stage debut at Covent Garden. He was a member of the Metropolitan Opera (1917-24), making his debut as Manrico in *Il Trovatore*. In New York he specialized in heroic roles in the Italian repertory. Later he returned to England, where he frequently appeared in productions at Covent Garden. In England, as in America, he was highly successful as an oratorio tenor.

Records: Columbia* records, some made in England, others in the United States. *U.S. re-recording:* Eterna.

KIPNIS, ALEXANDER, bass, b. Feb. 1, 1891, Shitomire, Russia. At first he planned to be a merchant, but then studied singing at the Conservatories in Warsaw and Berlin. In Berlin he was overtaken by World War I and as a Russian was interned. Later freed, he made his debut at the Hamburg Opera 1916. He sang at Wiesbaden (1916-19) and at the German Opera House in Berlin-Charlottenburg (1919-30). He became internationally famous through concerts and guest appearances. He traveled through the United States with the German Opera Company in 1929 and sang regularly at the Chicago Opera (1924-32), also making guest appearances at La Scala, the Paris Opéra, the Teatro Colón, and the opera houses in Vienna and Munich. He was principal bass at the Berlin State Opera (1932-35) and was highly successful in his appearances at the Bayreuth Festivals (1927-33). At the Salzburg Festivals he was particularly admired as Sarastro in *Die Zauberflöte*. Concert tours brought him additional triumphs in Germany, England, North and South America, Australia, and New Zealand. He was engaged by the Metropolitan Opera in 1940, where he made his debut as Gurnemanz in *Parsifal* and remained an honored member of the company until 1952. He lives on his estate at Westport, Connecticut, and teaches at the New York College of Music. A large and beautifully developed bass voice. He was admired particularly in the Russian repertory, but also in many other roles, on account of his skillful acting ability. Also a great lieder singer.

Records: Homochord, Polydor, Columbia*, HMV (The Hugo Wolf Society), as well as RCA Victor* (*Boris Godounov*). There are also private recordings taken at performances at the Metropolitan Opera. *U.S. re-issue:* RCA Victor. *U.S. re-recording:* RCA Victor, TAP, Continental, Seraphim.

KIRCHNER, ALEXANDER, b. 1880, Vienna. He studied singing with Alfred Robinson in Brünn, with Amalie Materna in Vienna, and made his debut at the Vienna Imperial Opera (1909) as Des Grieux in *Manon*. From Vienna he went to the Stockholm Royal Opera (1911-12); he sang at the German Opera House in Berlin (1913-14) and at the Berlin Imperial (later the State) Opera (1915-35). He appeared as guest at the Bayreuth Festival (1914) as Erik in *Der Fliegende Holländer;* his later guest appearances were made in London, Holland, Switzerland, Paris, and Vienna.

Records: Acoustics for Pathé*, Homochord, and Polyphon; electrics for Homochord.

KIRCHOFF, WALTER, tenor, b. Mar. 17, 1879, Berlin; d. Mar. 26, 1951, Wiesbaden. At first a cavalry officer, he turned to singing at the instigation of the intendant of the Berlin Imperial Opera, Count von Hülsen. He studied singing in Berlin with Robert Weiss and Lilli Lehmann and finally in Milan; he made his debut (1906) at the Berlin Imperial Opera as Faust in Gounod's work by that name. He remained in Berlin until 1920 and was specially known as a Wagner singer. He was greatly admired at the Bayreuth Festivals (1911-14) as Walther in *Die Meistersinger* and as Parsifal. At the outbreak of World War I he volunteered for service and became the personal adjutant to the Crown Prince of Germany. After the end of the war guest appearances brought him great success; he sang at Covent Garden, the Paris Opéra, the Teatro Colón, in Rio de Janeiro, Brussels, and Amsterdam. He was admired at the Vienna State Opera (1927-28) and in 1929 was a guest with the German ensemble under Von Hoesslin in Paris. He was a member of the Metropolitan Opera (1926-31). After the end of his stage career, he lived and taught in

Berlin. A powerful tenor voice, particularly outstanding in Wagner roles.

Records: Pathé, HMV, Odeon (*Tannhäuser*, Act II, 1908); electric records for Pathé (Paris, 1930) and Parlophone. *U.S. re-issue:* Columbia.

KIRKBY-LUNN, LOUISE, contralto, b. Nov. 8, 1873, Manchester, England; d. Feb. 2, 1930, London. She studied with Greenwood and Alberto Antonio Visetti in London. She made her concert debut in 1893 and then sang at the Harris Opera House and with the Carl Rosa Opera Company. After her marriage in 1899 at first she gave up her career, but in 1901 again appeared on the stage in London. In 1902 she was engaged by the Metropolitan Opera, her debut role being Ortrud in *Lohengrin*. She remained at the Metropolitan for two seasons and then undertook an American tour with the Savage Opera Company; on this tour she sang Kundry in *Parsifal*. She was again a member of the Metropolitan (1906-08). She sang regularly as guest at Covent Garden and there she created Dalila in the first performance of *Samson et Dalila* in England (1909). She was highly successful in operatic guest appearances in Budapest, as well as in concert halls in England and America. In 1919 she sang again at Covent Garden, this time as Amneris in *Aïda*. Thereafter she sang in only a few concerts. She later lived and taught in London.

Records: G & T (London, 1901), Columbia*, HMV, and Pathé*. *U.S. re-issue:* Opera Disc, IRCC. *U.S. re-recording:* TAP, FRP, ASCO, Cantilena, Rococo.

KIRSTEN, DOROTHY, soprano, b. 1917, Montclair, N.J. She at first became a telephone operator, then studied singing with Louis Dornay and Betsy Dornay-Culp in New York. In 1938 she was noticed by Grace Moore, who assisted her with her career. After further study with Astolfo Pescia in Italy, she sang in a concert at the New York World's Fair in 1940. She made her stage debut in the same year at the Chicago Opera at Poussette in *Manon*. In 1942 she sang with the San Carlo Opera Company and made a highly successful appearance in New York in *The Merry Widow*. After she had appeared at the New York City Opera, in San Francisco, and in Montreal, she came to the Metropolitan Opera (1945), first singing Mimi in *La Bohème*. Since then she has been a member of this company and has made guest appearances in South America, particularly at the Teatro Colón. She also sang as guest in England (1952) and made a tour of Russia (1962).

Records: RCA Victor* and Columbia*. *U.S. re-issue:* Capitol.

KITTEL, HERMINE, contralto, b. 1876 (?), Vienna; d. Mar. 4, 1938, Vienna. At first an actress, she made her acting debut (1897) in Laibach. In 1898 she came to Graz and, after the discovery of her voice, studied with Amalie Materna in Vienna. In 1900 she was called to the Vienna Imperial Opera, where she stayed for thirty years. At the beginning of her career she was substantially helped by Gustav Mahler. She sang at the Bayreuth Festivals in 1902 and 1908, and was greatly admired as Erda in the *Ring* cycle. She appeared at the Salzburg Festivals in 1922 and 1925 as Marzelline in *Le Nozze di Figaro*. She was particularly admired in the concert hall as the contralto soloist in Mahler's *Das Lied von der Erde*, which she sang in Amsterdam in 1913 as well as elsewhere. In 1931 she gave up her stage career and taught singing in Vienna. She was married to the baritone Alexander Haydter (1872-1919), who was engaged at the Vienna Imperial Opera at the same time that she was. A distinguished artist with a beautiful contralto voice, she mastered a very large opera and concert repertory.

Records: A great many valuable records for G & T (the oldest from Vienna, 1903), Odeon, and HMV. *U.S. re-issue:* Victor. *U.S. re-recording:* Belcanto.

KIURINA, BERTA, soprano, b. 1882, Linz, Austria; d. May 3, 1953, Vienna. She studied the piano at first with Fischof, at the Conservatory of the City of Vienna then studied singing with Geiringer. Her debut (1904) was quickly followed by a call to the Vienna Imperial Opera, of which she remained a member until 1927. In 1906 she sang Cherubino in *Le Nozze di Figaro* at the Mozart Festival in Salzburg; she again sang the same role at the Salzburg Festival in 1927. She sang as guest at Brünn, Wagram, Belgrade, Budapest, Trieste, Wroclaw, and at the Berlin City Opera. In 1928 she was feted in a long guest season at the Teatro Colón. Great success as a concert soprano also came to her, particularly as an interpreter of the *Gurrelieder* of Arnold Schoenberg. Her first marriage was to the tenor Hubert Leuer (b. 1880, Cologne), who was engaged at the Vienna Imperial Opera at the same time that she was. She possessed a coloratura voice of uncommon beauty and was particularly admired for her effortless flexibility in the upper ranges.

Records: Odeon, Zonophone, Polydor, Pathé*, Parlophone, and Ultraphone. *U.S. re-recording:* IRCC, Scala, Eterna.

KLARWEIN, FRANZ, tenor, b. Mar. 8, 1914, Garmisch, Germany. He studied at the Music High School in Frankfurt a. M. and in Berlin. He made his debut (1937) as a lyric tenor at the Berlin Volksoper, where he remained until 1942. Since then he has sung at the Bavarian State Opera in Munich, appearing there in the world *première* of *Capriccio* on Oct. 28, 1942; in 1949 he sang the title role there in the first German performance of *Raskolnikov*. He appeared at the Salzburg Festivals (1942-43) and sang as guest at Covent Garden (1953). During the course of his career his voice changed from lyric to heroic tenor; as the latter he sang Aegisthus in *Elektra* in 1957 at the Maggio Musicale Festival. He is married to the soprano Sari Barabas.

Records: During World War II he recorded for Imperial, later for Nixa, Cetra* (Aegisthus in *Elektra*), and Columbia (*Der Waffenschmied*). *U.S. re-issue:* Turnabout.

KLEIN, PETER, tenor, b. Jan. 25, 1907, Zündorf, Germany. He studied at the Music High School in Cologne and made his debut there (1930). After singing in Düsseldorf and Kaiserslautern, he was engaged at Zürich in 1933, where he excited great attention in *buffo* roles, such as David in *Die Meistersinger*. He sang again at Düsseldorf (1936-37) and at the Hamburg State Opera (1937-42). In 1942 he went to the Vienna State Opera, where he has remained. He appeared repeatedly after 1946 at the Salzburg Festivals. Guest appearances have brought him important successes on all the large European stages, for example, at Covent Garden in 1947-49 and again in 1955. An admirable *buffo* tenor.

Records: Decca (*Die Entführung aus dem Serail*, *Die Zauberflöte*, and *Der Rosenkavalier*) and Columbia (*Eine Nacht in Venedig*). *U.S. re-issue:* Vox, London, DGG.

KLINE, OLIVE, soprano, b. 1885 (?), New York State. The career of this singer was limited to appearances in church concerts and oratorios; she never sang on the operatic stage. She was engaged as a singer by the Victor Company in 1912, and from then until the 1930's a great many records of her voice appeared, ranging from operatic arias to popular songs. She sang popular numbers for the most part under the name Alice Green.

Records: Among her records, ranging from the acoustic to the electric era of recording, there are many beautiful ones which show a technically outstanding and expressive soprano voice. She recorded exclusively for Victor*. *U.S. re-recording:* RCA Victor.

KLOSE, MARGARETE, contralto, b. Aug. 6, 1902, Berlin, d. Dec. 14, 1968. After starting out in another occupation, later she studied singing at the Klindworth-Scharwenka Conservatory in Berlin, where her teachers included Franz Marschalk. She made her debut (1927) in Ulm, sang at Mannheim (1928-31), and was then called to the Berlin State Opera, where she sang until 1949 with brilliant success. She appeared as guest at all the leading opera houses of the world, including La Scala, Covent Garden, the Vienna State Opera, the opera houses in Hamburg, Dresden, and Munich, the Teatro Colón, and in San Francisco and Los Angeles. She sang Adriano in *Rienzi* at the 1935 Zoppot Festival, and demonstrated that she was a great Wagner contralto at the Bayreuth Festivals. She was under contract to the Berlin City Opera (1949-59), but returned to the East Berlin State Opera (1958-61). She had a wide-ranging, deep-textured contralto voice, with an unusual range of expressiveness and deep musicality.

Records: HMV, Urania*, and DGG (Fricka in *Die Walküre*, Ortrud in two recordings of *Lohengrin*, the title role in *Orphée et Eurydice*, and Maddalena in *Rigoletto*). *U.S. re-issue:* RCA Victor.

U.S. re-recording: Rococo, Electrola, Telefunken, Heliodor, RCA Victor, Seraphim, Vox.

KMENTT, WALDEMAR, tenor, b. Feb. 2, 1919, Vienna. He planned to become a pianist at first, but after 1949 studied singing at the Music High School in Vienna. As early as 1950 he sang the tenor solo in Beethoven's *Ninth Symphony* in Vienna under Karl Böhm. He came to the Vienna State Opera in 1951 as a lyric tenor and has remained a member of that organization ever since. Since 1958 he has sung regularly at Düsseldorf-Duisberg between his engagements at Vienna. He has also sung at the Salzburg Festivals and has appeared as guest at La Scala, the Rome Opera, the Vienna Volksoper, and in Paris, Amsterdam, Brussels, Munich, and Stuttgart. He is also a successful concert solist.

Records: A great many recordings, mostly for Philips* and Decca (complete recordings of *Così fan tutte*, two versions of *Salome*, *Das Rheingold*, et cetera). *U.S. re-issue:* SPA, Bach Guild, Westminster, Angel, Lyrichord, Vox, London, Epic, Urania, Vanguard-Everyman.

KNOTE, HEINRICH, tenor, b. Nov. 26, 1870, Munich; d. Jan. 12, 1953, Garmisch, Germany. He had his voice training in Munich with Cantor Emanuel Kirschner. The intendant of the Munich Royal Opera, Baron von Perfall, signed him to a contract for that house, where he made his debut (1892) as Georg in *Der Waffenschmied*. At the beginning of his career he sang *buffo* parts, but his voice soon developed into a heroic tenor and he then specialized in Wagner roles. He was an admired member of the Metropolitan Opera (1904-08). He came to the Hamburg Opera in 1908, later joined the Wiesbaden Royal Theater, then returned to Munich, where he was especially popular. He made a North American tour with the German Opera Company (1923-24) and in 1931 gave his farewell stage performance in Munich as Siegfried in the opera of the same name. He lived and taught in Munich thereafter. A heroic tenor voice of penetrating quality and an uncommon intensity of expression. He was principally noted as a Wagner singer.

Records: A great many acoustics for Edison* cylinders, G & T, HMV, and Anker; electrics for Odeon. *U.S. re-issue:* Opera Disc, American Decca.

KNÜPFER, PAUL, bass, b. June 21, 1865, Halle, Germany; d. Nov. 4, 1920, Berlin. After he had originally studied medicine, he undertook vocal studies at the Conservatory in Sondershausen with Günsburg. His debut occurred at Sondershausen (1887) and he then sang at Leipzig (1888-98). In 1898 he went to the Berlin Imperial Opera, where his career reached its climax. He sang there in 1904 in the unfortunate world *première* of *Der Roland von Berlin,* and in 1911 he sang Baron Ochs in the Berlin *première* of *Der Rosenkavalier,* as he had by that time become a noted *buffo* bass. He sang in the Bayreuth Festivals (1901-12) in all the heroic bass parts. After 1904 he was often a guest at Covent Garden. He was married to the soprano Maria Knüpfer-Egli (1872-1924). He possessed one of the finest bass voices of his time, and was consummate in both serious and *buffo* parts, but was particularly admired in Wagner roles.

Records: Valuable records for G & T and HMV. *U.S. re-issue:* Opera Disc, IRCC. *U.S. re-recording:* TAP, FRP, Eterna.

KOENEN, TILLY, contralto, b. Dec. 25, 1873, Salatiga, Java; d. Jan. 4, 1941, The Hague. When she was six years old, she returned with her parents to their Dutch homeland and in 1892 began studying voice at the Amsterdam Conservatory with Cornélie Van Zanten. When her teacher moved to Berlin, Tilly Koenen accompanied her. In 1898 she made her debut in a concert in Berlin. She very soon achieved great success in both Germany and Holland and sang before the Kaiser and before Queen Wilhelmina of Holland. After she had completed very successful concert tours in central Europe, she settled down in London. She toured Canada and the United States (1909-10), appearing as an oratorio singer. She never sang on the stage, except the title role in a performance of *Orphée et Eurydice* in Amsterdam, produced by Cornélie Van Zanten. In 1939 she returned to Holland and lived with her former teacher. She had a deep contralto voice and her best performances were in lieder.

Records: Four discs for G & T (London, 1907), four for Pathé, and one for Zonophone, all of Dutch songs.

KOHN, KARL-CHRISTIAN, bass, b. May 21, 1928. He had his first great success at Düsseldorf-Duisberg in 1958. He was a member of the Bavarian State Opera in Munich after 1958. He created great excitement there when he sang the title role in *Le Nozze di Figaro* at the opening performance in the newly rebuilt Cuvilliés Theater in the Residenz. He has made highly successful guest appearances in Vienna, Berlin, Hamburg, and in other music centers in Germany and abroad. While he is particularly noted as a Mozart interpreter, he is also a fine concert bass.

Records: HMV (*Der Freischütz* and *Don Giovanni*) and DGG* (*Don Giovanni* and *Arabella*). *U.S. re-issue:* Electrola, Telefunken, Turnabout, Seraphim.

KOLASSI, IRMA, mezzo-soprano, b. May 28, 1918, Athens. She studied piano at the Royal Conservatory in Athens and received her diploma as a piano teacher at the age of sixteen. She then studied singing with Maggie Karadja in Athens and later became a pupil at the Accademia di Santa Cecilia in Rome. She taught at the Hellenic Conservatory in Athens (1940-49) and after World War II also began a brilliant career as a concert singer, which brought her great success in various European musical capitals. Since 1949 she has lived in Paris, and from there she has embarked on her worldwide concert activities, including appearances in France, England, Germany, Holland, Belgium, Italy, and the United States. Although she has never sung in opera on the stage, she has taken part in performances on records and on the radio. She is known especially as a concert and lieder singer, and in these fields she has dedicated herself particularly to contemporary music.

Records: Decca*. *U.S. re-issue:* Monitor, Westminster, London.

KONETZNI, ANNY, soprano, b. Feb. 12, 1902, Weisskirchen, Austria; d. Sept. 6, 1968, Vienna. She studied at the Conservatory of the City of Vienna and with Jacques Stückgold in Berlin. She then made her debut (1927) at the Vienna Volksoper in the contralto role of Adriano in *Rienzi*. After singing in Augsburg and Eberfeld she came to Chemnitz as first dramatic soprano in 1929 and held the same position at the Berlin State Opera (1931-34). In the latter year she transferred to the Vienna State Opera. She had great triumphs in appearances at La Scala, the Rome Opera, the Paris Opéra, Covent Garden, and in Brussels, Amsterdam, and Buenos Aires. She was engaged at the Metropolitan Opera (1934-35). At the Salzburg Festival in 1935 she sang Isolde in *Tristan und Isolde* and alternated with her sister, Hilde Konetzni, in the role of the Marschallin in *Der Rosenkavalier*. Other outstanding performances at festivals include appearances as Ortrud in *Lohengrin* at the Arena Festival of 1949 and the title role in *Elektra* at the Maggio Musicale Festival in 1951. She married a physician and later became a professor at the Music Academy in Vienna. From 1955 till her death in 1968 she was partially paralyzed and lived in Vienna. She had a strong dark-timbred soprano voice.

Records: A few Telefunken records; she sang the title role in *Elektra* on Cetra*.

KONETZNI, HILDE, soprano, b. Mar. 21, 1905, Vienna. Her voice was discovered by her older sister, Anny Konetzni, and she studied at the Conservatory of the City of Vienna with Hess and Rudolf Nillius. In 1929 at Chemnitz she made her first appearance on the stage as Sieglinde in *Die Walküre* in a performance with her sister. After further study she sang at Gablonz (1931-32) and at the German Theater in Prague (1932-35). Engaged by the Vienna State Opera in 1935, she remained there for a starring career lasting more than twenty-five years. After 1936 she appeared regularly at the Salzburg Festivals, as Donna Elvira in *Don Giovanni*, Leonore in *Fidelio*, Elisabeth in *Tannhäuser*, and the Marschallin in *Der Rosenkavalier*, alternating in this last role with her sister. She made guest appearances at La Scala, Covent Garden, the Teatro Colón, and the most important opera houses in Germany. She toured the United States (1937; 1939). Since 1949 she has taught at the Vienna Music Academy and has also continued her career. A splendid soprano voice of special lightness of timbre and an uncommon warmth of delivery.

Records: Telefunken, Nixa (Elvira in *Don Giovanni*), Vox* (title role in *Fidelio*). She also sang a small role in 1965 in *Der Zigeunerbaron* for Eurodisc. *U.S. re-issue:* Vox.

KÓNYA, SANDOR, tenor, b. Sept. 23, 1923, Sarkád, Hungary. He began his vocal studies at the Budapest Conservatory, but they were interrupted by the war. While he was being held in a prisoner-of-war camp in Germany, he continued his studies at the Conservatory in Detmold and later in Milan. He made his debut as Turiddu in *Cavalleria Rusticana* in Bielefeld (1951) and sang there until 1954; then, after a season in Darmstadt, he changed to the Berlin City Opera, where he has appeared since 1955. He sang at the 1956 Edinburgh Festival and at the 1958 Bayreuth Festival in the title role in *Lohengrin*. Since then he has been greatly admired in this role both at Bayreuth and on all the most important stages of the world. Guest appearances have taken him to La Scala, the Paris Opéra, the Rome Opera, Budapest, and the larger German stages. He sang in 1960 at the San Francisco Opera and made concert tours in Spain, Portugal, and the United States. He was under contract to the Metropolitan Opera after 1961. A full and brilliant tenor voice.

Records: DGG* (*La Bohème*, *Madama Butterfly*, and *Tosca*) and RCA Victor (*Die Fledermaus*). *U.S. re-issue:* MGM.

KORJUS, MILIZA, soprano, b. Aug. 18, 1912, Warsaw, Poland (?). She is supposed to have passed her youth in Kiev and to have first appeared at the age of seventeen in a concert in Latvia. It is, however, closer to the truth to say that she was born in a Swedish colony in Wisconsin and later went to Europe to study singing. In 1932 she undertook a tour through Scandinavia and was then invited to the Berlin State Opera by Max von Schillings; she was very successful in guest appearances there in 1933. Later she also appeared as a guest at the most important opera houses in Europe, including the Vienna State Opera, Paris, Brussels, and Stockholm, but she became better known as a concert singer. In 1936 she returned to the United States; here she specialized in films, with great success in *The Great Waltz*. She appeared only occasionally in concert and on the stage. She had a technically brilliantly managed coloratura voice and was noted for her high range. In addition to her operatic repertory, she was outstanding in coloratura showpieces.

Records: HMV and RCA Victor*. In 1967 coloratura arias for the Venus* label appeared in the United States. *U.S. re-issue:* Electrola, Camden.

KOROLEWICZ-WAYDA, JANINA, soprano, b. 1875, Warsaw; d. 1957, Cracow, Poland. She studied at the Conservatory in Lemberg with Valerie Wysocki and A. Myszuga and made her debut (1893) at the Warsaw Opera with great success. Although she began by singing coloratura roles, she soon changed to lyric and dramatic parts. She appeared as a guest at Covent Garden in 1904 and 1906, later at La Scala, and in Venice, Lisbon, Madrid, Budapest, Moscow, Chicago, and Boston. In 1911 she made a tour of Australia with an opera troupe which Nellie Melba had collected. During World War I she sang in Poland and later directed the Warsaw Opera (1917-25). After living for a few years in the United States, she resumed the directorship of the Warsaw Opera (1934-37). In her foreign guest appearances she sang mostly under the name Giannina Wayda. She had a sumptuous and expressive voice.

Records: Very rare records for G & T, Syrena, Nicole (London, 1904), and HMV (Warsaw, 1908).

KORSOFF, LUCETTE, soprano, b. Feb. 1, 1876, Genoa; d. Feb. 14, 1955, Brussels. She was born in Italy of Russian parents; her father traveled as the impresario of an opera troupe in Russia. In a presentation of this company (1892) in St. Petersburg she first appeared before the public in *La Serva Padrona*. She then studied singing with Frédéric Boyer in Paris and made a second debut (1901) in Toulouse. After a tour of Egypt she came to the Brussels Opera in 1903 and was very successful there. She sang the role of Marie in the first production there of *The Bartered Bride* in 1905. She sang at the Opéra-Comique (1905-08) and was particularly admired as the Queen of the Night in *Die Zauberflöte*. She then came to the United States, where she appeared at the New Orleans Opera. In 1912 she gave several concerts in New York City and sang with the Boston Opera (1912-13). Following a year of further study with Teresa Arkel in Milan she sang as guest in London (1914) and thereafter at several theaters in Italy and at the Monte Carlo Opera (1918). In 1921 she ended her career and lived as a teacher in Paris; after 1926 she lived in Brussels, where she died in great poverty. A coloratura soprano of polished technique and exquisite tonal shading.

Records: G & T (Paris, 1906), Zonophone (Paris, 1905-06), HMV, Vocalion, Edison*, and Pathé*. *U.S. re-issue:* Victor.

KOSHETZ, NINA, soprano, b. Dec. 12, 1894, Kiev; d. May 15, 1965, Santa Ana, Calif. Following her studies with Igumov in Moscow and with Sergei Taneyev, she made her debut (1913) as Donna Anna in *Don Giovanni* at the St. Petersburg Imperial Opera. She remained in Russia until 1920 and then came to the United States with the Ukrainian Chorus, which her brother conducted. In America she was greatly helped by the conductor-pianist Ossip Gabrilowitsch. In 1921 she sang at the Chicago Opera and in that year appeared in the world *première* there of *The Love of Three Oranges*. Her greatest successes in America, however, were as a concert singer. She studied further with Felia Litvinne in Paris and sang in Paris, Brussels, and Amsterdam. Her appearances at the Teatro Colón in 1924 were very successful and she was highly admired in South America thereafter. In 1926 she gave a series of song recitals in New York, presenting the works of modern Russian composers; in these she was accompanied by Rachmaninov, Glazounov, or Gretchaninov at the piano. Toward the end of her career she sang frequently in opera in Los Angeles. She appeared in the American film *Algiers* with Charles Boyer. Later she lived in Hollywood. Her daughter, Marina Koshetz, was also a successful soprano. She had a well-trained and expressive soprano voice, particularly noted in the concert and song repertory.

Records: Brunswick*, Victor*, and Schirmer* records. *U.S. re-recording:* Belcanto, Veritas.

KOSLOWSKI, IVAN, tenor, b. 1900, in Marjanovka, Russia. He studied at the Kiev Conservatory with N.V. Lysenko and Murjavova and made his debut (1920) in Poltava. He came to the Kharkov Opera in 1924 and to Sverdlovsk in 1925. In 1926 he was engaged at the Bolshoi Opera and for the next thirty years was one of the most prominent singers at this famous Russian opera house. He made successful concert and guest appearances in all the centers of Russian musical life. He won the Stalin Prize in 1941 and 1949 and was later awarded the Order of Lenin and the title "People's Artist of the USSR." He had a well-trained lyric tenor voice, and the extraordinary quality of his expressive art was admired equally with the fine shading of his delivery.

Records: Russian State Record Trust. *U.S. re-issue:* Columbia.

KÖTH, ERIKA, soprano, b. Sept. 15, 1927, Darmstadt, Germany. She studied at the Music High School in Darmstadt and in 1947 won a singing contest conducted by the Hessian radio. Her debut occurred (1948) in Kaiserslautern as Philine in *Mignon.* After singing at Karlsruhe (1950-53), she was called to the Munich State Opera in 1953. She soon developed a brilliant international career and made regular guest appearances in Vienna and Hamburg. After 1955 she had sensational successes at the Salzburg Festivals, particularly as Konstanze in *Die Entführung aus dem Serail.* Other guest appearances included La Scala, Covent Garden, the Rome Opera, and in Hollywood, San Francisco, and Budapest. She had a triumphal tour of Russia in 1961 and in 1965 she sang the Forest Bird in *Siegfried* at the Bayreuth Festival. She has a coloratura voice of the highest technical virtuosity and exquisite tonal beauty.

Records: Columbia, Electrola*, and Ariola. *U.S. re-issue:* Bruno, London, Angel, Turnabout, DGG, Seraphim.

KOUSNETZOFF, MARIA, soprano, b. 1880, Odessa, Russia; d. Apr. 26, 1966, Paris. She became a ballet dancer and appeared at the St. Petersburg Imperial Opera. After studying singing with Joachim Tartakov in St. Petersburg, she made her debut as an opera singer (1905) at the Maryinsky Theater in St. Petersburg. About 1906 she made guest appearances at the Paris Opéra and the Opéra-Comique, followed by brilliantly successful guest appearances at Covent Garden, the Nice Opera, and particularly the Monte Carlo Opera. In the United States she sang with the Manhattan Opera (1909) and the Chicago Opera (1916-17). She was also active as a dancer and, among others, created the Richard Strauss ballet *Josephslegende* at the Théâtre des Champs-Elysées in 1914. During World War I she returned to Russia but after the 1917 Revolution fled to Sweden in an adventure-filled journey. She gave concert recitals (1917-19) together with the tenor Georges Pozemofsky, wherein she also appeared as a dancer. She then came to Paris in 1920, where she first appeared as a film actress, and in 1927 founded the Opéra Russe there. This operatic venture, which lasted until 1939, was very successful and introduced the Russian operatic repertory to France and the western musical world. Maria Kousnetzoff was the true prima donna of this company, with which she appeared not only in Paris, but also in Barcelona, Madrid, London, Milan, and South America. In 1936 she toured Japan. After her retirement she lived in Paris.

Records: One record for G & T (St. Petersburg, 1905) and other acoustics for Pathé*; electrics for Odeon.

KOZUB, ERNST, tenor, b. 1925, Duisburg, Germany. At first he pursued a commercial career, but then he studied singing at the Music High School in Weimar and made his debut (1950) at the Komische Oper in *Zar und Zimmermann.* He remained there until 1954, then sang at the Frankfurt a.

M. Opera (1954-62) and since 1962 at the Hamburg Opera. His guest appearances include the Vienna State Opera, Covent Garden, and opera houses in Rome, Naples, Genoa, Cairo, and Montevideo. He appeared at the Maggio Musicale Festival and in 1963 at La Scala, singing Siegmund and Siegfried in the *Ring* cycle. Besides these Wagner roles, he includes heroic parts in the Italian repertory among his particular starring roles.

Records: Electrola, Philips, one record for DGG*. *U.S. re-issue*: London.

KRAAYVANGER, HEINZ, tenor, b. Mar. 14, 1904, Essen, Germany. After his studies at the Music High School in Cologne and in Berlin, he made his debut at Lübeck (1933) as Lohengrin. His sequence of later engagements included Essen (1934-35), Kiel (1935-36), Königsberg (1936-37), Nuremberg (1938-39), the Vienna State Opera (1940-41) Danzig (1942-43), and Breslau (1943-44). After the war he took up his career again at Weimar in 1947; from there he moved to the Berlin City Opera (1947-50) and he sang at Bielefeld (1951-52) and at Krefeld (1953-54). He also made guest appearances in Munich and Stuttgart and at the Zoppot Festivals.

Records: Kristall and Siemens Special (recordings from Zoppot).

KRÁSOVÁ, MARTA, contralto, b. Mar. 16, 1901, Protovin, Austria. She started her studies in a teachers college in České Budějovice, but then studied singing with Valouska and Ludmilla Prochazkova-Neumannova in Prague as well as with Ulanowsky in Vienna. She made her debut (1924) in Bratislava. From there she was called in 1927 to the National Theater in Prague, where she was one of the most prominent artists for the next thirty years, making triumphant guest appearances in Vienna, Berlin, Hamburg, Dresden, Madrid, Paris, Moscow, and Warsaw. She made two long tours in the United States (1938; 1939), during which she displayed her Wagner repertory. Since 1935 she has been married to the composer Karel Boleslav Jirák. Her contralto voice was outstanding both for her tonal volume and for the range of her expressiveness in the operatic and concert repertories.

Records: Supraphon. *U.S. re-issue:* Colosseum, Artia.

KRAUS, ALFREDO, tenor, b. 1927, Las Palmas, Canary Islands. He was the son of an Austrian-Spanish family. He made a very successful debut (1951) at the Cairo Opera as the Duke in *Rigoletto*. In 1961 he was admired at the Rome Opera as Alfredo in *La Traviata* and soon thereafter he reached La Scala. Since then he has had a brilliant career all over the world, with tours in Europe and in North and South America. He has appeared at Covent Garden and at the Edinburgh Festival. In 1962 he sang at the Chicago Opera, appearing as Nemorino in *L'Elisir d'Amore*. He sang at the Metropolitan Opera in 1965-66 and subsequently. He possesses a lyric tenor voice of uncommonly subtle expressive skill.

Records: RCA Victor* (*Rigoletto*), Ricordi (*Rigoletto*), and a great many Spanish labels. *U.S. re-issue:* London, Angel, Mercury, Columbia, Montilla, Everest-Cetra.

KRAUS, ERNST, tenor, b. June 8, 1863, Erlangen, Germany; d. Sept. 9, 1941, Walchstadt, Germany. He was the father of the conductor Richard Kraus. At first he worked in his father's brewery, but on the advice of the Wagner tenor Heinrich Vogl he studied singing with Frau Schimon-Regan in Munich and later in Milan. He made his debut (1893) in Mannheim, where he stayed for three years. He then signed a contract (1898) with the Berlin Imperial Opera and was a member of that company until 1924. He was particularly noted as a Wagner tenor and he appeared regularly at the Bayreuth Festivals (1899-1909), as Walther in *Die Meistersinger*, Siegmund in *Die Walküre*, Erik in *Der Fliegende Holländer*, but, above all, Siegfried in the *Ring* cycle. His most successful guest appearances were at Covent Garden, La Scala, the Paris Opéra, and in Vienna, Munich, Dresden, and Brussels. During the 1903-04 season he appeared at the Metropolitan Opera. After his farewell to the stage, he was active as a teacher in Munich. He had a voice of inexhaustible vocal power and a special intensity of expression, making his perhaps the most voluminous tenor voice ever recorded. He was noted particularly as a Wagner tenor.

Records: G & T, HMV (Berlin, 1901-08), Edison* cylinders, and Vox. *U.S. re-issue:* Opera Disc. *U.S. re-recording:* Veritas, Cantilena.

KRAUS, FELIX VON, bass, b. Oct. 3, 1870, Vienna; d. Oct. 30, 1937, Munich. He was the son of the Austrian general staff physician Carl von Kraus. He first studied philology and music history in Vienna; then he studied harmony with Anton Bruckner and theory with Eusebius Mandyczewski, among others, and was graduated from the university in 1894 with a thesis on Caldara. He studied singing only briefly with Julius Stockhausen and he was, in general, a self-taught singer. After 1896 he appeared as a concert singer, at first in Vienna, then also in Leipzig and Berlin, and had brilliant successes both in the field of oratorio and song. His interpretation of the *Vier Ernste Gesänge* of Johannes Brahms was held to be incomparable. On the advice of Cosima Wagner, Von Kraus, by now a famous concert bass, first appeared on the opera stage at the Bayreuth Festival of 1899. As both Hagen in *Götterdämmerung* and Gurnemanz in *Parsifal* he was greatly admired, in general, and he continued to sing there until the summer of 1909, adding the roles of the Landgraf in *Tannhäuser* and King Mark in *Tristan und Isolde*. With the exception of a few guest appearances, he confined himself to the concert hall. He had his residence first in Leipzig, but from 1908-25 he was a professor at the Munich Academy of Music. He was married to the contralto Adrienne von Kraus-Osborne.

Records: A few excessively rare Odeon records (Vienna, 1906).

KRAUS, OTAKAR, baritone, b. Dec. 10, 1909, Prague. He studied in Prague and with Fernando Carpi in Milan and made his debut (1935) in Brno as Amonasro in *Aïda*. He then sang at Bratislava (1938-39), at the National Opera in Prague (1939-41), and after 1941 lived in London. After World War II he had a highly successful career at Covent Garden. In 1946 he sang at the Glyndebourne Festival in the world *première* of *The Rape of Lucretia*. Guest appearances followed in Belgium, in Holland, at the Vienna State Opera, at La Scala, in Scandinavia, and at the opera houses in Rome and Rio de Janeiro. He sang Nick Shadow in the world *première* of *The Rake's Progress* at the Teatro Fenice (1951). He has had great successes since 1961 at the Edinburgh, Glyndebourne, and Holland Festivals as Alberich in the *Ring* cycle.

Records: Columbia. *U.S. re-issue:* Angel.

KRAUSE, TOM, baritone, b. 1934, Helsinki. During his medical studies in Helsinki he played the piano and guitar in a jazz band. He began his serious study of singing at the Vienna Music Academy in 1956. He made his debut under the name Thomas Krause as a lieder singer in Helsinki (1957) and his stage debut (1958) at the Berlin City Opera. Since then he has been very successful in guest appearances in Switzerland, Germany, and Scandinavia. He has been engaged at the Hamburg State Opera since 1961. He sang the role of the Herald in *Lohengrin* at the 1962 Bayreuth Festival and in 1963 sang the baritone solo in Benjamin Britten's *War Requiem* in London. His Metropolitan Opera debut occurred in the 1967-68 season. He has a well-developed and rich voice.

Records: Ariola-Bertelsmann and Decca (including Kurwenal in a complete *Tristan und Isolde*). U.S. re-issue: London.

KRAUS-OSBORNE, ADRIENNE VON, contralto, b. Dec. 2, 1873, Buffalo, N.Y.; d. June 15, 1951, Zell-an-der-Ziller, Austria. Originally Adrienne Eisbein. She was the daughter of a German physician. She went to Germany to study singing and first became a pupil of Auguste Götze in Leipzig; she then studied with the bass Felix von Kraus, whom she married in 1899. She made her debut at the Leipzig Opera House (1893) and remained there until 1908, after which she was a member of the Royal Opera in Munich. Her fame came partly as a result of her singing of Wagner roles on the stage and partly from her activity in the concert hall, especially her performances of the *Alto Rhapsody* of Brahms. She sang at the Bayreuth Festivals (1902-09) and was admired as Erda and as Waltraute in the *Ring* cycle. Guest appearances and concerts took her to England, Holland, and the United States as well as to the centers of German musical life. On the stage her most brilliant performance was in the title role in *Carmen*.

Records: She made five exceedingly rare records for Odeon (Vienna, 1906); three of them are duets with her husband.

KRAUSS, FRITZ, tenor, b. June 16, 1883, Lehenhammer, Germany. After studies in Munich, Milan, and Berlin, he made his debut (1911) in Bremen. In 1912 he went to Leipzig and from there to Kassel. (1914-15). He sang at the Cologne Opera (1915-21) and then moved to the Munich State Opera, where he remained for over twenty years. He became internationally famous, particularly as a Wagner singer, through guest appearances at the Vienna State Opera (1931-33; 1939), the Frankfurt Opera, and the Berlin State Opera. He was frequently a guest at Covent Garden, including performances as Don Ottavio in *Don Giovanni* under Bruno Walter in 1926. In 1943 he gave up his stage career and taught in Munich. He lives in Öberlingen on the Bodensee. A brilliant tenor voice.

Records: Vox, Homochord, and HMV.

KREBS, HELMUT, tenor, b. Oct. 8, 1913, Dortmund, Germany. He studied theory and singing at the Berlin Music High School. After his first activity as a concert singer, he made his stage debut (1938) at the Berlin City Opera. He sang at Düsseldorf (1945-47) and since then again at the Berlin City Opera. He became internationally known through his guest appearances. These included the Festivals at Salzburg, Glyndebourne (as Belmonte in *Die Entführung aus dem Serail* and Idamantes in *Idomeneo*), and at Edinburgh; he has also made seasonal sojourns as guest at La Scala, Covent Garden, the State

Operas in Vienna, Munich, and Hamburg, as well as in Holland, Belgium, and Switzerland. He is additionally famous as a concert singer, particularly as an oratorio tenor; in this capacity he is noted as an interpreter of Bach and especially as the Evangelist in the *St. Matthew Passion.* In 1954 he sang Aron in the world *première* of *Moses und Aron* on the Hamburg radio. He has also composed songs, piano numbers, and chamber music. A beautifully cultivated lyric tenor voice of outstanding expressiveness.

Records: Decca, DGG* (*Orfeo*), Vox, and Columbia (*Die Fledermaus* and *Ariadne auf Naxos*). *U.S. re-issue:* Cantate, Epic, Westminster, Bach Guild, Angel, Nonesuch, Decca.

KREMER, MARTIN, tenor, b. Mar. 23, 1898, Geisenheim, Germany. After his studies with W. Fuhr in Wiesbaden and with Giuseppe Borgatti in Milan, he made his debut (1924) in Kassel and remained there until 1927. He sang in Wiesbaden (1927-29) and then came to the Dresden State Opera, where he remained until 1941. In Dresden he sang in several world *premières* of Richard Strauss' operas: *Arabella* on July 1, 1933, *Die Schweigsame Frau* on June 26, 1935, and *Daphne* on Oct. 15, 1938. His roster of guest appearances included London, Barcelona, Berlin, Vienna, Munich, and Zoppot Festivals. At the Bayreuth Festival he was much admired as David in *Die Meistersinger.* He was first lyric tenor at the German Theater in Oslo (1941-44). After World War II he was engaged as heroic tenor at Wiesbaden. He lives in Reit-im-Winkel. A noted *buffo* tenor.

Records: Orchestrola and HMV. *U.S. re-issue:* RCA Victor.

KRENN, FRITZ, bass-baritone, b. Dec. 11, 1887, Vienna; d. July 17, 1964, Vienna. He was at first a drawing teacher and then studied singing at the Vienna Music Academy. After his military service in World War I, he made his debut (1918) at the Vienna Volksoper in *Cavalleria Rusticana.* His next engagements were at Reichenberg in Bohemia (1919-20) and at the Vienna State Opera (1920-25). After he had sung briefly in Wiesbaden, he came in 1927 to the Berlin State Opera, where he was highly successful. He was particularly admired as Baron Ochs in *Der Rosenkavalier,* and he sang this part at the Salzburg Festivals after 1936 as successor to the great Richard Mayr. In 1938 he returned to the Vienna State Opera and remained there during the next twenty years. His guest appearances included Covent Garden, La Scala, and opera houses in Holland, Belgium, Spain, France, Hungary, and South America. He sang at the Metropolitan Opera (1951-52). He was married to the singer Luise Kornfeld and lived during his last years in Vienna.

Records: A few records for Remington* and MMS. *U.S. re-issue:* Period.

KREPPEL, WALTER, bass, b. 1923, Nuremberg. He at first planned to become an actor, but then studied singing at the Nuremberg Conservatory and made his debut there (1945) as Tommaso in *Tiefland.* After singing there until 1948 and at Würzburg (1948-50), he sang concurrently at Heidelberg and Gelsenkirchen (1950-53). The Hannover Opera was his base (1953-56), then the Frankfurt Opera (1956-59), and in this latter year he joined the Munich State Opera. After 1955 he appeared as guest at the Vienna State Opera, which he joined in 1960. Zürich, Amsterdam, London, and the Salzburg Festivals (1963-64) have had him as a guest. He has a volumi-

nous dark-timbred bass voice and has mastered a wide-ranging repertory.
Records: DGG (*Don Giovanni*), Decca (*Das Rheingold*), and Ariola. *U.S. re-issue:* Westminster, London.

KRUKOWSKI, ERNST, baritone, b. 1918, Gevelsburg, Germany. He studied at the Music High School in Cologne and made his debut in Bremen (1939), but his career was interrupted by the war. After the war he began again as a concert singer, then sang in opera at Göttingen (1948-53). Since 1953 he has sung at Basel and has also been a member of the Berlin City Opera. At this latter house he has had great success, especially in the title role of *Nabucco*. He is married to the ballerina of the Berlin City Opera Lilo Herbeth.
Records: HMV (small roles in complete operas), Opera, and Ariola (*Le Postillon du Longjumeau*).

KRULL, ANNIE, soprano, b. Jan. 12, 1876, near Rostock, Germany; d. June 14, 1947, Schwerin, Germany. She studied with Hertha Brämer in Berlin and made her stage debut (1898) in Plauen. In 1900 the intendant of the Dresden Royal Opera, Count von Seebach, heard her and engaged her for his house. There she went from one success to another (1901-10). In 1901 she sang Diemuth in the world *première* of *Feuersnot* and later in the same year sang the role of Ulana in the world *première* of *Manru*. Richard Strauss wanted her for the title role in the first performance of his opera *Salome*, but, by the tradition of the house, Marie Wittich, as prima donna of the Dresden company, claimed the right of creating the role. The part of Salome, however, later became one of Annie Krull's starring roles. On Jan. 25, 1909, at Dresden she created the title role in *Elektra* at its world *première*. She sang at Mannheim (1910-12), Weimar (1912-14), and finally at Schwerin. She had a dramatic soprano voice of special tonal volume and overpowering intensity of expressiveness.
Records: Odeon (Act II of *Tannhäuser*, Berlin, 1909). She also made Edison cylinders and Pathé* discs.

KRUSZELNICKA, SALOMEA, soprano, b. 1872, Tarnopol, Russia; d. Nov. 14, 1952, Lvov, Russia. After her studies with W. Wysocki in Lvov and Milan, she made her debut (1892) at the Lvov Opera and then sang in Cracow and Odessa. She appeared as guest (1896) at the Trieste Opera as Leonora in *La Forza del Destino*, sang in Chile (1897), and at Cremona and Parma (1898). In Italy she always sang under the name Kruszeniski, in Poland and Russia under her real name Kruszelnicka. She was the greatly admired prima donna of the Warsaw Opera (1898-1903) and made guest appearances at the Maryinsky Theater in St. Petersburg and (1902) in Paris. As a Ukrainian she became entangled in political intrigue in 1903 and became very unpopular first in Russia and then in Poland. She therefore returned to Italy and in May, 1904, sang the title role in the newly revised version of *Madama Butterfly* at Brescia and led the work from its previous unfortunate *première* to success. In 1907 she created the role of Salome at its La Scala *première* and in 1909 she created the role of Elektra for the Milan House. She was greatly admired at La Scala, where she also appeared as Isolde in *Tristan und Isolde* and in the world *première* of *Gloria* in 1907. She sang Brünnhilde in *Götterdämmerung* at the Teatro Massimo in 1911, and in 1913 she made guest appearances at the Teatro Colón. In that year she also married the Italian lawyer and political figure Cesare Rizzone, and lived thereafter in Viareggio. In 1915 she sang at La Scala in the world *première* of *Fedra*. After she had long since ceased to appear in public, she undertook an American tour in 1927, during which she sang especially for Ukrainian emigrant groups. She then settled down as a teacher in Milan. In 1939 she visited her family in Lvov and, because of the outbreak of the war, was unable to return to Italy. She then taught at the Lvov Conservatory and in 1945 sang at a charity concert there. One of the most beautiful soprano voices of her time. The volume and dark luster of her vocal timbre, the perfection of her phrasing, and the feeling for style in her delivery make her records of great value to connoisseurs.

Records: Fonotipia and G & T labels much-sought by all collectors. In 1927 she made American Columbia* records of Ukrainian folk songs, *U.S. re-issue:* Victor, Columbia-Fonotipia, HRS, IRCC. *U.S. re-recording:* TAP, Belcanto, Rococo.

KRUYSEN, BERNARD, baritone, b. Switzerland of Dutch parents. He grew up in Provence and studied with his guardian, Herbert Raideck. He gave his first concert at the age of seven. After studying painting, he joined the Royal Conservatory of Music in The Hague and graduated in 1957. While studying on a scholarship in Paris with Pierre Bernac, he won the Gabriel Fauré Prize. He has sung at the Amsterdam Opera House and elsewhere in Europe. In 1962 he was awarded the first of three Grand Prix du Disque for his singing of Debussy songs.

U.S. records: Epic, Westminster, Philips.

KUEN, PAUL, tenor, b. Apr. 8, 1910, Sulzberg, Germany; d. May 20, 1966, New York. He had planned to become an organ builder, but studied singing with Heinrich Knote and Adalbert Ebner in Munich. His debut (1933) in Konstanz was followed successively by engagements in Bamberg, Freiburg im Br., and Nuremberg. He was engaged at the Dresden State Opera (1944-47) and came to the Munich State Opera in the latter year; he was highly successful there. He was greatly admired at the Bayreuth Festivals as Mime in the *Ring* cycle (1951-57), and this particular role as well as many others for *buffo* tenor were features of his guest appearances in Holland, Belgium, France, Italy, Spain, and South America. He was applauded at the Metropolitan Opera as Mime (1961-62).

Records: DGG* (*Der Freischütz* and *Le Nozze di Figaro*), Columbia (*Die Kluge*), Decca (*Das Rheingold*). *U.S. re-issue:* Angel, London.

KULLMAN, CHARLES, tenor, b. Jan. 13, 1913, New Haven, Conn. He studied singing at the Juilliard School of Music in New York, then at the American Conservatory at Fontainebleau, before making his debut (1929) with the American Opera Company, which he joined for a two-year tour. He then came to the Kroll Opera (1931), was engaged at the Berlin State Opera (1932-36) with a simultaneous membership in the Vienna State Opera (1934-36). He appeared at the Salzburg Festivals (1934-36) as Belmonte in *Die Entführung aus dem Serail*, as Walther in *Die Meistersinger*, and as Huon in *Oberon*; and in the same years he was very successful at Covent Garden in London. Upon his return to the United States he joined the Metropolitan Opera and made his debut as Faust in Gounod's opera. He remained at the Metropolitan until 1956 and made guest appearances in Chicago, San Francisco, and Los Angeles. During his career in Germany and later in the United States he was successful as a singer in films. Since 1956 he has been a singing teacher at Indiana University School of Music. A voice with brilliant timbre and a flexibility of delivery that distinguished his interpretations.

Records: Columbia* and private recordings for the Metropolitan Opera. *U.S. re-recording:* Rococo.

KUNZ, ERICH, baritone, b. May 20, 1909, Vienna. Following his studies with Theodor Lierhammer and Hans Duhan in Vienna, he made his debut (1933) at Troppau as Osmin in *Die Entführung aus dem Serail*. Engagements in Plauen (1936-37) and Wroclaw (1937-41) preceded his call to the Vienna State Opera, where he acquired an extraordinary popularity. After 1942 he appeared almost annually in productions at the Salzburg Festivals. He was a special favorite in such Mozart roles as the title role in *Le Nozze di Figaro*, Leporello in *Don Giovanni*, Guglielmo in *Così fan tutte*, and particularly Papageno in *Die Zauberflöte*. In 1943 he sang Beckmesser in *Die Meistersinger* at the Bayreuth Festival. After World War II he had a brilliant international career singing at the Glyndebourne and Edinburgh Festivals, at La Scala, Covent Garden, and the Teatro Colón and during the 1952-53 season at the Metropolitan Opera.

Records: Many records for Columbia*, Vanguard*, Decca, RCA Victor* (including *Le Nozze di Figaro*, *Così fan tutte*, *Die Zauberflöte*, *Die Meistersinger*, *Die Fledermaus*, *The Merry Widow*). *U.S. re-issue:* London.

KUPPER, ANNELIES, soprano, b. Aug. 21, 1906, Glatz, Silesia, Austria. After studying musicology and pedagogy at the University of Wroclaw, she passed her examinations as music teacher and worked as such at the Lyceum of the Ursulines in Wroclaw (1929-35). She then became active as a concert singer before she made her stage debut at the Wroclaw Opera (1935). By way of Schwerin and Weimar she came (1940) to the Hamburg State Opera. Her stay there lasted until 1945 and since then she has been an esteemed member of the Munich State Opera, while making regular guest appearances at the Vienna State Opera and the City Opera in Berlin. Other guest appearances have also brought her success in London, Paris, Stockholm, Brussels, and Amsterdam. At the Bayreuth Festivals she sang Eva in *Die Meistersinger* (1944) and Elsa in *Lohengrin* (1960), while at the Salzburg Festival she created the chief role in *Die Liebe der Danaë* at its world première (1952). She has been married since 1936 to the music critic and pianist Joachim Herrmann, and he often accompanies her. Even while continuing her singing career, she has been a teacher at the Music Academy in Munich since 1956. Both the musical beauty of her voice and the fine animation of her delivery are greatly admired.

Records: DGG (including Elsa in *Lohengrin* and Senta in *Der Fliegende Holländer*) and Philips. *U.S. re-issue:* Electrola, Remington.

KURENKO, MARIA, soprano-contralto, b. 1890, Tomak, Siberia. She studied at Moscow University and at the same time undertook vocal studies with Masetti. Her debut occurred (1914) at the Kharkov Opera and in 1918 she came to the Bolshoi Theater in Moscow. However, she left Russia in 1923.

After 1925 she lived in the United States and was particularly active here in the concert hall and noted as an interpreter of Russian songs. She sang Rosina in *Il Barbiere di Siviglia* for a single performance at the Chicago Opera in 1927 and she later appeared in opera a few times in Los Angeles and at the Lewisohn Stadium in New York, where she sang in *A Life for the Czar* in 1936. Records of her voice which were made in 1955 show scarcely any change from her younger days.
Records: Columbia*. *U.S. re-issue:* Lyrichord, RCA Victor, Capitol. *U.S. re-recordings:* Collectors Guild.

KURT, MELANIE, soprano, b. Jan. 8, 1880, Vienna; d. Mar. 11, 1941, New York. She first studied piano with Theodor Leschetizky in Vienna, then singing with Fanny Müller and Marie Lehmann in Berlin. Her debut as Elisabeth in *Tannhäuser* took place in Lübeck (1902) and she remained there until 1905. She sang at Braunschweig (1905-08) before becoming a member of the Berlin Imperial Opera (1908-12) and then of the German Opera House in Berlin-Charlottenburg (1912-15). She became internationally famous through guest appearances, particularly in Wagner roles, at such houses as Covent Garden, La Scala, the Budapest Opera, and the opera houses in Dresden and Munich. She sang at the Metropolitan Opera (1914-17) and was esteemed in Wagner parts. After 1919 she became a teacher in Berlin, later in Vienna. In 1938 she emigrated to the United States. A sumptuous dramatic soprano voice, filled with expressiveness and overpowering dramatic ability.
Records: HMV, Columbia*, Beka, and Parlophone. *U.S. re-issue:* Opera Disc, Victor, IRCC. *U.S. re-recording:* Veritas.

KURZ, SELMA, soprano, b. Nov. 15, 1874, Biala, Galicia, Austria; d. May 10, 1933, Vienna. Her voice was discovered by Cantor Goldmann as she sang in his synagogue in Biala and a patron then financed her study of singing with Johannes Ress in Vienna; she completed her studies with Mathilde Marchesi in Paris. In 1895 she made her debut at the Hamburg Opera as Mignon in Thomas' opera. In 1896 she came to the Frankfurt Opera, where she stayed until 1899. Although she sang lyric soprano roles at the beginning of her career, she soon became a celebrated coloratura. In 1899 she was engaged by Gustav Mahler for the Vienna Imperial Opera, where she had sensational successes and where she sang until the end of her career in 1929. She had great triumphs in her guest appearances: Covent Garden (1904-07), where she was again a guest in 1924, the Paris Opéra, and the opera houses in Monte Carlo, Budapest, Prague, Ostend, Amsterdam, Warsaw and Cairo. In 1921 she traveled to America, but gave only a single concert in New York before returning to Europe. In 1922 she sang Konstanze in *Die Entführung aus dem Serail* at the Salzburg Festival. She was married to the Viennese gynecologist Professor Joseph Halban; her daughter, Desi Kurz-Halban, also appeared as a soprano and is especially remembered for her recording of Mahler's *Fourth Symphony*. Selma Kurz was one of the greatest coloratura sopranos of all time. She demonstrated an effortless mastery of the most difficult passages, a delicacy of feeling for style, and entirely unsurpassed minutes-long trills.
Records: Edison* cylinders and discs for G & T (Vienna, 1902-07), Polydor, and HMV. *U.S. re-issue:* Opera Disc, IRCC. *U.S. re-recording:* TAP, Scala, Eterna, Rococo, Belcanto, FRP, HRS.

KUSCHE, BENNO, baritone, b. Jan. 30, 1916, Freiburg im Br., Germany. After he had studied singing at the Academy of the Baden National Theater in Karlsruhe, he made his debut at the Heidelberg Opera Festival (1939). He was then engaged at Koblenz (1938-39), Augsburg (1939-44), and at the Bavarian State Opera in Munich (1944-58). Since 1958 he has been a member of the German-Opera-on-the-Rhine at Düsseldorf-Duisburg. His successful guest appearances include the State Operas in Vienna and Stuttgart, La Scala, and in London and Brussels. Although he is highly regarded as both a Mozart and a Wagner singer, he is also esteemed in the concert hall. He is married to the soprano Christine Görner.

Records: DGG, Columbia (*Die Meistersinger* and *Die Kluge*), Vanguard, and Decca. *U.S. reissue:* Angel, Electrola.

L

LABIA, MARIA, soprano, b. Feb. 14, 1880, Verona, Italy; d. Feb. 10, 1953, Como, Italy. She came from an old patrician family and her sister, Fausta Labia (1872-1935), was also a noted opera singer. After Maria Labia had become a concert singer, she made her stage debut (1905) at the Stockholm Royal Opera as Mimi in *La Bohème*. In 1906 she was engaged at the Komische Oper in Berlin through Hans Gregor. In her debut there as Tosca she had a sensational success. After she had remained there for two years, she sang with equally great success at the Manhattan Opera House (1908-10). She appeared as guest at the Paris Opéra (1909) and at the Vienna Imperial Opera (1911). In 1913 she sang the title role in *Salome* in its first presentation at La Scala; this was the basis for a brilliant career at the larger Italian opera houses. In 1919 she sang in *Il Tabarro* at the Teatro Costanzi on the occasion of the Italian *première* of the work; she also sang at La Scala in 1922 in the world *première* of *I Quattro Rusteghi*. After leaving the stage she was first a teacher in the Conservatory in Warsaw, but later became active in the Accademia Chigiana in Siena and in Rome. She was famed for the melodiousness of her voice and for the dramatic passion of her delivery; she was also esteemed as a great actress.

Records: Odeon (1907-10), Edison* cylinders and discs, Victor* records; unpublished electric records for Telefunken. *U.S. re-recording:* Scala.

LABÓ, FLAVIANO, tenor, b. 1926, Borgonovo, Italy. He began vocal studies at seventeen, but then became a soldier. During his military service his voice was discovered by the conductor Antonio Votto, who later permitted him to join the singing school of La Scala for training. He also studied with Campogalliani in Milan and he made his debut in Piacenza (1953) as Cavaradossi in *Tosca*. In the following years he sang at the most important Italian opera houses, including, after 1960, La Scala and Rome, and made guest appearances at the Vienna State Opera and in Paris, Lisbon, and Zürich. He was engaged by the Metropolitan Opera in 1957, making his debut as Don Alvaro in *La Forza del Destino*. Since then he has had an important career all over the world.

Records: DGG* (including *Don Carlos*), RCA Victor*, and Philips. *U.S. re-issue:* London.

LAFITTE, LÉON, tenor, b. Jan. 28, 1875, Saint-Geniès, France; d. September, 1938, Paris. Following his studies at the Paris Conservatory, he made his debut (1898) at the Paris Opéra as David in *Die Meistersinger*. In 1899 he went to the Opera in Brussels, where he sang for fifteen consecutive seasons with brilliant success. There he sang, among other roles, that of Jean in the first performance there of *Le Jongleur de Notre-Dame*. He also sang the same role in its first performance at Covent Garden. Before World War I he appeared as guest in Germany, Russia, Finland, and at The Hague. In 1908 he sang Mime in the first Paris performance of *Siegfried* opposite Ernest Van Dyck. In 1916 he went to South America, where he sang dramatic roles especially at the Teatro Colón and in Rio de Janeiro. In 1923 he appeared again at the Paris Opéra in *Samson et Dalila* and in *Le Damnation de Faust*.

Records: A few rare records for G & T (Paris, 1902), Columbia (Paris, 1902), and Zonophone (Paris, 1903).

LAHOLM, EYVIND, tenor, b. 1894, Eau Claire, Wis.; d. July, 1958, New York City. He came from a Swedish family; his name originally was Jon Edwin Johnson. After he had served in the American navy in World War I, he studied singing with William S. Brady in New York. At first he sang in operettas in the United States, and then began his operatic career in Europe. He made his debut in Essen (1927) as Canio in *I Pagliacci*, sang at Wiesbaden (1928-30), Stuttgart (1930-31), and at the Frankfurt Opera (1932-38). He was especially known as a Wagner tenor. He was a guest in Amsterdam in 1934, singing Rienzi in Wagner's opera, at the Zoppot Festival (1937), and at the Arena Festival as Tannhäuser (1938). In 1939 he gave a highly successful concert in New York and was then engaged by the Metropolitan Opera, where he sang until 1941.

Records: He left only a single Parlophone-Odeon record of arias from *Fidelio* and *Otello*, but there are private recordings at the Metropolitan Opera, including one of *Tannhäuser* with Rose Pauly. U.S. re-issue: American Decca.

LAMONT, FORREST, tenor, b. Jan. 26, 1881, Athlone, Canada; d. Dec. 17, 1937, Chicago. As a boy he came to Chicopee Falls, Massachusetts where he sang in a church choir. He studied in Italy and made his debut (1914) at the Teatro Adriano in *Poliuto*. In the same year he sang as guest in Moscow and later appeared as guest in Budapest, Vienna, and on various Italian stages. He came to the Chicago Opera in 1917, making his debut as Xalca in the world *première* of *Azora*. Until 1930 he was an esteemed member of the Chicago company, but he had his greatest success in 1920-21 when he sang in *I Gioielli della Madonna* opposite Rosa Raisa. After 1922 he also sang Wagner roles. He appeared in the Cincinnati Summer Opera after 1930 and then taught in Chicago.

Records: Okeh* (early 1920's).

LANCE, ALBERT, tenor, b. 1925, Adelaide, Australia. Originally Albert Lance Ingram. He studied in Australia, where he first appeared in operetta. In 1952 he sang Cavaradossi in *Tosca* in Sydney and in 1954 the title role in *Les Contes d'Hoffmann* in a gala performance for Queen Elizabeth of England. In 1954 he went to Europe for further study and was engaged in 1956 at the Opéra-Comique, making his debut as Cavaradossi. Since then he has been highly successful at that house as well as at the Paris Opéra, especially in 1960 as Don José in

Carmen with Jane Rhodes. In 1961 he made guest appearances at Covent Garden and completed an American tour.
Records: Columbia. *U.S. re-issue:* Angel.

LANDI, BRUNO, tenor, b. 1905 (?), Turin, Italy, d. May 8, 1968, Buenos Aires. He began his career in 1929 and soon found great success on the leading Italian stages, specializing in the lyric repertory. He sang at the Italian Opera in Holland (1934-35) and had special success at La Scala (1936-37). He was greatly admired at the Teatro Colón in 1937. During the 1938-39 season he was engaged at the Metropolitan Opera, his debut role being that of the Duke in *Rigoletto* and he toured the United States (1938-40). He was again a member of the Metropolitan (1941-47) and appeared once more as guest in 1951. He is married to the soprano Hilde Reggiani. A clear lyric voice of great subtlety of expression.
Records: HMV, RCA Victor*, and Allegro Royale*.

LANDOUZY, LISE, soprano, b. 1861, Le Cateau, France; d. 1943, Aix-les-Bains, France. Originally Elise Besville. She first appeared publicly at the Casino in Blankenburghe and then made her debut (1889) at the Opéra-Comique as Rosina in *Il Barbiere di Siviglia*. Thereafter she had great successes and sang Anne Ford in *Falstaff* there in 1894 in the presence of the composer on the occasion of the French *première* of the work. She sang Clorinde in *La Fille de Tabarin* at its world *première* in 1901. After 1895 she appeared regularly as guest at the Théâtre de la Monnaie and she also sang at the opera houses in Nice, Monte Carlo, and Aix-les-Bains. After giving up her stage career, she lived and taught in Paris. Possessing a distinguished and thoroughly trained soprano voice, she showed marked expressive ability in both coloratura and lyric roles.
Records: A great many records for Odeon De Luxe (Paris, 1905-07) and Columbia.

LANGENDORFF, FRIEDA, soprano-contralto, b. Mar. 24, 1868, Breslau, Germany; d. June 11, 1947, New York City. She studied with Jenny Meyer, Mathilde Mallinger, and August Iffert. Her debut occurred (1901) at Strasbourg, where she remained for four years. Her later engagements were at the German Theater in Prague (1905-07), the Metropolitan Opera (1907-08; 1910-11), the Kroll Opera (1909-11), and the Dresden Royal Opera (1914-16). She made very successful guest appearances in Amsterdam, Berlin, Brussels, and Helsinki. She sang at the Bayreuth Festival (1904). She was esteemed particularly in dramatic roles, but also as a concert singer. After the end of her career she lived in the United States.
Records: Three very rare duets with Gertrude Förstel on G & T (Prague, 1906).

LANKOW, EDWARD, bass, b. 1883, Tarrytown, N.Y.; d. Jan. 29, 1940, New York City. Originally Edward Rosenberg. He was a pupil in New York of Anna Lankow, whose name he took. He made his debut (1904) as a concert singer and in 1905 made a tour of the United States as assisting artist with Adelina Patti. He then went to Europe and was a member of the Dresden Royal Opera (1906-08). He sang at the Frankfurt Opera (1908-10) and at the Vienna Imperial Opera (1910-11). He was invited to join the Boston Opera in 1912, but a stronger bid from the Metropolitan Opera caused him to appear there instead. He made his debut in New York as Sarastro in *Die Zauberflöte* with Emmy Destinn, Leo Slezak, and Otto Goritz.

He sang this same role three times in the 1912-13 season and after 1913 he became active as a concert bass. In 1922 he appeared as King Mark in *Tristan und Isolde* at the Chicago Opera and during the same season he sang as guest at the Opéra-Comique. He gave up his career relatively early and became a teacher in New York. He had a large bass voice of special beauty in the lower ranges.

Records: Rare records for HMV (Frankfurt, 1908) and one electric record for HMV. *U.S. re-recording:* IRCC.

LANZA, MARIO, tenor, b. Jan. 31, 1921, New York; d. Oct. 7, 1959, Rome. Originally Alfredo Cocozza. In Philadelphia, where his parents had moved, he first worked as a truck driver and studied singing in his free time. The conductor Sergei Koussevitsky arranged for him to study at the New England Conservatory of Music, but his studies were interrupted by his army service in World War II. After the end of the war he made a precarious living as a casual laborer before he finally undertook a concert tour as part of the Bel Canto Trio with George London and Frances Yeend. He became world-famous overnight for his appearance in such American films as *The Louisiana Fisherman*, *Old Heidelberg*, and *Serenade*. In 1951 his fame spread throughout the world with the film *The Great Caruso*. This wildly intensified public adulation and the unsteadiness of his living habits brought him and his career to a sudden end. After 1956 he lived in Rome and only rarely appeared in concert; he died of a heart attack at age thirty-eight.

Records: RCA Victor*. *U.S. re-issue:* Camden.

LAPELLETRIE, RENÉ, tenor, b. 1883, Libourne, France. He studied with Leopold Ketten and at the Geneva Conservatory; he made his debut (1908) at the Théâtre Trianon-Lyrique. He sang in Dijon (1909-11), Nice (1911-12), and Marseilles (1912-14). After 1911 he appeared as guest almost annually at Vichy, where he was greatly admired, particularly in the 1920's. He was engaged at the newly opened Théâtre des Champs-Elysées in 1914 and had a great triumph there in *Benvenuto Cellini*. He was an admired member of the Opéra-Comique in Paris (1920-24); he made guest appearances in Marseilles, Nîmes, Toulouse, and Montpellier. Although he sang in Amsterdam in 1928 and 1929 as Don José in *Carmen* and in other roles, he otherwise rarely appeared outside of France. After World War II he was again active at the Opéra-Comique, where he first sang *buffo* roles and, until 1958, *comprimario* parts. He lives and teaches in Paris.

Records: Acoustic records for Odeon and HMV. His electric records included the title role in an abbreviated version of *Faust* for Polydor in 1931 and Spalanzani in *Les Contes d'Hoffmann* for Columbia in 1946.

LAPEYRETTE, KETTY, contralto, b. July 23, 1884, Oloron, France; d. Oct. 2, 1960, Paris. Having studied at the Paris Conservatory under Masson, Hettich, and Bouvet, she made her debut at the Opéra there (1908) as Dalila in *Samson et Dalila*. She remained for thirty years the first contralto of this house, and scarcely ever sang outside the French capital. In 1908 she appeared in the first performance at the Opéra of *Götterdämmerung* and sang Annina in the French *première* of *Der Rosenkavalier* in 1914 as well as the Voice from on High in the 1914 *première* of *Parsifal*. She sang in the world *première* of *Antar* in 1921 and on the occasion of the centenary festivities for Saint-Saëns in 1935 she sang Dalila. Her guest appearances were in Amsterdam (1936) and at Covent Garden (1937). In 1939 she left the stage and taught thereafter at the Paris Conservatory.

Records: Unfortunately, she sang only on Pathé* discs, which cannot be played on the equipment we use today *(La Favorita, Rigoletto,* and *Il Trovatore).*

LAPPAS, ULYSSES, tenor, b. 1881, Athens. He studied at the Athens Conservatory and after his debut there (1913) he continued studying singing in Italy and developed a highly successful stage career there. He sang at La Scala in *Il Macigno* in 1917 and at the Teatro Regio in Parma in *La Fanciulla del West* in 1918. Covent Garden heard him in 1919, Cairo in 1920, and he sang in 1925 again at Covent Garden, this time opposite Maria Jeritza in *Fedora.* His last appearance at this London house was as the title hero in *Don Carlos* in 1933. He was greatly admired during the 1920's at the Monte Carlo Opera and he was a member of the Chicago Opera (1921-22; 1928-29). Among his guest appearances on Italian stages should be included that at La Scala in 1934, where he sang in Felice Lattuada's *Don Giovanni.* He sang at the Royal Opera in Athens (1935-53); thereafter he taught singing in the Greek capital.

Records: Columbia*.

LARSÉN-TODSEN, NANNY, soprano, b. Aug. 2, 1884, Hagby, Sweden. She studied at the Royal Conservatory in Stockholm and in both Berlin and Milan before she made her debut at the Royal Opera in Stockholm (1906) as Agathe in *Der Freischütz.* After beginning with lyric roles, she later changed to dramatic parts. She undertook her first foreign guest appearance in 1916, but she became world-famous only after she began to specialize in Wagner roles in 1922. She was greatly admired at La Scala (1923-24) and sang at the Metropolitan Opera (1925-27). Later she made guest appearances at the Paris Opéra and at the principal opera houses in Berlin, Vienna, Munich, Hamburg, Copenhagen, Amsterdam, and Brussels. She was the center of attraction at the Bayreuth Festivals (1927-31) and she was admired particularly as Isolde and as Brünnhilde. After the end of her stage career she taught in Stockholm. The splendor of her vocal equipment and the dramatic intensity of her expressiveness put her in the first rank of Wagner singers.

Records: Parlophone, Favorite, Columbia* (including *Tristan und Isolde,* Bayreuth, 1928). *U.S. reissue:* American Decca.

LASSALLE, JEAN, baritone, b. Dec. 14, 1847, Lyons, France; d. Sept. 7, 1909, Paris. He studied at the National Conservatory in Paris and with Novelli before his debut (1868) at the Opera in Liège. After appearing in Lille, Toulouse, The Hague, and Brussels, he came to the Paris Opéra in 1872, making his debut in the title role of *Guillaume Tell.* He remained for many years one of the brightest stars of this house. He was an annual guest in London, where he was greatly admired (1879-93). During his tenure at the Paris Opéra he appeared in many important *premières: Le Roi de Lahore* (1877), *Polyeucte* (1878), *Henry VIII* (1883), and *Sigurd* (1884). In 1892 he sang in the first performance at the Opéra of *Samson et Dalila.* He was an esteemed member of the Metropolitan Opera (1891-98), where he sang, in addition to roles in the French and Italian repertories, Hans Sachs in *Die Meistersinger* and Wolfram in *Tannhäuser.* After his return to France he sang for a few years in Paris, then devoted himself to teaching. In 1903 he became a professor at the Conservatory. His baritone voice was famous not only because of his consummate mastery of singing technique but also because of the flexibility of his expressiveness.

Records: A few Pathé* cylinders, a few rare Odeon discs. *U.S. re-recording:* Pathé discs, IRCC, TAP, FRP, Rococo, Cantilena.

LASZLÓ, MAGDA, soprano, b. 1919 (?), Marosvasarhély, Hungary. She studied at the Franz Liszt Conservatory in Budapest and made her debut at the National Opera there (1943). In 1946 she left her Hungarian homeland and took up residence in Rome. In Italy she first gave concerts with the pianist Luigi Cortese and then appeared on the most important Italian stages, including La Scala and the Rome Opera. Guest appearances brought her more fame from her successes in Germany, Austria, France, England, Holland, and Switzerland. At the Glyndebourne Festivals she was admired as Alcestis in Gluck's opera and in 1964 in *L'Incoronazione di Poppea*. In 1954 she appeared at Covent Garden, where she had been a frequent guest, in the world *première* of *Troilus and Cressida*, singing the role of Cressida. She is greatly admired as an interpreter of contemporary music.

Records: Nixa (Bach cantatas and the *St. Matthew Passion*), Capitol, and HMV (*L'Incoronazione di Poppea*). *U.S. re-issue:* Westminster, Bartók, Angel.

LATTERMANN, THEODOR, bass-baritone, b. July 29, 1886, Frankfurt a. M.; d. Mar. 4, 1926, Seehof, near Berlin. He studied in Frankfurt and appeared publicly there at the age of nineteen. He was a man of many-sided artistic interests and occupied himself also with painting and sculpture. He made his stage debut in Barmen (1907) and came in 1908 to the Hamburg Opera, of which he remained a member until his death. His highly successful guest appearances at the Gura Opera in Berlin (1909-10) and in Cologne, Amsterdam, Brussels, and the Vienna State Opera (1920-21) all added to his fame. In 1923-24 he undertook a tour of the United States with the German Opera Company, to which his wife, the noted contralto Ottilie Metzger-Lattermann, also belonged. The breadth of his tonal range permitted this artist to sing both baritone and bass parts; he was esteemed as an admirable Mozart and Wagner interpreter.

Records: Edison* cylinders, Parlophone, and Polydor discs.

LAUBENTHAL, RUDOLF, tenor, b. Mar. 10, 1886, Düsseldorf, Germany. After he had studied medicine at the Universities of Munich, Strasbourg, and Berlin, he took up singing. When the director of the German Opera in Berlin heard him, he engaged him at once for his house and Laubenthal made his debut there (1913). He stayed until 1918 and then sang at the Munich State Opera (1919-23). In 1923 he made successful appearances at Covent Garden and was thereupon engaged by the Metropolitan Opera, where he made his debut singing Walther in *Die Meistersinger*. He remained at the Metropolitan until 1933, taking part in a number of important *premières*; he sang Stewa in *Jenufa* (1924), Menelaus in *Die Ägyptische Helena* (1928), and Babinski in *Schwanda* (1931). He also made guest appearances at Covent Garden, at the principal opera houses in Berlin and Vienna, and at the Chicago and San Francisco Operas. After World War II he lived on his estate in Upper Bavaria. With his heroic tenor voice he was particularly famous in Wagner roles.

Records: Parlophone and HMV.

U.S. re-issue: RCA Victor. *U.S. re-recording:* Angel.

LAURENTI, MARIO, baritone, b. 1890, Verona, Italy; d. Mar. 7, 1922, New York City. Originally Luigi Cavadani. He was sent to Germany to study engineering and while he was in Dresden his voice was discovered. He then began to study singing. In 1914 he came to the United States and first sang in the chorus of the Metropolitan Opera. After being brought forward in small roles, he made his solo debut as the Innkeeper in *Manon Lescaut* (1916). He remained at the Metropolitan for six more years, the importance of his roles being constantly increased. He sang as first baritone with the Scotti Opera Company (1920-21). At the Metropolitan he sang the part of Fritz in the first performance there of *Die Tote Stadt* with Maria Jeritza in 1921. His last appearance was on Feb. 20, 1922, at the Metropolitan as Fléville in *Andrea Chénier*. Two weeks later he died of meningitis.

Records: Many Edison* cylinders and discs. *U.S. re-recording:* Odyssey.

LAURI-VOLPI, GIACOMO, tenor, b. Dec. 11, 1892, Lanuvio, near Rome. He first studied jurisprudence, then singing at the Accademia di Santa Cecilia in Rome, his teachers being Enrico Rosati and later Antonio Cotogni. He made his debut (1919) at Viterbo in *I Puritani*. In the following years he had great success at the Teatro Costanzi, in Florence, Genoa, the Teatro Colón, and at the Rio de Janeiro Opera. He first sang at La Scala in 1922 and in 1923 he was engaged by the Metropolitan Opera, making his debut as the Duke in *Rigoletto*. He remained a member of this company until 1933. Guest appearances which brought him great success occurred at Covent Garden, the Paris Opéra, in Brussels, Monte Carlo, at the Teatro Colón, and the most important Italian opera houses. He was admired at the Arena Festivals, at the Maggio Musicale Festival, but most of all at La Scala. Since 1935 he has had his residence at Burjasot, near Valencia, in Spain. During World War II he appeared principally in Italy and Spain. The great beauty of his voice permitted him to have an uncommonly long career on the stage; he did not give up his career until 1965. He published several autobiographical writings: *L'equivovo* (Milan, 1930), *Cristalli viventi* (Rome, 1948), and *A visa aperto* (Milan, 1953). He also published a comparative presentation of voices of the present and past, *Voci parallele* (Milan, 1955). He is married to the Spanish singer Maria Ros. He had a powerful heroic tenor voice, especially at home in the Italian repertory. Also admired as an actor, he was generally held to be one of the greatest tenors of his time.

Records: Many records for Fonotipia, HMV, Brunswick*, Victor*, Cetra* (including *Il Trovatore* and *Luisa Miller*), and Remington* (including *La Bohème*). *U.S. re-issue:* Okeh-Fonotipia. *U.S. re-recording:* TAP, Eterna, Scala, Rococo, Harvest.

LAUTE-BRUN, ANTOINETTE, soprano, b. July 1, 1876, Nîmes, France. She studied at the Paris Conservatory with Duvernoy, Léon Melchissèdec, and Mangin and made her debut (1904) at the Paris Opéra under the name Mlle. Laute, singing Helmwige in *Die Walküre*. She remained a member of this institution until 1927. At first she sang small roles and developed an uncommon versatility; for example, in the production of *Armide* in 1905 she sang six different parts. She married the composer Georges Brun in 1907 and thereafter appeared under the name Mme. Laute-Brun. In 1907 she undertook a tour through Belgium with the baritone Jean Noté, but otherwise she did not appear outside France. She had a highly successful career, however, on the stages in the French provinces, often singing dramatic soprano roles. She was equally admired as an oratorio soprano.

Records: Many records for G & T (Paris, 1904-05), Favorite (Paris, 1906), and Odeon, as well as Edison* cylinders.

LAWRENCE, MARJORIE, soprano, b. Feb. 17, 1909, near Melbourne, Australia. A pupil of Cécile Gilly in Paris, she made her debut at Monte Carlo (1932) as Elisabeth in *Tannhäuser*. In the same year she came to the Paris Opéra, where she appeared with great success until 1935. In that year she was engaged by the Metropolitan Opera and remained there until 1941. Her guest appearances at Covent Garden and at the Zoppot Festivals testified to her ability. In 1941 she appeared as guest in Mexico City and fell ill there of poliomyelitis, which led to a paralysis of both legs. By what seemed like superhuman effort she was able to continue her career as a concert soprano in the United States. In 1943 she sang the role of Venus in *Tannhäuser* in a production at the Metropolitan Opera which did not require her to move about the stage. In a similar situation she later sang Amneris in *Aïda*. In 1948 in New York she sang the title role in a concert presentation of *Elektra*. She published her memoirs under the title *Interrupted Melody, the Story of My Life* (New York, 1949), and in 1954 this was filmed as *Interrupted Melody*.

Records: HMV, RCA Victor*, and Decca records. *U.S. re-issue:* IRCC.

LÁZARO, HIPÓLITO, tenor, b. Dec. 13, 1887, Barcelona. His voice was discovered during his military service and he made his debut (1911) at the Teatro Novedades without special study of singing. After study with Ernesto Colli in Milan, he sang in 1913 in London and Manchester under the name Antonio Manuele. He first created a sensation when he sang at La Scala in 1913 in the world *première* of *Parisina*. The critics compared the voice of this young singer with its brilliantly metallic high notes to that of the unforgettable tenor Giovanni Battista Rubini (1795-1854). In Italy his career subsequently was assisted by Pietro Mascagni. In 1918 he came to the Metropolitan Opera, making his debut as the Duke in *Rigoletto*. He had a sensational success there in 1918 as Arturo in *I Puritani*. There followed guest appearances all over the world, in which he was especially admired in Spain and South America. He was also applauded in his appearances at the Vienna State Opera, the Budapest National Opera, the Teatro Colón, the Teatro Real, the Teatro Liceo, the Mexico City and Havana Operas, and on all the important Italian stages. He also appeared at the Verona Festivals in 1921 and 1929. In 1920 he sang at the Teatro Costanzi in the world *première* of *Il Piccolo Marat*, and on Dec. 24, 1924, he sang at La Scala in the world *première* of *La Cena delle Beffe*. During the Spanish Civil War he was for a short time the director of the Teatro Liceo. He gave his farewell concert in New York in 1940, but appeared again at the Teatro Liceo in 1944 and at the Havana Opera in 1950. He lives in Barcelona.

Records: HMV and Columbia*. *U.S. re-issue:* Victor. *U.S. re-recording:* TAP, Eterna, FRP, Scala, Rococo.

LAZZARI, VIRGILIO, bass, b. Apr. 20, 1887, Assisi, Italy; d. Oct. 4,

1953, Castel Gandolfo, Italy. He began as an operetta singer with the Vitale Company, then studied singing with Antonio Cotogni in Rome (1911-13). He made his debut there (1914), followed by successful appearances in South America in 1915 and at the Havana Opera in 1916, after which he came to the Boston Opera Company. His career reached its high point in North America. From 1918-32 he was the celebrated principal bass of the Chicago Opera Company and sang almost every summer at the Ravinia Summer Opera nearby. Guest appearances took him to the Teatro Colón in 1920 and in 1926 to the Havana Opera. In 1932 he returned to Italy, where he had not sung since 1915. At La Scala he was admired in *L'Amore dei Tre Re*. In 1933 he was engaged at the Metropolitan Opera, making his debut as Don Pedro in *L'Africaine* with Rosa Ponselle. He sang at the Metropolitan until 1940 and again in 1943-50. He also had brilliant success at the Salzburg Festivals, singing Leporello in *Don Giovanni* (1934), Pistol in *Falstaff* (1936), and repeating both these roles plus Dr. Bartolo in *Le Nozze di Figaro* (1937-39). In 1950 he officially left the stage after an appearance as Leporello at the Metropolitan, but later he sang a few performances at Philadelphia and in April, 1953, at the Genoa Opera he sang Archibaldo in *L'Amore dei Tre Re*, one of his specialties.

Records: A few records for Edison* and Vocalion*; there are, however, a great many private recordings from the Metropolitan Opera which have not been released. *U.S. re-recording:* TAP, ASCO, FRP.

LEAR, EVELYN, soprano, b. 1931 (?), New York. She first studied piano and horn, then studied singing at the Juilliard School of Music in New York. After she had already begun to appear in concert in the United States, she went to Germany with her husband, the baritone Thomas Stewart, and in 1958 again took up her vocal studies at the Music High School in Berlin. In 1959 she sang Strauss' *Four Last Songs* in London's Royal Festival Hall. In the same year she made her stage debut at the Berlin City Opera as the Composer in *Ariadne auf Naxos*. She has been a much-honored member of the Berlin company ever since and has been a guest at the Vienna State Opera, the Munich State Opera, the San Francisco Opera, and the Salzburg Festivals, where she has demonstrated that she is an outstanding Mozart interpreter. She sang at the Metropolitan Opera after 1965, making her debut there as Rosina in *Il Barbiere di Siviglia*. The richly trained soprano voice of this artist has proved itself in a widely inclusive opera and concert repertory.

Records: DGG* (Pamina in *Die Zauberflöte*, Marie in *Wozzeck*, Bach's *St. John Passion*, and Janáček's *Slavonic Mass*). *U.S. re-issue:* Angel.

LEFFLER-BURCKHARD, MARTHA, soprano, b. June 16, 1865, Berlin; d. May 14, 1954, Wiesbaden, Germany. She studied with Anna von Meixner in Dresden and Pauline Viardot-Garcia in Paris and made her debut in Strasbourg (1888). She sang in Breslau (1889-90), Cologne (1891-92), and Bremen (1893-97). In Bremen she married the actor Hermann Leffler. Her further engagements included Weimar (1891-99), Wiesbaden (1900-12), and the Berlin Imperial Opera (1913-18). She made a highly successful American tour (1892-93). She was especially admired as a Wagner interpreter and she demonstrated her skill in her appearances at the Bayreuth Festivals, where she sang Kundry in *Parsifal*, Sieglinde in *Die Walküre*, and Ortrud in *Lohengrin* (1906-08). In 1908 she came for a season to the Metropolitan Opera and sang at the German Opera House in Berlin (1918-19). She was later active as a teacher in Berlin.

Records: One exceedingly rare record for Berliner (Wiesbaden, 1900-01).

LEHMANN, LILLI, soprano, b. Nov. 24, 1848, Würzburg, Germany; d. May 17, 1929, Berlin. Her mother, Maria Theresia Lehmann-Löw (1809-1885), was a singer and harpist; her father was the tenor Karl August Lehmann. Her younger sister, Marie Lehmann (1851-1931), was, like Lilli, a noted opera singer. Lilli Lehmann passed her childhood in Prague and was trained by her mother. In 1867 she made her debut at the Landestheater there as First Boy in *Die Zauberflöte*. In 1868 she sang at Danzig and in 1869 at Leipzig. She appeared as guest at the Berlin Imperial Opera in 1870, her role being Queen Marguerite in *Les Huguenots*. Thereafter she became a member of the Berlin house, where she enjoyed great triumphs. At the first Bayreath Festival in 1876 Richard Wagner assigned her the roles of Woglinde, Ortlinde, and the Forest Bird in the *Ring* cycle. She sang again at Bayreuth in 1896, this time as Brünnhilde. During her guest appearances in London, Paris, Stockholm, and Vienna she was given the homage due a queen. In 1886 she was engaged at the Metropolitan Opera, making her debut as Sulamith in *Die Königin von Saba*. By doing this she broke her Berlin contract. She stayed at the Metropolitan until 1891 and there joined dramatic roles to her otherwise limitless repertory. She sang altogether one hundred and seventy roles, ranging from coloratura to Wagner heroines. In 1888 she married the tenor Paul Kalisch (1855-1946). In 1891 she returned to Berlin and again became a member of the Imperial Opera, in spite of her broken contract, through the influence of the Kaiser. The influence of this artist on the musical life of her time was extraordinary. The Salzburg Mozart Festivals of the years 1901-10 took their stimulus from her and she both appeared in them as a singer and led them as *régisseur*. After 1926 she held famous singing courses at the Salzburg Mozarteum. Her singing career is one of the longest known. Even at the age of seventy she was still appearing, although at the last only as a lieder singer. She wrote works on the teaching of singing and an autobiography, *Mein Weg* (Leipzig, 1913). One of the most important figures in the history of singing, she was unsurpassed in the universality of her vocal endowments and in the deep artistic seriousness with which she dedicated herself to each performance.

Records: There are two valuable series of records, totaling thirty-eight sides, by her for Odeon (Berlin, 1905-07); these appeared with a special blue label. *U.S. re-issue:* Columbia-Fonotipia, IRCC, HRS. *U.S. re-recording:* TAP, Eterna, FRP, Scala, Cantilena, Rococo.

LEHMANN, LOTTE, soprano, b. Feb. 27, 1888, Perleberg, Germany. She studied in Berlin with Erna Thiele, Helene Jordan, and Mathilde Mallinger and made her debut (1910) in Hamburg, where she had her first great success as Elsa in *Lohengrin*. In 1914 she was engaged by the Vienna Imperial Opera and there she found her true artistic home. Although not a Viennese by birth, she became for an entire generation "the most Viennese of all

Leider

singers." On Oct. 10, 1919, in Vienna she sang the part of the Dyer's Wife in the world *première* of *Die Frau ohne Schatten*. On Nov. 4, 1924, she sang at the Dresden State Opera in the world *première* of *Intermezzo*. In 1922 she undertook a South American tour. She was a regular guest at Covent Garden, and in Paris, Stockholm, Berlin, and Dresden she received honors due a great artist. She sang for the first time in America at the Chicago Opera in 1930. In 1934 she was called to the Metropolitan Opera, making her debut as Sieglinde in *Die Walküre* opposite Lauritz Melchoir. Until she gave up the stage in 1945 she remained a highly honored member of this opera company. In 1938 she broke her contract with the Vienna State Opera and lived thenceforth in the United States. In 1945 she retired from the stage and in 1951 gave her farewell concert. She then lived and taught in Santa Barbara, California. She published several pedagogical and autobiographical works: *Anfang und Aufsteig* (Vienna-Leipzig-Zürich, 1937), *My Many Lives* (New York, 1948), *More Than Singing* (New York, 1945), *Five Operas and Richard Strauss* (New York, 1964), and a novel, *Orplid, Mein Land*. Lotte Lehmann possessed one of the most beautiful voices of the twentieth century. She was equally famous for the measured and tasteful musicality of her delivery and for the fresh naturalness of her singing. Beside her brilliant career as an opera singer stands a second, and not less brilliant, career as an interpreter of lieder.

Records: Polydor (including an abbreviated version of *Der Rosenkavalier*), Odeon, HMV (Act I of *Die Walküre*), RCA Victor*, and American Columbia*, as well as private recordings for the Metropolitan Opera. *U.S. re-issue:* Opera Disc, Vocalion, American Odeon, American Decca. *U.S. re-recording:* TAP, Angel, Columbia, Electrola, RCA Victor, Camden, Seraphim, Rococo.

LEIDER, FRIDA, soprano, b. Apr. 18, 1888, Berlin. She worked at first as an employee in a bank and studied singing in her free time. After she had completed her training with Otto Schwarz in Berlin, she made her debut (1915) at Halle as Venus in *Tannhäuser*. She was engaged at Rostock (1916-19), then at Königsberg, and next at Hamburg. In 1924 she sang at the Berlin State Opera, where she enjoyed great triumphs. She appeared as guest at La Scala, the Paris Opéra, in Vienna, Munich, Stuttgart, Stockholm, Amsterdam, Brussels, and the Chicago Opera. She was an annual guest at Covent Garden (1924-38) and was greatly admired there; she sang at the Zoppot Festivals (1921; 1924-27). Although she was considered the most famous Wagner soprano of her generation, she also had brilliant successes in other roles for dramatic soprano. She sang at the Metropolitan Opera (1932-34). Toward the end of her career she had great difficulties in Germany because her husband, the violinist Rudolf Deman, was Jewish; he finally fled to Switzerland. In spite of all menaces the singer refused to consider a separation from him. After World War II she gave occasional concerts, staged operas at the Berlin State Opera, and busied herself with teaching. She directed the voice studio at the Berlin State Opera (1945-52) and was a professor at the Music High School in Berlin (1950-58). She published her memoirs under the title *Das War Mein Teil* (Berlin, 1959). She had a dramatic soprano voice of great beauty.

Records: Polydor and HMV labels. *U.S. re-issue:* RCA Victor. *U.S. re-recording:* TAP, Eterna, Scala, Angel, RCA Victor, Rococo.

LEISNER, EMMI, contralto, b. Aug. 8, 1885, Flensburg, Germany; d. Jan. 12, 1958, Flensburg. After she had studied in Berlin with Helene Breest, she gave her first concert and lieder recital, which attracted uncommon attention, in Berlin (1911). In 1912 she sang Orphée in Jacques-Dalcroze's famous production of Gluck's opera at Hellerau. She was a member of the Berlin Imperial Opera (1913-21). She sang at the Berlin Volksoper (1921-24) and was engaged at the German Opera House in Berlin-Charlottenburg in 1925. In general, however, she was especially known as a concert contralto and was counted as one of the most famous song interpreters of her generation as well as a great Bach and Handel singer. Her concerts and recitals were reckoned among the high points of any year's musical events all over the world. At the Bayreuth Festivals she was greatly admired for her art in singing Wagner, particularly the part of Erda. After 1939 she lived in Kampen on the island of Sylt. A deep and highly musical contralto voice, whose dark tones were admired equally with the stylistic security of her delivery.

Records: Odeon, Polydor, HMV, and DGG; unpublished Edison discs. *U.S. re-issue:* RCA Victor. *U.S. re-recording:* TAP, Eterna, Rococo.

LELIO, UMBERTO DI, bass, b. 1890 (?); d. 1946, Milan. He began his career in the smaller Italian opera houses and had his first great success at Palermo in 1920. In 1921 he sang Pistol in *Falstaff* at the re-opening of La Scala after World War I and had a long and brilliant career there. In 1922 he sang in the *première* of *Debora e Jaele* there and in 1927 he was greatly admired in *Ariane et Barbe-Bleue*, as Baron Ochs in *Der Rosenkavalier*, and in 1929 in the first performance there of *The Tale of Tsar Saltan*. In 1923 he sang at the Arena Festival and as guest at the Teatro Colón in 1932. He was heard at Covent Garden in 1937 as Don Pasquale and as Ramfis in *Aïda*. Although he had his greatest success in *buffo* parts, he was well-liked as Klingsor in *Parsifal* and as King Henry in *Lohengrin*. His daughter, Loretta di Lelio, had a notable career as a soprano.

Records: Acoustics for HMV (including Basilio in *Il Barbiere di Siviglia*, 1920) and electrics for Columbia*.

LELIVA, TADEUSZ, tenor, b. 1867, in Teplik, in the Ukraine; d. Nov. 19, 1929, in Warsaw. He first studied medicine and law at the University of Kiev, then turned to vocal studies with Mme. Masini. After his debut at Saratov (1902) he continued his studies with Jean de Reszke in Paris. After early successes at the Warsaw Opera he sang at La Scala (1904), appearing as Radames in *Aïda* and as Raoul in *Les Huguenots*. Guest appearances took him to the opera houses in Boston, Chicago, and Buenos Aires. In 1909 he sang at Covent Garden as Pinkerton in *Madama Butterfly* and as Canio in *I Pagliacci*. After singing again in Italy, he returned in 1914 to Poland and later sang again in Kiev. He was forced to give up his career on account of increasing deafness and made his last stage appearance in Kiev in 1919. After 1922 he taught singing in Warsaw, where Jan Kiepura was one of his pupils. He sang abroad under the name Enzo de Leliva.

Records: A few rare records for Columbia* (St. Petersburg, 1904) and Fonotipia (1905-06). *U.S. re-issue:* Victor.

LEMESHEV, SERGEI, tenor, b.

1902, Stare Knjazewo, Russia. At first he wanted to become a military officer and attended a military academy. There his voice was noticed and he was sent to the Moscow Conservatory, where he became a pupil of N.C. Raiskis (1921-25) and later of Stanislavski in the voice classes at the Bolshoi Theater. He made his debut in Sverdlovsk (1926). By way of the Tiflis Opera he came (1931) to the Bolshoi Theater and remained there for over thirty years. He was soon considered the most famous Russian tenor of his time, and he gave concerts and made guest appearances in all the larger Russian cities. He was singled out by the Russian Government for both the Order of Stalin and the Lenin Prize and held the title "People's Artist of the U.S.S.R." Later he became a professor at the Moscow Conservatory. His well-trained and expressive lyric tenor voice was particularly admired in Russian roles.

Records: Russian State Record Trust (including *Eugen Onégin*). *U.S. re-issue:* RCA Victor. *U.S. re-recording:* Colosseum, Eterna, Monitor.

LEMNITZ, TIANA, soprano, b. Oct. 26, 1897, Metz, Germany. She studied both at the Music High School in Metz and at Hoch's Conservatory in Frankfurt with Anton Kohmann. Her debut occurred (1920) in Heilbronn, after which she sang at Aachen (1921-28) and at the Hannover Opera (1928-34). After 1931 she was a regular guest at the Dresden State Opera. She was a celebrated member of the Berlin State Opera (1934-35) and appeared there in the world *première* of *Der Prinz von Homburg* in 1935. Her highly successful guest appearances included Vienna, Munich, Covent Garden (1936; 1938), the Teatro Colón (1936; 1950), Amsterdam, Warsaw, Brussels, and Prague. In 1938 she was invited to join the Metropolitan Opera, but was unable to do so. She was greatly admired at the 1939 Salzburg Festival for her performance as Agathe in *Der Freischütz,* and she was highly esteemed as a concert singer. She lives in Berlin. Owning one of the most beautiful soprano voices of her time, she was famed for the delicate and sincere skill of her delivery as well as for her subtlety of expression.

Records: Polydor, HMV (*Die Zauberflöte*), DGG, Urania* (*Die Meistersinger* and *Der Rosenkavalier*). *U.S. re-issue:* RCA Victor, Brunswick. *U.S. re-recording:* Electrola, Vox, RCA Victor, Eterna, Rococo.

LENZ, FRIEDRICH, tenor, b. 1926, Westerwald, Germany. During World War II he was held in a Russian prisoner-of-war camp. After his return he studied singing with Clemens Glettenberg in Cologne. He made his debut in Düsseldorf (1953) as a lyric and *buffo* tenor. After staying two years at Düsseldorf, he sang at Wuppertal (1955-57) and since then he has been engaged at the Munich State Opera. He is also a noted concert singer.

Records: Electrola (*The Merry Wives of Windsor*), DGG* (*Fidelio*), and Ariola (David in *Die Meistersinger*). *U.S. re-issue:* Angel, RCA Victor.

LEONARD, LOTTE, soprano, b. Dec. 3, 1884, Hamburg. At first a pupil at the Stern Conservatory in Berlin, she began her career in 1910 and almost immediately had great success as a concert soprano. Some admired her most as an interpreter of Bach and Handel, others for her ability with contemporary music. Her real fame, however, came from her art in singing lieder. She lived in Berlin, but extended concert tours took her to Holland, Belgium,

France, Italy, Switzerland, Sweden, and Poland. She was also highly successful in both North and South America. She never appeared on the stage. In 1933 she and her husband, the music publisher and writer Henrich Lewy (d. 1940), had to leave Germany and she became a professor at the National Conservatory in Paris (1933-40). In 1940, when France was invaded by German troops, she fled to the United States, where she became a teacher at the Juilliard School of Music and the Mannes College of Music in New York. She had an outstandingly well-trained and expressive soprano voice.

Records: Homochord, Ultraphon, and Odeon. *U.S. re-issue:* American Decca.

LEONHARDT, ROBERT, baritone, b. 1877; d. Feb. 2, 1923, New York City. He made his debut (1898) at Linz and sang at the German Theater in Prague (1905-09), at Brünn (1909-11), and at the Vienna Volksoper (1911-13). He made guest appearances in 1909 at the Vienna Imperial Opera and in 1910 at the Gura Summer Opera in Berlin as Beckmesser in *Die Meistersinger* and as Alberich in the *Ring* cycle. In 1913 he was engaged by the Metropolitan Opera, making his debut as the Father in *Hänsel und Gretel*. Although he sang mostly small roles there, he also appeared as Alberich and Papageno. In 1915 he sang at the Metropolitan in the world *première* of *Madame Sans-Gêne*. Upon the outbreak of World War I, he changed his name to Robert Leonard, but in 1918 he had to give up his contract at the Metropolitan Opera because of his Austrian citizenship. He returned to the Metropolitan in 1920 and sang *comprimario* roles there until shortly before his death.

Records: He is primarily known because he left countless phonograph records. He made more records than any other artist of the acoustic era. These were not only of popular music, but included many arias. These records appeared on G & T (Berlin, 1901-05) and Columbia* (Berlin, 1903-05); in America he sang for Columbia* and Victor*, as well as on Edison* cylinders. *U.S. re-issue:* RCA Victor.

LEPRESTRE, JULIEN, tenor, b. Apr. 27, 1864, Paris; d. 1909, Paris. He studied with Bussine at the Paris Conservatory (1887-90) and made his debut as Faust in Gounod's opera at Rouen (1890). He then sang at Brussels before coming to the Opéra-Comique in 1894. There he sang the role of Jean Gaussin in the world *première* of *Sapho* in 1897. In 1899 he left the Opéra-Comique and in the following years sang at the Théâtre Lyrique and in opera houses in the French provinces.

Records: A few very rare records for Odeon (Paris, 1905).

LEWIS, MARY, soprano, b. Jan. 7, 1900, Hot Springs, Ark.; d. Dec. 31, 1941, New York City. At the age of eighteen she left the home of her parents, a Methodist family, and joined a vaudeville troupe. She then sang in cabarets in San Francisco and joined the Bathing Beauties of the Christie Comedies. She finally appeared in New York in operettas and revues before studying singing seriously there with William Thorner and with Jean de Reszke in Paris. She made her operatic debut (1923) at the Vienna Volksoper as Marguerite in *Faust*. Guest appearances followed in Berlin and Monte Carlo. In 1924 she was a member of the British National Opera Company, and with them she sang in London that year in the world *première* of *Hugh the Drover*. In 1925 she appeared at the Opéra-Comique, and she was a

member of the Metropolitan Opera (1926-30), making her debut as Mimi in *La Bohème*. For a short time she was married to the bass-baritone Michael Bohnen. It was thought that when sound films were developed she would have a great career in them, but this did not happen.
Records: HMV and RCA Victor*.

LEWIS, RICHARD, tenor, b. May 10, 1914, Manchester, England. As a child he sang in a boys' choir and studied at the Royal Conservatories in Manchester and in London. He made his debut (1939) with the Carl Rosa Opera Company as Count Almaviva in *Il Barbiere di Siviglia*. He was a soldier in World War II and continued his career in 1945 when he undertook a concert tour of Belgium. In 1948 he joined the Sadler's Wells Opera Company and in the same year had great success at Covent Garden as the title hero in *Peter Grimes*. At the Edinburgh Festival of 1948 he sang Don Ottavio in *Don Giovanni*; at the Glyndebourne Festivals he sang Don Ferrando in *Così fan tutte* in 1950 and the title role in *Idomeneo* in 1951. Guest appearances followed in Holland, Belgium, and France. In 1954 he created the role of Troilus for the world *première* production of *Troilus and Cressida* opposite Magda Laszló. In 1955 he sang for the first time at the San Francisco Opera and has appeared there frequently since then. The great musicality of his voice and the subtlety of his expressive art are especially demonstrated in the Mozart repertory; he is also greatly admired as an oratorio and lieder singer.
Records: Many recordings for HMV, RCA Victor* (including *Der fliegende Holländer*), and Columbia*. *U.S. re-issue:* Bartók, Capitol, Columbia, Epic, Angel, Monitor, L'Oiseau-Lyre, London, Nonesuch, Vox, Seraphim.

LICETTE, MIRIAM, soprano, b. Sept. 9, 1892, Chester, England. She came of a French-English family and studied singing with Mathilde Marchesi and Jean de Reszke in Paris and with Sabatini in Milan. She made her debut in Rome (1913) as Butterfly and then sang at the Genoa Opera. During World War I she was the real prima donna of the Beecham Opera Company and she appeared with this ensemble as guest at Covent Garden in 1919. In 1920 she sang Eurydice in *Orphée et Eurydice* at Covent Garden opposite Dame Clara Butt. After 1922 she belonged to the British National Opera Company, with which she had her greatest success as Desdemona in *Otello*. She sang again at Covent Garden (1928-29). In 1938 she gave up her stage career and founded an opera school in London.
Records: Acoustic records for HMV and electric records for Columbia.*

LICHTEGG, MAX, tenor, b. 1910, Buczacz, Poland. He made his debut (1936) in Bern, where he remained until 1938. He sang in Basel (1938-40) and after 1940 at Zürich, where he was very popular. He made guest appearances at the Vienna State Opera and in 1948 performed at the San Francisco Opera. In 1951 he sang in the first Swiss performance of *The Rake's Progress* in Zürich. Although he was highly successful in operetta, he was particularly noted as a lieder singer. He was admired in the concert halls in Holland, Belgium, England, North America, and Switzerland. He had a beautiful lyric tenor voice.
Records: Operetta arias and lieder for Decca. *U.S. re-issue:* London. *U.S. re-recording:* Scala.

LICHTENSTEIN, EDUARD, tenor,

b. Apr. 1, 1889, Karlsbad, Austria; d. Jan. 9, 1953, Hamburg. The son of the baritone Joseph Lichtenstein, he studied at Stern's Conservatory in Berlin with Nikolaus Rothmühl and made his debut (1908) at the Hamburg Opera as Georg in *Der Waffenschmied*. He stayed at Hamburg until 1915 and was particularly admired there as a *buffo* tenor, his particular starring role being David in *Die Meistersinger*, a part which he also sang in 1910 at Covent Garden. In 1910 he studied further with Jean de Reszke in Paris. He sang in the Gura Summer Opera in Berlin and in 1915 was engaged at the City Opera there. In the 1920's he transferred to operetta and was admired in various operetta productions in Berlin. He was the favorite singer of the operetta composer Eduard Künnecke. In 1933 he was forced to leave Germany because he was Jewish. He emigrated to Holland and became a teacher in the Conservatory of Amsterdam. He also undertook successful tours of Holland, Belgium, and Switzerland. After the invasion of Holland by the German army in 1940, he was unable to continue his teaching activity. In 1950 he again appeared in operetta and in the concert hall, giving concerts in Hamburg and in Switzerland.

Records: HMV, Pathé*, Edison cylinders, Odeon, Parlophone, Ultraphon.

LIEBAN, JULIUS, tenor, b. Feb. 19, 1857, Lundenburg, Moravia, Austria; d. Feb. 1, 1940, Berlin. Several of his brothers were also singers. He first played the violin in a gypsy orchestra, then studied singing with Joseph Gänsbacher in Vienna. In 1878 he made his debut at the Leipzig Opera, where he remained until 1881. In 1882 he undertook a tour with Angelo Neumann's traveling Wagner troupe. In the same year he was engaged at the Berlin Imperial Opera, where he remained as a celebrated *buffo* tenor until 1912. He was especially admired for his unforgettable performance as Mime in the *Ring* cycle. At the Mozart Festival in Salzburg in 1910 he sang Monostatos in *Die Zauberflöte*. He was engaged at the Berlin City Opera (1912-15), and sang then and later as a frequent guest at the Berlin Imperial Opera. He sang Mime there as late as 1933. He was successful in guest appearances at many of the great opera houses all over Europe. Although he was Jewish, he was not molested during the period of Nazi domination. He was married to the soprano Helene Lieban-Globig.

Records: G & T (Berlin, 1903-07), Odeon (Berlin, 1905), HMV, Beka, and Polydor. *U.S. re-issue:* Brunswick.

LIEBENBERG, EVA, contralto, b. Feb. 15, 1890, Stettin, Germany. She studied with Hugo Rasch in Berlin and was engaged as a singer at Coburg (1921-23). She then took up her residence in Berlin and became a noted concert and oratorio singer. In these areas she had great success, both in Germany and abroad. She appeared only rarely on the stage; for example, she sang Erda and one of the three Norns in the *Ring* cycle at the Bayreuth Festivals (1927-28). In 1933 she had to give up her career in Germany because she was Jewish. Since 1947 she has lived in Hilversum, Holland. Her voice was sumptuous and expressive.

Records: Ultraphon (Telefunken). *U.S. re-recording:* Eterna, Telefunken.

LIGABUE, ILVA, soprano, b. 1928, Reggio Emilia, Italy. She studied at the opera school at La Scala in Milan. After her first successes in Italian theaters she made guest appearances in Germany and England. From 1957-60 she was a much-admired Fiordiligi in *Così fan tutte* at the Glyndebourne Festivals. In 1961 she was honored for her singing of the title role in *Beatrice di Tenda* at La Scala; in the same year she sang Margherita in *Mefistofele* in Chicago. She sang later in Dallas, at the Teatro Colón, in Brussels, and at the Wiesbaden and Aix-en-Provence Festivals. She was engaged in 1963 by the American Opera Society in New York and in November of that year she fulfilled a guest engagement at the Vienna State Opera. She is married to the *buffo* bass Paolo Pesani. She is admired in opera both for her beautiful lyric soprano voice and for her uncommon stage presence.

Records: Philips, Bertelsmann, Decca, RCA Victor* (*Falstaff*), Harmonia Mundi (*Ascanio in Alba*). *U.S. re-issue:* London, Columbia.

LINDERMEIER, ELISABETH, soprano, b. 1925, Munich. At first she worked as an employee in a bank, then studied at the Munich Music High School and made her debut at the Bavarian State Opera there (1946) as the Sandman in *Hänsel und Gretel*. She has been a member of this company ever since and has had great success there. She is married to the conductor Rudolf Kempe. She has appeared as guest at Covent Garden, in Vienna, Frankfurt, and Amsterdam, and has sung annually at the Munich Festivals.

Records: DGG* and Electrola.

LINDI, AROLDO, tenor, b. 1889, Sweden; d. Mar. 8, 1944, San Francisco. Originally Arnold Lindfors. He studied in Italy and made his debut at the Teatro dal Verme (1923). He then appeared on various Italian stages, including the Teatro Costanzi and made guest appearances at Covent Garden in 1925 and 1929. He was a member of the Chicago Opera (1926-27) and during the same seasons sang in San Francisco. His guest appearances included those in Venice, Palermo, Barcelona, Monte Carlo, Cairo, Stockholm, and the Paris Opéra. He toured Germany with the opera troupe of Max Sauter. In the 1930's he was first tenor of the San Carlo Opera Company and undertook long tours of the United States with them. He also sang in opera seasons in Cincinnati and Philadelphia. His death was a tragic one; during a performance of *I Pagliacci* in San Francisco he was stricken by a fatal heart attack just after he had sung the aria "Vesti la giubba." He possessed a magnificent tenor voice.

Records: He recorded exclusively for Columbia* (including *Aida* opposite Giannina Arangi-Lombardi). *U.S. re-recording:* ASCO, FRP, TAP.

LINDSAY, JULIA, soprano, b. 1878, Paris, where her American parents had gone after the Civil War. She studied in Paris and made her debut at the Opéra there (1903). She was greatly admired there in 1905 as Sidonie in *Armide* and as Konstanze in *Die Entführung aus dem Serail*. She remained at the Opéra until 1907, but had her greatest successes at the Monte Carlo Opera, with whom she made guest appearances in 1907 in Berlin in *La Damnation de Faust* and as Elisabeth in *Don Carlos*. This artist, for whom a world-wide career was predicted, appears to have withdrawn from musical life about 1910. Nothing is known of her thereafter.

Records: HMV (Paris, 1907-10).

LIPKOWSKA, LYDIA, soprano, b. May 10, 1882, Babino, Bessarabia; d. Jan. 23, 1955, Beirut. She studied at the St. Petersburg Conservatory and made her debut (1907) at the Maryinsky Theater there as Gilda in *Rigoletto*. In 1910 she was highly successful at the Opéra-Comique as Lakmé and as Violetta in *La Traviata*; she remained there until 1912. She appeared as guest at the Chicago Opera in 1911 and was greatly admired in *Il Segreto di Susanna*. She also made guest appearances at the Vienna Volksoper, in Monte Carlo and Paris, as well as annual appearances at the Imperial Opera Houses in St. Petersburg and Moscow. In the years before World War I she married the baritone Georges Baklanoff. In 1914 they sang with Giovanni Martinelli at the Monte Carlo Opera in the world *première* of *I Mori di Valenza*. In 1919, after the Revolution, she fled from Russia to Paris by way of China. During the 1920's she was one of the most prominent singers of the Opéra Russe in Paris. She sang *La Traviata* at the Odessa Opera as late as 1941. After her retirement she lived first in Paris and finally in Beirut, Lebanon. She had a technically brilliant, thoroughly trained coloratura voice; her special starring role was that of the heroine in *The Snow Maiden*.

Records: HMV in Russia, and Columbia* in the U.S. *U.S. re-recording:* TAP, Angel, Columbia.

LIPP, WILMA, soprano, b. Apr. 26, 1925, Vienna. She studied with Friedel Sindel and Paola Novikova in Vienna, but finished her studies with Toti dal Monte in Milan. She was engaged at the Vienna State Opera in 1945 and has remained a member of that institution ever since. After singing small roles at the start, she was enormously successful in 1948 as the Queen of the Night in *Die Zauberflöte*. She also reaped brilliant success from guest appearances at La Scala, Covent Garden, in Paris, Brussels, Hamburg, Munich, and at the Berlin City Opera. In 1951 she appeared at the Bayreuth Festival. At the Salzburg Festivals she has been particularly admired in such Mozart roles as the Queen of the Night and Konstanze. She sang the latter role with special success at La Scala in 1950. In 1956 she was the starring attraction at the Copenhagen Mozart Week and she has also toured both North and South America with great success. Since 1958 she has been adding lyric roles to her repertory of coloratura parts.

Records: Many records for DGG*, Philips, Decca*, Vox*, and Ariola (including *Die Zauberflöte, Die Entführung aus dem Serail, Die Fledermaus*). *U.S. re-issue:* London, Angel, Richmond, Epic, Turnabout.

LISITZIAN, PAVEL, baritone, b. 1911, St. Petersburg, of an Armenian family. At the age of nine he sang in a church choir, but later turned to the study of the cello. Finally he became a worker in a factory in Leningrad. In 1932 he entered the Musical Institute of the Leningrad Conservatory and completed his course there in 1935. In the same year he made his debut at the Little Opera Theater in Leningrad. In 1937 he went to the opera house in Erivan, Armenia. He became a member of the Bolshoi Theater in 1948 and had great success there after that time. He was awarded the title "People's Artist of the U.S.S.R." After World War II he made guest appearances in Prague and Budapest and undertook a western European tour. In 1960 he toured the United States, where he was highly successful and appeared at the San Francisco Opera. In 1963 he again toured western Europe. He has a warm-timbred and expressive baritone voice.

Records: Russian State Record Trust. *U.S. re-issue:* New York, Colosseum, Period, Monitor, Bruno.

LIST, EMANUEL, bass, b. Mar. 22, 1891, Vienna; d. June 21, 1967,

Vienna. Originally a tailor, he sang also in the chorus of the Theater am Westens and studied singing with Emil Steger in Vienna. He then traveled all over Europe as the bass in a quartet. In 1914, after appearing in a vaudeville theater in London, he went to the United States, where he studied in New York with Josiah Zuro, but he sang only in film theaters and small vaudeville houses. In 1921 he returned to Austria and made his stage debut (1922) at the Vienna Volksoper as Mephistopheles in *Faust*. He went to the Berlin City Opera in 1923 and remained there until 1934, an honored member of the company. He sang at the Salzburg Festivals (1931-35) in such roles as Osmin in *Die Entführung aus dem Serail*, the Commandant in *Don Giovanni*, both the Minister and Rocco in *Fidelio*, and King Mark in *Tristan und Isolde*. At the 1933 Bayreuth Festival he was greatly admired in the roles of Fafner, Hunding, and Hagen in the *Ring* cycle. Because he was Jewish, he was required to leave Germany in 1934 and became a member of the Metropolitan Opera (1934-39). He made guest appearances at Covent Garden as Ochs in *Der Rosenkavalier* in 1936 and later appeared in San Francisco and Chicago. He was also noted in the United States for brilliant lieder concerts. He sang again at the Berlin State Opera (1950-52) and thereafter lived in Vienna.

Records: Vox, Christschall, Parlophone, HMV, and Remington*; he made many private recordings. *U.S. re-issue:* RCA Victor, American Decca. *U.S. re-recording:* Angel, Electrola, Rococo.

LITTLE, VERA, contralto, b. Dec. 10, 1928, Memphis, Tenn. She first studied in the United States, then in Paris, Rome, Copenhagen, and Vienna and made her debut (1950) at the New York City Center Opera as Preziosilla in *La Forza del Destino*. In the following years she sang in Italy, Germany, and Israel. In 1957 she astonished the audience at the Pau Music Festival by her delivery of Mozart arias. She was greatly admired as Carmen at the Berlin City Opera in 1958. In March, 1959, she sang a Bach cantata at a concert in the Vatican in the presence of Pope John XXIII. Later guest appearances took the contralto to the Vienna State Opera and to the Salzburg Festivals. Her voice is large and expressive.

Records: DGG* (Gaia in *Daphne*). *U.S. re-issue:* London.

LITVINNE, FELIA, soprano, b. Aug. 31, 1860, St. Petersburg; d. Oct. 12, 1936, Paris. Originally Francoise-Jeanne Schütz; her father was Russian and her mother of Canadian extraction. At the age of fifteen she came to Paris and studied with Mme. Barthe-Banderali, Victor Maurel, and Pauline Viardot-Garcia. She first appeared publicly in Paris in 1880, and in 1882 she sang under the name Litvinova at the Théâtre Italien there. After guest appearances in Barcelona and Genoa she undertook her first American tour in 1885. She sang at the Brussels Opera (1886-88) and in 1889 came to the Paris Opéra, where she made her debut singing Valentine in *Les Huguenots*. Triumphant guest appearances all over the world followed; she sang at La Scala in 1890 and in the same year at the Imperial Opera Houses in St. Petersburg and Moscow. In 1896-97 she sang at the Metropolitan Opera, after having added a number of Wagner roles to her repertory. From 1899-1910 she made annual guest appearances at Covent Garden. In 1906 she sang in the world *première* of *L'Ancêtre* at the Monte Carlo Opera.

World-wide guest and concert activity marked the last part of her career. In 1917 she made her farewell stage appearance in Paris. In 1927 she accepted a professorship at the American Conservatory at Fontainebleau. She published her memoirs under the title *Ma vie et mon art* (Paris, 1933). She had an outstanding dramatic soprano voice.

Records: G & T (Paris, 1903). Fonotipia (Paris, 1905), Odeon De Luxe (Paris, 1907), and Pathé*, all extremely rare. *U.S. re-issue:* Victor, IRCC. *U.S. re-recording:* FRP, TAP, Eterna, IRCC, Belcanto, Rococo.

LJUNGBERG, GÖTA, soprano, b. Oct. 4, 1893, Sundsvall, Sweden; d. June 30, 1955, Lidingö, Sweden. She studied at the Royal Academy in Stockholm with Gillis Bratt and Mme. Charles Cahier. She finished her studies with Fergusson in London, with Vittorio Vanza in Milan, and with Louis Bachner and Oscar Daniel in Berlin. She made her debut at the Royal Opera House in Stockholm (1918) as Elsa in *Lohengrin*, and remained there until 1926. She made regular guest appearances at Covent Garden (1924-28). In 1922 she sang at the Salzburg Festival and she appeared at the Zoppot Festivals (1928; 1929; 1933; 1936; 1937). In 1926 she was engaged by the Berlin State Opera, where she had great success until 1932. She was a member of the Metropolitan Opera (1931-35) and was highly successful in the United States, particularly as a Wagner singer. She gave her farewell performance at the Metropolitan in 1935 and worked thereafter as a teacher at the New York College of Music until she returned later to her native Sweden. She was married to the *régisseur* Harry Stangenberg. A dramatic soprano with a large-dimensioned voice, she was greatly admired in Wagner roles, but also in many others, including Salome and Elektra.

Records: HMV. *U.S. re-issue:* Victor. *U.S. re-recording:* Eterna, Angel, Rococo.

LLACER, MARIA, soprano, b. 1889, Valencia, Spain; d. July 5, 1962, Madrid. After her vocal studies, she began her career on the opera stages of Italy. As early as 1910 she sang the role of Suor Pazienza in the world *première* of *Mese Mariano* at the Teatro Massimo. In 1914 she was greatly admired at the Teatro Costanzi and in the 1920's at La Scala. In 1924 she appeared at the Arena Festival and in the same year at the Teatro dal Verme as Amelia in *Un Ballo in Maschera*. She made guest appearances in all the leading theaters in Italy, Spain, and South America. After her marriage she sang in Italy under the name Maria Casali Llacer. She appeared for the last time in 1930 at La Scala. She taught later in Milan and finally in Madrid.

Records: Only a single record exists of her highly expressive and dramatic voice, a duet from *Les Huguenots* with John O'Sullivan as partner. *U.S. re-recording:* TAP, FRP.

LLOYD, DAVID, tenor, b. Feb. 29, 1920, Minneapolis, Minn. He studied at the Minneapolis College of Music, then at the Curtis Institute in Philadelphia and the Berkshire Music Center. He began his career in 1947 and in 1949 sang at the New York City Center Opera and later was engaged by the New England Opera Company. He had his greatest success as a concert and oratorio singer, and thereby became well known in the United States, Canada, and England.

Records: He made records for both RCA Victor* and American Columbia*. He is not to be confused with the English oratorio tenor David Lloyd, who sang for

Lloyd · Lo Giudice

LLOYD, EDWARD, tenor, b. 1845, London; d. May 31, 1927, Worthing, England. From 1852-60 he was a choirboy at London's Westminster Abbey, but he never completed a course of formal vocal study. He was a member of the choir of Trinity and King's College in Cambridge (1866), of the St. Andrew's Choir in London (1867), and a Gentleman of the Chapel Royal (1869). He sang solo parts for the first time (1871) at the Gloucester Festival, when he took the tenor part in the *St. Matthew Passion*. After a sensational success at the Norwich Festival of 1872 he was considered the outstanding English concert singer of his time. His greatest successes were at the numerous English music festivals, where he created many parts in oratorios: at the Leeds Festival in *The Martyr of Anitoch* (1880), at Birmingham in Gounod's *Redemption* (1882), at Norwich in *The Rose of Sharon* by Mackenzie (1884), at Birmingham in Gounod's *Mors et Vita* (1885), at Leeds in Sullivan's *Golden Legend* (1886), at Birmingham in Sir Charles Parry's *Judith* (1888), again at Birmingham in Parry's *King Saul* (1894), and again at Leeds in Edward Elgar's *Caractacus* (1898). He never appeared in opera, but sang many opera arias at his concerts. Outside England he appeared at the Cincinnati Festival (1888) and made two American tours (1890; 1892). The high point of his career was reached when he sang the tenor solo at the world *première* of Elgar's *Dream of Gerontius* at the Birmingham Festival (1900). Later in the same year he gave his official farewell concert, but he appeared at charity concerts during World War I.

Records: G & T (London, 1904-07) and HMV, all of them rare. *U.S. re-issue:* Victor. *U.S. re-recording:* Belcanto.

LOEFFEL, FELIX, bass, b. July 25, 1892, Niederwangen, Switzerland. He was first a teacher in an elementary school, then studied singing with Heinrich Nahm in Bern, with Otto Freund in Prague, and with Felix von Kraus in Munich. He made his stage debut in Bern (1921) as King Mark in *Tristan und Isolde*, and appeared there for over thirty years. In 1928 he made guest appearances at the Berlin State Opera as the Commandant in *Don Giovanni*. The true fame of this artist, however, was in oratorio and lieder singing. He was greatly admired for his singing of Bach, especially Christus in the *St. Matthew Passion*, and as an interpreter of the songs of Othmar Schoeck. He was greatly admired in 1935 at the Salzburg Festival in Mozart's *Requiem*, as well as in his appearances in Rome, Paris, Vienna, Leipzig, Cologne, Hamburg, Budapest, Amsterdam, and at the World Exposition in Brussels in 1935; he was particularly well liked in his homeland, Switzerland.

Records: Polydor and lesser labels, including Die Cantorei.

LO GIUDICE, FRANCO, tenor, b. 1895, Paternò, Sicily. He was the older brother of the tenor Silvio Costa Lo Giudice and was related to the Portuguese soprano Maria Giudice. He studied first with Benianimo Carelli in Naples and Adernò in Catania, followed by further study after 1914 with Luigi Lucenti and Di Cagno in Milan. During World War I he was a soldier in the Italian army. He made his debut in Tortona (1920) in *La Fanciulla del West*. He had successful appearances at the Teatro Costanzi in 1922 and in the 1920's he often sang at La Scala, where he was given parts in important productions by Arturo Toscanini. At La Scala he sang the part of Gösta Berling in the world première of *I Cavalieri di Ekebù*, on Mar. 3, 1925. The same year he sang Pinkerton in *Madama Butterfly* as guest at Covent Garden. In the 1930's he was greatly applauded at La Scala and in the following decade he was to be heard on the more important provincial stages in Italy. Later he became a teacher at the Conservatory in Catania.

Records: Acoustic for HMV (including selections from Boito's *Nerone*); electrics for HMV (Verdi's *Requiem*), for Parlophone, and for Pathé. *U.S. re-issue:* RCA Victor.

LOHFING, MAX, bass, b. May 20, 1870, Blankenheim, Germany; d. Sept. 9, 1953, Hamburg. He was at first a teacher in an elementary school and then studied singing with Bodo Borchers in Leipzig and made his debut (1894) at Metz as the Hermit in *Der Freischütz*. He remained at Metz until 1896, then sang at Stettin (1896-97). After 1898 he was the honored first bass of the Hamburg Opera, where he appeared until the 1930's. In 1899 he made guest appearances at the Berlin Imperial Opera and later sang in Vienna, Dresden, Amsterdam, and The Hague. He was much admired at the 1902 Bayreuth Festival as Hunding in *Die Walküre* and as Daland in *Der fliegende Holländer*. In 1930 he sang Alfonso in *Così fan tutte* in a guest appearance in The Hague. He had a voluminous but very flexible bass voice and was admired both in Wagner and Mozart roles.

Records: HMV, Parlophone, and Pathé. *U.S. re-issue:* Victor.

LONDON, GEORGE, bass-baritone, b. May 30, 1919, Montreal, Canada. Originally George Burnstein. His family was of Russian origin. He first studied with R. Lert in Los Angeles, and made his debut under the name George Burnnon at the Hollywood Bowl (1942) as Dr. Grenvil in *La Traviata*. This was followed by further study in New York and by appearances in operettas and musicals. In 1947 a manager put together the Bel Canto Trio, consisting of George London, Mario Lanza, and Frances Yeend, which undertook tours throughout the world. Karl Böhm engaged him in 1949 for the Vienna State Opera and he made his debut there as Amonasro in *Aïda* without any rehearsal. He has appeared there annually since then with brilliant success. In 1950 he sang the title role in *Le Nozze di Figaro* at the Glyndebourne Festival, and since 1951 he has been admired as a Wagner singer of true genius at the Bayreuth Festivals in such roles as Amfortas in *Parsifal* and as the Dutchman. In 1951 he was engaged by the Metropolitan Opera, making his debut as Amonasro, and he has retained his membership in this company ever since. A world-wide operatic and concert activity has distinguished the later career of this artist. He has appeared as a guest in many opera houses, including La Scala, Covent Garden, the Teatro Colón, the Bolshoi Theater, and the opera houses in Chicago, San Francisco, Amsterdam, and Brussels, and at the Salzburg Festivals. With his warm-timbred and highly expressive voice, he has proved his worth in a wide-ranging repertory, climaxed by Wagner, Mozart, and many other roles. He is also admired for his great acting talent.

Records: Many recordings—mostly of complete operas—for Philips (*Don Giovanni*), RCA Victor* (*Der fliegende Hollander* and *Die Fledermaus*), Decca (*Arabella, Das Rheingold, Parsifal,* and *Tosca*), and Columbia (*Le Nozze di Figaro*). *U.S. re-issue:* Epic,

Electrola, Angel, Columbia, London, Haydn Society.

LOOSE, EMMY, soprano, b. 1914, Karbiz, Bohemia. She studied at the Conservatory in Prague and made her debut (1939) as Blondchen in *Die Entführung aus dem Serail* at Hannover. A guest appearance in 1941 as Ännchen in *Der Freischütz* at the Vienna State Opera led to her engagement by that company, with which she has since remained. She has specialized in the lighter soprano roles in Mozart operas and in other soubrette parts. She has sung almost yearly at the Salzburg Festivals and has appeared at both the Glyndebourne and Maggio Musicale Festivals, singing Mozart especially. She has been greatly applauded at the Aix-en-Provence Festivals as Blondchen, as Zerlina in *Don Giovanni*, and as Elisetta in *Il Matrimonio Segreto;* she has sung as guest at La Scala, Covent Garden, and in South America.

Records: Columbia (*Die Fledermaus*), Decca (*Die Entführung aus dem Serail, Così fan tutte, Der Freischütz*, and *Die Frau ohne Schatten*, among others), Vanguard, and Telefunken. *U.S. re-issue:* Westminster, Angel, Electrola, London.

LORENGAR, PILAR, soprano, b. 1928, Saragossa, Spain. She studied at the Conservatory of Barcelona, in which city she made her debut (1949) as a mezzo-soprano. In 1951 she won a voice competition in Barcelona and changed to soprano parts. At first she sang in Spanish theaters, but became internationally known through her guest appearances. She sang as guest in Paris and London in 1954. In 1955 she came to the United States, where she sang in opera in San Francisco and Chicago and gave concerts. She sang Pamina in *Die Zauberflöte* for her debut at the Glyndebourne Festival in 1957 and she sang the Countess in *Le Nozze di Figaro* there in 1958-59. Later guest appearances include the State Operas in Vienna and Munich, the Aix-en-Provence Festival, Barcelona, and Madrid. Since 1959 she has been engaged at the Berlin City Opera. In 1961 she sang in *Idomeneo* at the Salzburg Festival and in 1963 she sang Pamina there. She first sang at the Metropolitan Opera in the 1965-66 season.

Records: HMV (*The Bartered Bride*), Pathé, DGG* (*La Bohème*), and London*. *U.S. re-issue:* Angel, Electrola, Vox, Bruno.

LORENZ, MAX, tenor, b. May 17, 1902, Düsseldorf, Germany. At first he was an employee of an industrial firm in Düsseldorf and then he went to Berlin to study singing under Ernst Grenzebach. After he had won a singing contest, he made his debut (1926) at the Dresden State Opera and remained there until 1931. In that year he came to the Berlin State Opera, where he soon became a famous Wagner tenor. He was a member of the Metropolitan Opera (1931-34) and was later engaged at the Chicago Opera (1939-40). He made guest appearances at La Scala, the Paris Opéra, the Teatro Colón, and in Rome, Munich, and Hamburg. He was also active at international music festivals, appearing at Zoppot (1930), at the Maggio Musicale Festival (1941) as Tristan, and annually at Salzburg (1953-61); there he sang in the following world premières: *Der Prozess* (1953), *Penelope* (1954) *Irische Legend* (1955), and *Das Bergwerk von Falun* (1961). From the summer of 1933 on, he was involved in the Bayreuth Festivals, where he was particularly admired as Siegfried and Tristan. He also sang at the Salzburg Festivals. After 1941 he was a member of the Vienna State Opera. In 1949-50 he appeared as guest at the Paris Opéra in several roles, and in 1957 he sang at Salzburg; finally he even appeared at the Vienna Opera in 1962. He had a big, heroic tenor voice, which found its true expression in the Wagner repertory.

Records: Parlophone, HMV, DGG*, and Telefunken. U.S. reissue: RCA Victor. U.S. re-recording: Electrola, Eterna, Telefunken.

LUART, EMMA, soprano, b. Aug. 14, 1892, Brussels. Originally Emma Luwaert. She studied at the Conservatory in Brussels and made her debut (1914) at the Théâtre de la Haye, remaining there until 1917. In 1919 she began a starring career at the Brussels Opera. In 1922 she came to the Opéra-Comique and for many years was counted among the great prima donnas of the French metropolis. In 1927 she sang the title role at the Opéra-Comique in the world première of Sophie Arnoult; in 1930 at the same house she sang in the world première of Le Roi d'Yvetot. In addition to appearances in Paris, she sang very successfully in Brussels, Nice, and Monte Carlo. After her retirement from the stage she lived as a teacher in Brussels. The brilliance of her technique and the flexibility of her expressiveness made the coloratura voice of this artist outstanding.

Records: Pathé and Odeon. U.S. re-recording: American Decca.

LUBIN, GERMAINE, soprano, b. Feb. 1, 1890, Paris. She completed her education at the Collège de Sévigné in Paris and planned to become a physician, but she entered the Conservatory of Paris instead and studied singing there with Isnardon and Martini. In 1912 she made her debut at the Opéra-Comique as Antonia in Les Contes d'Hoffmann. She was engaged at the Paris Opéra in 1914 and she remained there as principal dramatic soprano for over twenty-five years. She was especially admired as a Wagner singer. Her guest appearances brought her great international fame; she was very often in demand at Covent Garden and sang, for example, Kundry in Parsifal there in 1927. She was also admired at the Bayreuth Festivals as Kundry (1938) and as Isolde (1939); at the Salzburg Festivals she sang Donna Anna in Don Giovanni. She later appeared as guest in Vienna, Prague, and Brussels. Because of the texture of her voice and the expressive qualities of her presentations she was one of the greatest dramatic sopranos of her time; she was called by some the best-known Wagner soprano in France in the twentieth century.

Records: Relatively few records for Odeon. U.S. re-recording: IRCC.

LUCA, GIUSEPPE DE, baritone, b. Dec. 25, 1876, Rome; d. Aug. 28, 1950, New York. He first studied with Ottavio Bartolini in Rome, then at the Accademia di Santa Cecilia with Venceslao Persichini. He made his debut (1897) at Piacenza as Valentin in Faust. He then appeared at various Italian opera houses and during the 1900-01 season sang at the Teatro São Carlos. He sang in several important world premières: Michonnet in Adriana Lecouvreur at the Teatro Lirico (Nov. 6, 1902), Gleby in Siberia (La Scala, 1903), and Sharpless in the disastrous first performance of Madama Butterfly (La Scala, Feb. 17, 1904). Guest appearances, however, made the name of this artist world-famous: in Santiago de Chile (1905), the Teatro Colón (1906-10), the Bucharest Opera (1907), the Vienna Imperial Opera (1909). He also appeared regularly at La Scala and the Teatro Costanzi, as well as in London, Paris, and Brussels. He was engaged at the Metropolitan Opera in 1915 and was a principal baritone there for more than thirty years. There he sang in the world *première* of *Goyescas* in 1916 and the title role in the world *première* of *Gianni Schicchi* on Dec. 14, 1918. In 1946 he gave up the stage and became a voice teacher in New York. His last will requested that he be buried in Rome. Among the baritones of his epoch he is the true *bel canto* singer; he was famous for the noble beauty of his voice and for the quality of his diction.

Records: Fonotipia, Victor*, and many private and club recordings from his last years, including one record of arias and songs on Continental (U.S.). *U.S. re-issue:* ASCO. *U.S. re-recordings:* RCA Victor, Belcanto, Rococo, Scala, TAP, FRP, Eterna.

LUCA, LIBERO DE, tenor, b. Mar. 13, 1913, Solothurn, Switzerland. After originally studying architecture, he studied singing in the Music High Schools in Stuttgart and Zürich, as well as with Alfredo Cairati in Zürich. In 1937 he won a prize in a competition held in connection with the Paris World Exposition and in 1941 he won first prize in a singing competition in Geneva. He made his stage debut (1942) at Solothurn-Biel, sang one season at Berne, and was first tenor at the Zürich Opera (1943-49). After World War II he had great success in guest appearances. In 1948 he appeared at the Teatro Colón and the Teatro San Carlo, as well as in Brussels, Vienna, and Munich. In 1949 he was chosen first lyric tenor at the Paris Opéra. He was particularly distinguished in parts from the French repertory.

Records: Decca (including *Lakmé* and *Carmen*). *U.S. re-issue:* London.

LUCCIONI, JOSÉ, tenor, b. Oct. 14, 1903, Corsica. He studied with Léon David in Paris and made his debut (1932) at Rouen. In 1933 he was engaged at the Opéra-Comique and had great success there in 1934 as Don José in *Carmen*. In 1935 he sang the same role at Covent Garden opposite Conchita Supervia and in 1936 he appeared in the same role in Amsterdam. From 1935-37 he sang particularly in Italy, both at the Rome Opera and at other important theaters. In 1936 he created the title role in *Cirano di Bergerac* at the Rome Opera. He was engaged at the Chicago Opera (1937-38). In 1941 he had a notable success at the Paris Opéra in *Esclarmonde*; he specialized in heroic roles at this house.

Records: Polydor, HMV, and Columbia (*Samson et Dalila*). *U.S. re-issue:* Pathé-Marconi, London International, Vox, Columbia.

LUCIA, FERNANDO DE, tenor, b. Oct. 11, 1860, Naples; d. Feb. 23, 1925, Naples. He first studied bassoon and contrabass at the Conservatory of San Pietro a Majella in Naples; then he studied singing with Beniamino Carelli and Lombardi and made his debut there at the Teatro San Carlo (1885) in *Faust*. After engagements in Bologna and Florence, he sang in 1887 in Buenos Aires and Montevideo. In the same year he made a guest appearance at the Drury Lane Theater as Alfredo in *La Traviata*. Starring guest appearances followed at all the leading opera houses in Europe: Madrid, Barcelona, Brussels, Paris, Lisbon, but particularly at Covent Garden, where he was a guest almost every year. He was famous in tenor roles in *verismo* operas and took part in the world *premières* of many of them; he sang Kobus in *L'Amico Fritz* at the Teatro Costanzi (Oct. 31, 1891), in *Silvana* at La Scala (Mar. 23, 1895), Osaka in *Iris* at the Teatro Costanzi (Nov. 22, 1898). In 1893 he came to the Metropolitan Opera for a season, making his debut as Don José in *Carmen* opposite Emma Calvé, and he also sang in Chicago. Abandoning his guest-appearance activity in 1910, he became a professor at the Conservatory of San Pietro a Majella in Naples, but continued singing, particularly in concert. He continued to make records as late as 1922. The exquisite musical beauty of his voice and his stylistic control of execution made him one of the most famous Italian tenors of the generation before Enrico Caruso.

Records: His first records appeared in 1903 for G & T; later he sang for HMV, Fonotipia, and his last records appeared in 1920 for Phonotype, a firm which he directed in Naples (*Rigoletto* and *Il Barbiere di Siviglia*). *U.S. re-issue:* Victor, IRCC, HRS. *U.S. re-recording:* IRCC, FRP, Eterna, TAP, Scala, ASCO, Belcanto, Classic, Cantilena, Rococo.

LUDIKAR, PAVEL, bass, b. Mar. 3, 1882, Prague. Originally Pavel Vyskočil. He first studied law and philosophy at the University of Prague, but then decided to become a pianist, and he appeared as such in the United States. He finally settled on a singing career and made his debut (1904) at the National Theater in Prague as Sarastro in *Die Zauberflöte*. After his first great successes in Prague, he came as guest to the Vienna Volksoper, the Royal Opera in Dresden, and La Scala. He sang Baron Ochs in the first performance of *Der Rosenkavalier* at La Scala in 1911, and he was particularly admired there as a *buffo*. In the 1913-14 season he sang with the Boston Opera Company and was highly successful in guest appearances at the Teatro Colón. He was a member of the Metropolitan Opera (1926-32). Here he sang in the *première* of *La Rondine* in 1928 and in a brilliant production of *Luisa Miller* in 1929. During World War II he appeared as a guest in Germany. He lives in Vienna.

Records: Private recordings for HMV; otherwise only records made in Czechoslovakia.

LUDWIG, CHRISTA, contralto-soprano, b. Mar. 16, 1928, Berlin. Her father, Anton Ludwig, was a tenor and later the general director of the theater in Aachen; while her mother, Eugenie Ludwig-Besalla, had a very successful career as a contralto. She was trained by her mother and at the Music High School in Frankfurt. She made her debut there (1946) as Orlovsky in *Die Fledermaus*. She remained at Frankfurt until 1952 and then sang in Darmstadt (1952-54), in Hannover (1954-55), and was engaged at the Vienna State Opera in 1955. She quickly became internationally known. Since 1956 she has been greatly admired at the Salzburg Festivals, particularly as Dorabella in *Così fan tutte*, Cherubino in *Le Nozze di Figaro*, and Octavian in *Der Rosenkavalier*. Guest appearances at La Scala, the Berlin City Opera, in Munich, Hamburg, Brussels, Rome, and Chicago have marked the brilliant later career of this artist, who is equally famous as a concert contralto. Since about 1960 she has had great success as a dramatic soprano. She made her debut at the Metropolitan Opera in 1959. She is married to the bass-baritone Walter Berry. She has a musical and masterfully trained voice of great tonal range and stylistic expressiveness.

Records: Beautiful performances for Columbia (*Fidelio, Carmen*, and *Der Rosenkavalier*), Decca (*Così fan tutte* and *Die Zauberflöte*), Philips (*Le Nozze di Figaro*), and HMV. *U.S. re-issue:* Angel, London, Vox, Epic, Electrola, DGG,

Ludwig · Luppi

LUDWIG, WALTHER, tenor, b. Mar. 17, 1902, Bad Oeynhausen, Germany. He studied jurisprudence first, then medicine, but during his days at the university in Königsberg he began to study singing. He made his debut in Königsberg (1928) and sang in Schwerin (1929-32); in 1931 he sang the title role there in the world *première* of *Friedemann Bach*. In 1932 he became first lyric tenor at the Berlin City Opera and remained there until 1945. In 1935 he excited great comment at the Glyndebourne Festival by his singing of Belmonte in *Die Entführung aus dem Serail* and Tamino in *Die Zauberflöte*. He made guest appearances at La Scala, Covent Garden, the Rome Opera, and the Teatro Liceo, as well as performing regularly at the Vienna State Opera. He was highly successful at the Salzburg Festivals, particularly as a Mozart singer. Brilliant concert tours, particularly as a lieder singer, brought him fame even as far away as South America. In 1955 he accepted a contract as professor in the Music High School in Berlin. He had a lyric tenor voice of highly varied expressiveness and a fine feeling for style.
Records: HMV, Urania*, DGG* (*Zar und Zimmermann* and Haydn's *The Seasons*), Decca (*Die Entführung aus dem Serail*), Columbia. *U.S. re-issue:* Victor, London, Richmond, American Decca. *U.S. re-recording:* Eterna.

LUGO, GIUSEPPE, tenor, b. 1890, near Verona, Italy. He began the study of singing with Tenaglia in Milan, but then moved to Belgium. There he worked in a mine in Charleroi and continued his vocal studies with Gaudier. After he had won a singing competition in Roubaix, he made his debut at the Opéra-Comique (1930) as Rodolfo in *La Bohème*. Until 1936 he sang at this institution as well as at the Brussels Opera, where he was greatly admired. In 1936 he was highly successful at La Scala as Nadir in *Les Pêcheurs de Perles* and he sang at the Arena Festival. Since he was, however, not equally successful as a singer in Italy, he returned to the Paris and Brussels opera houses.
Records: Polydor and HMV. *U.S. re-issue:* RCA Victor. *U.S. re-recording:* Eterna.

LUISE, MELCHIORRE, bass, b. Dec. 21, 1898, Naples; d. Nov. 22, 1967, Milan. He made his debut (1925) as a baritone, but after a few years changed to bass. In 1935 he had a brilliant success as Bartolo in *Il Barbiere di Siviglia* at the Teatro San Carlo. He soon became one of the best Italian *buffo* basses then on the stage. In 1938 he came to La Scala, where he appeared regularly until 1943 and again after 1951. Guest appearances followed at the Rome Opera, the Teatro Fenice, and the Arena Festival. He was particularly active at the Florence opera house (1944-46) and he was engaged by the Metropolitan Opera (1947-50). He was extremely successful there, as well as in guest appearances at Covent Garden, in France, Germany, Austria, and Spain. He was outstanding as a *buffo* bass for his masterly ability in characterization.
Records: He made electric records of Italian songs for Fonotipia-Odeon; in the LP era he sang mostly minor roles in a great many complete operatic recordings for HMV, Columbia, and RCA-Victor* (including *Il Barbiere di Siviglia*, *Tosca*, and *L'Elisir d'Amore*). *U.S. re-issue:* Richmond, Angel, Capitol.

LUPPI, ORESTE, bass, b. 1870, Rome; d. 1952, Milan. He studied at the Conservatory of the City of

Rome and made his debut (1892) at Foligno. He had a famous career on the more important stages in Italy and sang at the Teatro Costanzi, La Scala, the Teatro Regio in Turin, and in Genoa, Florence, Venice, and Naples. In 1907 he appeared as guest at Covent Garden. He was greatly admired in South America, where he appeared particularly at the Teatro Colón. In 1919 he sang at the Arena Festival. After the close of his career he taught in Milan and lived out his last years there in the Casa di Riposo founded by Verdi.

Records: A great many records of his large bass voice were made for Fonotipia (Milan, 1905-06); he also made two Odeon records. *U.S. re-issue:* Columbia-Fonotipia. *U.S. re-recording:* Eterna, TAP, IRCC, Belcoco, Rococo.

LURIA, JUAN, baritone, b. Dec. 20, 1862, Warsaw; d. 1942, Auschwitz, Poland. Originally Johannes Lorié. He was a pupil of Joseph Gänsbacher in Vienna and made his debut (1885) in Stuttgart. From there he went to the Metropolitan Opera (1890-91). He then settled down in Berlin and began a great many guest performances. He sang frequently at the Theater am Westens and in 1902 he sang in the world *première* of *Die Rose vom Liebesgarten* in Elberfeld. His guest appearances included those at La Scala (where in 1893 he created Wotan in the first performance there of *Die Walküre*) and Vienna, Munich, Paris, Turin, Genoa, and Brussels. In 1908 he sang again at the Theater am Westens and then dedicated himself entirely to his teaching activity. His end was a tragic one. In 1937 he had to leave Germany, since he was Jewish, and he fled to Holland, where he taught in the Conservatories in Amsterdam and The Hague. After the occupation of Holland by the German troops, the almost eighty-year-old artist was sent to the concentration camp at Auschwitz in 1942.

Records: Favorite (Berlin, 1905-07), Odeon, G & T, Pathé, Parlophone, HMV, and Anker. *U.S. re-issue:* Okeh-Odeon.

LUSSAN, ZÉLIE DE, mezzo-soprano, b. 1861, Brooklyn; d. Dec. 18, 1949, London. She studied with her mother and gave concerts when she was sixteen. She made her stage debut (1884) in Boston; she made her first appearance as a guest in London (1889) and was highly successful at Covent Garden (1895-1902). In 1894 she was engaged by the Metropolitan Opera, first singing Carmen with Jean de Reszke and Nellie Melba in the cast. In 1895 she sang there in the first performance of *Falstaff* with Victor Maurel. She returned to the Metropolitan (1898-1900). In 1907 she married the pianist Angelo Fronani and thereafter made only a single guest appearance as Carmen in 1910 at Covent Garden. With her wide-ranging and expressive voice, she was able to sing a great many soprano and mezzo-soprano roles.

Records: Rare records for Victor* (1903) and Beka (1906). *U.S. re-recording:* Belcanto, Cantilena.

M

MACBETH, FLORENCE, soprano, b. 1891, Mankato, Minn. After studying in New York and Paris, she first appeared in public in a concert in Scheveningen. She gave a concert in London in 1913 and in the same year made her stage debut as Rosina in *Il Barbiere di Siviglia* at the Royal Theater in Braunschweig. After guest appearances in Darmstadt and Dresden she was engaged at the Chicago Opera in 1914 and remained there as first coloratura soprano until 1930. She appeared annually at the Summer Opera in Ravinia near Chicago. She sang in San Francisco in 1926-27 and also undertook an American tour with the Commonwealth Opera Company, in which she appeared in Gilbert and Sullivan operettas. After her retirement from the stage, she busied herself with teaching. In 1950 she married the novelist James M. Cain.
Records: American Columbia*. *U.S. re-recording:* IRCC.

MACCHI, MARIA DE, soprano, b. 1870, Peruzzaro, Italy; d. Jan. 16, 1909, Milan. She studied with Virginia Boccabadati in Milan and made her debut as a contralto (1889) at Brescia as Laura in *La Gioconda*. Her voice then developed into a dramatic soprano. She sang in Malta (1892-93); she had an enormous success at the Moscow Imperial Opera (1893) and then appeared in Kiev and Venice (1894), at the Teatro São Carlos (1894-95), the Teatro Costanzi and Teatro dal Verme (1900). She was greatly applauded at La Scala in *Die Königin von Saba* in the 1900-01 season. Guest appearances followed in Prague, Bucharest, Berlin, and at the Teatro San Carlo. In 1904 she came for a season to the Metropolitan Opera, where she sang the title role in *Lucrezia Borgia* with Enrico Caruso and Edyth Walker in the cast. She also sang Valentine in *Les Huguenots* and *Aida* there. She last appeared on the stage in Rome in 1908 as Lucrezia Borgia. Her voice was regal and dark.
Records: Eight very rare Fonotipia Records (Milan, 1905-08). *U.S. re-recording:* Eterna, FRP, TAP, Rococo.

MACDONALD, JEANETTE, soprano, b. 1907, Philadelphia; d. Jan. 14, 1965, Houston. She sang and danced as a child and made her first public appearance at a charity ball when she was four years old. She first sang in musical comedy in New York before appearing in highly successful musical motion pictures in Hollywood. She starred opposite Maurice Chevalier in a number of films, notably *The Merry Widow*. Earlier she appeared with Dennis King in *The Vagabond King* and Ramon Novarro in *The Cat and the Fiddle*. In 1935 she and Nelson Eddy began a successful series of operettas with *Naughty Marietta*, which was an international success. In the 1940's she made her operatic debut as Juliette in *Roméo et Juliette* in Canada and as Marguerite in *Faust* in Chicago. She also sang the latter role in her native Philadelphia at the Academy of Music. Although she was active as a concert singer and made frequent radio and television appearances, she is best remembered for her motion pictures and recordings in a repertory of operettas and popular songs. In 1937 she married the motion picture actor Gene Raymond.

Records: RCA Victor.

MACLENNAN, FRANCIS, tenor, b. Jan. 7, 1879, Bay City, Mich.; d. July 17, 1935, Port Westminster, N.Y. He studied with Sir George Henschel in London, then with Von Emmerich in Berlin, and made his debut (1902) at Covent Garden as Faust in Gounod's opera. He sang first with several American traveling opera companies and in 1906 with the Savage Opera Company, which was touring the United States, presenting *Parsifal*. On this tour he came to know the soprano Florence Easton, whom he later married. In 1907 they were both engaged at the Berlin Imperial Opera and sang there very successfully until 1913. They were engaged by the Hamburg Opera (1913-15). In 1915 they returned to the United States, where they later were separated. He was a member of the Chicago Opera Company (1915-17), and later lived and taught music in New York City.

Records: Four very rare records for HMV (Hamburg, 1908).

MACNEIL, CORNELL, baritone, b. Sept. 24, 1922, Minneapolis, Minn. He first became a machinist and later studied singing at the Hartt School in Hartford, Connecticut, and later with Friedrich Schorr. He made his debut (Mar. 1, 1950) in Philadelphia as John Sorel in the world *première* of *The Consul*. He sang next with several small opera companies and then with the New York City Center Opera (1952-55). In 1955 he had outstanding successes at the San Francisco Opera as the Herald in *Lohengrin* and as Sharpless in *Madama Butterfly*. He made guest appearances in Caracas, Mexico City, and at the Chicago Opera in 1957. In 1959 he had a sensational success at La Scala in *Ernani*. Since 1959 he has been an admired member of the Metropolitan Opera, where he made his debut as Rigoletto. He has been especially noted there for his singing of the title role in *Nabucco*.

Records: Decca (*Un Ballo in Maschera, Rigoletto, Aïda, Cavalleria Rusticana, I Pagliacci,* and *La Fanciulla del West*) and RCA Victor* (*Luisa Miller*). U.S. re-issue: London.

MADEIRA, JEAN, contralto, b. Nov. 14, 1924, Centralia, Ill. Originally Jean Browning. She studied piano and singing in St. Louis, New York, and Vienna with the intention of becoming a pianist. At the age of fifteen she gave a concert with the St. Louis Symphony Orchestra. She made her debut as a singer (1948) at the Metropolitan Opera, singing the First Norn in *Götterdämmerung* and she has been a member of that company ever since. She has also sung with the San Carlo Opera Company, but her first great success came, after her marriage to the conductor Francis

Madeira, in Europe. Since 1955 she has been a member of the Vienna State Opera and she has appeared as guest at La Scala, Covent Garden, in Munich, and at the Salzburg Festivals. She sang Erda and Waltraute in the *Ring* cycle at the Bayreuth Festivals (1956-58). She is also a well-known concert contralto. Her particular starring role is Carmen.

Records: Columbia*, Philips (including Suzuki in *Madama Butterfly*), DGG* (Klytämnestra in *Elektra*), and Vox* (*Carmen*). *U.S. re-issue:* London.

MAGINI-COLETTI, ANTONIO, baritone, b. 1855, Iesi, Italy; d. July 21, 1912, Rome. After his debut (1880) he had a highly successful career on the most important Italian stages, singing both at La Scala and at the Teatro Costanzi. After making guest appearances in various European opera houses, he was engaged by the Metropolitan Opera in 1891; there he sang for his debut the role of Nevers in *Les Huguenots* with Lillian Nordica and Jean and Edouard de Reszke. In 1892 he had a huge success at the Metropolitan as Amonasro in *Aida* with Lilli Lehmann and Jean de Reszke. He often appeared as guest at Covent Garden and Monte Carlo.

Records: Zonophone (Milan, 1902), Fonotipia (Milan, 1905), and Columbia. *U.S. re-issue:* Columbia-Fonotipia, HRS. *U.S. re-recording:* Eterna, TAP, Scala, FRP, Belcanto, Rococo.

MAIKL, GEORG, tenor, b. Apr. 4, 1872, Zell-an-der-Ziller, Austria; d. 1951, Vienna. His father was a famous yodeler from the Tyrol and the son first appeared with a yodeling troupe. His voice was discovered by Bernhard Pollini and he studied with Anton Hromada in Vienna. He made his debut (1899) at Mannheim as Tamino in *Die Zauberflöte*. After great success at Mannheim he was engaged (1904) at the Vienna Imperial Opera, where he remained for forty years. He sang Don Ottavio in *Don Giovanni* at the Salzburg Festivals (1906; 1910). He also appeared very successfully at the later Festivals there, for example, as Aegisthus in *Elektra* in 1937. His career is one of the longest that any singer ever had. He remained a member of the Vienna State Opera until 1944, but even in 1950 he made a guest appearance in *Palestrina*. He had a beautiful tenor voice and was especially famous for lyric parts at the peak of his career.

Records: He made two records for Columbia, one for Odeon, seven for Favorite (all from 1905-06), one for HMV (a quartet with Hans Breuer, Carl Rittmann, and Lorenz Corvinus), and Pathé records. He also made electric records for Columbia*, including Beethoven's *Ninth Symphony* under Weingartner.

MAISON, RENÉ, tenor, b. Nov. 24, 1895, Frameries, Belgium; d. July 11, 1962, Mont d'Or, France. He studied singing in Brussels and Paris and made his debut (1920) in Geneva as Rodolfo in *La Bohème*. He had his first great successes at the opera houses in Nice and Monte Carlo. After 1925 he appeared at the Paris Opéra and the Opéra-Comique, and was particularly noted as a Wagner tenor. He was engaged at the Chicago Opera (1928-31) and sang at the Teatro Colón (1934-37). He made guest appearances at Covent Garden, the Brussels Opera, and in San Francisco. A member of the Metropolitan Opera (1935-43), he made his debut there as Walther in *Die Meistersinger*. After leaving the stage he taught singing, first in New York and, after 1957, in Boston. The brilliance and expressiveness of his tenor voice were ad-

mired in the French and Italian, but especially in the Wagner repertory.
Records: Odeon, Columbia*, and private recordings for the Metropolitan Opera. *U.S. re-issue:* American Decca.

MAJKUT, ERICH, tenor, b. Feb. 3, 1907, Vienna. After his vocal studies at the Music High School in Vienna, he joined the chorus of the Vienna State Opera. In 1928 he was named a soloist of this ensemble and specialized particularly in acting roles for tenor. He was heard there in such roles for more than thirty years. He made guest appearances, mostly with the ensemble of the Vienna State Opera, in Milan, London, Berlin, and Brussels. He appeared almost annually at the Salzburg Festivals and in 1951 at the Bayreuth Festival. He also had an important career as lieder singer and as an oratorio singer.
Records: Columbia (*Le Nozze di Figaro, Die Zauberflöte,* and *Der Rosenkavalier*), Philips (*Salome*), Decca (*Die Meistersinger*), and Vox (*St. Matthew Passion* and *Missa Solemnis* by Beethoven). *U.S. re-issue:* Lyrichord, Epic, Angel, Amadeo, Electrola, Music Guild, RCA Victor, Remington, Seraphim.

MALANIUK, IRA, contralto, b. Jan. 29, 1923, Stanislau, Poland. Her family was of Ukrainian extraction. She studied with Adam Didur in Lvov and then in Vienna with Anna Bahr-Mildenburg. In 1944 she studied at the summer academy of the Mozarteum in Salzburg and in 1945 she made her debut at Graz. In 1947 she came to the Municipal Theater in Zürich and took up her residence there. While under contract at Zürich, she became a member of the Munich State Opera in 1952; after 1956 she was concurrently a member of the Vienna State Opera. She has been highly successful in her guest appearances on all the leading European stages: at Covent Garden, La Scala, the Paris Opéra, and in Stuttgart, Hamburg, Brussels, and Amsterdam. She sang at the Bayreuth Festivals (1951-53) as Brangäne in *Tristan und Isolde,* Magdalena in *Die Meistersinger,* and Fricka in the *Ring* cycle. After 1956 she was highly successful at the Salzburg Festivals, and she has also had a noted career as a concert singer.
Records: Columbia, Decca, and Philips* (including *Così fan tutte, Arabella,* and *Die Meistersinger*). *U.S. re-issue:* DGG, London.

MANN, JOSEPH, tenor, b. 1879, Lemberg, Austria; d. Sept. 9, 1921, Berlin. He first studied law and established himself as a lawyer in Lemberg. Then he studied singing with Kicki in Lemberg and made his debut there (1910). He was a member of the Vienna Volksoper (1911-18). In 1918 he was engaged at the Berlin State Opera, where he had great success. Guest appearances brought him to the Vienna State Opera (1912; 1915; 1920), to the Munich State Opera (1921), as well as to the opera houses in Frankfurt and Bucharest. At the peak of his career he fell dead on the stage of the Berlin State Opera during a performance of *Aida.*
Records: Pathé and Odeon. *U.S. re-recording:* Eterna.

MANOWARDA, JOSEF VON, bass, b. July 3, 1890, Cracow, Poland; d. Dec. 23, 1942, Berlin. He came of a noble Austrian family and completed the Diplomatic School in Vienna, after which he studied philosophy at the University of Graz. In Graz he took singing lessons and in this way his voice was discovered. He made his debut in Graz (1911) and sang at the Vienna Volksoper (1915-18); during this time he continued his study of singing with Otto Iro. He sang at Weisbaden (1918-19) and then was engaged at the Vienna

State Opera, where on Oct. 10, 1919, he sang the Spirit Messenger in the world *première* of *Die Frau ohne Schatten*. After 1922 he appeared almost annually at the Salzburg Festivals, where he was especially admired as Alfonso in *Così fan tutte*. From 1931 until the time of his death he was one of the mainstays of the Bayreuth Festivals. He made successful guest appearances in Amsterdam, Brussels, Rome, Budapest, and at La Scala. He remained at the Vienna State Opera until 1935, after which he joined the Berlin State Opera. He was active as a professor at the National Academy for Music in Vienna (1932-35). He was married to the singer Nelly Pirchhof. The volume and quality of his voice and the dramatic force of his acting made him famous; on account of the exceptional range of his voice he was able to sing parts for heroic baritone as well as bass roles. He was also admired in concerts.

Records: Polydor and Telefunken (Bayreuth, 1936).

MANSKI, DOROTHEA, soprano, b. Mar. 11, 1891, New York; d. Feb. 24, 1967, Bloomington, Ind. She studied in Berlin and made her debut at the Komische Oper there (1911). She sang in Mannheim (1914-20) and in Stuttgart (1920-24). She was engaged by the Berlin State Opera (1924-27). In 1927 she accepted a bid to the Metropolitan Opera, making her debut as the Witch in *Hänsel und Gretel*. She remained a member of this company until 1941. Although she appeared mostly in small roles, she substituted for Frida Leider in 1933 as Brünnhilde in *Die Walküre*. In 1933 she sang Isolde at the Salzburg Festival in a performance of *Tristan und Isolde* under Toscanini. In 1934 she appeared as guest at the Vienna State Opera. After 1942 she taught singing at Indiana University. She was married to the Swedish music critic Walter Brandon, and her daughter, Inge Manski, became a singer.

Records: Many records for Vox, HMV, and Tri-Ergon; private recordings for the Metropolitan Opera.

MANTELLI, EUGENIA, contralto-soprano, b. 1860; d. Mar. 3, 1926, Lisbon. She made her debut (1883) at the Teatro São Carlos as Urbain in *Les Huguenots*. She then made long guest-appearance tours in Germany, Italy, and South America with the famous Spanish tenor Julien Gayarré. In 1894 she sang at the Imperial Opera in Moscow opposite Francesco Tamagno. About the turn of the century she appeared regularly as guest at Covent Garden. She was a member of the Metropolitan Opera (1894-1900) and was particularly admired there as Dalila in *Samson et Dalila*. She sang again at the Metropolitan (1902-03). In 1904 she took up her residence in Lisbon, but appeared there only once at the Teatro São Carlos before becoming a teacher. The repertory of this artist reached from coloratura-contralto parts to that of Brünnhilde.

Records: Zonophone* (U.S. 1904-07). *U.S. re-issue:* IRCC. *U.S. re-recording:* Scala, Belcanto, TAP.

MAŘÁK, OTTOKAR, tenor, b. Jan. 5, 1872, Esztergom, Hungary; d. July 2, 1939, Prague. He originally planned to be a painter, but studied singing at the Prague Conservatory and made his debut in Brünn (1899) as Faust in Gounod's opera. In 1900 he came to the German Theater in Prague, where in 1901 he sang the part of the Prince in the world *première* of *Rusalka* at the National Theater. In 1903 he was chosen by Gustav Mahler for the Imperial Opera in Vienna. In 1906 he came to the Komische Oper, where he was enormously successful; in 1911 he sang the role of Gennaro there in the world *première* of *I Gioielli della Madonna*. He was admired in highly successful guest appearances in London, Paris, Brussels, and Munich. He was engaged at the Chicago Opera (1913-14), and he married the American soprano Mary Cavan. In 1914 he became the first tenor at the National Opera in Prague and remained there as a celebrated star for the next twenty years, appearing over fifteen hundred times. In 1934 he left the stage and became a teacher of voice in Chicago. There he soon fell into complete poverty and was finally reduced to selling newspapers on the streets. As soon as this became known in Czechoslovakia, a fund was collected to allow him to return to his homeland, but this great artist died soon after his return. He had in his lyric tenor voice both tonal volume and tonal beauty as well as a rare quality of expressiveness.

Records: For Odeon he sang Canio in a complete performance of *I Pagliacci*. Later he recorded for HMV, Ultraphon, Polydor, and Pathé. He made records of Polish folk songs for American Columbia*. *U.S. re-issue:* Victor.

MARCEL, LUCILLE, soprano, b. 1887, New York; d. June 22, 1921, Vienna. Originally Lucille Wasself. She studied first in the United States, then with Jean de Reszke in Paris. She made her debut quite unexpectedly (1908) at the Imperial Opera in Vienna as Elektra in Strauss' opera of the same name when she replaced Anna Bahr-Mildenburg in this role. She was a member of the Vienna Imperial Opera (1908-10) and was greatly assisted by the director of the house at that time, the conductor Felix Weingartner, whom she married in 1911. In 1910 she went with him to the Hamburg Opera and during the following years she appeared with the Boston Opera Company (1911-14), being particularly admired there as Tosca. She made guest appearances at the Théâtre des Champs-Elysées in 1914. When her husband accepted an engagement at Darmstadt in 1914, she went with him but rarely appeared on the stage there.

Records: Rare records for HMV and American Columbia*. *U.S. re-issue:* RCA Victor. *U.S. re-recording:* Columbia.

MARCHESI, BLANCHE, soprano, b. Apr. 4, 1863, Paris; d. Dec. 15, 1940, London. She was the daughter of a famous singing couple; her mother, Mathilde Marchesi, *née* Graumann (b. 1821, Frankfurt; d. 1913, London) was considered to be the finest voice teacher of her time; her father, Salvatore Marchesi, Cavaliere de Castrone, Marchese della Rajata (1822-1908), had settled down in Paris with his wife to teach after a successful career in the concert hall. Blanche Marchesi was trained according to the celebrated method of her mother and made her debut as a concert singer in Paris (1895). In 1896 she gave concerts in London and Berlin. She chose London for her residence and was soon active there as a much-sought-after teacher. She also undertook long concert tours which brought her great success, particularly in the United States. She did not make her stage debut until 1900, when she appeared at the German Theater in Prague as Brünnhilde in *Die Walküre*. She also appeared with the Moody Manners Opera Company in London, but her greatest successes were as a concert singer. She sang before Queen Victoria of England and Kaiser Wilhelm II of Germany at court concerts. She was married to Baron André Anzon Caccamisi. The beauty of her voice remained for an uncommonly long time. She gave a concert in London on her seventy-fifth birthday. Her memoirs appeared under the title *A Singer's Pilgrimage* (London, 1923) and she also published an instruction book on the art of singing, *The Singer's Catechism* (London, 1932). Her voice, which was trained entirely according to the classical method of her mother, was outstanding for her total mastery of technique, her clear tone production, and a completely artistic control of phrasing.

Records: Her first records appeared for G & T (Berlin, 1906). She made electric records for HMV (London, 1936). *U.S. re-issue:* IRCC. *U.S. re-recording:* IRCC, Rococo, Belcanto, Audio Rarities.

MARCHI, EMILIO DE, tenor, b. 1861, Voghera, Italy; d. Mar. 20, 1917, Milan. At first he trained for a military officer's career and was a lieutenant in the Bersaglieri. After the discovery of his voice, he made his debut (1886) at the Teatro dal Verme. He next sang in Palermo, at the Teatro Costanzi, and at the Teatro Argentina, and appeared as guest at the Teatro Liceo (1888-93). After 1891 he was successful at the Teatro Real and at La Scala. On Jan. 14, 1900, at the Teatro Costanzi, he sang Cavaradossi in the world *première* of *Tosca*. He sang one guest season at Covent Garden (1901) and was a member of the Metropolitan Opera (1901-03). He appeared as guest at the Opéra-Comique in 1904. In 1909 he ended his stage career and lived as a teacher in Milan.

Records: The voice of this artist is unfortunately not known through disc records but only through a few fragments preserved on Mapleson cylinders, which scarely gave a true impression of its beauty. *U.S. re-recording:* IRCC.

MARCONI, FRANCESCO, tenor, b. May 14, 1853, Rome; d. Feb. 5, 1916, Rome. Originally a cabinetmaker by trade, he studied singing with Ottavio Bartolini in Rome and made his debut (1878) at the Teatro Reale as Faust in Gounod's opera. He then had a successful career on the biggest stages in Italy, particularly at La Scala and the Teatro Costanzi. After starring guest appearances in Spain, Portugal, and Russia, he sang Enzo in *La Gioconda* in the first performance in England at Covent Garden (1883). In 1888 he sang the title role in the American *première* of *Otello* at the New York Academy of Music, but was not otherwise successful in the United States. Thereafter until his death he made Rome, where he resided, the center of his guest-appearance activity. Musical beauty and dramatic strength were joined in a fortunate manner in his tenor voice.

Records: G & T (Milan, 1903-04) and HMV (Milan, 1908), all very rare. *U.S. re-issue:* RCA Victor. *U.S. re-recording:* Belcanto, Rococo, TAP.

MARCOUX, VANNI-, bass-baritone, b. June 12, 1877, Turin, Italy; d. Oct. 21, 1962, Paris. Originally Jean-Émile Vanni-Marcoux, the son of French parents. He studied law at the University of Turin, then studied singing with Taverna and Collino there as well as with Frédéric Boyer at the Paris Conservatory. He made his debut (1899) in Bayonne as Friar Lawrence in *Roméo et Juliette*. He then sang with the Nice and Brussels Operas and at the Théâtre de La Haye, being especially well liked at the latter. He sang every year (1904-15) as guest at Covent Garden and on June 28, 1905, appeared there in the world *première* of *L'Oracolo*. In 1909 he came to the Paris Opéra, where he made his debut as Guido Colonna in the world *première* of *Monna Vanna*. Thereafter he had one triumph after another in Paris and in 1913 he created the title role in *Panurge*. He sang with the Boston Opera Company in 1912 and in 1913 came to Chicago, making his debut as Scarpia to Mary Garden's Tosca. During World War I he returned to France. In 1919 he was applauded at the Teatro Colón and in 1922 he sang Boris Godounov, one of his starring roles, at La Scala. He appeared regularly as guest at Monte Carlo and Covent Garden as well as the two great Paris opera houses and at La Scala. He was again a member of the Chicago Opera (1926-32) and also appeared successfully in sound films. As late as 1947 he sang Don Quichotte in Massenet's opera at the Opéra-Comique. He was director of the Opera in Bordeaux (1948-52), but lived thereafter in Paris. A sumptuous and dark-toned voice of great expressive quality. He was considered one of the noted actors among the opera singers of his time.

Records: HMV, his first records appearing in 1924. *U.S. re-issue:* RCA Victor. *U.S. re-recording:* TAP, FRP, Pathé-Marconi.

MARDONES, JOSÉ, bass, b. 1869, Fontecha, Spain; d. May 4, 1932, Madrid. He studied at the Royal Conservatory in Madrid and made his debut (1891) in South America, where he had his first great successes at the Rio de Janeiro Opera and at the Teatro Colón. About the turn of the century he appeared as guest at various famous theaters in Europe, for example, Covent Garden, the Teatro São Carlos, La Scala, and in Madrid and Barcelona. In 1913 he came for three seasons to the Boston Opera Company; he was then a member of the Metropolitan Opera, where he was equally successful (1917-26). After his retirement from the stage he lived in his native Spain. He had a bass voice of great size and volume; connoisseurs say he had the most voluminous bass voice ever to be recorded.

Records: American Columbia* and Victor*. *U.S. re-recording:* Columbia, Eterna, Scala, FRP, TAP.

MARÉCHAL, ADOLPHE, tenor, b. Sept. 26, 1867, Liège, Belgium; d. 1935, Brussels. He studied at the Conservatory in Liège and made his debut (1891) at Dijon. He then sang at the opera houses in Rheims, Bordeaux, and Nice. In 1895 he was engaged at the Opéra-Comique, where he had great success during the next decade. He sang there in a number of important world *premières*: Julien in the first performance of *Louise* (Feb. 2, 1900), in *Grisélidis* (1901), in *Le Reine Fiammette* (1903) opposite Mary Garden, and in *Le Chemineau* (1907). On Feb. 8, 1902, at the Monte Carlo Opera he sang Jean in the world *première* of *Le Jongleur de Notre-Dame*. He appeared regularly as guest at the Brussels Opera and also made guest appearances at Nice, Monte Carlo, and the Imperial Opera in Moscow. In 1907 he gave up his career because of poor health and lived in retirement in Brussels thereafter. He had a beautifully trained lyric tenor voice and was especially famed in the interpretation of French roles for his voice range.

Records: G & T (Paris, 1905), Zonophone (Paris, 1907), and Pathé. *U.S. re-recording:* IRCC.

MARHERR, ELFRIEDE, soprano, b. 1885, Berlin. She studied with Juan Luria and made her debut (1916) at the Berlin Imperial Opera, where she remained active throughout her entire career of more than thirty years. At the outset she became known through her performances

Marié De L'Isle · Marsh

as Cherubino in *Le Nozze di Figaro* and as Octavian in *Der Rosenkavalier*. In 1932 she sang Fatime in *Oberon* at the Salzburg Festival and she appeared at the Bayreuth Festivals as Wellgunde and as the Third Norn in the *Ring* cycle (1936-46). She appeared at the Berlin State Opera in 1946. She also sang under the name Marherr-Wagner; she lived and taught in Berlin.

Records: There are only electric records by this artist, but none of them are solo discs. She first worked for Polydor in various abbreviated operas; then she sang the First Lady in *Die Zauberflöte* for HMV and in duets with Frida Leider. Finally she sang in scenes from *Der Rosenkavalier* with Elisabeth Ohms and Adele Kern. *U.S. re-issue:* Brunswick. *U.S. re-recording:* Angel, Turnabout.

MARIÉ DE L'ISLE, JEANNE, contralto, b. 1872, Paris; d. 1926, Paris. Originally Jeanne Beugnon. She was trained by her aunt, the celebrated contralto Célestine Galli-Marié (1840-1905), who had sung both Carmen and Mignon in the world *premières* of these operas. She made her debut at the Opéra-Comique (1896) and in 1900 she sang the role of Camille there in the world *première* of *Louise*; in 1903 she had an overwhelming success as Charlotte in *Werther*. She also became the great successor to her aunt in the role of Carmen at the Opéra-Comique. A few guest appearances took her to the opera houses in Bucharest and Sofia, among others, in 1910. At the end of her life she lived and taught in Paris.

Records: Rather rare discs for G & T (Paris, 1904), Odeon (Paris, 1904), and Zonophone (Paris, 1905), including scenes from *Carmen*; these last are of importance in that she probably approached the original interpretation of the role. *U.S. re-recording:* IRCC.

MARIO, QUEENA, soprano, b. 1896, Akron, Ohio; d. May 28, 1952, New York. Originally Queena Mario Tillotson. She was a journalist first and wrote under the names Queena Tillotson and Florence Bryan. On the advice of Enrico Caruso she studied singing in New York with Oscar Saenger and Marcella Sembrich. She made her debut (1918) with the San Carlo Opera Company in *Les Contes d'Hoffmann*. She sang with that company until 1921, then, until 1922, with the Scotti Opera Company. She was a member of the Metropolitan Opera (1922-39) and made guest appearances in Chicago and San Francisco. She was especially famous as Gretel in *Hänsel und Gretel*. In 1938 she became a teacher at the Curtis Institute of Music and included both Rose Bampton and Helen Jepson among her pupils. She also began writing again and published the famous mystery novel *Murder in the Opera House*.

Records: No records of her beautiful coloratura soprano voice were released during her lifetime, except a course of singing lessons which she made for American Columbia*. Interesting private records for the Metropolitan Opera were made and later published.

MARSH, LUCY ISABELLE, soprano, b. Apr. 10, 1878, Ithaca, N.Y.; d. Jan. 20, 1956, Providence, R.I. She studied with Walter Hall in New York and with Trabadello in Paris and became a church singer in the United States. She then made a few records for Columbia*, but shortly thereafter she was engaged by the Victor* Company and remained for many years their stock soprano. As a singer on records she was highly successful, but she never appeared on the stage and only rarely in concert. She later became a teacher of singing. She had a well-trained and expressive voice.

Records: Of her many records the duets with John McCormack were especially well known. She later made electric records for Victor*, including masterfully conceived recordings of arias from *The Messiah* and the oratorios of Mendelssohn and Rossini. *U.S. re-recording:* Rococo.

MARSHALL, LOIS, soprano, b. 1928 (?), Toronto, Canada. She began her study of singing at the age of twelve at the Royal Conservatory in Toronto and was giving concerts by the age of fifteen. In 1952 she came to New York and had brilliant success in concerts in Town Hall; Toscanini thereupon engaged her for the soprano solo in a performance of Beethoven's *Missa Solemnis* in New York. In 1956 she made a trip to England, where she gave very successful concerts and made records of operas and oratorios. Concerts in Amsterdam, Brussels, and Hamburg established her as one of the great concert sopranos of her time. In 1957 she was admired at the Edinburgh Festival and in a production of *The Messiah* in Dublin. In 1958 she completed a successful concert tour in Russia. She has occasionally appeared in opera in Canada as Mimi in *La Bohème* and as Donna Anna in *Don Giovanni*.

Records: RCA Victor* (*The Messiah*) and Columbia (*Die Entführung aus dem Serail*). *U.S. re-issue:* Epic, Angel.

MARTAPOURA, JEAN, baritone, b. 1860 (?), Belgium; d. February, 1929, Brussels. Originally Jean, Baron von Heekeren. He had his first brilliant success in his eight-year tenure at the Paris Opéra. He sang there in the world *première* of *Ascanio* in 1890 and in *Le Mage* in 1891. He was engaged at the Metropolitan Opera in 1891, making his debut as Mercutio in *Roméo et Juliette* with Victor Capoul and Jean and Edouard de Reszke. He remained at the Metropolitan until 1894 and in April of that year sang Albert in the *première* there of *Werther*. Later he sang in the opera houses in Brussels, Monte Carlo, and Nice. He also appeared in operetta.

Records: Very rare records for Zonophone (Paris, 1900).

MARTEN, HEINZ, tenor, b. Jan. 17, 1908, Schleswig, Germany. He first was taught by his father to be a skilled cabinetmaker and then studied singing with Albert Fischer and Oscar Rees in Berlin. He made his debut (1928) as a concert and oratorio tenor. In 1934 he first sang the Evangelist in the *St. Matthew Passion* in Leipzig under Karl Straube. Thereafter he often sang with the St. Thomas Church choir in Leipzig. He won the Music Prize of the City of Berlin in 1938. He resided in Schleswig (1945-50) and in Bielefeld (1950-56). Since 1956 he has been a professor at the Music High School in Cologne. This artist, so highly esteemed as an interpreter of Bach, appeared on the stage only once, in Bielefeld in 1953.

Records: Relatively few records for DGG*, including the Bach *Magnificat*. *U.S. re-issue:* Vox, L'Oiseau-Lyre.

MARTIN, RICCARDO, tenor, b. Nov. 18, 1874, Hopkinsville, Ky.; d. Aug. 11, 1952, New York. Originally Hugh Whitfield. He studied violin in Nashville and then became a pupil of Edward MacDowell at Columbia University. At this time he was composing songs, choral pieces, and other musical works. In 1901 he decided to become a singer; among his teachers were Jean de Reszke, Léon Escalais, and Giovanni Sbriglia in Paris, as well as Lombardi in Florence. In 1904 he made his debut as Faust in Gounod's opera in Nantes. In 1906 he sang with Henry Russell's opera company in New Orleans. In 1907 he came to the Metropolitan Opera, where he made his debut as Faust in *Mefistofele* opposite Feodor Chaliapin. He remained at the Metropolitan until 1915, appearing there in 1913 in the world *première* of *Cyrano de Bergerac*. In 1910 he sang as guest at Covent Garden and in Mexico City. He belonged to the Boston Opera Company (1916-17) and undertook an American tour with that company. In 1917 he returned to the Metropolitan, but sang only a single performance as Rodolfo in *La Bohème*. He sang at the Chicago Opera (1920-23). For a long time after giving up his singing career he lived in Paris and there became a correspondent for the magazine *Opera News*. He later lived in Bermuda.

Records: Edison* cylinders and Victor* records. *U.S. re-issue:* IRCC, HRS. *U.S. re-recording:* IRCC, TAP.

MARTINELLI, GIOVANNI, tenor, b. Oct. 22, 1885, Montagnana, Italy; d. February 2, 1969, New York. During military service he was a clarinetist in a military band; the band leader was astonished at his vocal talents and, with this encouragement, Martinelli studied singing with Mandolini in Milan. He made his debut (1911) at the Teatro dal Verme there, singing the title role in *Ernani*. His career developed very quickly; in 1912 Toscanini chose him for the role of Dick Johnson in the La Scala *première* of *La Fanciulla del West* and in the same year he had a sensational success at Covent Garden. In 1913 he was engaged by the Metropolitan Opera and he remained until 1946 as esteemed principal tenor of this famous house. In 1915 he sang there in the world *première* of *Madame Sans-Gêne* and, on Jan. 28, 1916, in the world *première* of *Goyescas*. In 1914 he sang at the Monte Carlo Opera in the world *première* of *I Mori di Valenza*. After the death of Enrico Caruso he was generally esteemed as the leading operatic tenor, especially in the Caruso roles. From New York he undertook very successful guest tours to all the principal European musical centers, particularly to Covent Garden, where he sang the role of Otello during the Coronation Season of 1937. After 1946 he lived and taught in New York City. A masterfully trained, voluminous tenor voice. In the passionate quality of his characterizations and the moving intensity of his expressiveness he was outstanding, particularly in heroic roles.

Records: Many recordings for Victor*, Edison*, and Allegro Royale*. Private records for the Metropolitan Opera. *U.S. re-recording:* Scala, RCA Victor, TAP, ASCO, FRP, Cantilena.

MARTINIS, CARLA, soprano, b. 1924, Danculovice, Yugoslavia. She studied at the Conservatory in Zagreb with, among others, Professor Martinis, whom she later married. After she had first sung in the opera houses in Zagreb and Prague, she won an international singing contest in Geneva in 1949. She had an outstanding success at the New York City Center Opera (1950-53), making her debut there as Turandot. In 1951 she first appeared at the Vienna State Opera and has returned there regularly ever since. In the same year she sang Aïda in a concert performance in Vienna under Herbert von Karajan and, also in 1951, she sang Desdemona in *Otello* under Furtwängler at the Salzburg Festival. Since 1953 she has lived in Vienna and has undertaken an extraordinary amount of guest activity from there.

Records: Decca and HMV. *U.S. re-issue:* London.

MASCHERINI, ENZO, baritone, b. 1916, Florence. He began studying singing in Florence in 1937 and included among his teachers Titta Ruffo and Riccardo Stracciari. He made his debut (1938) there as the elder Germont in *La Traviata*. He sang at the Teatro San Carlo, as well as in Parma and Genoa, in 1939. In 1940 he came to La Scala, where he has sung repeatedly since then. After World War II he made guest appearances in Vienna and Prague, at the New York City Opera, and in Chicago, Philadelphia, and San Francisco. He was engaged at the Metropolitan Opera in 1950. In 1951 he was greatly admired at the Maggio Musicale Festival as Montfort in *I Vespri Siciliani*.

Records: Decca (Scarpia in *Tosca* with Renata Tebaldi), Cetra, and Columbia. *U.S. re-issue:* London, Richmond.

MASINI, GALLIANO, tenor, b. 1902, Livorno, Italy. He studied in Milan with Maestro Laura; then he made his debut in Livorno (1923) as Cavaradossi in *Tosca*. He had a famous career in Italian opera houses and sang at La Scala. He made successful guest appearances in Rio de Janeiro in 1933. He also sang at the Arena and Maggio Musicale Festivals. In the United States he was first engaged at the Chicago Opera and then at the Metropolitan Opera (1938-39). Later he made guest appearances at the Teatro Colón and at the Paris Opéra. He also appeared in films.

Records: Columbia and Odeon, but especially for Cetra*, (including *La Forza del Destino*). *U.S. re-issue:* FRP.

MASON, EDITH, soprano, b. Mar. 22, 1893, St. Louis, Mo. She studied in Paris with Enrico Bertram and then in Boston. She made her debut unexpectedly as Nedda in *I Pagliacci* with the Boston Opera Company (1912). After further study with Edmond Clément in Paris she sang at Nice, Marseilles, and Monte Carlo. She studied repeatedly with Vanzo and Cottone in Milan and with Victor Maurel in New York. In 1915 she was engaged by the Metropolitan Opera, making her debut as Sophie in *Der Rosenkavalier*. After 1917 she sang almost annually at the Ravinia Summer Opera near Chicago. She made a tour with the Bracala Opera Company through Central America. In 1919 she made guest appearances at the Théâtre Lyrique and the Opéra-Comique. She sang at the Monte Carlo Opera in 1920 and was a member of the Chicago Opera (1921-23; 1934-42); here her career reached its high point. She married the Italian conductor Giorgio Polacco, but later was separated from him. In Italy she appeared in 1924 in Rome and Turin and in 1927 sang Marguerite in *Faust* at La Scala under Toscanini. She made guest appearances at Covent Garden in 1930 and at the Maggio Musicale Festival as Nanetta in *Falstaff* in 1933. She sang the same part at the Salzburg Festival in 1935. After her marriage to the American millionaire, Ragland, she gave up her career. She lives in Chicago. She had a technically first-rate voice, thoroughly trained and of beautiful sound quality.

Records: A few recordings for Brunswick*.

MASSARY, FRITZI, soprano, b. Mar. 31, 1882, Vienna; d. Jan. 31, 1969, Los Angeles. Originally Friederike Massaryk. She began her career in 1902 with an Austrian operetta troupe that had undertaken a tour of Russia. In 1904 she came to the Metropol Theater in Berlin and had sensational success in a revue there. She was soon feted as an operetta diva and she had triumphs in this field in Berlin like those of no other artist of her time. In 1915 she created in Berlin the title role in *Die Kaiserin*, and this was followed by *premières* in operettas by Lehár, Oscar Strauss, and Robert Stolz. In 1911 she sang in *La Belle Helène* opposite Maria Jeritza at the Munich Opera Festival. At the City Opera in Berlin she sang Adele in *Die Fledermaus* and Hanna Glowari in *The Merry Widow*, both under Bruno Walter, who treasured her voice. Walter also suggested to her that she sing the role of Carmen, but Massary declined. She was greatly admired as Adele in *Die Fledermaus* at the Salzburg Festival of 1926. After 1917 she married the actor Max Pallenburg, who was the greatest comedian of the German stage of his day. In 1933 she moved to the United States, where she lived in Beverly Hills, California. As an operetta singer Fritzi Massary became the idol of an entire generation; she raised the art of operetta singing to an entirely new artistic level, without losing the sparkling lightness of the genre.

Records: G & T, Polydor, and HMV. *U.S. re-recording:* Scala, Rococo.

MATHIS, EDITH, soprano, b. 1933, Lucerne, Switzerland. She studied at the Conservatory of Lucerne and made her debut there (1956). She came to the Cologne Opera in 1959 and was very successful; in 1963 she moved to the Berlin City Opera. Her guest appearances include the Salzburg Festival in 1960, the Glyndebourne Festival in 1962 (in *Le Nozze di Figaro*), and the Vienna State Opera. She has been admired on the stage in the lyric repertory and in the concert hall.

Records: HMV and Electrola. *U.S. re-issue:* Electrola, DGG, Angel, Vox, Seraphim.

MATZENAUER, MARGARETHE, contralto-soprano, b. June 1, 1881, Temesvár, Hungary, where her father was bandmaster; d. May 19, 1963, Van Nuys, Calif. She studied with Georgine von Januschowsky in Graz, then with Antonie Mielke and Franz Emmerich in Berlin. She made her debut (1901) at Strasbourg and remained there until 1904. She was a greatly admired member of the Munich Royal Opera (1904-11) and during that time she appeared as guest in Vienna, Berlin, Hamburg, London, and Paris. In 1911 she sang several roles at the Bayreuth Festival: Waltraute, Flosshilde, and the First Norn in the *Ring* cycle. In 1911 she was called to the Metropolitan Opera, making her debut there as Amneris in *Aida* with Enrico Caruso and Emmy Destinn. She had a great many successes at the Metropolitan until 1930. After 1911 she made many successful guest appearances at the Teatro Colón. She was first married to the Munich singing teacher Ernst Preuse, next to the tenor Edoardo Ferrari-Fontana, and finally to her chauffeur. Toward the end of her career she undertook dramatic soprano roles, particularly in the Wagner repertory. After 1930 she lived and taught in New York City and later in Santa Monica, California.

Records: A great many records for G & T, HMV, Columbia*, and Pathé, as well as Edison discs. After 1912 she recorded exclusively for Victor*. *U.S. re-issue:* RCA Victor, Opera Disc, IRCC. *U.S. re-recording:* Pathé Actuelle, FRP, Collectors Guild, TAP.

MAUGERI, CARMELO, baritone, b. July 16, 1889, Catania, Sicily. He studied at the Conservatory in Trieste with Tartine, then with Matteo Adernò in Catania, where he made his debut (1913) as Alfio in *Cavalleria Rusticana*. After guest appearances on the southern Italian stages and in Lisbon, he became a soldier in the Italian army in World War I. During the years 1917-21 he sang at the Teatro Carcana and the Teatro dal Verme and in 1918-19 made guest appearances in Madrid and Barcelona. In 1931 he had great success at the Teatro Massimo. He first became famous as an interpreter of the baritone parts in the operas of Riccardo Zandonai. In 1922 he sang Tebaldo in *Giulietta e Romeo* at its world *première* at the Teatro Costanzi under the direction of the composer. In 1929 he sang the same role at La Scala and had great success during the following decade at that house. Later he specialized in *buffo* roles and was for many years one of the leading performers in this type.

Records: Beautiful electric records for Columbia about 1930. After he had made no records for more than twenty years, he sang for Vox* on LP recordings of *Il Signor Bruschino* and Cimarosa's *Il Maestro di Capella.*

MAURANE, CAMILLE, baritone, b. Nov. 29, 1911, Rouen, France. A student of his father, who was himself a singing teacher, he later studied at the Conservatory Saint-Évode in Rouen and at the Paris Conservatory with Claire Croiza. He made his debut (1940) at the Opéra-Comique, where he first appeared under the name Camille Moreau. There he was highly successful in the part of Pelléas in *Pelléas et Mélisande*; this role remained his specialty and he interpreted it on many stages. He was also a concert singer of the first rank. His voice is bright-timbred and is a typically French baritone.

Records: Columbia, Philips, and Decca (including two versions of *Pelléas et Mélisande*). *U.S. re-issue:* Epic, DGG, Pathé-Marconi, London.

MAUREL, VICTOR, baritone, b. June 17, 1848, Marseilles, France; d. Oct. 22, 1923, New York. He studied at the Conservatories in Marseilles and Paris and he made his debut (1868) at the Paris Opéra, where he immediately had brilliant success. By 1870 he was singing at La Scala in the world *première* of *Il Guarany.* He was especially famous as an interpreter of Verdi roles and was chosen by Verdi himself for the role of Posa at the first Italian performance of *Don Carlos* at the Teatro San Carlo in 1871. In 1873 he made his first guest appearance in the United States, singing Amonasro in the American *première* of *Aida.* By the age of twenty-five he had become the most famous baritone of his generation in the Italian repertory. In the course of the following three decades he went from triumph to triumph in all the great opera houses of the world. His chief centers of activity were La Scala, the Paris Opéra, and the Metropolitan Opera, of which he was a member (1894-99). He also appeared as guest in London, Madrid, Lisbon, Barcelona, Cairo, Naples, St. Petersburg, and Moscow. He was a member of the directorate of the Théâtre des Italiens in Paris (1883-85). On Feb. 5, 1887, he sang the role of Iago in the brilliant world *première* of *Otello* at La Scala and on Feb. 9, 1893, he created the title role in *Falstaff* there. On May 22, 1892, at the Teatro dal Verme he sang the role of Tonio in the world *première* of *I Pagliacci.* In 1904 he ended his triumphal stage career. He had some experience as an actor; then he lived and taught singing first in Paris, then in New York. He wrote several essays on the teaching of singing and an autobiographical work, *Dix ans de carrière* (Paris, 1897). He was celebrated as a singer for the outstandingly thorough training of his voice, the depth and brilliance of his vocal quality, and the strongly realistic and expressive quality of his characterizations.

Records: Very rare records for

G & T (Paris, 1903) and Fonotipia (Milan, 1905-07), including fragments from *Otello* and *Falstaff*. *U.S. re-issue:* IRCC, HRS. *U.S. re-recording:* IRCC, TAP, Scala, FRP, Belcanto, HRS, Cantilena, Rococo.

MAYNOR, DOROTHY, soprano, b. Sept. 3, 1910, Norfolk, Va. The daughter of a Negro Methodist preacher, she first sang in her parish church choir. At the age of fourteen she was a pupil at the Hampton Institute and made a tour of Europe with the famous choir of the school. A gift from an unknown patron made it possible for her to continue her vocal studies. After 1933 she joined the Westminster Choir School in Princeton, New Jersey. After her marriage to a Methodist minister she studied with the teachers W. Klamroth and H. Houghton. Beginning in 1936, she led a church choir in Brooklyn. In 1939 she made her debut at the Berkshire Festival and had a brilliant success there. Serge Koussevitsky invited her to record arias by Handel and Mozart with the Boston Symphony Orchestra. Concert tours, first in the United States and then in Europe, brought her great success. She never appeared on the stage, but she sang a great many operatic arias in her concerts. She enchanted the musical public in Holland, Belgium England, France, and Italy. She has been the director of Bennett College in Greensboro, North Carolina, and now directs a school of music in Harlem, New York City. Dorothy Maynor, without doubt, possessed the most beautiful soprano voice of her generation in the United States; to some it was most outstanding for its sumptuous quality, to others for the variety of shading which she could bring to bear in her presentations. *Records* RCA Victor*. *U.S. re-recording:* RCA Victor.

MAYR, RICHARD, bass, b. Nov. 18, 1877, Henndorf, Austria; d. Dec. 1, 1935, Vienna. At first he studied medicine at the University of Vienna, but studied voice at the same time at the Conservatory of the City of Vienna. In 1902 he was engaged by Gustav Mahler for the Vienna Imperial Opera before making his formal debut. He remained a member of this company until his death. During this long period he became one of the best-loved artists of the Austrian capital. In 1902 he also appeared at the Bayreuth Festival, where he subsequently specialized in the roles of Hagen in *Götterdämmerung* and Gurnemanz in *Parsifal*. He was admired as a Mozart interpreter of genius at the Salzburg Festivals in 1906 and 1910, and from the very beginning of the regular Salzburg Festivals in 1922 he was at the center of this artistic endeavor. He was applauded there for his Mozart roles and for his incomparable Baron Ochs in *Der Rosenkavalier*. On Oct. 10, 1919, he sang Barak at the Vienna State Opera in the world *première* of *Die Frau ohne Schatten*. Guest appearances also brought him great fame and success in opera houses all over the world. He was a member of the Metropolitan Opera (1927-30), making his debut as Pogner in *Die Meistersinger*. A dark, sumptuous voice which he handled with great resourcefulness in both serious and *buffo* roles; he was also esteemed as an outstanding actor.

Records: G & T (Vienna, 1905), HMV, Christchall, Polydor, including an abbreviated *Der Rosenkavalier* (1934), and Beethoven's *Ninth Symphony* under Weingartner. *U.S. re-issue:* Opera Disc, Victor, Columbia. *U.S. re-recording:* Angel, Eterna, Scala, Belcanto, TAP.

MAZZOLENI, ESTER, soprano, b. 1884, Sebenico, Dalmatia. At first she planned to be a painter, but her voice was discovered during a sojourn in Italy and she made her debut at the Teatro Costanzi (1904) as Leonora in *Il Trovatore*. She quickly developed an important career on various Italian stages. She came to La Scala in 1908 and was highly successful there until 1917. She was greatly admired there in 1908 as Giulia in Spontini's *La Vestale* and in 1909 she sang the title role in Cherubini's *Medea* so well that the opera seemed newly discovered after long oblivion. She sang Aïda opposite Giovanni Zenatello in the first Arena Festival in 1913. She was enormously successful in Spain and South America and she also appeared as guest in other western European countries. She had a dramatic soprano voice in which were joined both great mastery of singing technique and forceful intensity of expression.

Records: Many recordings for Fonotipia. *U.S. re-recording:* Eterna.

McCORMACK, JOHN, tenor, b. June 14, 1884, Athlone, Ireland; d. Sept. 16, 1945, Dublin. He began his vocal studies with Vincent O'Brien in Dublin and in 1902 he won a singing competition there. About 1904 he sang at the World Exposition in St. Louis. After further study with Vincenzo Sabatini in Milan, he made his debut under the name Giovanni Foli in Savona as the hero in *L'Amico Fritz*. In 1906 he gave successful concerts in London and in 1907 he sang for the first time at Covent Garden, making his debut as Turiddu in *Cavalleria Rusticana*. He continued his triumphs by singing there annually until 1914. In 1909 he appeared as guest at the Teatro San Carlo, but without particular success. In 1910 he sang at the Teatro Regio in Parma opposite Luisa Tetrazzini in *La Fille du Régiment*. In 1909 he was engaged at the Manhattan Opera House in New York and thereafter he was extraordinarily successful in the United States. In 1910 he belonged to the Chicago-Philadelphia Opera Company and in the same year he made his debut at the Metropolitan Opera, of which he was a member (1912-14; 1917-18). In 1912 he began long concert tours and thereafter was celebrated in the concert halls of the entire world. Towards the end of his career he appeared rarely on the operatic stage, for example, in Monte Carlo in 1921 and 1923. In 1919 he applied for American citizenship and he was later made a Papal Count. In 1938 he gave his farewell concert in London and lived thereafter in Ireland. He made a number of successful motion pictures in the thirties. After Enrico Caruso he was esteemed the most famous tenor of his time. His voice was of exquisite tonal quality, equally polished in technical characteristics and in stylistic subtlety. He was admired on the stage in lyric roles and in the concert hall especially in Irish songs. His widow, Lily, wrote his biography, *I Hear You Calling Me* (1949).

Records: G & T (London, 1904), Odeon (London, 1906-08), HMV, Victor*, Edison* cylinders, and Pathé discs. *U.S. re-issue:* Columbia-Fonotipia, Okeh, CRS, American Odeon, IRCC, Victor, American Gramophone Society. *U.S. re-recordings:* RCA Victor, Camden, Angel, Eterna, TAP, ASCO, Scala, Avoca, FRP, CRS, Audio Rarities, Jay, Rococo, Cantilena.

McCRACKEN, JAMES, tenor, b. 1927, Gary, Ind. He first appeared in the United States in musicals and operettas. Then he was a pupil at the Metropolitan Opera, where he sang small roles (1952-56). In 1957 he went to Europe and studied for two years with Conati in Milan. After singing briefly in Bonn, he went to Zürich in 1959 and soon was enormously successful there. In 1960 he appeared as guest in Vienna, singing the role of Bacchus in *Ariadne auf Naxos*. Since then he has been engaged as a regular guest at the Vienna State Opera. He developed his voice into that of a heroic tenor and he has been especially admired in the title role of *Otello*. In 1963 he sang Manrico in *Il Trovatore* at the Salzburg Festival. He became a member of the Metropolitan Opera in 1965. He is married to the contralto Sandra Warfield.

Records: Allegro Royale* and Decca in *Fidelio*. U.S. re-issue: London.

MEADER, GEORGE, tenor, b. July 6, 1888, Minneapolis, Minn. He sang in a boys' choir in Pittsburgh, then studied law at the University of Minnesota. His voice was discovered during a vacation stay in Germany. He studied with Anna Schoen-Rene and made his concert debut in London (1908). After further study with Pauline Viardot-Garcia in Paris, he made his stage debut (1910) at the Leipzig Opera as the Steersman in *Der Fliegende Holländer*. He was engaged at the Stuttgart Opera in 1911 and there, on Oct. 25, 1912, he sang Scaramuccio in the world *première* of *Ariadne auf Naxos*. He was a highly successful concert singer; in 1913 he sang the tenor solo in Mahler's *Das Lied von der Erde* under Willem Mengelberg in Amsterdam. In the same year he sang the tenor part in a brilliant performance of Haydn's *Creation* in Berlin. He remained at Stuttgart until 1919 and then returned to the United States. He was engaged by the Metropolitan Opera in 1921 and remained there until 1932. He was especially admired in *buffo* roles, but also appeared in lyric parts. After he had had a brilliant success in 1931 opposite Maria Jeritza in *Boccaccio*, he turned to operettas and musicals and became well known in these circles in New York. Later he lived in Hollywood and took small parts in films there.

Records: HMV and Columbia*.

MEI-FIGNER, MEDEA, soprano-contralto, b. 1858, Florence, Italy; d. July 16, 1952, Paris. She was trained by Bianchi, Heinrich Panofka, and Carlotta Zucchi in Florence. She made her debut (1874) in Sinaluga, near Florence, as Azucena in *Il Trovatore*. She then had a successful career in Italy, including appearances at La Scala and guest appearances followed in Madrid, Barcelona, Bucharest, and South America. In 1887 she met the Russian tenor Nicolai Figner in Milan and later they were married. Both of them joined the Imperial Opera in St. Petersburg and she made her debut there (1887), singing Valentine in *Les Huguenots*. Thereafter the couple had brilliant careers in St. Petersburg, the society of Czarist Russia loading them both with honors. Peter Ilyich Tchaikovsky belonged to their circle of friends and he completed his opera *The Queen of Spades* while staying on their estate near Tula. In the world *première* of this opera on Dec. 7, 1890, at St. Petersburg, Medea Mei-Figner sang Lisa and Nicolai Figner sang Hermann. Further world *premières* in which this celebrated soprano sang were *Iolanthe* (1892), *Doubrovsky* (1895), and *Francesca da Rimini* by Napravnik (1902), all in St. Petersburg. In 1912 she made her farewell stage appearance at a gala presentation of *Carmen* in St. Petersburg, but after the Russian Revolution of 1917 she was forgotten. From 1919 on, she lived in Paris. She had a dark-timbred expressive voice, with which she could sing both soprano and contralto parts.

Records: Very rare records for G & T (St. Petersburg, 1900-01), including several duets with Nicolai Figner. *U.S. re-recording:* Belcanto.

MEISLE, KATHRYN, contralto, b. Oct. 12, 1899, Philadelphia. She began her music study at the age of five and gave concerts at the age of nine. When she was fifteen she played the piano in a silent film theater in Philadelphia. In 1912 she was soloist at Christ Episcopal Church there and then sang in a vocal quartet. In 1920 she made her debut as a concert contralto with the Minneapolis Symphony Orchestra. Her stage debut followed (1923), when she appeared as Erda in *Siegfried* with the Chicago Opera Company. She remained in Chicago until 1935 with great success and made guest appearances during this time in Los Angeles and San Francisco. In 1930 she undertook a concert tour of Europe. In the same year she was engaged by the Metropolitan Opera, making her debut there as Amneris in *Aida*. She remained at the Metropolitan until 1938. She also sang in operettas and in 1950 sang in a revival of *Roberta*.

Records: Brunswick*, Victor* (*St. Matthew Passion* under Koussevitsky), and American Columbia*. She also made private recordings for the Metropolitan Opera.

MELANDER, STINA BRITT, soprano, b. June 12, 1924, Stockholm. She began her studies with Adelaide von Skilondz and Karl Nygren-Kloster in Stockholm. After 1945 she became a pupil at the Opera School in Stockholm, where she studied under Dobrowen; she made her debut there (1947). After she had great success at the Stockholm Opera and at the Gothenburg Lyric Theater, she became more widely known as a member of the Hamburg Opera. She has been a regular guest at the Berlin City Opera. She sings both coloratura and lyric roles.

Records: Ariola (*L'Elisir d'Amore*) and Electrola* (*Si j'étais roi*).

MELANDRI, ANTONIO, ténor, b. Feb. 11, 1891, Bologna, Italy. He studied the oboe at the Bologna Conservatory. His voice was discovered relatively late and he made his debut in Novara (1924). He quickly became known, particularly after Pietro Mascagni chose him to sing the role of Folco in a production of *Isabeau*, which was given in the Piazza San Marco in Venice. In 1926 he came to La Scala, making his debut as Kalaf in *Turandot*. He was highly successful at that house thereafter, singing in 1928 in the world *première* of *La Maddalena*. In 1927 he was applauded at the Teatro Colón and in 1937-38 at the Italian Opera in Holland. He made guest appearances in Germany, Belgium, Switzerland, and Chile and appeared regularly at the most important opera houses in Italy.

Records: He sang exclusively for Columbia* (including *Mefistofele* and *Cavalleria Rusticana* with Giannina Arangi-Lombardi, *Fedora*, and an abbreviated version of *Ernani*).

MELBA, NELLIE, soprano, b. May 19, 1861, near Melbourne, Australia; d. Feb. 23, 1931, Sydney. Originally Helen Mitchell. She took the name Melba in memory of her native city. Her family was of Scottish extraction and she was married to Captain Charles Porter Armstrong when she was quite young. Although she had appeared in the concert hall when she was only six years old, she did not decide to become a singer until after her separation from her husband in 1883. In 1885 she sang the soprano solo in a production of Handel's *Messiah* in Sydney and in 1886 she came to Europe for further study. She gave a concert in London and then went to Paris to study with the famous Mathilde Marchesi. She made her debut (1887) at the Brussels Opera as Gilda in *Rigoletto* and had great success in this role. In 1888 she was noted as Lucia di Lammermoor at Covent Garden. Her guest appearances, all outstanding successes, included the Paris Opéra (1889), St. Petersburg (1890), La Scala (1893), and the Metropolitan Opera (1893-96; 1898; 1902-03; 1905-06; 1911-12). She was honored as if she were a queen at the New York house. She sang at the Chicago Opera (1913-14). In 1904 she created the title role in *Hélène* at Monte Carlo. Guest appearances and concerts brought her triumph after triumph all over the world. She was for many years the prima donna of Covent Garden and at this house she made her last appearance at a gala performance in 1926. Even then her voice retained the fresh youthfulness of timbre which had marked it at the outset of her career. She was awarded the title Dame of the British Empire by the King of England. After 1926 she was president of the Melbourne Conservatory. She wrote her memoirs under the title *Melodies and Memories* (London, 1925). She had a legendary soprano voice of great beauty and a silvery timbre. Her coloratura roles were admirable for her technical mastery, and in lyric parts her voice was admired for its splendid tonal quality.

Records: Mapleson cylinders and records for G & T (London, 1904-06), Victor* (New York, 1907-09), and later for HMV. *U.S. re-issue:* RCA Victor, IRCC. *U.S. re-recording:* RCA Victor, IRCC, Belcanto, Scala, Angel, TAP, FRP, Design, Olympic, Rococo, ASCO, Fidelio, Cantilena.

MELCHERT, HELMUT, tenor, b. Sept. 24, 1910, Kiel, Germany. He first studied piano and musicology at the Music High School in Hamburg, but after 1934 he changed to the study of singing. He made his debut as a concert singer in 1936 and began his stage career in 1939 in Wuppertal. In 1943 he went to the State Opera in Hamburg, where he had great success, especially as a Wagner tenor. After World War II he appeared as guest at the Berlin City Opera, at Covent Garden, and in Vienna, Düsseldorf, Amsterdam, and Munich. In 1956 he sang the title role in *Oedipus Rex* at the Edinburgh Festival and in 1958 he appeared at the Salzburg Festival.

Records: HMV and Philips, including *Moses und Aron*. *U.S. re-issue:* Vox, Electrola, Telefunken.

MELCHIOR, LAURITZ, tenor, b. Mar. 20, 1890. Copenhagen. Originally Lebrecht Hommel. He began his vocal studies in 1908 with Paul Bang in Copenhagen and made his debut (1913) as a baritone in the role of Silvio in *I Pagliacci* at the Royal Opera in Copenhagen. During his engagement at this theater he studied with Vilhelm Herold (1917-18). After 1918 he sang tenor roles. He remained at the Copenhagen Opera until 1921 and often appeared there later as a guest. Further study followed with Victor Beigel in London, Ernst Grenzebach in Berlin, and with Anna Bahr-Mildenburg in Munich. He appeared with sensational success at Covent Garden in 1924 and thereafter was an annual guest in London. He was the chief attraction at the Bayreuth Festivals (1924-31) and was esteemed to be uncontestedly the greatest Wagner tenor of his time. He developed a great friendship with Cosima and Siegfried Wagner. He was a regular guest at the Berlin State Opera (1935-39) and he also appeared as guest in Vienna, Munich, Paris, Brussels, Milan, Stockholm, Chicago, and San Francisco. In 1926 he was engaged at the Metropolitan Opera, making his debut as Tannhäuser. He -experienced triumph after triumph at this house until he left in 1950. After 1949 he also appeared in films in America. After he had given up his operatic career, he appeared in operettas, musicals, and revues. He lives in Beverly Hills, California. The voice of Lauritz Melchior incorporated the ideal qualities of the heroic tenor: its baritone warmth, its brilliance in dramatic conception—all of which gave his Wagner roles something unmatchable. He also sang other roles.

Records: Polydor, Parlophone, Brunswick*, HMV, and RCA Victor*. *U.S. re-recording:* ASCO, RCA Victor, Camden, Angel, Electrola, TAP, Columbia.

MELCHISSÈDEC, LÉON, baritone, b. May 7, 1843, Clermont-Ferrand, France; d. Mar. 23, 1925, Paris. He studied at the National Conservatory in Paris and made his debut (1866) at the Opéra-Comique there, remaining until 1877. In that year he changed to the Théâtre Lyrique where he sang in the world *première* of *Le Timbre d'Argent* in 1877. In 1879 he was engaged at the Paris Opéra, making his debut as Nevers in *Les Huguenots*. He was highly successful and sang there until 1891, returning from 1905-12. At the Paris Opéra he sang in the world *première* of *Le Tribut de Zamora* in 1881 and in 1888 in the newly revised version of *Roméo et Juliette*, with a cast including Adelina Patti and Jean and Edouard de Reszke. After 1894 he was a professor at the Paris Conservatory; he published several writings on the teaching of singing. He possessed a technically finished and outstandingly expressive voice.

Records: A few rare records were made for APGA and Odeon. There is also one for Zonophone (Paris, 1902). *U.S. re-recording:* Rococo.

MELIS, CARMEN, soprano, b. Apr. 14, 1885, Cagliari, Sardinia; d. Dec. 19, 1967, Italy. She first studied in Milan and then with Jean de Reszke in Paris and made her debut (1905) singing the title role in *Thaïs* in Novara. Her first success came when she sang *Iris* at the Teatro San Carlo in 1906. She made a guest-appearance tour of Russia in 1907. In 1909 she came to the Manhattan Opera House, making her debut as Tosca. She sang with the Boston Opera Company (1911-13) and also sang in Philadelphia, Chicago, and San Francisco. She was highly successful in the United States as a concert soprano. She made a starring guest appearance at the Teatro Colón in 1917. In Europe she was particularly admired at the Paris Opéra, where in 1913 she sang in the first Paris production of *La Fanciulla del West* with Enrico Caruso and Titta Ruffo in the cast. In the 1920's she was one of the great prima donnas both of La Scala and of the Teatro Costanzi. At the latter in 1923 she sang in the world *première* of *Petronio* and at the former in *La Cena delle Beffe* in 1924. In 1929 she again appeared as guest at Covent Garden. She lived and taught later in Milan, where she included Renata Tebaldi among her pupils.

Records: Fonotipia, Columbia, HMV (*Tosca*), Edison* cylinders and discs, and Zonophone*. *U.S. re-issue:* Victor. *U.S. re-recording:* IRCC, FRP, Rococo.

MELMS, HANS, baritone, b. 1869, Berlin; d. Aug. 28, 1941, Berlin. He made his debut in Altenburg in 1892. His later engagements included: Würzburg (1893-94), Olmütz (1894-95), Chemnitz (1895-

97), Cologne (1897-98), the Vienna Imperial Opera, where he made his debut as Tonio in *I Pagliacci* (1898-1902), the Berlin National Theater (1903-05), the Vienna Volksoper (1905-07). In 1907 he returned to the Vienna Imperial Opera and remained there until 1918. He sang in Lucerne (1919-20). Later he lived in Berlin where, completely reduced to poverty, he played small roles in films. A strong, expressive baritone voice.

Records: Odeon (Vienna, 1906-08) and Zonophone (Vienna, 1908-09); also Edison cylinders.

MELTON, JAMES, tenor, b. Jan. 2, 1904, Moultrie, Ga.; d. Apr. 21, 1961, New York. As a student he played the saxophone in a dance band, then studied singing with Gaetano de Luca in Nashville, later with Enrico Rosati in New York. In 1927 he joined the "Roxy's Gang" troupe of performers. Later he undertook a tour of both the United States and Europe with a male quartet, "The Revellers." After renewed study with Michael Raucheisen in Berlin, he gave his first serious concert in New York's Town Hall (1932). He became known later as a radio singer, singing popular music, and sang in a number of motion pictures. He made his stage debut (1938) as Pinkerton in *Madama Butterfly* in Cincinnati. He sang with the San Carlo Opera Company (1939) and made very successful appearances at the Chicago Opera (1940-42). He was engaged at the Metropolitan Opera in 1942, making his debut as Tamino in *Die Zauberflöte*, and he remained there until 1950.

Records: RCA Victor*. *U.S. re-recording:* RCA Victor.

MENOTTI, TATIANA, soprano, b. June 24, 1911, Boston. She was the daughter of the Italian baritone Delfino Menotti, who at that time was engaged by the Boston Opera Company. She lived later in Trieste, where she was trained by her father. After further study in Vienna, she made her debut at the Vienna Volksoper (1931) as Olympia in *Les Contes d'Hoffmann*. She sang the same part in Berlin in a famous production of the opera by Max Reinhardt. During the following years she again appeared in Vienna and in Italy, particularly in operetta theaters. In 1935 she again returned to the operatic stage and specialized in soubrette parts. After 1935 she sang for several seasons at La Scala, making her debut there as Oscar in *Un Ballo in Maschera*. In 1938 she appeared as guest in Amsterdam as Cherubino in *Le Nozze di Figaro*. In 1939 she sang Despina in *Così fan tutte* at the Glyndebourne Festival. After World War II she sang in Switzerland and at the Edinburgh Festivals. She is married to the Spanish tenor Juan Oncina.

Records: She made one Columbia record about the time of her debut and later records for HMV (including Musetta in *La Bohème* with Beniamino Gigli). *U.S. re-issue:* RCA Victor.

MENZINSKY, MODEST, tenor, b. Apr. 29, 1875, Novosiolki, Galicia; d. Dec. 11, 1935, Stockholm. The son of a Russian Orthodox priest, he first studied theology at the University of Lemberg; he then studied singing with Julius Stockhausen in Frankfurt a. M. (1899-1903) and made his debut (1902) in Elberfeld. He was a member of the Stockholm Royal Opera (1904-10) and was engaged at the Cologne Opera (1910-26). Guest appearances took him to the Vienna Imperial Opera, Covent Garden, and other famous opera houses, all with great success. In 1924 he sang the part of Christobald in the world *première* of *Irrelohe* at Frankfurt. After 1926 he

lived in Stockholm, where he gave concerts and taught singing.
Records: Pathé and HMV.

MEO, CLÉONTINE DE, soprano, b. 1904, Paris; d. Aug. 1930, Paris. She studied at the National Conservatory in Paris, where she won several prizes and made her debut (1927) at the Opéra there. She had great success in dramatic parts, such as Aïda, Agatha in *Der Freischütz*, Tosca, and Sieglinde in *Die Walküre*. Everything appeared to point toward a great artistic career for this singer, when, in a fit of melancholy, she shot herself.
Records: One record for Columbia.

MERLI, FRANCESCO, tenor, b. Jan. 27, 1887, Milan. He studied with Borghi there and made his debut (1914) as Elisero in *Mosè*. After first singing in the Italian provinces, he made very successful guest appearances in 1916 at the Teatro Colón. In 1922 he made his La Scala debut as Walther in *Die Meistersinger*. Thereafter he was heard regularly at La Scala until 1946, his career there being greatly helped by Arturo Toscanini. In the 1920's he appeared regularly at the Teatro Colón and from 1926-30 at Covent Garden. He sang with great success at the Teatro Costanzi and on other important Italian stages. In 1932 he was engaged at the Metropolitan Opera, but after a month he fell ill and returned to Italy. He appeared in Italy until 1950, and thereafter was a teacher in Milan. With a large and well-managed heroic tenor voice, he was admired in the Italian repertory and in a few Wagner parts.
Records: Columbia* (*Il Trovatore* and *I Pagliacci*) and Cetra* (*Norma* and *Turandot*). *U.S. re-recording:* Eterna, TAP.

MERREM-NIKISCH, GRETE, soprano, b. July 7, 1887, Düren, Germany. She studied with Schulz-Dornburg in Cologne, with Marie Hedmont at the Leipzig Conservatory, and made her debut in the latter city (1910), remaining there until 1913. In 1911 she made a guest appearance at the Berlin Imperial Opera as the Goose Girl in *Königskinder*. She sang at the Dresden Opera (1913-30) and she was admired there in soubrette parts, in lyric roles, and in youthful dramatic parts, such as Eva in *Die Meistersinger* and Sophie in *Der Rosenkavalier*. In 1916 she sang the role of Arsinoë in the world *première* of *Die Toten Augen* in Dresden. After 1914 she was married to Arthur Nikisch, Jr., the lawyer and eldest son of the famous conductor-pianist. Her father-in-law frequently accompanied her in the lieder recitals that she gave after 1918 with increasing success. She lives in Kiel, where her husband is a professor at the university.
Records: Odeon-Parlophone and Polydor. *U.S. re-issue:* Columbia, American Decca.

MERRILL, ROBERT, baritone, b. 1919, New York. He completed his vocal studies in New York and then sang for various radio stations. He was engaged by the Metropolitan Opera in 1945 and made his debut as the elder Germont in a production of *La Traviata* with Jan Peerce and Licia Albanese. Since then he has had a highly successful career there as a principal baritone. Guest appearances in Chicago, San Francisco, Europe—principally in Italy—and in South America have made him one of the most famous American singers of his time. In 1945 he sang before both Houses of Congress at the memorial services for President Franklin Delano Roosevelt. In 1960 he had brilliant successes in guest appearances in Milan and Venice. He was married for a time to the soprano Roberta Peters. He published his autobiography, *Once More from the Beginning* (New York, 1965). The warmth and volume of his baritone voice are greatly admired as well as his variety of characterizations; his starring roles are in the Italian repertory.

Records: A great many complete opera recordings for RCA Victor*, HMV, and Decca (including *Cavalleria Rusticana, I Pagliacci, Rigoletto, La Bohème, La Traviata, Carmen, Il Barbiere di Siviglia,* and *Manon Lescaut*). *U.S. re-issue:* Columbia, London, Everest, Camden, Seraphim.

MERRIMAN, NAN, contralto, b. Apr. 28, 1920, Pittsburgh. She was brought up in Los Angeles, where she studied and where (1940) she made her debut as a concert singer. She became famous through her concerts and in 1943 had great success in opera production on the radio under Toscanini. After World War II she began an extraordinary concert and guest-appearance activity, particularly in Europe. She was greatly admired at the Festivals in Edinburgh and Glyndebourne in *The Rake's Progress* (1952) as well as the Aix-en-Provence and Holland Festivals. Her operatic guest appearances included the Vienna State Opera, the Paris Opéra, La Scala (1955), Brussels, Amsterdam, Chicago, and San Francisco. She is celebrated for a wide-ranging stage repertory, her starring role being Dorabella in *Così fan tutte,* as well as for her work as a concert contralto.

Records: RCA Victor* (*Falstaff* under Toscanini), Columbia* (*Così fan tutte*), HMV (*Falstaff, Rigoletto,* and *Otello*), and Philips. *U.S. re-issue:* Westminster, Epic, Angel, Electrola, DGG.

METCALFE, SUSAN, contralto, b. 1884 (?). Although this American singer belonged to the most famous interpreters of lieder of her time, scarcely any details of her artistic career are known. She first excited great attention during a tour of Holland in 1909, which included appearances with the Concertgebouw Orchestra of Amsterdam under Willem Mengelberg. This was followed in 1910 by a long concert tour through Germany and Denmark. She had notable success in London in the autumn of 1910. In 1914 she married Pablo Casals, from whom she was later separated. After she had not been seen or heard from in a long time, she appeared again as a lieder singer in France and Holland in 1929. She then took up her residence in France and in 1936 sang in a series of concerts for the British Broadcasting Corporation. The voice of this artist was one of the most beautiful ever captured on records, both for the expressiveness of her vocal shading and the delicacy of her phrasing in the singing of art songs.

Records: A few private recordings for HMV.

METTERNICH, JOSEF, baritone, b. June 2, 1915, Hermühlheim, Germany. He worked as a violinist in a dance orchestra to pay for his singing lessons, and he graduated from the chorus of the opera houses in Bonn and Cologne to the singing of solo parts. In 1945 he made his debut at the Berlin City Opera as Tonio in *I Pagliacci.* He also continued his studies with the intendant of the City Opera Michael Bohnen. He reached international fame through his guest appearances, which included Covent Garden, La Scala, the Vienna State Opera, and the Edinburgh Festivals. He was a member of the Metropolitan Opera (1953-56), and there he sang both Wagner roles and those in the Italian repertory. After 1954 he was engaged simultaneously by the State Operas in Munich and Hamburg. In 1957 he created the role of Johannes Kepler in *Harmonie die Welt* in Munich. He is married to the soprano Liselotte Losch.

Records: HMV, Philips (*Salome*), but mostly for DGG (including *Lohengrin, Der Fliegende Holländer,* and *Fidelio*). *U.S. re-issue:* Angel, Electrola.

METZGER-LATTERMANN, OTTILIE, contralto, b. July 15, 1878, Frankfurt a. M.; d. Feb. 1943 (?), Auschwitz, Poland. She studied with Frau Nicklass-Kempner and Emanuel Reicher in Berlin and made her debut (1898) at Halle. She then sang at the opera houses in Cologne (1900-03) and Hamburg (1903-15). Her important career began in Hamburg. She made guest appearances in Berlin, Vienna, St. Petersburg, Covent Garden, and in Brussels, Ostend, Budapest, and Munich. During 1901-12 she was greatly admired for her singing at the Bayreuth Festivals, particularly Erda and Waltraute in the *Ring* cycle. In 1902 she married the novelist Clemens Froitzheim, and in 1910 her second marriage was to the baritone Theodor Lattermann. She sang at the Dresden State Opera in 1917-21 and in 1922-23 undertook an American tour with the German Opera Company. Thereafter she lived in Berlin, made guest appearances, and gave concerts. In 1934 she was forced, because she was Jewish, to leave Germany, and she became a teacher in Brussels. After the invasion of Belgium she was arrested by the German authorities and sent to the concentration camp at Auschwitz, from which she never emerged.

Records: G & T, Parlophone, and Odeon records, as well as Edison* discs. There are also unpublished Homochord records. *U.S. re-issue:* Opera Disc, Columbia, American Odeon.

MEYER, KERSTIN, contralto, b. Apr. 3, 1928, Stockholm. She began her vocal studies at the age of fourteen and at sixteen entered the opera classes at the Royal Conservatory in Stockholm. She later studied in Milan and Vienna and made her debut (1952) at the Stockholm Royal Opera as Carmen, which has become one of her specialties. After 1954 she was frequently a guest at the Hamburg Opera, where she was particularly admired as a Wagner singer. Guest appearances also took her to Vienna, Covent Garden, Munich, and Copenhagen, as well as to the Salzburg Festivals after 1956. In 1959 she toured the United States. Since 1961 she has sung at the Metropolitan Opera. In 1956 she sang at the Bayreuth Festival.

Records: HMV. *U.S. re-issue:* Angel, Turnabout.

MEYER-WELFING, HUGO, tenor, b. Mar. 25, 1905, Hannover, Germany. He studied at the Conservatory in Hannover and made his debut (1928) in Osnabrück. In 1934 he came from Aachen to the Königsberg Opera, where he stayed until 1938. He was engaged by the Vienna Volksoper in 1938 and after 1945 he was a member of the Vienna State Opera. He has appeared at the Salzburg Festivals and was a respected concert and oratorio singer. Since 1956 he has been a professor at the Conservatory of the City of Vienna.

Records: Solo records for Odeon, later LP records of smaller roles in complete opera recordings for Decca. He has also recorded for Remington*, Counterpoint, and MMS. *U.S. re-issue:* Bach Guild, Haydn Society, Richmond.

MICHAELIS, RUTH, contralto, b. Feb. 27, 1909, Posen, Poland. She studied with Hans Beltz and Jeanne Robert in Berlin, as well as with Anna Bahr-Mildenburg in Munich, and she made her debut in Halberstadt (1933). She then sang in Kottbus and Augsburg and in 1937 came to the Munich State Opera. There she had a successful career for over twenty years. In 1942 she appeared at the Salzburg Festival. After the close of her active singing career, she taught in Munich and since 1956 has been a professor at the National Opera School in Istanbul, Turkey. This singer was greatly admired both on the stage and in the concert hall, especially as an interpreter of Bach.

Records: DGG* and Remington* (including Christmas Oratorio of Bach). U.S. re-issue: Baroque.

MICHAILOWA, MARIA, soprano, b. 1864, Kharkov, Russia. Originally Maria van Puteren. She came of a family of Dutch origin. She began her singing studies with Mme. Groewing-Wilde in Kharkov and at the Conservatory in St. Petersburg; she then studied with Bakst in Paris and Rauzzoni in Milan and made her debut (1892) at the Maryinsky Theater in St. Petersburg as Queen Marguerite in Les Huguenots. In 1892 she sang a small role in the world première there of Iolanthe. During her entire career she remained in St. Petersburg, where she was enthusiastically admired by the society of Czarist Russia. She became world-famous through her phonograph records, which first appeared in 1900 and stirred up great excitement everywhere. Despite the international acclaim, she would not leave her native land. Oscar Hammerstein tried in vain to sign her up for his Manhattan Opera House. She did, however, make one concert tour of Japan. In 1912 she left the stage after singing Antonida in A Life for the Czar at a performance in the Maryinsky Theater in St. Petersburg. She lived later in Leningrad, but the date of her death is uncertain. Her voice was one of the most beautiful captured on the early phonograph. In her interpretations, mastery of vocal technique, and fine sense of style in her delivery were equally balanced.

Records: A great many records, the oldest for Berliner (1900-01), then G & T (1900 and later), Columbia*, Lyrophone, HMV, and Pathé; she made one record for Amour. U.S. re-issue: Victor. U.S. re-recording: Scala, Belcanto, TAP.

MICHALSKY, ANNE, soprano, b. July 19, 1908, Prague. She studied at the Music Academy in Vienna and made her debut at the State Opera there (1928) as Micäela in Carmen, remaining at this house until 1953. She made successful guest appearances in Barcelona, Paris, Dresden, and Stuttgart. She sang at the Salzburg Festivals (1928, 1931-37, 1939, and 1941) in such parts as Zerlina in Don Giovanni and Barbarina in Le Nozze di Figaro. She sang in operetta at the Neuen Lustspielhaus in Berlin (1942-43). In 1951 she sang a small role in Elektra at the Maggio Musicale Festival. Since 1953 she has lived and taught in Vienna. She is married to the chief literary editor of the Vienna State Opera, Wilhelm Jarosch.

Records: Polydor (the Duenna in Der Rosenkavalier, 1934), Remington* (Kate in Madama Butterfly, 1953), and Cetra (a small part in Elektra, 1951). U.S. re-issue: RCA Victor. U.S. re-recording: Angel.

MICHEAU, JANINE, soprano, b. Apr. 17, 1914, Toulouse, France. She studied at the Conservatories in Toulouse and Paris and made her debut at the Opéra-Comique in 1933, singing Cherubino in Le Nozze di Figaro. She subsequently had great success at both the principal opera houses in the French capital. At the Paris Opéra she sang the title role in the world première of Médée in 1938 and in 1950 the role of Manuela and in the world *première* of *Bolivar*. In 1941 at the Opéra-Comique she created the role of Caroline in *Comme ils s'aiment*. She also appeared with success on opera stages in France, Italy, Belgium, and Holland and made a long South American tour. She was the most important French coloratura soprano of her generation.

Records: Decca, HMV, Philips (including *Pelléas et Mélisande, Carmen* twice, *Roméo et Juliette, Les Pêcheurs de Perles*). *U.S. re-issue:* London, Angel, Epic, Pathé-Marconi.

MICHELETTI, GASTON, tenor, b. Jan. 5, 1892, Tavaco, Corsica; d. May 21, 1959, Ajaccio, Corsica. He studied at the National Conservatory in Paris and after he had sung in the French provinces, he was engaged at the Opéra-Comique in 1925, making his debut as Des Grieux in *Manon*. For the next two decades he remained one of the most prominent singers at that house. Although he made guest appearances in Brussels, Monte Carlo, and Nice, the Opéra-Comique remained the true center of his artistic activity. In 1946 he gave up his career and lived first as a teacher in Paris, then in Ajaccio.

Records: A great many records for Odeon. *U.S. re-issue:* American Decca.

MILANOV, ZINKA, soprano, b. May 17, 1906, Zagreb, Yugoslavia. She studied at the Music Academy in Zagreb with Milka Ternina, then with Carpi in Milan and with Jacques Stückgold in Berlin, finally completing her studies in Zagreb with B. Kunc, whom she married. She made her debut (1927) in Ljubljana and after 1931 sang at the Zagreb Opera. She was engaged at the Prague Opera (1936-37) and Arturo Toscanini chose her for the soprano solo in Verdi's *Requiem* for the Salzburg Festival in 1937; she had an overwhelming success there. After brilliant guest appearances at Covent Garden and the Vienna State Opera, she was engaged by the Metropolitan Opera in 1938, making her debut as Leonora in *Il Trovatore*. She had a highly successful career there for over twenty years; she made guest appearances in Chicago and San Francisco and was a very successful concert soprano. Her wide-ranging and expressive soprano voice was at its best in parts from the Italian repertory; she not only sang Verdi and Puccini roles, but also Norma and Giulia in Spontini's *La Vestale*.

Records: She sang exclusively for RCA Victor* (including *Tosca, Aïda, La Forza del Destino, Rigoletto* under Toscanini, *Un Ballo in Maschera, La Gioconda, Il Trovatore,* and *Cavalleria Rusticana*). *U.S. re-issue:* Victrola. *U.S. re-recording:* Halo.

MILDMAY, AUDREY, soprano, b. Dec. 19, 1900, Vancouver, Canada; d. May 31, 1953, Glyndebourne, England. She studied in London and sang coloratura parts with the Carl Rosa Opera Company. In 1931 she married John Christie, the English art dealer and landowner. They then built a small theater seating three hundred and fifty on their estate at Glyndebourne. After the famous conductor Fritz Busch had been won over to the idea, the Glyndebourne Festivals were launched in 1934. In the opening performance she sang Susanna in *Le Nozze di Figaro*. From 1934-39 she appeared on the stage at the Festivals as Susanna, Zerlina in *Don Giovanni*, and as Norina in *Don Pasquale*. She was able to witness the growth of Glyndebourne to a musical festival of the first rank. After World War II she was occupied in planning the productions at Glyndebourne. She died after a long illness.

Records: HMV (*Le Nozze di Fi-*

garo, Don Giovanni, and The Beggars' Opera from Glyndebourne). U.S. re-issue: RCA Victor. U.S. re-recording: Electrola, Vox.

MILINKOVIČ, GEORGINE VON, contralto, b. July 7, 1913, Prague. She came of a Croatian family and, after study in Zagreb and Vienna, made her debut (1937) in Zürich. From there she came in 1940 to the Bavarian State Opera in Munich. She caused great excitement when she sang Kundry in a performance of *Parsifal* which was broadcast in 1941 from the Dutch station in Hilversum. She was engaged at the Prague Opera House (1945-48), but also continued to make guest appearances during that time in Munich and Vienna. After 1948 she was a member of both the Vienna and Munich Operas. After 1951 she had great successes at the Bayreuth Festivals, the Salzburg Festivals, and those at Edinburgh and in Holland as well. In Salzburg she sang in the world *première* of *Die Liebe der Danaë* on Aug. 15, 1952, and later she sang Octavian in *Der Rosenkavalier* and Marcellina in *Le Nozze di Figaro* there. She was also highly successful in guest appearances at Covent Garden and in concert tours.

Records: DGG, Vox (*Der Rosenkavalier*, 1940) and Philips (*Salome*). U.S. re-issue: Haydn Society, Vox, Epic.

MILL, ARNOLD VAN, bass, b. Mar. 26, 1921, Schiedam, Holland. He completed the courses at the Conservatories in Amsterdam and The Hague and finished his studies with Beyk. He made his debut (1946) at the Brussels Opera. In the following years he sang as guest in Holland and Belgium and in 1950 was engaged at the Antwerp Opera. He sang at Wiesbaden (1951-53) and since 1953 has been a highly successful member of the Hamburg State Opera. He has sung at the Bayreuth Festivals since 1951 in various roles. He has also sung as guest at the Vienna State Opera, the Paris Opéra, the Teatro São Carlos, the Rio de Janeiro Opera, and has made very successful appearances at the Holland and Edinburgh Festivals. His bass voice has been admired both for its size and for the forceful quality of his dramatic expressiveness.

Records: Decca (King Mark in *Tristan und Isolde*, Hunding in *Die Walküre*, Titurel in *Parsifal*, and Ramfis in *Aïda*) and RCA Victor* (*Don Giovanni*). U.S. re-issue: London, Electrola.

MILLIGAN, JAMES, bass, b. Apr. 5, 1928, Halifax, Nova Scotia; d. Nov. 28, 1961, Basel. After original activity as a concert singer, he made his stage debut in Toronto (1955). In 1957 he won first prize in a singing competition in Geneva. After 1960 he was under contract to the Municipal Theater in Basel. In 1960 he sang at the Glyndebourne Festival and in 1960-61 at Covent Garden. In the same year he was greatly admired at the Bayreuth Festival as the Wanderer in *Siegfried*. The great international career which had been anticipated for him was suddenly ended by his death.

Records: Bass soloist in *The Messiah* for Canadian Victor. U.S. re-recording: Angel.

MÍNGHETTI, ANGELO, tenor, b. Dec. 6, 1889, Bologna, Italy; d. April 1957, Milan. He made his debut about 1920 and had his first great success in that year at the Teatro Massimo. In 1921 he sang at the Opera in Rio de Janeiro and 1922-24 at the Chicago Opera. In 1923 he came to La Scala, his debut role being Rodolfo in *La Bohème* and he was also successful there in 1925 and again in 1932. In 1924 he sang as guest at the Teatro Colón and in 1926, 1930, and 1933-34 at Covent Garden. He had a famous career in the Italian opera houses, where he was especially admired in

La Bohème. At the end of the 1930's he gave up his career.

Records: Three electric HMV records (London, 1926).

MINGHINI-CATTANEO, IRENE, contralto, b. Apr. 12, 1892, near Ravenna, Italy; d. Mar. 24, 1944, Rimini, Italy, from an airplane attack on her villa there. She studied with Ettore Cattaneo, the director of the Ricordi music publishing firm in Milan, whom she later married, and made her debut (1918) at Savona as Azucena in *Il Trovatore*. She made guest appearances at the Teatro dal Verme, in Turin, at the Teatro Costanzi, and in Nice and Zürich and sang at the Arena Festivals (1925-27). She first appeared at La Scala in 1928 and had great success there. She made guest appearances at Covent Garden (1928-30) and was greatly beloved in South America; her other guest appearances were in Germany, Austria, and Egypt. After 1935 she sang dramatic soprano roles. The almost boundless size of her voice and the expressive skill of her characterizations made her one of the most famous contraltos of her generation.

Records: Columbia and HMV (including *Aïda* and *Il Trovatore*). *U.S. re-issue:* RCA Victor.

MIURA, TAMAKI, soprano, b. 1884, Tokyo; d. May 26, 1946, Tokyo. She studied at the Tokyo Music Academy and in Germany and made her debut at the Tokyo Opera (1914) as Santuzza in *Cavalleria Rusticana*. She came to England in 1915 and had a sensational success there in the title role of *Madama Butterfly* under Sir Thomas Beecham. She also sang this role with success in Boston (1915), in Chicago (1918), and in Monte Carlo and Barcelona (1920). She was very successful in Italy, where she appeared in 1921 at the Teatro Costanzi and on other important stages. In 1924 she made a tour of the United States with the San Carlo Opera Company. In 1926 she sang in San Francisco in the world *première* of *Namiko San*, which was composed especially for her. In 1930 she returned to Japan, but toured Italy again in 1932. Thereafter she remained in Japan until her death and occupied herself as a radio singer. Tamaki Miura was the first and most famous of a long line of Japanese and Asiatic singers who excited great comment in the roles of Madama Butterfly and Iris in Mascagni's opera, both by their authentic costumes and by their correct acting of the parts. Among her successors may be named Toshiko Hasegawa, Nobuko Hara, Theiko Kiwa, Hizi Koyke, Yovita Fuentes, and Isang Tapales.

Records: Acoustic records for American Columbia*, including Japanese folk songs; electric records for Victor* which were never published in Japan.

MÖDL, MARTHA, soprano, b. Mar. 22, 1913, Nuremberg. She worked first for a Nuremberg transportation firm and then became a bookkeeper. She was able to begin her vocal studies at the age of twenty-eight at the Conservatory in Nuremberg. She made her debut in Remscheid (1943) as Hänsel in *Hänsel und Gretel*. In the early years of her career she sang contralto parts. She was engaged as a contralto at the Düsseldorf Opera (1945-49), but her voice changed there to a dramatic soprano. In 1949 she came to the Hamburg Opera and developed into a celebrated Wagner singer. In 1951 she sang Kundry in *Parsifal* and Gutrune in the *Ring* cycle at the first Bayreuth Festival after World War II. Later she was particularly admired as Brünnhilde and she has sung at Bayreuth every year since 1951. In 1952 she accepted an engagement at the Vienna State Opera and after 1953 she was simultaneously a member of the Stuttgart Opera. Guest appearances brought her great successes at La Scala, Covent Garden, the Paris Opéra, and on the most important German stages; she has also sung at the Salzburg Festivals. In 1956 she first sang at the Metropolitan Opera. She sang Leonora in *Fidelio* at the first performance in the newly reconstructed Vienna State Opera on Nov. 5, 1955. Her sumptuous voice and fascinating characterizations made her interpretations—particularly of the great Wagner heroines—unforgettable.

Records: HMV (*Die Walküre* and *Fidelio*), Cetra* (*Elektra*), Philips (*Oedipus Rex*), Decca (*Parsifal*), DGG* (*Die Frau ohne Schatten*) and Telefunken. *U.S. re-issue:* Electrola, Columbia, London, Seraphim.

MÖDLINGER, JOSEF, bass, b. Feb. 3, 1848, Leoben, Austria; d. Apr. 14, 1927, Berlin. As a boy soprano he sang in the choir of the Benedictine Abbey of St. Lamprecht; then he studied philology at the university in Graz and played the cello in the orchestra of the theater there. After studying singing with Frau Weinlich-Tipka in Graz, he made his debut (1869) in Zürich as the Cardinal in *La Juive*. At the time of the conquest of Bosnia by Austria, he broke off his career and took part in that campaign as an officer in the Austrian army. He sang in Mannheim (1876-90) and was principal bass at the Berlin Imperial Opera (1890-1912). After the end of his stage career he lived and taught in Berlin. His brother, Ludwig Mödlinger, was also a successful singer and an operatic *régisseur*.

Records: Very rare records for Odeon (Berlin, 1905) and one duet with Hermann Jadlowker which was recorded in 1910. There is a cylinder, made about 1901, on which he was announced as the singer, but it is a forgery.

MOEST, RUDOLF, bass, b. Apr. 22, 1872, Karlsruhe, Germany; d. Apr. 28, 1919, Vienna. He studied with Franz Krükl in Strasbourg and with Carl Hermann in Frankfurt. He made his debut in Strasbourg (1892) as Ruggiero in *La Juive*. He sang in Strasbourg until 1896 and was an esteemed member of the Hannover Opera (1896-1914). In 1914 he was engaged by the Vienna Imperial Opera, where he had already appeared as a guest in 1900. At the Bayreuth Festival of 1909 he sang King Henry in *Lohengrin*. He possessed a strong, expressive bass voice.

Records: Parlophone, Odeon, and Pathé records, all from his Hannover period.

MOFFO, ANNA, soprano, b. June 27, 1933, Wayne, Pa. Her family was of Italian extraction and she studied at the Curtis Institute of Music in Philadelphia before going to Italy to study at the Accademia di Santa Cecilia in Rome. Her debut occurred (1955) at the Rome Opera. After she had great success at the Teatro San Carlo, she appeared at La Scala, the Vienna State Opera, in Munich, and in Paris. In 1957 she sang Ann Ford in *Falstaff* at the Salzburg Festival, and she has sung there repeatedly since; in the same year she also appeared at La Scala. She is married to the *régisseur* Mario Lanfranchi. In 1959 she came to the Metropolitan Opera, making her debut as Violetta in *La Traviata*. There, as well as at the opera houses in Chicago and San Francisco and at the Teatro Colón, she continued her series of triumphs. In 1962 she was greatly admired at the Metropolitan as Mélisande in *Pelléas et Mélisande* under Ernest Ansermet. She has a beautiful coloratura voice, perfectly trained. Her success in the concert hall has equalled that of her stage appearances.

Records: Columbia* (*La Bohème* and *Falstaff*) and RCA Victor* (*Madama Butterfly*, *La Bohème*, and *Rigoletto*). U.S. re-issue: Angel, Vox, Victrola.

MOJICA, JOSÉ, tenor, b. Apr. 14, 1896, Mexico City. He made his debut (1919) at the Chicago Opera. At first he sang small roles there, but later assumed more important parts with great success. In 1921 he sang in the world *première* there of *The Love of Three Oranges*. He was very successful as partner to Mary Garden in *Pelléas et Mélisande*, and he remained at the Chicago Opera until 1930. He sang only once in Europe—at a concert in the Mexican Embassy in Berlin. After 1930 he had success in American films (*One Mad Kiss*) and in Spanish films; he was particularly well liked in South America. In 1940 he sang Fenton in *Falstaff* a few times at the Chicago Opera. When his mother died in 1943, he made her a deathbed promise to become a priest. He then entered a religious order, took priestly vows, and went as a missionary to the Andes region of Peru. In 1954 he undertook a concert tour through Mexico and Central America for his religious order. He lives on his missionary station in Peru. He is now completely deaf. A lyric tenor voice greatly admired for its expressive use and for the richness of shading in his handling of it.

Records: Edison* and Victor* records. *U.S. re-recording:* IRCC.

MOLINARI, ENRICO, bass-baritone, b. 1883; d. Apr. 4, 1956, Milan. He studied at the Liceo Musicale Marcello in Venice and made his debut (1907) as a bass; he sang as such for several years on Italian stages. After renewed study he made his debut as a baritone (1916) in Palermo as King Alfonso in *La Favorita*. He had great success in the years after World War I at the Teatro Costanzi and in guest appearances at the Teatro Liceo. He came to La Scala in 1924 and was equally successful there, as he was also in guest appearances in Budapest, Bucharest, Lisbon, Monte Carlo, and Madrid. In the 1930's his voice changed again and he appeared as a *buffo* bass at all the leading Italian opera houses, particularly as Lunardo in *I Quattro Rusteghi*. In 1950 he gave up his career and retired to the Casa di Riposo which Verdi founded in Milan.

Records: His first records, made as a bass, appeared on HMV; as a baritone he sang for Columbia* (including *Tosca* and *Il Trovatore*); he also made Edison cylinders. *U.S. re-issue:* RCA Victor.

MOLLET, PIERRE. baritone, b. Mar. 23, 1920, Neuchâtel, Switzerland. He studied first in his home city, then at the Conservatories in Lausanne and Basel. He began his career as a concert singer in 1948. After successful concerts in Paris and Switzerland, he was engaged by the Opéra-Comique in 1952; he was especially admired there as Pelleás in *Pelléas et Mélisande*. He is also the most admired concert singer in France in his generation. On the one hand, he is a famous oratorio singer—a particularly great Bach interpreter—and on the other, an esteemed singer of lieder and art songs. Not the least of his accomplishments is his dedication to contemporary music; he was helped in the study of Arthur Honneger's works by the composer himself.

Records: Decca (*Pelléas et Mélisande*) and Pathé (*Iphigénie en Tauride*). *U.S. re-issue:* DGG, London.

MONTESANTO, LUIGI, baritone, b. Nov. 23, 1887, Palermo, Sicily; d. June 14, 1954, Milan. He studied with Santorno in Palermo and made his debut there (1909) as Escamillo in *Carmen*. His career developed very quickly in Italy; in 1912 he sang in Palermo in the world *première* of *Il Battista*. In 1913 he was admired as Figaro in *Il Barbiere di Siviglia* at the opening season of the Théâtre des Champs-Elysées. In 1913 he was also a member of the Western Metropolitan Opera Company, with which he toured the United States. Still in 1913 he sang as guest at the Teatro Colón, where he created the role of Jochanaan in the first performance there of *Salome*. In 1918 he came to the Metropolitan Opera, making his debut as Marcello in *La Bohème*. There, on Dec. 14, 1918, he sang Michele in the world *première* of *Il Tabarro*. In 1920 he sang as guest at Monte Carlo and he was a member of the Chicago Opera (1926-29). He also had a very important career at La Scala, the Teatro Costanzi, and other important Italian opera houses. In 1937 he appeared at the Italian Opera in Holland. In 1940 he retired from the stage and lived and taught in Milan; Giuseppe di Stefano was one of his pupils.

Records: Columbia, Fonotipia, HMV, and Pathé, *U.S. re-recording:* Pathé Actuelle, Pathé Perfect, Eterna.

MONTI, NICOLA, tenor, b. Nov. 21, 1920, Milan. Since his family was poor, he had to choose a practical calling and studied singing at night. In 1940 he gave his first concert, in Sardinia, and made his debut at the Cagliari Opera as the Duke in *Rigoletto* in the same year. After World War II he took a job in an apothecary shop, but in 1950 he entered the opera classes at La Scala in Milan. In 1951 he assumed his first important roles at the Teatro San Carlo and in 1955 he was brilliantly successful at La Scala. He also made guest appearances in Paris, Brussels, and the United States. He was greatly admired at the Arena and Maggio Musicale Festivals. At the Holland Festival in 1957 he sang Ernesto in *Don Pasquale*. A clear and beautiful lyric tenor voice.

Records: HMV (*Il Barbiere di Siviglia* and *L'Elisir d'Amore*), Columbia (*La Sonnambula*), DGG* (*Il Barbiere di Siviglia*) and Decca (*La Sonnambula*). *U.S. re-issue:* Angel, London, Mercury, Capitol, RCA Victor.

MOORE, GRACE, soprano, b. Dec. 5, 1901, Jellicoe, Tenn.; d. Jan. 26, 1947, Copenhagen, in an airplane accident at Kastrup Airport. She studied first in Nashville and Washington and after 1919 with Marafiori in New York. She then appeared in operettas and revues. In 1926 she went to Europe, studied further in Paris and Milan, and made her debut (1928) at the Metropolitan Opera as Mimi in *La Bohème*. From 1928-32 and from 1934 until her death she was a member of the Metropolitan Opera. She had great success through concerts and guest appearances all over the world. She appeared as guest in Paris, London, Amsterdam, Vienna, Berlin, and Stockholm. In 1930 she began one of the most brilliant careers any singer ever had in films. Her most famous film was *One Night of Love* (1935) and she also starred as the heroine in a film version of *Louise*. She had her greatest successes in the lyric parts of the French and Italian repertories.

Records: Brunswick* and Victor*. Private recordings for the Metropolitan Opera (including *L'Amore dei Tre Re*, *Tosca*, and *Manon*). *U.S. re-recording:* American Decca, TAP, RCA Victor, Camden.

MORENA, BERTA, soprano, b. Jan. 27, 1878, Mannheim, Germany; d. Oct. 7, 1952, Rottach-Egern, Germany. Originally Berta Meyer. She studied with Frau Röhr-Brajnin and with Aglaia von Origeni in

Munich and made her debut at the Royal Opera there (1898) as Agathe in *Der Freischütz*. She remained a member of this institution during her entire career. Guest appearances brought her voice before audiences all over the world, particularly as a dramatic and Wagner soprano. She had great success at the Metropolitan Opera (1908-12) and in 1914 at Covent Garden. She also appeared as guest at the Imperial Operas in Berlin and Vienna, at the Hamburg Opera, in London, Amsterdam, Barcelona, and in 1912 at the Budapest National Opera. In 1925 she again sang at the Metropolitan, appearing as Brünnhilde in *Götterdämmerung*. In 1927 she left the stage and lived as a teacher in Munich.

Records: G & T (Munich, 1907) and HMV.

MORESCHI, ALESSANDRO, castrato soprano, b. Nov. 11, 1858, Montecompatrio, Italy; d. Apr. 21, 1921, Rome. He was a student of Capocci in Rome. After 1883 he was the soprano soloist of the Capella Sistina and was believed to be the last *castrato* singer in Italy. He appeared with the Capella Sistina until 1913; he also was occupied as a teacher in Rome and was given the title "professor."

Records: In 1902 and 1904 his voice, with that of the Capella Sistina, was put on a few records by G & T. These very rare records are of the highest interest since the voice of a *castrato* soprano is documented on them. *U.S. re-issue:* Victor. *U.S. re-recording:* ASCO, Belcanto.

MOSCISCA, MARIA, soprano, b. 1885 (?), Poland. Originally Maria Mokrzycka. She began her career under her own name in her Polish homeland. She made her debut there (1908) at the Warsaw Opera in *Wanda*. Mattia Battistini, who was appearing as a guest at this time in Warsaw, advised the young singer to go to Italy. She sang there with him under the name Maria Moscisca on various operatic stages. In 1913 she undertook an American tour with the Western Metropolitan Opera Company. Nothing is known of her later career. Hers was a delicately spiritual, lyric soprano voice.

Records: In 1912, five duets by Moscisca and Battistini were recorded for HMV; these are—so far as is known—the only records she ever made. *U.S. re-issue:* Opera Disc, Victor, Columbia (one imported solo record). *U.S. re-recording:* Cantilena.

MOSCONA, NICOLA, bass, b. Sept. 23, 1907, Athens, Greece. He studied at the Athens Conservatory with Elena Theodorini and made his debut there (1929). In the following years he sang especially in Greece and Egypt and under the name Nicolai Mosconas. In 1937 he was given a scholarship for further study in Italy. However, he was immediately engaged in Italy by Edward Johnson for the Metropolitan Opera, where he made his debut as Ramfis in *Aida*. He was for twenty-five years a principal bass at the Metropolitan. He also sang at the San Francisco Opera and in 1938 made appearances in Florida; in 1938-39 he appeared at La Scala as the Minister in *Fidelio* and in *Loreley*.

Records: Columbia* (*La Bohème*) and RCA-Victor* (under Toscanini in *La Bohème, Mefistofele, Rigoletto*, the Verdi *Requiem*, and the *Ninth Symphony* of Beethoven).

MOSER, ANTON, baritone, b. Aug. 13, 1872, Reinsdorf, near Vienna; d. Nov. 29, 1909, Vienna. He studied with Wilhelm von Willen in Vienna and made his debut (1895) at Heidelberg as the title hero in *Hans Heiling*. He sang in Aachen

Mount · Munteanu

(1896-97), in Zürich (1897-1900), in Bremen (1900-02). In 1902 he was engaged at the Vienna Imperial Opera, where he was greatly admired. He had already been chosen for the role of Papageno in *Die Zauberflöte* for the Salzburg Festival of 1910 when he suddenly died. His was a dark-timbred baritone voice.

Records: Columbia* (Vienna, 1905) and Oden (Vienna, 1906-07).

MOUNT, VIOLET, soprano (*see* L'Incognita)

MÜLLER, MARIA, soprano, b. Jan. 29, 1898, Theresienstadt, Bohemia; d. Mar. 15, 1958, Bayreuth, Germany. She studied at the Conservatory in Prague and with Erik Schmedes in Vienna. She made her debut at Linz (1919) as Elsa in *Lohengrin*. She sang at Brno (1919-21) and at the German Theater in Prague (1921-23); she was then engaged at the Munich State Opera (1924-25). In 1925 she signed a contract with the Metropolitan Opera and, after making her debut as Sieglinde in *Die Walküre*, she sang there until 1935, appearing particularly in Wagner roles. In 1926 she sang at the Berlin City Opera and in 1927 she had a huge success at the Berlin State Opera. She also appeared regularly at the Vienna State Opera, as well as at La Scala, the Paris Opéra, Covent Garden, and in Hamburg, Dresden, Brussels, and Amsterdam—all very successfully. She first sang at the Bayreuth Festivals in 1930 and appeared there annually until 1944 to great applause in such roles as Elsa, Eva in *Die Meistersinger*, and Sieglinde in *Die Walküre*. She also sang at the Salzburg Festivals and was active at the Berlin State Opera until 1945. After World War II she appeared there only rarely and lived later in Bayreuth. She had a soprano voice of light tone quality and delicate expressiveness; she appeared both on the stage and in the concert hall in a wide-ranging repertory.

Records: HMV, Columbia* (*Tannhäuser*, Bayreuth, 1930), Telefunken (Bayreuth, 1936), and DGG (Act I of *Die Walküre*). *U.S. re-issue:* RCA Victor. *U.S. re-recording:* Telefunken.

MUNSEL, PATRICE, b. May 12, 1925, Spokane, Wash. She studied with W. Herman and G. Spadoni in New York and she made her debut at the Metropolitan Opera (autumn of 1943)—the youngest singer who had ever appeared there—in the role of Philine in *Mignon*. In 1948 she undertook her first European tour. In 1950 she had an overwhelming success at the Metropolitan as Adele in *Die Fledermaus*. Her film debut was in *Melba*, based on the life of the Australian soprano. A coloratura voice of soaring lightness of tonal production and silver-bright quality.

Records: RCA Victor*, *U.S. re-issue:* Philips.

MUNTEANU, PETRE, tenor, b. Nov. 26, 1919, Campina, Rumania. He studied singing and the violin at the Conservatory in Bucharest and made his debut at the Royal Opera there (1940), but he went to Germany for further study and became a pupil of Weissenborn in Berlin. After World War II he caused great excitement in his appearances in concerts in Italy. In 1947 he came to La Scala, where he appeared in the first performances there of Stravinsky's *Persephone*, *Credulo*, and *Wozzeck*. He also appeared as guest at Covent Garden, at the State Operas in Vienna and Munich, and in Rome, Trieste, Florence, and Naples. In 1961 he sang in the world *première* of *Intolleranza 60* at the Teatro Fenice. Besides his complete mastery of the Italian *bel canto* operas of Bellini, Rossini, and Donizetti, he is an outstanding interpreter of Mozart; in

the concert hall he is famous both as an oratorio tenor in Bach and Handel and as a lieder singer.
Records: DGG, Philips (*Don Pasquale*), and Nixa (*St. Matthew Passion*). U.S. re-issue: Music Guild, Westminster, Epic.

MURATORE, LUCIEN, tenor, b. Aug. 29, 1878, Marseilles; d. July 16, 1954, Paris. He was at first an actor and appeared at the Odeon in Paris, among other theaters. He was discovered as a singer by Emma Calvé. She taught him a role in *La Carmélite*, and he sang opposite her in the world *première* of this work at the Opéra-Comique on July 16, 1902. After this extraordinary debut he had great success at both great Paris opera houses in the next decade. In 1909 he sang the part of Prinzavalle in the world *première* of *Monna Vanna* at the Paris Opéra. He experienced one success after another in his guest appearances in Brussels, Monte Carlo, Bordeaux, Marseilles, Nice, and at Covent Garden. In 1913 he married the soprano Lina Cavalieri, from whom he was later separated. He was a celebrated principal tenor at the Chicago Opera (1913-29). In 1917 he had a triumphant guest season at the Teatro Colón. After his retirement from the stage he lived and taught in Paris, where in 1944 he took over the direction of the Opéra-Comique for one week. Easily the most famous French tenor of his generation through the brilliance of his voice and the intensity of his expression.
Records: Edison* cylinders and discs for G & T, Zonophone, and Pathé*. U.S. re-recording: Pathé Actuelle, Scala, FRP, TAP, IRCC.

MURO, BERNARDO DE, tenor, b. 1881, Tempio Pausanio, Sardinia; d. Oct. 27, 1955, Rome. He completed his studies at the Accademia di Santa Cecilia in Rome and originally appeared as a baritone, but after further study with Alfredo Martino he changed to tenor roles. He made his debut at the Teatro Costanzi (1911) as Turiddu in *Cavalleria Rusticana*. In the same year he sang Folco in the world *première* of *Isabeau* at the Teatro Coliseo; this remained one of his starring roles. In 1912 he came to La Scala, where he first appeared in the title role of *Don Carlos*. Thereafter he had a starring career on the important Italian stages, particularly as Otello. He made guest appearances in Madrid, Barcelona, Buenos Aires, Rio de Janeiro, Montevideo, and Havana. He married the American soprano Barbara Wait. He appeared principally in the United States in the 1920's, but sang there only with smaller companies, such as the San Carlo Opera Company. A large, heroic tenor voice, whose expressiveness and bright luster are notable even on records.
Records: HMV. U.S. re-issue: Victor. U.S. re-recording: TAP, Eterna.

MURO LOMANTO, ENZO DE, tenor, b. 1902, Canosa di Puglia, Italy; d. 1952, Naples. Originally Vincenzo de Muro. He studied at the University of Naples and undertook vocal training at the Conservatory of San Pietro a Majella there. He made his debut (1925) at Catanzaro as Alfredo in *La Traviata*. His first great success was at the Teatro San Carlo as Cavaradossi in *Tosca* and as the Duke in *Rigoletto*. After guest appearances at the most important opera houses in France and Switzerland, he sang at La Scala in the world *première* of *Il Re* in 1929. Thereafter he was often heard at La Scala and in 1929 he went with the ensemble of this house for a guest season in Berlin. From 1929-32 he was married to the coloratura soprano Toti dal Monte, with whom he had undertaken a tour through Australia and

Japan. In 1934 and again in 1936-37 he sang at the Italian Opera in Holland. Thereafter he appeared chiefly at the leading Italian opera houses. A well-trained, lyric tenor voice, which was best displayed in *bel canto* parts and in Italian songs.

Records: Columbia*. *U.S. re-recording:* Eterna, Rococo.

MUSZELY, MELITTA, soprano, b. 1928, Vienna. Her family was of Hungarian origin. She entered the Conservatory of the City of Vienna, where she first studied piano and singing. She made her debut at Regensburg (1952) and sang at Kiel (1953-54). Since 1954 she has been a much-admired member of the Hamburg Opera. Guest appearances have taken her to the Berlin City Opera, the Cologne Opera, the Vienna State Opera, to Zürich, the Paris Opéra, the Teatro São Carlos, and to many other important opera houses. She has sung at the Edinburgh and Holland Festivals. In 1960 she made a brilliantly successful concert tour through Russia. She has a wonderfully trained and expressive lyric voice.

Records: for Electrola* (*I Pagliacci* and *Carmen*). *U.S. re-issue:* Telefunken, Nonesuch.

MUZIO, CLAUDIA, soprano, b. Feb. 7, 1889, Pavia, Italy; d. May 24, 1936, Rome. Her father worked as a *régisseur* at Covent Garden and at the Metropolitan Opera; her mother was a chorister at the latter house. Claudia Muzio studied with Signora Casaloni in Turin. In 1911 she made her debut in Arezzo as the heroine in *Manon Lescaut*, and in 1912 she had a brilliant success in the same role at the Teatro dal Verme. She was greatly admired in the 1913-14 season at La Scala as Desdemona in *Otello* and as Fiora in *L'Amore dei Tre Re*. She sang brilliantly in a guest season at Covent Garden in 1914. In 1916 she was engaged by the Metropolitan Opera, making her debut as Tosca, and she remained one of the leading sopranos there until 1921. She sang the role of Giorgietta in *Il Tabarro* at its world *première* there on Dec. 14, 1918. She was a leading star at the Chicago Opera (1922-32). During this time she completed guest appearances at the Teatro Colón as well as at the Operas in Havana and Rio de Janeiro. In 1926 she returned to Italy, where she went from one triumph to another at the leading opera houses. In 1934 she was again engaged at the Metropolitan, but sang only Violetta in *La Traviata* and Santuzza in *Cavalleria Rusticana*. In February, 1934, she created the title role in Rome in *Cecilia*. She undertook a South American tour in 1935-36, but fell ill in the spring of 1936. The interpretations of this artist were unforgettable experiences through her uncommon skill of expression, through the psychological depths of her understanding of her roles, and through the sumptuous musicality of her presentations. Because of her eminence in the art of acting, she was called "the Duse of opera."

Records: There are two HMV records by her, which were followed by Edison* and Pathé* recordings as well as electric records for Columbia*. *U.S. re-issues:* IRCC, Victor. *U.S. re-recordings:* RCA Victor, IRCC, Pathé Actuelle and Perfect, Scala, Angel, FRP, TAP, Davega, HRS, Belcanto.

MYSZ-GMEINER, LULA, contralto, b. Aug. 16, 1876, Kronstadt, Germany; d. Aug. 7, 1948, Schwerin, Germany. She came from a musical family: her sister, Ella Gmeiner, and her brother, Rudolf Gmeiner, had successful careers as concert singers; another sister, Luise Gmeiner, was a pianist in Berlin. After first studying with Ludwig Lassel in Kronstadt, she worked under Gustav Walter in Vienna after 1895 and after 1896 with Emilie Herzog, Etelka Gerster, and Lilli Lehmann in Berlin. In 1911-12 she was again a pupil, this time in London under Raimund von zur Mühlen. She gave her first concert in Berlin (1899) and excited great comment by her beautiful singing. She was one of the most famous concert singers of her epoch and had brilliant successes on extraordinary concert tours in both Europe and North America. After 1900 she was married to the Austrian naval officer Ernst Mysz. She was a professor at the Berlin High School of Music (1920-45); among her pupils was the tenor Peter Anders, who married her daughter.

Records: Polydor.

N

NADALOVITCH, JEAN, tenor, b. Sept. 6, 1875, in the province of Wallachia in Rumania; d. Sept. 22, 1966, Berlin. The son of a peasant, he first studied medicine at the Universities of Bologna, Paris, and Vienna. After passing his professional examinations, he worked in German clinics and was an assistant to Professor Schröder in Vienna. Even during his medical studies he had also been studying singing at the Conservatory in Jassy with Mezetti and Ernesto Rossi, as well as with Jean Faure and Gabrielle Ferrari in Paris. He then studied with Joseph Gänsbacher in Vienna. He made his debut (1904) in Graz in *Faust*. After guest appearances at the Vienna Volksoper, in Klagenfurt, and in Belgrade, he was engaged in 1905 by Hans Gregor for his newly founded Komische Oper. In the opening performance at this new house, he sang the title hero in *Les Contes d'Hoffmann*. He remained the esteemed first tenor there until 1911. Later he busied himself mostly with his medical calling and in 1912 opened an Institute for the Physiology of the Voice in Vienna. This Institute was closed by the Nazis in 1935 and he was sent to the Theresienstadt concentration camp during World War II, but he was one of the few to survive.
Records: Parlophone.

NANI, ENRICO, baritone, b. Nov. 4, 1873; d. Dec. 22, 1940, Rome. He studied literature at the University of Rome, then singing with Antonio Cotogni, and made his debut (1899) in Codogno as Alfio in *Cavalleria Rusticana*. He next sang in Bologna, Piacenza, Livorno, and La Valetta, Malta, before coming to La Scala in Milan in 1902. During the years 1902-22 he appeared almost annually at the Teatro San Carlo. He made many successful guest appearances, particularly in Spain and in South America; other guest appearances included the Imperial Opera in St. Petersburg (1908-09), the Vienna Imperial Opera (1908), the Brussels Opera (1911), and the Monte Carlo Opera (1919). In 1924 he became a singing teacher in Rome.
Records: Fonotipia and Fonografia Nazionale records.

NASH, HEDDLE, tenor, b. June 14, 1894, London; d. Aug. 14, 1961, London. His voice was discovered by the famous soprano Maria Brema. His debut was hindered by the outbreak of World War I, but in 1923 he made a world tour with the marionette theater of Podrecca, the "Teatro dei Piccoli." He then completed his studies with Giuseppe Borgatti in Milan and (1924) made his debut at the Teatro Carcano there as Count Almaviva in *Il Barbiere di Siviglia*. After singing in Turin, Genoa, and Bologna, he returned to England in 1925. He first appeared there at the Old Vic Theater in London and with the British National Opera Company. In 1929 he made his Covent Garden debut as Don Ottavio in *Don Giovanni*. Thereafter he had a long and successful career at that opera house, where he appeared until 1947. After 1934 he also appeared very successfully at the Glyndebourne Festivals and was a famous oratorio tenor. His son, John Heddle Nash, had a successful career as a baritone.

Records: Before World War II he made records for Columbia* and HMV (*Le Nozze di Figaro* and *Così fan tutte* at Glyndebourne); after the war for HMV. *U.S. re-issue:* American Decca, RCA Victor, Electrola, Capitol, Turnabout, Seraphim.

NAST, MINNIE, soprano, b. Oct. 10, 1874, Karlsruhe, Germany; d. June 20, 1956, Füssen, Germany. She studied at the Conservatory in Karlsruhe and made her debut in Aachen (1897). From there she went (1898) to the Dresden Royal Opera, where she was an honored member until the end of her career in 1919. She was particularly admired for her artistic skill in Mozart roles. In the unforgettable world *première* of *Der Rosenkavalier* in Dresden on Jan. 26, 1911, she sang the role of Sophie. After 1919 she lived and taught in Dresden until her home was destroyed in a bombing raid in 1945 and she was forced to leave the city. A well-trained and highly expressive coloratura voice.

Records: G & T (Dresden, 1902-08), Odeon (Dresden, 1907-08), HMV, Beka, and Pathé. For HMV she sang Micaëla in a complete recording of *Carmen* in 1908. *U.S. re-issue:* Victor, IRCC. *U.S. re-recording:* Rococo, Belcanto.

NAVAL, FRANZ, tenor, b. Oct. 20, 1865, Laibach, Austria; d. Aug. 9, 1939, Vienna. Originally Franz Pogacnik. He began his voice study with A. Nedred in Laibach and completed it with Joseph Gänsbacher in Vienna; he made his debut (1888) at Frankfurt a. O. as Lionel in *Martha*. He remained in Frankfurt for seven years and then in 1895 came to the Imperial Opera in Berlin, where he sang until 1898. In that year he was engaged at the Vienna Imperial Opera and was highly successful there also. He made guest appearances at the Paris Opéra in 1900 and sang at the Metropolitan Opera, mostly in roles in the French repertory (1903-04). He again sang at the Berlin Imperial Opera (1903-08) and was greatly admired there as partner to Geraldine Farrar. In 1908 he shifted to the Komische Oper. After the end of his stage career he lived and taught singing in Vienna. He had a well-trained lyric tenor voice.

Records: G & T (Vienna, 1901-09) and Odeon (Vienna, 1906); on the latter he sang in complete recordings of *Cavalleria Rusticana* and Schubert's *Die Schöne Müllerin*. *U.S. re-issue:* Victor.

NAVARINI, FRANCESCO, bass, b. 1855, Cittadella, Italy; d. Feb. 23, 1923, Milan. He studied with Carlo Boroni in Milan and made his debut (1878) in Treviso in *Lucrezia Borgia*. After he had appeared as guest at the opera houses in Malta, Venice, Trieste, Florence, and Turin, he sang at the Teatro São Carlos (1881-83). He first came to La Scala in 1883 and was highly successful both there and at the Teatro Costanzi. On Feb. 5, 1887, he sang the role of Ludovico in the world *première* of *Otello* at La Scala. He also appeared as guest in London in 1887 and later in St. Petersburg, Madrid, Barcelona, Buenos Aires, Moscow, Odessa, and Seville. He was particularly successful in Russia. He ended his career in 1912 at the Narodny Theater in St. Petersburg. His was one of the most beautiful bass voices of his time; he was noted both for the sumptuous quality of his midrange and for the maturity of his expressive art.

Records: Extremely rare recordings for Fonotipia (Milan, 1906-07). *U.S. re-issue:* HRS. *U.S. re-recording:* FRP, Belcanto.

NEATE, KEN, tenor, b. July 27, 1914, Cessnock, NSW, Australia. He studied at the University of Melbourne and during this time he sang with an amateur troupe which undertook a tour of Australia performing *Madama Butterfly* and *Carmen*. On the advice of John Brownlee he studied singing with Emilio de Gogorza in New York. In 1940 he entered the Royal Canadian Air Force. After the war he appeared at Covent Garden (1946-51) and made guest appearances in Paris, Bordeaux, Lyons, Bologna, Turin, Palermo, and Trieste. In 1954 he appeared as guest in Madrid. In 1956 he sang in Bordeaux in the world *première* of *Sampiero Corsi*. In 1954 he had resumed his studies with Lucien Muratore in Paris and made successful concert tours in the United States, Canada, Australia, and England. He sang Loge in the *Ring* cycle at the 1956 Bayreuth Festival.

Records: Le chant du monde. *U.S. re-issue:* Monitor.

NEBE, CARL, bass, b. 1858, Braunschweig, Germany; d. Feb. 7, 1908, Berlin. The son of the actor Richard Nebe, he was a pupil of Staudigl, Sedlmayer, and Felix Mottl; he made his debut at Wiesbaden (1878), remaining there until 1881. He sang at Dessau (1881-90) and at Karlsruhe (1890-1900). In 1900 he was engaged at the Berlin Imperial Opera, where he was greatly admired in *buffo* roles, but also as Alberich in the *Ring* cycle. He sang Beckmesser at the Bayreuth Festival in 1892 and made guest appearances at Covent Garden, in Brussels, Amsterdam, and at the Wiesbaden Festivals. He starred in the concert hall as the leader of a male quartet which he founded, the Nebe Quartet.

Records: He made a great many records for G & T (Berlin, 1903-06), Columbia* (Berlin, 1904), and one record for Favorite (Berlin, 1906). He also made Edison* cylinders. *U.S. re-issue:* Victor.

NEGRI, GIOVANNI BATISTA DE, tenor, b. Apr. 3, 1850, Nizza Monferrato, Italy; d. 1923, Turin. He planned at first to become a merchant, but his voice was discovered when he sang at a party in 1876. After two years of study he made his debut in Bergamo (1878) in the title role in *Poliuto*. He sang at first on smaller stages in northern Italy, Austria, and Hungary. In 1884 he was a guest at the Teatro San Carlo; 1885 at the Teatro Fenice, the Teatro Regio in Turin, and the Teatro Real. He was particularly famous for his singing of the title role in *Otello* and was held to be next to Francesco Tamagno in the part. He appeared in this role at La Scala and on other famous stages. In 1896 he was forced to undergo an operation and in 1898 he gave up his career and taught singing in Turin.

Records: Rare records for G & T (Milan, 1902) and Zonophone. *U.S. re-recording:* TAP, HRS, Rococo.

NEIDLINGER, GUSTAV, bass-baritone, b. Mar. 21, 1912, Mainz,

Germany. He studied at the Conservatory in Frankfurt, made his debut in Mainz (1931), and remained there until 1934. His later engagements included: Plauen (1934-35), the Hamburg Opera (1935-50), and after 1950 the Stuttgart Opera. Guest appearances earned him great international success at the Paris Opéra, at the Teatro San Carlo, and repeatedly after 1953 at La Scala. After 1953 he held membership in the Vienna State Opera in addition to being an honored member of the Stuttgart Opera. He sang at the Bayreuth Festivals after 1952, where he was particularly admired in his starring specialty, Alberich in the *Ring* cycle. His voice was characterized by an imposing volume of tone and he had great skill in acting, particularly in the Wagner repertory.

Records: DGG (*Zar und Zimmermann* and *Fidelio*), HMV (*Die Meistersinger*), Decca (*Das Rheingold* and *Siegfried*), and Columbia (*Die Kluge*). *U.S. re-issue:* Westminster, Bruno, Electrola, Period, Angel, London, Philips, Everest-Cetra.

NELEPP, GEORGII, tenor, b. 1904, Bobruika, Russia; d. 1957, Moscow. He first entered the School of Military Topography in Leningrad and completed the course there in 1926. In 1927 he began the study of singing at the Leningrad Conservatory with I.S. Tomar and made his debut at the Opera there (1930), remaining until 1944. In 1944 he was engaged at the Bolshoi Theater, where he was highly successful. He won the Stalin Prize (1941, 1949, and 1950), was later awarded the Order of Lenin, and (1951) was given the title "People's Artist of the U.S.S.R." He made guest appearances in all the centers of Russian musical life and abroad. A powerful tenor voice, particularly admired in the Russian operatic repertory.

Records: Russian State Record Trust. *U.S. re-issue:* Ultraphone, Colosseum, Bruno, Period.

NEMETH, MARIA, soprano, b. Mar. 13, 1897, Körment, Hungary; d. Dec. 28, 1967, Vienna. She first attended a commercial school in Pressburg and after 1921 studied with Georg Anthes in Budapest, followed by further studies with László in Budapest, with Fernando de Lucia in Naples, and after 1925 with Felicie Kaschovska in Vienna. She made her debut (1923) at the National Opera in Budapest and by 1924 she had been engaged at the Vienna State Opera, where she was highly successful. From Vienna she went on to guest appearances at Covent Garden, La Scala, Paris, Rome, Budapest, Prague, Berlin, and Munich. She was greatly admired as Donna Anna in *Don Giovanni* at the Salzburg Festivals. The career of this artist lasted until the end of World War II. In 1945 she lost her estate in Hungary, including her castle and her valuable costume collection. Thereafter she lived and taught in Vienna. With a dramatic soprano voice of rare tonal volume and beauty, she was distinguished for the special musicality of her presentations.

Records: Her performances, much-sought-after by connoisseurs, are found on Polydor and HMV. *U.S. re-recording:* RCA Victor, FRP.

NERI, GIULIO, bass, b. 1909, Turrita di Siena, Italy; d. Apr. 21, 1958, Rome. He studied one year with Ferraresi in Florence, then for three years at the Conservatory of the City of Rome and made his debut there (1935). After he had sung small parts at first on various Italian stages, he slowly became one of the most celebrated Italian basses of his generation. He sang at La Scala, in Rome, Venice, Florence, and Catania. After World War II he made guest appearances at Covent Garden, the Teatro Liceo, the Munich State Opera, the Teatro Colón, and the Rio de Janeiro Opera. Just as he was about to leave for a guest appearance in London, he died in Rome of a heart attack.

Records: Cetra* (including *Mefistofele* and *La Gioconda*), HMV (*Don Carlos*), Urania* (*Mefistofele*), and Columbia. *U.S. re-issue:* Capitol, Vox.

NESHDANOVA, ANTONINA, soprano, b. July 17, 1873, near Odessa, Russia; d. May 26, 1950, Moscow. She was a teacher at first and her voice was not discovered until she was thirty years old. She then studied at the Moscow Conservatory with Mazetta, whom she married. She made her debut at the Moscow Imperial Opera (1903) as Antonida in *A Life for the Czar*, and in a short time she was the celebrated prima donna of that opera house. Guest appearances in St. Petersburg, Kiev, and Odessa brought her further brilliant successes. She rarely appeared outside Russia, but in 1913 she sang Gilda in *Rigoletto* with Enrico Caruso and Titta Ruffo at the Théâtre des Champs-Elysées. She remained in Russia after the October 1917 Revolution and was to be heard until about 1930 as an esteemed coloratura soprano of the Bolshoi Opera. Thereafter she was a teacher of singing there. One of the most beautiful coloratura voices of her time; toward the end of her career she sang dramatic roles such as Tosca, Elsa, and Desdemona.

Records: G & T (Moscow, 1906-08), HMV, and Pathé. *U.S. re-recording:* Rococo, TAP, Collector's Guild, Angel, Rococo.

NESPOULOS, MARTHE, soprano, b. May 1, 1894, Paris; d. Aug. 6, 1962, Paris. She studied with Mme. Billa-Azéma in Paris and made her debut (1920) at the Nice Opera. In 1922 she sang the soprano solo in the Fauré *Requiem* at a church concert in Paris. She was engaged at the Paris Opéra in 1923, making her debut in a small role in *Hérodiade*. She soon took over the most important parts for her voice range and had great success both at the Paris Opéra and at the Opéra-Comique. She was repeatedly a guest at the Operas in Brussels, Monte Carlo, Nice, and Bordeaux. Her guest appearances at the Teatro San Carlo, the Teatro Liceo, the Teatro Colón, and in Amsterdam quickly established her as one of the greatest lyric sopranos of her generation. Her particular starring part was Mélisande in Debussy's opera. She also appeared in several films. After she had given up her career in 1934, she taught singing and in 1949 became a professor at the Bordeaux Conservatory.

Records: Columbia* (including *Pelléas et Mélisande*, 1928).

NESSI, GIUSEPPE, tenor, b. Sept. 25, 1887, Bergamo, Italy; d. Dec. 16, 1961, Milan. He made his debut as Alfredo in *La Traviata* and sang lyric roles on Italian provincial stages for several years. The conductor Tullio Serafin advised him to specialize in smaller character parts. He thus made a second debut as a character-tenor (1911) at the Teatro Lirico, where he sang Nick in *La Fanciulla del West*. He had great success in this role for the next decade. He was so greatly admired, particularly at La Scala, that people could scarcely imagine an operatic performance there without him. For almost forty years, from 1921 until his death, he sang at La Scala; on April 25, 1926, he created the role of Pang in *Turandot* there and in 1924 he sang in the world *première* of Boito's *Nerone*. He appeared at the Salzburg Festivals of 1935-39 as Bardolph in *Falstaff* and in 1937-39 as Don Curzio in *Le Nozze di Figaro*. Although he made guest appearances at the

Vienna State Opera and the Teatro Colón (1917), La Scala remained his artistic home.

Records: He sang particularly for Columbia*, where he took *comprimario* roles in almost all the recordings of complete operas; he sang similar parts for HMV (*I Pagliacci* with Beniamino Gigli), and Cetra* (*Falstaff*). *U.S. re-issue:* RCA Victor. *U.S. re-recording:* RCA Victor, Electrola, Telefunken, Seraphim, Rococo.

NEVADA, MIGNON, soprano, b. Aug. 14, 1888, Paris. She was the daughter of the famous American soprano Emma Nevada (1859-1940), and her godparents were the composer Ambroise Thomas and her mother's teacher, Mathilde Marchesi. Trained by her mother, Mignon Nevada made her debut (1907) at the Teatro Costanzi. After successful appearances on various Italian stages and in Lisbon, she had a brilliant debut (1910) as Ophelia in Thomas' *Hamlet* at Covent Garden, where she was greatly admired thereafter. She made guest appearances in Brussels and in 1923 at La Scala. She lives in Liverpool.

Records: There is but a single private recording for IRCC* made in 1938; she sings a song by Ambroise Thomas and is introduced by her mother, Emma Nevada.

NEWAY, PATRICIA, soprano, b. 1920, New York. She studied in New York with Morris Gesell, whom she later married. After she had sung in concerts and on the radio, she caused great excitement in her stage debut at the Chautauqua Festival (1946) as Fiordiligi in *Così fan tutte*. In 1948 she sang in *The Rape of Lucretia* at the New York City Opera. In March, 1950, she created the role of Magda Sorel in the world *première* of *The Consul* at the opera house in Philadelphia, and this has remained one of her starring roles; she has sung it in London, Paris, and other European centers. In 1951 she appeared again in a world *première*, this time in *The Dybbuk* at the New York City Opera. In the summer of 1952 she sang the title heroine in *Iphigénie en Tauride* at the Aix-en-Provence Festival. She was engaged at the Opéra-Comique (1952-54). In 1958 she created the title role in *Maria Golovine* at the World Exposition in Brussels. She is also a very successful concert soprano.

Records: Columbia* (in Menotti's works) and Pathé (*Iphigénie en Tauride* from Aix-en-Provence). *U.S. re-issue:* Vanguard, Lyrichord, American Decca.

NEŽADÁL, MAŘIA, soprano, b. Feb. 21, 1897, Pardubice, in what is now Czechoslovakia. She studied with Joseph Böhm and at the Prague Conservatory with Eugen Fuchs, Ferdinand Pujman, and Albín Síma. She made her debut (1924) in Olomouc, sang at the Vienna Volksoper (1925-26) and in Bern (1926-27). She was highly successful as principal dramatic soprano at the Munich State Opera (1927-33). She made guest appearances at the Vienna State Opera (1926, 1930, and 1934) and later at Covent Garden, in Amsterdam, Basel, Prague, Brno, and Bratislava. She was especially admired in Wagner roles at the Bayreuth Festival in 1927. After 1933 she was rarely able, for political reasons, to appear in Germany. After 1935 she was married to the conductor and composer Clemens Franckenstein (1875-1942). She lives in Hechendorf.

Records: Columbia (from Bayreuth, 1927).

NICHOLLS, AGNES, soprano, b. July 14, 1876, Cheltenham, England; d. 1959, London. She studied at the

Royal College of Music in London with Alberto Antonio Visetti and made her stage debut in 1895 and her concert debut in 1897. In 1904 she married the conductor Sir Hamilton Harty, and in the same year she undertook a successful concert tour of North America. In 1904 she also sang at Covent Garden, where she was particularly admired in Wagner roles; in 1908 she sang Sieglinde in *Die Walküre* there under Hans Richter and in 1910 sang Elsa in *Lohengrin* with Ernst Kraus. She appeared in performances at Covent Garden until the 1920's and was also engaged by the Carl Rosa Opera Company. She was a highly successful concert and oratorio singer.

Records: HMV.

NICOLAI, ELENA, mezzo-soprano, b. Sept. 26, 1912, Sofia, Bulgaria. She studied at the Conservatory in Milan with Pintorno and made her debut at the Teatro San Carlo (1938). During World War II she became famous in Italy, appearing at La Scala and the Rome Opera among others. After 1946 she was greatly admired for her almost annual appearances at the Arena Festivals, particularly as Amneris in *Aida*, Laura in *La Gioconda*, and as Ortrud in *Lohengrin*. She excited great comment for her singing in *Olympia* at the Maggio Musicale Festival, and she sang Cornelia in Handel's *Giulio Cesare* at the Pompeii Festival. In 1954 she sang in the world *première* of *La Figlia di Jorio* at La Scala. She has appeared as guest at both the great opera houses in Paris, at the Teatro Colón, at the Rio de Janeiro Opera, and in Spain and Switzerland.

Records: Decca (*Cavalleria Rusticana*), Colosseum (*Adriana Lecouvreur*), HMV (*Orfeo* and *Don Carlos*), and Cetra* (*La Vestale* by Spontini). *U.S. re-issue:* London,

Nicolai · Nikolaidi

American Decca, Capitol, Angel, Richmond, Seraphim.

NIELSEN, ALICE, soprano, b. June 7, 1876, Nashville, Tenn; d. Mar. 8, 1943, New York. She came of a Danish-Irish family and as a child sang in a church choir in Kansas City. She went on tour with this choir in 1893 and when it broke up for financial reasons, she undertook small roles with the Burton Opera Company, which was just then appearing in St. Paul, and thereby earned her fare home. Later she sang with the Tivoli Opera Company in San Francisco, but changed to operetta. While she was appearing in operetta at the Shaftesbury Theater in London in 1901, she was advised by the impresario Henry Russell to direct her steps toward opera. After study in Rome, she made her debut (1903) at the Teatro Bellini as Marguerite in *Faust*. In the same season she appeared as guest at Covent Garden as Zerlina in *Don Giovanni*. In 1905 she was greatly admired when she sang Norina in *Don Pasquale* at the Casino Theater in New York. She toured the United States in 1908 with the San Carlo Opera Company. She was a celebrated prima donna of the Boston Opera Company (1909-13) and at the same time a member of the Metropolitan Opera. At the latter house she made her debut as Mimi in *La Bohème*. In 1917 she appeared for the last time, singing at the Casino Theater in New York in *Kitty Darling*. Thereafter she lived and taught in New York. She had a well-trained and expressive voice.

Records: American Columbia* and Victor*. *U.S. re-issue:* HRS. *U.S. re-recording:* TAP, Columbia, Rococo.

NIKOLAIDI, ELENA, contralto, b. June 29, 1909, Smyrna, Turkey, the daughter of Greek parents. She studied in Athens with Tanos Mellos, and married him in 1936. At the conclusion of her studies she came to Vienna and made her debut there at the State Opera, of which she remained a member until 1947. She was highly successful there as well as at the Salzburg Festivals. She appeared as guest at Covent Garden, La Scala, the Prague Opera, and she made a tour of Egypt. In 1949 she was highly successful on an extended tour of the United States and Canada. She was a member of the Metropolitan Opera (1950-56). She was frequently a guest in Chicago, San Francisco, and on the leading opera stages of South America.

Records: American Columbia*.

NILSSON, BIRGIT, soprano, b. May 17, 1918, on a small farm near Karup, Sweden. She studied at the Royal Conservatory in Stockholm (1941-46) and made her debut there (1944) at the Royal Opera; the first important role she sang there was Agathe in *Der Freischütz*. In 1948 she undertook a successful tour of Germany and Italy. In 1951 she caused a great stir by her singing of Elektra in *Idomeneo* at the Glyndebourne Festival. Her voice gradually changed from a lyric to a dramatic soprano and she became the most famous Wagner soprano of her time. She had great triumphs in her guest appearances at La Scala, Covent Garden, the State Operas in Vienna and Munich, and at the Düsseldorf Opera. In 1954 she sang Elsa in *Lohengrin* at the Bayreuth Festival. Since then she has had great triumphs in her annual appearances there, particularly as Brünnhilde in the *Ring* cycle and as Isolde in *Tristan und Isolde*. Finally this celebrated soprano, who makes her home in Zürich, was highly successful in the United States, particularly as Turandot. She appeared as guest in 1956 at the opera houses in San Francisco and Los Angeles, and later in Chicago. She was engaged at the Metropolitan Opera in 1959, making her debut there as Isolde. This artist is world-famous. The dramatic skill and emotionality of her characterizations, the beauty and clarity of her intonation, and her brilliant stage presence combine to put her in the first rank of Wagner singers.

Records: HMV, Decca (including *Salome, Tristan und Isolde, Un Ballo in Maschera*, and *Siegfried*), Columbia (*La Fanciulla del West*), and RCA Victor* (*Turandot*). *U.S. re-issue:* London, Angel, DDG.

NILSSON, SVEN, bass, b. May 11, 1898, Gävle, Sweden. He first studied engineering and followed this occupation from 1923-28. He then studied singing in Stockholm and Dresden. He was an honored member of the Dresden State Opera (1930-44). Although he was especially admired for his Wagner characterizations, he was also esteemed for his Sarastro in *Die Zauberflöte*, Osmin in *Die Entführung aus dem Serail*, and Baron Ochs in *Der Rosenkavalier*. He appeared annually in productions of the Zoppot Festival (1935-42). In 1946 he became a member of the Royal Opera in Stockholm, where he had great success for many years.

Records: Very few records, some for Swedish Columbia and Swedish HMV; among the latter, Pogner in a recording of Act III of *Die Meistersinger. U.S. re-issue:* RCA Victor.

NISSEN, HANS HERMANN, baritone, b. May 20, 1896, Danzig, Germany. At first he became a businessman, but studied singing with Julius von Raatz-Brockmann in Berlin after 1916. In 1920 he gave his first concerts and for the next four years busied himself as a concert singer. In 1924 he made his

Noni · Noordewier-Reddingius

stage debut at the Berlin Volksoper. In 1925 he was engaged at the Bavarian State Opera in Munich, where he sang for more than thirty-five years. He was especially admired as a Wagner baritone. Guest appearances took him to Covent Garden, the Paris Opéra, the Royal Opera in Stockholm, the Vienna State Opera, and the opera houses in Brussels, Antwerp, and Barcelona. He was a guest at La Scala (1936-38). In 1936 he sang Hans Sachs at the Salzburg Festival under Toscanini and in 1943 he sang the same role at the Bayreuth Festival. He sang at the Zoppot Festivals (1938-42). He was a member of the Chicago Opera (1930-32) and in the 1938-39 season sang at the Metropolitan Opera, particularly in Wagner roles.
Records: Homochord and HMV (*Die Meistersinger*). U.S. re-issue: RCA-Victor.

NONI, ALDA, soprano, b. June 30, 1916, Trieste. She studied piano first and then singing at the Trieste Conservatory and made her debut (1937) at the opera there as Rosina in *Il Barbiere di Siviglia*; she then sang principally in Zagreb and Belgrade. She was engaged at the Vienna State Opera in 1942, where she was particularly admired in the works of Mozart, Rossini, and Donizetti. After 1945 she had a very successful career in Italy, above all at La Scala, but also in Rome, Venice, and Turin, as well as at the Arena and Maggio Musicale Festivals. Her guest appearances included Covent Garden, the Berlin State Opera, the Opéra-Comique, the Teatro São Carlos, and in Madrid, Buenos Aires, and Rio de Janeiro. In 1949 she sang at the Edinburgh Festival, in 1950 at Glyndebourne. She has also had great success as a concert soprano. She possesses a charming coloratura voice, outstanding for the technical thoroughness of her vocal training.
Records: DGG* (*Ariadne auf Naxos*), Cetra* (*Don Pasquale, L'Elisir d'Amore, Il Matrimonio Segreto, I Quattro Rusteghi, Le Cantatrice Vilane*, and *Le Nozze di Figaro*), and HMV (*La Cenerentola*).

NOORDEWIER - REDDINGIUS, AALTJE, soprano, b. Sept. 1, 1868, Deurne, Holland; d. Apr. 6, 1949, Hilversum, Holland. She was the daughter of a Protestant pastor and began her study of singing in 1886 at the Conservatory of Amsterdam as a pupil of Johannes Messchaert. She made her debut in Utrecht (1888) in a production of Mendelssohn's *St. Paul*. As an oratorio and lieder singer she soon became world-famous. She never appeared in operatic productions. She was to be heard regularly in Amsterdam and The Hague, often with the Concertgebouw Orchestra. On the one hand, she was treasured as an outstanding interpreter of Bach and Handel; on the other, as an interpreter of contemporary music. She was also considered the definitive interpreter of the vocal compositions of the Dutch composer Alfons Diepenbrock. Concert tours brought her great success in England, France, and Belgium, and in 1926 she made a brilliant tour of North America. She married the painter M. Noordewier in 1893. In 1921 she became a professor at the Music Lyceum in Amsterdam and in 1923 a professor at the Conservatory in The Hague. She appeared on the concert platform until 1929 and thereafter lived and taught in Hilversum. One of the most famous concert sopranos of her epoch, she was outstanding both for the beauty of her voice and for the delicacy of her presentations.
Records: Rare records for Edison; a few electric records for Columbia*.

Norbert · Nordmo-Lövberg

NORBERT, KARL, bass, b. Oct. 3, 1893, Prague; d. Aug. 6, 1938, Vienna. He studied with Konrad Wallerstein in Prague and made his debut at the German Theater (1914); he remained at that house until 1920. From then until his death he was an esteemed member of the Vienna State Opera. He experienced great success, particularly as a Mozart singer, at the Salzburg Festivals from 1922 on. He sang Bartolo in *Le Nozze di Figaro*, Osmin in *Die Entführung aus dem Serail*, and Don Alfonso in *Così fan tutte* there. He made successful guest appearances in Paris, Prague, Berlin, and Munich.
Records: Vox.

NORDICA, LILLIAN, soprano, b. May 12, 1857, Farmington, Me.; d. May 10, 1914, Batavia, Java. Originally Lillian Norton. She studied at the New England Conservatory of Music in Boston. She gave her first concerts at the age of seventeen. In 1877-78 she traveled with an opera troupe through the United States, England, and on the Continent. She then studied further with Sangiovanni in Milan and made her Milanese debut (1879) as Donna Elvira in *Don Giovanni*. In the same year she was greatly admired in Brescia for her Violetta in *La Traviata*. In 1880 she appeared as guest in St. Petersburg, traveled through Germany, and was very successful at the Paris Opéra. In 1883 she married the American Frederick A. Gower and gave up her career. After her husband was killed in a balloon trip in 1885, she returned to the stage. She had great success after 1887 at Covent Garden. In 1888-89 she toured the United States with the Henry Abbey Company, and in 1891 she was engaged at the Metropolitan Opera, making her debut as Leonora in *Il Trovatore*. She remained a prima donna there until 1909. In 1894 she sang Elsa in *Lohengrin* at the Bayreuth Festival. In 1896 she married the Hungarian baritone Zoltan Döme, from whom she was, however, soon separated. She was an annual guest at Covent Garden. In 1907 she was celebrated for her performance in the title role in *La Gioconda* at the Manhattan Opera and she sang the same role in 1909 in Boston. In that year she contracted her third marriage, this time to the London banker George H. Young. In 1913 she gave a concert in Carnegie Hall in New York and began a farewell tour around the world. The ship on which she traveled was wrecked on the coast of New Guinea; Mme. Nordica was rescued and brought to a hospital in Batavia, Java, where she died. Lillian Nordica, like Lilli Lehmann, was one of those universal artists who mastered the entire soprano repertory from coloratura parts to Wagner roles. People marveled at her complete technical mastery and at the dramatic expressiveness of her characterizations.
Records: Rare records for American Columbia* (1907-11), as well as fragments on Mapleson cylinders. *U.S. re-issue:* IRCC. *U.S. re-recording:* IRCC, Columbia, TAP, FRP, Rococo, Cantilena.

NORDMO-LÖVBERG, AASE, soprano, b. June 10, 1923, Maalselv, Norway. She appeared in church concerts as a small child and studied singing with Hjaldis Ingebjart in Oslo, where she made her concert debut (1948). After a concert in Stockholm, she made her stage debut at the Royal Opera there (1952). She had her first great success in 1957 as Sieglinde in *Die Walküre* at the Vienna State Opera and has appeared frequently in Vienna since that time. Later guest appearances in London, Hamburg, Munich, and at La Scala and the Rome Opera added to her fame. In 1959 she came to the Metropolitan

Opera, making her debut as Elsa in *Lohengrin*. She made a successful tour of the United States, singing with the Philadelphia Symphony Orchestra. She sang Elsa and Sieglinde at the Bayreuth Festival in 1960. She is also greatly admired as an interpreter of songs.

Records: Columbia and one for HMV. *U.S. re-issue:* Angel.

NORENA, EIDÉ, soprano, b. Apr. 26, 1884, Oslo, Norway; d. Nov. 19, 1968, Switzerland. Originally Karolina Hansen. She began her career as a concert soprano in 1904. In 1907 she made her stage debut at the Oslo opera house as Amor in *Orphée et Eurydice*. In 1909 she married the actor Egel Naess Eidé and sang under the stage name of Kaja Eidé at the Oslo Opera. After World War I she became a student again, this time under Raimund von zur Mühlen in London, followed by further study in Paris and Milan. She began a really brilliant international career at the age of forty. She sang in 1924 at La Scala under the name Eidé Norena and was highly successful there as Gilda in *Rigoletto* under Toscanini. In the same year she appeared as guest at Covent Garden. She sang at the Chicago Opera (1926-28). After 1928 she made her home in Paris and went from one great success to another at the two opera houses there. From 1933-39 she sang every year in the Cathedral Concerts in connection with the Salzburg Festivals. She was a greatly admired member of the Metropolitan Opera (1933-38). In 1939 she gave up her career and returned to live in Norway. She was admired for the thoroughness of her technical training and the stylistic correctness of her characterizations; she was a famous coloratura singer in oratorio and concert performances.

Records: Pathé and Swedish HMV as Kaja Eidé; electric records for Odeon and HMV. *U.S. re-issue:* American Decca, RCA Victor.

NOTÉ, JEAN, baritone, b. May 6, 1859, Tournai, Belgium; d. Apr. 1, 1922, Brussels. The voice of this artist was discovered during his military service and a patron financed his studies at the Conservatory of Ghent. He first appeared publicly in a concert there (1883) and made his debut as an opera singer a little later. After he had sung in opera in Ghent and Antwerp, he came in 1887 to the Brussels Opera. He was very successful there and in 1893 was engaged at the Paris Opéra, where he had a brilliant career for over thirty years. Guest appearances took him to Covent Garden and the Berlin Imperial Opera. During the 1908-09 season he was a member of the Metropolitan Opera. He was also a very successful concert singer and often sang in church concerts at the Madeleine in Paris. In 1921 he appeared in the world *première* of *Antar* at the Paris Opéra. The most famous baritone of his generation on the French operatic stage.

Records: He left a great many phonograph records: these included Edison cylinders, discs for G & T (Paris, 1902-04), Odeon (Paris, 1904-07), Zonophone (Paris, 1906-07), Anker, Chandal, Lyrophone, and Pathé*. *U.S. re-issue:* Victor, Columbia. *U.S. re-recording:* IRCC, Pathé Actuelle.

NOVOTNÁ, JARMILA, soprano, b. Sept. 23, 1907, Prague. She studied at the Conservatory in Prague and in Milan and made her debut at the Prague Opera (1926) as Violetta in *La Traviata*. The young singer quickly became well known. By 1928 she was singing Gilda in *Rigoletto* at the Arena Festival and in 1929 she appeared at the Berlin Volksoper as guest. She appeared regularly at the Vienna State Opera after 1929 and became a member of the company in 1933. In 1934 she sang the title role there in a brilliant world *première* of *Giuditta*. After 1935 she was much admired at the Salzburg Festival, particularly in Mozart roles, but also as Eurydice in *Orphée et Eurydice* and as Frasquita in *Der Corregidor*. She made guest appearances in Berlin, Munich, Milan, Rome, Paris, Brussels, and at the Maggio Musicale Festival. In 1938 she left Vienna and in 1940 began a brilliant career at the Metropolitan Opera, making her debut as Mimi in *La Bohème*. She was a much-admired member of this company until 1957 and also scored triumphs in her guest appearances and concerts elsewhere in the United States. After World War II she briefly returned to her Czech homeland, but then resumed her career in the United States. In 1957 she made guest appearances at the Vienna Volksoper. She had a starring career in films in Europe and the United States. A beautifully trained and expressive soprano voice, particularly successful in lyric parts. She was a famous interpreter of Czech and Slovakian folk songs.

Records: Parlophone and RCA Victor*; also private recordings for the Metropolitan Opera. *U.S. re-recording:* Scala.

NUIBO, AUGUSTIN, tenor, b. May 1, 1874, Marseilles; d. April, 1948, Nice. He studied at the Marseilles Conservatory with Boudouresque, then in Paris with Victor Capoul. He made his debut at the Paris Opéra (1900) as the Fisherman in *Guillaume Tell*. Until 1908 he was an esteemed member of the Opéra, particularly in lyric roles. In 1906 he sang David in *Die Meistersinger* there. In 1904-05 he was a member of the Metropolitan Opera, his debut role being Turiddu in *Cavalleria Rusticana;* he also completed an American concert tour. At the request of the board of directors of the Metropolitan Opera, he changed his Christian name to Francesco, so that he is also known as Francesco Nuibo. In 1908 he returned to Paris and sang at the Opéra-Comique and later at the Théâtre Lyrique. In 1913 he sang at the Théâtre des Champs-Elysées. He made guest appearances at Covent Garden, in Lisbon, Mexico City, San Francisco, and Havana and also toured South America. All this was in addition to his brilliant career in the larger French opera houses. In 1923 he founded a conservatory in the Montmartre section of Paris to which students without resources could come to receive free voice training.

Records: There are only five records for Victor* (1905) and five for Columbia* (1905), all of which were published in the United States; in France some Pathé records were issued later, but all are very rare. *U.S. re-recording:* IRCC.

O

OBBERGH, LUCIEN VAN, bass, b. 1887, Schaerbake, Belgium; d. October, 1959, Brussels. He studied at the Brussels and Paris Conservatories and made his debut in Nice (1913). In 1914 he came to the Brussels Opera, where he had a brilliantly successful career for more than forty-five years. Guest appearances took him to the Opéra-Comique and the Operas in Monte Carlo and Nice. Even after his seventieth birthday this well-beloved singer appeared on the stage in Brussels. At the last he taught in Brussels and headed an organization for the assistance of needy stage artists. He had a beautiful and well-managed voice.

Records: Electrics for Polydor.

OBER, MARGARETHE, contralto, b. Apr. 15, 1885, Berlin. She undertook vocal studies in Berlin with Benno Stolzenberg and Arthur Arndt, whom she later married. She made her debut at Frankfurt a. d. O. (1906) as Azucena in *Il Trovatore*. After a short engagement in Stettin, she was promptly engaged by the Berlin Imperial Opera, where she remained a member practically until the end of her career; in 1908 she had a great triumph there as Amneris in *Aïda* with Enrico Caruso. She was a member of the Metropolitan Opera (1913-16) and made guest appearances in Spain, Holland, Norway, and the largest German opera houses. She appeared almost every year at the Zoppot Festival (1922-42). She sang at the Berlin State Opera until 1945 and lives in Bad Sachsa in the Harz Mountains. She had a warm and highly expressive contralto voice with which she mastered a wide-ranging repertory.

Records: There are a great many records of her voice, especially acoustic examples on HMV, Odeon, Parlophone, Pathé*, and, in the United States, on Victor*. Her electric records include a single record for HMV, 1928; the Meistersinger Quintet from Zoppot, 1942, on DGG; and *Hänsel und Gretel*, 1944 (?), on Urania*. Her European records appeared under the name Margarethe Arndt-Ober. *U.S. re-issue:* Opera Disc, Okeh, American Odeon. *U.S. re-recording:* IRCC, TAP, ASCO.

OBERLIN, RUSSELL, countertenor, b. Oct. 11, 1925, Akron, Ohio. He studied in Cleveland, Chautauqua, N.Y., and at the Juilliard School of Music in New York City. He made his concert debut in New York (1951) and sang with the New York Pro Musica group (1953-59).

He has appeared with the New York Philharmonic, the Chicago Symphony, and the National Symphony Orchestras, among others. He has sung with the American Opera Society, the Cantata Singers, the Collegiate Chorale, the American Concert Society, and at the Vancouver, Edinburgh, Caramoor, and American Shakespeare Festivals. He has given recitals and appeared in plays. His opera appearances include those in San Francisco and in an NBC television production of *Die Zauberflöte*. He has sung in *A Midsummer Night's Dream* both on BBC television and at Covent Garden.

Records: Philips (complete *Messiah*), Decca, Columbia*. U.S. re-cordings: Counterpoint, Urania, Telemann, Decca, Expériences Anonymes, Everest, and Odyssey.

OBOUKHOVA, NADESHA, contralto, b. Feb. 22, 1886, Moscow; d. Aug. 15, 1961, Feodosia, Russia. She studied at the Conservatory in Moscow and made her debut at the Opera there (1917). She was for many years the first contralto at the Bolshoi Theater and was particularly admired in such contralto roles as Orphée in Gluck's opera, Dalila in *Samson et Dalila*, Carmen, Amneris in *Aida*, and in the contralto roles in the Russian repertory. She was also highly successful in concerts and recitals. The career of this artist, who was awarded the title "People's Artist of the U.S.S.R.," lasted until after World War II. In her later years she was a professor at the Moscow Conservatory. Her dark-timbred beautiful contralto voice was exceptional.

Records: Russian State Record Trust. *U.S. re-issue:* Colosseum, Westminster.

ÖDMANN, ARVID, tenor, b. 1850, Karlstadt, Sweden; d. July 15, 1914, Stockholm. He studied at the Conservatory in Stockholm with J. Gunther, Arlberg, and Hallström. He made his debut there (1873) as Tamino in *Die Zauberflöte*, and was thereafter highly successful at the Royal Opera House. In 1875-76 he studied in Paris with Massenet. He was engaged at the Copenhagen Opera (1887-89), but then returned to the Stockholm Opera, where he gave his last performance in 1911 after a brilliant career. His flexible tenor voice was brilliant in its upper ranges.

Records: G & T (Stockholm, 1904), Favorite (Stockholm, 1905-08), and Edison cylinders.

OEGGL, GEORG, baritone, b. 1900, Innsbruck, Austria; d. July 17, 1954, Vienna. Originally he was an actor at the Exl-Theater in Innsbruck, where plays in the Tyrolean dialect were performed. He then studied singing with Cairone in Milan and made his debut (1927) in Munich. After singing in Coburg and Würzburg, he appeared at the Vienna Volksoper (1934-54). After 1948 he was also a member of the Vienna State Opera.

Records: Telefunken, Remington*, and Counterpoint.

OEHME-FOERSTER, ELSA, soprano, b. Sept. 23, 1899, New York. Her father was a clarinetist in the orchestra of the Metropolitan Opera and as a child she sang in performances there. She sang the daughter of the Broommaker in the 1910 world *première* of *Königskinder*, and she continued to sing children's roles at the Metropolitan until 1915. She then studied singing with Frank Dossert and after 1918 at the Grauberry Conservatory in New York. She made her debut (1920) with the Ossining Opera Company and in 1920-21 made an American tour with the Fleck Opera Company. She went to Germany, where she sang in the opera houses in Düsseldorf (1922-24) and Cologne (1924-38). She made guest appearances at the State Operas in Berlin and Vienna. After 1938 she taught singing and appeared as a concert soprano in Cologne. She had a richly expressive lyric soprano voice.

Records: A few HMV records.

OESTVIG, KARL AAGARD, tenor, b. May 17, 1889, Oslo; d. July 21, 1968, Oslo. He studied in Germany with W. Kloed, F. Wüllner, and Fritz Steinbach in Cologne and made his debut (1914) in Stuttgart; he sang there in the world *première* of *Mona Lisa* on Sept. 9, 1915. He remained at Stuttgart until 1919 and from then until 1925 was a celebrated member of the Vienna State Opera, where he sang the role of the Emperor in the world *première* of *Die Frau ohne Schatten* on Oct. 10, 1919. He was engaged at the Berlin City Opera (1927-30). After 1923 he undertook extensive concert tours, which brought him great success both in Europe and in America. He was married to the soprano Maria Rajdl, and their daughter, Lillimarie Oestvig, also appeared on the stage as a soprano. After 1932 he lived and taught in Oslo, where he was also *régisseur* of the Opera. After the occupation of Norway by German troops in 1941 he took over the direction of the opera houses in Oslo. After the end of the war he was imprisoned for a time as a collaborator.

Records: Polydor.

OFFERS, MAARTJE, contralto, b. Feb. 27, 1892, Koudekerke, Holland; d. Jan. 28, 1944, on the Dutch island of Tholen. She studied at the Conservatory in The Hague with Arnold Spoel and Frau Hekking, then with Pauline de Haan-Manifarges in Rotterdam. She made her debut as a concert singer in Leyden (1910) and made her stage debut (1917) at the Théâtre de la Haye as Dalila in *Samson et Dalila*. She sang with several opera associations in Holland and in 1920 appeared in Paris as a guest with Jacques Urlus, again as Dalila. She had great success at La Scala as Erda and Fricka in the *Ring* cycle under Toscanini (1924-25). She also appeared as guest at the Teatro Fenice and toured Australia. In 1926 she sang the contralto solo in Mahler's *Second Symphony* in New York under the direction of Willem Mengelberg; she also had great success as a concert singer in London. In 1928 she returned to Holland and thereafter appeared only rarely in the concert hall. She was married to the jurist Van Buuren, but was separated from him in 1928. She died during World War II on the island of Tholen, to which she had been evacuated. She had a contralto voice of luxurious volume and strong dramatic expressiveness.

Records: Artiphone and HMV. *U.S. re-issue:* RCA Victor.

ÖHMANN, CARL MARTIN, tenor, b. Sept. 4, 1887, Floda, Sweden, the son of a Lutheran pastor. He first decided to become a military officer and was made a lieutenant in 1907 upon completion of the military academy course. He then began to study piano and organ as well as music theory at the Royal Academy of Music in Stockholm. He studied singing with Gentzel in Stockholm and finally with Giuseppe Oxilia and Quadri in Milan and made his debut as a concert singer in 1914 and on the stage in 1917 at the Storatheater in Gothenburg, where he remained until 1923. After 1919 he was also engaged at the Royal Opera in Stockholm. He sang at the Metropolitan Opera (1924-25). In the years 1925-37 he was highly successful at the Berlin City Opera and after 1928 was a regular guest at the State Opera there. He made guest appearances particularly in London and Stockholm. In 1937 he ended his stage career but continued to appear in concert; in 1940 he sang Mahler's *Das Lied von der Erde* in Amsterdam. He had a large brilliant voice and was famous both in Wagner roles and in the heroic tenor parts in the Italian repertory.

Records: Parlophone, Polyphon, Ultraphon, and HMV. *U.S. reissue:* RCA Victor, American Decca. *U.S. re-recording:* Telefunken.

OHMS, ELISABETH, soprano, b. May 17, 1888, Arnhem, Holland. She began her musical studies in 1908 with Jacob Heuckeroth in Arnhem, studying both violin and piano. In 1916 she decided to study singing and became a pupil of C.H. van Oort and Rose Schönberg at the Amsterdam Conservatory. In 1919 she went to Frankfurt a. M., where she concluded her study with Eduard Bellwidt. She made her debut (1921) in Mainz. From there she went (1923) to the Munich State Opera, where she had a brilliant career for over twenty years. In 1927 and 1929 she was a guest at La Scala, singing Kundry in *Parsifal* and Isolde in *Tristan und Isolde* under Toscanini; these appearances gave her a reputation of being a great Wagner soprano. She also had success at the Metropolitan Opera (1929-31), particularly as Brünnhilde in the *Ring* cycle and as Ortrud in *Lohengrin*. She made guest appearances at the Vienna State Opera, the Berlin State Opera, in The Hague, and in Amsterdam. She sang Kundry at the Bayreuth Festival in 1931. She is married to the scene designer Leo Pasetti and lives in Munich. Her dark-timbred soprano voice, managed with great dramatic skill and completely controlled, made her most famous in the Wagner repertory.

Records: Polydor. *U.S. re-issue:* Brunswick.

OLEJNITSCHENKO, GALINA, soprano, b. Feb. 23, 1929, near Odessa, Russia. She first studied harp at the Stoliarski Music School in Odessa and after 1946 studied singing with Urbana Natalia Arkadievna in Odessa. Further study followed at the Conservatory in Odessa (1949-53) and she made her stage debut (1952) at the opera house there, remaining until 1955. In 1953 she won first prize in a singing competition held in connection with the World Youth Festival in Bucharest. She sang at the Kiev Opera (1955-57) and since then she has been an honored member of the Bolshoi Theater. She won first prize in 1957 in a singing competition in Toulouse. She has made guest appearances and has given concerts in France, England, Austria, Greece, Belgium, Rumania, Poland, Hungary, Czechoslovakia, and China. She has an outstandingly beautiful and technically brilliantly managed coloratura voice.

Records: Russian State Record Trust.

OLITZKA, ROSE, contralto, b. Sept. 6, 1873, Berlin; d. Sept. 29, 1949, Chicago. Her family was of Polish extraction and she began the study of singing at the age of fourteen and completed it with Julius Hey in Berlin and with Desirée Artôt de Padilla in Paris. She made her stage debut (1892) in Brünn. In 1894 she came to Covent Garden, where her first role was that of the Page in *Les Huguenots*; she sang regularly at Covent Garden until 1897. She was a member of the Metropolitan Opera (1895-1901), making her American debut as Siebel in *Faust*. In 1898 she appeared with triumphant success at the Imperial Opera in St. Petersburg. Until 1910 she made guest appearances at the leading German opera houses and the two great Paris houses. She sang with the Chicago Opera (1910-11) and later with the Boston Opera. She was celebrated through her guest appearances and concerts in both Europe and North America. She later taught singing in Chicago. Her nephew, Walter Olitski (1899-1949), was very successful as a baritone at the Metropolitan (1939-47).

Records: Her phonograph records are all very rare; G & T (London, 1901, and Paris, 1902), Zonophone (Paris, 1905), Lyrophone (London, 1905), American Columbia* (1911-12), and both Edison* cylinders and discs. *U.S. reissue:* HRS. *U.S. re-recording:* IRCC, TAP.

OLIVIERO, MAGDA, soprano, b. 1912, Turin. She first studied at the Turin Conservatory, then joined classes for soloists given by the Italian radio. She made her stage debut (1935) at the Teatro Vittorio Emmanuele as Lauretta in *Gianni Schicchi*. Later in the same year she made her first appearance at La Scala, singing Anna in *Nabucco*. She had great success on the principal Italian stages until 1941, when she married and gave up her career. In 1950, however, at the request of the composer Cilea, she sang the title role in a revival of his opera *Adriana Lecouvreur*; her success was so great that after a ten-year silence she began a second, and even more successful, operatic career. This time she appeared particularly at La Scala and the Rome Opera, but made guest appearances in Paris, Brussels, Amsterdam, Buenos Aires, and at Covent Garden as well as at the Maggio Musicale and Arena Festivals in 1951-54 and 1960-62. In 1966 she was highly successful in Cherubini's *Medea* in Dallas.

Records: Cetra* (including Liu in *Turandot*).

OLLENDORFF, FRITZ, bass, b. Mar. 24, 1912, Darmstadt, Germany. He studied at the Mozarteum in Salzburg with H. Graf, later in Milan, and made his debut in Basel (1937), remaining there until 1951. He became widely known through his guest appearances after World War II. He was regularly a guest at the Netherlands Opera in Amsterdam and also at La Scala, the Vienna State Opera, and many other opera houses of the first rank. In 1954 he sang Doctor Bombasto in *Arlecchino* at the Glyndebourne Festival. He has been engaged at the Düsseldorf Opera since 1951 and held a simultaneous contract with the Stuttgart Opera (1956-58). He is particularly noted as a *buffo* bass.

Records: Columbia (*Il Barbiere di Siviglia* with Maria Callas and *Le Nozze di Figaro*), HMV, and MMS. *U.S. re-issue:* Angel, Turnabout.

OLSZEWSKA, MARIA, contralto, b. Aug. 12, 1892, Ludwigsschwaige, Germany. Originally Maria Berchtenbreiter. After studying at the University of Munich, she was first active as an operetta singer. In 1915 she made her operatic debut at Krefeld. After an engagement at the Leipzig Opera, she sang at the Hamburg Opera (1917-20). There in 1920 she created the role of Brigitte in the world *première* of *Die Tote Stadt*. She was engaged at the Vienna State Opera in 1921 and sang at the Munich State Opera (1923-25), but then returned to the Vienna house, where she had great triumphs. In 1925 she married the baritone Emil Schipper, but was later separated from him. She had brilliant successes in her guest appearances all over the world, singing at La Scala, Covent Garden, the Brussels Opera, and making successful tours in South and Central America. She was a member of the Chicago Opera (1928-32) and then was engaged by the Metropolitan Opera, making her debut there as Brangäne in *Tristan und Isolde*; she remained at the Metropolitan until 1935. Since 1947 she has taught at the State Academy of Music in Vienna and in 1948 she became a lecturer there at the State Opera. She lives in Baden, near Vienna. Her voice was outstanding for its wide tonal range, for the musicianship with which it was handled, and for the dramatic variety of her presentations.

Records: Odeon, Polydor (including a famous abbreviated version of *Der Rosenkavalier*, 1934), and HMV. *U.S. re-issue:* RCA Victor. *U.S. re-recording:* Angel, Eterna.

OLTRABELLA, AUGUSTA, soprano, b. 1901, Savona, Italy. She studied with Bavagnoli and Caffo in Milan and made her debut at the Teatro dal Verme there (1923). She then sang for five years at the smaller Italian houses and in 1929 was engaged at the Metropolitan Opera, making her debut as Musetta in *La Bohème*. In 1931 she sang at La Scala and had a sensational success there as the Goose Girl in *Königskinder*. During the next decade she was a principal soprano at La Scala. She sang in the world *premières* of the operas *The Dybbuk* (1934) and *Le Morte di Frine* (1937), but her particular starring role was that of the title character in *Suor Angelica*. She appeared in 1936 as guest at Covent Garden and sang at the Salzburg Festivals under Toscanini (1936-38), first appearing as Ann Ford, then as Alice Ford in *Falstaff*. In the years after World War II she had great success in the title role of *Salome*. Her career lasted a long time; she sang her last performance in Como in 1960, appearing in *Colloquio de Tajo*. Her voice was admired for the lightness of its timbre and for the musical beauty of her interpretations.

Records: HMV. *U.S. re-issue:* RCA Victor. *U.S. re-recording:* Eterna.

ONEGIN, SIGRID, contralto, b. June 1, 1889, Stockholm; d. June 16, 1943, Magliaso, Switzerland. The daughter of German parents, she was named Elisabeth Elfriede Sigrid Hoffmann. She began her vocal studies with Luise Resz in Frankfurt a. M. and then studied with Eugen Robert Weiss in Munich and with Ranieri in Milan. Not least, she studied with her husband, the Russian pianist and composer Eugen B. Onegin (1883-1919). She made her debut as a concert singer (1911) under the name of Lilly Hoffmann. In 1912 she made her stage debut in Stuttgart as Carmen. She remained in Stuttgart until 1919 and sang the role of the Dryad there in the world *première* of *Ariadne auf Naxos* on Oct. 25, 1912. She was a member of the Bavarian State Opera in Munich (1919-22) and of the Metropolitan Opera (1922-24), making her debut there as Amneris in *Aïda*. She sang with great success as guest at the Paris Opéra, at Covent Garden, and at the State Operas in Vienna and Berlin. After 1920 she was married to the physician and writer Fritz Pentzoldt. She was engaged at the Berlin City Opera (1926-31) and held a guest-appearance contract with the City Theater in Zürich (1931-35). In 1931 she was notable for her unforgettable acting in the role of Orphée in Gluck's opera at the Salzburg Festival. At the Bayreuth Festivals (1933-34) she sang Fricka, Waltraute, and the First Norn in the *Ring* cycle. After 1931 she lived mostly in Switzerland. Her husband wrote the story of her life in his book *Alt-Rhapsodie*,

Sigrid Onegins Leben und Werk (Magdeburg, 1939). One of the most finished contraltos of the twentieth century, she was as famous for the sculptural breadth of her expressiveness as for her complete mastery of technique and for the flexible ease shown in her interpretations.
Records: Polydor, Brunswick*, HMV, and Victor*. *U.S. re-recording:* Scala, FRP, Electrola, TAP, RCA Victor, IRCC.

OSTEN, EVA VON DER, soprano, b. Aug. 19, 1881, on the island of Helgoland, Germany; d. 1936, Dresden. She studied with August Iffert in Dresden, and, after making her debut there (1902), she remained in the Saxon capital until the end of her career. She was one of the best-loved artists at the Dresden Royal Opera. Her husband, the baritone Friedrich Plaschke, was also a singer there. On Jan. 26, 1911, she sang Octavian in the brilliant world *première* of *Der Rosenkavalier* there. In 1916 she sang there also in the world *première* of *Höllisch Gold*. After 1906 she made regular guest appearances at the Komische Oper, and she was also highly successful in guest appearances in Milan, London, and Munich. In 1914 she sang Kundry in the English *première* of *Parsifal* at Covent Garden. In 1923-24 she and her husband joined the German Opera Company and traveled with it throughout the United States. In 1930 she gave her farewell stage performance, singing Brünnhilde in *Die Walküre* to the Wotan of her husband. She later was *régisseur* at the Dresden State Opera and managed the production of the world *première* of *Arabella* there in 1933.
Records: G & T (Dresden, 1905), HMV, Columbia, and Pathé*. *U.S. re-issue:* Opera Disc, IRCC. *U.S. re-recording:* Rococo, Belcanto.

O'SULLIVAN, JOHN, tenor, b. 1878, County Cork, Ireland; d. Feb. 9, 1948, Paris. He studied at the National Conservatory in Paris and made his debut in England (1909). He sang in Toulouse (1910), Geneva (1912), Lyons (1913), and (1914) came to the Paris Opéra, where he sang with great success until 1919. He appeared at the Chicago Opera (1918-20). In 1922 he sang in Parma as Raoul in *Les Huguenots* and began a brilliant singing career in Italy. In the following five years he was celebrated on all the leading Italian stages in such parts as Manrico in *Il Trovatore*, Otello, and Arnold in *Guillaume Tell*. In 1923 he appeared as guest at the Teatro Colón and sang concurrently in Spanish and South American theaters. He was greatly admired at La Scala as Otello and as Raoul (1924) and he sang at the Arena Festival (1926). He appeared as guest at Covent Garden in 1926 and undertook an extensive tour of Germany, Poland, Hungary, and the Balkan countries. In 1928 and again in 1932-34 he appeared at the Paris Opéra, and he lived and taught in Paris after 1929. He had a brilliant heroic tenor voice of astonishing size in the upper ranges.
Records: Columbia, Parlophone, and Pathé. *U.S. re-recording:* TAP, FRP.

OTAVÁ, ZDENEK, baritone, b. Mar. 11, 1901, Vitejeves, in what has become Czechoslovakia. He first wanted to become a teacher like his father and entered a teacher-training institution in Brno, where he also worked with the composer Leos Janáček as a music teacher. He then studied singing with Bohumil Benoni in Prague and made his debut in Bratislava (1925) as Iago in *Otello.* He sang in Brno (1926-29) and thereafter for over thirty years he was one of the most prominent artists at the National Theater in Prague. In 1959 he was named a National Artist. He made some guest appearances abroad.

Records: Before World War II for HMV; later for Ultraphon, Esta, and particularly for Supraphon (including *The Bartered Bride* and *The Bride of Messina*). *U.S. re-issue:* Colosseum.

OTTO, LISA, soprano, b. Nov. 14, 1919, Dresden. The daughter of the concert singer Karl Otto, she studied with Susanne Steinmetz-Prée at the Music High School in Dresden and made her debut in Beuthen (1941) as Sophie in *Der Rosenkavalier*, remaining at that theater until 1944. She sang in Nuremberg (1945-46) and at the Dresden State Opera (1946-51). Since 1951 she has been a member of the Berlin City Opera. She made very successful guest appearances at La Scala, the Vienna State Opera, and in Paris. At the Salzburg Festivals she sang Blondchen in *Die Entführung aus dem Serail* and Despina in *Così fan tutte* (1953-54). She is an outstanding Mozart singer, but is also admired for other soubrette roles in her voice range.

Records: HMV, Columbia, MMS (including *Die Zauberflöte* and *Così fan tutte*). *U.S. re-issue:* Electrola, DGG, Angel.

OXILIA, GIUSEPPE, tenor, b. 1865, Montevideo, Uruguay; d. May 1, 1939, Milan. He studied in Italy and made his debut there (1888). In 1889 he sang at La Scala in the world *première* of *Asrael*. He was famous for his interpretation of the title role of *Otello* and was held to be, next to Francesco Tamagno, the greatest Otello of his time. He was particularly admired in the part when he sang it at La Scala with Victor Maurel as Iago. His guest appearances on the most important Italian stages, in Spain, and in South America brought him great successes in heroic parts for his voice range. After he left the stage, he lived and taught in Milan.

Records: Very rare records for G & T (Milan, 1902-03) and one record for Zonophone.

P

PAALEN, BELLA, contralto, b. July 9, 1881, Paszthó, Hungary; d. July 28, 1964, New York City. She studied with Rosa Papier-Paumgartner and Johannes Ress and made her debut in Düsseldorf (1904) as Fidès in *Le Prophète*. After singing in Graz (1905-06), she was a member of the Vienna Imperial Opera (1906-37). She earned great success by her guest appearances in Holland, Spain, England, and Czechoslovakia. She also appeared at the Salzburg Festivals. In 1939 she emigrated to the United States and taught singing in New York.

Records: Acoustics for Pathé and Polydor; for the latter she sang in an abbreviated version of *Der Rosenkavalier*, 1934. *U.S. re-issue:* RCA Victor. *U.S. re-recording:* Angel.

PACAL, FRANZ, tenor, b. Dec. 24, 1865, Leitomischl, Austria; d. 1938, Nepomuk, Czechoslovakia. He first studied violin at the Prague Conservatory and became a violinist in the orchestra of the National Theater there. He then studied singing with Gustav Walter in Vienna and sang in the chorus at the Cologne Opera (1892-93), at Bremen (1893-94), and at Graz (1894-95); after 1895 he joined the Vienna Imperial Opera. He had a sensational success there in 1897, singing the small role of the Fisherman in *Guillaume Tell*. He was then chosen as a soloist and had a brilliant career there until 1905. He sang at the National Theater in Prague (1905-09), at the Riga Opera (1909-11), and at Posen (1911-13). During World War I he was the chief official of the grain exchange in Prague. He had a lyric voice, outstanding in its upper register.

Records: G & T (Vienna, 1902, and Prague, 1904), as well as two duets with the soprano Ella Renard on Favorite (Prague, 1907), all rare.

PACETTI, IVA, soprano, b. 1898 (?), Prato, Italy. She studied in Florence and Milan and made her debut in Prato (1920) as Aïda. In 1922 she had great success in Genoa, and in 1925 at the Teatro Costanzi, where she sang the title role in the first performance there of *Turandot*. She was engaged at La Scala in 1927, making her debut under Toscanini as Ariane in *Ariane et Barbe-Bleue*. She was one of the leading singers at La Scala until 1942. She sang as guest at Covent Garden (1930-31; 1938) and at the Teatro Colón (1930). She was an esteemed member of the Chicago Opera (1931-32). At La Scala she was particularly admired as partner to Beniamino Gigli. After her retirement from the stage, she lived and taught singing in Milan. She had a light soprano voice of wide range and she was famous for her dramatic expressiveness and for her acting ability as well.

Records: Columbia and HMV (including *I Pagliacci* with Gigli). *U.S. re-issue:* RCA Victor. *U.S. re-recording:* Electrola, Angel, Seraphim.

PACINI, REGINA, soprano, Jan. 6, 1871, Lisbon; d. Sept. 18, 1965, Buenos Aires. Her father, a well-known baritone, was the director of the Teatro São Carlos. She first studied with him, then with Valani in Lisbon, and made her debut there (1888) as Amina in *La Sonnambula*. In Lisbon she soon came to be greatly admired and was a celebrated singer there until 1904. Guest appearances took her to the first-rank opera houses elsewhere: in 1889 to the Teatro Manzoni, to the Majestic Theater in London, and to Palermo, and in 1890 to the Spanish opera houses. She was a regular guest at the Teatro Real (1890-1905). She was admired in St. Petersburg and Warsaw (1894-95), at Montevideo and the Teatro Politeamo (1899). She was also successful at Covent Garden, where she appeared opposite Enrico Caruso. After the turn of the century she sang at the Teatro San Carlo, in Florence, Rome, and at La Scala. In 1905 she was one of the stars of the Sonzogno-Season at the Théâtre Sarah Bernhardt. At the peak of her career in 1907 she married the Argentine diplomat Marcelo T. de Alvear, who later became president of his country. She then gave up her career and lived in Buenos Aires, where she had great influence on Argentine musical life. She had one of the most beautiful coloratura soprano voices of her time, because the brilliance and exactitude of her vocal ornamentation were intelligently applied to the shadings of her interpretations.

Records: Fonotipia (Milan, 1905-06). *U.S. re-issue:* Columbia-Fonotipia. *U.S. re-recording:* FRP.

PAGLIUGHI, LINA, soprano, b. 1910, San Francisco. The daughter of Italian immigrants, she was reared in an entirely Italian milieu. As a child prodigy she gave concerts at the age of eleven. She was discovered by Luisa Tetrazzini, who took her with her to Milan, where the young San Franciscan studied with Gaetano Bavagnoli. At the age of seventeen she made her debut at the Teatro Nazionale there, singing Gilda in *Rigoletto*. In the same year she married the tenor Primo Montanari. In 1928 she undertook an Australian tour. She appeared with her husband at the Italian Opera in Holland (1929-30). In Italy she sang at all the largest opera houses, but particularly at La Scala, where in 1940 she was greatly admired as Gilda. Up to 1956 she was one of the most famous coloratura sopranos appearing on the operatic stages of world rank. She sang at Covent Garden, in Paris, Brussels, South America, and undertook several tours of the United States. She also appeared at the Arena and Maggio Musicale Festivals, but especially at the Baths of Caracalla Festival in Rome. She lives and teaches in Milan. Her coloratura soprano was outstanding for its delicate tonal beauty and for the technical brilliance of her management of it.

Records: HMV (including *Rigoletto*) and Cetra* (including *La Sonnambula, Rigoletto, La Fille du Régiment, Un Giorno di Regno, Lucia di Lammermoor,* and *Falstaff*). *U.S. re-issue:* RCA Victor, American Decca. *U.S. re-recording:* Rococo.

PALET, JOSÉ, tenor, b. 1878, Barcelona; d. 1946, Milan. He entered the Barcelona Conservatory and made his debut there (1901) as Fernando in *La Favorita*. After appearing in Barcelona and Madrid, he came to Italy, where in 1913 he sang Don José in *Carmen* at La Scala and appeared as guest at the Teatro Costanzi and on other important stages. In 1915 he was much admired as Radames in *Aïda* at the Havana Opera. He made a tour of the United States in 1921 with the Scotti Opera Company. In 1927 he sang at the Italian Opera in Holland, appearing as Raoul in *Les Huguenots*. He was highly successful in repeated guest appearances in Madrid, Barcelona, and Lisbon. Later he lived and taught singing in Milan. He had a brilliant heroic tenor voice of famous expressive qualities.
Records: Fonotipia and HMV. *U.S. re-issue:* Victor. *U.S. re-recording:* Eterna, TAP.

PAMPANINI, ROSETTA, soprano, b. Sept. 2, 1900, Milan. She studied with Sga. Molajoli in Milan and made her debut in Biella (1923) as Musetta in *La Bohème*. In 1925 she came to La Scala, where she sang the title role in the first performance there of *Madama Butterfly* since the unfortunate *première* of the opera at that theater in 1904. The career of this young singer was assisted by Arturo Toscanini and she appeared under him with the La Scala ensemble in Berlin in 1929, singing the roles of Butterfly and Manon Lescaut in the Puccini work. She made guest appearances at Covent Garden (1928-29; 1933); she appeared regularly after 1926 at the Teatro Colón. She was engaged at the Chicago Opera (1931-32), but La Scala was the artistic center of her career. After 1937 she sang dramatic roles in her voice range, such as Aïda, Madeleine in *Andrea Chénier*, and Leonora in *La Forza del Destino*. Her voice was musical, very beautifully handled, and highly expressive.
Records: Fonotipia, Columbia* (*La Bohème*, *I Pagliacci*, and *Madama Butterfly*) and Cetra.

PANDOLFINI, ANGELICA, soprano, b. 1871, Spoleto, Italy; d. July 15, 1959, Lenno, Italy. The daughter of the famous Verdi baritone, Francesco Pandolfini (1827-1916), she made her debut without special study of singing (1894) in Modena as Marguerite in *Faust*. She sang at the Royal Opera in Malta (1894-95) and came to La Scala in 1897; there she sang Mimi in the first performance at that house of *La Bohème*. Thereafter she had a brilliant starring career at La Scala and at the other leading Italian opera houses. On Nov. 6, 1902, she sang the title role in the world *première* of *Adriana Lecouvreur* opposite Enrico Caruso at the Teatro Lirico. She made guest appearances at the Teatro São Carlos, in Madrid, Barcelona, and at the Teatro Colón. In 1909, after her marriage, she withdrew from musical life.
Records: Five extremely rare records for G & T (Milan, 1904). *U.S. re-recording:* IRCC.

PANERAI, ROLANDO, baritone, b. Oct. 17, 1924, near Florence, Italy. He studied at the Conservatory in Florence with Frazzi, then in Milan with Armani and Giulia Tess. In 1947 he won first prize in a singing competition in Spoleto. He made his debut (1947) at the Teatro San Carlo. After he had appeared with great success at the most important Italian opera houses, he came (1951) to La Scala and has been a member of that company ever since. He has made guest appearances at Covent Garden, the Vienna State Opera, and in Paris and Brussels. He has appeared with equal success at the Salzburg Festivals since 1957 and at the Edinburgh and Glyndebourne Festivals. In 1955 he was engaged at the Metropolitan Opera. In 1958 he sang the title role in the first performance at La Scala of *Mathis der Maler*; in the same year he sang in San Francisco. He has a deep baritone voice of great musicality and extraordinary flexibility of expression.

Records: Columbia* (including *I Puritani, I Pagliacci, Cavalleria Rusticana, Così fan tutte, Amelia Goes to the Ball, Il Trovatore*, and *Falstaff*), HMV, Cetra* (*La Battaglia di Legnano*), and Odeon. *U.S. re-issue:* Angel, Mercury, DGG, Seraphim, Everest-Cetra, London. *U.S. re-recording:* TAP.

PANZÉRA, CHARLES, baritone, b. Feb. 16, 1896, Geneva, Switzerland. He volunteered for the French army in World War I and was twice wounded. He then studied singing at the National Conservatory in Paris and made his debut (1919) at the Opéra-Comique as Albert in *Werther*. In 1922 the composer Gabriel Fauré dedicated his song cycle *L'horizon chimérique* to Panzéra. The initial performance of this work in Paris brought the singer huge success and since then he has been esteemed as one of the great song interpreters of his time. Concert tours brought him further triumphs in all the musical centers of Europe and America. He was friendly with such composers as Arthur Honneger, Darius Milhaud, Albert Roussel, Vincent d'Indy, and Guy Ropartz, and he created many of their songs. He appeared only rarely on the stage, mostly in the role of Pelléas, which he sang in Amsterdam and Florence, among other cities. At his song recitals he was frequently accompanied at the piano by his wife, the pianist Madeleine Panzéra-Baillot. After he had taught for a time at the Juilliard School of Music in New York, he become a professor at the National Conservatory in Paris in 1951. The warmth and rich expressiveness of his voice permitted him to give very impressive performances in his song recitals, particularly in songs by the French Impressionist composers.

Records: HMV. *U.S. re-issue:* RCA Victor. *U.S. re-recording:* RCA Victor, Pathé-Marconi.

PAOLI, ANTONIO, tenor, b. 1870, San Juan, Puerto Rico; d. Sept. 14, 1946, San Juan. Originally Ermogene Imleghi Bascaran. He came to Spain at the age of twelve and began the study of singing there; after 1895 a stipend from the Spanish Queen, Maria Christina, permitted him to continue his studies in Italy. He made his debut (1889) at the Paris Opéra as Arnold in *Guillaume Tell*. He next had great success singing in the largest Italian opera houses. In 1902 he traveled through the United States and Canada with an opera troupe which the composer Pietro Mascagni had put together. He sang as guest at the Teatro Colón in 1908, appearing in the roles of Manrico in *Il Trovatore* and Otello. He was admired at La Scala in 1910 as Samson and as Vasco di Gama in *L'Africaine*. He was very successful in his regular guest appearances in South and Central America and in Spain and Portugal. He sang at the Cairo Opera in 1921. He later received an honorary pension from the government of his homeland, Puerto Rico, and he lived there and taught in San Juan. He had a powerful heroic tenor voice and was greatly admired as Otello.

Records: HMV (including Canio in *I Pagliacci* under the composer's direction, 1907). *U.S. re-issue:* Victor, HRS. *U.S. re-recording:* Eterna, TAP.

PAOLIS, ALESSIO DE, tenor, b.

Mar. 5, 1893, Rome; d. Mar. 9, 1964, New York. He studied singing at the Accademia di Santa Cecilia in Rome. He served in the Italian air force in World War I and made his debut in Bologna (1919) as the Duke in *Rigoletto*. In 1921 he first sang at La Scala, appearing as Fenton in *Falstaff*. Until 1932 he had a highly successful career as first lyric tenor at La Scala and sang in Rome, Buenos Aires, and on other Italian stages as well. He undertook a tour of Germany and Switzerland with Claudia Muzio. In 1933 he gave up lyric roles and turned to *buffo* parts, particularly *comprimario* parts, which he sang first in Italy and at the Metropolitan Opera from 1938 until his death. In this second career he was notably successful.

Records: Solo records in the 1920's for Polydor. Twenty-five years later he sang a great many *comprimario* parts in complete operas for Columbia*. Also on Columbia there appeared a record of Ljuba Welitsch singing Donna Anna's scene from *Don Giovanni*, in which he sang the replies of Don Ottavio—a role which he had not sung on the stage for decades. He also sang small roles on private records for the Metropolitan Opera. *U.S. re-issue:* Victor, Odyssey.

PAPROCKI, BOGDAN, tenor, b. 1919, Thorn, Poland. He studied at the Conservatory in Lublin (1943-44), then with Ignazius Dygas in Warsaw, and made his debut in Bytom (1946). He became first tenor at the Warsaw Opera in 1947 and has had great success there since then. In 1965 he was awarded a National Prize by the Polish Government. He has made guest appearances and given concerts in Russia, Hungary, Czechoslovakia, Israel, Canada, France, the United States, West Germany, Korea, and China. In 1960 he appeared successfully in London.

Records: Polish labels and DGG*. *U.S. re-issue:* Bruno.

PARETO, GRAZIELLA, soprano, b. Mar. 6, 1889, Barcelona. She studied with Vidal in Milan and made her debut (1908) in Madrid. By 1909 she was already singing at the Teatro Colón, where (1910) she was greatly admired as Ophelia in Thomas' *Hamlet*. She sang as guest in 1911 at the Havana Opera and in 1912 at the Teatro Regio in Turin, appearing there as Queen Marguerite in *Les Huguenots*. She had other brilliant successes as guest singer in the largest opera houses in Spain and Italy, at the Imperial Opera in St. Petersburg, and at La Scala, where she sang Gilda in *Rigoletto* in 1914. In 1920 she was admired at Covent Garden and in 1921 at Monte Carlo, where she appeared opposite John McCormack. She was engaged by the Chicago Opera (1921-22), but sang only once, appearing with the Chicago ensemble in New York as Violetta in *La Traviata*. She was re-engaged by the Chicago company (1923-25) and also sang at nearby Ravinia in the summer (1922-24). She returned as guest to the Teatro Colón in 1926. She sang Carolina in *Il Matrimonio Segreto* at the Salzburg Festival in 1931. She was married to the composer Gabriele Sibella, and she lived in Naples after she left the stage. With one of the most beautiful coloratura voices of her time, she was admired greatly both for her mastery of vocal technique and for the elegance of her characterizations.

Records: HMV. *U.S. re-issue:* Victor. *U.S. re-recording:* Scala, Cantilena.

PARKINA, ELIZABETH, soprano, b. June 11, 1882, Kansas City, Mo.; d. June 11, 1922, Colorado Springs, Colo. She studied with Mathilde Marchesi in Paris and made her debut at the Opéra-Comique there (1902), singing the title role in

Lakmé. In 1904 she went to Covent Garden, where she remained until 1907. She toured Australia in 1905, but apparently never sang in the United States. She was supposed to be a protégée of Nellie Melba, but the truth is that the latter really hindered Parkina's advancing career. She ended her career early on account of illness. She had an outstandingly beautiful coloratura soprano, trained in the classic Marchesi method.

Records: Twelve rare records for G & T (London, 1904-07).

PARMEGGIANI, ETTORE, tenor, b. 1895, Milan; d. March, 1960, Milan. His voice was discovered during World War I. He studied with Mandolini in Milan and made his debut at the Teatro dal Verme there (1922) as Cavaradossi in *Tosca*. In 1923 he sang with the Italian Opera in Holland. He made his debut as Max in *Der Freischütz* at La Scala in 1927; during the next decade he was regularly to be heard there and he turned more and more to the Wagner repertory. He sang at La Scala in the world *premières* of Mascagni's *Nerone* in 1935, *Lucrezia* in 1937, and made guest appearances at all the ranking Italian opera houses. He sang in France, England, and Holland. After the end of his singing career he taught in Milan and at the last was the claque leader at La Scala.

Records: Relatively few records for Columbia* about 1930. *U.S. re-recording:* Eterna.

PARSI-PETINELLA, ARMIDA, contralto, b. Aug. 30, 1868, near Rome; d. Sept. 1, 1949, Milan. She made her debut in 1893 and had a highly successful career in Italian opera houses. She often appeared at La Scala, where in 1896 she was greatly admired as Dalila in Saint-Saën's opera. In 1895 she also sang at La Scala in the world *premiére* of *Guglielmo Ratcliff*. She was married to the conductor Petinella. She sang as guest in London, Paris, Madrid, and Buenos Aires. She passed her last days in the Casa di Riposo, founded by Verdi in Milan.

Records: Fonotipia (Milan, 1905-06) and Columbia. *U.S. re-issue:* Columbia-Fonotipia. *U.S. re-recording:* Eterna.

PARVIS, TAURINO, baritone, b. Sept. 15, 1879, Turin. He studied law and became an attorney, but then studied singing, made his debut in Italy, and quickly acquired international fame. He was engaged at the Metropolitan Opera in New York (1904-06), making his debut as Enrico in *Lucia di Lammermoor*. He appeared at Covent Garden in 1906 and made other brilliant guest appearances later, particularly in London, but also in Budapest, Russia, Spain, South America, and on the leading Italian stages. In 1911 he sang the Spielmann in the first production of *Königskinder* at La Scala. He returned there in 1917 and in the same year sang at the Teatro Colón. About this time he toured the United States with the San Carlo Opera Company and sang at the opera house in Boston. He was a guest at the Havana Opera in 1920. In the 1920's he was very much admired at the Teatro Costanzi, where he appeared in 1921 in the world *première* of *Il Piccolo Marat*. In 1925 he sang at La Scala in the world *première* of *I Cavalieri di Ekebù*. In 1929 he gave up his singing career and settled in Milan, where he practiced law.

Records: After making cylinders for Columbia and Edison, he made a great many records for Zonophone* (New York, 1905-06), Columbia*, Pathé*, and Edison*.

PASERO, TANCREDO, bass, b. Jan. 11, 1893, Turin. He studied with Pessina in Turin and made his debut (1917) at Vicenza as Count

Rodolfo in *La Sonnambula*. By 1918 he was already appearing at La Scala, where he returned frequently. Guest appearances took him in the 1920's to all the great Italian opera houses, to Covent Garden, the Paris Opéra, and to Brussels and Barcelona. He was highly successful at the Metropolitan Opera (1929-34). In 1935 he sang in the world *première* of Mascagni's *Nerone* at La Scala and in Florence at the world *première* of *L'Orsèolo*. He then appeared at the Arena and Maggio Musicale Festivals. His career lasted about forty years. With Ezio Pinza he was considered the most famous Italian bass of his generation; he was particularly admired for his interpretations of Verdi roles.

Records: Odeon, Fonotipia, Columbia* (including *Aïda*), HMV (*Aïda* and *Un Ballo in Maschera*), and Cetra* (*Norma*). U.S. re-issue: American Decca.

PASINI, LAURA, soprano, b. Jan. 28, 1894, Gallarate, Italy; d. June 30, 1942, Rome. She studied piano at the Milan Conservatory with Appiani and made her debut as a concert pianist in 1912. Then she studied singing at the Accademia di Santa Cecilia in Rome with Di Pietro and made her singing debut (1921) at the Teatro dal Verme in *Fra Diavolo*. In 1922 she had her first great success at the Teatro Costanzi and at the Teatro Regio in Parma. In 1923 she came to La Scala, first singing the Queen of the Night in *Die Zauberflöte* under Toscanini. Thereafter she had great success at La Scala and sang, among others, in the world *première* of *Le Rossignol* in 1926 under the direction of the composer. She made guest appearances at the Teatro Colón in 1925. In 1925 and 1927 she sang in Turin with Conchita Supervia in the memorable productions of *L'Italiana in Algeri* and *Così fan tutte*. At the Maggio Musicale Festival in 1933 these two artists again joined forces in *La Cenerentola*. She sang Elisetta in *Il Matrimonio Segreto* at the Salzburg Festival in 1931. Along with her work on the operatic stage, she was a celebrated concert and oratorio singer and sang the *St. Matthew Passion* in German in Rome. She had one of the most beautiful Italian coloratura voices of her generation, and was outstanding for the musical taste of her presentations.

Records: Her voice is preserved on only three acoustic records for Columbia.

PASINI-VITALE, LINA, soprano, b. 1876, Rome; d. November, 1959, Rome. She made made her debut at the age of sixteen at the Teatro dal Verme in the title role of *La Tilda*. She then had a distinguished career at the leading Italian opera houses, chiefly La Scala, the Teatro Costanzi, and the Teatro Regio in Turin. She was especially loved in South America, particularly at the Teatro Colón. Although she sang only lyric roles at the outset of her career, she later developed into one of the most celebrated Italian Wagner sopranos. In 1914 she sang Kundry in *Parsifal* in the first production of this work on several stages in Italy and in South America. In 1926 she sang Brünnhilde in the *Ring* cycle at the Rome Opera. She was married to the conductor Edoardo Vitale (d. 1957).

Records: Fonotipia. U.S. re-recording: Eterna, Rococo.

PASQUALI, BERNICE DE, soprano, b. 1880, Boston; d. Apr. 3, 1925, New York. Originally Bernice James. She studied with Oscar Saenger in New York and in Milan. Just before her stage debut in Milan (1900) as Gilda in *Rigoletto*, she married the Italian tenor Pietro de Pasquali. She appeared in Italian theaters until 1907 and made guest appearances at Covent Garden, in Berlin, and in Paris. In 1907 Pietro de Pasquali put together his own opera troupe, with his wife as prima donna, with which they toured the United States. In 1909 she replaced Marcella Sembrich, who was ill, as Susanna in *Le Nozze di Figaro* at the Metropolitan Opera; she was thereupon engaged at that house and remained there as a principal coloratura soprano until 1917. In 1915 she sang at the Havana Opera.

Records: Two discs for G & T (London, 1902); including a duet with Pietro de Pasquali; she later recorded for American Columbia*. *U.S. re-recording:* TAP.

PATAKY, KOLOMAN VON, tenor, b. Nov. 14, 1896, Alsó Neudra, Hungary; d. March, 1964, Los Angeles. He planned at first to become a military officer and completed the military academy course in Budapest. After World War I he studied singing at the Budapest Music Academy and made his debut at the National Opera there (1921). After singing there for five years he was engaged at the Vienna State Opera, where he remained until 1938. He had a brilliant career in Vienna and made guest appearances at La Scala and in Berlin and Munich. He was highly applauded at the Glyndebourne and Salzburg Festivals as a Mozart tenor; in 1936 at Salzburg he sang Florestan in *Fidelio*. He sang at La Scala (1939-40) and in the latter year was engaged at the Teatro Colón. Thereafter he remained in South America and later taught singing in Santiago de Chile.

Records: Polydor, Parlophone, and HMV (including *Don Giovanni* from Glyndebourne). *U.S. re-issue:* RCA Victor. *U.S. re-recording:* Rococo, Vox-Turnabout.

PATTI, ADELINA, soprano, b. Feb. 19, 1843, Madrid; d. Sept. 27, 1919, Brecknock, Wales. A daughter of the Italian tenor Salvatore Patti and the soprano Caterina Bareli, her two sisters, Amelia and Carlotta Patti, were also celebrated opera singers. As a child she came to the United States, where her father was *régisseur* of the Italian Opera in New York. She was trained by her brother-in-law, Moritz Strakosch, the husband of her sister Amelia. At the age of eight she sang a concert in New York and she made her stage debut there at sixteen as Lucia di Lammermoor. Her success was sensational and, after an extended tour of the United States, she went to Europe. She had a further and equally sensational success at Covent Garden as Amina in *La Sonnambula*. She was idolized in Paris, Milan, Brussels, Monte Carlo, St. Petersburg, Moscow, Berlin, Vienna, Madrid, and Lisbon. She was the last in a long line of great prima donnas, so characteristic of the operatic culture of the nineteenth century. In 1868 she married the Marquis de Caux, from whom she was separated in 1885. She then married the Italian tenor Nicolini (originally Ernst Nicholas, 1833-99), who accompanied her on her tours. She made brilliant guest appearances in 1892 at the Metropolitan Opera. In 1899 she married the Swedish baron Cederström. In the same year they settled down on their estate, the castle of Craig-y-Nos, near Brecknock in Wales, which she had built for herself. From this center she continued her triumphal career. After the turn of the century she kept announcing her impending retirement from musical life, but was forced by the public to return again and again. She was last heard in a charity concert in London in 1914. The voice of Adelina Patti was a coloratura soprano of special musical beauty; technical difficulties did not exist for her and she also bewitched the listener with the complete musical maturity of her characterizations.

Records: She made two series of records which appeared on G & T under special labels (the first was made at Craig-y-Nos in 1905; the second in London in 1906). IRCC* has issued a re-recording of a cylinder made privately in 1895. *U.S. re-issue:* Victor, Opera Disc, IRCC. *U.S. re-recording:* TAP, Scala, Rococo, Belcanto, Audio Rarities, IRCC.

PATTIERA, TINO, tenor, b. June 27, 1890, Cavtat, near Dubrovnik, Yugoslavia; d. 1966, Cavtat. He first studied medicine, then law, in Vienna; he next studied singing (1912-14) at the Vienna Music Academy with Ranieri, after he had had his first success singing with an operetta company. Through an agent, William Frankfurter, he was engaged by the Dresden Opera, where he made his debut as one of the Armed Men in *Die Zauberflöte.* After he had been given more important roles, he went from triumph to triumph at Dresden. The Verdi renaissance, which in the 1920's spread outward through Germany from Dresden, depended for the most part on this great singer. From 1924-29 he was also a member of the Berlin State Opera. He was often a guest at the Vienna State Opera and he appeared in Paris, Brussels, and Budapest. In 1922-23 he sang at the Chicago Opera, but never appeared in Italy. He continued his starring career in Dresden until 1941. After singing a few times at the National Theater in Prague, he settled down as a teacher in Vienna. In 1948 he again gave very successful concerts in Dresden. After 1950 he was a professor at the Vienna Music Academy. He was esteemed for the gleaming brilliance of his voice and the supple quality of his vocal material as well as for the maturity of his presentations. He was also a noted actor in his roles.

Records: Odeon, Parlophone, Polydor, HMV, Brunswick*, Kristall. *U.S. re-recordings:* Rococo, Eterna, TAP.

PATZAK, JULIUS, tenor, b. Apr. 9, 1898, Vienna. He wanted to become a conductor and studied counterpoint and composition in Vienna with Mandyczevski and with Franz Schmidt. He was then occupied as a church musician, but in 1923 took up a singing career, being entirely self-taught. He made his debut (1923) in Liberec as Radames in *Aida.* After singing at Brno (1927-28), he was then engaged at the Munich State Opera, where he stayed until 1945. He became internationally famous for his interpretations of Mozart roles at the Munich Festivals in the 1930's. In 1945 he was engaged at the Vienna State Opera, where he had equally great successes. From his extensive concert and guest appearances he was accepted as one of the leading tenors of his generation. He sang almost every year at the Salzburg Festivals, including (1947) a role in the world *première* of *Dantons Tod.* In 1948 he became a professor at the Vienna Music Academy, but continued his singing career as well. He had an outstandingly well-managed voice musically, full of expressive richness, and he was equally noted in the operatic and oratorio repertory; for the Evangelist roles in Bach's *Passions,* and in the art of song. Besides his Mozart roles, he was admired for his unexcelled performance in the title role of *Palestrina.*

Records: Polydor, Decca (*Die Fledermaus* and *Salome*), MMS* (*Fidelio* and Haydn's *Creation*), and Philips. *U.S. re-issue:* Remington, Amadeo, Vox, London, Harmony, Richmond, Epic, Haydn Society. *U.S. re-recording:* Eterna, Scala.

PAULY, ROSE, soprano, b. Mar. 15, 1894, Eperjes, Hungary. She studied with Rosa Papier-Paumgartner in Vienna and made her debut (1918) at the Vienna State Opera as Desdemona in *Otello*. She sang at Hamburg (1918-19), Gera (1919-20), Karlsruhe (1921-22), Cologne (1923-25), and Mannheim (1926-27). In 1927 she was engaged at the Kroll Opera in Berlin, where she remained until 1931. In Berlin she was highly successful and often appeared as guest at the State Opera there; she was also a member of the Vienna State Opera (1929-35). After singing the Dyer's Wife in *Die Frau ohne Schatten* at the Salzburg Festival in 1933, she was an unequalled Elektra there in 1934 and 1937. She appeared at La Scala and the Rome Opera (1935-39). In 1937 she came to the United States for the first time and sang Elektra in a concert performance in New York City. In 1938 she was greatly admired in the same role at the Metropolitan Opera and remained there until 1940. She also sang Elektra in 1938 at Covent Garden and in San Francisco. In 1939 she was a guest at the Teatro Colón. She sang Carmen at the Lewisohn Stadium concerts in New York in 1940, and her other guest appearances included Moscow, Leningrad, and Odessa. After the end of her singing career she lived and taught singing in Israel. One of the most famous dramatic sopranos of her time, she was equally noted for her interpretations of Wagner and Richard Strauss roles.

Records: Rare performances for Kristall, Odeon, Parlophone; private recordings for the Metropolitan Opera and unpublished recordings for Vox. *U.S. re-issue:* American Decca (as Rose Pauly-Dreesen). *U.S. re-recording:* IRCC, Rococo.

PEARS, PETER, tenor, b. June 22, 1910, Farnham, England. He studied at the Royal College of Music in London, after he had first been occupied as organist and choir leader of the Grange School. After completing his studies, he joined the Choir of the BBC about 1935 and the New English Singers (1936-39). He appeared in America (1939-42). In 1943 he was engaged at Sadler's Wells in London; there, on June 7, 1945, he sang the title role in the world *première* of *Peter Grimes*. Since then he has been associated with the composer Britten and has appeared in the world *premières* of several of the latter's works: in 1946 at the Glyndebourne Festival as the Male Chorus in *The Rape of Lucretia*; in 1947 at Glyndebourne in *Albert Herring*; in 1951 at Covent Garden as Captain Vere in *Billy Budd*; in 1953 as Essex in the Coronation opera *Gloriana*; and in 1954 at the Venice Festival as Prologue and as Quint in *The Turn of the Screw*. He has sung many times at Covent Garden and has made guest appearances in La Scala, in Vienna, Zürich, Munich, Rome, and the United States. He has had great successes as a concert singer, as well as in oratorio, particularly as an interpreter of Bach's works. Together with Britten he founded the Aldeburgh Festival, in the town where he also has his residence. He has published, also with Britten, editions of old English vocal music.

Records: Decca (*Peter Grimes* and *The Turn of the Screw*), HMV (*The Rape of Lucretia*), Philips (*Oedipus Rex*), and L'Oiseau Lyre (*Acis and Galatea*). *U.S. re-issue:* London, Epic, Angel, Columbia, RCA Victor.

PEASE, JAMES, baritone, b. Jan. 9, 1916, Indianapolis, Ind.; d. Apr. 26, 1967, New York. He originally studied law, then voice at the Academy of Vocal Arts in Philadelphia. He was under contract to the Metropolitan Opera in 1943-44, but before the opening performance of the season he had been inducted into the American army. He made his debut (1946) at the New York City Center Opera and had his first successes there as Figaro in *Le Nozze di Figaro* and as Don Giovanni. In 1948 he went to Europe, made guest appearances at English and German opera houses, and undertook concert tours. In 1952 he was engaged at the Hamburg Opera. In 1956 he appeared at the Edinburgh Festival and in 1959 he was admired at Covent Garden as Hans Sachs in *Die Meistersinger*. Later he sang as guest in Brussels, Amsterdam, San Francisco, Los Angeles, Chicago, Munich, Zürich, and Stuttgart. His Mozart roles, Hans Sachs, and Baron Ochs in *Der Rosenkavalier* were counted as his starring specialities. He was married to the soprano Adele Leigh.

Records: Allegro Royale* and DGG. *U.S. re-issue:* RCA Victor, London, Nonesuch.

PECHNER, GERHARD, baritone, b. 1903, Berlin. He began his career in 1927 at the German Opera in Berlin and his first great success there was the title role in *Don Pasquale* with Maria Ivogün and Karl Erb. In 1933, because he was Jewish, he was forced to leave Germany. After working at the German Theater in Prague, he made guest appearances at the Teatro Colón in 1937. He was engaged in 1941 by the Metropolitan Opera and remained there for more than twenty years. He sang small roles at first, but was also given the part of Alberich in the *Ring* cycle, Klingsor in *Parsifal*, and Fra Melitone in *La Forza del Destino*. He also had a very successful career as a lieder singer.

Records: His first records appeared on Ultraphon in 1927, but he later sang for HMV. He made many records, mostly lieder, for Allegro Royale*. He sang a small part in *Macbeth* for RCA Victor*.

PEDERZINI, GIANNA, contralto, b. Feb. 10, 1906, Trento, Italy. She was the last pupil of Fernando de Lucia in Naples and she made her debut against her teacher's advice about 1923 at the Messina Opera as Preziosilla in *La Forza del Destino*. By her highly successful guest appearances she came to the leading Italian opera houses. She also appeared at the Arena and Maggio Musicale Festivals and made a guest appearance as Preziosilla at Covent Garden in 1931. She was particularly well liked in South America, where she appeared almost annually at the Teatro Colón and in other important houses. After the death of Conchita Supervia she added the difficult coloratura contralto parts to her repertory and had great success with them. She was greatly admired at La Scala in 1937 in *La Cenerentola*. She also appeared in films. Her career lasted a long time; in 1957 she appeared at La Scala in the world *première* of *Les Dialogues des Carmélites*.

Records: HMV, Colosseum (*L'Arlesiana*), and Cetra*.

PEERCE, JAN, tenor, b. June 3, 1904, New York. Originally Jacob Pinkus Perelmuth. He sang as a boy in a synagogue in New York, then studied the violin and worked as a violinist and popular singer in a cabaret. The fine quality of his voice was noticed when he sang concert songs on the radio for the Radio City Music Hall (1933-38). He first appeared on the operatic stage in Philadelphia (1938). In 1940 he was engaged at the Metropolitan Opera, making his debut as Alfredo in *La Traviata*, and from there he went from one triumph to another. He was substantially assisted in his career by Arturo Toscanini, who chose Peerce as tenor for the brilliant opera productions which Toscanini presented on radio (1944-54). He appeared as guest in Chicago, San Francisco, Los Angeles, and in South America with brilliant success. In 1955 he was the first American singer to appear on the stage of the Bolshoi Theater. Concert tours took him to Sweden, Austria, South Africa, Japan, Australia, and New Zealand. He is admired for the steadiness of his voice, for the expressiveness of his singing in Italian and French operas.

Records: RCA Victor* (including *Fidelio, Un Ballo in Maschera,* and *Rigoletto* under Toscanini; later he sang in *La Bohème, Ariadne auf Naxos, Carmen,* and *Lucia di Lammermoor*), DGG (*Fidelio*), and Westminster*. *U.S. reissue:* American Decca, United Artists, Desto, Bach Guild, Vanguard, Columbia.

PENNARINI, ALOYS, tenor, b. 1870, near Vienna; d. June 23, 1927, Ústi, Czechoslovakia. He studied with Joseph Gänsbacher and Johannes Rees in Vienna and made his debut (1893) in Pressburg, singing Turiddu in *Cavalleria Rusticana.* He then sang at Olmütz (1895-96), Elberfeld (1896-97), and Graz (1898-1900), where he began to specialize in heroic roles, particularly in the Wagner repertory. In 1900 he was engaged as first heroic tenor at the Hamburg Opera and he sang there until 1913 with brilliant success. In 1904 he toured the United States with the Savage Opera Company in a production of *Parsifal.* He later made guest appearances at Covent Garden, in Amsterdam, and at The Hague. From 1913-20 he held the post of director of the Municipal Theater in Nuremberg, where he also frequently appeared as a singer. In 1920 he became the director of the Municipal Theater in Liberec, Czechoslovakia.

Records: Odeon (Hamburg, 1905-08).

PEREA, EMILIO, tenor, b. May 25, 1894, Milan. He originally wanted to be an engineer and attended the Polytechnic University in Milan. After studying singing, he made his debut in Varese (1904). He then had a very successful career as a lyric tenor on the leading Italian stages, including La Scala and the Teatro Costanzi. In 1916 he sang Count Almaviva in *Il Barbiere di Siviglia* on the occasion of the centenary of its composition. Guest appearances brought him great successes at the Teatro Liceo, the Teatro Real, the Teatro Colón, and in Rio de Janeiro, Montevideo, and Cairo. He was married to the soprano Fausta Labia (1872-1935), sister of the famous Maria Labia. Their daughter, Gianna Perea-Labia, had a successful career as a soprano.

Records: G & T (1905-06). *U.S. re-issue:* Victor.

PÉRIER, JEAN, baritone, b. Feb. 2, 1869, Paris; d. Nov. 6, 1954, Paris. His parents came originally from Belgium. He studied at the Paris Conservatory with Taskin and Bussine and made his debut at the Opéra-Comique (1892) as Monostatos in *Die Zauberflöte.* He spent his entire career at this house and only rarely made guest appearances. The number of world *premières* in which he appeared at the Opéra-Comique would fill many pages: Apr. 30, 1902, he sang Pelléas in the world *première* there of *Pelléas et Mélisande;* 1903 in *La Reine Fiammette;* 1907 in *Le Chemineau;* 1901 in *La Fille de Tabarin;* 1904 in *La Fille de Roland;* he created the role of Ramiro in *L'Heure Espagnole* on May 19, 1911; and on May 5, 1914, the title role in *Marouf.* He appeared not only on the operatic stage, but also at such operetta theaters in Paris as the Bouffes-

Parisiennes and the Folies-Dramatiques; he was also an actor and later appeared in films. His voice was that of a typical French *bariton-martin*, half tenor and half baritone; he was admired mostly as an actor.

Records: He made a few extremely rare Pathé cylinders; he also sang on disc records for APGA, but these were never officially published.

PERINI, FLORA, contralto, b. 1887, Rome. She studied at the Accademia di Santa Cecilia in Rome and made her debut at La Scala in Milan (1908) as Anaconda in *Cristoforo Colombo*. In 1910 she sang at the Teatro Colón and appeared there each year thereafter. In 1915 she was called to the Metropolitan Opera, making her debut there as Lola in *Cavalleria Rusticana*. On Jan. 28, 1916, she sang there the role of Pepe in the world *première* of *Goyescas* and on Dec. 14, 1918, sang the Princess opposite Geraldine Farrar in the world *première* of *Suor Angelica*. In 1920 she was admired at the Havana Opera with Enrico Caruso. She remained at the Metropolitan until 1924 and was engaged at the Chicago Opera (1924-25). She returned to Italy in 1925 and sang particularly at the Teatro Costanzi. She lives in Rome.

Records: A few recordings for Victor*, including the Quartet from *Rigoletto* with Caruso, Amelita Galli-Curci, and Giuseppe de Luca. *U.S. re-recording:* RCA Victor.

PERNERSTORFER, ALOIS, bass-baritone, b. June 3, 1912, Vienna. He began his study of singing in 1933 at the Vienna Music High School with Lierhammer and Josef Krips. He made his debut in Graz (1936) as Biterolf in *Tannhäuser*. After three years at Graz, he came to the Vienna Volksoper in 1939 and in 1945 was engaged at the Vienna State Opera, where he has since remained. He was briefly engaged at the Municipal Theater in Zürich (1947-48). He has sung in the Festivals in Edinburgh and Glyndebourne and almost annually at Salzburg. Guest appearances have taken him to La Scala, the Teatro Liceo, the Paris Opéra, and the Brussels Opera. During the 1951-52 season he sang at the Metropolitan Opera. He has also been a successful concert singer. He is married to the soprano Henny Herze.

Records: Nixa (*Don Giovanni*), MMS*, Philips (*La Finta Semplice*), and Columbia. *U.S. re-issue:* Bach Guild, Angel.

PERNET, ANDRÉ, bass-baritone, b. Jan. 6, 1894, Rambersville, France; d. June 23, 1966, Paris. He served as an officer in the French army in World War I. After the end of the war he first studied law, but then turned to singing. He studied at the National Conservatory in Paris and made his debut in Nice (1921). During the next seven years he sang in the French provinces and was engaged at the Paris Opéra in 1928. He was soon considered one of the best French singers in his vocal range. In 1935 he sang the role of Shylock at the Opéra in the world *première* of *Le Marchand de Venise*. He appeared as a guest in Amsterdam, Brussels, London, and Monte Carlo and was also successful in the United States. He sang the role of the Father in the film version of *Louise* with Grace Moore and Georges Thill. He remained a member of both the Opéra and the Opéra-Comique until 1948. After 1949 he suffered from progressive paralysis.

Records: Odeon, HMV, and Columbia (abbreviated versions of *Louise* and *Les Contes d'Hoffmann*). *U.S. re-recording:* Pathé-Marconi.

PERRAS, MARGHERITA, soprano,

b. Jan. 15, 1908, Saloniki, Greece. She studied in Berlin with Oscar Daniel and made her debut there (1927) in a school performance of *Don Pasquale*, singing the role of Norina. She was immediately offered a contract by Bruno Walter for the Berlin City Opera, where she sang in 1927-30. In 1931 she transferred to the Berlin State Opera and in 1936-40 was concurrently active at the Vienna State Opera. She made a highly successful tour of Spain (1928-29) and appeared as guest in South America, particularly at the Teatro Colón and in Rio de Janeiro. She sang in Zürich (1934-35) and was a guest at Covent Garden and the Glyndebourne Festival. In 1935 she sang Konstanze in *Die Entführung aus dem Serail* at the Salzburg Festival. After her marriage to the Swiss psychiatrist Dr. Rothpletz, she lived in Zürich and gave only concerts and song recitals. She had a technically well-schooled and expressive coloratura voice.

Records: Ultraphon and HMV. *U.S. re-issue:* RCA Victor and American Decca. *U.S. re-recording:* Rococo.

PERTILE, AURELIANO, tenor, b. Nov. 3, 1885, Montagnana, Italy; d. Jan. 23, 1952, Rome. He studied for four years with Vittorio Orefice in Padua and made his debut (1911) in Vicenza as Lionel in *Martha*. His career was interrupted by World War I and in 1919 he made his first guest appearances abroad. He was engaged at the Metropolitan Opera (1921-22). In 1922 Toscanini engaged him at La Scala and he had enormous success in his debut role, Faust in *Mefistofele*. He then remained the celebrated first tenor at La Scala until he left the stage in 1940. He appeared there in several world *premières:* the title role in Boito's *Nerone* in 1924, the title role in *Sly* in 1927, and the title role in Mascagni's *Nerone* in 1935. His guest appearances were made at Covent Garden, the Paris Opéra, and the opera houses in Vienna, Berlin, and Brussels; he was admired at the Arena and Maggio Musicale Festivals, but La Scala remained the artistic center of his career. After 1940 he lived and taught in Rome. With his large well-managed voice, his best performances were attained in the heroic roles in the Italian repertory, such as Radames, Manrico, and Otello, but he also sang Lohengrin and Walther in *Die Meistersinger*.

Records: Pathé, Columbia* (including *Carmen*), HMV (*Il Trovatore* and *Aida*), and Fonotipia. *U.S. re-issue:* RCA Victor and American Decca. *U.S. re-recording:* Scala, TAP, Eterna, ASCO, Telefunken, FRP, HRS.

PETERS, ROBERTA, soprano, b. May 4, 1930, New York. Her family came originally from Austria. She studied with William Hermann in New York City and made her debut (1950) at the Metropolitan Opera when she replaced an indisposed colleague in the role of Zerlina in *Don Giovanni*. Her success was so great that in 1951 she became a member of the company and has remained there ever since. She was particularly admired there as the Queen of the Night in *Die Zauberflöte*. She has had great success in guest appearances in Chicago and San Francisco and in her concert appearances. In 1951 she sang at Covent Garden and in 1957 on various Italian stages. She has made successful concert tours through Russia. She was admired as Queen of the Night at the Salzburg Festivals (1963-64). For a short time she was married to the baritone Robert Merrill. She has a brilliant coloratura voice, which she manages with great virtuosity.

Records: RCA Victor (including *Il Barbiere di Siviglia, Rigoletto, Un Ballo in Maschera, Orphée et*

Eurydice, Ariadne auf Naxos, and *Lucia di Lammermoor*). *U.S. reissue:* Command, DGG, Columbia.

PETINA, IRRA, contralto-soprano, b. 1907, St. Petersburg. Her father, General Stepan Petina, was personal adjutant to the last Russian Czar. After the 1917 Revolution she and her family fled to China. There she first appeared on the stage in a small part in *Eugen Onégin*. In 1930 she came to the United States and began her vocal training at the Curtis Institute of Music in Philadelphia. After some appearances in concert, she made her debut at the Metropolitan Opera (1934); her first role was that of Desire Annable in the world *première* of *Merry Mount*. She remained at the Metropolitan until 1950, having undertaken many small roles there, but also some important ones. She was highly regarded as Marfa in *Khovantchina* in 1950. She made guest appearances in Los Angeles and San Francisco and after 1950 was outstandingly successful in operetta, notably *Song of Norway*, based on the life of Grieg. She was also esteemed as an interpreter of Russian songs.

Records: RCA Victor* and private recordings for the Metropolitan Opera. *U.S. re-issue:* Columbia, ASCO.

PETRELLA, CLARA, soprano, b. 1918 (?). She studied with Giannina Russ in Milan and made her debut (1941) in Alessandria as Liu in *Turandot*. She then sang in the Italian provinces until she was engaged at La Scala in 1947, where she first sang Giogietta in *Il Tabarro*. Thereafter she caused a great stir by her overwhelming interpretations of parts in such contemporary operas as *The Consul, Debora e Jaele,* and *L'Uragano*. In 1953 she sang Maliella at the Rome Opera in the *première* there of *I Gioielli della Madonna*. In 1958 she created the role of Anna in the world *première* of *Il Vortice* at the Teatro San Carlo. She has appeared as guest at all the important opera houses in Europe and America and is well known as a concert soprano.

Records: Cetra* (*Manon Lescaut, Il Tabarro,* and *L'Amore dei Tre Re*) and Decca (*I Pagliacci*). *U.S. re-issue:* Richmond.

PETROV, IVAN, bass, b. 1920, Irkutsk, Russia. He came in 1938 to the Glazounov Music School in Moscow, where he became a pupil of Miniiev. His stage debut followed (May, 1943) at the Bolshoi Theater. After he had first sung in small roles there, he enchanted the public in the Russian capital in such parts as the title hero in *A Life for the Czar*, as Russlan in *Russlan and Ludmilla*, but particularly as Boris Godounov. After World War II he had great triumphs at the Paris Opéra and undertook extensive concert tours in western European countries. He was awarded the Stalin Prize, the Order of Lenin, and the title of "People's Artist of the U.S.S.R." He has a typical Russian bass voice, whose powerful depth and volume and overwhelmingly forceful characterizations recalled the unforgettable Feodor Chaliapin.

Records: Russian State Record Trust (including *Eugen Onégin* and *Russlan and Ludmilla*) and Philips (Verdi *Requiem*). *U.S. re-issue:* Monitor, Period, Parliament.

PFLANZL, HEINRICH, bass, b. Oct. 9, 1903, Salzburg, Austria. He studied at the Music High School in Vienna and made his debut in Bern (1929) as Beckmesser in *Die Meistersinger*. His later engagements included: Breslau (1930-36), Nuremberg (1936-39), Kassel (1939-42), and after 1942 the Dresden State Opera. Guest appearances brought him great success at the opera houses in Vienna, Munich, and Stuttgart; he also appeared on the leading stages in Italy and

Spain. In 1951 he sang Alberich in the *Ring* cycle at the Bayreuth Festival; he was especially admired as a Wagner singer.

Records: DGG, Columbia, Urania* (*Die Meistersinger*), and MMS. *U.S. re-issue:* Telefunken, Electrola.

PHILIPP, ROBERT, b. Nov. 21, 1852, Offenbach a. M., Germany; d. Aug. 12, 1933, Berlin. He was at first an actor and as such appeared after 1877 at the Belle-Alliance Theater in Berlin. He then became an operetta tenor and in the decade 1880-90 appeared at the Friederich-Wilhelm Theater in Berlin. In 1882 he undertook an American tour with the Hasse Operetta Association. The intendant of the Berlin Imperial Opera, Count Hochberg, persuaded him to turn toward grand opera. In 1890 he became a member of the Imperial Opera and remained at this theater for forty years, becoming one of the best-loved lyric tenors there. Guest appearances included St. Petersburg and Moscow, but he had his greatest successes in the German capital. He was married to the soprano Marie Dietrich, who was also a member of the Imperial Opera in Berlin. He appeared until 1930 on the stage, but at the last took only small roles. He also occupied himself in Berlin as a teacher.

Records: G & T (Berlin, 1904), Odeon (Berlin, 1905), Anker, and HMV. He sang for G & T in a complete *Die Fledermaus* (1907).

PHILIPPI, MARIA, contralto, b. July 26, 1875, Müllheim, Germany; d. June 16, 1944, Zürich. She began her study of singing at the Basel Conservatory with Emil Hegar, then continued with Julius Stockhausen in Frankfurt a. M. and with Pauline Viardot-Garcia in Paris. She made her debut as a concert contralto (1901) and dedicated herself entirely to oratorio and lieder singing; she never appeared on the stage. She was particularly admired as an interpreter of genius in the works of Bach and Mozart. Concert tours brought her the greatest success in Germany, Austria, Holland, Switzerland, France, Italy, Russia and England. She was also a very highly regarded teacher. She was a professor at the Music High School in Cologne (1925-36) and after 1936 lived in Zürich. Her contralto voice was as much admired for the sumptuousness of her vocal equipment as for the stylistic maturity of her conceptions.

Records: Vox.

PICCALUGA, NINO, tenor, b. 1893, Bologna. He made his debut (1918) at Novara and then sang in Genoa and Parma. In 1919 he married the soprano Augusta Concato, but was later separated from her. They appeared together, however, in the 1920's on the leading Italian stages. In 1922 he came with his wife to La Scala, where he made his debut as Luigi in *Il Tabarro*. They had already sung together in the world *première* of *Sakuntala* in Bologna in 1921. He had great success on the stage of La Scala for many years. He appeared as guest at the Teatro Colón in 1928, and in 1930 toured the United States with the Columbia Opera Company. He sang at the Italian Opera in Holland (1931-32). The composer Riccardo Zandonai especially prized his voice and assigned him tenor parts in his operas. In 1934 he gave concerts in Holland and Belgium, but a year later was forced to give up his career on account of illness. This artist is particularly famous for his interpretations of *verismo* roles.

Records: Fonotipia, Parlophone, Columbia*, Pathé, and Homochord (sometimes as Filippo Piccaluga). *U.S. re-issue:* Okeh-Fonotipia, Oddeon. *U.S. re-recording:* Eterna, TAP.

PICCAVER, ALFRED, tenor, b. Feb. 5, 1883, Long Sutton, England; d. Sept. 23, 1958, Vienna. His family was of Spanish extraction. In New York, where his family had emigrated, he studied electricity and worked for a time in the laboratory of the famous inventor Thomas A. Edison. His voice was discovered while he was on a European trip by Angelo Neumann, who engaged him for the German Theater in Prague, of which Neumann was then the director. Piccaver studied with Frau Prochazková-Neumannova in Prague and with Rosario in Milan. He made his debut (1907) at the German Theater in Prague as Roméo in *Roméo et Juliette*. In 1910 he came with an Italian company to Vienna, where he was so successful that in 1912 he was called to the Vienna Imperial Opera. Until 1937 he was the celebrated first tenor of that house and was loved by the public of the Austrian capital as was scarcely any other singer of his time. He appeared as guest in Berlin, Munich, London, Paris, and at the Salzburg Festivals. Three long American tours also brought him great success. In 1923 he sang at the Chicago Opera. Shortly before the outbreak of World War II he left Vienna and worked in London until 1955 as a concert singer and later as a teacher, but he finally returned to Vienna. Possessing one of the most beautiful tenor voices of his generation, he was outstanding also for the wideness of his tonal range; he was effective particularly in Verdi and Puccini roles.
Records: Odeon, Polydor, and Decca. *U.S. re-issue:* Vocalion, Brunswick, Okeh. *U.S. re-recording:* Eterna, Scala, ASCO, TAP.

PILARCZYK, HELGA, soprano, b. Mar. 12, 1925 Schöningen, Germany. After she had given up her original ambition to become a pianist, she studied singing in Braunschweig and Hamburg. At first she sang in operetta, but after 1951 she appeared in opera. After singing at Braunschweig (1951-54) she was a member of the Hamburg Opera. She specializes in contemporary music. In 1956 she sang in the world *première* of *König Hirsch* at the Berlin City Opera; in 1958 she sang the dramatic monologue *Erwartung*, by Arnold Schoenberg, at the Holland Festival; and in 1959 she sang Renata in the Cologne Music Festival production of *The Flaming Angel*. In 1959 she sang in *Salome* in a guest appearance at Covent Garden and guest appearances and concerts followed in Amsterdam, Brussels, at the Paris Opéra, and at the major opera houses in Vienna, Munich, and Stuttgart.
Records: Opera and American Columbia*. *U.S. re-issue:* Mercury.

PILINSKY, SIGISMUND, tenor, b. Dec. 19, 1891, Budapest. He studied at the Conservatory in Budapest, then with Frau Böhme-Köhler in Leipzig, and finally with Konrad von Zawilovski in Berlin; he made his debut (1913) at the National Opera in Budapest and remained there until 1927. In 1928 he was engaged by the Berlin City Opera and was thus able to become internationally known, particularly as a Wagner tenor. He sang the title role in *Tannhäuser* at the Bayreuth Festivals in 1930 and 1931. He made successful guest appearances in Vienna, London, Chicago, and San Francisco. At the end of his career he returned to the National Opera in Budapest and taught singing there.
Records: Odeon, Columbia* (*Tannhäuser*, Bayreuth, 1930). *U.S. re-issue:* American Decca.

PILTTI, LEA, soprano, b. Jan. 2, 1904, Rautjärvi, Finland. Originally

Lea Maire Killinen. She began her vocal studies at the Helsinki Conservatory in 1926 and made her debut there in the same year as the title heroine in *Lakmé*. She then completed her studies in Paris and Berlin. She sang at Königsberg (1929-31), Danzig (1931-33), Darmstadt (1933-34), and Weimar (1934-38). In 1938 she appeared with the Düsseldorf Opera ensemble as guest in Amsterdam and sang Konstanze in *Die Entführung aus dem Serail*. In the same year she was engaged by the Vienna State Opera and had great success there until 1944. She was greatly admired at the Salzburg Festival in 1941 as the Queen of the Night in *Die Zauberflöte*. Guest appearances and concerts brought her further laurels in Europe and in both North and South America. Since 1954 she has lived in Finland; in 1954 she gave her last concert and is now a teacher in Helsinki. An outstandingly trained coloratura soprano voice.

Records: HMV.

PINI-CORSI, ANTONIO, baritone, b. June, 1859, Zara, Austria; d. Apr. 21, 1918, Milan. His brother Gaetano Pini-Corsi (b. 1868) also became a well-known opera singer. Antonio Pini-Corsi made his debut (1878) at Cremona as Don Magnifico in *La Cenerentola*. After first having succeeded on smaller Italian stages, he came in 1892 to La Scala, where he made his debut in the world *première* of *Cristoforo Colombo*. On Feb. 9, 1893, he sang Ford there in the world *première* of *Falstaff*. His first guest appearance at Covent Garden in London in 1894 was the beginning of a brilliantly successful series that lasted for more than twenty years. On Feb. 1, 1896, he sang at the Teatro Regio in Turin in the world *première* of *La Bohème*. He was a member of the Metropolitan Opera (1899-1901) and made his debut there as Masetto in *Don Giovanni*. He then specialized more and more in *buffo* roles, and, in spite of the fact that he was a baritone rather than a bass, he became the best-loved *buffo* singer on the Italian stage. He was also very successful in South America, where he appeared regularly after 1908 at the Teatro Colón. He returned to the Metropolitan (1909-14), but thereafter he confined his activity to La Scala and other important Italian theaters until 1916.

Records: G & T (Milan, 1904-07), Columbia (Milan, 1904), HMV, and Pathé. *U.S. re-issue:* Victor. *U.S. re-recording:* TAP.

PINKERT, REGINA, soprano, b. 1869, Warsaw; d. 1931, Milan. After studying in Poland and Milan, she made her debut (1892) in Milan. She then had a brilliant career on all the important Italian stages, but particularly at La Scala, where in 1897 she had a great success in *I Puritani* opposite Alessandro Bonci. She was equally admired at La Scala in 1901 as Adina in *L'Elisir d'Amore* with Enrico Caruso. She sang as guest in Prague, Paris, and Warsaw and was extremely successful in South America. In 1906 she was greatly admired for her singing in *I Puritani* at the opening performance of the newly built Manhattan Opera House. After the end of her career she lived in Milan.

Records: Very rare records for Fonotipia (Milan, 1905). *U.S. re-issue:* HRS. *U.S. re-recording:* TAP, Rococo.

PINTO, AMELIA, soprano, b. 1878, Palermo, Sicily; d. 1946, Palermo. She studied at the Accademia di Santa Cecilia in Rome and made her debut (1899) at Brescia as the title heroine in *La Gioconda*. By 1900 she had arrived at La Scala, where she was particularly admired as Isolde, as Brünnhilde in *Die Walküre*, as Tosca, and as the Queen of Sheba in Goldmark's opera of the same name. In 1902 she sang opposite Enrico Caruso in Milan in the world *première* of *Germania*. She appeared as guest at the Teatro Colón in 1908. After her marriage to a Sicilian physician, she gave up her career, but appeared again in 1914 at La Scala as Isolde. Later she lived in Palermo.

Records: Rare records for G & T (Milan, 1902) and Columbia. *U.S. re-issue:* HRS, TAP.

PINZA, EZIO, bass, b. May 18, 1892, Rome; d. May 9, 1957, Stamford, Conn. He originally wanted to be a professional bicycle rider, but studied singing at the Conservatories in Ravenna and Bologna with Ruzza and Vizzani and made his debut in Spezia (1914) as Oroveso in *Norma*. After he had served in the Italian army in World War I, he took up his career again in 1919 at the Teatro Verdi in Florence. In 1921 he came to La Scala, where he was highly successful. He sang there in several world *premiéres:* in 1922 in *Debora e Jaele* and in 1924 in Boito's *Nerone*. Toscanini was a great admirer of his voice and saw to it that he was assigned important parts at La Scala. In 1926 he was engaged by the Metropolitan Opera, making his debut as the High Priest in Spontini's *La Vestale*. Until 1948 he was the principal bass of the Italian wing of this house. He was highly successful in his guest appearances at Covent Garden, the Paris Opéra, the Vienna State Opera, the Arena and Maggio Musicale Festivals, and on many other stages. At the Salzburg Festivals he was celebrated for his singing in memorable productions of *Don Giovanni* and *Le Nozze di Figaro* under the direction of Toscanini. He also sang in American films and after 1948, when he had given up his operatic career, appeared in musicals and operettas, such as *South Pacific*, and in popular concerts. A warm-timbred and very flexible bass voice with great affective powers. He sang over seventy operatic roles and was also noted for his acting ability.

Records: HMV, Victor*, RCA Victor*, and Columbia*. *U.S. re-recording:* Harmony, Eterna, Camden, Angel, RCA Victor, Rococo.

PIRAZZINI, MIRIAM, contralto, b. 1918, Vicenza, Italy. She studied at the Canneti Musical Institute in Vicenza and with Luigi Ricci in Rome; she made her debut in Rome (1944) as Laura in *La Gioconda*. She then had a very successful career on the stage in Italy, particularly at La Scala, the Rome Opera, the Arena and Baths of Caracalla Festivals. Guest appearances also took her to France, Germany, England, Spain, Portugal, Holland, Egypt, Switzerland, and Japan. She had a large contralto voice of great flexibility.

Records: Nixa (*La Gioconda*), HMV (*Il Tabarro*), Cetra* (*Il Trovatore* with Giacomo Lauri-Volpi), and Philips (*Rigoletto*). *U.S. re-issue:* Mercury, Angel, Urania, RCA Victor, Columbia, DGG, Heliodor, Everest-Cetra.

PIROGOV, ALEXANDER, bass, b. June 22, 1899, Novoselki, Russia; d. June 24, 1966, Moscow. He studied singing in the Musical-Dramatic Institute of the Moscow Philharmonic Association with V.C. Tjutunik and made his debut (1919) at the Theater of the Revolutionary Military Soviet in Moscow. He was a member of the Moscow Free Opera (1922-24), but then he was engaged by the Bolshoi Opera and remained with this house for over thirty-five years. He made guest appearances in all the Russian music centers, but particularly in Leningrad and Odessa. He won the Stalin Prize in

1943 and 1949 and in 1937 was named "People's Artist of the U.S.S.R." He was a deputy in the Russian Supreme Soviet. He had a powerful, typically Russian bass voice and was particularly esteemed in the role of Boris Godounov.

Records: Russian State Record Trust (including *Boris Godounov* and *Prince Igor*). *U.S. re-recording:* Colosseum, Period, Bruno, TAP, Vanguard.

PISO, JON, tenor, b. 1926, Kronstadt, Rumania. He studied at the Conservatory in Cluj and made his debut at the Municipal Opera there (1949). A short time later he was called to the Bucharest Opera. In 1953 he won a prize at a singing contest held in conjunction with the World Youth Festival in Bucharest. After great successes in concerts and guest appearances, he was applauded at La Scala (1958) as Faust, as the Duke in *Rigoletto*, and as Edgardo in *Lucia di Lammermoor* opposite Anna Moffo. He made a very successful debut at the Metropolitan Opera in New York. He has also been successful in guest appearances at the Bolshoi Theater in Moscow.

Records: Supraphon and some for the Russian State Record Trust.

PISTOR, GOTTHELF, tenor, b. Oct. 17, 1887, Berlin; d. Apr. 4, 1947, Cologne. He was at first an actor and in 1922, when he was appearing in Berlin in *Wallensteins Lager* and had to sing a song on the stage, his voice was discovered by Juan Luria, who later taught him. He made his singing debut in Nuremberg (1923) and then engagements followed in Würzburg (1924-25), Darmstadt (1925-27), and Magdeburg (1928-29). After 1929 he was engaged as first heroic tenor at the Cologne Opera and became internationally known as a Wagner tenor. By 1925 he was alreading singing Froh in the *Ring* cycle at the Bayreuth Festivals and in 1927-31 he sang Tristan, Siegmund, Siegfried, and Parsifal there, all with great success. He sang almost every year from 1930-38 at the Zoppot Festivals. In 1931 he appeared as guest at the San Francisco Opera. After the end of his stage career he lived and taught singing in Cologne.

Records: HMV and Parlophone. *U.S. re-issue:* Columbia and RCA Victor.

PITZINGER, GERTRUDE, contralto, b. Aug. 15, 1904, Mährisch-Schönberg, Austria. She passed her youth in Olmütz and first taught in an elementary school. She then entered the Vienna Academy of Music and in 1926 obtained her diploma as a music teacher. She resided in Liberec, Czechoslovakia, and soon became a greatly admired concert and oratorio contralto. Long tours in Europe and America brought her international fame and she was held in the highest esteem as an interpreter of Bach and of lieder. In 1945 she had to give up her Bohemian estate; she then lived on another in the Black Forest. In 1959 she became a professor at the Music High School in Hannover and in 1960 at the Music High School in Frankfurt, but she still continued her concert activity.

Records: Relatively few records for DGG*. *U.S. re-issue:* Heliodor.

PLAICHINGER, THILA, soprano, b. Mar. 13, 1868, Vienna; d. Mar. 19, 1939, Vienna. Her father was a school director and choir leader for one of the largest churches in Vienna. She studied at the Conservatory of the City of Vienna with Joseph Gänsbacher, later with Luise Dustmann and Frau Mampe-Babbnigg. The director of the Hamburg Opera House, Bernhard Pollini, engaged her for his company and she made her debut there (1893). She sang next at Strasbourg

in a wide variety of roles, since she was the only dramatic soprano in the company (1894-1901). She sang at the Bayreuth Festival in 1897. In 1899 she appeared as guest at the Opera in Frankfurt a. M. as Isolde and in 1900 in the same role during a guest season at the Berlin Imperial Opera; her success there caused her to be offered a contract and she remained until 1914 a greatly admired singer there. She made guest appearances in 1904 and 1910 at Covent Garden and later in Vienna, Munich, and Amsterdam. She later lived and taught singing in Rodaun, near Vienna.
Records: Rare Pathé* discs.

PLANÇON, POL, bass, b. June 12, 1854, Fumay, France; d. Aug. 11, 1914, Paris. Originally Paul-Henri Plançon. He studied with Gilbert Duprez and Giovanni Sbriglia in Paris and made his debut at Lyons (1877) as St. Bris in *Les Huguenots.* He stayed two years in Lyons and then sang in French provincial theaters. He was engaged at the Paris Opéra in 1883 and made his debut as Mephistopheles in *Faust.* During the next decade he had many triumphs at the Opéra and sang there in 1885 in the world *première* of *Le Cid,* among others. His guest appearances included La Scala, Covent Garden, Brussels, and Nice. In 1893 he was called to the Metropolitan Opera, making his debut as Vulcain in *Philémon et Baucis.* He was a celebrated principal bass there until 1908 and had great success as a concert singer in the United States. In 1908 he gave his farewell performance, appearing at the Metropolitan as Plunkett in *Martha.* Thereafter he lived and taught in Paris. His sumptuous-sounding and true *bel canto* bass voice, both large and technically well-handled, is to be heard on G & T (London, 1902-03), Zonophone (Paris, 1902-08), and Victor* records. *U.S. re-issue:* RCA Victor, IRCC, HRS. *U.S. re-recording:* RCA Victor, TAP, FRP, Rococo, Belcanto, Audio Rarities, Cantilena.

PLASCHKE, FRIEDRICH, bass-baritone, b. Jan. 7, 1875, Jaromer, Bohemia; d. Nov. 20, 1951, Prague. He originally wanted to become a painter. His voice was discovered by Julius Marak and trained by Leontine von Dötscher and Ottilie Sklenar-Mala in Prague. He first sang in the chorus of the Dresden Opera. The famous baritone Karl Schiedemantel having arranged for his debut as a soloist, he sang the part of the Herald in *Lohengrin* at the Dresden Opera (1900) and remained a member of that house during his entire career. After 1911 he was married to the soprano Eva von der Osten, who also sang with the Dresden company. In 1911 he sang Pogner in *Die Meistersinger* at the Bayreuth Festival. He appeared as a guest in Vienna and Munich as well as at Covent Garden. He and his wife were engaged by the German Opera Company for a tour of North America (1923-24). He sang at the Zoppot Festivals (1924-25; 1928-29). At Dresden he appeared in several world *premières: Die Toten Augen* in 1916, *Die Ägyptische Helena* in 1928, and *Die Schweigsame Frau* in 1935; on July 1, 1933, he sang Waldner in *Arabella.* After his retirement he lived on his estate, Medingen, near Dresden, but at the last returned to Prague.
Records: G & T (Dresden, 1902-08) and HMV (including five duets with Eva von der Osten).

PLÜMACHER, HETTY, contralto, b. 1922, Solingen, Germany. She studied at the Music High School in Cologne and made her debut in Stuttgart (1946); she remained a member of that company thereafter. She has appeared as guest at the leading opera houses in Italy,

France, Spain, Norway, and Switzerland and has made frequent guest appearances in Munich and Vienna. She sang at the Bayreuth Festivals (1953-54; 1959) and in 1959 at the Salzburg Festival. She has also had a successful career as a concert singer.

Records: DGG, Columbia, Vox*, and Decca. *U.S. re-issue:* Electrola, Period, Amadeo, Angel, Dover, Remington, London, Everest-Cetra.

PODVALOVÁ, MARIE, soprano, b. 1912, Cakovice, in what is now Czechoslovakia. She originally studied the violin, then took up vocal studies with A. Fatossova and Doubravka Brambergova in Prague. She made her debut in Brno (1935) as Marina in *Boris Godounov*. She came to the National Theater in Prague in 1935 and remained there for more than twenty years. From the first she distinguished herself in dramatic parts and she adopted the title role in *Libuse* as her particular starring role. She sang this part in 1959 when the National Opera made a tour throughout Czechoslovakia.

Records: Supraphon. *U.S. re-issue:* Urania.

POELL, ALFRED, baritone, b. 1900, Linz, Austria; d. Jan. 20, 1968, Vienna. The son of a physician, he also studied medicine at the University of Innsbruck, passed his state examination, was graduated there, and then became a specialist in diseases of the throat and larynx. He finally began to study music at the Music Academy in Vienna with Philipp Forstén and Josef von Manowarda. He made his debut (1929) at Düsseldorf and remained there for the next decade. In 1940 he was engaged at the Vienna State Opera, where he remained. He appeared as guest at La Scala, Covent Garden, the Paris Opéra, and on other leading European stages—all of which brought him great fame, especially as a Mozart singer. He was also highly successful at the Salzburg and Glyndebourne Festivals. Not the least of his accomplishments was his success as a concert and lieder singer.

Records: A great many records—HMV (*Fidelio*), Nixa (*B Minor Mass* of Bach), Vox*, Decca (*Die Frau ohne Schatten, Der Rosenkavalier, Le Nozze di Figaro, Die Fledermaus, Die Meistersinger,* and *Der Freischütz*), and Vanguard*. *U.S. re-issue:* London, Westminster, Lyrichord, Electrola, Haydn Society, Seraphim.

POGGI, GIANNI, tenor, b. 1924, Piacenza, Italy. He began his studies in 1942 with Valeria Mann, but then entered the Italian air force. After the end of the war he studied with Emilio Ghirardini in Milan and made his debut (1947) as Rodolfo in La Bohème at the Teatro Massimo. By 1948 he had already been engaged at La Scala, where he has appeared repeatedly since. He has made successful guest appearances in Spain, Portugal, France, and Switzerland. He is very well liked in South America, where he has appeared almost annually at the Teatro Colón and the Opera in Rio de Janeiro. He has been an admired singer at the Arena and Maggio Musicale Festivals. In 1956 he was engaged at the Metropolitan Opera and since then has sung there very successfully. He has a typical Italian tenor voice and he is especially noted in lyric roles.

Records: Nixa (*Mefistofele* and *Lucia di Lammermoor*), Decca (*La Favorita* and *La Traviata*), Cetra* (*La Gioconda* and *Tosca*), DGG* (*Un Ballo in Maschera* and *La Bohème*), Columbia and Philips. *U.S. re-issue:* Urania, London, Vox.

POLESE, GIOVANNI, baritone, b. 1873; d. January, 1952, near Varese, Italy. He began his career at the smaller Italian opera houses and had his first great success in 1904 at Bergamo and at the Teatro Massimo. He was engaged by the Manhattan Opera Company (1909-10) and also sang in Parma with Luisa Tetrazzini. He had his greatest successes in the United States, however—in 1911 with the Boston Opera Company and with the Chicago Opera (1912-14; 1916-17; 1926-28). In the 1930's he taught singing in Boston, but finally returned to Italy. He planned to enter the Casa di Riposo founded by Verdi in Milan, but he died suddenly.

Records: Except for Edison* cylinders and discs, his voice is preserved only on G & T in a single duet with Antonio Pini-Corsi (1905). *U.S. re-issue:* Victor.

POLI, AFRO, baritone, b. 1907, Pisa. He made his debut (1930) at Pisa as the elder Germont in *La Traviata* and quickly developed a reputation by singing on the leading Italian stages, including La Scala and the Rome Opera. In 1938 he sang at the Italian Opera in Holland, his roles including Don Giovanni and Alfio in *Cavalleria Rusticana*. In 1947 he was admired at the Cambridge Theater in London. He made guest appearances with great success at the Teatro São Carlos and in Spain, Germany, Switzerland, and South America. In 1955 he undertook an Australian tour. He has also appeared in films, including a version of *Aïda* with Sophia Loren; there he acted the part of Amonasro, while Gino Bechi sang the part. Toward the end of his career he appeared especially as a character singer. His rich and expressive voice was constantly compared by the critics with that of Mariano Stabile.

Records: His first records appeared on HMV (including duets with Adelaide Saraceni, *Don Pasquale*, 1933, and *La Bohème*, 1938). During World War II he made records for Telefunken* and later for Cetra* (Ping in *Turandot*), Urania* (*Don Pasquale*) and Decca (*I Pagliacci*). *U.S. re-issue:* RCA Victor. *U.S. re-recording:* Pathé-Marconi, Vox, London.

POLI-RANDACCIO, TINA, soprano, b. 1877, Ferrara, Italy; d. Feb. 1, 1956, Milan. She studied with Ortisi in Pesaro and made her debut (1901) at Bergamo as Amelia in *Un Ballo in Maschera*. She soon attained brilliant successes at La Scala and other leading Italian theaters; she was greatly assisted in her career by the composer Mascagni. In 1910 she sang Brünnhilde in *Siegfried* at La Scala; in 1912 she sang in the world *première* of *Abisso*, and in 1913 in the world *première* of *Parisina*. She sang as guest at the Teatro Colón in 1915 and at the Havana Opera in 1916; later she made guest appearances in Barcelona and Madrid. She was uniformly successful in her appearances in Italy. She retired from the stage in 1931. Her highly expressive soprano voice was demonstrated in a many-sided repertory.

Records: HMV, Odeon, and Fonotipia. *U.S. re-recording:* ASCO, Eterna.

PONS, LILY, soprano, b. Apr. 13, 1904, near Cannes, France. She entered the Paris National Conservatory at the age of thirteen and first studied piano there. She studied voice in Paris with Albert di Gorostiaga and made her stage debut in Mulhouse (1928), singing the title role in *Lakmé*. She then sang in French provincial opera houses and was heard in a performance in Montpellier by Giovanni Zenatello and Maria Gay; through their efforts she came in 1931 directly to the Metropolitan Opera. Her debut there as Lucia di Lammermoor was a sensational success, as was her appearance in 1932 as Lakmé. For thirty years she was one of the most prominent singers at the Metropolitan. She also was highly successful in guest appearances at Covent Garden, the two great Paris opera houses, the Teatro Colón, and in Brussels, Chicago, and San Francisco. Her concert tours took her through Europe, North and South America, and to Mexico and Cuba. Her second marriage in 1938 was to the conductor André Kostelanetz. They have since been divorced. She also had a successful film career in Hollywood. In 1956 she was honored by a gala presentation celebrating her twenty-fifth anniversary at the Metropolitan Opera. Although her coloratura soprano voice was not of large dimensions, she was one of the most famous coloraturas of her time for the effortlessness and virtuosity of her vocal ornamentation.

Records: Odeon, RCA Victor*, and American Columbia* (including *Lucia di Lammermoor*). U.S. *re-issue:* American Decca. U.S. *re-recording:* RCA Victor.

PONSELLE, CARMELA, contralto, b. June 7, 1892, Schenectady, New York. She was the elder sister of the famous soprano Rosa Ponselle. They sang together as the Ponzillo Sisters in vaudeville theaters in New York, but she began her serious study of singing before her sister. After Rosa's sensational debut in 1918, Carmela waited until 1923 to begin her own stage career. Her debut was as Amneris in *Aïda* in a summer performance at the Polo Grounds in New York. In 1925 she made her debut at the Metropolitan Opera, also as Amneris. She sang at the Metropolitan until 1934, but did not appear regularly. She sang once at a Sunday Night Concert in a duet with her famous sister in 1925 and appeared once in *La Gioconda* in 1932. After 1934 she gave concerts on the American radio and taught singing in New York. She had a richly cultivated contralto voice, outstanding in the higher register, and otherwise comparable to that of her sister.

Records: A few acoustic records for American Columbia* of songs and ballads, including four interesting duets with Rosa Ponselle.

PONSELLE, ROSA, soprano, b. Jan. 22, 1897, Meriden, Conn. Originally Rosa Ponzillo. Her parents were Italians who had emigrated to the United States. She sang with her sister, Carmela Ponselle, in American vaudeville under the name the Ponzillo Sisters. The impresario William Thorner heard her by chance and obtained an audition for her at the Metropolitan Opera. There she was helped by Enrico Caruso and the completely unknown young singer made her debut with him (1918) as Leonora in *La Forza del Destino*. Her success was overpowering and at a stroke Rosa Ponselle became world-famous. She was thereafter a principal singer at the Metropolitan and had numerous triumphs there. Her greatest were as Rachel in *La Juive* in 1919, as Giulia in Spontini's *La Vestale* in 1925, as Norma in 1927, and as the title heroine in *Luisa Miller* in 1929. She appeared at Covent Garden, in Chicago, and in San Francisco and had a brilliant career as a concert singer. In 1933 she sang Giulia in *La Vestale* at the Maggio Musicale Festival. In 1936 she married the American industrialist Carle A. Jackson and withdrew from musical life. Since then she has lived in Baltimore; in 1954 she permitted the publication of later records in which her voice retained all of its beauty. Rosa Ponselle's voice possessed an extraordinary volume and beauty of tonal production because of her secure grasp of the technique of singing, and this in turn permitted her to master the most difficult *bel canto* roles without any strain. She had the rare gift of coloratura singing with dramatic life.

Records: American Columbia* (including duets with her sister), Victor*, and RCA Victor* records; she also made records for collectors' club labels (the Baltimore Opera Fund). *U.S. re-issue:* IRCC. *U.S. re-recording:* Camden, Scala, TAP, RCA Victor, FRP, ASCO.

POPP, LUCIA, soprano, b. 1940, Bratislava, Czechoslovakia. She studied singing at the Conservatories in Brno and Prague. She made her stage debut (1963) at the Theater an der Wien and in the same year she was engaged at the Vienna State Opera, where she has since remained and has sung with great success, particularly the roles of the Queen of the Night in *Die Zauberflöte*, Konstanze in *Die Entführung aus dem Serail*, and Zerbinetta in *Ariadne auf Naxos*. She has appeared as guest at the National Opera in Prague and on other important stages. She made her Metropolitan debut in *Die Zauberflöte* on Feb. 19, 1967. She is married to the conductor Georg Fischer.

Records: Columbia (Queen of the Night in *Die Zauberflöte*), Amadeo (*Jonny Spielt Auf*), and Decca (*Götterdämmerung*). *U.S. re-issue:* Westminster, Angel, London, RCA Victor.

PRANDELLI, GIACINTO, tenor, b. 1920, near Brescia, Italy. He sang as a boy in a church choir and then studied singing with Fornarini in Rome and Grandini in Brescia. He made his debut in Bergamo (1942) as Rodolfo in *La Bohème* and then sang in Bologna and on the Italian radio. In 1944 he was successful at the Genoa Opera with Toti dal Monte. Engagements at the leading Italian opera houses, including La Scala, followed. When Toscanini decided to direct Beethoven's *Ninth Symphony* in May, 1945, at the re-opening of La Scala, he offered the tenor solo part to Prandelli. After the war he appeared as guest in London, Madrid, Barcelona, Buenos Aires, and Rio de Janeiro, as well as at the Arena, Maggio Musicale and Edinburgh Festivals. In 1951 he was engaged at the Metropolitan Opera in New York. He had a tenor voice of special tonal beauty and mastered over fifty roles in the lyric repertory.

Records: Decca (*Amelia Goes to the Ball* and *La Bohème*), Cetra* (*Adriana Lecouvreur* and *Francesca da Rimini* by Zandonai), HMV (*Mefistofele* and *Il Tabarro*), Columbia, and Urania. *U.S. re-issue:* Angel, London, Harmony, RCA-Victor, Vox.

PREGER, KURT, baritone, b. 1907, Berlin; d. Sept., 1960, Vienna. He was the son of Miksa Preger, who was later the director of the Carl-Theater in Vienna. Kurt Preger made his debut (1933) at the German Theater in Prague, then sang in Basel. He toured Holland and Belgium with the Franz Hirsch Operetta Company (1938-40). He was in Holland at the time of the German invasion in 1940 and had to flee, since he was Jewish. After an adventure-filled flight to Switzerland, he sang again in Basel. In 1945 he was engaged at the Vienna Volksoper. He was highly successful there and at the Vienna State Opera until his death, and was particularly noted as a *buffo* baritone and operetta singer.

Records: Decca, Philips, Bertelsmann, MMS, and Amadeo (Ollendorff in *Der Bettelstudent*). *U.S. re-issue:* Urania, Vanguard, Epic, Richmond.

PREOBRASHENSKAJA, SOFIA, contralto, b. Sept., 1904, Leningrad. She began her study of singing in 1923 at the Leningrad Conservatory with Ivan Erschov and N. N. Zajcová. In 1928 she was called to the Leningrad Opera, where she remained for more than twenty years. In 1928 she appeared as guest with the Leningrad Opera under Boris Assafiev at the Salzburg Festival. Later she was often a guest at various Russian musical centers and had a celebrated career as a concert contralto. She was awarded the Stalin Prize in 1946 and 1951 and was made a "People's Artist of the U.S.S.R." From 1948-53 she was a professor at the Leningrad Conservatory.

Records: Russian State Record Trust. *U.S. re-issue:* Colosseum. *U.S. re-recording:* TAP.

PREUSS, ARTHUR, tenor, b. Feb. 23, 1878, Königsberg, Germany; d. Aug. 20, 1944, Vienna. He studied in Berlin with Benno Stolzenberg and Franz Krolop and made his debut (1899) at the Vienna Imperial Opera, where he specialized in *buffo* parts. He was greatly admired by the opera-going public in Vienna. He sang at the Mozart Festival in Salzburg in 1906; in 1908 in Vienna he appeared in the world *première* of *Ein Wintermärchen*. He remained at the Imperial Opera until 1915 and during this time often sang as guest at the Cologne Opera. In 1915 he transferred to the Vienna Volksoper, where he became celebrated in the role of Schubert, which he sang there at the world *première* in 1916 of *Die Dreimäderlhaus*, known later in the United States as *Blossom Time*. He also had great success as a concert tenor, for example, for his singing of Schoenberg's *Gurrelieder* in Vienna in 1919. He appeared as guest at the Vienna Volksoper until 1930 and sang both on the Austrian radio and in concerts. He also busied himself as a composer and wrote film music, songs, and other vocal works. He then lived and taught singing in Vienna. He had a beautiful, expressive tenor voice.

Records: G & T (Vienna, 1905-07) and HMV. *U.S. re-issue:* Victor.

PREVEDI, BRUNO, tenor, b. Dec. 21, 1928, Rovere, Italy. He made his debut (1958) at the Teatro Nuovo as a baritone, singing the role of Tonio in *I Pagliacci*. After he had sung baritone parts for a season, he made his debut as a tenor (1960) after further study. His career took a sharp upward turn through his brilliant successes at the leading opera houses in Italy; he sang at La Scala in Milan and in 1964 was engaged at the Metropolitan Opera. In 1965 he sang the role of Pollione in *Norma* at the Arena Festival. The brilliance of his voice and the richly expressive interpretations of this artist have proven his ability in many roles, particularly in the Italian repertory.

Records: Decca. *U.S. re-issue* London.

PREY, HERMANN, baritone, b. July 11, 1929, Berlin. He studied at the Berlin High School of Music with Günther Baum and Harry Gottschalk. In 1952 he won a singing competition conducted by the Hessian radio and in the same year he made his stage debut in Wiesbaden. In 1953 he became a regular member of the Hamburg Opera and after 1956 was concurrently a regular guest at the Vienna State Opera and the Berlin City Opera; since 1959 he has had similar arrangements with the Operas in Munich and Cologne. In 1956 he undertook a highly successful American tour, in which he was especially admired as a singer of lieder. Since 1959 he has garnered many laurels at the Salzburg Festivals. He has appeared as guest at La Scala, in Copenhagen, Amsterdam, and Brussels. In 1960 he was engaged at the Metropolitan Opera, making his debut there as Wolfram in *Tannhäuser*, the same role which

he had sung at the Bayreuth Festival in 1956. His warm, expressive baritone voice is inspiring on the stage, particularly in lyric roles, and in the concert hall in his superior interpretations of songs.
Records: Particularly for Columbia (*Der Barbier von Bagdad, Die Kluge, Ariadne auf Naxos, Carmen, Le Nozze di Figaro,* and song cycles, such as Schubert's *Die Winterreise*); also Odeon. *U.S. re-issue:* Electrola, London, Angel, Turnabout, DGG, Vox, Seraphim.

PRICE, LEONTYNE, soprano, b. 1929, Laurel, Miss. This young Negro artist was trained at the Juilliard School of Music and by Florence Page Kimball in New York. In 1950 she made her debut as a concert singer and in 1951 her stage debut in *Four Saints in Three Acts.* Also in 1951 she joined a company to make a tour through Europe with *Porgy and Bess.* She appeared as Bess with great success in London, Paris, Berlin, and Moscow; her partner was the baritone William Warfield, whom she married and from whom she was later separated. In 1954 she greatly moved the audience at a concert in Town Hall in New York by her spectacular singing. She then sang Aïda at the Chicago and San Francisco Opera Houses. In 1957 she was very successful in a concert tour of Italy and in her appearances at La Scala as Aïda. She triumphed in the same role in 1958 at the Arena Festival. She has appeared regularly as guest at the Vienna State Opera, Covent Garden, the Paris Opéra, and the Berlin City Opera. In 1960 she was celebrated for her portrayal of Donna Anna in *Don Giovanni* at the Salzburg Festival. In 1960 she was also engaged at the Metropolitan Opera, making her debut as Leonora in *Il Trovatore.* She has sung there since. In 1966 she created the role of Cleopatra in *Anthony and Cleopatra,* which had its world *première* as the opening production at the Metropolitan Opera's new home in Lincoln Center. One of the most beautiful soprano voices of her time; her tonal beauty and intelligent portrayals are remarkable. In addition to her stage roles, she is a famous singer of songs.
Records: RCA Victor* (*Aïda, Don Giovanni,* and *Il Trovatore*); she has made two records for Decca. *U.S. re-issue:* Columbia, London.

PROHASKA, JARO, baritone, b. Jan. 24, 1891, Vienna; d. Oct. 2, 1965, Munich. At the age of seven he was singing with the Vienna Sängerknaben and later was an alto soloist with this group. He first wanted to be an elementary school teacher, but in 1907 he began the study of music at the Conservatory of the City of Vienna with Otto Müller. There he studied music theory, piano, and conducting. In 1909 he became choir leader at St. Teresa's Church in Vienna. In 1912 he joined the army and took part in World War I. In 1915 he was captured and confined in a Russian prison near Przemysl until 1919. After 1920 he was busy as a concert singer. In 1922 he made his stage debut at Lübeck and remained there for three years. He sang in Nuremberg (1925-31) and was one of the most prominent singers at the Berlin State Opera (1931-52). There in 1935 he sang in the world *première* of *Der Prinz von Homburg.* In 1933 he was admired at the Bayreuth Festival for his singing of Hans Sachs in *Die Meistersinger* and he appeared there regularly until 1944, particularly as Wotan in the *Ring* cycle, but also as the Flying Dutchman, as Telramund in *Lohengrin,* Amfortas in *Parsifal,* Kurwenal in *Tristan und Isolde,* and Donner in the *Ring* cycle. He also appeared in productions at the Salzburg Festivals and made guest appearances in the leading opera houses in Europe and South America. In 1947 he became a teacher and in 1949 a professor at the Berlin Music High School. He had a well-managed heroic baritone voice; he was a singer of the first rank as a Wagner interpreter.

Records: Telefunken (Bayreuth, 1936) and Urania. *U.S. re-recording:* Telefunken, London.

PROTTI, ALDO, baritone, b. 1926 (?). He made his debut (1948) on the Italian radio and in the same year made his stage debut at Pesaro as Figaro in *Il Barbiere di Siviglia*. By 1949 he was already appearing at La Scala, where he excited great comment by his performance as Amonasro in *Aïda* and as Gérard in *Andrea Chénier*. In the following years he sang at all the important Italian opera houses, but particularly at La Scala and the Rome Opera; he made guest appearances at the Paris Opéra, in Spain, the United States, and Switzerland. At the Arena Festivals he sang Egberto in *Aroldo* and Don Carlos in *La Forza del Destino*. Since 1957 he has been a regular guest at the Vienna State Opera; he has also appeared in productions at the Salzburg Festivals. He is a baritone of exceptionally voluminous tone and is especially known as an interpreter of Verdi.

Records: A great many records for Philips, but particularly for Decca (including *I Pagliacci, Cavalleria Rusticana, Aïda, Otello, Rigoletto,* and *La Traviata*). *U.S. re-issue:* London, Richmond.

PÜTZ, RUTH-MARGRET, soprano, b. Feb. 26, 1931, Krefeld, Germany. She studied in Krefeld with Berthold Pütz. In 1950 she came to the Cologne Opera as a beginner and made her debut as Nuri in *Tiefland*. She was engaged at the Hannover Opera (1951-57) and studied there with Otto Köhler. In 1957 she sang as guest at the Stuttgart Opera as Gilda in *Rigoletto* and was engaged for the company. In 1958 she had a spectacular success as Zerbinetta in *Ariadne auf Naxos* there. She sang at the Glyndebourne Festival in 1958 and appeared at the Bayreuth Festival as the Forest Bird in *Siegfried*. In addition to guest appearances at the Hamburg Opera, she held a second guest contract with the Vienna State Opera. After 1961 she was highly successful at the Salzburg Festivals, particularly as Konstanze in *Die Entführung aus dem Serail*. She made a triumphal tour of Russia in 1961.

Records: Her first records appeared on the Opera label (*The Magnificat*, by J.S. Bach); she then sang for Electrola (*The Merry Wives of Windsor*), Telefunken, and Columbia (*Il Barbiere di Siviglia*). *U.S. re-issue:* Electrola, Angel.

Q

QUARTARARO, FLORENCE, soprano, b. May 31, 1922, San Francisco. She studied singing with Elizabeth Wells in San Francisco and with Pietro Cimini in Los Angeles. She earned a diploma as a teacher of singing and then made her debut as a concert singer (1945) at the Hollywood Bowl. After successful concerts on the radio, her stage debut followed (1946) at the Metropolitan Opera, where she was introduced as Micaëla in *Carmen*. She remained a valuable member of this company until 1949 and sang such parts there as Pamina in *Die Zauberflöte*, Desdemona in *Otello*, Violetta in *La Traviata*, and Nedda in *I Pagliacci*. She made guest appearances in opera in San Francisco and Philadelphia. In 1953 she appeared at the Arena Flegrea in Naples as Margherita in *Mefistofele*. Thereafter she was heard only occasionally in the concert hall.

Records: RCA Victor*.

R

RAATZ-BROCKMANN, JULIUS VON, baritone, b. Apr. 29, 1870, Hamburg; d. Oct. 23, 1944, Perleberg, Germany. He studied law at the Universities of Bonn and Innsbruck and then completed his study of singing in Berlin and Milan. Through Cosima Wagner he was induced to study Wagner's operas, while at the same time he was occupied as a concert singer. He was admired as a soloist in oratorio and in sacred music as well as in lieder and ballads, but he was especially well liked as an interpreter of Bach. He had enormous success in the concert halls of both Germany and foreign countries. After 1907 he lived and taught singing in Berlin and after 1923 he was a professor at the Berlin Music High School. A highly expressive baritone voice.

Records: Edison cylinders, Anker, Kalliope, and HMV discs; he made ten sides of Loewe ballads for Odeon (Berlin, 1909).

RADEV, MARIANNA, contralto, b. Nov. 21, 1911, Constantza, Rumania. She studied until 1936 at the Music Academy in Zagreb, then in Milan and Trieste and made her debut in the latter city at the Teatro Verdi (1937) as Marina in *Boris Godounov*. She sang very successfully in 1938 at the Rome Opera and then became a member of the Opera in Zagreb. After World War II she appeared as guest at La Scala, in Rome, and in Vienna and earned a great reputation as a concert contralto. In 1955 she sang Carmen at Covent Garden and in 1965 she appeared at the Salzburg Festival. She possesses a dark-timbred contralto voice.

Records: DGG (Verdi's *Requiem*, Rossini's *Stabat Mater*, and Beethoven's *Missa Solemnis*). U.S. re-issue: American Decca.

RADFORD, ROBERT, bass, b. May 13, 1874, Nottingham, England; d. Mar. 3, 1933, London. He studied at the Royal Academy of Music in London with Albert Randegger, Battison Haynes, and Frederick King. He made his concert debut (1899) at the Norwich Festival and his stage debut (1904) at Covent Garden as the Commandant in *Don Giovanni*. He was very successful at Covent Garden and in 1910 appeared in Mozart roles at His Majesty's Theater also. In 1921 he became one of the founders of the British National Opera Company and took over its direction. In 1929 he was made a professor at the Royal Academy of Music in London. He never appeared outside England.

Records: G & T (London, 1903-06), Columbia (London, 1904), Zonophone (London, 1914); after 1908 he made a great many acoustical and electric records for HMV. *U.S. re-issue:* Victor.

RAIMONDI, GIANNI, tenor, b. Apr. 17, 1923, Bologna, Italy. He made his stage debut in Budrio (1947) as the Duke in *Rigoletto*. In 1948 he sang Ernesto in *Don Pasquale* at Bologna. After he had been successful on most of the larger Italian stages, he came to La Scala in 1956, being introduced as Alfredo in *La Traviata* with Maria Callas. In 1958 he again appeared with her, this time singing Lord Percy in *Anna Bolena*. In 1957 he sang as guest at the Arena Festival, his role being that of Pollione in *Norma*. A world-wide career quickly developed for this singer; since 1959 he has frequently appeared at the Vienna State Opera and since 1960 at the Munich State Opera. In 1959 he was very successful in the United States; he was also admired at Covent Garden and at the Teatro Colón. In 1965 he made his debut at the Metropolitan Opera. A strong and brilliant tenor voice.

Records: Cetra* (*La Favorita*) and DGG*.

RAINS, LEON, bass, b. Oct. 1, 1870, New York; d. July 11, 1954, Los Angeles. He began studying singing in 1890 at the National Conservatory in New York, then became a pupil of Oscar Saenger. In 1896 he went to Paris for further study with Jacques Bouhy. He made his debut (1897) with the Damrosch-Ellis Opera Company and toured the United States with them in 1899. In the same year he was engaged for a guest appearance with the Dresden Royal Opera and he remained there for eighteen years. In 1904 he sang Hagen in *Götterdämmerung* at the Bayreuth Festival and in the same year he also sang as guest at Covent Garden. He was greatly admired at the Metropolitan Opera as Hagen and as Mephistopheles in *Faust* (1909-10). Upon the entry of the United States into World War I, he was required to leave Dresden and he returned to the United States, where he appeared only rarely in the concert hall. He was especially admired as a lieder singer. After 1924 he lived and taught in Los Angeles.

Records: G & T (Bayreuth, 1904; Dresden 1905-07); he sang the Landgrave in a recording of Act II of *Tannhäuser* for Odeon and later recorded for HMV and Columbia.

RAISA, ROSA, soprano, b. May 30, 1893, Bialystok, Poland; d. Sept. 28, 1963, Los Angeles. She studied at the Conservatory of San Pietro a Majella in Naples and then became a pupil of Barbara Marchisio in Milan. She made her debut in Parma (1913) and in the same year she also sang at La Scala. In 1914 she was highly successful at the Teatro Costanzi and in 1916 at the Teatro Colón. She was engaged at the Chicago Opera in 1916 and there her career reached its high point. In 1920 she married the baritone Giacomo Rimini, who was also on the roster of the Chicago company. From Chicago she undertook brilliant guest-appearance tours to Covent Garden, the Paris Opéra, and the opera houses in Brussels, Rio de Janeiro, Montevideo, and São Paulo. She frequently sang at La Scala, where she was particularly admired by Toscanini. On May 1, 1924, she sang the role of Asteria there in the world *première* of Boito's *Nerone* and on Apr. 25, 1926, the title role in *Tur-*

andot. She was highly successful at the Arena Festival and at the Maggio Musicale Festival where in 1933 she sang in *Les Huguenots* with Giacomo Lauri-Volpi. In 1937 she opened an opera studio in Chicago with her husband and after his death she directed it alone. At the last she lived in California. A dark-timbred soprano voice of overflowing tonal volume.

Records: Acoustic records for American Pathé*, Vocalion*, and Brunswick*; electric records for HMV. *U.S. re-issue:* RCA Victor, IRCC. *U.S. re-recording:* TAP, Scala, FRP, RCA Victor.

RALF, TORSTEN, tenor, b. Jan. 2, 1901, Malmö, Sweden; d. Apr. 27, 1954, Stockholm. His two older brothers, Oscar Ralf and Einar Ralf, were both highly admired opera singers. Torsten Ralf studied first at the Royal Conservatory in Stockholm and then in Berlin with Hertha Dehmlow. He made his debut in Stettin (1930) as Cavaradossi in *Tosca*. By way of Chemnitz and Frankfurt he came to Dresden in 1935. He was highly successful at the State Opera there until 1943. On Oct. 15, 1938, he sang the role of Apollo there in the world *première* of *Daphne* with Margarethe Teschemacher. He was particularly celebrated as a Wagner tenor and often appeared as guest in Munich, Vienna, and at Covent Garden. After 1941 he was a member of the Royal Opera in Stockholm and in 1952 was named Swedish Court Singer. He was a member of the Metropolitan Opera (1945-47). In 1946 he toured South America, where he was particularly applauded at the Teatro Colón. After 1948 he lived in Sweden and until 1952 he appeared on the stage and in concert there.

Records: HMV, Vox* (*Fidelio*), and Columbia*. *U.S. re-issue:* RCA Victor. *U.S. re-recording:* Rococo.

RANCZAK, HILDEGARD, soprano, b. Dec. 20, 1895, Witkowitz, Moravia. She studied at the Conservatory of the City of Vienna and made her debut in Düsseldorf (1920), singing there until 1923. She sang at the Cologne Opera (1923-24) and at Stuttgart (1926-28). In 1928 she was called to the Munich State Opera and remained there until 1944. She made very successful guest appearances, particularly in The Hague and Amsterdam. She appeared as Salome at Covent Garden in 1936 and at the Paris Opéra in 1937 as Octavian in *Der Rosenkavalier*. In 1940 she sang at the Rome Opera and also at the Berlin State Opera, where she was particularly successful. In 1942 she sang the role of Clairon in the world *première* of *Capriccio* at Munich. She lives in Berg-am-Starnbergersee.

Records: Telefunken and DGG. *U.S. re-recording:* Telefunken.

RANKIN, NELL, contralto, b. 1925, Montgomery, Ala. She studied singing for four years with Jeanne Lorraine and Karin Branzell in New York. She gave her first concerts in 1947 and made her stage debut (1948) at Zürich as Ortrud in *Lohengrin*. In 1949 she came to Basel and in 1950 won an international singing competition in Geneva. In the same year she appeared as guest at La Scala and in 1951 sang at the Verdi Festival there, taking the contralto solo part in the Verdi *Requiem*. In 1951 she came to the Metropolitan Opera, where she has appeared very successfully.

Records: Decca (Suzuki in *Madama Butterfly* with Renata Tebaldi). *U.S. re-issue:* Columbia, Richmond, London.

RAPPOLD, MARIE, soprano, b. 1873, London; d. May 12, 1957, Los Angeles. Originally Marie Winterroth. She appeared in children's roles in London at the age of five and later came with her parents when they immigrated to the United States. She studied with Oscar Saenger in New York and made her debut (1905) at the Metropolitan Opera, singing Sulamith in *Die Königin von Saba*. She remained at the Metropolitan until 1909, then went to the Bucharest Opera and concurrently appeared as guest in German opera houses. Her first marriage was to the American physician Julius Rappold; in 1913 she married the tenor Rudolf Berger. She was again engaged at the Metropolitan in 1910 and remained there until 1920. In the 1920's she appeared as guest at the Havana Opera and at the Teatro San Carlo. She was a member of the Chicago Opera (1927-28) and made a concert tour through Europe in 1929. At the end of her life she was a teacher in Los Angeles.

Records: Edison* cylinders and discs. *U.S. re-recording:* IRCC, TAP.

RASKIN, JUDITH, soprano, b. June 21, 1932, New York. She studied at Smith College and with Anna Hamlin in New York. She made her debut on NBC television in *Les Dialogues des Carmélites*. She appeared with the Washington Opera Society and was well liked in the role of Susanna in *Le Nozze di Figaro* in Santa Fe. She has also sung with the American Opera Society in New York and appeared at Central City in Colorado in the title role in *The Ballad of Baby Doe*. She has sung at the Dallas opera, including performances of Chérubini's *Medea* with Maria Callas. Her principal appearances have been as a leading soprano with the New York City Opera, where she first sang Despina in *Così fan tutte*. On television she has appeared as Marzellina in *Fidelio* and as Zerlina in *Don Giovanni*. In addition to other concert and opera appearances, she made her debut at the Glyndebourne Festival in 1962 as Pamina in *Die Zauberflöte*, and in the same year she came to the Metropolitan Opera, where her debut role was that of Susanna in *Le Nozze di Figaro*.

Records: Decca*. *U.S. re-recordings:* Columbia, RCA Victor, Epic, London.

RATTI, EUGENIA, soprano, b. 1933, Genoa, Italy. She first studied voice with her mother. In 1952 Tito Schipa heard this young singer and engaged her for a concert tour with him. She made her stage debut in Sestri Levanti (1954). In 1955 she sang Lisa in *La Sonnambula* at La Scala. Since then she has had great success there and she sang the role of Constance in the world *première* there of *Les Dialogues des Carmélites* in 1957. In 1955 she appeared at the Holland Festival in *L'Italiana in Algeri*. She has appeared at all the great Italian opera houses and in 1959 at the San Francisco Opera. Hers is a beautiful coloratura voice.

Records: Columbia (*Falstaff*, *La Bohème*, *Un Ballo in Maschera*, *Aida*, and *La Sonnambula*) and RCA Victor (*Don Giovanni*). *U.S. re-issue:* Angel.

RAUTAWAARA, AULIKKI, soprano, b. May 2, 1906, Helsinki, Finland. Her father, Eino Rautawaara, was a singing teacher in Helsinki. She studied first with him, then with Olga Eisner in Berlin, and made her debut (1932) at the Helsinki Opera. She became internationally known through her brilliant guest appearances. She was the center of attraction at the Glyndebourne Festivals (1934-38), particularly for her remarkable Countess in *Le Nozze di Figaro*. She also sang very successfully at the Salzburg Festival in 1937. Other guest appearances included the State Operas in Berlin, Munich, and Vienna, Amsterdam, Brussels, and the Royal

Opera in Stockholm. She appeared in films and was a well-known operetta singer. After World War II she resumed her residence in Helsinki and undertook her guest-appearance and concert activity from there. She sang at the Visby Festivals (1946-50) and gave concerts at the Edinburgh Festival in 1949. She is now a voice teacher in Helsinki.

Records: Telefunken and HMV (*Le Nozze di Figaro*, Glyndebourne, 1934). *U.S. re-issue* RCA Victor, Vox, Westminster. *U.S. re-recording:* Eterna, Telefunken, Turnabout.

RAVEAU, ALICE, contralto, b. 1884 (?); d. 1945, Paris. She studied at the National Conservatory in Paris with Dubulle and made her debut at the Opéra-Comique there (1908) in the title role of *Orphée et Eurydice*; this role remained her particular starring part and she was held to be unsurpassed in it within her generation. In 1911 she was applauded for her singing of this part at the Arena in Orange. At the Opéra-Comique she sang in 1910 in the world *premières* of *Leone* and Ernest Bloch's *Macbeth*. After successful appearances at the Paris Opéra, as well as in Marseilles, Toulouse, and Bordeaux, she dedicated herself more and more to concerts and song recitals. She was considered one of the most famous French song interpreters of her time and sang particularly the songs of Henri Tomasi. She made a concert tour through Scandinavia, Belgium, and Holland in 1934. The voice of this artist was notable for its rich tone and delicately expressive shading.

Records Odeon and Pathé records; she made electric records for Columbia-Pathé (including *Orphée et Eurydice* under Henri Tomasi, 1936). *U.S. re-recording:* Vox, Scala.

RAYNER, SIDNEY, tenor, b. 1895, New Orleans, La. He studied in the United States and in Milan and made his debut in Italy (1927). He sang at the Opéra-Comique very successfully (1930-35). During this time he also appeared as guest in the opera houses in Marseilles, Lyons, and Tunis. In 1936 he was engaged at the Metropolitan Opera and stayed there until 1938. He was particularly admired for his interpretations of lyric roles in the Italian and French repertories. A famous concert singer, he lives and teaches in New York.

Records: Decca. *U.S. re-issue:* American Decca. *U.S. re-recording:* Eterna.

REALI, ANTENORE, baritone, b. June 17, 1897, Verona, Italy; d. January, 1960, Milan. He made his debut in 1925 and in 1926 undertook a tour of Indonesia; he then sang on various Italian stages and was highly successful at the Italian Opera in Holland (1930-35). In 1936 he was called to La Scala and appeared there regularly until 1949. He also sang at the Rome Opera and at the Arena and Maggio Musicale Festivals, as well as in London, Vienna, and Brussels. In 1952 he again gave concerts in Holland. In the winter of 1958 he suffered a stroke and had to give up his career.

Records: Cetra* (*Il Tabarro* and *La Gioconda*).

REGGIANI, HILDE, soprano, b. Nov. 26, 1911, Modena, Italy. She studied at the Conservatory in Bologna and made her debut in Modena (1933) as Gilda in *Rigoletto*. She sang at the Italian Opera in Holland (1933-34) and at the Teatro Reale with Beniamino Gigli in 1935. She sang next in Budapest and at the Teatro Colón (1935-38). She was engaged at the Chicago Opera (1938-39) and at the Metropolitan Opera in 1939, making her debut there as Gilda. She remained at the Metropolitan until 1943 and in 1940-41 toured the United States with the opera company of Charles L. Wagner. She returned to the Teatro Colón as guest in 1947 and thereafter sang especially in Italy. She was married to the tenor Bruno Landi. Hers was a musical and intelligently managed coloratura voice.

Records: RCA Victor (*Il Barbiere di Siviglia*) and Allegro Royale*.

REHFUSS, HEINZ, baritone, b. May 25, 1917, Frankfurt a. M. His father was the concert singer and teacher Carl Rehfuss (1885-1946) and his mother, Florentine Rehfuss-Peichert, was an admired concert contralto. The son spent his youth in Neuchâtel, Switzerland, where his parents had moved and where he was trained by his father. He made his debut (1938) at Biel-Solothurn and in 1939 came to Zürich, where he was highly successful. From there he made guest appearances at La Scala, the Paris Opéra, the State Operas in Vienna and Munich, and the Operas in Chicago and Amsterdam. He also appeared at the Festivals in Verona and Venice and at the Maggio Musicale Festival. In 1961 he sang at the Teatro Fenice in the world *premiére* of *Intolleranza 60*. Concert tours brought him brilliant success in Germany, France, England, Italy, Austria, Belgium, Holland, and North America. He teaches singing in Zürich. He had a wide-ranging and highly flexible baritone voice; among his starring roles were Don Giovanni and Boris Godounov; he was especially famous in the concert hall as an interpreter of Bach.

Records: MMS (including *Fidelio, Les Contes d'Hoffmann, Carmen,* and *The Messiah*), Nixa (*St. Matthew Passion* and *B Minor Mass* of Bach), Decca (*L'Heure Espagnole, Pelléas et Mélisande,* and *Roméo et Juliette*) and Philips (*Oedipus Rex*). *U.S. re-issue:* DGG, Angel, Westminster, Epic, London, Perfect, Harmony, Columbia, Nonesuch, Mercury, Vanguard.

REHKEMPER, HEINRICH, baritone, b. May 23, 1894, Schwerte, Germany; d. Dec. 12, 1949, Munich. At first a machinist, he studied singing in the Conservatories in Hagen and Düsseldorf and then at the Munich Music Academy. He made his stage debut (1919) in Coburg. He then sang at Stuttgart (1921-24) and after 1925 at the Munich State Opera, where he was one of the best-liked singers of his time. He sang there in 1931 in the *première* of *Das Herz*. After 1924 he was especially noted as a concert singer and was held to be one of the great interpreters of lieder in his time. His art and genius in this field were acknowledged both in Germany and abroad. During the period 1940-45 in addition to his singing career he was a teacher at the Mozarteum in Salzburg. His warm and beautifully expressive baritone voice was best displayed in Mozart roles on the stage, but also in the Italian and Wagner repertories. He was also a lieder singer of the first rank.

Records: Polydor. *U.S. re-issue:* Vox. *U.S. re-recording:* Scala, TAP, Rococo.

REIMERS, PAUL, tenor, b. Mar. 14, 1877, Lunden, Germany; d. Apr. 14, 1942, New York City. He came of a German-Danish family. He studied with Spengel in Berlin, with Sir George Henschel and Raimund von zur Mühlen in England, and with Jean Criticos in Paris. He made his stage debut as Max in *Der Freischütz* at Hamburg (1903). He soon gave up his stage career and dedicated himself exclusively to oratorio and particularly to lieder singing. He was especially treasured in Germany as an interpreter of the tenor solo part in Beethoven's *Ninth Symphony*. He sang also in Holland, Belgium, England, and France and was the first German singer to bring the songs of the French Impressionist composers before the public. In 1913 he came to the United States, where he was highly successful in the concert hall and where he remained thereafter. During the 1920's he gave master courses for lieder singers each summer in Baden-Baden. After 1914 he was a professor at the Juilliard School of Music in New York. One of the most accomplished lieder singers of the twentieth century, he was a constant source of wonder for both the rich coloration of his expressive art and for the masterful skill he had in phrasing.

Records: Odeon (Berlin, 1907) including duets with Julia Culp; Victor*, including (about 1927) duets with Hulda Lashanka, and both Edison* cylinders and discs.

REINHARDT, DELIA, soprano, b. Apr. 27, 1892, Elberfeld, Germany. She entered Hoch's Conservatory in Frankfurt a. M., where she was a pupil of Strakosch and of Hedwig Schako. She made her debut in Breslau (1913) and from there went to the Munich State Opera (1916-23) She had great success at the Metropolitan Opera (1923-24). She was a member of the Berlin State Opera (1924-33) and made guest appearances at Covent Garden, the Paris Opéra, and in Copenhagen, Budapest, Amsterdam, and Brussels, as well as in Italian and Spanish opera houses. She was very successful at the Teatro Colón. She was first married to the baritone Gustav Schützendorf and then to the conductor Georges Sebastian. After 1937 she was not allowed, for political reasons, to appear in Germany; she immigrated to the United States then and lives in California. She was admired both for the natural freshness of her characterizations and for the musicality of her voice management.

Records: Polydor.

REINING, MÁRIA, soprano, b. Aug. 7, 1903, Vienna. At first an employee in the foreign exchange department of a bank in Vienna, she began her study of singing at the age of twenty-five. In 1931 she made her debut at the Vienna State Opera, where she sang soubrette roles until 1933. She sang at Darmstadt (1933-35) and at the Munich State Opera (1935-37). In 1937 she returned to the Vienna State Opera, at first as a youthful dramatic soprano, and had brilliant success there. After 1937 she appeared almost every year at the Salzburg Festivals: as Eva in *Die Meistersinger* under Toscanini in 1937, as the Marschallin in *Der Rosenkavalier*, and in the title role in *Arabella*. Both at Salzburg and on many another famous operatic stage she sang Mozart roles particularly. She was highly successful both in guest appearances at Covent Garden, La Scala, the New York City Opera, and the Chicago Opera and also as a concert singer. She was admired for the lightness and strength of her soprano voice, for her intelligent conception of her roles, and for her delicate sense of style.

Records: Telefunken, HMV, and Decca (the Marschallin in *Der Rosenkavalier*). *U.S. re-issue:* London, Telefunken, DGG, Electrola, Richmond.

REINMAR, HANS, baritone, b. April 11, 1895, Vienna; d. Feb. 6, 1961, Berlin. He studied at the Vienna Academy of Music and with Vittorio Vanza in Milan and made his debut (1919) at Olomouc. His later engagements included:

Zürich (1921-23), the Dresden State Opera (1923-26), Hamburg (1926-28), and finally the Berlin City Opera (1928-45). Guest appearances took him to the Vienna State Opera, La Scala, the Paris Opéra, and the opera houses in Brussels and Rome. He was an admired Wagner singer at the Bayreuth Festivals (1938-41) where he sang Donner and Gunther in the *Ring* cycle and Amfortas in *Parsifal*. At the Salzburg Festival he sang Mandryka in *Arabella* (1942-43). He appeared at the Munich State Opera (1945-47), the Berlin State Opera (1947-52), and from 1952 until his untimely death he was again a well-liked member of the Berlin City Opera. He was famous both for the tonal volume and for the artistic skill of his characterizations, particularly in heroic baritone roles.

Records: Odeon and Telefunken. *U.S. re-recording:* Telefunken.

REISS, ALBERT, tenor, b. Dec. 31, 1870, Berlin; d. June 20, 1940, Nice. He was first an actor in Hamburg (1889-97). His voice was discovered by Bernhard Pollini and Ernestine Schumann-Heink. Thereupon he studied with Wilhelm Vilmar, Benno Stolzenburg, and Julius Lieban in Berlin and made his debut (1897) as Ivanov in *Zar und Zimmermann* at Königsberg in East Prussia. He sang at Posen (1898-99), at Wiesbaden, and at the Munich Royal Opera (1899-1901). In 1901 he was engaged at the Metropolitan Opera and remained there until 1919 as principal *buffo* tenor. He was especially pleasing as David in *Die Meistersinger* and as Mime in the *Ring* cycle. In 1910 he sang Nick in the world *première* of *La Fanciulla del West;* on Dec. 28, 1910, the Broommaker in the world *première* of *Königskinder;* and in 1917 he appeared in the world *première* of *The Canterbury Pilgrims*.

In 1919 he returned to Germany, where he was engaged at the Berlin Volksoper (1923-25) and later made guest appearances at the Berlin City Opera.

Records: Victor*, HMV, and Polydor. *U.S. re-issue:* IRCC. *U.S. re-recording:* RCA Victor, Cantilena.

REIZEN, MARK, bass, b. June 21, 1895, Kharkov, Russia. He studied at the Conservatory in Kharkov with Bugamell (1917-19) and made his debut at the Opera there in 1921. He sang at the Leningrad Opera (1925-30) and was then engaged at the Bolshoi Theater, where he was considered one of the most prominent singers thereafter. He appeared there for over thirty years. He earned great international success by his guest appearances at the Paris Opéra, at the State Operas in Berlin and Dresden, and at the National Opera in Budapest. He made concert tours both in Russia and in western Europe. He was awarded the Stalin Prize, the Order of Lenin, and was named a "People's Artist of the U.S.S.R." He had a sumptuous, typically Russian bass voice; he was especially noted for the dignified manner of his characterizations.

Records: Russian State Record Trust (including *Boris Godounov*). *U.S. re-issue:* Colosseum, Monitor, Bruno.

RENAUD, MAURICE, baritone, b. 1861, Bordeaux; d. Oct. 16, 1933, Paris. He studied at the Paris National Conservatory and made his debut (1883) at the Théâtre de la Monnaie, where he remained until 1890; he sang there in 1884 in the world *première* of *Sigurd*. In 1890 he was engaged at the Opéra-Comique, where he first appeared in the role of Karnac in *Le Roi d'Ys*. He immediately had great success at the two great Paris opera houses, and was also highly successful in guest appearances at La Scala, Covent Garden, and the Brussels and Monte Carlo Operas. In 1902 he sang the role of Boniface at Monte Carlo in the world *première* of *Le Jongleur de Notre-Dame*, and in 1905, again at Monte Carlo, he sang in the world *première* of *Chérubin*; in 1906 at the Théâtre Nouveau in Paris he had a part in the world *première* of *Le Clown*. In 1906 he was engaged by the Metropolitan Opera, but due to a change in management the contract fell through and he became a highly successful singer on the roster of the Manhattan Opera Company (1906-10). He was a member of the Metropolitan Opera (1910-12) and appeared as guest with the Chicago and Boston companies. In 1912 he returned to France and ended his career in Paris; at the last he taught singing there. He united a completed mastery of the techniques of singing, a deeply founded musicality, and a rare stylistic delicacy of portrayal. He was particularly famous in the role of Don Giovanni.

Records: G & T (Paris, 1901-06; London, 1902), HMV, and Pathé. *U.S. re-issue:* Victor, HRS, IRCC. *U.S. re-recording:* IRCC, RCA Victor, FRP, TAP, Eterna, Belcanto, Rococo.

RESNIK, REGINA, soprano-contralto, b. Aug. 30, 1923, New York. She studied music at Harvard University with Fritz Busch and others, and won a prize in the Metropolitan Opera Auditions of the Air contest. She made her debut in 1942 at the New York City Opera as Santuzza in *Cavalleria Rusticana*. In 1943 she appeared as guest at the Mexico City Opera and in 1945 she was engaged at the Metropolitan Opera. There, in 1948, she sang Ellen Orford in the first New York performance of *Peter Grimes*. Guest appearances in Chicago, San Francisco, London, and Paris followed and in 1953 she sang Sieglinde in *Die Walküre* at the Bayreuth Festival. Her voice then changed to contralto and after further study with Giuseppe Danise she made her debut at the Metropolitan Opera (1956) as Marina in *Boris Godounov*. Outstanding success attended her performances at Covent Garden in 1957; since 1958 she has appeared regularly as a guest at the Vienna State Opera. In 1960 she was applauded at the Salzburg Festival as Princess Eboli in *Don Carlos* and at Bayreuth as Fricka in the *Ring* cycle. She later made guest appearances at the Teatro Colón and at the leading Italian opera houses. The dark tonal quality of her voice and the fascinating drama of her portrayals have rightly caused her to be repeatedly admired for her art; her particular starring role is Carmen.

Records: As a soprano she recorded for Columbia* and as a contralto for Decca (*Tristan und Isolde*). *U.S. re-issue:* RCA Victor, Westminster, London, Everest.

RESZKE, EDOUARD DE, bass, b. Dec. 22, 1855, Warsaw; d. Apr. 25, 1917, Gurek, Poland. Originally Edouard Mieczislav. He was the brother of both the famous tenor Jean de Reszke and the soprano Joséphine de Reszke (1845-91). He did not originally plan to become a singer, but his voice was discovered by his brother Jean. Thereupon he studied with Steller and Alba in Milan, with Coletti in Naples, and finally with Giovanni Sbriglia in Paris. He first appeared in 1875 in Warsaw. He had great success at the Théâtre Italien in Paris in 1876 as the King in *Aida* in a performance given in the presence of Verdi, and he sang at that house until 1880. In 1879 he appeared as guest at La Scala; in 1880 he was successful at Covent Garden, later in Trieste, Turin, and Lisbon. He sang at Covent Garden (1880-84), where he returned again and again as a guest. He was first bass at the Paris Opéra (1885-98) and during this time completed many starring guest performances in all the great international music centers, particularly in St. Petersburg, Warsaw, Vienna, Berlin, Monte Carlo, Madrid, and Barcelona. In 1891 he came to the Metropolitan Opera, making his debut as Friar Lawrence in *Roméo et Juliette*. Until 1903 he was a greatly admired member of the Metropolitan roster. After a short period of teaching in Paris, he was engaged in 1906 by the Manhattan Opera Company, but he never appeared there. He taught singing in London (1906-08) and in 1909 founded a school for singers in Warsaw. Later he lived on his estate, Gurek, in Polish Silesia. During the invasion by German troops in World War I, he fell into pressing poverty.

Records: The strength and volume of his expressive bass voice can only be guessed at from poorly made records for American Columbia* in 1903. He is also heard on Mapleson cylinders. *U.S. re-recording:* Columbia, IRCC, TAP, Cantilena, Rococo.

RESZKE, JEAN DE, tenor, b. Jan. 14, 1850, Warsaw; d. Apr. 3, 1925, Nice. Originally Jan Mieczislav. He came from a very musical family; his brother Edouard and his sister Joséphine were both world-famous singers. He studied first with Ciaffei in Warsaw and then with Antonio Cotogni in Venice. He made his debut as a baritone under the name Giovanni di Reschi (1874) at the Teatro Fenice as Alfonso in *La Favorita*. In the following years he sang baritone parts on Italian stages and in Paris and London. After renewing his studies with Giovanni Sbriglia in Paris, he made his debut as a tenor at the Teatro Real in the title role of *Robert le Diable* in 1879. In 1884 he had a sensational success at the Paris Opéra as Jean in *Hérodiade*; at the same theater in 1885 he created the title role at the world *première* of *Le Cid*. He had a triumphal career at the Opéra until 1889 and was soon esteemed as the greatest tenor of his time. Guest appearances on the leading stages of Italy, France, Russia, England, and Austria confirmed this estimate of the artist. In 1890, at the climax of his career, he was engaged by the Metropolitan Opera. In America he added to his already extensive repertory the heroic Wagner tenor roles. Until 1902 he was the admired principal tenor of the Metropolitan. In that year he appeared occasionally in a few roles at the Paris Opéra, then gave up his career. He lived in Paris and became a much-sought-after teacher of singing. He married the French contralto Marie de Goulain; his only son, a French officer, died in World War I. Jean de Reszke was one of the greatest personalities known in the history of the art of singing. Aside from the universality of his repertory, the critics of the time celebrated the breadth of expressiveness of his art, the absolute mastery of his singing technique, and the overpowering force of his acting. He confined himself strictly to stage performances and never appeared in the concert hall.

Records: In the year 1905 two records by Jean de Reszke were announced by Fonotipia. Whether these will ever appear is questionable; in any case, they have not turned up; the voice of this famous singer is preserved only on a few fragmentary Mapleson cylinders of great technical inadequacy. *U.S. re-recording:* IRCC.

RETHBERG, ELISABETH, soprano, b. Sept. 22, 1894, Schwarzenberg, Germany. Originally Lisbeth Sättler. She studied first piano and then singing at the Dresden Conservatory (1912-13) and finally with Otto Watrin. She made her singing debut (1915) at Dresden as Agathe in *Der Freischütz*. She remained at Dresden until 1922, when she was called to the Metropolitan Opera. There she had great triumphs as a singer (1922-42). Toscanini remarked that she had the most beautiful soprano voice that he had ever heard. Guest appearances brought her one success after another wherever she appeared: at Havana (1923; 1928), at Covent Garden (1925), at La Scala and the Rome Opera (1929). She was also heard in her native Germany. In 1928 she sang at Dresden in the world *première* of *Die Ägyptische Helena*; at the Salzburg Festivals she sang Konstanze in *Die Entführung aus dem Serail* in 1922, Leonora in *Fidelio* in 1933, and Donna Anna in *Don Giovanni* in the same year. She was first (1923) married to the merchant Albert Doman and then (1957) to the baritone George Cehanovsky. She gave up her career in 1942 and lives in New York City. The soprano voice of Elisabeth Rethberg was equally outstanding for its exquisite tonal beauty, for the complete mastery she had of the technique of singing, and for the musical maturity of her interpretations.

Records: Odeon, Brunswick*, HMV, and Victor*. *U.S. re-issue:* American Decca. *U.S. re-recording:* ASCO, TAP, RCA Victor, Scala, Camden.

RÉTHY, ESTER, soprano, b. Oct. 22, 1912, Budapest. After study in Budapest and Vienna she made her debut (1935) at the Budapest National Opera. In 1937 she was engaged by the Vienna State Opera and she sang there until 1949. She became celebrated through her appearances at the Salzburg Festivals, where she sang Susanna in *Le Nozze di Figaro* and Sophie in *Der Rosenkavalier* (1937-39). During this time she often appeared as guest at the Budapest Opera. Since 1949 she has sung principally at the Vienna Volksoper and has had great success in operetta. She is married to the conductor Anton Paulik.

Records: HMV records, some of them conducted by Franz Lehár. *U.S. re-issue:* Columbia (*Eine Nacht in Venedig*).

REUSS-BELCE, LUISE, soprano, b. Oct. 24, 1862, Vienna; d. March, 1945, Aichach, Germany. Originally Luise Baumann. She studied with Joseph Gänsbacher in Vienna and made her debut (1881) at Karlsruhe as Elsa in *Lohengrin*. On June 26, 1882, she sang the role of a Flower Maiden in the world *première* of *Parsifal* at the Bayreuth Festival. She appeared as guest at the Munich Royal Opera in 1884. She married the conductor and composer Eduard Reuss (1851-1911), who had been a pupil of Franz Liszt. After fifteen years at Karlsruhe, she sang at Weisbaden (1897-1901). During the period 1896-1912 she sang at the Bayreuth Festivals, where she was particularly admired as an unequaled Fricka in the *Ring* cycle. Later she became a dramatic assistant at Bayreuth. She was the last living artist who had sung under Richard Wagner himself. In 1900 she sang Sieglinde in *Die Walküre* at Covent Garden and was a member of the Metropolitan Opera (1902-03). Thereafter she lived in Berlin and made guest appearanecs and gave concerts until 1916. She was the director of staging at the German Opera House in Berlin (1916-25) and she was also *régisseur* at the Nuremberg Festivals. She lived at the last in Dresden, but had to flee from there during the destructive bombing attacks of the last weeks of the war; she died on this flight.

Records: While it is safe to say that she made records for G & T in 1904 at Bayreuth, none of them have thus far been published; therefore there are only fragments on Mapleson cylinders. *U.S. re-recording:* IRCC.

RÉVY, AURELIE, soprano, b. 1879, Kapsovar, Hungary; d. Oct. 30, 1957, Toronto, Canada. She originally wanted to be a violinist, but also studied singing in Budapest and made her debut there (1897) at the Volkstheater. In 1898 she came to England and resumed her studies at the Royal Academy of Music with Alberto Visetti. She sang with the Carl Rosa Opera Company and also at Covent Garden (1898-1900); at the same time she gave concerts as a violinist. In 1900 she transferred her activity to Vienna, where she appeared particularly as an operetta singer at the Carl Theater and at the Theater an der Wien. In 1901 she made a tour of Russia with a Viennese operetta company. After 1901 she lived in Berlin and undertook concert tours and guest appearances. She sang Nedda in *I Pagliacci* at Covent Garden in 1902 and 1904. In 1906 she sang the three leading feminine roles in *Les Contes d'Hoffmann* at Zürich. Still later she married Major George Alexander Chapman and gave up her career early. She then was active as a teacher and as an impresario of opera companies. She spent her last years in Canada.

Records: Zonophone, Odeon (Berlin, 1905-06, and London, 1907-08), and G & T (Berlin, 1906).

RHODES, JANE, soprano, b. 1930, Paris. She made her debut (1953) at Nantes in *La Damnation de Faust* and in 1954 appeared in Brussels in a musical. On Nov. 25, 1954, she sang the role of Renata in Paris in the world *première* of *The Flaming Angel*. She became world-famous in 1959 when she created the role of Carmen in its first performance (with dialogue) at the Paris Opéra. Since then she has had a brilliant career at the Opéra, particularly as Tosca and Salome. In 1963 she made her debut at the Metropolitan Opera in the latter role. She is married to the conductor Roberto Benzi.

Records: Philips, Pathé, and Vega. *U.S. re-issue:* Westminster.

RIAVEZ, JOSÉ, tenor, b. 1890, Gradisca, Italy; d. 1958, Ljubljana, Yugoslavia. Originally Josip Rijavec. He first studied in Görz and Laibach, then in Vienna with Franz Schreker and H. Graedner. He made his debut at the Zagreb Opera (1916) and remained there until 1926. During this time he made guest appearances at the opera houses in Belgrade and Ljubljana. In 1926 he appeared as guest in Berlin and was engaged at the City Opera there (1928-32). Guest arrangements took him to the Vienna State Opera (1931-32) and after 1931 he was a regular guest at the Teatro Colón, where he was greatly admired. He was a member of the German Theater in Prague (1934-37). In 1937 he returned to his native Yugoslavia and for the next decade sang at the opera houses in Zagreb, Belgrade and Ljubljana. After 1948 he became a professor at the Music Academy in Belgrade and at the last lived in Ljubljana. His tenor voice was especially admired in the Italian repertory.

Records: HMV (including a Siciliana from *Cavalleria Rusticana* under Mascagni).

RIMINI, GIACOMO, baritone, b. Mar. 22, 1888, Verona, Italy; d. Mar. 6, 1952, Chicago. He studied at the Verona Conservatory and made his debut there (1910). After he had appeared on various Italian stages, he sang in 1915 at the Teatro Colón in *La Battaglia di Legnano* with Rosa Raisa. In 1920 he married this famous soprano. In 1916 he was engaged at the Chicago Opera and remained there until the end of his career, a very successful singer. Guest-appearance tours took him, often with his wife, to various countries, but especially to Italy. He created the role of Ping at La Scala on Apr. 25, 1926, in *Turandot*, while his wife sang the title role. In 1932 he was applauded at La Scala as Don Pasquale and as Gianni Schicchi. He made guest appearances in 1933 at Covent Garden. In 1937 he gave up his career and with his wife founded an opera studio in Chicago. He had a well-developed baritone voice and was particularly famous in *buffo* roles; his starring part was Falstaff.

Records: Jumbo Records, Brunswick*, Pathé*, Vocalion*, and Columbia* (*Falstaff*).

RITTER, RUDOLF, tenor, b. Jan. 19, 1878, Brüx, Austria. He at first became an officer in the Austro-Hungarian army (1898-1908). He then studied singing at the Vienna Music Academy and made his debut (1910) at the Vienna Volksoper, where he remained until 1913. There he sang the role of Primus Thaller in the world *première* of *Der Kuhreigen* in 1911. Called to the Stuttgart Opera in 1913, he remained there singing very successfully for the next thirty years. In 1923-24 he made a tour of the United States with the German Opera Company. He was especially admired as a Wagner interpreter and sang Siegfried in the *Ring* cycle in 1924 and 1925 and Tannhäuser in 1930 at the Bayreuth Festivals. In 1928-29 he again toured the United States, this time with the German Opera Company collected by Johanna Gadski. His later guest engagements included Covent Garden, the Paris Opéra, and the most important houses in Germany. In 1933 he gave up his career and taught in Stuttgart; at the last he retired to Sulzbach-am-Kocher.

Records: Vox, Odeon, and Polydor.

RITTER-CIAMPI, GABRIELLE, soprano, b. Nov. 2, 1886, Paris. She came from a French-Italian family; her father was the tenor Ezio Ciampi and her uncle was Théodore Ritter, the famous pianist. She also wanted to become a pianist at first and at the age of sixteen she gave piano recitals, but she changed to the study of singing and completed the course at the Paris Conservatory. She made her debut (1917) at the Théâtre Lyrique. In 1919 she was engaged at the Opéra-Comique and after 1921 concurrently at the Paris Opéra. She was especially admired in the Mozart repertory, but also in French and Italian parts. She sang with great success as a guest at La Scala, the Brussels Opera, and the State Operas in Berlin and Vienna. In 1932 she sang Konstanze in *Die Entführung aus dem Serail* at the Salzburg Festival. After she had given up her singing career, she lived and taught singing in Paris. In her soprano voice a sovereign vocal technique and a mastery of character shading were happily joined.

Records: Pathé and Polydor. *U.S. re-recording:* FRP, Eterna, TAP.

ROBESON, PAUL, bass, b. Apr. 9, 1898, Princeton, N.J. His father, who had been a Negro slave in his youth, held a high office with the Quakers. The son first studied law at Columbia University and opened a law office. He gave up this profession, however, and became an actor. He made his acting debut in 1921 in Eugene O'Neill's play *All God's Chillun Got Wings*. He gave his first concert in 1925, singing Negro spirituals particularly. In 1926 he made a long concert tour through the United States. Later his concert tours took him all over the world, but he also continued to act and he specialized particularly in the role of Shakespeare's *Othello*. He also made a number of motion pictures. After World War II he lived in England. After he had undertaken a successful concert tour of Russia in 1945, he became more and more attracted to the idea of Communism and often appeared in Russia. His was a dark, deep bass voice and he was admired both for his art of expression and for his vocal power; he was particularly noted as a singer of Negro spirituals and as a lieder singer.

Records: HMV, RCA Victor*, Columbia*, Vanguard*, and Philips. *U.S. re-issue:* Monitor, Verve.

ROBIN, MADO, soprano, b. Dec. 29, 1918, Tours, France; d. Dec. 10, 1960, Paris. Her naturally phenomenal voice was discovered by Titta Ruffo when she was sixteen years old. She studied at the Paris Conservatory and first sang publicly in 1942, when she gave a recital of songs and arias at the Salle Gaveau in Paris. In 1945 she was engaged by the Paris Opéra and made her debut there as Gilda in *Rigoletto*. She was very successful thereafter both at the Opéra and at the Opéra-Comique. She had special successes in Marseilles in 1950 as Lucia di Lammermoor and in 1951 in *Le Rossignol* at the Monte Carlo Opera. Guest appearances at the most important theaters in France and Italy followed and she sang at the San Francisco Opera (1954-56). She died at the height of her career. A brilliant coloratura soprano, she was equally admired for the exactitude of her vocal ornaments and for her effortlessness in the highest registers.

Records: Decca (including *Lakmé*) and Pathé (*Rigoletto* and *La Traviata*). *U.S. re-issue:* London, Pathé-Marconi.

RODE, WILHELM, baritone, b. Feb. 17, 1887, Hannover, Germany; d. Sept. 2, 1959, Ikking, Germany. He was first an insurance-company employee, then studied voice with Moest in Hannover. He made his debut in Erfurt (1909) as the Herald in *Lohengrin*; he sang at Bremerhaven (1912-14), Breslau (1914-21), Stuttgart (1921-22), at the Munich State Opera (1922-30), and the Vienna State Opera (1930-32). He then sang at the Berlin City Opera (1932-45) and after 1945 was general intendant there. He was regularly a guest at the Vienna State Opera and also appeared at the Paris Opéra and in Berlin, Dresden, Amsterdam, Budapest, Prague, Bucharest, Madrid, and Barcelona. In 1928 he sang Wotan at Covent Garden and he frequently appeared at the Salzburg Festivals, both as Count Almaviva in *Le Nozze di Figaro* and as Pizarro in *Fidelio*. In 1945 he retired to Ikking. He had a powerful heroic baritone of overpowering impressiveness, particularly in Wagner roles.

Records: Odeon, Ultraphon, and Polydor. *U.S. re-issue:* American Decca. *U.S. re-recording:* Telefunken, DGG.

ROESELER, MARCELLA, soprano, b. 1890, Berlin; d. Jan. 29, 1957, Berlin. She made her stage debut in Wiesbaden (1910) and in 1911 went to Kassel, later to Dessau, and made guest appearances in Munich. She belonged to the Breslau Opera (1919-21) and went to the Berlin Volksoper (1922-23). In 1923 she toured the United States with the German Opera Company. She was then engaged by the Metropolitan Opera and remained there until 1927. She sang mostly small parts there, but she did sing Elsa in *Lohengrin*, Elisabeth in *Tannhäuser*, and Aïda. After 1928 she lived in Berlin and made guest appearances in Vienna, Dresden, Hamburg,

Leipzig, at the Berlin City Opera, and frequently sang on the German radio. Her guest appearances and concert activity also took her to Holland, Belgium, and France. After her retirement she became a teacher of singing in Berlin.

Records: Acoustic records for Polydor and Odeon; electric for Kristall.

ROGATSCHEWSKY, JOSEPH, tenor, b. 1891, Mirogorod, Russia. He came to Paris when he was eighteen and studied at the Conservatory there with Isnardon and Hettich. In World War I he volunteered for the French army and was twice wounded. At the end of the war he did not return to Russia but completed his vocal studies in Paris and made his debut (1922) in Toulouse. In the same year he was engaged by the Opéra-Comique. After 1924 he was principal lyric tenor at the Théâtre de la Monnaie, where he was greatly admired. During this time he was a regular guest at the Opéra-Comique and other important theaters in France and Belgium. In 1929 and 1930 he fulfilled guest engagements brilliantly at the Vienna State Opera. He was the director of the Brussels Opera (1953-59) and lived as a teacher there. One of the most beautiful lyric tenor voices of his time.

Records: Columbia* (including *Manon*). *U.S. re-recording:* Rococo, Eterna.

ROGGEN, MICHAEL VON (see Gitowsky, Michael)

ROHR, OTTO VON, bass, b. Feb. 24, 1916, Berlin. He studied at the Berlin Music High School with Weissenborn and made his debut (1938) at Duisburg as Sarastro in *Die Zauberflöte.* He came from there in 1941 to the Stuttgart State Opera, where he sang for over twenty years. After 1946 he made regular guest appearances at the Frankfurt Opera and was highly successful in guest appearances at La Scala, the Paris Opéra, the Teatro São Carlos, the Teatro San Carlo, and at the Maggio Musicale Festival. In 1960 he was highly applauded at the Teatro Colón. He has also been heard at the Berlin City Opera and the Vienna State Opera and has had great success as a concert singer.

Records: DGG* (*Lohengrin, 1 Vespri Siciliani,* and *Tannhäuser*), Urania* (*Tannhäuser*), and Philips.

ROHS, MARTHA, contralto, b. 1909, Saarbrücken, Germany; d. July 27, 1963, Vienna. She made her debut (1932) at Aachen, came to the Dresden Opera in 1934, and finally to the Vienna State Opera in 1937. From Vienna she made brilliant guest appearances at La Scala, Covent Garden, Munich, Paris, Brussels, Amsterdam, and Rome. After 1938 she had outstanding successes at the Salzburg Festivals, where she was greatly admired as Octavian in *Der Rosenkavalier* and as Cherubino in *Le Nozze di Figaro.* She returned to Salzburg in 1949 as Sesto in *La Clemenza di Tito.* On the grounds of health she then gave up her career and appeared only occasionally in the concert hall. She was married to the operetta tenor Fred Liewehr. She had a dark-timbred and beautifully expressive voice and was equally renowned in the concert and recital hall and on the stage.

Records: Very few records for DGG; she later made operetta records for minor labels. *U.S. reissue:* Period.

ROMAN, STELLA, soprano, b. 1910, Rumania. She completed her study of singing with Giuseppina Baldassare-Tedeschi in Rome and made her debut in Italy (1934). She had her first success at the Rome Opera and other Italian theaters. In 1940 she sang the role of the Empress in the first performance at La Scala of *Die Frau ohne Schatten.* She was a

member of the Metropolitan Opera (1940-50), where she shared with Zinka Milanov the dramatic soprano roles in the Italian repertory. Guest appearances and concerts brought her noted success in Europe and America.
Records: Capitol*.

ROOY, ANTON VAN, baritone, b. Jan. 1, 1870, Rotterdam; d. Nov. 28, 1932, Munich. Originally Antonius Maria Josephus van Rooy. He studied with Julius Stockhausen in Frankfurt and appeared as a concert and oratorio singer in 1894. Felix Weingartner and Cosima Wagner then urged him to turn to the operatic stage. He made his stage debut as Wotan in the *Ring* cycle at the 1897 Bayreuth Festival and had an overwhelming success, which made him at a stroke the most famous Wagner singer of his voice range. Besides his Wotan, he was admired at Bayreuth as Hans Sachs in *Die Meistersinger* (1899) and as the Dutchman (1901). He made annual guest appearances at Covent Garden (1898-1913). In 1898 he joined the Metropolitan Opera and remained there until 1908. For his appearance in New York in 1903 in the production of *Parsifal*, which Bayreuth had forbidden, he became persona non grata at the Festivals and appeared there no more. In 1907 he sang Jochanaan in the first New York production of *Salome* at the Metropolitan. Guest appearances and concerts brought him additional laurels in Berlin, Munich, Brussels, Amsterdam, and many other music centers. After 1909 he was engaged by the Frankfurt Opera, but he rarely sang there. Toward the end of his career he lived in Munich. With a powerful baritone voice of a moving dramatic quality, he was particularly admired in Wagner roles.
Records: Rare records for G & T (London, 1902), Columbia*, and HMV (London, 1908); Edison* and Mapleson cylinders. *U.S. reissue:* Victor, HRS, IRCC. *U.S. re-recording:* IRCC, Rococo, TAP, CRS.

ROSELLE, ANNE, soprano, b. Mar. 20, 1894, Budapest. Originally Anna Gyenges. She came as a child to the United States and completed her study of singing here. She made her debut (1920) at the Metropolitan Opera as Musetta in *La Bohème* and sang small parts there until 1922; she then traveled through the country with the Scotti Opera Company, with which she sang such roles as Tosca and Madama Butterfly. In 1925 she went to Europe and was engaged by the Dresden State Opera. In 1926 she sang the title role in *Turandot* at Dresden in the first German performance of the opera. In 1929 she was applauded at Covent Garden for her singing of Donna Anna in *Don Giovanni*. She returned to America in 1930 and sang with the San Carlo Opera Company and the Philadelphia Opera. In 1931 in the latter city she sang Marie in the first American production of *Wozzeck* under Leopold Stokowski. Since her retirement from the stage she has lived in Philadelphia and she teaches singing there.
Records: Polydor and Remington*. *U.S. re-recording:* Eterna, TAP.

ROSING, VLADIMIR, tenor, b. 1890, St. Petersburg, Russia; d. Nov. 23, 1963, Los Angeles. His father, a lawyer, owned a large collection of phonograph records, which was the stimulus for the son to study music. This he did along with his legal studies, with Joachim Tartakov in St. Petersburg. He made his debut there (1910) at a salon concert with the violinist Jascha Heifetz. After further study with George Power in London and with both Jean de Reszke and Giovanni Sbriglia in Paris, he made his stage debut (1912) as the St. Petersburg Art Opera as Lenski in *Eugen Onégin*. He gave successful concerts in London in 1913 and in 1915-16 sang at the Drury Lane Theater and also staged a production of *The Queen of Spades*. In the winter of 1917-18 he gave forty recitals in London. He came to the United States in 1921 and became the director of the Eastman School of Music in Rochester, New York. In 1927 he founded the American Opera Company and toured the United States with it. In the 1930's he lived for a time in England, but returned to the United States in 1939. Here he lived in Hollywood, California, and occupied himself as a teacher and opera *régisseur*. His expressive lyric tenor voice was proved both on the stage and in song recitals.

Records: Acoustic records for Vocalion* and electric for Parlophone. *U.S. re-issue:* American Decca. *U.S. re-recording:* TAP.

ROSSI-LEMENI, NICOLA, bass, b. Nov. 6, 1920, Istanbul, Turkey. His father was Italian and his mother, Xenia Lemeni-Macedon, had been a voice teacher at the Conservatory in Odessa. He was brought up in Italy and studied jurisprudence. Without special vocal training he made his debut (1946) at the Teatro Fenice as Varlaam in *Boris Godounov*. In the same year he excited great comment for his singing of King Philip in *Don Carlos* at Trieste. He was substantially assisted in his career by the conductor Tullio Serafin, whose daughter Vittoria he married in 1949. He was admired at the Arena Festival in 1949 and after 1950 he sang regularly at La Scala and at the Rome Opera. In 1951 he made guest appearances in the United States and was applauded for his singing of Boris Godounov in San Francisco. In 1953 he became a member of the Metropolitan Opera, where he was very successful. In 1958 he sang the part of Thomas à Becket at La Scala in the world *première* of *L'Assasinio nella Cathedrale*. In 1958 he married for the second time; his present wife is the soprano Virginia Zeani. World-wide concert and stage activity have marked his career. He has also appeared before the public as a poet, having published two collections, *Impeti* and *Le Orme*, and has been a contributor to literary periodicals. He has a large and sumptuous bass voice; he is outstanding in both the Russian and Italian repertories and he sings the former in the original language.

Records: Cetra* (*Don Carlos*), Philips* (*Mosé*) and Columbia (*Norma, I Puritani,* and *La Serva Padrona*). *U.S. re-issue:* Angel, Capitol, Vox, ASCO.

ROSSI-MORELLI, LUIGI, baritone, b. 1890, Cesena, Italy; d. January, 1941, Rome. A pupil of Antonio Cotogni in Rome, he made his debut in 1912. He had his first great success in 1914 as Amfortas in *Parsifal* in Palermo and others followed at the Teatro Costanzi (1920-21), the Teatro Massimo (1923), and the Teatro dal Verme (1924). He was greatly admired at the Costanzi in 1926 as Wotan in the *Ring* cycle and also in the same part at La Scala in 1927 with Frida Leider. Thereafter he was considered one of the most famous Italian Wagner baritones. He was regularly engaged at La Scala and sang as guest at the Italian Opera in Holland in 1935 and 1937. In the latter year his Amfortas was admired at the Rome Opera.

Records: Rare records for Columbia.

RÖSSL-MAJDAN, HILDE, contralto, b. Jan. 21, 1921, Moosbirbaum, Austria. A daughter of the bass Karl Rössl-Majdan, she studied music at the Vienna Music Academy and in 1946 began her career as a concert contralto. In 1947 she unexpectedly replaced an ill singer in a production of the St. Matthew Passion in Vienna under Wilhelm Furtwängler and had a brilliant success. She was called to the Vienna State Opera in 1950 and since then has been a member of that institution. Guest appearances have taken her to La Scala, Covent Garden, and many other important theaters in the course of a highly successful career. She has been equally rewarded in her appearances at the Festivals in Salzburg, Edinburgh, and Aix-en-Provence. She has proved herself as an oratorio and concert singer in the music centers of Germany, Austria, and Italy.

Records: She has recorded for many companies including Nixa (*St. Matthew Passion*), Decca (*Der Rosenkavalier, Die Frau ohne Schatten, Le Nozze di Figaro,* and *Die Zauberflöte*), and RCA Victor*. *U.S. re-issue:* Remington, Bach Guild, Westminster, Lyrichord, Vanguard, Vox, SPA, London, Epic, DGG, and Columbia.

ROSWAENGE, HELGE, tenor, b. Aug. 29, 1897, Copenhagen. At first he wished to become a chemist and he studied this subject at the Technical High School in Copenhagen. He then studied singing there and in Berlin. After he had already appeared in concerts and in small theaters in Denmark, he made his debut in Neustrelitz (1921). He sang at Altenburg (1921-24), Basel (1924-26), and at the Cologne Opera (1926-29). In 1929 he was engaged at the Berlin State Opera, had a successful career there, and after 1930 was concurrently a member of the Vienna State Opera. He sang guest performances in London, Milan, Copenhagen, Stockholm, Brussels, Amsterdam, Munich, Hamburg, and Dresden. After 1932 he appeared at the Salzburg Festivals almost every year and was held to be one of the great Mozart interpreters. He also appeared at the Bayreuth Festival. Since 1949 he has lived in Vienna, where he is a frequent guest at the State Opera and particularly at the Volksoper. He was a member of the State Opera in East Berlin after 1955; during this time he also sang in Zürich as well as at the Festivals in Bregenz and Bad Hersfeld. He managed an operetta theater in Vienna temporarily, but now appears only in the concert hall. He was married for a time to the soprano Ilonka Holndonner. He was treasured as much for the volume and beauty of his voice as for the rich expressiveness of his characterizations and for his bravura and often daring voice management. He was admired on the stage in a many-sided repertory.

Records: Parlophone, HMV (including *Die Zauberflöte*), Polydor, Urania*, DGG (*Rigoletto* and *I Vespri Siciliani*). In the United States he has made one recording for Record Album of his 1963 and 1964 concerts in New York. *U.S. re-issue:* RCA Victor, London. *U.S. re-recording:* Eterna, Rococo, Scala, TAP, Electrola, Telefunken, Vanguard, Classic.

ROSZA, ANNA, soprano, b. 1898, Temesvar, Rumania. As a child she came to the United States and studied singing at the Milwaukee Conservatory, but in 1921 she returned to Rumania, where she continued her studies with Jenny Czolak in Krajova. She finally became a pupil of Tina Scognamiglio in Milan and made her debut as a mezzo-soprano (1921) in Cluj as Siebel in *Faust*. In 1928 she returned to Italy and sang as a soprano, at first in lyric and coloratura roles but later she appeared in dramatic parts also. She was heard as Freia in *Das Rhein-*

gold at La Scala in 1931, but otherwise she appeared only in provincial houses. In 1932 she sang Violetta in *La Traviata* as guest in Bucharest and was later engaged there (1934-44); during this time she also sang as guest in Temesvar, Cluj, Czernowitz, and Jassy; in 1942 she sang as guest in Odessa. She lives in Cluj.

Records: HMV (including *La Traviata*). *U.S. re-issue:* RCA Victor.

ROTHAUSER, THERESE, contralto, b. June 10, 1865, Budapest; d. 1942 (?), Auschwitz, Poland. She studied with Emmerich Bellovicz in Budapest and appeared first as a concert singer. She was engaged at the Leipzig Opera in 1887, where she first sang in *Die Loreley*. In 1889 she joined the Imperial Opera in Berlin and sang there for over thirty years, including the memorable *première* there of *Der Rosenkavalier* in 1911, in which she sang Annina. She made successful guest appearances at all the great German opera houses. After the close of her active career she taught in Berlin. Because she was Jewish, she was persecuted by the Nazi regime; she was finally imprisoned and died in the concentration camp at Auschwitz.

Records: Columbia (Berlin, 1904-05) and one for HMV.

ROTH-EHRANG, PETER, bass, b. 1920, Ehrang, France; d. Dec. 28, 1966, Hamburg. He first learned to be a surveyor, then studied singing with Paul Lohmann and Kurt Frasse in Berlin and made his debut (1950) at Trèves as the Hermit in *Der Freischütz*. In 1952 he came to the Leipzig Opera and also sang regularly at Dessau. In 1954 he joined the Berlin City Opera, where he was especially esteemed as a Wagner singer. He appeared at the Bayreuth Festivals after 1960, particularly as Fafner in the *Ring* cycle. He was a true basso profundo.

Records: Opera and DGG records (on the latter in a small part in *Orfeo*). *U.S. re-issue:* Westminster, Electrola.

ROTHENBERGER, ANNELIESE, soprano, b. June 19, 1924, Mannheim, Germany. She studied at the Music High School in Mannheim and began her career (1943) at Koblenz, where she was also required to appear as an actress. She was a member of the ensemble of the Hamburg Opera (1946-56) and with this company she made very successful guest appearances at the Edinburgh Festival of 1953; during her years at Hamburg she often sang on the German radio. In 1956 she was engaged at the Düsseldorf Opera and after 1953 she appeared regularly as guest at the Vienna State Opera, of which she became a regular member in 1958. Since 1954 she has appeared every year at the Salzburg Festivals and in 1957 she created there the part of Agnes in the *première* of *Die Schule der Frauen*. She was applauded at La Scala in 1960 and in the autumn of that year she made her debut as Sophie in *Der Rosenkavalier* at the Metropolitan Opera. Guest appearances have brought her to every major musical metropolis in the world and concert tours in Europe and both North and South America have brought her great honors. She has recently been acclaimed for her performances in the title role of *Lulu*. She has also been successful in musical films, such as the English operetta film *Fledermaus* (1955). One of the most amiable performers among the sopranos of her time, she is outstanding in both coloratura and lyric roles.

Records: Columbia (*Le Nozze di Figaro*), HMV, DGG* (*Arabella*), and RCA Victor (*Die Fledermaus*). *U.S. re-issue:* Electrola, Telefunken, Angel, Seraphim.

ROTHIER, LÉON, bass, b. July 26, 1874, Rheims, France; d. July 6, 1951, New York. He studied at the Conservatory in Paris and made his debut at the Opéra-Comique there (1899) as Vulcain in *Philémon et Baucis*. He then had famous successes at both of the great Paris houses as well as in Brussels, Nice, and Monte Carlo. In 1900 he sang a small role at the Opéra-Comique in the world *première* of *Louise*. In 1910 he was engaged by the Metropolitan Opera and he was one of three singers who remained for over thirty years as members of that tradition-rich house. By the time of his farewell performance there in 1940 he had sung in more than twelve hundred performances in five different languages. He had also appeared as guest in San Francisco and at the summer opera festival at Ravinia. The beauty of his voice remained for a long time; he made phonograph records as late as 1950. He was first married to the soprano Mariette Mazarin, from whom he was later separated; his second marriage was to the contralto Maria Duchêne, but they were also separated. He had a splendidly cultivated voice of beautiful expressiveness, especially admired in the French repertory.

Records: Columbia* and Victor*, the latter with Enrico Caruso; he made private recordings in the last years of his career. *U.S. re-recording:* RCA Victor, TAP, IRCC, FRP.

ROTHMÜLLER, MARKO, baritone, b. Dec. 31, 1908, Zagreb, Yugoslavia. He studied in Zagreb, then in Vienna with Franz Steiner. He next studied composition with Alban Berg and later wrote chamber music, a symphony, and some songs. He made his debut (1932) at the Hamburg Opera, but he was released in 1933 because he was Jewish, and he then sang at the Zagreb Opera (1933-35) and at the Zürich Opera (1935-47). There the critic Desmond Shawe-Taylor discovered his voice and in 1947 he began a brilliant career with the New London Opera Company at the Cambridge Theater in London; he substituted there in the same year for Paul Schöffler, who was ill, with the visiting ensemble of the Vienna State Opera, singing Jochanaan in *Salome*. In 1948 he was applauded at Covent Garden as Rigoletto and as Scarpia, and also in that year he appeared at the Edinburgh Festival in *Così fan tutte*. He sang as guest at the Vienna State Opera (1946-47) and joined the New York City Opera (1948-49). After 1950 he sang regularly at Covent Garden and created the title role in *Wozzeck* in the first performance there in 1952. That year he sang the title role in *Macbeth* at the Glyndebourne Festival. He now lives in New York, where he teaches singing.

Records: HMV published first in Switzerland, then in England. A *Macbeth* record from Glyndebourne has appeared on Allegro Royale* on which a false name is used. *U.S. re-issue:* Bartók, London.

ROUARD, EDOUARD, baritone, b. Nov. 22, 1876, Nice, France; d. Mar. 13, 1962, Nice. He studied in Marseilles and made his debut in Nice (1900). After great successes at the opera houses in Lyons, Liège, and Geneva, he sang at the Opera in Nice (1910-11) and at the Brussels Opera (1911-14), where he was very well liked. In 1914 he sang Amfortas in *Parsifal*, both at the first production at the Brussels Opera and at the first production at the Paris Opéra. He became a member of the Opéra in 1914 and remained there until 1936. In 1921 he appeared there in the world *première* of *Antar* and in 1934 sang Valentin in the jubilee production of *Faust*. After his retirement from the stage he lived and taught in Nice.

Records: HMV and Odeon.

ROUSSELIÈRE, CHARLES, tenor, b. Jan. 17, 1875, St. Nazaire, France; d. May 11, 1950, Joue-les-Tours, France. He was originally a smith by trade, but he studied at the National Conservatory in Paris and made his debut at the Opéra there (1900). He sang particularly in Paris and Monte Carlo, and appeared in many world *premières:* at the Opéra in *Les Barbares* in 1901; in Monte Carlo in *Amica* in 1905; also in Monte Carlo in *L'Ancêtre* in 1906; again in Monte Carlo in *Pénélope* in 1913; at the Opéra-Comique in *Julien* in 1913. He sang during the 1906-07 season at the Metropolitan Opera, where he was particularly admired as Roméo in *Roméo et Juliette*. His other guest appearances included La Scala in 1909, the Teatro Massimo in 1910, and the Teatro Colón, where he sang the title role in the first performance there of *Parsifal* in 1914. Toward the end of his career he was especially active on various stages in France and he later lived and taught in Paris. He had a powerful, but well-managed, heroic tenor voice admired in Wagner roles.

Records: Acoustic records for G & T (Paris, 1903), HMV, Beka, and Pathé*; electric records for Polydor. *U.S. re-issue:* IRCC, HRS.

ROUX, MICHEL, baritone, b. 1924 (?), Angoulême, France. He began his study of singing at the Bordeaux Conservatory in 1944, but in 1945 he transferred to the National Conservatory in Paris, where he made his debut (1948) and soon had great success at both the Opéra and the Opéra-Comique. In 1952 he appeared as guest in Dublin and in 1953 at La Scala as Golaud in *Pelléas et Mélisande*. In 1956 he was applauded at the Glyndebourne Festival in *Le Comte Ory* and at the Aix-en-Provence Festival as well. He sang Athanaël in *Thaïs* at the Chicago Opera in 1959.

Records: HMV (*Le Comte Ory* from Glyndebourne), Nixa, Philips (*Pélleas et Mélisande*), Columbia (*Le Devin du Village* and *Le Rossignol*) and London International. *U.S. re-issue:* DGG, Vox, Epic, Urania, Pathé-Marconi.

RUBIO, CONSUELO, soprano, b. 1928 (?). She studied at the Conservatory in Madrid and won a prize there in 1948 before making her debut there later that year. She had her first success in Spain, including the Granada Festival and the Teatro Liceo. In 1953 she won a singing competition in Geneva. In 1954 she had brilliant successes at the Teatro Colón as Mimi in *La Bohème* and as Eva in *Die Meistersinger*. Guest appearances and concerts brought her fame and success in Italy, France, Sweden, Switzerland, England, and Holland, as well as at the Paris Opéra and at the Aix-en-Provence Festival; at the latter she sang Donna Elvira in *Don Giovanni* (1958). She then added dramatic roles to her repertory—she sang the title role in *Alceste* at the Glyndebourne Festival in 1957 and in 1959 was applauded at the Teatro Massimo for her singing of the title role in *Beatrice di Tenda* and Rosario in *Goyescas*. She appeared as guest at the Vienna State Opera (1960-61) and at the Chicago Opera in 1962. She is greatly admired for her singing of songs, particularly Spanish art songs by De Falla and others.

Records: Decca (*Goyescas*), Philips, and MMS (*Carmen*). U.S. reissue: DGG, Epic.

RUFFO, TITTA, baritone, b. June 8, 1877, Pisa, Italy; d. July 5, 1953, Florence. Originally Ruffo Cafiero Titta. His brother, Ettore Titta, was an esteemed composer and his sister, Fosca Titta, was a well-known singer. Titta Ruffo originally planned to be an engineer and prepared himself in this field at the University of Rome, but he gave it up for the study of singing, which he completed with Persichini and with Lelio Casini in Rome. He made his debut (1898) at the Teatro Costanzi there as the Herald in *Lohengrin*. He then sang in Rio de Janeiro and soon became well known in Italy at the most important opera houses. He was highly successful in guest appearances at Covent Garden, the Paris Opéra, the Teatro Liceo, the Teatro Colón, and at the Imperial Opera Houses in Berlin and Vienna. He became finally the most noted baritone of his time. In 1912-13 and in 1919-20 he was highly applauded at the Chicago Opera, where in 1920 he sang in the world *première* of *Edipo Re*. He was a member (1921-29) of the Metropolitan Opera, where he went from one triumph to another. Guest appearances and concerts in all the best-known music centers of the world marked the later career of this artist. In 1936 he retired from the stage and lived as a singing teacher in Florence. He published *La mia parabola* (Milan, 1937). Titta Ruffo possessed one of the most beautiful baritone voices preserved on records. The dark but warm timbre of his voice, the captivatingly dramatic characterizations, and the vocal security with which he mastered light parlando passages were all worthy of high praise. He was especially well liked in Verdi roles and as Figaro in *Il Barbiere di Siviglia*.

Records: Many performances for G & T (Milan, 1907), HMV, Victor*, and Pathé*. U.S. re-issue: Victor, RCA Victor, Opera Disc, HRS. U.S. re-recording: TAP, Scala, RCA Victor, FRP, Eterna, Rococo, Olympus, Belcanto, HRS.

RUNGE, GERTRUD, soprano, b. 1880, Brandenburg, Germany; d. Aug. 7, 1948, Weimar. She studied in Berlin and made her debut in 1902. In 1903 she came to the Weimar Court Theater and remained there until 1913, after which she sang at Mannheim (1913-25). In 1902 she was married to Captain-Lieutenant von Einem, son of the Prussian minister of war. She passed the end of her days in the Marie Seebach Foundation in Weimar.

Records: While this artist had no brilliant international career, it is significant that she left a great number of phonograph records. Her coloratura soprano is to be heard on Berliner records (Berlin, 1900-01), G & T (Berlin and Weimar, 1901-06), Zonophone* (Berlin, 1905), Pathé*, and Edison* cylinders. U.S. re-issue: Victor.

RÜNGER, GERTRUDE, contralto-soprano, b. 1899, Posen, Germany; d. June 10, 1965, Berlin. She made her debut in Erfurt (1924) and remained there until 1927. She then sang at Magdeburg (1927-28) and at the Vienna State Opera (1928-35). She was concurrently engaged at the Berlin State Opera (1932-38) and was under concurrent contract at Munich and Vienna again (1938-44). After 1949 she appeared at the East Berlin State Opera. At the beginning of her career she sang contralto parts, but later her voice changed to a dramatic soprano. She was very successful at the Salzburg

Festivals, where she sang the Nurse in *Die Frau ohne Schatten* (1932-33), Klytemnestra in *Elektra* (1934), and Leonora in *Fidelio* (1938). She also sang as guest at La Scala, Munich, and Dresden and was engaged at the Metropolitan Opera (1937-38). She later taught singing in Berlin. She was admired for the sumptuous quality of her voice and the effective acting in her presentations, particularly in Wagner roles such as Brünnhilde, Venus, Isolde, and Brangäne.

Records: Very few records for DGG.

RÜSCHE-ENDORF, CÄCILIE, soprano, b. Apr. 8, 1873, Dortmund, Germany; d. Mar. 13, 1939, Leipzig. She studied at the Conservatory in Cologne, with Alberto Selva in Milan, and made her debut (1894) in Zürich as Agathe in *Der Freischütz*. She was a member of the Cologne Opera (1896-1902). In 1898 she married the opera singer Hermann Endorf. Her career continued at Elberfeld (1904-05) and at Hannover (1905-10). In 1910 she was engaged as first dramatic soprano at the Leipzig Opera, where she remained until 1919. She sang the role of Kundry in the *première* there of *Parsifal* in 1914. She sang Gutrune in *Götterdämmerung* at the Bayreuth Festivals (1906-09). She also sang Wagner roles as guest at Covent Garden in 1908 and 1911-14. Other cities which heard her as guest were Amsterdam, Brussels, Zürich, and Dresden. She later lived and taught at Leipzig.

Records: G & T and Odeon. *U.S. re-issue:* Opera Disc.

RUSS, GIANNINA, soprano, b. 1878, Lodi, Italy; d. 1951, Milan. She originally studied piano at the Milan Conservatory with Fumagalli and then studied singing with Alberto Leoni and Giacosa. She made her debut in 1903 and in the same year was singing at La Scala. In 1904 she was admired in Paris in productions with Adelina Patti, and in 1905 she sang at Monte Carlo with Enrico Caruso. Guest appearances in opera theaters all over the world distinguished her later career. In Italy she sang at La Scala and at the Teatro Costanzi. She appeared as guest in London and Paris, at the Imperial Operas in St. Petersburg and Vienna, at the Teatro São Carlos, and at the Athens Opera. In 1908 she sang with equal success at the Manhattan Opera House. She was particularly admired in South America, where she sang regularly at the Teatro Colón and on other important stages. After the end of her stage career she lived in Milan as a teacher; she passed her last days at the Casa di Riposo, founded by Verdi there. She had a large dramatic soprano voice of such expressiveness that she could evoke great emotional heights with it; she was particularly admired as Norma.

Records: G & T (Milan, 1903-04), Fonotipia (Milan, 1905-09), and Columbia. *U.S. re-issue:* Columbia-Fonotipia, Okeh. *U.S. re-recording:* TAP, Eterna, Scala, FRP.

RUSZKOWSKA, ELENA, soprano, b. 1878, Cracow, Poland; d. Nov. 3, 1948, Cracow. She made her debut (1900) in Lemberg after her studies there and in Warsaw. She had great success at the opera houses in both these cities. She appeared as guest at La Scala as Gutrune in *Götterdämmerung* with Felia Litvinne as the Brünnhilde (1907), and in 1909 she was admired there as Elena in *Mefistofele* with Feodor Chaliapin singing the title role. Her other guest appearances included Palermo in 1909 and on the most important stages in Italy, Spain, and South America about 1910; at the same time she was the great prima donna of the Warsaw Opera. In

Poland she sang under the name Helena Zboinska-Ruszkowska. Although she often sang at the opera houses in Prague and Budapest, after 1914 she appeared only in Poland, particularly in Warsaw, but also in Cracow and Lvov. Her career lasted a long time; in 1938 she sang in concerts on the Polish radio.

Records: A few exceedingly rare records for HMV which were published in Italy (Milan, 1908-10). *U.S. re-issue:* Victor.

RUZDAK, VLADIMIR, baritone, b. Sept. 21, 1922, Zagreb, Yugoslavia. He studied at the Conservatory in Zagreb and was a member of the Opera there (1947-54). In 1954 he became a member of the Hamburg State Opera. Since then he has had great success there and in guest appearances in Munich, Vienna, Amsterdam, London, and Brussels. He is also an esteemed concert singer and has been active as a composer, having written piano and orchestral works as well as choral pieces. He is especially admired in the Italian and Slavic repertories.

Records: Supraphon. *U.S. re-issue:* Columbia.

RUZICZKA, ELSE, contralto, b. 1898 (?), Vienna. She began her operatic career in Düsseldorf in 1920 and remained there until 1924. After singing at Cologne until 1927, she became a member of the Berlin State Opera (1927-34). There she had great success in a many-sided repertory. After 1934 she called herself Else Tegetthoff. She was married to the *régisseur* Hans Strobach, of the Dresden Opera. After World War II she appeared as guest at Frankfurt a. M. and on other German stages. Her technically excellent and cultivated voice had great expressive qualities.

Records: Polydor (in so-called "Opera High Lights"), HMV, Columbia*, Telefunken, and Urania (*Martha*); she made no solo recordings. *U.S. re-issue:* RCA Victor. *U.S. re-recording:* RCA Victor.

RYSANEK, LEONIE, soprano, b. Nov. 24, 1926, Vienna. She studied at the Conservatory of the City of Vienna, as did her younger sister, Lotte Rysanek (b. Mar. 18, 1928), also a well-known singer. Her teachers were Alfred Jerger and Rudolf Grossmann, whom she later married. She made her debut (1949) at Innsbruck, sang at Saarbrücken (1950-52) and at the Munich State Opera (1952-54). In 1954 she was engaged at the Vienna State Opera, where she had great success. She sang Sieglinde in *Die Walküre* at the Bayreuth Festival in 1951 and has since been very successful in Wagner roles. She also sang as guest at La Scala, Covent Garden, the Paris Opéra, and the State Operas in Hamburg, Munich, and Berlin, as well as at the Salzburg and Munich Festivals. She was engaged at the Metropolitan Opera in 1954 and won fame there in 1959 when she replaced Maria Callas in the role of Lady Macbeth in Verdi's opera. A world-spanning guest-appearance and concert activity distinguish the later career of this artist. Dramatic intensity of expression and a large tonal volume form the basis for her individualized interpretations. She is well known for her singing of Wagner roles.

Records: Columbia; RCA Victor* (*Der Fliegende Holländer, Ariadne auf Naxos, Macbeth,* and *Otello*), HMV (*Die Walküre*), DGG (*Fidelio*), and Decca (*Die Frau ohne Schatten*). *U.S. re-issue:* Electrola, London, Seraphim.

S

SACK, ERNA, soprano, b. Feb. 6, 1903, Berlin-Spandau, Germany. Originally Erna Weber. She studied singing in Prague and Berlin and in 1928 became a pupil at the Berlin State Opera, where she sang small contralto roles. In 1930 she went to Bielefeld and there her voice changed to that of a coloratura. She then sang at Wiesbaden (1932), Wroclaw (1934), and at the Dresden State Opera (1935). At the latter she sang Isotta in the world première of *Die Schweigsame Frau* in 1935. Since 1933 she has appeared with great success as guest at the Berlin State Opera and has also been admired in Milan, London, Paris, Vienna, Hamburg, and Munich, as well as at the Salzburg Festival. In 1936 she toured the United States very successfully and during World War II she appeared in Sweden, Switzerland, and Turkey. In 1947 she began a five-year world tour, which took her to South America, Canada, South Africa, and Australia. Again in 1954-55 she was applauded on two long American tours. Since 1953 she has returned each year to sing in her native Germany. For a time after World War II she lived in California, but since 1956 she has lived in Murnau in Upper Bavaria. She has appeared in several films. The coloratura voice of Erna Sack is noted for a special kind of phenomenon; she can sing G in alt and is called "the German nightingale." So far as her records show, she has not attained this height. A similar range was reported of the soprano Lucrezia Agujari (1743-83). Erna Sack has attained her best performances in songs and showpieces for the coloratura soprano voice.

Records: Telefunken* and Decca. *U.S. re-issue:* Richmond, Capitol-Telefunken.

SADOVEN, HÉLÈNE, contralto, b. 1894, Finland. She studied and made her debut during World War I in Russia, but in 1917 she came to Paris by way of Finland. In Paris she appeared as guest several times at the Opéra and at the Opéra-Comique. In 1922 at the Opéra she sang in *Aïda* with Claudia Muzio. She was a frequent guest at the Monte Carlo Opera and the Teatro Liceo. When the Opéra Russe was founded in Paris in 1927, she became the first contralto of the company and she visited La Scala, London, Holland, and South America with it. She made guest appearances in Vienna in 1928 and was also greatly successful as a song recitalist. She lives in Paris.

Records: Two acoustic records for HMV (both duets with Fernand Ansseau); electric records for HMV and Polydor. *U.S. re-recording:* TAP.

SAILER, FRIEDERIKE, soprano, b. 1926, Regensburg, Germany. She originally planned to become a kindergarten teacher and lived after her marriage in Ansbach. Her voice was discovered by accident when she sang in an operetta theater, and she was first presented in operatic roles from the Nuremberg studio of the Bavarian radio. In 1952 she was engaged at the Stuttgart Opera, where she still sings. She has appeared as guest, particularly in lyric roles, at the Munich State Opera and on other important stages; she sang at the Salzburg Festival in 1959 and is also admired as an oratorio and lieder singer.
Records: Opera and Eurodisc. *U.S. re-issue:* Vox, Epic, Columbia, Electrola, Period, Lyrichord, Dover, Turnabout.

SALAZAR, MANUEL, tenor, b. Jan. 3, 1887, San José, Costa Rica; d. Aug. 6, 1950, San José. At the age of nineteen he went to Italy to study singing and later came to New York for a time, but then returned to Italy. He made his debut in Vicenza (1913) as Edgardo in *Lucia di Lammermoor*. He had his first great success in 1914 at the Teatro dal Verme. He then sang in Padua, Fiume, Catania, Palermo, and in 1917 in Havana with Titta Ruffo. In 1919-21 he made North American tours with the San Carlo Opera Company. He was a member of the Metropolitan Opera (1921-23), making his debut as Alvaro in *La Forza del Destino* with Rosa Ponselle. He was applauded at the Metropolitan as Canio in *I Pagliacci*, as Radames in *Aïda*, and as the title hero in *Andrea Chénier*. After 1923 he traveled with small companies throughout the United States. He later lived in his native Costa Rica.
Records: Electrics for Columbia* (c. 1930). *U.S. re-recording:* FRP.

SALÉZA, ALBERT, tenor, b. 1867, Bruges, near Bayonne, France; d. Nov. 26, 1916, Paris. He made his debut (1888) after studying at the National Conservatory in Paris, and he sang Mylio in *Le Roi d'Ys* at the Paris Opéra as his debut role. In the same year he sang the title role in *Otello* in its first production in France, also at the Opéra. He sang as guest in Nice (1892), at the Monte Carlo Opera (1895-97), and the Théâtre de la Monnaie (1898). He also made successful guest appearances at Covent Garden. In 1899 he was engaged by the Metropolitan Opera, making his debut as Faust with Nellie Melba and Edouard de Reszke. He remained at the Metropolitan until 1901 and returned again in 1904-05. Thereafter he resumed his activity at the Paris Opéra, where he continued to appear until 1911.
Records: He left fragments on Mapieson cylinders. *U.S. re-recording:* IRCC.

SALIGNAC, THOMAS, tenor, b. Mar. 19, 1867, Générac, France; d. 1945, Paris. Originally Eustace Thomas. Salignac was the family name of his wife. At the Paris Conservatory he was a pupil of Duvernoy; he originally thought his voice was that of a baritone, but it changed to a tenor during his study. He made his debut at the Opéra-Comique (1893), where he sang small roles at first. By 1896 he had been engaged at the Metropolitan Opera, making his debut as Don José to Emma Calvé's Carmen. He remained in New York until 1904 and then returned to the Opéra-Comique, where he sang in several world *premières: Les Pêcheurs de St. Jean* (1905), *Le Chemineau* (1907), *Habanera* (1908), *La Jota* (1911), and

Saltzmann-Stevens · Salvatini

La Brebis Égarée (1923). In the latter year he sang the title role in El Retablo de Maese Pedro at the world première in the private theater of the Princesse de Polignac in Paris. He appeared as guest at Covent Garden and in Nice, Monte Carlo, and Brussels. He was the director of the Nice Opera (1913-14) and he taught at the American Conservatory in Fontainebleau (1922-23). In 1922 he founded the musical journal Lyrica, which he edited until 1939.

Records: Mapleson cylinders. U.S. re-recording: IRCC.

SALTZMANN-STEVENS, MINNIE, soprano, b. 1879, Bloomington, Ill. Her father was French and her mother was German. She first studied in the United States, then with Jean de Reszke in Paris; she made her debut (1908) at Covent Garden as Brünnhilde in Die Walküre. She achieved a reputation as a Wagner singer when she later sang as guest in Paris, Berlin, Brussels, Madrid, and Lisbon. She was applauded at the Bayreuth Festivals as Sieglinde in Die Walküre and as Kundry in Parsifal (1911-12). After being engaged at the Chicago Opera (1914-16), she gave only occasional concerts and guest appearances. She lived later in Milan.

Records: A few records for HMV (London, 1908-09). U.S. re-recording: Belcanto.

SALVANESCHI, ATTILIO, tenor, b. Nov. 25, 1873, near Livorno, Italy; d. July 18, 1938, The Hague. He made his debut in 1902 and had a successful career at the leading opera houses in Italy, but never appeared at La Scala. He sang with the Lombardi Opera Company in the United States (1907), Prague (1908), and Havana (1910 and 1914). His other guest appearances included Odessa and Stockholm. Engaged for the 1914-15 season at the Italian Opera in Holland, he remained there upon the outbreak of World War I; he sang with the French Opera in The Hague (1915-19). In 1919 he returned to Italy, where he had great success at the Teatro Adriano and in Padua. In 1924 he gave up his career and after 1928 he lived and taught in The Hague. After a throat operation in the last years of his life, he lost his speech. One of the most beautiful voices which Italy produced in his generation.

Records: Odeon, Jumbo Records, Edison Amberola Cylinders (1912), and HMV (Cavaradossi in Tosca, 1921).

SALVAREZZA, ANTONIO, tenor, b. 1906. He made his debut in 1935. He became generally known after singing Arturo in I Puritani at La Scala in 1939. During World War II he sang in the leading Italian opera houses, specializing in heroic tenor parts in the Italian repertory, and he caused geat admiration for the brilliance of his voice in the highest registers. He made a guest appearance at the Cambridge Theater in London in 1948 and sang in France, Holland, Belgium, and Austria in both opera and concert. He sang at the Arena Festival in 1948 and also at the Maggio Musicale Festival.

Records: Cetra*. U.S. re-recording: TAP.

SALVATINI, MAFALDA, soprano, b. Oct. 17, 1888, near Naples, Italy. She studied with Jean de Reszke and Pauline Viardot-Garcia in Paris. She became well known through her appearances at the Berlin Imperial Opera (1908-12). She had brilliant success in a guest appearance at the Paris Opéra (1914). She sang at the opera house in Berlin-Charlottenburg (1914-23) and was extremely well liked there. She sang again at the Berlin State Opera (1924-32). Guest appearances in 1922 and 1928 at the Vienna State

Opera and on the operatic stages of France, Belgium, and Holland were very successful, but she never sang in her native Italy. She lives on her estate in Tessin, Switzerland. Besides the wide tonal range of her voice, her intensely dramatic characterizations and her great acting talent made her famous.

Records: Polydor, Odeon, and HMV (one duet from *Madama Butterfly* with Hermann Jadlowker). *U.S. re-issue:* Opera Disc.

SALVI, MARGHERITA, soprano, b. 1904, Milan. She studied with Avelina Carrera in Barcelona, then with Torati in Milan, and made her debut in Florence (1925) as Gilda in *Rigoletto*. She appeared very successfully at the Teatro Colón in 1926 and sang with the Italian Opera in Holland (1926-27). In 1927 she undertook a long guest tour through Germany, appearing on the leading opera stages. In 1928 she was again to be heard in Holland. She was a member of the Chicago Opera (1929-31) and made her debut there as Rosina in *Il Barbiere di Siviglia*. She sang as guest at Monte Carlo in 1929 and returned once more to the Italian Opera in Holland (1933). For a time she lived in Paris and after 1936 in New York. In 1937 she sang the title role in *La Traviata* at the Chicago Opera. She now lives in South America. A musically outstanding and thoroughly trained coloratura soprano.

Records: Parlophone, HMV, and Victor*.

SAMMARCO, MARIO, baritone, b. Dec. 13, 1873, Palermo, Sicily; d. Jan. 24, 1930, Milan. He studied with Antonio Cantelli in Milan and made his debut there (1894) at the Teatro dal Verme in *Le Villi*. Within the same year he was appearing at La Scala. There, on Mar. 28, 1896, he sang the role of Gérard in the world *première* of *Andrea Chénier*, and on Nov. 10, 1900, at the Teatro Lirico he sang Cascart in the world *première* of *Zaza*. In 1902 in Milan he sang in the world *première* of *Germania* with Enrico Caruso and Amelia Pinto in the cast. He was a highly successful annual guest at Covent Garden (1900-1914). In 1907 he was engaged by the Manhattan Opera, and he sang there with great success until 1910. During this time he also sang in Chicago and Philadelphia. Sammarco was very well liked in South America, particularly at the Teatro Colón. In 1918 he was made a member of the management at La Scala, but he also continued to appear there as a singer, as he did elsewhere, including Covent Garden in 1919. Mario Sammarco possessed one of the most beautiful baritone voices of his generation. He was equally famed for the richness of his vocal material and for the great musicality with which he managed his voice. He was especially noted for his interpretation of Verdi roles.

Records: G & T (Milan, 1902-04), Fonotipia (Milan, 1905), HMV, Victor*, and Pathé*. *U.S. re-issue:* Opera Disc, Victor, Columbia-Fonotipia, IRCC. *U.S. re-recording:* Eterna, TAP, FRP, ASCO, Olympus, Belcanto, Rococo, Cantilena.

SANCHIONI, NUNU, soprano, b. Sept. 17, 1908, Cairo, Egypt. The daughter of an Italian consular secretary, she studied with Sra. Molajoli in Milan and made her debut in 1929, singing with great success at the Italian Opera in Holland (1930-32). After equal success at the Teatro San Carlo in 1932, she became ill and had to abandon her career for two years. In 1934 she sang Adele in a production of *Die Fledermaus* by Max Reinhardt in Milan. She sang again in Holland (1935-36). After guest appearances in Spain, she settled down with her husband, who was German, in Batavia, Java, as a teacher. She often gave concerts there over Radio Bandung, which she was able to continue during the Japanese occupation of Java. Since 1946 she has lived and taught in Rome. The coloratura soprano of this artist was one of the finest produced in Italy in her generation, but it never reached its former height after her illness.

Records: Her Columbia and HMV records all come from the earliest period of her career.

SANDEN, ALINE, soprano, b. Nov. 26, 1876, Berlin; d. May 8, 1955, Berlin. Originally Aline Kelch. She sang first in Berlin operetta and vaudeville theaters. Then she studied singing with Frau Albrecht-Fraude and Valeska von Facius and made her debut as a coloratura soprano there (1899). She sang at Plauen (1903-06), the Cologne Opera (1906-08), and with great success as a dramatic soprano at the Leipzig Opera (1909-21). She moved to the Grossen Volksoper in Berlin (1923-24) and finally to the Munich State Opera (1924-26). Guest appearances and concerts, all highly successful, took her to Berlin, Vienna, London, Paris, Amsterdam, and Brussels, as well as to the United States. Her first marriage was to the baritone Walter Soomer and the second, in 1927, to the composer Charles Flick-Steger. After her retirement in 1930 she lived and taught in Berlin. Along with the passionately dramatic delivery of this singer, she was admired for her brilliant acting ability.

Records: Edison cylinders and Odeon and Homochord disc records.

SANTLEY, SIR CHARLES, baritone, b. Feb. 28, 1834, Liverpool, England; d. Sept. 22, 1922, Hove, near London. He studied first with Gaetano Nava in Milan, then with Manuel Garcia in London, and made his debut in Pavia (1858). His first great successes came from his guest appearances in Italy, France, and England, particularly at the Paris Opéra and at Covent Garden. In 1863 he sang the role of Valentin in *Faust* at Her Majesty's Theater in London on the occasion of the first performance in England of the work and in the presence of the composer. After this production Gounod composed for Santley the air for Valentin, "Avant de quitter ces lieux," which had not appeared in the original score of the opera and which is not even now sung in Paris. In 1871 and 1891 he undertook highly successful American tours. He appeared on the stage until 1900, but thereafter gave only concerts. In 1907 he was knighted by King Edward VII. He wrote two autobiographical works, *Student and Singer* (London, 1892) and *Reminiscences of My Life* (London, 1909). His voice was outstanding both in opera and concert for his complete technical mastery and for the great musicality with which he used it. His particular starring roles were Don Giovanni and Valentin.

Records: A few very rare records on G & T (London, 1903) and Columbia. *U.S. re-recording:* Rococo, Belcanto.

SARACENI, ADELAIDE, soprano, b. 1898, Rosario, Argentina. She studied in Italy and made her debut as Rosina in *Il Barbiere di Siviglia* at the Teatro Verdi in Bologna (1920). She then had a famous career on the best-known Italian stages, including La Scala, the Teatro San Carlo, and at the Arena Festival. In 1926 she sang as guest in Holland and in 1928 at the Teatro Colón. On Mar. 15, 1931, she sang in the world *première* of *Le Vedova Scaltra* at the Rome Opera. She often sang on the Italian radio.

After she had retired from the stage, she lived and taught in Milan.

Records: HMV (including *Don Pasquale*). *U.S. re-issue:* RCA Victor. *U.S. re-recording:* Pathé-Marconi.

SARI, ADA, soprano, b. June 30, 1888, Lemberg, Germany. Originally Jadwiga Szajerowna. She studied in Milan and made her debut at the Teatro Costanzi as Marguerite in *Faust* (1912). She had her first great successes at the Teatro San Carlo in 1912-14, at the Teatro dal Verme, and in Trieste and Parma. In 1914 she was admired at the Warsaw Opera as Thaïs and in *The Demon* with Mattia Battistini. Although she sang lyric roles at the outset of her career, after 1914 she specialized in coloratura parts. After the war she sang a great deal in South America, particularly at the Teatro Colón, and toured the United States. In 1932 she excited great comment for her singing of the role of the Queen of the Night at La Scala. In the following years she sang regularly at the Vienna State Opera and the Budapest and Prague Operas, as well as at the Paris Opéra. Since 1939 she has lived in Warsaw; but she sang again as guest at the Vienna State Opera in 1947, appearing as Gilda in *Rigoletto*. She teaches singing at the Warsaw Conservatory. Her incomparable staccato technique was greatly admired in her coloratura singing.

Records: Polydor and HMV.

SATTLER, JOACHIM, tenor, b. Aug. 21, 1899, Affoltersbach, Germany. His voice was discovered by Siegfried Wagner and he studied with Beines in Darmstadt. He made his debut in Wuppertal (1926) as Claudio in *Das Liebesverbot*. He remained at Wuppertal until 1929 and then sang at Darmstadt (1929-37) and was engaged at the Hamburg State Opera (1937-52). In 1928-31 he sang Melot in *Tristan und Isolde* and Froh in *Das Rheingold*, as well as smaller roles at the Bayreuth Festivals. He made guest appearances at the Vienna State Opera (1935-41), at Amsterdam (1931), and was also a guest at the Dresden State Opera, the Teatro Liceo, and the Zoppot Festivals (1914-20), as well as in Switzerland. He was esteemed as a Wagner singer and heroic tenor of the first rank. His career lasted a long time; he sang Tristan in Kassel as late as 1957.

Records: Polydor. *U.S. re-issue:* Columbia.

SAVILLE, FRANCES, soprano, b. Jan. 6, 1862, San Francisco; d. Nov. 8, 1935, Burlingame, Calif. A pupil of Mathilde Marchesi in Paris, she made her debut as Juliette in *Roméo et Juliette* at the Brussels Opera (1892). In 1895 she sang the title role in *La Traviata* at the Opéra-Comique. She was a member of the Metropolitan Opera (1895-99) and during this time made regular guest appearances at Covent Garden. Her later guest appearances included the Imperial Opera in St. Petersburg and in Warsaw and Monte Carlo. She was engaged at the Vienna Imperial Opera (1899-1903). She was celebrated there for her singing of Fiordiligi in 1899 in a memorable production of *Così fan tutte*. Later she gave only isolated guest appearances and concerts and then lived in complete retirement in California. She was the aunt of the soprano Frances Alda. A brilliant coloratura voice; her total mastery of technique demonstrated her training in the Marchesi method.

Records: G & T (Vienna, 1902-03). *U.S. re-issue:* IRCC.

SAYAO, BIDU, soprano, b. May 11, 1902, Niteroi, Brazil. Originally Balduina Sayao. She came to Italy at the age of fourteen and studied singing with Elena Theodorini. She made her debut (1920) in Rumania and then completed her studies with Jean de Reszke in Paris. In 1926 her true debut followed, when she sang Rosina in *Il Barbiere di Siviglia* at the Teatro Costanzi. She had great success in Italy and France, particularly in Paris. In 1937 she was engaged by the Metropolitan Opera, her debut role being Manon in Massenet's opera; she was esteemed in New York as a worthy successor to Lucrezia Bori and she had brilliant success during her fifteen year stay there. From New York she made guest appearances in the leading opera houses in North and South America, particularly in Rio de Janeiro. In 1947 she married the baritone Giuseppe Danise. After 1952 she appeared only in concerts. She lives near Rio de Janeiro. She was outstanding both in coloratura and lyric roles; she was also a celebrated interpreter of Spanish and French songs.

Records: RCA Victor* and Columbia*. *U.S. re-recording:* Camden, United Artists.

SCACCIATI, BIANCA, soprano, b. 1894, Faenza, Italy. She studied with Ernesto Bruschino in Milan and made her debut (1917) at the Teatro della Pergola as Marguerite in *Faust*. She was soon noted as one of the leading dramatic sopranos of Italian opera. She was celebrated at La Scala, the Teatro Costanzi, and on other great stages in Italy, as well as for her appearances at the Arena and Maggio Musicale Festivals. In 1926 she created the title role in the first performance of *Turandot* at the Rome Opera, and also sang the same part at the Covent Garden *première* in 1927. She often appeared as guest at the Teatro Colón, as well as at the Paris Opéra and the Cairo Opera. Her career came to a close in the years after World War II. She had a dramatic soprano voice of luxurious tonal quality and great flexibility.

Records: Columbia* (including *Tosca* and *Il Trovatore*). *U.S. re-recording:* Eterna.

SCAMPINI, AUGUSTO, tenor, b. 1880; d. 1939, Barcelona. He made his debut about 1905 in Italy and in 1907 he sang as guest at the Teatro del Opera in Buenos Aires in *Hérodiade*; in the same year he sang Radames in *Aida* and Samson in *Samson et Dalilia* at the Teatro Massimo. He made highly successful guest appearances at the largest theaters in Italy, Spain, South America, and Russia. In 1910-11 he was applauded at La Scala for his singing in *Simone Boccanegra* and in *Saffo*. He sang at the German Theater in Prague (1913-14) and the critics there designated him as a probable successor to Enrico Caruso. In World War I he volunteered for service in the Italian army and lost a leg in the campaign in the Alps. This ended his singing career and he then became a singing teacher in Barcelona. He had a strong heroic tenor voice.

Records: HMV (1908-09) and Pathé* (1913). *U.S. re-issue:* Victor. *U.S. re-recording:* Eterna, Rococo.

SCANDIANI, ANGELO, baritone, b. 1872, Venice; d. June 2, 1930, Milan. At first in the civil service, he began his singing career around 1900 in the smaller Italian theaters. In 1903 he sang Amfortas in a concert production of *Parsifal* at La Scala. In the first decade of the century he was frequently a guest at Covent Garden, where he is particularly remmbered in *Madama Butterfly* with Emmy Destinn. In 1916 he sang Lothario in *Mignon* at La Scala with Ninon Vallin in the title role; in the same year he sang at the Teatro Colón as Hans Sachs in *Die Meistersinger*. In 1923 he

joined the management at La Scala.
Records: Edison* Amberola cylinders (c. 1912).

SCARAMBERG, ÉMILE, tenor, b. 1863, Besançon, France; d. Feb. 26, 1938, Besançson. He studied singing with Pellin in Paris, but then became a horn player in a military band. After further voice study with Charles Nicot in Paris, he made his debut at the Opéra-Comique in *Richard-Coeur-de-Lion* (1893). He remained at the Opéra-Comique for two years and then sang in Nantes, Nice, Marseilles, Bordeaux, and Vichy. Guest appearances took him to Covent Garden and the Operas in Brussels, Antwerp, Monte Carlo, and Moscow. He was a member of the Paris Opéra (1903-07), where his debut role was Lohengrin. He suddenly lost his voice and lived thereafter as a teacher in Besançon. He had a well-formed tenor voice with which he mastered not only the French repertory but also Wagner roles.
Records: Odeon De Luxe (Paris, 1905-06). *U.S. re-recording:* Rococo.

SCATTOLA, CARLO, bass, b. 1878 (?); d. 1947, Milan. Of the early career of this artist little is known, but around the turn of the century he sang serious bass parts on Italian operatic stages. After World War I he began a second career as a *buffo* bass and was highly successful. In 1922 he came to La Scala, where he had brilliant success, particularly as Lunardo in *I Quattro Rusteghi*. When Conchita Supervia began to revive Rossini's almost completely forgotten *bel canto* operas, he belonged to the group of artists who took part in this Rossini renaissance. In 1926 he sang Taddeo in *L'Italiana in Algeri* with her at the Teatro Argentina. In 1929 he sang both this part and Don Magnifico in *La Cenerentola* with her at the Théâtre des Champs-Elysées. In 1933 he appeared with her again at the Maggio Musicale Festival and also in 1936 at Covent Garden. In 1930 he made an American tour with the Columbia Grand Opera Company. Until about 1943 he sang regularly at La Scala and appeared in other important Italian opera houses in his celebrated *buffo* roles.
Records: About 1903 he made three records for G & T; in 1919 he sang in one duet with Beniamino Gigli for HMV. He made electric records for Odeon-Parlophone (1927) with Conchita Supervia and sang a small part in *La Bohème* with Gigli and Licia Albanese for HMV (1938). *U.S. re-issue:* American Decca, RCA Victor. *U.S. re-recording:* Washington.

SCHÄRTEL, ELISABETH, contralto, b. 1890 (?), Weiden, Germany. She studied singing first with Helena Rödiger and Wilma Kaiser, then with Anna Bahr-Mildenburg in Munich, and finally with Henny Wolff in Hamburg. After her debut in Regensburg, she sang at Freiburg i. Br. until 1951, Braunschweig (1951-57), Nuremberg (1957-59). She was selected as principal contralto for the Cologne Opera in 1960. She has appeared almost every year since 1954 at the Bayreuth Festivals, particularly as Mary in *Der Fliegende Holländer* and as Magdalena in *Die Meistersinger*.
Records: Decca (Mary in *Der Fliegende Holländer* at Bayreuth). *U.S. re-issue:* London, DGG.

SCHECH, MARIANNE, soprano, b. Jan. 8, 1915, Geitau, Germany. She studied at the Trapp Conservatory in Munich and made her debut (1937) at Coblenz as Marta in *Tiefland*. She then sang at the Munich State Opera (1939-41), the Düsseldorf Opera (1941-44), and the Dresden State Opera (1944-51). Since 1945 she has also been a member of the Bavarian State Opera in Munich. She has sung as guest at Covent Garden, the Paris Opéra, the Teatro Liceo, the Teatro São Carlo, and the opera houses in Rio de Janeiro, Brussels, Hamburg, Stuttgart, and the Vienna State Opera. She has mastered a large operatic and concert repertory and is esteemed as an interpreter of both Wagner and Richard Strauss roles.

Records: DGG* (including *Der Rosenkavalier, Elektra, Hänsel und Gretel,* and *Die Zauberflöte*), HMV, Urania* (*Tannhäuser*), and Decca. *U.S. re-issue:* Angel, London, Vox.

SCHEFF, FRITZI, soprano, b. Aug. 30, 1879, Vienna; d. Apr. 8, 1954, New York City. She was the daughter of the opera singer Anna Jäger and was first taught by her mother; she then studied with Frau Schröder-Hanfstaengl in Munich. She completed her studies at the Conservatory in Frankfurt a. M. and made her debut (1897) at the Munich Royal Opera as Marie in *La Fille du Régiment,* after which she remained in Munich for three years. In 1898 she sang as guest at the Theater an der Wien and in 1900 she sang Nedda in *I Pagliacci* at Covent Garden. In the same year she was engaged at the Metropolitan Opera, making her debut as Marzelline in *Fidelio.* She sang there successfully for the next three seasons but in 1904 she gave up her operatic career and turned entirely to operettas. In 1906 she had a sensational success in New York in *Mlle. Modiste.* She completed a long American tour with this piece and became one of the most celebrated American operetta stars. She appeared in the United States on the operetta stage until 1930. She was first married to Baron Fritz von Bardeleben and then to the novelist John Fox, Jr., from whom she was separated in 1913.

Records: No records of her voice exist, only a fragment on a Mapleson cylinder. *U.S. re-recording:* IRCC.

SCHEIDEMANTEL, KARL, baritone, b. Jan. 21, 1859, Weimar, Germany; d. June 21, 1923, Weimar. He studied with Bodo Borchers in Weimar and with Julius Stockhausen in Berlin and made his debut in Weimar (1878) as Wolfram in *Tannhäuser.* He remained at Weimar until 1886, but during this time he sang as guest at various German opera houses and in London. In 1886 he was selected for the Dresden Royal Opera, where he sang for thirty-four years. In 1888 at the Bayreuth Festivals he sang Amfortas in *Parsifal,* in 1888-89 Hans Sachs in *Die Meistersinger,* and in 1891 Wolfram in *Tannhäuser.* At the Dresden Opera he appeared in several world *premières* of Richard Strauss' operas: as Kunrat in *Feuersnot* (1901), as Faninal in *Der Rosenkavalier* (1911). In the same year he retired from the stage and then lived in Weimar. He was director of the Dresden State Opera (1921-22). He was also active as opera *régisseur* and he published (1909) a newly edited text of *Così fan tutte* under the title *Dame Kobold.* In 1914 his translation into German of *Don Giovanni* was awarded a prize by the German Stage Society. He published two textbooks on singing: *Stimmbildung* (Leipzig, 1907) and *Gesangsbildung* (Leipzig, 1913).

Records: Nine rare records for G & T (Dresden, 1902 and 1907-08).

SCHEIDL, THEODOR, baritone, b. Aug. 3, 1880, Vienna; d. Apr. 22, 1959, Tübingen, Germany. After completing schooling in a commercial school, he became a druggist;

then he began the study of singing in Vienna in 1906 and made his debut there at the Volksoper (1910) as the Herald in *Lohengrin*. He sang at Olmütz (1911-12), Augsburg (1912), and Stuttgart (1913-21). He came to be known as an important Wagner singer through his appearances at the Bayreuth Festivals: Klingsor in *Parsifal* and Donner in the *Ring* cycle (1914), Amfortas in *Parsifal* (1924-25), and Kurwenal in *Tristan und Isolde* (1927). He was a celebrated member of the Berlin State Opera (1921-32) and made highly successful guest appearances in Milan, London, Paris, Brussels, Vienna, Prague, Amsterdam, and Munich. In 1932 he spent one year at the German Theater in Prague. He was named professor at the Music High School in Munich in 1937, and after 1947 he lived and taught in Tübingen. He was particularly noted as a Wagner singer, but was also famous for his interpretations of lieder and ballads.

Records: Polydor and Parlophone. *U.S. re-issue:* Odeon-Okeh. *U.S. re-recording:* Rococo.

SCHEIDT, JULIUS VOM, baritone, b. Mar. 29, 1877, Bremen, Germany; d. Dec. 10, 1948, Hamburg. He made his debut at the opera house in Cologne (1899) and remained there until 1916. He sang at the German Opera in Berlin (1916-24) and then went to the Hamburg State Opera as principal baritone (1924-30). There he was especially admired as Hans Sachs in *Die Meistersinger* and as Falstaff. After 1930 he sang only in guest appearances and was particularly active as a teacher.

Records: G & T (Cologne, 1904; Bayreuth, 1904; Berlin, 1906), including duets with Selma vom Scheidt.

SCHEIDT, ROBERT VOM, baritone, b. Apr. 16, 1879, Bremen, Germany; d. Apr. 10, 1964, Frankfurt a. M. Originally an actor, he was the brother of Julius and Selma vom Scheidt. He studied at the Conservatory in Cologne and made his debut (1897) at the opera house there, remaining until 1903. He sang at the Hamburg Opera (1903-12) and then at the Opera in Frankfurt a. M. (1912-40). In Frankfurt he sang Tamare in the world *première* of *Die Gezeichtneten* (1918) and Vogt in the world *première* of *Der Schatzgräber* (1920). At the Bayreuth Festival (1904) he appeared as Biterolf in *Tannhäuser*, Donner in the *Ring* cycle, and Klingsor in *Parsifal*.

Records: Odeon (Hamburg, 1908-09), Pathé, and Polyphon.

SCHEIDT, SELMA VOM, soprano, b. June 26, 1874, Bremen, Germany; d. March, 1959, Weimar, Germany. She was the sister of the two opera singers Julius and Robert vom Scheidt, and she began her study of singing with Heinrich Böllhof in Hamburg, then studied with Theodor Bertram. She made her debut (1891) at Elberfeld as Agathe in *Der Freischütz* and sang at Essen (1892-94) and Düsseldorf (1894-95). She came to Weimar in 1900 by way of Aachen, Bonn, and the Theater am Westens. She appeared at Weimar for more than twenty-five years. In 1958 she was made an honorary citizen of that city.

Records: G & T (Weimar, Cologne, and Bayreuth, 1904; Berlin, 1906) including duets with Julius vom Scheidt.

SCHELLENBERG, ARNO, baritone, b. June 16, 1908, Berlin. He began his study of singing in 1926 at the Berlin Music High School with Julius von Raatz-Brockmann and made his debut (1929) at the Düsseldorf Opera. After singing at the Cologne Opera (1931-32), he was engaged at the Munich State

Opera, where he remained until after World War II. He made guest appearances in Paris (1935), at the Vienna State Opera (1937), Rome Opera (1938), the Royal Opera in Stockholm (1941), and Maggio Musicale Festival. In 1950 he took up a professorship at the Berlin Music High School, but continued to appear as a singer—for example, at the Salzburg Festival in 1953. He also led a continuation course at the Mozarteum in Salzburg.

Records: HMV. *U.S. re-issue:* Urania.

SCHEPPAN, HILDE, soprano, b. Sept. 17, 1908, Forst, Germany. She studied at the Berlin Music High School and with Erny von Stetten there and made her debut (1934) at Darmstadt. She was engaged at the Berlin State Opera (1935) and she sang there with great success until 1954. Her guest appearances in Amsterdam, Vienna Hamburg, Munich, and Dresden were equally successful. She appeared annually at the Bayreuth Festivals (1937-43) and was especially admired there as Eva in *Die Meistersinger.* After World War II she resided in Bayreuth and sang at the Festivals after their resumption in 1951, but took only small roles. She was a member of the Stuttgart Opera (1952-57) and in the latter year accepted a professorship at the Nuremberg Conservatory.

Records: Telefunken, HMV, DGG (*Cavalleria Rusticana* and *I Pagliacci*). *U.S. re-issue:* RCA Victor.

SCHEY, HERMANN, bass, b. Nov. 8, 1895, Bunzlau, Germany. He studied singing with Franz von Dulong in Berlin (1913-15). In 1915 he was put in the German army and resumed his vocal studies at the end of the war. After 1922 he was occupied in Berlin as a concert and oratorio singer, in which he was particularly admired for his interpretations of Bach. He was highly successful in his concert tours to various European musical centers. In 1934, because he was Jewish, he emigrated to Holland and in 1936 became a professor at the Amsterdam Conservatory and continued his successful concert activity. When Holland was occupied by the German army in 1940, he was forced to go into hiding until the end of the war. He then resumed his career and sang at the Holland Festival and at the Salzburg Festival. Concert tours took him to Germany, England, Austria, and Switzerland; thereafter he worked as a singing teacher.

Records: A great many records for Vox, Ultraphon, Odeon, Philips (*St. Matthew Passion* under Mengelberg), and MMS. *U.S. re-issue:* DGG.

SCHEYRER, GERDA, soprano, b. July 18, 1925, Vienna. She studied at the Music Academy in Vienna. After her debut at Graz, she sang first at the Vienna Volksoper, but since 1959 she has been a member of the Vienna State Opera. She has also made guest appearances at Düsseldorf and Stuttgart among others, and she is a well-known oratorio singer.

Records: Philips, Ariola, Columbia (*Die Fledermaus*), and Amadeo. *U.S. re-issue:* Angel, Seraphim.

SCHIAVAZZI, PIERO, tenor, b. 1878, Cagliari, Sardinia; d. May 25, 1949, Rome. The city of Cagliari financed his study of singing at the Conservatory in Pesaro. He made his debut in 1898 and on November 22 of that year he appeared at the Teatro Costanzi in Rome as the Ragpicker in the world *première* of *Iris.* Later the role of Osaka in this opera became his particular starring part, which he sang in 1903 at Parma, in 1904 at Fiume, and in 1906 in Florence and Rome. In

1907, at the Teatro dal Verme, he sang in the world *première* of *Amica*. In 1906 he was applauded at La Scala in *Risurrezione*, and in 1911 at the Teatro dal Verme in the world *première* of *Conchita*. He made very successful guest appearances at the Teatro São Carlos and at the Teatro Coliseo, as well as on other famous stages. He took part in World War I as a soldier. After the war he sang on provincial stages in Italy and then opened a voice studio in Rome. At the end of his life he again lived in Sardinia, where after World War II he busied himself in political activity for the Monarchist party. He had a voice that was outstandingly handled from the musical point of view and one that was very expressive.

Records: One record for G & T (Milan, 1904), others for Fonotipia (1905-06), and Pathé.

SCHIØTZ, AKSEL, tenor-baritone, b. Sept. 1, 1906, Roskilde, Denmark. Originally an elementary school teacher, he first studied singing at the Royal Conservatory in Copenhagen in 1938. He completed his studies with John Forsell in Stockholm, made his debut as a concert tenor (1938) and his operatic debut at the Royal Opera in Copenhagen (1939), singing Ferrando in *Così fan tutte*. After the occupation of Denmark, he objected to appearing under the German occupation forces. Thereupon he gave secret concerts for the Resistance and became a symbol of the Danish Resistance Movement. His career reached its high point in the early years after the war. In 1945 he undertook a tour of Sweden and Norway and sang on the English radio. At the Glyndebourne Festival of 1946 he alternated with Peter Pears in *The Rape of Lucretia*. He was highly applauded at the Edinburgh Festival in 1947 and in 1948 on a tour of the United States. He was particularly admired for his singing of Mozart. In 1950 he developed a brain tumor and underwent an operation whose aftereffects were a partial paralysis of the speech and sight organs. With almost superhuman energy he was able to sing again—but as a baritone. Thereafter he had brilliant successes in the United States as a concert and oratorio singer. After 1955 he was a professor at the University of Minnesota, but later returned to Denmark.

Records: As both tenor and baritone he recorded for HMV; as baritone he made a record for Dyer-Bennett in the United States. *U.S. re-issue:* RCA Victor, London International, Seraphim.

SCHIPA, TITO, tenor, b. Jan. 2, 1889, Lecce, Italy; d. Dec. 16, 1965, New York City. The bishop of Lecce first recognized his beautiful voice and Schipa began his studies with Alceste Gerunda in Lecce and then with Emilio Piccoli in Milan. He made his debut in Vercelli (1911) and sang on small stages for the next two years. In 1913 he sang as guest at the Teatro Colón and at the Opera in Rio de Janeiro. The next year, 1914, saw him at the Teatro Costanzi and in 1915 he made his debut at La Scala as Vladimir in *Prince Igor*. On Mar. 27, 1917, he created the role of Ruggiero in the world *première* of *La Rondine* at Monte Carlo. He was admired as one of the great singers at the Chicago Opera (1919-32), and after 1927 he was an almost annual guest at the Teatro Colón and was highly successful at the Ravinia Summer Opera, near Chicago. In 1929 he returned to La Scala and enjoyed continuous triumphs there for twenty years. He was engaged at the Metropolitan Opera (1933-35; 1940-41). His debut there was as Nemorino in

L'Elisir d'Amore. His career lasted a long time; he sang at the Teatro Colón in 1954 and in 1957 was idolized on his guest appearances in Moscow, Leningrad, and Riga; even at the age of seventy he still gave concerts. He was also a composer; besides church music and songs he wrote an operetta, *Principessa Liana,* first produced in Rome in 1935. The voice of Tito Schipa was the ideal of the *bel canto* lyric tenor; its velvety melodic line, the fine shadings of characterizations, and the effortlessness of his singing cannot be admired too much.

Records: Many records for Pathé*, HMV (including *Don Pasquale*), Victor*, and Durium. *U.S. re-issue:* National. *U.S. re-recording:* RCA Victor, TAP, Pathé-Marconi, Scala, Eterna, Canto, Design, FRP, Angel, Capitol, Richmond, Pathé-Actuelle, and Pathé-Perfect.

SCHIPPER, EMIL, baritone, b. 1882, Vienna; d. July 20, 1957, Vienna. He first studied law and completed his J.D. degree. Then he studied singing with Guarino in Milan and made his debut (1904) at the German Theater in Prague as Telramund in *Lohengrin.* In 1911 he went from there to Linz; he sang at the Vienna Volksoper (1912-15) and the Munich Royal Opera (1916-22). He was then chosen for the Vienna State Opera. He sang with brilliant success in his guest appearances in Madrid, Barcelona, Amsterdam, Brussels, Paris, and Budapest. He made regular guest appearances at Covent Garden (1924-30) and was heard at the Berlin State Opera. He undertook very successful tours of the United States (1922-23; 1928) and he sang in opera in Chicago and Boston. At the Salzbug Festival of 1930 he was greatly applauded as Agamemnon in *Alceste* and in 1935 as Kurwenal in *Tristan und Isolde* under Toscanini. He gave his farewell stage performance in 1938. He was for a time married to the contralto Maria Olszewska. A heroic baritone, he was particularly admired in Wagner roles.

Records: Polydor, Odeon, and HMV. *U.S. re-issue:* RCA Victor. *U.S. re-recording:* Eterna, Belcanto.

SCHIRP, WILHELM, bass-baritone, b. July 27, 1906, Elberfeld, Germany. He studied at the Cologne Conservatory and with Theile there and made his debut at the Cologne Opera (1928) as a bass. He remained in Cologne until 1934, then sang at Mainz (1934-35) and the Berlin City Opera (1935-49). He appeared as guest at the Vienna State Opera (1938-39) and sang Hagen in *Götterdämmerung* at Covent Garden in 1938. He later appeared in Hamburg, Munich, and Leipzig. He was a member of the Cologne Opera (1949-52) and there he turned to baritone roles; since 1952 he has been a member of the Stuttgart Opera.

Records: Telefunken.

SCHLEMM, ANNY, soprano, b. Feb. 22, 1929, Neu-Isenburg, Germany. She studied with Erna Westberger in Berlin and made her debut (1946) at Halle. In 1949 she came to the Berlin State Opera and was also engaged at the Komische Oper there under a simultaneous contract. She then sang at the Cologne Opera (1950-51) and after 1951 at the Opera in Frankfurt. She has frequently been a guest at the State Operas in Hamburg and Munich. In addition to a wealth of stage parts, mostly lyric roles, she is also famous as a concert and lieder singer.

Records: DGG (*Madama Butterfly*) and HMV. *U.S. re-issue:* Bach Guild, Heliodor.

SCHLUSNUS, HEINRICH, baritone, b. Aug. 6, 1888, Braubacham-Rhein, Germany; d. June 19, 1952, Frankfurt a. M. He worked first as a postal employee in Frankfurt and studied singing at the same time. In 1914 he was drafted into the army and suffered a leg wound at the front. He then began his career as an opera singer and made his stage debut (1915) at the Hamburg Opera as the Herald in *Lohengrin*. He sang at Nuremberg (1915-17) and was then engaged at the Berlin Imperial Opera, where he remained until 1945. After further study with Louis Bachner in Berlin he gave his first lieder recital in 1918 in Berlin's Blüthner Hall. He quickly became the most famous singer of German lieder of his generation. He appeared in Holland, Belgium, England, France, Austria, Italy, the United States, and Canada. He frequently made guest appearances at Covent Garden in London and at the Vienna State Opera. He was engaged at the Chicago Opera (1927-28) and in 1934 he sang Amfortas in *Parsifal* at the Bayreuth Festival. After World War II he appeared at the Opera in Frankfurt, where in 1948 he sang Rigoletto as his final stage role. He gave his last recital in 1951. His baritone voice was distinguished by an entirely personal and warm sound. On the stage he was held to be an outstanding Verdi interpreter and in the concert hall a lieder singer of the highest artistic rank.

Records: A great many records for Polydor, Urania*, and DGG (including *Rigoletto*, *La Traviata*, *Tannhäuser*, and *I Vespri Siciliani*). *U.S. re-issue:* Brunswick, American Decca. *U.S. re-recording:* TAP, Eterna, HRS, Rococo.

SCHLÜTER, ERNA, soprano, b. Feb. 5, 1904, Oldenburg, Germany. She made her debut in Oldenburg (1922) as a contralto. In 1925 she moved to Mannheim, where her voice changed to a dramatic soprano, and then to Düsseldorf (1930-40). By this time she was experiencing great successes in guest appearances, for example, in 1936 at the Teatro Liceo. In 1940 she was engaged by the National Opera in Hamburg, where she sang until 1956. In 1947 she sang Ellen Orford in the German *première* of *Peter Grimes*. She was the first German singer to appear (1946-47) after World War II at the Metropolitan Opera; her roles there were Brünnhilde in *Die Walküre* and Isolde. She was also applauded in guest appearances at Covent Garden, the Vienna State Opera, in Amsterdam and Brussels, and she was admired as Leonora in *Fidelio* at the 1948 Salzburg Festival. She lives and teaches in Hamburg. She was the most celebrated German dramatic soprano of her time.

Records: A few for HMV (including *Elektra*) and unpublished records for DGG. *U.S. re-issue:* RCA Victor (*Elektra*).

SCHMEDES, ERIK, tenor, b. Aug. 27, 1868, Gjentofte, Denmark; d. Mar. 23, 1931, Vienna. His brother, Haakon Schmedes, later became a well-known violinist. Erik Schmedes studied with Rothmühl in Berlin and with Johannes Ress in Vienna; he made his debut (1891) at Nuremberg as a baritone, remaining there until 1894. The director of the Hamburg Opera, Bernhard Pollini, discovered that he really had a tenor voice and after renewed study with August Iffert in Dresden, he sang at the Dresden Royal Opera (1894-97) as a heroic tenor. In 1898 he was engaged at the Vienna Imperial Opera and there he found his true artistic home; for more than twenty-five years he was the declared darling of the opera-going public in Vienna. Famous for his Wagner roles, he sang annually at the Bayreuth Festivals (1899-1906); there he was particularly applauded as Siegfried in the *Ring* cycle and also as Parsifal. He sang at the Metropolitan Opera (1908-09), making his debut as Siegmund in *Die Walküre*. He later appeared at Covent Garden, the Paris Opéra, and in Berlin, Munich, and Prague. In 1924 he left the stage and then taught in Vienna. A strong expressive tenor voice, particularly admired in Wagner roles.

Records: G & T (Vienna, 1903-06), HMV, Favorite (Vienna, 1905), and Pathé. *U.S. re-issue:* Victor. *U.S. re-recording:* HRS, Eterna, TAP, FRP.

SCHMIDT, JOSEPH, tenor, b. Mar. 4, 1904, Davidende, Rumania; d. Nov. 16, 1942, Gyrenbad, Switzerland. He sang as a boy in the choir of a synagogue in Czernowitz; his uncle, Leo Engel, who later became his manager, made it possible for him to study singing in Vienna. In 1928 he made his debut in Berlin in a radio performance of *Idomeneo*. On account of his small size it was hardly possible for him to aspire to a career on the operatic stage; therefore he developed an astounding career in the concert hall and particularly as a singer in radio and films as well as on records. After the release of the film *Ein Lied Geht um die Welt* (1932) his popularity in Germany reached its highest point. In 1933 because he was Jewish he was required to leave Germany. He then undertook very successful concert tours in Holland, Belgium, Switzerland, the United States, Mexico, and Cuba. In 1937 he attempted to return to Germany, but again had to flee. Upon the occupation of Belgium in 1940 by German troops, he escaped under adventuresome circumstances through France to Switzerland. There he was put into an internment camp at Gyrenbad, near Zürich, where he soon died. Joseph Schmidt possessed one of the most beautiful lyric tenor voices of his generation. Its brilliance in the higher ranges and its expressive power, filled with tonal nuances, brought him great admiration for his many records.

Records: Ultraphon (Telefunken), Odeon, and HMV. *U.S. re-issue:* American Decca. *U.S. re-recording:* Scala, Eterna, TAP, Telefunken, Bruno, Capitol, Rococo.

SCHMITT-WALTER, KARL, baritone, b. July 23, 1900, Germersheim-am-Rhein, Germany. He studied at the Nuremberg Conservatory, with Richard Trunk in Munich, and made his debut at Nuremberg (1923); he then sang at Oberhausen (1924), Saarbrücken (1925), Dortmund (1926-28), Wiesbaden (1929-35), and after 1935 at the German Opera in Berlin. He appeared as guest at the State Operas in Vienna and Hamburg, at the Paris Opéra, the New York City Opera, and in Brussels, Amsterdam, and Barcelona. He sang with great success at the Salzburg and Bayreuth Festivals. Upon the resumption of the Bayreuth Festivals after World War II he was greatly admired there as Beckmesser in *Die Meistersinger*; he sang this same part again at Bayreuth in 1961. After 1950 he was a member of the Munich State Opera and also a professor at the Music High School there. Since 1962 he has taught in Copenhagen. He had a dark-timbred voice and was equally admired in Mozart and Wagner on the stage and as an oratorio and lieder singer in the concert hall.

Records: Telefunken, Decca and DGG (*I Pagliacci*). *U.S. re-recording:* Telefunken, London.

SCHNABEL-BEHR, THERESE, contralto, b. Sept. 14, 1876, Stuttgart, Germany; d. Feb. 2, 1959, Lugano, Switzerland. She studied with

Julius Stockhausen in Frankfurt a. M. (1893-95), then with Schulz-Dornburg in Cologne, and finally with Etelka Gerster in Berlin. She began her career as a concert singer (1898). In 1905 she married the famous pianist Artur Schnabel (1882-1951); his accompaniments to her singing were brilliant and inspiring. She gave lieder recitals in all the important music centers of the world; several tours of the United States brought this pair of artists great success. She worked as a teacher in Berlin, where her husband was also a professor at the Music High School (1925-33). In 1933 Schnabel, who was Jewish, had to leave Germany, and he and his wife then lived in England. After 1939 they moved to New York City and finally to Switzerland. She was especially known as a lieder singer; she never appeared on the stage.

Records: G & T and HMV, mostly lieder, accompanied by Artur Schnabel.

SCHOCK, RUDOLF, tenor, b. Sept. 4, 1915, Duisburg, Germany. After overcoming grave hardships, he studied singing in Cologne and Hannover and at the age of eighteen sang in the chorus at Duisburg. His first engagement as soloist was in Braunschweig (1937) and remained there until 1940. He then became a soldier and resumed his career in 1945 at the opera house in Hannover. In 1946 he came to the State Opera in Berlin and sang as guest at the Berlin City and Hamburg Operas. He had great success at Covent Garden (1949-50) and in 1949 he was very successful on an Australian tour. In 1948 he first sang at the Salzburg Festival and since 1952 he has appeared several times at the Edinburgh Festival, where he was especially liked in 1956 as Tamino in *Die Zauberflöte*. Since 1951 he has been under contract to the Vienna State Opera, at the same time making guest appearances at the Düsseldorf Opera and the State Operas in Munich and Hamburg. He was highly successful as Walther in *Die Meistersinger* at the 1959 Bayreuth Festival. He was also one of the most famous German film singers of his generation. In the film *Du bist der Welt für Mich* he portrayed Richard Tauber. His later film successes were *Die Stimme der Sehnsucht, Der Fröhliche Wanderer*, and the Lehár film *Schön ist die Welt*. He possessed a tenor voice of rare brilliance in the higher registers and expressiveness. He found suitable expression in both opera and operetta, as well as in art songs and popular songs.

Records: HMV (*Fidelio, Lohengrin, Die Meistersinger, Ariadne auf Naxos*, and *Der Freischütz*), Columbia (*Carmen*), and Ariola (*L'Elisir d'Amore, Tiefland*, and *Die Fledermaus*). *U.S. re-issue:* Electrola, Bruno, Angel, Fiesta, Capitol, Seraphim. *U.S re-recording:* TAP.

SCHOEPFLIN, ADOLF, bass, b. July 9, 1884, Appenweier, Germany; d. Mar. 3, 1956, near Karlsruhe, Germany. He studied with F. Schuberg in Karlsruhe, made his debut (1909) at Olmütz, then sang at Posen (1910-11). He appeared at the German Opera in Prague (1911-19) and at the German Opera in Berlin (1919-23). In 1923 he made an American tour with the German Opera Company. In 1924 he sang Pogner in *Die Meistersinger* and Gurnemanz in *Parsifal* at the Bayreuth Festival. After singing at the Dresden State Opera (1924-29), he was engaged at the Municipal Theater in Karlsruhe, where he appeared until 1945. He sang at the Zoppot Festivals (1930-36).

Records: Vox.

SCHÖFFLER, PAUL, bass-baritone, b. Aug. 15, 1897, Dresden, Germany. He studied singing, piano, violin, and music theory at the Dresden Conservatory. After further study of singing with Mario Sammarco in Milan, he was engaged in 1925 by Fritz Busch for the Dresden State Opera. After he had sung there until 1937, he was called to the Vienna State Opera and remained there for more than twenty-five years. At the Bayreuth Festivals he sang Hans Sachs in *Die Meistersinger* (1943-44) and the title role in *Der Fliegende Holländer* (1956). He appeared almost annually at the Salzburg Festivals, where he was particularly admired for his Mozart roles; in 1947 he sang the title role there in the world *première* of *Dantons Tod*. In 1952 he created the role of Jupiter at Salzburg in the world *première* of *Die Liebe der Danaë*. He made highly successful guest appearances at the Paris Opéra, Covent Garden, La Scala, the Teatro Colón, the Rome Opera, and the State Operas in Munich and Hamburg. He sang successfully at the Metropolitan Opera (1949-51). His career lasted a long time; he was still appearing on the stage and in the concert hall at the age of sixty-five. The magnificence of his vocal ability and the expressive skill which he put into his characterizations brought him great admiration in a wide-ranging repertory.

Records: Many records for Ultraphon, Polydor, Philips, Decca (*Die Zauberflöte, Così fan tutte, Die Frau ohne Schatten,* and *Die Meistersinger*), and Vanguard. *U.S. re-issue:* Vox, Vanguard, London, Epic, DGG, Everyman, Remington, RCA Victor.

SCHÖNE, LOTTE, soprano, b. Dec. 15, 1894, Vienna. Originally Charlotte Bodenstein. She began her vocal studies at the age of fifteen with Johannes Ress in Vienna and also studied there with Luise Ress and Marie Brossement. In 1912 she made her debut at the Vienna Volksoper as a Bridesmaid in *Der Freischütz*. In 1917 she was engaged by the Vienna Imperial Opera and was very successful there. She sang at the Salzburg Festivals (1922-28; 1935; 1937) and was particularly noted in such Mozart roles as Despina in *Così fan tutte*, Susanna in *Le Nozze di Figaro*, and Pamina in *Die Zauberflöte*. In 1926 she was engaged by the Berlin City Opera and there she added lyric parts to her repertory. In 1929 she sang as guest at The Hague as Mélisande in *Pelléas et Mélisande* and she had outstanding success in the same role at the Opéra-Comique. In 1927 she created the role of Liu in *Turandot* at the *première* of the work at Covent Garden. She was successful at The Hague and Amsterdam (1930-31). In 1933 because she was Jewish she was required to leave Germany. She was then engaged at the Opéra-Comique and undertook concert tours in France, Belgium, Holland, and Switzerland. When the German army invaded France, she was forced to conceal herself in a village in the French Alps. In 1945 she resumed her singing career, but confined herself almost exclusively to concert appearances. In 1948 she again appeared as guest at the Berlin City Opera. In 1953 she gave up her career and taught singing in Paris. Her soprano voice possessed an uncommon musical beauty.

Records: Vox, Odeon, and HMV. *U.S. re-issue:* RCA Victor, American Decca. *U.S. re-recording:* Rococo.

SCHORR, FRIEDRICH, baritone, b. Sept. 22, 1888, Nagyvárád, Hungary; d. Aug. 14, 1953, Farmington, Conn. He planned to become a jurist, but studied singing with Adolph Robinson in Brünn and made his debut at Graz (1911) as

Wotan in *Die Walküre*. After remaining in Graz until 1916, he sang in the German Theater in Prague (1916-18) and at the Cologne Opera (1918-23). In 1923 he toured the United States with the German Opera Company and in 1924 he was engaged at the Metropolitan Opera, making his debut as Wolfram in *Tannhäuser*. He remained a celebrated member of the Metropolitan until 1943 and was treasured all over the world, particularly as a magnificent Wagner baritone. He appeared annually as a guest at the Berlin State Opera (1922-33) and also sang regularly at the Vienna State Opera. He first sang at the Bayreuth Festivals in 1925 and was greatly admired there until 1931 as Wotan in the *Ring* cycle. In 1943 he gave up the stage but continued to appear in concert, and he produced Wagner operas at the New York City Opera. At the same time he conducted an opera studio at the Hartt School in Hartford, Connecticut. He was one of the most famous Wagner baritones of his time. With his large, beautifully controlled voice, he shaped such parts as Hans Sachs and Wotan in an unforgettable manner.

Records: Polydor, Brunswick*, HMV, Victor*, and Vocalion*. *U.S. re-recording:* Scala, Angel, Rococo, TAP, FRP, Veritas.

SCHRAMM, HERMANN, tenor, b. Feb. 7, 1871, Berlin; d. Dec. 14, 1951, Frankfurt a. M. He first began a business career, but then studied singing and made his debut (1895) at Breslau as Gomez in *Ein Nachtlager von Granada*. He sang as a lyric tenor at the Cologne Opera (1896-1900) but then turned to *buffo* parts. He was a highly prized member of the Frankfurt Opera (1900-33). He was the finest Mime in the *Ring* cycle and the finest David in *Die Meistersinger* on the German stage in his time. In 1899 he appeared as guest at Covent Garden and sang there frequently thereafter; he also sang successfully in Brussels and Paris and, above all, in Holland. In 1899 he sang David at the Bayreuth Festival. In 1920 he sang the Chancellor in the Frankfurt *première* of *Der Schatzgräber*. As late as 1946 he appeared as Eisenstein in *Die Fledermaus* at Frankfurt. His son, Friedrich Schramm, was for many years the director of the Basel City Theater and is now the intendant of the Wiesbaden Theater.

Records: Berliner (Frankfurt, 1901) and G & T (Frankfurt, 1904-07). *U.S. re-recording:* Belcanto.

SCHREIER, PETER, tenor, b. 1935, Gauernitz, near Meissen, Germany. He sang as a boy contralto in the choir of the Holy Cross Church in Dresden; then with the same group as a tenor until 1954. He studied singing in Leipzig and at the Music High School in Dresden. While studying, he made his debut at the Berlin State Opera as Paolino in *Il Matrimonio Segreto*. He was a pupil for three years at the Berlin State Opera and sang beginner's roles there. His formal debut followed there (1959) as Belmonte in *Die Entführung aus dem Serail*. Guest appearances followed in Hamburg, Vienna, London, Munich, Bucharest, Lausanne, Warsaw, Moscow, and Leningrad. In 1966 he sang at the Bayreuth Festival. In 1967 he was engaged by the Metropolitan Opera, making his debut there as Tamino in *Die Zauberflöte*. He is also an outstanding oratorio tenor. He has a well-trained lyric tenor voice.

Records: Eterna (including records as a boy contralto) and Columbia (*Il Barbiere di Siviglia* and *Zar und Zimmermann*). *U.S. reissue:* Seraphim, Nonesuch.

SCHRÖDTER, FRITZ, tenor, b. Mar. 15, 1855, Leipzig; d. Jan. 16, 1924, Vienna. He completed both the course at the Music Academy in Düsseldorf and the one at a music school in Cologne. He began his career as an operetta singer with small companies in Cologne, Hamburg, and Bremen. While he was singing at the Friedrich-Wilhelmstädtischen Theater in Berlin, he was heard by Johann Strauss, Jr., who obtained an engagement for him in 1876 at the Budapest National Theater. In 1877 he came to Vienna as an operetta singer, but also studied operatic roles with Stolz in Prague. His debut as an opera singer took place in Prague at the German Theater in 1879 and he remained there until 1886. In 1884 he appeared as guest under Hans Richter at Covent Garden. In 1886 he was engaged at the Vienna Imperial Opera, where he was particularly admired in *buffo* parts, but also sang lyric roles. He remained at the Vienna Opera until 1915 and sang at the Bayreuth Festivals (1898-1900). After his retirement he lived and taught in Vienna. He was the father-in-law of the bass Wilhelm Hesch. He possessed a tenor voice of special musical beauty.

Records: G & T (Vienna, 1902-03) and HMV.

SCHUBERT, RICHARD, tenor, b. Dec. 15, 1885, Dessau, Germany; d. Oct. 12, 1959, Oberstaufen, Germany. He studied with Rudolf von Milde and made his debut as a baritone (1909) at Strasbourg. He soon showed, however, that he was really a tenor and he renewed his studies with Rudolf von Milde and with Hans Nietan in Dresden. He sang as tenor in Nuremberg (1911-13) and Wiesbaden (1913-17). Beginning with the 1916-17 season he held a five-year contract with the Metropolitan Opera, but the entry of the United States into World War I canceled it. In 1917 he was engaged at the Hamburg Opera, where he remained until 1935. There, on Dec. 4, 1920, he sang the role of Paul in the world *première* of *Die Tote Stadt*. He was also concurrently a member of the Vienna State Opera (1920-29). He appeared successfully as guest at the Paris Opéra, the Teatro Liceo, and the State Operas in Munich and Dresden. In the 1922-23 season he sang at the Chicago Opera. In 1937 he went to Opera in Stettin and in 1938 he was both singer and *régisseur* at Osnabrück. At the last he lived and taught in Hamburg. One of the most important Wagner tenors of his time.

Records: Polydor. U.S. re-recording: Eterna.

SCHUMANN, ELISABETH, soprano, b. June 13, 1885, Merseburg, Germany; d. Apr. 23, 1952, New York. She studied in Dresden, Berlin, and Hamburg and made her debut at the Hamburg Opera (1909), remaining there until 1919. In the latter year she was engaged by the Vienna State Opera, where she had triumphal successes in the following twenty-three years. She was one of the most loved singers there, especially appreciated for her singing of Mozart roles. She was a chief star of the Salzburg Festivals (1922-35), where she was admired for her singing of Mozart and of Sophie in *Der Rosenkavalier*. She sang as guest at Covent Garden, La Scala, and in Berlin, Dresden, and Munich. She was a member of the Metropolitan Opera (1914-15). A world-wide reputation came to Elisabeth Schumann for her activity on the stage but especially as a lieder singer. Her lieder recitals were the high points of musical life in every world metropolis. On many of her concert tours of the United States she was accompanied at the piano by Richard Strauss, whose songs were among her specialties. In 1938 she left Austria and thereafter lived in New York, where she was a teacher. She was married to the conductor Karl Alwin (1891-1945). On the stage she delighted by the lightness and elegance of her coloratura voice; on the concert platform in art songs she pleased by the fine quality of her diction and the deep spirituality of her interpretations.

Records: Valuable records for Polydor (including an abridged version of *Der Rosenkavalier*, 1934), HMV, Victor*, Allegro, Brunswick*, Vocalion*, and Edison* discs. *U.S. re-recording:* Angel, Rococo, TAP, Seraphim.

SCHUMANN-HEINK, ERNESTINE, contralto, b. June 15, 1861, Lieben, Germany; d. Nov. 17, 1936, Hollywood, Calif. Originally Ernestine Rössler. She studied singing with Mariette von Leclair in Graz. At the age of fifteen she sang the contralto solo in Beethoven's *Ninth Symphony* in Graz. She made her stage debut (1878) at the Dresden Royal Opera as Azucena in *Il Trovatore*. Further study in Dresden with Karl Krebs and Franz Wüllner followed. In 1882 she married the secretary of the Dresden Opera, Ernst Heink, but was later separated from him. In 1882 she came to the Kroll Opera and in 1883 to the Hamburg Opera, where she sang for sixteen years. In 1892 she appeared as guest at Covent Garden with brilliant success in a production of the *Ring* cycle under Gustav Mahler. In 1894 she married the director of the Thalia Theater in Hamburg, Paul Schumann (d. 1904). During 1896-1914 she was especially successful at the Bayreuth Festivals. She was a regular guest at Covent Garden (1897-1900). In 1898 she sang in Chicago, making her first appearance in the United States. In 1899 she was engaged at the Metropolitan Opera, making her debut as Ortrud in *Lohengrin*, and she was to be heard there until 1932. In America her career reached its real climax; guest appearances and concerts brought her great triumphs in all the centers of international musical life. On Jan. 25, 1909, she created the role of Klytemnestra in the world *première* of *Elektra* at the Dresden Royal Opera. In 1905 she married the lawyer William Rapp, but was separated from him in 1914. In 1932 she gave her farewell performance as Erda in a performance of the *Ring* cycle at the Metropolitan. In 1935 the seventy-four-year-old singer had great success in the American film *Here's To Romance*. Ernestine Schumann-Heink was the most famous contralto of her generation. Her voice was outstanding for her perfect technique and for the overpowering expressiveness of her portrayals.

Records: Private records until 1898; later she sang for Columbia* (1903) and HMV, but particularly for Victor* (after 1905). She is also to be heard on re-recordings of Mapleson cylinders. *U.S. re-issue:* Opera Disc, IRCC. *U.S. re-recordings:* IRCC, Columbia, RCA Victor, TAP, Eterna, Rococo, Belcanto, Cantilena.

SCHÜRHOFF, ELSE, contralto, b. 1898, Wuppertal, Germany; d. Mar. 17, 1961, Hamburg. She was at first a teacher of singing and taught until 1928 at the Academy of Church and School Music in Berlin. She was engaged at the Hannover Opera (1929-36), the Munich State Opera (1937-41), and the Vienna State Opera (1941-53). After 1953 she was engaged as first contralto at the Hamburg State Opera, but remained under contract to the Vienna house through a guest-appearance arrangement. Concert tours and guest appearances brought her great successes both in Germany and abroad.

Records: Decca (*Die Meistersinger* and *Salome*), Columbia (*Hänsel und Gretel* and *Die Zauberflöte*), and Vox. *U.S. re-issue:* Vox, Angel, London, Remington, Richmond.

SCHÜTZ, HANS, baritone, b. Dec. 16, 1862, Vienna; d. Jan. 12, 1917, Wiesbaden, Germany. His father owned an art metal foundry and the son at first worked at this occupation. He then studied singing with Emmerich Katzmair, Normi and Joachim Sattler in Vienna. He made his debut at Linz (1891), remaining there until 1893. He sang at Zürich (1893-96), Düsseldorf (1896-98), Leipzig (1898-1908), and, from 1908 until his death, at Wiesbaden. He was especially admired as a Wagner singer. At the Bayreuth Festivals he sang Amfortas in *Parsifal* (1898), Donner in *Das Rheingold*, and Klingsor in *Parsifal* (1901-02). He sang as guest at Covent Garden (1902; 1904).

Records: One record for Nicole (London, 1904) and rare records for Kalliope (Wiesbaden, 1907-08).

SCHÜTZENDORF, GUSTAV, baritone, b. 1883, Cologne; d. Apr. 27, 1937, New York. Like several of his brothers he became an opera singer after studying at the Cologne Conservatory and in Milan. He made his debut as Don Giovanni in Düsseldorf (1905). He then sang successively at the Imperial Opera in Berlin, in Wiesbaden, and in Basel. He appeared as guest at the Teatro Liceo in 1912 and was engaged at the Munich Royal Opera (1914-20). He sang at the Berlin State Opera (1920-21) and at Leipzig (1921-22). In 1922 he was engaged at the Metropolitan Opera, remaining there until 1935. During these years he made several guest appearances in Europe—for example, as Don Giovanni in Amsterdam (1926). He was first married to the soprano Delia Reinhardt, from whom he was later separated; his second wife was the soprano Grete Stückgold.

Records: Vox.

SCHÜTZENDORF, LEO, bass-baritone, b. May 7, 1886, Cologne; d. Dec. 16, 1931, Berlin. He came from a family in which several of the sons took up careers as opera singers. He studied at the Cologne Conservatory and made his debut (1908) in Düsseldorf. He then sang in Krefeld (1909-13), Darmstadt (1913-17), and Wiesbaden (1917-20). In 1920 he was engaged by the Berlin Volksoper, where he enchanted the public particularly by his brilliant acting in *buffo* roles. On Dec. 14, 1925, at the Berlin State Opera he created the title role in the world *première* of *Wozzeck*. He had brilliant successes in guest appearances on leading operatic stages all over Europe. After 1922 he occupied himself as a very successful operetta singer in Berlin. When the directorate of the State Opera forbade him to do this—although it was a common practice among almost all artists in the 1920's—he turned entirely to operetta. His dark and uncommonly moving voice with his fine characterization and his brilliant acting ability proved his claims to greatness in serious, but particularly in *buffo*, roles.

Records: Ultraphon (Telefunken), Parlophone, Kristall, Homochord, Odeon (*Der Bettelstudent*), HMV, and Polydor. *U.S. re-recording:* Telefunken, ASCO.

SCHWAIGER, ROSL, soprano, b. Sept. 5, 1918, Saalfelden, Austria. She studied at the Salzburg Mozarteum and made her debut (1940) at the Landestheater there. She sang at the Vienna Volksoper (1942-45) and was a member of the Vienna State Opera (1945-52). At the Salzburg Festivals she sang Blondchen in *Die Entführung aus dem Serail*

(1945) and Sophie in *Der Rosenkavalier* (1946). In 1952 she was engaged as first coloratura soprano at the Munich State Opera. This artist, who is especially renowned as an interpreter of Mozart, undertook a highly successful tour of the United States in 1954.

Records: Among others, for Philips (*Le Nozze di Figaro*). *U.S. re-issue:* Bach Guild, DGG, Westminster, Haydn Society.

SCHWARZ, JOSEPH, baritone, b. Oct. 10, 1880, Riga, Russia; d. Nov. 10, 1926, Berlin. His study of singing at the Conservatory of the City of Vienna was financed by a wealthy Russian nobleman. His stage debut occurred (1900) at Linz. He then sang with small opera companies and with one of these appeared as guest in his birthplace, Riga, in 1901. After a guest appearance at the Imperial Opera in St. Petersburg, he was engaged at the Vienna Imperial Opera (1909) and was particularly admired there as a Wagner singer. He also made guest appearances at the Berlin Imperial Opera and in Dresden and after 1915 joined the Berlin house. During World War I he often sang in opera in the Scandinavian countries. In 1921 he gave highly successful concerts in New York. He joined the Chicago Opera (1922-23) and appeared with this company as guest in New York. He sang as guest in Berlin, Vienna, Prague, and Budapest in 1923. In 1924 he again accepted an engagement at the Berlin State Opera, but fell ill shortly thereafter. The colorful beauty of his voice and the dramatic skill he used in handling it proved his worth both on the stage and in the concert hall in a wide repertory.

Records: Polydor, Parlophone, Pathé*, and Vocalion*. (He is not to be confused with the bass Joseph E. Schwarz, who sang at the Prague Opera and made electric records for Tri-Ergon.) *U.S. re-issue:* Opera Disc, IRCC. *U.S. re-recording:* Eterna, Rococo.

SCHWARZ, VERA, soprano, b. July 10, 1888, Agram, Austria; d. Dec. 4, 1964, Vienna. She studied in Vienna with Philipp Forstén and made her debut (1912) at the Theater an der Wien. In 1914 she came to the Hamburg Opera, and went from there (1917) to the Imperial Opera in Berlin and finally (1921) to the Vienna State Opera. In 1925 she had an enormous success when she sang in Berlin in the first production of *Der Zarewitsch* with Richard Tauber. She was thereafter one of the great operetta sopranos of the German stage and was exceedingly popular as a co-star with Tauber and an interpreter of Lehár roles. At the same time she continued her operatic career. At the Salzburg Festival in 1929 she sang Octavian in *Der Rosenkavalier* and in 1939 she was greatly admired at the Glyndebourne Festival as Lady Macbeth in Verdi's opera. She made guest appearances in London, Paris, Amsterdam, and Munich. After 1938 she lived in the United States, where she appeared chiefly at the Chicago and San Francisco Operas and in the Hollywood Bowl. After 1948 she conducted an annual singing course at the Salzburg Mozarteum.

Records: Parlophone, Odeon, Polydor, and Homochord. *U.S. re-issue:* American Decca. *U.S. re-recording:* ASCO, Eterna, Rococo.

SCHWARZKOPF, ELISABETH, soprano, b. Dec. 9, 1915, Jarotschin, Poland. Her parents were of German origin. She completed her vocal studies at the Berlin Music High School and with Maria Ivogün there. In 1938 she made her debut at the Berlin City Opera as a Flower Maiden in *Parsifal*. After her first successes in Berlin she was engaged by the Vienna State Opera in 1943. Her international career started in Vienna after World War II. Year after year she enchanted the public at the Salzburg Festivals, both with her art in singing Mozart and with her portrayal of the Marschallin in *Der Rosenkavalier*. She was applauded at the Bayreuth Festival for her singing of Éva in *Die Meistersinger*. She created the role of Ann Trulove in the world *première* of *The Rake's Progress* at the Teatro Fenice in 1951. She joined the roster of Covent Garden by signing a guest-appearance contract in 1948, and in 1951 she took up residence in London. In 1953 she married Walter Legge, the director of the English Columbia Phonograph Record Company. She first appeared in the United States when she sang at the San Francisco Opera in 1953. Through concerts and guest appearances she has been enthusiastically applauded throughout the world. In 1964 she was engaged at the Metropolitan Opera, where she made her debut as the Marschallin. Elisabeth Schwarzkopf possesses one of the most beautiful soprano voices of her time, outstanding both for the fullness and texture of her vocal material and for the deeply felt animation of her portrayals. She is to be heard on the opera stage and as an operetta oratorio, and lieder singer in a repertory of the widest possible range.

Records: A great many records for Telefunken in operettas and for Urania* (*Abu Hassan*), but particularly for Columbia (*Le Nozze di Figaro, Così fan tutte, Der Rosenkavalier, Hänsel und Gretel, Die Kluge, Dido and Aeneas* with Kirsten Flagstad, *Die Fledermaus, Der Barbier von Bagdad, Capriccio*, and *Ariadne auf Naxos*). *U.S. re-issue:* Angel, Electrola, Vox, Seraphim.

SCHYMBERG, HJORDIS, soprano, b. Apr. 24, 1909, Almo, Sweden. She was giving concerts at an early age and sang on the Swedish radio in 1926. Her musical training followed at the Royal Music School in Stockholm with Britta von Vegesack. She made her debut at the Stockholm Royal Opera (1934) as Bertha in *La Poupée de Nuremberg*. For more than twenty-five years she was the first coloratura soprano there. After World War II she appeared as guest at the Copenhagen Opera, in Oslo, and at Covent Garden. In 1947 she was engaged at the Metropolitan Opera, where she sang in the following season, particularly in roles from the Italian repertory. Long concert tours also brought her great success. She lives in Stockholm.

Records: HMV and Telefunken. *U.S. re-issue:* RCA Victor. *U.S. re-recording:* Rococo.

SCIUTTI, GRAZIELLA, soprano, b. Apr. 7, 1932, Turin, Italy. She studied at the Accademia di Santa Cecilia in Rome and in 1949 gave her first concert in Venice, singing old Italian airs. Her stage debut occurred (1950) when she sang Elisetta in *Il Matrimonio Segreto* at the Aix-en-Provence Festival. At the same Festival, in 1951, she sang Lucy in *The Telephone*, and in 1952 she sang Susanna in *Le Nozze di Figaro*. In 1954 she sang again at Aix in the world *première* of *Les Caprices de Marianne*. In the same year she was admired at the Holland Festival, at the Glyndebourne Festival as Rosina in *Il Barbiere di Siviglia*, and at the Edinburgh Festival. In 1955 she appeared at La Scala as Papagena in *Die Zauberflöte* under Herbert von Karajan and had a sensational success. Since then she has been heard frequently at La Scala and she is a regular guest at the Vienna State Opera. She has sung at the Salzburg Festival every year since 1957. She was highly successful in her appearances at the opera houses in Brussels,

Rome, Paris, and London and since 1961 she has been a member of the Metropolitan Opera. She possesses a coloratura soprano voice with thorough technical training. Her true quality is that of a soubrette, in which roles she is a particularly outstanding interpreter of Mozart and Rossini. She is also a successful concert singer.

Records: Philips (*Don Giovanni*), Cetra*, Decca, RCA Victor (*La Scala di Seta*), Ricordi (*Il Barbiere di Siviglia* by Paisiello), and Columbia* (*Il Matrimonio Segreto* and *L'Italiana in Algeri*). *U.S. re-issue:* Angel, London, Epic, Mercury, Everest-Cetra.

SCOTNEY, EVELYN, soprano, b. July 11, 1896, Ballarat, Australia; d. Aug. 5, 1967, London. Her voice was discovered by Nellie Melba on one of her Australian tours. Melba took the young singer with her to Paris and put her under her own teacher, Mathilde Marchesi, for training. She made her debut at the Boston Opera (1912) in *Lucia di Lammermoor*, when she substituted for the indisposed Luisa Tetrazzini. After she had appeared successfully for several years in Boston, she was engaged at the Metropolitan Opera (1919-21), making her debut as Eudoxia in *La Juive*. Following this engagement she made concert tours in the United States, Canada, and Australia and was a highly successful concert singer in England until about 1935, appearing rarely on the stage. She had a coloratura voice which was entirely trained in the classic manner of the Marchesi school.

Records: Vocalion* (U.S. 1918-23) and acoustic and electric records for HMV.

SCOTTI, ANTONIO, baritone, b. Jan. 25, 1866, Naples; d. Feb. 26, 1936, Naples. He studied with Signora Trifari-Paganini in Naples and made his debut (1889) at the Opera in Malta as Amonasro in *Aïda*. He had his first successes on Italian operatic stages and appeared at both La Scala and the Teatro Costanzi. There followed years of traveling from one European stage to another while he made guest appearances in St. Petersburg, Moscow, Madrid, Lisbon, and Warsaw. In 1889 he excited great comment by his singing of Don Giovanni at Covent Garden, and in the same year he was engaged by the Metropolitan Opera. He sang there as principal baritone for over thirty-four years. No other artist sang so long at the Metropolitan. He was particularly admired there as a partner to Enrico Caruso. In the years after World War I he put together his own opera company, the Scotti Grand Opera Company, and toured the United States with it. From New York he also made guest tours, particularly to London, but also to the leading Italian theaters, all of which brought him great success. At Covent Garden he created the role of Chim-Fen in the world *première* of *L'Oracolo* (1905); this role remained one of his starring specialties. He was applauded at the 1910 Salzburg Festival as Don Giovanni. He sang his last performance in 1933, at the Metropolitan, in the role of Chim-Fen. He then retired to his native Italy, but quickly fell into great poverty. He had a sumptuous and highly musical baritone voice; he was admired on the stage especially as an actor.

Records: His first records were made for G & T (London, 1902) and Columbia* (New York, 1903), but thereafter he sang for Victor* and HMV; he also made Edison* and Mapleson cylinders. *U.S. re-recording:* IRCC, RCA Victor, FRP, TAP, Rococo, Olympus, CRS, Columbia, Belcanto, Cantilena.

SCOTTO, RENATA, soprano, b. Feb. 24, 1933, Savona, Italy. She made her debut at La Scala (1954) as Walter in *La Wally*. She quickly developed a great reputation for her singing at the largest Italian theaters, particularly at La Scala and the Rome Opera. After her Italian successes she appeared in guest appearances all over the world. She sang frequently at Covent Garden, where she appeared as Amina in *La Sonnambula* (1958). She was also admired in other coloratura roles from Italian operatic literature at the Vienna State Opera and in Chicago and San Francisco. She has sung at the Metropolitan since 1965-66 and is noted there for her singing of the title role in *Madama Butterfly*.

Records: Cetra, Columbia, Ricordi, HMV, and DGG* (*Lucia di Lammermoor*, *La Traviata*, *La Bohème*, and *Rigoletto*). *U.S. re-issue:* Mercury, Angel, Everest-Cetra.

SCUDERI, SARA, soprano, b. Dec. 11, 1906, Catania, Sicily. She made her debut in 1925 and then sang in small Italian opera houses before she was engaged by the Italian Opera in Holland (1926). In Holland she earned such popularity that in Italy she was called "la diva Olandese." After singing in Holland (1926-28), she toured Cuba, Venezuela, and Central America (1929-31). After 1931 she returned to the Italian Opera in Holland, where she went from one triumph to another. In 1936 she made a brilliant debut at La Scala as Fiora in *L'Amore dei Tre Re*. In the same year she sang in the world *première* of Malipiero's *Giulio Cesare* at the Genoa Opera. During World War II she remained in Italy, but in 1948 she sang as guest at the Cambridge Theater in London and in 1952 she sang again in Holland, appearing as Mimi in *La Bohème* at the Netherlands Opera. She lives and teaches in Milan.

Records: Decca and HMV.

SEDLMAIR, SOPHIE, soprano, b. Jan. 25, 1857, Hannover, Germany; d. 1939, Hannover. She began her career as an operetta singer at the Carola Theater in Leipzig. She sang at Mainz (1879-80), at the Residenztheater in Dresden (1880-85), and at the German Theater in Amsterdam (1886-87). In 1887 she came to the Thalia Theater in New York, but returned to Germany and sang—still as an operetta singer—at the Friedrich-Wilhemstädtischen Theater in Berlin (1888-92). After renewed study of singing with Schmidt in Vienna, she made her operatic debut (1893) as Leonora in *Fidelio* in Danzig. After guest appearances at the Leipzig Opera and the Kroll Opera, she sang in Breslau (1895-96) and was then engaged by the Vienna Imperial Opera. Until 1907 she was celebrated there as a successor to Amalie Materna, the famous dramatic soprano. She sang as guest at the Imperial Opera in St. Petersburg, at the National Opera in Budapest, and at Covent Garden. After the close of her career she taught singing in Hannover. Her large, dark-timbred soprano voice was admired in dramatic, and particularly in Wagner, roles.

Records: Her records are very rare; there are five titles for G & T (Vienna, 1903-04) and three for the Parsifal label. *U.S. re-recording:* Rococo.

SEEBÖCK, CHARLOTTE VON, soprano, b. 1886, Satoraljaujhely, Hungary. Originally Sará Sebeök von Lasztocz. She studied with Rosa Papier-Paumgartner and Frau Maleczky in Vienna and made her debut as a coloratura soprano at the Vienna Imperial Opera (1905), remaining there until 1907. She then sang as guest in various German opera houses and was engaged at the Opera in Frankrurt a. M. (1907-08). In 1908 she was engaged by the National Opera in Budapest and there she added many dramatic soprano roles to her repertory. She was one of the most prominent singers in the Budapest company until 1923, after which she retired and taught singing there. She had a most uncommon voice in which the effortless ease of performing the ornaments is perfectly matched with the intensity of dramatic presentation.

Records: Very rare records for Pathé.

SEEFRIED, IRMGARD, soprano, b. Oct. 9, 1919, Köngetried, Germany. She studied at the Conservatory in Augsburg with Albert Mayer and made her debut (1940) in Aachen, where she continued her studies with Herbert von Karajan and with the choirmaster of the Aachen Cathedral, Theodor Bernhard Rehmann. In 1943 she was engaged at the Vienna State Opera, making her debut as Eva in *Die Meistersinger*. She has sung annually at the Salzburg Festivals since 1946 and she is particularly admired in Mozart roles. In 1946 she married the violinist Wolfgang Schneiderhan, with whom she has frequently appeared in the concert hall. Her guest appearances include La Scala, Covent Garden, the opera houses in Munich, Brussels, and Amsterdam, and she has been so highly successful in the concert hall that she is esteemed as one of the most famous lieder interpreters of her time. Concert tours have brought her many triumphs in the United States, Canada, India, and Australia. A well-formed and richly expressive soprano voice, admired on the stage in Mozart roles and in the concert hall as a lieder and oratorio interpreter.

Records: Many records for DGG* (including *The Creation*, the *St. John Passion* of Bach, *Le Nozze di Figaro*, *Don Giovanni*, *Fidelio*, and *Der Freischütz*) and Columbia* (*Le Nozze di Figaro*, *Ariadne auf Naxos*, and *Die Zauberflöte*). *U.S. re-issue:* Remington, Vox, Angel, Electrola, Heliodor, American Decca, Seraphim.

SEGUROLA, ANDRES PERELLO DE, bass, b. 1873, Valencia, Spain; d. November, 1953, Barcelona. Born of a noble family, he studied singing with Varvaro in Barcelona and made his debut there (1898). After he had caused a sensation by his singing in Italy and France, he was engaged by the Metropolitan Opera for one season. After 1903 he had notable successes at La Scala. He sang in 1905 at the Havana Opera and in 1908 at the Manhattan Opera. In 1909 he was again engaged at the Metropolitan and remained there for fourteen years. During this time he sang there in the world *premières* of *La Fanciulla del West* (1910) and *Gianni Schicchi* (1918). He had a magnificent success as Leporello in *Don Giovanni* at the 1910 Salzburg Festival. Guest appearances and concert tours took him to all the important music centers of the world. In 1931 he became a singing teacher in Hollywood, and then appeared in films, including *One Night of Love* with Grace Moore. Toward the end of his life he became blind. His elegant manner and skillful acting were admired equally with the splendor and size of his dark bass voice.

Records: G & T (Barcelona, 1903; Milan, 1907), Victor*, Columbia*, and unpublished Edison Discs. Some of his Victor records appeared under the name Perello de Segurola. *U.S. re-recording:* RCA Victor, TAP, FRP, Rococo.

SEINEMEYER, META, soprano, b. Sept. 5, 1895, Berlin; d. Aug. 19,

1929, Dresden. She studied with Nikolaus Rothmühl and Ernst Grenzebach in Berlin and made her debut (1918) at the German Opera in Berlin, where she remained for seven years. In 1923 she undertook an American tour with the German Opera Company. In 1925 she was engaged by the Dresden State Opera, where she performed with artists such as Tino Pattiera and Ivar Andresen in the Verdi renaissance of the 1920's, a renaissance which began in Dresden. In 1926 she undertook a long South American tour and made guest appearances at the Vienna State Opera (1927) and Covent Garden (1929). She died at the height of her career from an incurable blood disease; on her deathbed she married the conductor Frieder Weissmann. One of the most beautiful soprano voices of her time, she was equally accomplished in the breadth of her expressive skill and in the noble and musical beauty of her presentations.

Records: Parlophone and Artiphone. *U.S. re-issue:* American Decca. *U.S. re-recording:* Rococo, Eterna.

SEMBACH, JOHANNES, tenor, b. Mar. 9, 1881, Berlin; d. June 20, 1944, Bremerhaven, Germany. Originally Johannes Semfke. He first studied singing in Vienna, then with Jean de Reszke in Paris. He made his debut at the age of nineteen at the Vienna Imperial Opera and remained there until 1905. He was engaged at the Dresden Royal Opera (1905-13) and on Jan. 25, 1909, he created the role of Aegisthus there in the world *première* of Decca. *U.S. re-recording:* Rococo, *Elektra*. In 1914 he went to the Metropolitan Opera, where he was especially admired as a Wagner tenor and where the critics compared his singing of Siegmund and Siegfried in the *Ring* cycle to that of the famous Jean de Reszke. He sang at the Metropolitan until 1917 and again in 1920-22. Guest appearances brought him great success in London and Paris and particularly in South America, where he most frequently appeared at the Teatro Colón. In 1925 he settled in Berlin as a singing teacher.

Records: Acoustic records for G & T, HMV, and Columbia*; electric records for Deutscher Bücher-Verband. *U.S. re-issue:* Victor. *U.S. re-recording:* TAP.

SEMBRICH, MARCELLA, soprano, b. Feb. 15, 1858, Wiesniewcyk, Poland; d. Jan. 11, 1935, New York. Originally Praxede Marcelline Kochánska; Sembrich was the family name of her mother. Her musical gift showed itself very early; at the age of four she began the study of the piano and at six, the violin. By the time she was twelve, she was a pupil at the Conservatory in Lemberg. Her piano teacher was Wilhelm Stengel (1846-1917), whom she later married. Although she had perfected her piano and violin playing, she took up the study of singing on the advice of Franz Liszt and in 1875 became a voice pupil of Viktor von Rokitansky in Vienna and later of Battista Lamperti in Milan. In 1877 she made her debut at the Opera in Athens as Elvira in *I Puritani*. She was a member of the Dresden Royal Opera (1878-80). In 1880 she went to London, where for the next five years she had enormous success. After 1878 she had her residence in Dresden and Berlin and later in Nice and Lausanne and from these cities she launched her world-wide concert and guest-appearance activities. She was idolized in Paris, Milan, Berlin, Vienna, Stockholm, and Brussels. After she had sung in the opening season of the Metropolitan Opera (1883), she was again engaged there in 1898 and remained a member of that house until her retirement from the stage in 1909. She then worked as a teacher of singing in Berlin and later in Lausanne. After 1924 she was the leader of the voice faculty at the Curtis Institute of Music in Philadelphia and also at the Juilliard School of Music in New York. Marcella Sembrich was one of the most famous coloratura sopranos of all time. The exactitude and brilliance of her coloratura and the security of her style in her presentations command the highest admiration even on records.

Records: Columbia* (1903), HMV, but especially Victor* (1904-08). There are fragments on Mapleson cylinders. *U.S. re-issue:* IRCC, HRS. *U.S. re-recording:* IRCC, Olympus, Scala, Rococo. TAP, RCA Victor, Belcanto, Columbia, Cantilena. The Stanford Archive of Recorded Sound has issued one re-recording of Johann Strauss' *Voce di Primavera* made in 1900 on a Bettini cylinder.

SENIUS, FELIX, tenor, b. Sept. 19, 1868, Königsberg, Germany; d. 1913, Königsberg. In 1872 his father became a director of the Azov Commerce Bank in St. Petersburg and the artist passed his youth there. He entered his father's bank, but sang at charity concerts in St. Petersburg in 1895. After study with Prianischnikov there, he gave his first lieder recital in 1900 and sang the tenor solo in a presentation of Handel's *Messiah*. He gave brilliantly successful concerts in the largest Russian cities, in Germany, Sweden, and Finland. He moved to Berlin and became one of the most noted concert tenors of his time; he was considered a worthy successor to the famous Gustav Walter. He married the soprano Clara Senius-Erler. He died of fish poisoning, contracted at a banquet which the city of Königsberg gave in his honor. A masterful tenor voice with which he earned great admiration for the beauty of his vocal sound as well as for the delicate nuances of his presentations.

Records: Rare records for Anker (Berlin, 1908-09), including two duets with Clara Senius-Erler. *U.S. re-recording:* Rococo.

SERENI, MARIO, baritone, b. 1931, Perugia, Italy. He studied at the Accademia di Santa Cecilia in Rome, at the Accademia Chigiana in Siena, and with Mario Basiola. He made his debut (1953) at the Maggio Musicale Festival in *Il Diavolo nel Campanile*. His career then developed very quickly on the important Italian stages. He sang as guest at the Teatro Colón (1956) and in 1957 came to the Metropolitan Opera, making his debut as Gérard in *Andrea Chénier*. He has been very successful at the Metropolitan as well as at La Scala and in guest appearances in London and Rome. His expressive voice is especially admired in the Italian repertory.

Records: HMV (*Madama Butterfly*, *Andrea Chénier*, and *Cavalleria Rusticana*). *U.S. re-issue:* Angel, RCA Victor.

SERGEI, ARTURO, tenor, b. 1927, New York. In 1947 he came to Germany as a soldier in the United States army of occupation. He completed his study of singing in Rome with the help of a scholarship from the United States army. He made his debut in Wuppertal as Otello (1954) and became a member of the Hamburg Opera (1958); later he became a member concurrently of the Frankfurt Opera. He has made successful guest appearances on the leading German stages and in 1960 he sang Alfredo in *La Traviata* at Covent Garden. He sang at the Metropolitan Opera after 1964. A powerful lyric-heroic tenor voice.

Records: Eurodisc and MMS.

SEYDEL, KARL, tenor, b. Dec. 14, 1879, Dresden; d. Aug. 7, 1947, Munich. He first studied Protestant theology at the University of Leipzig, then studied singing there with Emil Pinks. In 1901 he made his debut as a concert tenor and for the first six years of his career he appeared exclusively in the concert hall. His stage debut occurred (1907) at Altenburg in Thuringia and he remained there until 1910. He sang at Hannover (1910-17) and Karlsruhe (1917-20). In 1920 he was engaged at the Munich State Opera, where he sang for many years. He was especially admired as a great *buffo* tenor in such parts as David in *Die Meistersinger* and Mime in the *Ring* cycle. Guest appearances took him to Paris, Barcelona, Amsterdam, The Hague, and Switzerland. At the end of his life he taught singing in Munich.
Records: Vox.

SHERIDAN, MARGARET, soprano, b. Sept. 15, 1889, County Mayo, Ireland; d. Apr. 16, 1958, Dublin. She studied in Dublin and with Tina Scognamiglio in Milan; she made her debut (1918) at the Teatro Costanzi as Mimi in *La Bohème*. She then had great success at Italian theaters, particularly at the Teatro San Carlo. She sang for the first time at La Scala in 1920 and she was later to become a greatly admired artist there. She was also successful at the Arena Festival and in many guest appearances at Covent Garden. After her retirement from the stage, she returned to her native Ireland. She was admired for her expressive characterizations and for the richness of her vocal endowment; she was particularly applauded as a Puccini singer.
Records: HMV (including *Madama Butterfly*). *U.S. re-issue:* RCA Victor. *U.S. re-recording:* Eterna.

SHUARD, AMY, soprano, b. 1924, London. After she had already appeared in South Africa, she made her debut (1950) at Sadler's Wells in London as Marguerite in *Faust*. She came to Covent Garden in 1960, where she had a brilliantly successful career. Her best parts were held to be those of Turandot, Santuzza in *Cavalleria Rusticana*, the title role and Amneris in *Aida*, Lady Macbeth in Verdi's *Macbeth*, and Ortrud in *Lohengrin*. In both 1961 and 1963 she sang Brünnhilde in *Die Walküre* as guest at the Vienna State Opera.
Records: One record of arias, which demonstrate her large dramatic soprano voice, has been issued by HMV.

SIBIRIAKOV, LEO, bass, b. 1869, St. Petersburg, Russia; d. October, 1942, Antwerp, Belgium. He made his debut in 1895 and had great success at the Imperial Opera in St. Petersburg. He was under contract with the Boston Opera Company (1910-11) and was greatly admired there as Mefistofele in Boito's opera of the same name. In 1912 he made guest appearances in Berlin. During World War I he confined his activity to Russia, but emigrated to the West at the time of the Russian Revolution. Having settled as a teacher in Antwerp, he made occasional guest appearances in Paris, Brussels, and Antwerp. In 1938 he sang Pimen in *Boris Godounov* at the Brussels Opera. He had a broad, typically Russian bass voice.
Records: Rare records for G & T (St. Petersburg, 1905), Zonophone (St. Petersburg, 1905-06), and Sirena (St. Petersburg, 1907-08). *U.S. re-recording:* TAP, Rococo.

SIEBERT, DOROTHEA, soprano, b. 1921, Königsberg, Germany. She studied in Berlin and Vienna and made her debut in Marburg (1943). She sang at Klagenfurt (1945-48), Graz (1948-51), and at the Vienna State Opera (1951-55). Since 1956 she has been a member of the German-Opera-on-the-Rhine at Düsseldorf-Duisburg. She has sung as guest at Covent Garden, the Teatro San Carlo, and in Rome, Brussels, and Paris. In 1952 she sang at the Salzburg Festival and has appeared many times since 1954 at the Bayreuth Festivals, both as the Forest Bird and as Woglinde in the *Ring* cycle. A coloratura of the highest technical finish.

Records: Philips (*La Finta Semplice*), Vox, and Decca (*Die Zauberflöte*). *U.S. re-issue:* Bach Guild, Vox.

SIEGLITZ, GEORG, bass, b. Apr. 26, 1854, Mainz, Germany; d. Nov. 3, 1917, Munich. He studied at the Stern Conservatory in Berlin and made his debut (1880) at the Hamburg Opera as Masetto in *Don Giovanni*. His later engagements included Posen (1881), Düsseldorf (1882), Nuremberg (1883-86), the German Theater in Prague (1888-98), and, from 1898 to the time of his death, the Munich Royal Opera, where in 1899 he sang in the world *première* of *Der Bärenhäuter* and in 1903 in the world *première* of *Le Donne Curiose*. In 1906 he created the role of Lunardo in the world *première* of *I Quattro Rusteghi* in Munich. In 1887 he was notably successful at the Metropolitan Opera. He was also admired as a concert bass.

Records: Rare records for G & T (Munich, 1903-05).

SIEMS, MARGARETHE, soprano, b. Dec. 30, 1879, Breslau, Germany; d. May 13, 1952, Dresden. She first studied violin and piano, then, after 1899, voice with Aglaia von Orgeni in Dresden and later with Mattia Battistini in Milan. She made her debut (1902) at the German Theater in Prague, where she remained until 1908. In the latter year she was engaged by the Dresden Royal Opera as a successor to Irene Abendroth. There, on Jan. 25, 1909, she sang the role of Chrysothemis in the world *première* of *Elektra* and on Jan. 26, 1911, she created the role of the Marschallin in the world *première* of *Der Rosenkavalier*. In 1912, when the Stuttgart Opera produced the world *première* of *Ariadne auf Naxos*, she sang, as guest, the taxing role of Zerbinetta, which had been composed with her voice in mind. In the years before World War I she appeared as guest in Berlin, London, Milan, St. Petersburg, and Amsterdam. In 1920 she became a teacher at the Stern Conservatory in Berlin, but made guest appearances in both Dresden and Berlin. After 1926 she again resided in Dresden, but thereafter appeared only in the concert hall. In 1937 she accepted a professorship at the Wroclaw Conservatory and moved her residence to Bad Laneck; in 1946 she returned to Dresden. She united in her coloratura voice both virtuoso singing technique and true dramatic force of presentation.

Records: G & T, Pathé*, HMV (scenes from *Der Rosenkavalier*), Odeon, and Parlophone. *U.S. re-issue:* IRCC. *U.S. re-recording:* Rococo, Belcanto.

SIEPI, CESARO, bass, b. Feb. 10, 1923. Milan, Italy. He studied at the Conservatory in Milan and made his debut in Florence (1941) as Sparafucile in *Rigoletto*, but the continuance of his career was hindered by World War II. In 1943 he fled to Switzerland for political reasons. In 1945 he resumed his singing career and stirred up great excitement when he sang Zacharias in *Nabucco* at the Teatro Fenice; in 1946 he sang the same role with equally great success at La Scala. In 1948 Toscanini chose him for the title role in *Mefistofele* and the role of Simon Magno in *Nerone*, both produced in memory of the fortieth anniversary of the death of Boito. In 1949 he was engaged at the Metropolitan Opera, making his debut as King Philip in *Don Carlos*. Since that time he has been greatly admired, chiefly at the Metropolitan and at La Scala and he has also had great success in guest appearances and concerts in Spain, Austria, South America, and Switzerland. In 1951 he was a source of admiration for his singing of the role of Don Giovanni at the Salzburg Festival; he has since been heard there repeatedly. He is esteemed to be the most famous living interpreter of Mozart in his vocal range. He possesses a bass voice of uncommon beauty, and is easily the most famous bass produced in his time in Italy.

Records: Cetra* (*La Sonnambula*), RCA Victor (*Don Giovanni*), but especially Decca (*Le Nozze di Figaro, Don Giovanni, La Gioconda, Rigoletto, La Forza del Destino,* and *Il Barbiere di Siviglia*). *U.S. re-issue:* London, Columbia, Angel, Richmond.

SIEWERT, RUTH, contralto, b. 1911 (?), Viersen, Germany. She studied at the Folkwang School in Essen with Anna Erler-Schnaudt and made her stage debut in Bremen, but since 1946 she has been especially noted as a concert contralto. She has appeared in opera theaters in Karlsruhe, Cologne, and Düsseldorf and she has sung as guest at Covent Garden, La Scala, and in Paris, Rome, Naples, Madrid, and Amsterdam. She sang at the Bayreuth Festivals (1951; 1952; 1960) as Erda, Fricka, and Waltraute in the *Ring* cycle. She lives in Viersen.

Records: HMV (*Die Walküre* and *Das Rheingold*) and Columbia. *U.S. re-issue:* DGG, Electrola.

SIGNORINI, FRANCESCO, tenor, b. 1860, Rome; d. September, 1927, Rome. He studied at the Accademia di Santa Cecilia in Rome and made his debut (1882) at the Teatro Politeama in Florence. In contrast to many other singers, he had great difficulty in attaining any fame as a singer. His first success came in 1890 when he sang Turiddu in *Cavalleria Rusticana* in Florence. He finally reached La Scala in 1897, and about the turn of the century he had brilliant success at all the ranking Italian opera houses. In 1907 he sang in opera in San Francisco and Los Angeles and appeared in South America. In 1910 he gave up his career and lived thereafter as a singing teacher in Rome. A large heroic tenor voice of brilliant and metallic timbre.

Records: Very rare records for HMV (Milan, 1908), including scenes from *Chatterton*.

SILJA, ANJA, soprano, b. Apr. 7, 1940, Berlin. Both parents were actors and the vocal gifts of the daughter were discovered by her grandfather. She began to study singing at the age of eight and at ten gave a concert at the Titania Palast in Berlin, followed by others in Hamburg. At fifteen she gave lieder recitals in public. In 1956 she made her stage debut as Rosina in *Il Barbiere di Siviglia* at the Berlin City Opera. From Braunschweig, where she had been singing, she came to the Stuttgart State Opera in 1958 and to the Opera in Frankfurt in 1959. In the latter year she sang the Queen of the Night at the Aix-en-Provence Festival and made guest appearances in Vienna, Hamburg, and Paris. She excited great comment for her singing of Senta in *Der Fliegende Holländer* at the Bayreuth Festivals (1960-61). Since then she has had great success in various Wagner roles in her annual appearances at Bayreuth.

Records: Philips (Senta in *Der Fliegende Holländer*, 1961). *U.S. re-issue:* London.

SILVERI, PAOLO baritone, b. Dec. 28, 1913, Ofena, Italy. He began his study of singing with Perugini in

Milan, but in 1940 was called to the Italian army. In 1942 he was able to resume his studies, this time at the Accademia di Santa Cecilia in Rome. In 1943 he made his debut as a bass, but in the following years changed to a baritone. He first sang in southern Italy, particularly at the Teatro San Carlo. In 1946 he appeared as guest with the ensemble of the Naples company at Covent Garden in London. Since 1949 he has sung regularly at La Scala and the Rome Opera. His other guest appearances include Paris and London, the Vienna State Opera, and many others. He has sung at the festivals in Florence, Verona, and Edinburgh. He was engaged by the Metropolitan Opera (1951-52). Later he managed and led an Italian opera company; in a guest appearance with this troupe in Dublin in 1959 he sang the title role in *Otello*, but with no special success.

Records: Cetra* (*Simone Boccanegra, La Gioconda, Tosca, Il Barbiere di Siviglia, Don Carlos, L'Arlesiana,* and *Nabucco*) and Columbia.*

SIMÁNDY, JOSEF, tenor, b. 1916, Budapest. He was able to study at the Budapest Conservatory only after overcoming great difficulties; he made his debut (1938) in Szeged as Don José in *Carmen*. In 1939 he was called to the National Opera in Budapest, where he has since remained as principal tenor. After World War II he had great success in guest appearances, particularly in his frequent visits to the Vienna State Opera; since 1956 he has held a concurrent guest contract with the Munich State Opera. He specializes in Italian and French roles, but he also sings Wagner parts.

Records: DGG*. *U.S. re-issue:* Bruno, SS.

SIMIONATO, GIULIETTA, contralto, b. Dec. 15, 1910, Forli, Italy. She passed her childhood in Sardinia and studied with Ettore Lucatello in Rovigo and Guido Palumbo in Milan. In 1933 she won a singing competition in Florence and made her debut there (1938) in *L'Orsèolo*. By 1939 she was already singing at La Scala, where for more than twenty years she was a celebrated contralto. In 1942 she had sensational success there as Rosina in *Il Barbiere di Siviglia*. After World War II she made guest appearances all over the world; she sang at Covent Garden, the Teatro Colón, the Paris Opéra, the New York City Opera, and the State Operas in Berlin and Munich, as well as at the opera houses in Brussels, Chicago, Mexico City, and Rio de Janeiro. She sang as a special guest at the Vienna State Opera. She was greatly admired at the Arena, Edinburgh, Maggio Musicale, and Holland Festivals. After 1958 she sang at the Salzburg Festivals. In 1959 this famous singer was engaged at the Metropolitan Opera, where she was also brilliantly successful. In 1966 she gave up her stage career.

Records: A great many records for Cetra* (including *Il Matrimonio Segreto, La Favorita, Cavalleria Rusticana,* and *La Cenerentola*), HMV, and Columbia (*L'Italiana in Algeri*); but she has sung mostly for Decca (*Il Barbiere di Siviglia, Il Trovatore, La Favorita, Rigoletto, La Gioconda, Aida, Adriana Lecouvreur, Cavalleria Rusticana, Un Ballo in Maschera,* and *La Forza del Destino*). *U.S. re-issue:* London, Electrola, Angel, Richmond, Seraphim.

SIMONEAU, LÉOPOLD, tenor, b. 1921 (?), Montreal, Canada. He first sang in the choir of St. Patrick's Church in Montreal, then studied singing with Emile de la Rochelle. In 1943 he sang in a concert in Montreal under Sir Thomas Beecham, and in the same year he made his debut at the Variétés Lyriques there as Wilhelm Meister in *Mignon*. In 1945 he came to New York, where he continued his studies with Paul Althouse. In 1946 he made guest appearances with the New York City Opera, the Philadelphia Opera, and in New Orleans. In 1947 he married the soprano Pierette Alarie, and they both accepted an engagement at the Opéra-Comique. Through his singing at the Festivals in Aix-en-Provence and Glyndebourne, he became known as a leading Mozart tenor. He sang as guest at Covent Garden, La Scala, the Vienna State Opera, and the Rome Opera with huge success. In 1954 he undertook a brilliantly successful tour of North America with his wife. He has also been admired at the Salzburg Festivals. He has a lyric tenor voice of noble musical beauty; although he is particularly noted in the Mozart repertory, he is also well liked in parts from French operatic literature and in the concert hall.

Records: DGG*, Decca (*Die Zauberflöte*), Columbia* (*Die Entführung aus dem Serail* and *Così fan tutte*), Philips (*Don Giovanni*, *Orphée et Eurydice*, and *Idomeneo*), and MSS (Handel's *Messiah*). *U.S. re-issue:* Westminster, RCA Victor, Epic, Perfect, Angel, Electrola, London.

SINGHER, MARTIAL, baritone, b. Aug. 14, 1904, Oloron-Sainte-Marie, France. He first studied philology at St. Cloud, then studied singing at the Paris Conservatory with André Gresse. he made his debut (1930) during a guest appearance of the Paris Opéra in Amsterdam, where he sang Orestes in *Iphigénie en Tauride*. After 1937 he was a celebrated member of the Opéra-Comique and after 1940 a member of the Opéra. In 1932 he created in Paris the song cycle *Don Quichotte à la Dulcinée*, which had been dedicated to him by the composer, Maurice Ravel. He sang annually as guest at the Teatro Colón (1936-40). In 1940 he married Margareta Rut Busch, the daughter of the conductor Fritz Busch. They fled to the United States when the German army occupied France in 1940. Although he was engaged by the Metropolitan Opera, the immigration authorities caused him so many difficulties that he was unable to begin his engagement until 1943. Thereafter he was brilliantly successful both at the Metropolitan and in his American guest appearances and concerts. He has taught at the Curtis Institute of Music in Philadelphia and at the Mannes College of Music in New York. He had a superb baritone voice, equally outstanding in concert and operatic repertory.

Records: Columbia*, RCA Victor* (*La Damnation de Faust*). *U.S. re-issue:* Vanguard, Royale. *U.S. re-recording:* IRCC.

SINIMBERGHI, GINO, tenor, b. 1913, Rome. He studied at the Accademia di Santa Cecilia in Rome. Soon after his debut he came to Germany where he sang after 1937 at the Berlin State Opera and made guest appearances in Leipzig, Danzig, Hamburg, Vienna, and at the Théâtre des Champs-Elysées. In 1944 he returned to Italy and had a brilliant career there, particularly at the Rome Opera and at the Teatro Fenice. He appeared at La Scala and at the Festivals of the Baths of Caracalla. In 1960 he sang as guest at the Frankfurt Opera, appearing in the title role of *Orfeo*. He also sang in films. He had a clear, lyrical, and expressive tenor voice.

Records: DGG, Westminster*, Urania.

SISTERMANS, ANTON, baritone, b. Aug. 5, 1865, Hertogenbosch, Holland; d. Mar. 18, 1926, The Hague. After his study with Julius Stockhausen in Frankfurt a. M. he lived there as a concert singer; later he moved to Wiesbaden and soon became known as one of the most noted baritones in Europe. His presentation of the songs of Johannes Brahms, particularly the *Vier Ernsten Gesänge*, was held to be incomparable. In 1899 he first sang on the stage, appearing as Pogner in *Die Meistersinger* and Gurnemanz in *Parsifal* at the Bayreuth Festival, but thereafter he took stage roles only occasionally. From 1904-15 he taught at the Scharwenka Conservatory in Berlin. In 1916 he returned to Holland, but had no great singing triumphs there. In Holland he taught singing at the Blaauw Conservatory in The Hague.

Records: A few extremely rare records for G & T.

SKILONDZ, ADELAIDE VON, soprano, b. Jan. 21, 1888, St. Petersburg, Russia. She studied at the Conservatory in St. Petersburg and made her debut at the Imperial Opera (1904) with quick and brilliant success. On Oct. 7, 1909, she created the role of the Queen of Shemakan in the world *première* of *The Golden Cockerel* at the Moscow Opera. In 1910 she was engaged as a successor to Frieda Hempel at the Berlin Imperial Opera and remained there until 1914. Upon the outbreak of World War I she went to Stockholm and sang there for several years as principal coloratura soprano at the Royal Opera. She later lived and taught singing in Stockholm, where one of her pupils was the bass Kim Borg.

Records: HMV, Pathé, and Parlophone.

SLEZAK, LEO, tenor, b. Aug. 18, 1873, Mährisch-Schönberg, Austria; d. June 1, 1946, Rottach-Egern-am-Tegernsee, Germany. He first worked as a gardener and locksmith, before studying singing with Adolph Robinson in Brünn. He made his debut there (1896) as Lohengrin. In 1898 he came to the Imperial Opera in Berlin and in 1899 he was engaged at the Breslau Opera where he remained until 1901. After 1900 he was highly successful in guest appearances at Covent Garden. In 1901 Gustav Mahler engaged him for the Vienna State Opera, where he remained as a member until 1926. He also appeared as guest at the Paris Opéra, the Royal Operas in Munich and Dresden, before resuming his studies, this time with Jean de Reszke in Paris. He was called to the Metropolitan Opera in 1909 and sang there with huge success until 1912. He was particularly admired for his acting genius as Otello. Guest appearances and concerts in which he showed himself to be a brilliant interpreter of songs led him from one triumph to another in all the great musical centers of the world. After 1934 he sang only in the concert hall, and he also began an astounding second career as an actor of comic father roles in motion pictures. He was married to the actress Elsa Wertheim; his daughter, Margarethe Slezak, became a singer, and his son, Walter Slezak, was best known in the United States as a stage and film actor. Leo Slezak's humorous autobiographical writings are highly readable: *Mein Sämtlichen Werke* (Berlin, 1922), *Der Wortbruch* (Berlin, 1928), *Der Rückfall* (Berlin, 1930), *Mein Lebensmärchen* (Munich, 1948). Leo Slezak was one of the most important heroic tenors of the twentieth century. The size and brilliant quality of his voice, the maturity of his conceptions, and the artistic skill shown in his characterizations may still be admired on records.

Records: A great many records for almost all labels, the oldest for Zonophone (Vienna, 1901) and G & T (Vienna, 1901); later for Columbia*, Edison*, and Pathé*, including both cylinders and discs. Still later he recorded for Anker, HMV, Polydor, Odeon, Parlophone, et cetera. *U.S. re-issue:* Victor, Okeh, IRCC, HRS, Opera Disc, Odeon-Okeh. *U.S. re-recording:* Scala, Eterna, Design, Belcanto, Columbia, TAP, FRP, ASCO, Odyssey.

SLOBODSKAYA, ODA, soprano, b. Nov. 28, 1895, Vilna, Russia. She studied at the St. Petersburg Conservatory with Natalie Iretzkaya and made her debut at the Maryinsky Theater in Leningrad (1918) as Lisa in *The Queen of Spades*. After great success in Russian musical centers, she came to Paris (1922), where she sang the role of Parasha in the world *première* of *Mavra*. She never returned to Russia, but remained in Paris. She next undertook a long tour of North and South America with the Ukrainian Chorus. She then became one of the stars of the Opéra Russe in Paris. In 1931 she transferred her residence to London, and in that year sang at the Drury Lane Theater under Sir Thomas Beecham. In 1932 she was admired at Covent Garden as Venus in *Tannhäuser* and on the same stage she sang in the world *première* of *Koanga* (1935). She made guest appearances in 1934 at La Scala and sang in concerts in Belgium and Holland. In 1943 she was admired at the Savoy Theater in London in *The Fair at Sorotchinsk*. Even in 1960 she appeared in the concert hall and made phonograph records; these activities were in addition to her work as a teacher and *régisseur* in London. A dark-timbred and expressive soprano voice, particularly admired in the interpretation of Russian songs.

Records: A few records for HMV, later for Decca and Saga. *U.S. re-recording:* TAP.

SMIRNOV, DMITRI, tenor, b. Nov. 7, 1882, Moscow; d. Apr. 27, 1944, Riga, Latvia. He studied with E. K. Pavlovskaya in Moscow and made his debut at the Imperial Opera there (1904) as Prince Sinodal in *The Demon*. In 1907 he came to Paris with a Russian opera company and through Raoul Ginsberg was engaged at the Monte Carlo Opera where he appeared regularly as a guest thereafter. In 1910 he came to the Metropolitan Opera, making his debut as the Duke in *Rigoletto* opposite Lydia Lipkowska and Pasquale Amato. He was not so successful in the United States as in Europe, and in 1912 he returned to France and made very successful guest appearances at the Paris Opéra and later at the Teatro Colón, in Brussels, Berlin, Cologne, Milan, Rome, Madrid, and Barcelona. He sang every year at the Imperial Operas in St. Petersburg and Moscow. In 1914 he was admired at the Drury Lane Theater in London. During the war years (1914-17) he returned to Russia, but fled to Paris after the Revolution. From there he continued his world-wide concert and guest-appearance activity. In 1929 he again undertook a concert tour through Russia. He lived in London (1935-37) and appeared frequently on the radio, but especially occupied himself as a teacher. He taught singing at the Athens Conservatory (1937-41). He was married to the soprano Lydia Smirnova-Malzeva. He was undoubtedly the most famous Russian tenor of his generation and his highly musical voice attained its best performances in lyric roles.

Records: Acoustic records for HMV; electrics for Parlophone (1926). *U.S. re-issue:* Victor. *U.S. re-recording*: Rococo, Siena, Angel, Belcanto, TAP.

SMOLENSKAYA, EUGENIA, soprano, b. 1919, in an industrial area of the Donetz Basin of Russia. The daughter of a smith, she first completed a teacher-training course and taught Ukrainian language and literature. In 1939 she began to study voice at the Kiev Conservatory and made her debut (1945) at the opera house in Stalino. In 1947 she was engaged at the Bolshoi Theater, where she has sung successfully ever since. Aside from her stage activities she has also been successful as a concert and radio singer. She prefers to sing dramatic soprano roles.

Records: Russian State Record Trust (including *The Queen of Spades*). *U.S. re-issue:* Colosseum, Bruno.

SOBINOFF, LEONID, tenor, b. June 7, 1872, Jaroslavl, Russia; d. Oct. 14, 1934, Riga, Latvia. He studied law and became an attorney, but finally decided on a singing career; he then studied with Dodonov and Alexandra Alexandrovna Santagano-Gortschakova in Moscow. His first engagement was with an Italian opera troupe which was making appearances at the Shelapoutinsky Theater in Moscow and he appeared in small roles with them under the name of Sobonni. He had his first great success at the Imperial Opera in Moscow when in 1897 he sang Prince Sinodal in *The Demon*. Thereafter he had great triumphs at the Imperial Operas in Moscow and in St. Petersburg and he became the idolized tenor of Czarist society. He made guest appearances at the Monte Carlo Opera (1906), at La Scala (1910-11), and in London, Paris, and Berlin (1910). In Madrid he was admired as Nadir in *Les Pêcheurs de Perles*. In 1910, at the height of his career, he was awarded the title of Court Singer by the Czar. In 1911 he was *régisseur* and director of the Philharmonic Society in St. Petersburg. He was appointed director of the Bolshoi Theater in Moscow (1917-22); he was detained in southern Russia (1918-22) as a result of the post-war disorders. He still continued to appear as a singer and made a long tour singing in Warsaw, Helsinki, Riga, Reval, Berlin, and Paris (1930-31). His thirty-fifth anniversary on the stage was celebrated by a gala performance at the Bolshoi Theater in 1933. He had a marvelously trained lyric tenor voice of exceptionally beautiful expressiveness. His chief role was Lenski in *Eugen Onégin*.

Records: Pathé, G & T (Moscow, 1900-04), and HMV. *U.S. re-recording:* Rococo, Collectors Guild, Angel, Belcanto, TAP.

SÖDERSTRÖM, ELISABETH, soprano, b. May 7, 1926, Stockholm. She made her debut at the Drottningholm Court Theater near Stockholm (1950) as Bastienne in *Bastien und Bastienne*. She then sang at the Royal Opera in Stockholm. She has appeared at the Salzburg, Glyndebourne (1957), and Edinburgh (1959) Festivals and in the major European opera houses. She made her Metropolitan Opera debut (1959-60) as Susanna in *Le Nozze di Figaro*. Other important roles in her repertory are Marguerite in *Faust*, Marie in *Wozzeck*, Violetta in *La Traviata*, and Sophie, Octavian, and the Marschallin in *Der Rosenkavalier*.

Records: Decca. *U.S. re-issue:* Westminster, London, RCA Victor.

SOLARI, CHRISTY, tenor, b. 1894, Smyrna, Turkey. He was the son of Italian parents. He studied with Serafino de Falco in Milan and made his debut (1916) in Mantua. He was singing at Parma when he was called up for the Italian army. After World War I he sang in various Italian theaters and had a brilliant success at the Italian Theater in Holland (1926-27). Guest appearances followed in Bucharest, Sofia, Cairo, and he made a tour through Germany. In 1929 he sang at the Teatro Colón and in 1931 he appeared in *Il Matrimonio Segreto* at the Salzburg Festival. He recorded further successes in Genoa, Palermo, Naples, and at the Arena Festivals. In 1937 he made several guest appearances in Holland as Nadir in *Les Pêcheurs de Perles* and in 1939 he made a concert tour through Belgium and Holland. He made scarcely any appearances after World War II. The voice of this artist, though small in itself, was, through his art of shading, qualified as superior in the performance of lyric roles.

Records: Columbia*. *U.S. re-recording:* Eterna.

SOOMER, WALTER, bass-baritone, b. Mar. 12, 1878 Liegnitz, Germany; d. August, 1935, Leipzig. He first studied philosophy and then singing with Hermann Stoeckert and Anna Uhlig in Berlin and he made his debut in Colmar (1902). He sang at Halle (1902-06), where he began to sing Wagner roles. In 1906 he was engaged at the Leipzig Opera and he remained a member of that organization until the end of his stage career in 1927, except the period 1911-15, when he sang at the Dresden Royal Opera. In 1906 he appeared at the Bayreuth Festival as Kurwenal and Donner and at the Festivals in 1908-14 he was celebrated not only for his incomparable Wotan but also as the Flying Dutchman and as Hans Sachs in *Die Meistersinger*. He was a member of the Metropolitan Opera (1908-11) and also appeared in London, Paris, Berlin, and Dresden. After World War I he changed to Wagner bass roles and was equally successful. In 1924-25 he sang at Bayreuth as Hunding and Hagen in the *Ring* cycle. After 1927 he was the director of a singing and opera school in Leipzig. He was married to the soprano Aline Sanden.

Records: G & T (Leipzig, 1907), HMV-Vox, Edison* cylinders, and Pathé*. *U.S. re-recording:* Rococo.

SOOT, FRITZ, tenor b. Aug. 20, 1878, Neunkirchen, Germany; d. June 9, 1965, Berlin. He was active as an actor at the Royal Theater in Karlsruhe (1901-07); at the same time he studied singing and later became a pupil of Karl Schiedemantel in Dresden. He made his debut at the Dresden Royal Opera (1908) as Tonio in *La Fille du Régiment*. At the same house on Jan. 26, 1911, he created the role of the Italian Singer in the world *première* of *Der Rosenkavalier*. During World War I he served in the German army. In 1918 he resumed his career at the Stuttgart Opera, but changed from lyric to heroic roles and began to specialize in Wagner parts. He sang at Stuttgart until 1922 and was a celebrated member of the Berlin State Opera (1922-35). His guest appearances included Covent Garden and all the important German stages. After 1935 he worked as a stage director at the Berlin State Opera.

Records: Pathé and Polydor. *U.S. re-recording:* Rococo, Eterna, Scala, TAP.

SOUEZ, INA, soprano, b. 1908 Windsor, Canada. Originally Ina Rains. She took the name Souez from the family name of her grandmother. She studied with Florence Hinrichs in Denver, then with Sofia Del Campo in Milan and made her debut in Ivrea (1928) as Mimi in *La Bohème*. In 1929 she had her first success at the Teatro Massimo and in the same year she sang Liu in *Turandot* at Covent Garden. She was married to an Englishman and lived in London (1929-39). In England she was applauded at Covent Garden and especially at the Glyndebourne Festivals, where her singing of Donna Anna in *Don Giovanni* and of Fiordiligi in *Così fan tutte* caused her to be esteemed as a great interpreter of Mozart. She sang as guest at the Royal Opera in Stockholm and in 1939 was chosen as soprano soloist in Verdi's *Requiem* at The Hague. In 1939 she returned to the United States and during World War II was a leader in the Women's Auxiliary Corps of the army. In 1945 she sang Fiordiligi again with the New York City Opera, but then gave up her operatic career and became a popular singer with Spike Jones and His City Slickers band, with whom she undertook an American tour. She now lives in California.

Records: HMV (*Don Giovanni* and *Così fan tutte* from Glyndebourne) and Columbia. She recorded arias and songs for New Sound about 1960. *U.S. re-issue*: RCA Victor. *U.S. re-recording*: Vox, Electrola, RCA Victor, Turnabout.

SOUKOUPOVÁ, VĚRA, contralto, b. Apr. 12, 1932, Prague. She studied singing with L. Kadeřabek and A. Mustanová-Linková at the Music High School in Prague. In 1954 she won a singing competition in Prague and from 1955 on began to appear in concerts. In 1957 she was engaged in Pilsen and in 1960 came to the National Theater in Prague. Since then she has had a brilliant career. In 1961 she made a guest tour through the Soviet Union and in the same year sang Dalila in *Samson et Dalila* as guest at the Bordeaux Opera. She has made concert tours in France and Switzerland and has appeared as guest at the Vienna State Opera. In 1963 she took part in a tour which the Prague National Theater made through West Germany. In 1966 she sang Erda in the *Ring* cycle at the Bayreuth Festival. She has a magnificently trained and expressive voice.

Records: Supraphon and DGG*. *U.S. re-issue*: Parliament, Artia.

SOULACROIX, GABRIEL, baritone, b. Dec. 11, 1853, Villeneuve-sur-Lot, France; d. 1905, Paris. He studied at both the Toulouse and Paris Conservatories and made his debut at the Théâtre de la Monnaie (1878) in *Les Dragons de Villars*. After famous success in Brussels and the French provinces, he was engaged in 1885 at the Opéra-Comique. There he sang in the world *première* of *La Basoche* (1890), in the first performance there of *Les Pêcheurs de Perles* (1893), and the part of Ford in the French *première* of *Falstaff* (1894). In 1887 while he was singing Laertes in *Mignon* at the Opéra-Comique, a terrible fire broke out and he managed to save the lives of many people. He remained at the Opéra-Comique until 1894 and later sang there as a guest, but he then sang chiefly at the Théâtre Gaîté Lyrique and appeared there in the French *première* of *La Bohème* (1898). On Feb. 18, 1902, he sang in the world *première* of *Le Jongleur de Notre-Dame* at the Monte Carlo Opera. He died quite suddenly at the height of his career.

Records: G & T (Paris, 1903-04) and Odeon (Paris, 1904-05).

SOUZAY, GÉRARD, baritone, b. Dec. 8, 1918, Angers, France. He passed his youth in Paris and studied first with Pierre Bernac, then at the National Conservatory with Claire Croiza and Vanni-Marcoux, among others. In 1945 he made his debut as a concert singer. After he had appeared in small theaters he was engaged at the Paris Opéra and the Opéra-Comique (1947). He became best known, however, as a concert singer of the first rank and particularly as a song interpreter. In 1945 he gave his first song recital in Paris and in Germany to excitedly appreciative comments. He is generally esteemed as the leading French song interpreter of his time and as such had great success in London, Brussels, Amsterdam Helsinki, and in Italy and Switzerland. His concert tours took him to North America first in 1951 and

later to South America, South Africa, Egypt, Australia, New Zealand, India, and Japan. He also sang at the Festivals in Aix-en-Provence and in Salzburg. He had a warm-timbred and expressive voice and showed his extraordinary musicality in song interpretations.
Records: Philips* (*Pelléas et Mélisande*), Decca, and DGG*. *U.S. re-issue:* London, Angel, Epic, RCA Victor, Pathé-Marconi, Turnabout.

SPANI, HINA, soprano, b. Feb. 15, 1896, Puán, Argentina. Originally Higinia Tunon. She began the study of singing at the age of eight and at twelve gave a concert in the Argentine city of Cordoba. She then studied with Amanda Campodonico in Buenos Aires and after 1914 with Vittorio Moratti in Milan. She made her debut there at La Scala (1915) as Anna in *Loreley*. In 1915 she was engaged at the Teatro Colón, where she had great triumphs until 1919. In that year she returned to Italy and sang in Turin, the Teatro dal Verme, the Teatro San Carlo, and in Parma. In 1922 she appeared at the Teatro Colón in the world *première* of *Raquelo* and she was applauded at the opera houses in Rio de Janeiro and São Paulo. In 1924 she sang at the Puccini memorial services at the Milan cathedral. Until 1934 she sang as guest at all the leading Italian opera houses, particularly La Scala and the Rome Opera. She was admired in her guest appearances and concerts in Paris, London, Spain, and Switzerland as well as in Australia and South America. She sang again at the Teatro Colón (1934-40) and after 1946 she both taught and appeared in concerts there. After 1952 she became the director of the music school at the University of Buenos Aires. A superbly trained and darkly colored soprano voice of subtle expressiveness and an uncommon feeling for vocal style. She was particularly admired in Puccini roles.
Records: HMV and Columbia. *U.S. re-recording:* TAP, Scala, Rococo.

SPLETTER, CARLA, soprano, b. Nov. 9, 1911, Flensburg, Germany; d. Oct. 19, 1953, Hamburg. She began her study of singing in 1931 at the Leipzig Conservatory with Oscar Lassner. She made her debut at the German Opera House in Berlin (1932) and appeared there until 1935. In that year she transferred to the Berlin State Opera, to which she belonged until 1945. She made guest appearances at the Vienna State Opera, in Holland, and at the most important German opera houses; after 1945 she lived in Hamburg and appeared particularly at the Hamburg State Opera. In 1953 at Essen she created the title role in the first German performance of *Lulu* and, although already very ill, she sang the same part in the summer of 1953 at the Holland Festival.
Records: There are relatively few records of her voice; these are on DGG (*Die Zauberflöte* and *Der Freischütz*), Telefunken, and Imperial. *U.S. re-issue:* RCA Victor.

SPOORENBERG, ERNA, soprano, b. 1925, Djojakarta, Java. The daughter of Dutch parents, she studied with Aaltje Noordewier-Reddingius in Hilversum and with Berthe Seroen in Amsterdam. She also studied the violin at the Amsterdam Conservatory. In 1947 she made her debut in a radio concert in Hilversum, singing Mozart's *Exsultate, Jubilate*. In 1949 she made her stage debut at the Vienna State Opera. She then had great success both on the operatic stage and in the concert hall. She visited Germany, Austria, and the Scandinavian countries and appeared as guest at the Vienna State Opera, among others. In 1958 she was engaged at the Netherlands Opera in

Amsterdam. In 1962 she was greatly admired as Mélisande in *Pelléas et Mélisande* at the Hamburg State Opera. She had a technically well-trained and outstandingly beautiful soprano voice of great expressiveness.

Records: Philips and Decca (*Pelléas et Mélisande*). *U.S. re-issue:* London, Mercury.

STABILE, MARIANO, baritone, b. May 12, 1888, Palermo, Sicily. He made his debut in Palermo (1911) as Marcello in *La Bohème*. Although he had already become well known through his great successes in Italy before World War I he did not become world-famous until Toscanini gave him important assignments at La Scala in the 1920's. He was especially admired in the role of Falstaff. He had enormous successes through guest appearances in London, Paris, Amsterdam, Brussels, Berlin, and Vienna. He was engaged at the Chicago Opera (1928-29) and sang almost annually at the Teatro Colón as guest. He first sang at the Salzburg Festivals (1931) and he was greatly admired there as Don Giovanni (1934) and as Falstaff (1935). He also sang at the Arena and Maggio Musicale Festivals. He retained the beauty of his voice until an advanced age. In 1955 he sang at La Scala in *Il Turco in Italia* with Maria Callas; in 1958 he appeared at the Teatro Fenice as the title hero in *Gianni Schicchi*. He is married to the soprano Gemma Bosini. He joined in a fortunate combination an attractive baritone voice and a masterly art of characterization; he was admired as Don Giovanni and as Falstaff.

Records: Fonotipia, Columbia (*L'Italiana in Algeri*), Telefunken, and Nixa (*Don Giovanni*). *U.S. re-recording:* Eterna, Telefunken, Rococo.

STADER, MARIA, soprano, b. Nov. 5, 1918, Budapest. She moved to Switzerland in 1922 and studied (1933-39) with H. Keller in Karlsruhe and later with Ilona Durigo in Zürich, with Lombardi in Milan and with Therese Schnabel-Behr in New York City. Although she won first prize in a singing contest in Geneva in 1939, she was able to pursue her career only after World War II. She has made only occasional appearances on the operatic stage—for example, at Covent Garden as the Queen of the Night in *Die Zauberflöte* (1949-50), but she has had instead a brilliant career as a concert soprano. She has sung as guest in the centers of European musical life and has made several brilliant American concert tours. She has had very great success with her series of concerts at the Salzburg Festivals, and in 1960 the city of Salzburg awarded her the Lilli Lehmann Medal. Although she has rarely appeared on the operatic stage, she has in the concert hall, and especially on radio and records, sung a great many operatic roles. In this way she has established herself as an outstanding Mozart singer. She has taught at the Zürich Conservatory. She is married to the conductor Hans Erismann. She has a beautifully expressive and technically well-managed voice of a special clearness of intonation.

Records: HMV, MMS, Westminster*, but particularly for DGG* (*Die Entführung aus dem Serail, Die Zauberflöte, Orphée et Eurydice, Le Nozze di Figaro, Don Giovanni* and *Fidelio*). *U.S. reissue:* Decca, Turnabout, Vanguard-Everyman.

STAHLMANN, SYLVIA, soprano, b. March 5, 1929, Nashville, Tenn. She completed a course at the Juilliard School of Music in New York City and first sang in musicals on Broadway. She was engaged at the Théâtre de la Monnaie (1951-54) under the name Giulia Bardi; she made her debut there as Elvira in *I*

Puritani and sang many parts in the classic coloratura repertory. In 1956 she appeared under her own name at the New York City Opera as Blondchen in *Die Entführung aus dem Serail*. She sang with the San Francisco Opera (1958), with the Chicago Opera (1960), and was engaged by the Metropolitan Opera (1961), where she remains, still singing mostly soubrette parts. She has regularly appeared as guest with the Frankfurt Opera.

Records: Decca (*Un Ballo in Maschera*, a small role in *La Sonnambula*, and Gustav Mahler's *Fourth Symphony*). *U.S. re-issue:* London, Vanguard Vox, CRI.

STEBER, ELEANOR, soprano, b. June 17, 1916, Wheeling, W. Va. She studied first with her mother, then for six years at the New England Conservatory of Music in Boston, and finally with Paul Althouse in New York City. She made her debut at the Metropolitan Opera (1940) as Sophie in *Der Rosenkavalier*. She became well known when in 1945 she undertook a tour of the United States with the company of the San Francisco Opera. She sang at the Glyndebourne Festival in 1947 and in 1953 sang Elsa in *Lohengrin* at the Bayreuth Festival; she has also appeared with success at the Edinburgh Festival. In 1958 she sang at the Metropolitan Opera in the world *première* of *Vanessa* and she sang the same role at the Salzburg Festival in 1959. She had a strongly expressive and flexible soprano voice and she was admired in both Verdi and Wagner roles.

Records: RCA Victor*, Philips (*Faust*), Decca (*Lohengrin*), HMV (*Fidelio*), and Columbia* (*Così fan tutte*). *U.S. re-issue:* Angel, Amadeo, London RCA Victor, American Decca, Standard.

STEFANO, GIUSEPPE DI, tenor, b. July 24, 1921, near Catania, Sicily. At great financial sacrifice his family made it possible for him to study with Luigi Montesanto in Milan. He made his stage debut (1946) at Reggio Emilia as Des Grieux in *Manon Lescaut*, and made a guest appearance in the same year at the Teatro Liceo. In 1947 he sang at the Rome Opera, and in 1948 at La Scala. He appeared with huge success at the Metropolitan Opera (1948-50). Since 1951 he has had triumphs at La Scala and in guest and concert appearances all over the world: at the Vienna State Opera, Covent Garden, in Paris, Chicago, San Francisco, Mexico City, Buenos Aires, Rio de Janeiro, and Johannesburg. In 1950 he was applauded at the Arena Festival as Nadir in *Les Pêcheurs de Perles*, and he has appeared at the Edinburgh Festival. He is generally rated as one of the most consequential Italian tenors of his generation. He has a warm timbred and highly expressive voice best suited to lyric parts in the Italian repertory, but is also admired as an interpreter of Italian songs.

Records: He has made a great many records for HMV, Decca (including *L'Elisir d'Amore*), RCA Victor (*La Gioconda, La Forza del Destino*), DGG (*Lucia di Lammermoor*), and Columbia* (a great many operas with Maria Callas as partner, including *Lucia di Lammermoor, Cavalleria Rusticana, I Pagliacci, La Bohème, Madama Butterfly, Manon Lescaut, Un Ballo in Maschera, Tosca*, and *I Puritani*). *U.S. re-issue:* Angel, London, Mercury, Epic, Everest-Cetra.

STEFFEK, HANNY, soprano, b. Dec. 12, 1930, Biala, Poland. She studied at the Vienna Music Academy and at the Salzburg Mozarteum. After her concert debut (1949) she began her stage career in 1951 in Wiesbaden. In 1953 she came to Graz, later to the Frankfurt Opera, and in 1958 to the Munich State Opera. Through her successes at the latter and through her frequent guest appearances at the Vienna State Opera she became internationally known. In 1955 she sang Papagena in *Die Zauberflöte* at the Salzburg Festival. She sang Sophie in *Der Rosenkavalier* in a guest appearance at Covent Garden in 1959; in 1960 she sang at the Aix-en-Provence Festival and in 1962 at the Teatro Fenice and in Amsterdam. At the Salzburg Festival of 1962 she sang the soprano solo in the oratorio *Das Buch mit dem Sieben Siegeln*, by Franz Schmidt. She is married to the director of the Vienna Volksoper, Albert Moser. She has a well-trained soprano voice with complete mastery of coloratura technique and she is particularly admired in the operas of Mozart and Richard Strauss.

Records: DGG and Columbia (Despina in *Così fan tutte*). *U.S. re-issue:* Angel, Amadeo, Vanguard.

STEHLE, ADELINA, soprano, b. 1865, Trieste, Austria; d. 1945, Milan. She was the daughter of the director of an Austrian military band. She made her debut (1888) at the Bologna Opera. She married the tenor Edoardo Garbin and with him had a brilliant career on the leading Italian opera stages, particularly at La Scala and at the Teatro Costanzi. On May 22, 1892, she sang the part of Nedda in the world *première* of *I Pagliacci* at the Teatro dal Verme. On Feb. 9, 1893, at La Scala, she created the role of Ann Ford in *Falstaff*, while her husband sang the role of Fenton. She had also created the role of Walter in *La Wally* at La Scala (1892). In 1898 at the Teatro Massimo she sang, again with her husband, in *La Bohème*, and they led the work to a definite success. In 1902 she made a tour of South America with the Gran Compagnia Lirica Italiana. Outside Italy she appeared only a few times as guest. She did not sing in the United States or England. After her retirement from the stage she lived and taught singing in Milan until she withdrew to the Casa di Riposo, founded there by Verdi.

Records: Two records for Fonotipia (a duet with Edoardo Garbin and in the Quartet from *La Bohème*). *U.S. re-issue:* HRS. *U.S. re-recording:* HRS.

STEHMANN, GERHARD, baritone, b. 1861, Seiffen, Germany; d. July, 1926, Vienna. He studied with Lilli Lehmann in Berlin and with Karl Ress in Leipzig. He made his debut at Altenburg (1899) as General Lefort in *Zar und Zimmermann*. In 1890 he went to the United States, where he first sang in St. Louis and then with the Damrosch Opera Company; he remained with them until 1897 and then undertook another American tour (1898-99) with a troupe which Nellie Melba had gathered together. In 1899 he was engaged by the Vienna Imperial Opera, where he sang until his death. He appeared at the Salzburg Festivals (1906; 1910). His strong and expressive baritone voice was particularly admired in Wagner parts.

Records: Zonophone (Vienna, 1905-08), G & T (Vienna, 1906-07), HMV (Vienna, 1908), and Pathé; with one exception all are ensemble scenes. *U.S. re-issue:* Victor.

STEINER, FRANZ, baritone, b. 1876, Hungary; d. Oct. 23, 1954, Mexico City. A student of Ress in Vienna and Johannes Messchaert in Frankfurt, he had already left Vienna by 1906 and traveled through Europe and America as a concert, and particularly as a lieder, singer. He was considered a great interpreter of the songs of Richard

Strauss, who often accompanied him at the piano during his recitals. In 1938 he left Austria and became a singing teacher in Mexico City. He had a bright-timbred, almost tenor voice.

Records: A great many records for Anker, mostly in Strauss and Schubert songs; he made both acoustic and electric records for Polydor.

STEINGRUBER, ILONA, soprano, b. Feb. 8, 1912, Vienna; d. Dec. 12, 1962, Vienna. She first wanted to become a pianist, but then studied singing at the Music High School in Vienna and appeared on the Vienna radio (1938-42). In 1942 she had her first stage engagement at Tilsit. After World War II extended concert tours took her all over Europe and by this means she became a well-known interpreter of contemporary music. In 1948 she was engaged at the Vienna State Opera. She sang as guest in Prague and Brussels and appeared frequently at the Salzburg Festivals. She was particularly admired as a concert and oratorio soprano. After 1951 she was a teacher in the summer courses at the Darmstadt Music High School. She was married to Friedrich Wildgans, the son of the poet Anton Wildgans.

Records: Philips (*Lulu*), Vox*, Decca, and DGG* (*Der Rosenkavalier*). *U.S. re-issue:* Columbia, Lyrichord, SPA, MGM.

STELLA, ANTONIETTA, soprano, b. March 15, 1929, Perugia, Italy. She studied at the Accademia di Santa Cecilia in Rome and made her debut at the Rome Opera (1951); she had her first great success there in the same year, singing Leonora in *La Forza del Destino*. Guest appearances followed in Florence, Naples, and Perugia and she sang at the Arena Festival in 1953, which was also the year of her debut at La Scala. She often sang as guest at the Vienna State Opera and also at Covent Garden, as well as in Paris, Brussels, and Chicago, all very successfully. In 1959 she joined the Metropolitan Opera, making her first appearance as Leonora in *La Forza del Destino*. Dramatic talent, musical beauty, and a real mastery of singing technique are joined in her soprano voice.

Records: Cetra* (*Simone Boccanegra*), Philips (*Linda di Chamounix, La Bohème,* and *Tosca*), DGG* (*Un Ballo in Maschera, Don Carlos* and *Il Trovatore*), HMV (*Don Carlos*), and Columbia* (*La Traviata*). *U.S. re-issue:* Angel, Capitol, Seraphim.

STEVENS, RISE, contralto, b. June 11, 1913, New York. Her father was Norwegian. She sang on the American radio when she was very young and then began her vocal studies at the Juilliard School of Music in New York. In 1935 she went to Europe and studied in Vienna with Marie Gutheil-Schoder and Herbert Graf. In 1936 she made her debut at the Opera in Prague as Mignon. She remained in Prague until 1938 and during this time sang Octavian in *Der Rosenkavalier* as guest at the Vienna State Opera. She also sang the same role that year at the Teatro Colón. In 1939 she was applauded at the Glyndebourne Festival as Cherubino in *Le Nozze di Figaro*. In 1939 she signed a contract with the Metropolitan Opera, making her debut there as Mignon. She remained a member of the Metropolitan for over twenty years, an honored principal contralto of the house. In 1940 she had a sensational success there as Cherubino. She appeared as guest in Europe only rarely—for example, in Paris and London, among others; and in 1954 at La Scala in *La Figlia del Diavolo*. In 1956 she was admired as an unforgettable Orphée in Gluck's opera at the Festival of the Acropolis in Athens. After her farewell to the stage in 1964, she became the leader of the Metropolitan National Opera Company, a traveling troupe, which is no longer active. The volume of her voice, the richness of nuance of her expressive art, and her great grasp of style were demonstrated in a wide-ranging repertory, which reached its peaks as Carmen and Orphée.

Records: Columbia* and RCA Victor* (including *Carmen, Le Nozze di Figaro, Orphée et Eurydice,* and *Die Fledermaus*). *U.S. re-recording:* RCA Victor.

STEWART, THOMAS, baritone, b. 1923, Texas. He first studied mathematics and worked in a government laboratory for mathematical-physical research. Finally he turned to the study of singing, which he completed in part at the Juilliard School of Music in New York. He then sang with American orchestras and appeared as guest in American opera houses. In 1958 he was engaged by the Berlin City Opera and has had great success there ever since. Guest appearances followed in Cologne, Hamburg, Rome, Paris, Chicago, New York, and Monte Carlo. At the Bayreuth Festivals (1960-62) he sang Amfortas in *Parsifal,* Donner in *Das Rheingold,* and Gunther in *Götterdämmerung*; in 1965 he sang the title role in *Der Fliegende Holländer.* He made his Metropolitan Opera debut as Ford in *Falstaff* on Mar. 9, 1966. He is married to the soprano Evelyn Lear. He has a strong and heroic baritone voice.

Records: DGG*, Odeon, and Amadeo (*Jonny Spielt Auf*). *U.S. re-issue:* Electrola, Turnabout, Heliodor.

STICH-RANDALL, TERESA, soprano, b. Dec. 24, 1927, West Hartford, Conn. She studied at the Hartford Conservatory and at Columbia University. After appearing in the United States in concert, she transferred her activity to Europe. In 1951 she was a great sensation at the Festival in the Boboli Gardens in Florence with her singing of the Mermaid in *Oberon* while she swam in a great basin. In 1952 she was engaged by the Vienna State Opera, where she has since had great success. Her guest appearances brought her great triumphs, particularly in Italy, where she has sung at La Scala, the Teatro San Carlo, and in Genoa and Turin, as well as at the Maggio Musicale Festival. She has also been highly successful at the Salzburg Festivals and in guest appearances in Switzerland and Germany. She has sung at the Aix-en-Provence and Glyndebourne Festivals and has had a noted career as a concert soprano. In 1961 she sang at the Chicago Opera and made her Metropolitan Opera debut in the same season. Her voice is admired for the instrumental precision of her tone production and the well-balanced quality of her delivery. She is particularly noted as a Mozart singer.

Records: Philips* (*Così fan tutte*), HMV (*A Life for the Czar*), RCA-Victor* (*Falstaff* under Toscanini and *Aïda*), DGG*, MMS, Pathé (*Le Nozze di Figaro*), and Columbia (*Der Rosenkavalier*). *U.S. re-issue:* Bach Guild, Capitol, Music Guild, Epic, Angel, Westminster, Vox, Nonesuch, Everyman, Vanguard.

STIGNANI, EBE, contralto, b. July 11, 1904, Naples. She studied at the Conservatory of San Pietro a Majella at Naples with Agostino Roche. The director of the San Carlo Opera heard her at a school concert and engaged her for his house, where she made her debut (1925) as Amneris in *Aïda.* She was so successful that Toscanini also engaged her for La Scala; as her debut role there she sang Princess Eboli in *Don Carlos*. She remained the first contralto at La Scala until 1953. In 1927 she first sang as guest at the Teatro Colón and in 1938 was admired as Amneris at Covent Garden; in the same year she sang at the San Francisco Opera. At the Maggio Musicale Festival in 1940 she sang the difficult coloratura contralto part of Arsaces in *Semiramide*. Although this famous artist had magnificent triumphs in Europe and South America, she made surprisingly few appearances in the United States; she sang again in San Francisco in 1948 and followed this with concerts in Minneapolis and New York, but she was never offered a contract at the Metropolitan Opera. In the last years of her career she sang particularly on the larger Italian stages. Her contralto voice was admired for her powerful tonal quality, for the rich shading of her expression, and for her consummate vocal technique.

Records: Columbia (about 1930, including a complete *La Gioconda*; later she recorded *Norma* with Maria Callas and *Il Matrimonio Segreto*), HMV, and Cetra* (*Norma, La Forza del Destino,* and *Don Carlos*). *U.S. re-issue:* American Decca, RCA Victor, Angel, Richmond, Seraphim.

STOLZE, GERHARD, tenor, b. Oct. 1, 1926, Dessau, Germany. After serving in World War II as a soldier, he became an actor and worked as such in Bautzen, in the Komödienhaus in Dresden, and with a traveling company. He then studied singing with Willy Bader and Rudolf Dittrich in Dresden. He made his debut at the Dresden State Opera (1949) as Augustin Moser in *Die Meistersinger*. He had his first important successes at the Bayreuth Festivals, where he sang every year after 1951. He was especially admired there in the following decade as Mime in the *Ring* cycle and as David in *Die Meistersinger*. He remained in Dresden until 1953 and then was engaged at the Berlin State Opera (1953-61). After 1956 he was also under guest-appearance contracts with both the Vienna State Opera and the Stuttgart Opera. On Apr. 27, 1961, he sang the title role in the world *première* of *Oedipus der Tyrann* at the Vienna State Opera. Since 1959 he has sung at the Salzburg Festivals, and since 1961 has been a regular member of the Vienna State Opera. The flexibility of his voice and his great acting ability have allowed him to excel in *buffo* tenor parts.

Records: Decca (*Salome, Lohengrin,* and *Siegfried*) and DGG* (*Antigonae*). *U.S. re-issue:* London, Electrola, Philips, Columbia.

STOLZENBERG, HERTHA, soprano, b. 1889, Cologne; d. Mar. 20, 1960, Obertsdorf, Germany. After study in Cologne and Berlin, she made her debut in the latter city at the Komische Oper (1910). She sang at Kiel (1910-11) and at the German Opera in Berlin (1911-24), where she was exceptionally successful. She sang at the Hannover Opera (1924-32). She appeared as guest on the largest German stages and in Holland; she became well known through concerts which she gave on the German radio. In 1932 she gave up her career. She had a wonderfully trained and expressive soprano voice and she was especially admired in the lyric repertory.

Records: Homochord, Parlophone, and Polydor.

STORCHIO, ROSINA, soprano, b. May 19, 1876, Venice; d. July 24, 1945, Milan. She studied with Fatuo and Giovanni in Mantua and made her debut, before her seventeenth birthday, at the Teatro Lirico

(1892) as Micaëla in *Carmen*. In 1893 she sang in Padua and in 1895 appeared at La Scala, where she made her debut as Sophie in *Werther*. She quickly developed a brilliant career on the leading Italian stages. In 1897 she sang the role of Mimi Pinson in the world *première* of Leoncavallo's *La Bohème* at the Teatro Fenice. In 1900 she was admired in the title role of *Zaza* in the world *première* at the Teatro Lirico and in 1903 at the La Scala as Stephana in the world *première* of *Siberia*. At La Scala her career was assisted by Arturo Toscanini. There, on Feb. 17, 1904, she created the title role in the world *première* of *Madama Butterfly*. But the production was unfortunate; on account of the insult that she suffered from being hissed by the gallery, she decided never to sing the role of Butterfly in Italy again; she did, however, sing it a single time in Rome in 1920. After 1904 she sang repeatedly as guest in South America, especially at the Teatro Colón. She also undertook a tour of Russia. She sang the title role in *Lodoletta* in 1917 at the Teatro Costanzi at its world *première*. She was engaged by the Chicago Opera (1920-21) and she sang in Barcelona (1923), but then gave up her stage career. She lived later in Milan and in her last years was entirely paralyzed. She was famed for her sovereign mastery of singing technique in coloratura parts and for the fineness of her expressive art in lyric roles.

Records: Very rare records for G & T (Milan, 1904) and Fonotipia (Milan, 1905). *U.S. re-issue:* HRS, IRCC. *U.S. re-recordings:* FRP, TAP, HRS.

STOSKA, POLYNA, soprano, b. 1914, Worcester, Mass. Originally Apollonia Stoscus. She came of a Lithuanian family. She first studied violin and then sang with an amateur operetta society. She finally studied singing in Boston and at the Juilliard School of Music in New York. In 1938 she was a pupil of Charlotte Gadski-Busch in Berlin and she made her debut there at the German Opera House (1939). She remained there until 1941 and then returned to the United States and undertook long concert tours. She was engaged at the New York City Opera (1944-46), sang in operetta on Broadway (1946) and in California (1947). She was highly successful at the Metropolitan Opera (1947-53). In 1953 she sang as guest at the Teatro Liceo and at the Vienna State Opera; in that year she also appeared in Berlin in *Ariadne auf Naxos*. She was particularly admired on the stage in Mozart and Wagner roles.

Records: A few Columbia* records.

STRACCIARI, RICCARDO, baritone, b. June 26, 1875, Casalecchio, Italy; d. Oct. 10, 1955, Rome. He studied at the Liceo Musicale in Bologna. His concert debut took place there (1899) in a production of the oratorio *La Risurrezione di Cristo*, by Perosi. He made his stage debut there also (1900) as Marcello in *La Bohème*. Guest appearances followed on Italian stages, at the Teatro São Carlos, and in Egypt and Chile. After 1904 he sang regularly at La Scala. He was a member of the Metropolitan Opera (1906-08), making his debut as the elder Germont in *La Traviata*. In two seasons there he sang ten important roles. The center of gravity of his artistic career came in the following years at La Scala and the Teatro Costanzi. He was greatly admired in South America and sang regularly at the Teatro Colón and in other important theaters. He sang with the Chicago Opera Company (1917-19). In 1939 he gave up his brilliant career and lived as a teacher in Rome. He had one of the most beautiful baritone voices which Italy produced in his generation; he was especially admired for the elegance of his parlando singing. Of the seventy-eight roles which he sang on the stage, his particular starring part was that of Figaro in *Il Barbiere di Siviglia*, which he sang more than nine hundred times.

Records: Fonotipia and Columbia* (including *Rigoletto* and *Il Barbiere di Siviglia*). *U.S. re-issue:* Columbia-Fonotipia, Okeh. *U.S. re-recordings:* Eterna, Scala, Belcanto, Rococo, TAP, FRP.

STRALIA, ELSA, soprano, b. 1880, Adelaide, Australia; d. Aug. 5, 1945, Melbourne, Australia. She was the daughter of the German baritone Hugo Fischer. After studying with her father and at the Adelaide Conservatory, she appeared in concerts in Australia under her own name, Elsa Fischer. In 1910 she came to Milan and began her career there under the name Elsa Stralia. She made her stage debut at Covent Garden as Donna Anna in *Don Giovanni* (1913). During World War I she had great success at the Drury Lane Theater as Aïda under Sir Thomas Beecham. She sang the same part at Covent Garden (1919). She made long concert tours in England, North America, and Australia. In 1929 she made another long tour of the United States. At the end of her career she taught singing in Melbourne.

Records: Columbia (c. 1918).

STRATAS, TERESA, soprano, b. 1938, Toronto, Canada. She studied at the Toronto Conservatory and made her debut there (1958). In 1959 she won the Metropolitan Opera Auditions in New York and she has been engaged there since 1960, having become one of the principal prima donnas of this house. She has made successful guest appearances in Moscow, London, Munich, and elsewhere in Germany.

Records: Decca. *U.S. re-issue:* London.

STREICH, RITA, soprano, b. Dec. 18, 1920, Barbaul, Siberia, where her father was interned as a German prisoner of war. She came to Germany as a child and studied singing with Willi Domgraf-Fassbänder, Maria Ivogün, and Erna Berger in Berlin. She made her debut (1943) in Ustí and in 1946 was engaged by the Berlin State Opera; at the latter she had her first great successes as Olympia in *Les Contes d'Hoffmann* and as Blondchen in *Die Entführung aus dem Serail*. She remained at the Berlin State Opera until 1950, when she transferred to the Berlin City Opera, to which she belonged until 1953; at that time she became a member of the Vienna State Opera. In 1952 she sang at the Bayreuth Festival and since 1954 has sung each year at the Salzburg Festivals. She appeared as guest at the Rome Opera as Sophie in *Der Rosenkavalier* (1952). She has also sung with brilliant success at La Scala, Covent Garden, and the Chicago Opera, as well as at the Glyndebourne and Aix-en-Provence Festivals. In 1957 she toured the United States and made her debut at the Metropolitan Opera. A brilliant coloratura voice which she manages with great virtuosity; she is also a celebrated singer in the concert and song repertory.

Records: Many records for DGG* (*Orphée et Eurydice*, *Hänsel und Gretel*, *Die Entführung aus dem Serail*, *Die Zauberflöte*, *La Bohème*, and *Der Freischütz*), Decca (*Ariadne auf Naxos*), Columbia (*Die Fledermaus*), and Nixa (*Tannhäuser*). *U.S. re-issue:* Urania, Epic, Angel, Electrola, Heliodor, Vox, American Decca, Fiesta.

STRIENZ, WILHELM, bass, b. Sept. 2, 1900, Stuttgart, Germany. He began his vocal study in 1919 with

Strong · Stückgold

Theodor Scheidl and Oscar Schröter in Stuttgart and made his stage debut (1922) at the German Opera House in Berlin as the Hermit in *Der Freischütz*. After further study with Luise Reuss-Belce and Louis Bachner in Berlin, he sang in Wiesbaden (1923-24) and Bremen (1925-26). He was engaged as soloist by the West German radio in Cologne (1926-33). After 1933 he lived in Berlin and engaged in extraordinary concert and guest-appearance activity. In 1938 he was greatly admired on the occasion of a long series of guest appearances at Covent Garden; he was a very frequent guest in Holland, where he often sang with the Concertgebouw Orchestra. He also sang at the State Operas in Berlin, Hamburg, and Munich. After 1945 he lived in Frankfurt and had great success, particularly as a concert singer, in Germany, Austria, and Switzerland. A warm, dark bass voice which he demonstrated in a wide repertory.

Records: His first records appeared for Polydor; he then recorded for Electrola (including *Die Zauberflöte* under Sir Thomas Beecham). His last records were made for DGG and Urania. *U.S. re-issue:* RCA Victor. *U.S. re-recording:* Electrola, Eterna, Urania, Turnabout, Rococo.

STRONG, SUSAN, soprano, b. Aug. 3, 1870, Brooklyn; d. Nov. 3, 1946, London. She was the daughter of Dennis Strong, a state senator and the mayor of Brooklyn. She studied voice with no particular thought, at first, of becoming a singer, but she continued her studies with Francis Korbay at the Royal College of Music in London and made her debut there with the Hedmondt Opera Company (1893) as Sieglinde in *Die Walküre*. In 1895 she sang the same role and also Elsa in *Lohengrin* at Covent Garden. She was engaged to sing at the Bayreuth Festival of 1896, but did not appear. Later she sang as guest at the Teatro San Carlo. In 1896 she sang Elsa again and Marguerite in *Faust* with the Mapleson Opera Company in New York. She returned to Covent Garden to sing Wagner roles (1897; 1899). She sang with great success at the Metropolitan Opera (1899-1900), making her debut as Sieglinde. She made guest appearances at the Imperial Opera in Vienna in 1901. She then became a celebrated concert singer and was noted in England for her singing of lieder. After the end of her singing career she opened a de luxe laundry in London. She had a large and highly expressive voice.

Records: A few rare HMV records (London, 1907-08). *U.S. re-issue:* IRCC.

STROZZI, VIOLETTA DE, soprano, b. 1891, Zagreb. She studied at the Conservatory of Zagreb and with Irene Schlemmer-Ambros in Vienna and made her debut (1918) at the Zagreb Opera as Anne in *The Merry Wives of Windsor*. She was engaged in the Opera at Wroclaw (1921-24) and was a member of the Berlin State Opera (1924-33). She sang in a varied repertory there, but gave her best performances in Italian roles. In 1927 she sang as guest at the Vienna State Opera and later in Paris, Prague, and Rome. In 1933 she emigrated to the United States, where in 1934-35 she joined the Cosmopolitan Opera Company.

Records: Acoustics for Odeon and Homochord; a few electric records for Odeon and HMV.

STÜCKGOLD, GRETE, soprano, b. July 6, 1895, London. Her father, Ludwig Schneidt, a German, was the director of the cable works in Nordenham; her mother was English. The singer passed her youth in Nordenham and London and went to Germany in 1913. There she studied singing with Jacques Stückgold in Munich. She later married her teacher, but was separated from him in 1929. Her second marriage was to the baritone Gustav Schützendorf. She began her career as a concert and oratorio singer, then made her stage debut (1917) in Nuremberg; she remained there until 1922, when she transferred to the Berlin State Opera. During this time she often sang as guest with the Berlin City Opera and appeared with the Leipzig Gewandhaus Orchestra under Artur Nikisch. In 1927 she was engaged at the Metropolitan Opera, making her debut as Eva in *Die Meistersinger*. She remained there until 1940 and sang as guest in San Francisco, Philadelphia, and Chicago. She lives in New York. A very beautiful and expressive soprano voice; in addition to her stage roles, she was admired as an oratorio and lieder singer.

Records: Vox and Polydor; she also made private records in the United States.

STÜZNER, ELISA, soprano, b. 1888 (?), Thuringia, Germany. She studied music at the Leipzig Conservatory. In 1909 she was engaged as an apprentice at the Dresden Royal Opera, making her debut there as the Shepherd Boy in *Tannhäuser* and remaining there until she gave up the stage in 1935. After further study with Dora Erl in Dresden, she mastered the entire youthful-dramatic repertory. She was particularly admired in the operas of Richard Strauss and sang, among others, the role of Salome under the composer's baton at the Vienna State Opera. In 1932 she sang the part of the Mother in the world *première* of *Mr. Wu* at the Dresden State Opera. She was a highly prized concert and lieder singer; in 1930 she created the *Fiedellieder* of Ernst Křenek and in 1932 the same composer's *Gesänge des Späten Jahres*. In 1935 she gave her last stage performance as Elisabeth in *Tannhäuser* in Dresden. She then became a professor at the Music High School in Leipzig, later at the Carl Maria von Weber High School in Dresden; after she relinquished her teaching position, she was made an honorary senator of the school.

Records: Electric records for Polydor and Parlophone; one acoustic record for Schweizer Tonkunstplatte in a duet with Max Hirzel. *U.S. re-issue:* American Decca.

SULIOTIS, ELENA, soprano, b. 1943, Athens. Her mother was Russian and her father Greek. When she was five years old her parents moved to Buenos Aires. In 1962 she went to Italy to study singing and became a pupil of Mercedes Llopart in Milan. She made her debut as Santuzza in *Cavalleria Rusticana* at the Teatro San Carlo (1964). Since 1965 she has been successful in opera houses in Italy and Spain. In 1966 she appeared in opera in Mexico City and Chicago and made her New York debut in a concert performance of *Anna Bolena*. In 1966 she also had a great triumph at La Scala as Abagail in *Nabucco*. She has a large, dramatic soprano voice.

Records: Decca (*Nabucco* and *Cavalleria Rusticana*). *U.S. re-issue:* London.

SUNDELIUS, MARIE, soprano, b. Feb. 4, 1884, Karlsstadt, Sweden; d. June 27, 1958, Boston. Originally Marie Sandtvig. She came to Boston at the age of ten and her study of singing began after her marriage to a physician there. She made her concert debut there under Karl Muck (1910). In 1915 she sang in New York in the oratorio *Jeanne d'Arc*, by Bossi. In 1916 she made her stage debut at the Metropolitan Opera as a Priestess in *Iphigénie en Tauride*. She remained a member of the Metropolitan until 1928 and sang there in several world premières: *The Canterbury Pilgrims* (1917), *Shanewis* (1918), *Suor Angelica* and *Gianni Schicchi* on Dec. 14, 1918. For the most part she sang small roles at the Metropolitan, but she was entrusted also with some significant parts. In 1920 she made a tour of the United States with the Scotti Grand Opera Company. She sang with the Philadelphia Opera Company (1929-30). After the close of her career she taught at the Malbin Conservatory in Boston. She died following an automobile accident.

Records: Relatively few records for American Columbia*, Vocalion*, and Edison* Disc records.

SUPERVIA, CONCHITA, contralto, b. Dec. 9, 1895, Barcelona, Spain; d. Mar. 30, 1936, London. She came of an old Andalusian family and entered the Barcelona Conservatory at the age of twelve. She made her debut (1910) in Buenos Aires in *Los Amantes de Teruel*. In 1911 she sang in the first Italian performance of *Der Rosenkavalier* at the Teatro Costanzi; her role was that of Octavian opposite the Marschallin of Hariclea Darclée. In 1912 she was admired in Bologna as Carmen and as Dalila in *Samson et Dalila*. In 1914 she had a magnificent success at the Havana Opera and she was a member of the Chicago Opera Company (1915-20). After 1920 she sang chiefly on the most important Italian stages and in Barcelona; she was very successful in 1924 at La Scala. In 1925 she began the revival of the *bel canto* operas of Rossini, such as *L'Italiana in Algeri*, *La Cenerentola*, and *Il Barbiere di Siviglia*—singing the latter in its original form with Rosina as a coloratura contralto role. These operas were not being presented because the technical difficulties of their contralto coloratura were so great that twentieth-century singers of this voice range could not master them. With the help of her phenomenal singing technique, Conchita Supervia caused great excitement in her appearances in these roles, first at the Teatro Regio in Turin, then in Florence, Rome, London, Paris, and South America. In 1931 she married the British industrialist Sir Ben Rubenstein. She died in London as an aftermath of childbirth. With a contralto voice of unique beauty she displayed the greatest virtuosity in singing technique.

Records: Parlophone and Ultraphon. *U.S. re-issue:* American Decca. *U.S. re-recording:* Angel, TAP, Scala, Rococo, Washington.

SUTHAUS, LUDWIG, tenor, b. Dec. 12, 1906, Cologne, Germany. He studied at the Cologne Music High School (1922-28) and made his debut in Aachen (1928) as Walther in *Die Meistersinger*. He remained at Aachen until 1931 and then sang at the State Opera in Stuttgart (1932-41). In 1941 he was engaged at the Berlin State Opera and remained there until 1948. After 1948 he sang at the Berlin City Opera and after 1957 was concurrently a member of the Vienna State Opera. He created international attention as a Wagner tenor. He made several guest appearances at Covent Garden, the Paris Opéra, La Scala, and the State Operas in Munich and Hamburg. He sang at the Bayreuth Festivals as Siegmund and Loge in the *Ring* cycle and as Walther in *Die Meistersinger*. In addition to Wagner parts he has sung a range of other roles for heroic tenor.

Records: HMV (*Tristan und Isolde* and *Die Walküre*). *U.S. re-issue:* Angel, Electrola, Seraphim.

SUTHERLAND, JOAN, soprano, b. Nov. 7, 1926, Sydney, Australia. She studied with John and Aida Dickens in Sydney and sang the

Sutter · Svéd

title role in *Judith* there in 1950. In 1951 she came to London to study with Clive Carey; she made her debut there (1952) at Covent Garden as the First Lady in *Die Zauberflöte*. She was also highly successful there in such parts as Aïda, Amelia in *Un Ballo in Maschera*, Agathe in *Der Freischütz*, and Eva in *Die Meistersinger*. In 1958-59 her voice changed to coloratura soprano and she then sang Lucia di Lammermoor, Amina in *La Sonnambula*, and Violetta in *La Traviata* to rapturous applause. Guest appearances included the Vienna State Opera (1959) and Genoa, Parma, and Venice (1960); in 1961 she was ecstatically received at La Scala in *Beatrice di Tenda*. She has also sung with brilliant success at the Paris Opéra, the Glyndebourne and Edinburgh Festivals, in Cologne, Barcelona, and San Francisco. In 1961 she was engaged at the Metropolitan Opera, making her debut as Lucia. She is married to the conductor Richard Bonynge. She combines in a rare unity the highest virtuosity in florid singing with subtle expressiveness.

Records: Decca (*Lucia di Lammermoor*, *Rigoletto*, *Alcina*, and *The Messiah*), Columbia (*Don Giovanni*), L'Oiseau Lyre (*Acis and Galatea*), and HMV. *U.S. re-issue:* RCA Victor, Belcanto, London.

SUTTER, ANNA, soprano, b. Nov. 26, 1871, Wil, Switzerland; d. June 29, 1910, Stuttgart. She first studied piano at the Bern Conservatory and then singing in Munich. She made her debut at the Volkstheater there (1892). She sang at Augsburg (1893-98) and in the latter year came to the Royal Opera in Stuttgart, where she was very successful. She made guest appearances with the Stuttgart ensemble in Berlin. Her end was a tragic one; she was shot by the conductor Alois Obrist, who then committed suicide.

Records: A few records for HMV (Stuttgart, 1908-09).

SVANHOLM, SET, tenor, b. Sept. 9, 1904, Västerås, Sweden, where his father was a Lutheran pastor; d. Oct. 4, 1964, Stockholm. He was first an elementary school teacher and organist in his native town. He studied at the Royal Conservatory in Stockholm (1927-29) and passed his examinations as a music teacher. He studied singing with John Forsell in Stockholm (1930-31) and made his debut at the Royal Opera there (1930), singing baritone parts. He continued for six years as a baritone before his voice changed to tenor and he became a noted Wagner singer. The first tenor role he sang was Radames in *Aida* at the Royal Opera in Stockholm (1936). He was applauded at the 1938 Salzburg Festival as Walther in *Die Meistersinger* and as Tannhäuser. In 1940 he was offered a contract at the Metropolitan Opera, but was unable to accept it on account of the outbreak of World War II. In 1942 he sang as guest at La Scala and that summer he sang Siegfried in the *Ring* cycle at the Bayreuth Festival. He joined the Metropolitan Opera in 1946; guest appearances at Covent Garden, La Scala, and the Vienna State Opera distinguished his later career, which lasted for many years. In 1957 he was made director of the Royal Opera in Stockholm. He was married to the soprano Nini Högstedt. His powerful and flexibly expressive tenor voice found its best parts in the Wagner repertory.

Records: HMV and Decca (*Götterdämmerung* and Act I of *Die Walküre*). *U.S. re-issue:* RCA Victor, London, Electrola.

SVÉD, ALEXANDER, baritone, b. May 28, 1906, Budapest. He first studied violin at the Budapest Conservatory, then singing with Mario Sammarco and Riccardo Stracciari in Milan. He made his debut at the Budapest National Theater (1930). In 1935 he was engaged at the Vienna State Opera, through Felix Weingartner, and he sang there until 1939. In 1936 he appeared as guest at Covent Garden, in 1937 at the Salzburg Festival, and in 1938-40 at the Maggio Musicale Festival. During this time he was a regular guest at the Munich State Opera. After appearing at La Scala (1939-40), he came to the Metropolitan Opera, making his debut as Renato in *Un Ballo in Maschera.* For ten years he was very successful in New York and during this decade he also made frequent guest appearances in Italy. In 1951 he was admired as Hans Sachs in *Die Meistersinger* at the Rome Opera. After visiting his family in Hungary in 1951, he was denied permission to return to the United States. He then became a member of the Budapest National Opera. He made a concert tour of the United States subsequently in 1955. With a well-trained and expressive baritone voice, he was successful on the stage in both the Italian and French repertories and in Mozart parts.

Records: Polydor, Cetra, and RCA Victor*.

SWARTHOUT, GLADYS, contralto, b. Dec. 25, 1904, Deepwater, Mo.; d. July 7, 1969, Florence. She sang in church concerts when she was only thirteen years old. After her study at Bush Conservatory in Chicago, she made her debut at the Opera there (1924) as the Shepherd Boy in *Tosca.* At first she sang only smaller roles at Chicago, but in 1925 she sang Carmen in nearby Ravinia at the Summer Opera there. In 1929 she was engaged by the Metropolitan Opera, first singing La Cieca in *La Gioconda.* She stayed at the Metropolitan until 1945, a much-admired member of the company. She was especially liked as Carmen and Mignon. In 1934 she appeared at the Metropolitan in the world *première* of *Merry Mount.* She also had great success in films, the best-known of which was *Champagne Waltz.* After 1932 she was married to the baritone Frank Chapman (d. 1967). Guest appearances and concerts took her to San Francisco, Chicago, London, and Paris, all with great success. After 1940 she appeared chiefly as a concert singer and became known as one of the most famous interpreters of songs. A severe heart attack in 1954 required her to retire from musical life. She lived in Florence. Her autobiography appeared under the title *Come Soon, Tomorrow* (New York, 1945).

Records: RCA Victor*. *U.S. re-recording:* RCA Victor.

SWOLFS, LAURENT, tenor, b. 1867, Ghent, Belgium; d. Nov. 4, 1954, Ghent. He studied in Antwerp and Brussels and made his debut in Antwerp (1901) as Max in *Der Freischütz.* In 1903 he became principal tenor at the Théâtre de la Monnaie and sang there for over twenty years with great success. In 1908-09 he appeared at the Lyons Opera. In 1908, on the inducement of the composer-conductor Felix Weingartner, who had heard him in Antwerp, he sang the chief role in *Genesius* in its world *première* at the Vienna Imperial Opera. He had great success at the Paris Opéra as Samson in *Samson et Dalila* and as Siegmund in *Die Walküre* in 1910; in 1913 he repeated this success and also sang Loge in *Das Rheingold* there. Later he appeared as guest at the Opera in Nice. After the close of his career he lived in Ghent. He died as a result of a fall on the staircase of his house, caused by his great age and the fact that he was almost entirely blind. He had a strong and brilliant tenor voice.

Records: Pathé, Odeon, and Anker.

SYLVA, MARGUERITE, soprano, b. July 10, 1875, Brussels; d. Feb. 21, 1957, Glendale, Calif. She was the daughter of a Belgian physician of English origin. After her studies in Paris she made her debut in London as Carmen (1892). In the same year she was engaged at the Opéra-Comique, where she sang with great success, particularly as Carmen, until 1907. She was engaged at the Manhattan Opera (1909-11) and the critics compared her acting in the role of Carmen to that of the famous Emma Calvé. In 1911 she sang with the Chicago-Philadelphia Company, but in 1912 she returned to the Opéra-Comique. She made guest appearances in Berlin and Vienna and also became very successful in the field of operetta, appearing on Broadway in *Zigeunerliebe* (1908-09). She was a member of the Chicago Opera Company (1918-19) and in 1924 she opened the Hollywood Bowl with a performance of *Carmen.* Later she became a teacher and opera *régisseur* in New York, but also appeared on Broadway in small character parts and undertook appearances in films. After 1930 she lived in California, where she died as a result of an automobile accident. She had a powerfully expressive dramatic soprano voice and was especially noted as Carmen.

Records: Edison* cylinders (1901-12). The matrices of her two Edison discs were destroyed in a fire which swept the Edison plant in 1914.

SZABO, LUISA, soprano, b. 1904, Budapest; d. Nov. 19, 1934, Budapest. She studied at the Music Academy in her native Budapest and made her debut at the National Opera there (1927). In 1931 she sang as guest at the Berlin City Opera and had a magnificent success as the Queen of the Night in *Die Zauberflöte* under Bruno Walter. She sang the same role in Amsterdam in 1931 and on the German radio. Before her career had fully developed, she died during an operation. She had a coloratura soprano of extraordinary brilliance.

Records: Ultraphon and HMV. *U.S. re-issue:* RCA Victor.

SZANTHO, ENID, contralto, b. 1907, Budapest. After study at the Royal Academy of Music in Budapest, she made her debut (1928) at the Vienna State Opera and remained a member of that organization until 1939. She was especially famous as an interpreter of Wagner; at the Bayreuth Festivals she sang Erda and Waltraute in the *Ring* cycle (1930-37). In 1937 she was engaged by the Metropolitan Opera, but she sang there for only one year. She sang as guest and made concert appearances in all the noted music centers of the United States. She lives and teaches in New York. A highly expressive, dramatic contralto voice.

Records: One commercial record of her voice on Victor*; private recordings for the Metropolitan Opera.

SZEKÉLY, MIHÁLY, bass, b. 1900, Jaszherény, Hungary; d. Mar. 23, 1963, Budapest. He studied at the Budapest Conservatory with Geza Laszló and made his debut at the Opera there (1920) as Ferrando in *Il Trovatore.* He remained a celebrated member of this company until his death. He made guest appearances in Germany, Austria, and Italy, but particularly at the Vienna State Opera and at the 1937 Salzburg Festival. He was a member of the Metropolitan Opera (1946-50)

Székely

and made his debut there as Hunding in *Die Walküre*. After 1957 he sang at the Glyndebourne Festivals, particularly the roles of Osmin in *Die Entführung aus dem Serail* and Sarastro in *Die Zauberflöte*. He was applauded at the Holland Festivals as Bluebeard in *Duke Bluebeard's Castle*, which was his particular starring role. In 1957-58 he was briefly a member of the Munich State Opera, but he soon returned to Budapest.

Records: As early as 1929 he made records for Parlophone in Berlin; later he sang for Hungarian labels. In the LP era he sang for DGG and for Columbia (*Duke Bluebeard's Castle*). U.S. re-issue: Mercury, RCA Victor.

T

TACCANI, GIUSEPPE, tenor, b. 1885, Milan; d. May, 1959, Milan. He studied with Lelio Casini in Milan and made his debut (1905) at Bologna in the title role in *Andrea Chénier*. He was then very successful on the most important Italian stages, particularly at the Teatro dal Verme and at the Rome Opera, but he never sang at La Scala in Milan. He was highly applauded in guest appearances at the Teatro Colón, and in Madrid, Barcelona, and Rio de Janeiro. During the 1909-10 season he sang at the Metropolitan Opera. In 1916 he sang at the Teatro Lirico in the world *première* of *Suona la Ritrata* and in 1928 he sang the title role at the Genoa Opera in Boito's *Nerone*. His career lasted a long time; he appeared on the stage as late as 1940. He then lived and taught singing in Milan. He possessed a brilliant-sounding, heroic tenor voice.
Records: Columbia*, HMV, and Fonotipia. *U.S. re-issue:* Victor. *U.S. re-recording:* Eterna, Rocco, FRP, TAP.

TADDEI, GIUSEPPE, baritone, b. June 26, 1916, Genoa, Italy. He made his stage debut at the Rome Opera (1936) and even before World War II had his first successes on Italian stages, but his career was interrupted by the War. In 1946 he came to the Vienna State Opera, where he has since often appeared as guest. After guest appearances at the National Theater in Budapest, he developed a brilliantly successful career in the larger theaters in Italy, especially at La Scala, but also in Rome, Naples, Turin, and Venice. He sang at the Arena and Maggio Musicale Festivals. He has also had enormous success in his appearances at Covent Garden, at both opera houses in Paris, at the Teatro Colón, and at the Rio de Janeiro Opera. Since 1951 he has been a member of the Metropolitan Opera. He has a baritone voice of large volume and possesses a fine ability to use it in his characterizations, of which the most admired are Figaro in *Il Barbiere di Siviglia* and Don Giovanni.
Records: Cetra* (*La Bohème, Otello, Ernani, Un Ballo in Maschera, Gianni Schicchi*, and *Rigoletto*), Columbia* (*Le Nozze di Figaro* and *Don Giovanni*), and Philips (*Moïse et Pharaon* and *Tosca*). *U.S. re-issue:* Angel, Seraphim, Everest-Cetra, London.

TAGLIABUE, CARLO, baritone, b. Jan. 13, 1898, Mariano Comense, Italy. He made his debut (1920) at

Lodi as Amonasro in *Aïda*, and in 1924 had great success in the same role at the Genoa Opera. Thereafter he sang on the leading stages in Italy and at the Havana Opera (1929-30). In 1931 he made his first appearance at La Scala and remained there for more than twenty-five years as a principal baritone. His appearances at the Arena and Maggio Musicale Festivals were highly successful. In 1934 he appeared at the Rome Opera in the world *première* of *La Fiamma*. He was greatly admired in South America, where he made repeated appearances, especially at the Teatro Colón. He was a member of the Metropolitan Opera (1937-39). In 1938 he sang as guest at Covent Garden and during World War II on several German stages. After the war he concentrated his activity in the principal Italian opera houses.

Records: Cetra* (*La Forza del Destino, La Favorita, Martha, I Pagliacci, Il Trovatore*, and *Francesca da Rimini*, by Zandonai), and Columbia* (*Norma* and *La Forza del Destino*, both with Maria Callas). *U.S. re-issue:* Angel, Everest-Cetra.

TAGLIAVINI, FERRUCCIO, tenor, b. Aug. 14, 1913, Reggio Emilia, Italy. He studied at the Conservatory in Parma with Brancucci and in Florence with Amadeo Bassi and made his stage debut (1939) at the Florence Opera as Rodolfo in *La Bohème*. By 1940 he was already a source of admiration at La Scala. In 1941 he married the soprano Pia Tassinari, whom he had come to know during a guest engagement at the Teatro Massimo. In the years after World War II he was acclaimed in all the great opera houses of the world. He sang as guest at Covent Garden, the Teatro Colón, the Vienna State Opera, and in Rio de Janeiro, Brussels, Paris, Chicago, and San Francisco, as well as at the Arena and Maggio Musicale Festivals. He was very successful at the Metropolitan Opera (1946-50), making his debut as Rodolfo in *La Bohème*. Since 1951 he has lived in the United States. He had a well-trained and highly expressive lyric tenor voice and he specialized in the operas of Bellini, Donizetti, and Rossini.

Records: Cetra* (*La Sonnambula, Martha, La Bohème, L'Arlesiana, Tosca, Rigoletto*, and *Un Ballo in Maschera*), RCA Victor*, and Columbia (*Lucia di Lammermoor*). *U.S. re-issue:* Angel, Everest-Cetra.

TAJO, ITALO, bass, b. Apr. 25, 1915, Pinerolo, Italy. He made his debut (1935) at the Turin Opera as Fafnir in *Das Rheingold*, but then had to complete his military service. In 1939 he again appeared on the stage and had great success in the leading Italian theaters. He was applauded at La Scala and at the Rome Opera, as well as at the Arena and Maggio Musicale Festivals. After World War II he began his great international career with guest appearances at Covent Garden, the Paris Opéra, the Teatro Colón, and the leading German opera houses. After 1949 he was a member of the Metropolitan Opera and his concert tours also brought him great success in Europe and in both North and South America. He had a large-dimensioned bass voice, outstanding for his technical management of it. He has been heard in over eight roles, but is especially admired as an interpreter of Mozart.

Records: Cetra* (*Don Giovanni*), RCA Victor* (*Rigoletto*), and HMV. *U.S. re-recording:* Telefunken, Seraphim, Everest-Cetra.

TALÉN, BJÖRN, tenor, b. Nov. 8, 1890, Oslo, Norway; d. July 12, 1947, Bergen, Norway. He completed the military academy course in Oslo and was an officer in the Norwegian army. He studied singing (1914-15) with Sebastianini in Naples and made his debut in Oslo in the latter year. He sang in Norway until 1920 and then was a member of the Berlin State Opera (1921-28) and the Berlin City Opera (1929-32). He sang as guest in Copenhagen, Stockholm, Zürich, Hamburg, and in Spain; he appeared in parts from the Italian repertory as well as in such Wagner roles as Walther in *Die Meistersinger* and Lohengrin.

Records: Vox, Odeon, and Kristall. *U.S. re-issue:* American Decca.

TALLEY, MARION, soprano, b. Dec. 20, 1906, Nevada, Mo. She was a musical prodigy who began to sing at the age of five; by the time she was fifteen she had already given a concert in Kansas City. She then studied with Frank La Forge in New York City, where she also gave concerts. After a student trip through Europe, she made her debut at the Metropolitan Opera (1926) as Gilda in *Rigoletto*. She received sensational acclaim from the public and the critics. She was a member of the Metropolitan for the following three seasons and appeared in *Mignon, Le Rossignol, Il Barbiere di Siviglia,* and *Les Contes De Hoffmann* among others. A triumphal tour of the United States in 1928 marked the high point of her career, which ended as quickly as it had begun. In 1933 she sang Gilda at the Chicago Opera, but entirely without success. In 1934 she made a film, *Follow Your Heart,* and later had a weekly program on radio. She withdrew from musical life and lives in Hollywood. She had a well-trained and brilliant coloratura voice.

Records: Victor*.

TALVELA, MARTTI, bass, b. Feb. 4, 1935, Hiitola, Finland. At first an elementary school teacher, he studied singing at the Conservatory in Lahti and with Carl Martin Öhmann in Stockholm. He made his debut (1960) as a guest at the National Opera in Helsinki as Sparafucile in *Rigoletto*. He was a member of the Royal Opera in Stockholm (1961-62) and since 1962 has been engaged at the Berlin City Opera. In 1962 he sang Titurel in *Parsifal* at the Bayreuth Festival and in 1964 the Landgraf in *Tannhäuser*. He has sung at La Scala as the Grand Inquisitor in *Don Carlos* and in Helsinki, Rome, and Bordeaux. As a concert singer he has toured Germany, Sweden, Finland, and the Soviet Union.

Records: Philips (Titurel in *Parsifal*) and DGG*. *U.S. re-issue:* London.

TAMAGNO, FRANCESCO, tenor, b. Dec. 28, 1850, Turin, Italy; d. Aug. 31, 1905, Varese, Italy. He was one of fifteen children of an innkeeper in Turin and sang there first in the opera chorus at the Teatro Regio. After completing his military service, he studied singing with Perotti in Palermo, where he made his debut at the Teatro Massimo (1874). He then had great successes on the leading Italian stages, particularly at La Scala. Verdi admired his voice and called him "unique in the whole world." In 1881 he was acclaimed at La Scala for his singing of the title role in *Ernani* and in the same year he sang the role of Gabriele Adorno there in the newly revised version of *Simone Boccanegra*; in 1884 he also sang the title role in the newly revised *Don Carlos* there. He reached the high point of his career when he was chosen to create the role of Otello in the world *première* at La Scala on Feb. 5, 1887. In this role no successor has ever matched his performance. Guest appearances brought him enormous triumphs in all the largest opera houses; he sang in Paris, London, Monte Carlo, Vienna, St. Petersburg, and Moscow. In 1894-95 he was the marvel of New York in his performances as Otello and Samson at the Metropolitan Opera. In 1899 he sang at Monte Carlo in the world *première* of *Messaline*. A severe heart attack in 1898 left a noticeable mark on the great singer. In 1901 he sang Otello again at Covent Garden and in 1902 he appeared in a concert at La Scala. He then retired to his villa in Varese. The voice of Francesco Tamagno incorporated within it the ideal of the heroic tenor. The basic weight of the voice, its driving dramatic force, and the brilliance in the upper registers are, even on records, truly remarkable.

Records: G & T in 1903 and a few more in 1905; all are of great documentary value. *U.S. re-issue:* Victor, Opera Disc, IRCC. *U.S. re-recording:* RCA Victor, Rococo, Belcanto, Cantilena, Olympus, ASCO, TAP.

TÄNZLER, HANS, tenor, b. 1897, Berlin; d. Sept. 25, 1953, Berlin. He at first planned to become an architect, but then decided to study singing with Teresa Emrich in Berlin. He made his debut (1903) in Danzig and sang successively in Elberfeld (1905-06), Graz (1906-07), and Karlsruhe (1907-12). He appeared as guest at the Munich Royal Opera (1907-09) and at the Vienna Imperial Opera (1906; 1908; 1912). He also sang in Paris, Budapest, Warsaw, and (1914) at the Berlin Imperial Opera. During the 1920's he immigrated to the United States and settled as a teacher in Los Angeles. In 1928-30 he took part in the tour of the German Opera Company and again had great success, especially as a Wagner tenor. Later he returned to Los Angeles with the plan of building an opera house, the plan of which he had drawn himself. When this did not materialize, he returned to Germany in 1939 and worked as a singing teacher. He had a well-managed heroic tenor voice.

Records: Odeon and Pathé.

TASSINARI, PIA, soprano-contralto, b. Sept. 15, 1909, Modigliana, Italy. She studied with Cesar Vezzani in Bologna, with Marcantoni in Milan, and made her debut (1929) at Castel Monferrato as Mimi in *La Bohème*. She had arrived at La Scala by 1930 and she sang there for the next twenty years with great success. She sang there in such world *premières* as *Don Giovanni*, by Lattuada, *La Farsa Amorosa*, and *Notturno Romantico*. In 1940 she married the tenor Ferruccio Tagliavini, whom she had met when they were both making guest appearances at the Teatro Massimo. After World War II they sang a great deal in South America, especially at the Teatro Colón. She was engaged at the Metropolitan Opera (1947-48), and in 1948 she was applauded at the Chicago Opera as Marguerite in *Faust*. She also sang at the Arena and Maggio Musicale Festivals. After 1952 she sang contralto roles and had an important career in Italy as a contralto.

Records: As a soprano she recorded for HMV, Fonit, and Cetra; as a contralto for Cetra* (*Un Ballo in Maschera*, *L'Arlesiana*, and *Martha*). *U.S. re-issue:* American Columbia.

TAUBER, RICHARD, tenor, b. May 16, 1892, Linz, Austria; d. Jan. 8, 1948, London. He first studied at Hoch's Conservatory in Frankfurt and planned to become a conductor, but he then studied singing with Karl Beines in Freiburg im. Br. and made his debut (1913) at Chemnitz as Tamino in *Die Zauberflöte*. Through the intendant of the Dresden Royal Opera, Count von Seebach, he was engaged for that house in the same year. There the young singer had brilliant successes. In 1919 he became a member of the Berlin State Opera and after 1925 he was concurrently a member of the Vienna State Opera. He was acclaimed at the Festivals in Salzburg and Munich as a great interpreter of Mozart. In 1924 he met Franz Lehár in Berlin and a great friendship sprang up between them. Lehár wrote the tenor parts in many of his operettas for Tauber, including *Paganini, Der Zarewitsch, Friederike,* and *Das Land des Lächelns.* Tauber sang in the world *premières* of most of these and so gained not only in Germany but in the entire world an almost unbelievable popularity. In the role of Prince Sou-Chong in *Das Land des Lächelns* alone, he appeared more than nine hundred times. He also earned great success as a film singer. He made extremely successful American tours (1931; 1938; 1947), and he visited Canada, South Africa, South America, and Australia. Because he was Jewish, he was required to leave Germany in 1933 and Austria in 1938; he then lived in London. There he sang particularly in the concert hall, but after World War II he returned to opera. In 1947 Tauber, already seriously ill, sang Don Ottavio in *Don Giovanni* at Covent Garden. He was first married to the operetta soprano Carlotta Vanconti (1892-1964) and then to the actress Diana Napier. He had one of the most beautiful lyric tenor voices preserved on records. He was unmatched in the richness of nuance in his characterizations and in the ease of his tone production.

Records: Odeon. *U.S. re-issue:* Okeh, American Columbia, American Decca. *U.S. re-recording:* Capitol, American Decca, Scala, TAP, Design, Electrola, FRP, Eterna, ASCO, Seraphim, Rococo.

TAUBEROVÁ, MARIA, soprano, b. 1914, Vysoké Mýto, in what is now Czechoslovakia. She came as a child to Vienna, where she studied piano at the Vienna Academy of Music and singing with Ferdinand Rebay. In 1934 she concluded her singing studies with Fernando Carpo in Milan and made her concert debut in Prague (1934), singing the solo part in Mahler's *Second Symphony* under Bruno Walter. She made her stage debut also in Prague at the National Theater as Gilda in *Rigoletto* (1936). She remained thereafter a member of that company for over twenty-five years. She sang as guest at Monte Carlo (1937-38) and later in Geneva, Lausanne, Oslo, London, and Berlin. In 1946 she made guest appearances with her husband, the well-known conductor Jaroslav Krombholc, at the Rio de Janeiro Opera. She was a frequent guest at the Vienna State Opera and in 1957 she made a tour of Russia with the Czech Philharmonic Orchestra and appeared in Budapest, Bucharest, and Sofia. In 1959 she was named a National Artist by the Czechoslovakian government.

Records: Supraphon (*Rusalka, Two Widows,* and *The Storm*).

TAUBMANN, HORST, tenor, b. Feb. 14, 1912, Pirna, Germany. He studied in Dresden and made his debut (1935) at Chemnitz as Lionel in *Martha.* After engagements in Stuttgart and Freiburg im Br. he came to the Munich State Opera (1939). He had his first great success there as Lohengrin. In 1942 he sang the role of Flamand in the world *première* in Munich of *Capriccio;* in the same year he sang Matteo in *Arabella* at the Salzburg Festival. He remained a member of the Munich State Opera until 1945; after that he made guest appearances there and at the Vienna State Opera. In 1947 he created the role

of Camille in the world *première* of *Dantons Tod* at the Salzburg Festival. He later worked in a large electrical company in Munich.
Records: DGG. U.S. re-issue: Haydn Society, Vox.

TAUCHER, CURT, tenor, b. Oct. 25, 1885, Nuremberg, Germany; d. Aug. 7, 1954, Munich. A pupil of Heinrich Hermann in Munich he made his debut (1908) in Augsburg as Faust in Gounod's opera. He sang at Augsburg until 1912, at Chemnitz (1912-15), Hannover (1915-20), and in 1920 he went to the Dresden State Opera. On that stage he sang Menelaus in the world *première* of *Die Ägyptische Helena* (1928). He also became a well-known Wagner tenor and sang at the Metropolitan Opera (1923-27), making his debut as Siegmund in *Die Walküre*. In New York, on March 3, 1925, in a performance of *Siegfried*, he stepped into a stage trap door which had been left open accidentally after the exit of Erda and in spite of painful injuries he continued to sing the performance to the end. Guest appearances took him to Covent Garden, the Teatro Liceo, the State Operas in Berlin and Munich, and to Zürich and Helsinki. In 1935 he gave up his career and lived thereafter on his estate near Bad Aibling in Bavaria.
Records: Polydor and Parlophone.

TEBALDI, RENATA, soprano, b. Feb. 1, 1922, Pesaro, Italy. She was ill as a child with poliomyelitis, but studied singing at the Parma Conservatory and later with Carmen Melis. She made her debut (1943) in Rovigo as Elena in *Mefistofele*. After World War II she was assisted by Arturo Toscanini, who had heard her in 1946 and had engaged her for La Scala, where she has since been greatly admired. She became a world-famous singer and after 1950 appeared as guest at Covent Garden, the Vienna State Opera, in Paris, Rome, Naples, and Barcelona, being paid homage by the public everywhere. In 1951 she made a guest appearance in San Francisco, her first in the United States. She accepted an engagement at the Metropolitan Opera (1955) and has since gone from one triumph to another there as she has done at Chicago since 1956. She has been highly applauded in South America, particularly at the Teatro Colón and in Rio de Janeiro. Concert tours have taken her to Spain, Portugal, Germany, Holland, France, and to both North and South America. Renata Tebaldi possesses one of the most beautiful soprano voices of her time, outstanding both for her clean intonation and for the elegance of her portrayals. She is admired as a Verdi and Puccini interpreter of the first rank.

Records: She recorded first for Fonit, then made a great many records for Decca (including *La Bohème, Tosca, Madama Butterfly, Manon Lescaut, Turandot, Aïda, La Traviata, Il Trovatore, Otello, Adriana Lecouvreur,* and *Andrea Chénier*), and RCA Victor* (*Cavalleria Rusticana*). U.S. re-issue: London, Richmond, Everest-Cetra, United Artists, American Decca.

TEDESCHI, ALFIO, tenor, b. Jan. 4, 1882, Palermo, Sicily; d. March, 1967, Milan. He made his debut (1903) in Asti in *La Sonnambula*. In the next two decades he had a successful career as a lyric tenor on the larger Italian provincial stages. In 1915 and 1917 he sang as guest at the Teatro Colón. In 1925 he came to the Metropolitan Opera, his debut role being Léopold in *La Juive*; he remained there until 1935. He sang there under the name Alfio Tedesco and principally filled smaller roles; but he was also entrusted with important parts. In 1935 he returned to Italy and, under his real name, Alfio Tedeschi, came to La Scala, where he interpreted character parts, such as Dr. Caius in *Falstaff* and Pong in *Turandot*. He sang the former role at the Salzburg Festivals (1936; 1938-39). His career lasted a long time; in 1948 he was still singing at the Teatro Colón. In 1951 he retired to the Casa di Riposo, founded by Verdi in Milan.

Records: Pathé* and Beka from the beginning of his career; one electric record of an ensemble scene for Victor*.

TEGETHOFF, ELSE (*see* Rusiczka, Else)

TELLINI, INES ALFANI-, soprano, b. 1900 (?), Florence, Italy. She made her debut (1921) at the Teatro della Pergola. After she had scored a great success in 1923 at the Teatro Regio in Parma as Ann Ford in *Falstaff*, Toscanini engaged her for the same role in a production of the opera at La Scala in December, 1923. She had a great career thereafter at La Scala and in 1929 she joined with this company for a series of guest appearances in Berlin. She sang as guest at the Teatro Colón in 1928; her greatest honors, however, came in Italian theaters. She specialized in parts from the Mozartian and classic repertories. An admired concert soprano, she gave up her stage career in 1942 and thereafter sang in concerts and taught at the Accademia Chigiana in Siena.

Records: Columbia* (*Falstaff* under Toscanini and Micaëla in *Carmen*) and a few records for HMV. *U.S. re-recording:* Eterna.

TELVA, MARIAN, contralto, b. Dec. 26, 1897, St. Louis, Mo.; d. Oct. 23, 1962, Norwalk, Conn. Originally Marian Toucke. She first sang in church concerts in St. Louis and was discovered by Ernestine Schumann-Heink. After a single year of study in New York, she made her debut at the Metropolitan Opera (1920) as the Italian Singer in *Manon Lescaut*. She remained a member of that house until 1930 and, after first singing small roles, took over more important ones. She had her first great success in 1927 when she sang Adalgisa in *Norma* with Rosa Ponselle in the title role. After her marriage to an industrial magnate, the owner of the Wells-Fargo Company, she gave up her career at first, but she again signed a contract with the Metropolitan in 1933. She sang only one concert there, however. In 1923 she sang in the Summer Opera at Ravinia, near Chicago; she was also considered to be one of the most famous American oratorio and song interpreters of her time. She gave her last concert in New York in 1936.

Records: One record for Victor* (a duet from *Norma* with Rosa Ponselle). She made private recordings of songs, some with translations and piano accompaniments by Geraldine Farrar. *U.S. re-issue:* IRCC. *U.S. re-recording:* RCA Victor, Camden, IRC.

TERKAL, KARL, tenor, b. 1919, Vienna. He studied cabinetmaking, but when work was scarce he roamed Vienna as a street singer. In 1937 he won first prize in a competition among Viennese street singers, which was conducted by the Schubert Association. After the end of World War II he resumed his cabinetmaking, then decided to study singing. In 1949 the conductor Clemens Krauss took him to the State Opera, of which he has since been a member. He has frequently sung at the Vienna Volksoper and has also had success as an operetta singer.

Records: A great many records for Columbia, HMV, Decca, and Philips; on these he has sung in complete operas, but mostly in small roles. *U.S. re-issue:* Angel, Epic.

TERNINA, MILKA, soprano, b. Dec. 19, 1863, Vezicze, Austria; d. May 18, 1941, Zagreb, Yugoslavia. She studied with Joseph Gänsbacher in Vienna and made her debut (1882) in Agram. She sang at Leipzig (1883-84), Graz (1884-86), Bremen (1886-89), and at the Munich Royal Opera (1890-99), where she had great success. In 1899 she was a source of great admiration at the Bayreuth Festival for her Kundry in *Parsifal*. In 1900 she created the role of Tosca in its English *première* at Covent Garden. She was engaged at the Metropolitan Opera (1899) and sang New York's first Tosca there in 1900. In 1903 she sang Kundry in the first American performance of *Parsifal*, a production which had been forbidden in Bayreuth. She had great success at the Metropolitan until 1904, but in that year she was forced to give up her stage career on account of a paralysis of the nerves of the eye. She lived thereafter as a teacher of singing in Zagreb; among her pupils was the soprano Zinka Milanov.

Records: There are no disc records of the voice of this famous singer, only a fragment on a Mapleson cylinder. *U.S. re-recording:* IRCC.

TERVANI, IRMA, contralto, b. June 4, 1887, Helsinki, Finland; d. Oct. 29, 1936, Berlin. She was a daughter of the Finnish soprano Emmy Strömer-Ackté (1850-1924), and a sister of the famous soprano Aïno Ackté. She was trained by her mother and then studied in Paris and Dresden. She made her debut (1908) at the Dresden Royal Opera as Dalila in *Samson et Dalila*. Until her retirement from the stage in 1932 she was active as principal contralto at Dresden. She was married to the actor Paul Wiecke, and her daughter, Maria, also chose to become an actress. Irma Tervani had great success in her guest appearances, including the Frankfurt Opera (1910), when she sang her starring role, Carmen, opposite Enrico Caruso. She was frequently heard in Finland.

Records: One record for G & T (Helsinki, 1907) on it she sings a Finnish folk song under the name Irma Ackté.

TESCHEMACHER, MARGARETHE, soprano, b. Mar. 3, 1903, Cologne; d. May 19, 1959, Bad Weissee, Germany. She studied at the Conservatory in Cologne and made her debut at the Opera there (1924) as Micaëla in *Carmen*. She then sang successively at Aachen (1925-27), Dortmund (1927-28), Mannheim (1928-31), and the Stuttgart State Opera (1931-43). In 1934 she was engaged at the Dresden State Opera and had great international success. In 1938 she sang the title role in the world *première* there of *Daphne* opposite Torsten Ralf. She also sang at the Salzburg Festival. In 1934 she sang the title role in the first performance of *Arabella* at the Teatro Colón. She was greatly applauded at Covent Garden in 1936 for her singing of the Countess in *Le Nozze di Figaro* and Donna Elvira in *Don Giovanni*. She appeared as guest at La Scala, at the Teatro Liceo, the Chicago Opera, and at the State Operas in Berlin, Vienna, and Munich. In 1943 she married the painter Richard Panzer. After World War II she was engaged at the Düsseldorf Opera in a guest-appearance contract. She was admired for the lightness of her lyric-dramatic voice and for the wide range of her skillfully presented characterizations.

Records: HMV, Urania (*Der Corregidor* and *The Taming of the*

Tetrazzini · Teyte

Shrew), and DGG (*Don Giovanni*). *U.S. re-issue:* RCA Victor. *U.S. re-recording:* Eterna, Electrola.

TETRAZZINI, LUISA, soprano, b. June 28, 1871, Florence, Italy; d. Apr. 4, 1940, Milan. She first studied singing under her sister, Eva Tetrazzini-Campanini (1862-1938), who was also a highly successful opera singer, and her further training followed at the Liceo Musicale in Florence. In 1892 she made her debut there as Inez in *L'Africaine*. She was able to succeed only after great difficulty. After she had appeared in the smaller opera houses in Italy, she made a tour of South America (1898) and sang as guest in San Francisco (1903). In 1907 she finally had a sensational success at Covent Garden as Violetta in *La Traviata*. From there she went from one triumph to another in all the great musical centers of the world. In 1908 she came to the Manhattan Opera House and she was a member of the Metropolitan Opera (1911-12). In the following years she had her greatest successes at Covent Garden and at the Chicago Opera. Guest appearances and concerts took her to many countries. In 1925 she was the center of attraction in the first concert broadcast by the British radio. The career of this celebrated coloratura lasted a long time. She bade farewell to the stage in 1934 and then taught singing in Rome and Milan. She published her memoirs, *La mia vita di canto* (Milan, 1921) and a textbook on singing, *How to Sing* (New York, 1923). One of the most outstanding coloratura voices of the twentieth century; she cannot be admired enough for the exactitude of her ornamental singing and for her unmatchable staccato technique.

Records: Zonophone* (1904-05); after 1908 she made a great many records for HMV and Victor*. *U.S. re-issue:* Victor; RCA Victor, Opera Disc, HRS, IRCC. *U.S. re-recording:* Scala, Rococo, Angel, Belcanto, Olympus, FRP, TAP, ASCO.

TEYTE, MAGGIE, soprano, b. Apr. 17, 1889, Wolverhampton, England. Originally Maggie Tate. She studied at the Royal College of Music in London and after 1905 with Jean de Reszke in Paris. She made her debut (1907) at the Monte Carlo Opera as Zerlina in *Don Giovanni*. In 1908 she came to the Opéra-Comique, where she made her debut in the title role of *Circé* in the world *première* of this work. She had sensational success at the Opéra-Comique, where she remained until 1910, as Mélisande in *Pelléas et Mélisande*. Debussy himself, who often accompanied her at the piano in her song recitals, hailed her as the successor to Mary Garden, who had created the role. She sang as guest at Covent Garden (1910-11) and was a celebrated member of the Chicago Opera Company (1911-14) and, until 1917, the Boston Opera Company. After World War I she returned to England, giving only a few concerts, and, after her marriage, she withdrew from musical life. In 1930 she returned to Covent Garden as Mélisande and renewed her former triumphs there. In the next decade she was celebrated in England both on the stage and in the concert hall, and during World War II she gave concerts for soldiers in England. Her career lasted for many years. In 1946 she toured the United States and in 1948 sang Mélisande with the New York City Opera Company. Her last role on the stage was that of Belinda in *Dido and Aeneas* at London's Mermaid Theater in 1951. In 1954 she again undertook concert tours of England and the United States. She was made a Dame of the British Empire by Queen Elizabeth II. Her memoirs appeared as *Star on the Door* (London, 1958). She had a lyric soprano voice of exquisite beauty and was a great interpreter of French art songs.

Records: Edison* discs, American Columbia*, Decca, HMV, and RCA Victor*. *U.S. re-issue:* American Decca, Gramophone Shop. *U.S. re-recording:* Angel, London, RCA Victor, Seraphim.

THEBOM, BLANCHE, contralto, b. Sept. 19, 1918, Monessen, Pa. She came of a Swedish family and studied in New York with Margarethe Matzenauer and Edyth Walker. She made her debut (1941) as a concert contralto. In 1944 she made her stage debut at the Metropolitan Opera as Fricka in *Die Walküre*. She has since retained her membership at the Metropolitan. Her international fame sprang from guest appearances at Covent Garden, the Paris Opéra, and in Milan, Rome, and Brussels. She sang Dorabella in *Così fan tutte* at the Glyndebourne Festival in 1950 and in 1957 was greatly applauded at Covent Garden as Dido in *Les Troyens*. In 1958 she made a brilliantly successful tour of Russia. She is also well known as an interpreter of contemporary music.

Records: RCA Victor*, HMV (including *Tristan und Isolde* with Kirsten Flagstad), and Columbia* (*The Rake's Progress*). *U.S. re-issue:* Angel.

THEODORINI, ELENA, soprano, b. 1858, Krajova, Rumania; d. 1926, Rio de Janeiro. Her parents were actors. She studied singing at the Milan Conservatory with Sangiovanni and made her debut in Cuneo (1877) as a mezzo-soprano singing Gondi in *Maria di Rohan*. In the next two years she sang mezzo roles in Alessandria, Livorno, Pisa, Chieti, and at the Bucharest Opera. In 1879 she made her debut at the Teatro dal Verme as Marie in *La Fille du Régiment* and in the same season also sang Rachel in *La Juive* there. In 1880 she made her debut at La Scala as Marguerite in *Faust* and in 1881 sang Valentine in *Les Huguenots*. In the following decade she had a brilliant career, particularly at the most important Italian theaters. In 1890-91 she sang again at La Scala, this time in the *verismo* opera *Mala Pasqua*. Thereafter she gave only concerts. Later she lived and taught singing in Rio de Janeiro and counted among her pupils the soprano Bidu Sayao. Her wide-ranging and large soprano voice was used to master a repertory of unusual variety.

Records: In 1903 she made five titles for G & T in Milan; she then made two records for Odeon, which were published in Athens under the name Elena Theodorides. All are of the greatest rarity.

THILL, GEORGES, tenor, b. Dec. 14, 1897, Paris. He studied at the National Conservatory there and with Fernando de Lucia in Naples. He made his debut (1924) at the Paris Opéra as Nicias in *Thaïs*. In 1928 he had a sensational success there as Kalaf in *Turandot*, a part which he also sang that year at the Arena Festival. He was then called to La Scala, where he was greatly admired in tenor roles from both the French and Italian repertories. He was applauded, particularly in French parts, at the Metropolitan Opera (1930-32). He had many successes at the Teatro Colón, as he did generally in South America. He later sang as guest at Covent Garden, the Vienna State Opera, the Royal Opera in Stockholm, and he was successful as a concert singer in Brussels. He was to be heard at the two great Paris opera houses until after World War II. The most celebrated French tenor of his epoch, he was noted for the expressiveness of his voice and for its brilliant timbre.

Records: Columbia* (*Carmen Werther,* and *Louise*). *U.S. re-recording:* TAP, Pathé-Marconi, Rococo.

THOMAS, JESS, tenor, b. Aug. 4, 1928, San Francisco. He studied at Stanford University and became a child psychologist and an educational adviser. He then studied singing and made his debut in San Francisco (1957). In 1958 he was engaged by the City Theater in Karlsruhe. He worked at the Munich Festival in 1960; in 1961 he sang Parsifal at the Bayreuth Festival and the next year he sang the same role and added that of Lohengrin. He made guest appearances at the State Operas in Vienna, Munich, and Stuttgart. In the opening performance of the newly rebuilt Munich State Opera in 1963 he sang the Emperor in *Die Frau ohne Schatten.* Since 1963 he has been a member of the Metropolitan Opera, where he first sang Walther in *Die Meistersinger.* At the 1965 Salzburg Festival he sang Bacchus in *Ariadne auf Naxos.* He has a heroic tenor voice, admired in Wagner roles.

Records: Electrola (*Lohengrin*), DGG* (*Die Frau ohne Schatten*), and Ariola. *U.S. re-issue:* RCA Victor, Angel, Philips.

THOMAS, JOHN CHARLES, baritone, b. Sept. 6, 1891, Meyersdale, Va.; d. December, 1960, New York. He studied with Adelin Fermin in New York City and was first an extremely successful operetta singer. In 1924 he went to Europe and after a single concert in Brussels was engaged by the Brussels Opera, where he sang with great success until 1928. In that year he returned to the United States and first gave concerts and sang at the opera houses in Philadelphia, San Francisco, and Chicago. He was engaged at the Metropolitan Opera in 1934, making his debut there as the elder Germont in *La Traviata* and remaining until 1943. During this time he increased his international reputation by concerts and guest appearances abroad. In 1950 he made a tour of Australia. He spent his last years as a teacher in New York City. He had a luxuriant baritone voice of great power and intensity of expression. He was especially admired in the Italian repertory.

Records: Vocalion*, Brunswick*, and RCA Victor*. One unpublished Edison disc. *U.S. re-recording:* RCA Victor, Word.

THORBORG, KERSTIN, contralto, b. May 19, 1896, Venjan, Sweden. She studied at the Royal Conservatory in Stockholm and made her debut at the Royal Opera there (1924) as Ortrud in *Lohengrin.* She remained in Stockholm until 1930 and then sang at the Prague Opera (1930-32) and at the Berlin City Opera (1933-35). In 1935 she was engaged at the Vienna State Opera, where she had great success. She frequently appeared at the Salzburg Festivals, where she sang Brangäne in *Tristan und Isolde* (1935), Orphée in *Orphée et Eurydice,* Magdalena in *Die Meistersinger* (1936), and Eglantine in *Euryanthe* (1937). She remained at the Vienna State Opera until 1938, when she came to the Metropolitan Opera; there she made her debut as Fricka in *Die Walküre* and she remained until 1950. She made very successful guest appearances at Covent Garden, in Paris, Brussels, Berlin, and Munich. She also made concert tours of the United States, Canada, and Europe. Since 1950 she has lived and taught in Stockholm. Her contralto voice was noted for the beauty of her singing and for the exciting quality of her acting. She was particularly admired as an interpreter of Wagner.

Records: HMV, Odeon, Columbia* (*Das Lied von der Erde*, by Mahler), and RCA Victor*. *U.S. re-issue:* American Decca.

THORNTON, EDNA, contralto, b. 1875, Bradford, England; d. 1958, Brighton, England. She began her studies with Mme. Lemmens-Sherrington in Manchester and then studied with Sir Charles Santley in London. She made her debut (1899) at Daly's Theater in London. In 1904 she sang at Covent Garden and was thereafter very successful there; she sang there in the first complete production of the *Ring* cycle (1910). During World War I she was one of the important artists of the Beecham Opera Company and her voice was highly esteemed by Sir Thomas. In 1919 she was again applauded at Covent Garden in *Prince Igor*. She undertook a long tour with the Quinlan Opera Company through Canada, Australia, and Africa. After the close of her career she taught singing in London.

Records: Zonophone, Odeon, G & T, and HMV (including ensembles with Nellie Melba and John McCormack). *U.S. re-recording:* ASCO.

TIBBETT, LAWRENCE, baritone, b. Nov. 16, 1896, Bakersfield, Calif.; d. July 15, 1960, New York. He passed his youth in Los Angeles, where he studied singing with Basil Ruysdael. After 1921 he appeared as a concert singer and in 1923 he continued the study of singing with Frank La Forge in New York. That year he was engaged by the Metropolitan Opera and made his debut there in a small role in *Boris Godounov*. When he sang Ford in *Falstaff* there on Jan. 2, 1925, the public accorded him a stormy ovation. Thereafter he had brilliant successes on this stage. He sang there in the world *première* of various operas *The King's Henchman* (1927), *Peter Ibbetson* (1931), *The Emperor Jones* (1933), and *Merry Mount* (1934). In 1937 he sang Scarpia in *Tosca* as guest at Covent Garden and his concerts and guest appearances took him to all the international music centers and as far as Australia and New Zealand. As early as 1930 he was appearing in sound films and was highly successful in this medium. After a vocal crisis in 1940 he was to be heard only rarely, but remained a member of the Metropolitan Opera until 1949. He died as a result of a traffic accident. He had a baritone voice of great power and impressive dramatic skill.

Records: Victor*. *U.S. re-issue:* RCA Victor. *U.S. re-recording:* RCA Victor, TAP, Camden, RCA Victrola, Rococo.

TIKALOVÁ, DRAHOMIRA, soprano, b. May 9, 1915, Berlin. A child of Czech parents, she passed her youth in the Moravian city of Hodonin and then studied medicine at the University of Brno. She gave up these studies, however, and studied singing with Theodor Cernik there. In 1937 she began her stage career at an operetta theater in Brno. In 1942 she appeared as guest at the National Theater in Prague, singing the role of Vendulka in *The Kiss*; in the same year she was engaged there and has since remained at that theater. She is especially admired as an interpreter of the classic soprano roles in the Czech repertory, namely, Marie in *The Bartered Bride* and the title role in *Jenufa*. She sang the role of Jenufa very successfully in guest appearances in Vienna and Amsterdam in 1961.

Records: Supraphon. *U.S. re-issue:* Bruno, Artia, Colosseum

TOBIN, EUGENE, tenor, b. 1925 (?), Philadelphia. After his study of singing in New York, he had his first success during his engagement at the Düsseldorf Opera (1952-54). Since 1954 he has been a member of the Stuttgart State Opera and in

1961 he sang Cavaradossi in *Tosca* opposite Renata Tebaldi there. He sang small roles at the Bayreuth Festivals (1953-54) and Canio in *I Pagliacci* at the Vienna State Opera (1959); in the same year he appeared as Erik in *Der Fliegende Holländer* at the Chicago Opera and in 1960 he sang Riccardo in *Un Ballo in Maschera* at the Cologne Opera. He has a powerful tenor voice and is especially at home in the heroic roles in the Italian repertory.
Records: Telefunken.

TOKATYAN, ARMAND, tenor, b. June 16, 1895, Plovdiv, Bulgaria; d. July 12, 1960, Pasadena, Calif. His family was of Armenian extraction and later moved to Alexandria, Egypt, where he made his debut (1914). In 1921 he went to Italy and had great success at theaters there. In 1923 he was engaged by the Metropolitan Opera, remaining a member of that organization until 1946. During these years he sang also in San Francisco, Chicago, and Los Angeles. In 1934 he was greatly admired as Kalaf in *Turandot* at Covent Garden. In the course of his career he sang in Germany, Austria, Italy, Hungary, and Czechoslovakia. He was a greatly admired tenor in both the French and Italian repertories.
Records: Vocalion* and Victor*. *U.S. re-recording:* Record Album.

TÖPPER, HERTHA, contralto, b. Apr. 19, 1924, Graz, Austria. She completed her studies at the Graz Conservatory and made her debut there (1945), remaining until 1951. Since 1951 she has been a member of the Bavarian State Opera in Munich. She sang Brangäne in *Tristan und Isolde* and several contralto parts in the *Ring* cycle at the Bayreuth Festivals (1951-52); she has also sung at the Salzburg Festival. Guest appearances have taken her to La Scala, Covent Garden, Brussels, Amsterdam, Rome, and Zürich with great success. In 1960 she appeared as Octavian in *Der Rosenkavalier* at the San Francisco Opera and in 1961 she was engaged at the Metropolitan Opera. Since 1949 she has been married to the composer Franz Mixa. In addition to her highly successful stage appearances, she has been much-sought-after as a concert and oratorio contralto, and is considered a great interpreter of Bach.
Records: DGG* (*Die Meistersinger* and *Le Nozze di Figaro*), Eurodisc, Philips, HMV (*Die Walküre*), and Opera. *U.S. re-issue:* Epic, Bruno, Electrola, Telefunken, Amadeo, Seraphim.

TORRI, ROSINA, soprano, b. Dec. 20, 1898, Guastalla, Italy. She first studied violin, then singing, at the Parma Conservatory and made her debut in Valenza (1919) as Mimi in *La Bohème*. In 1922 she sang with the Italian Opera in Holland. In 1925 she appeared in San Francisco in the title role of *Manon*. She made successful guest appearances at Covent Garden as Mimi and as Lauretta in *Gianni Schicchi* in 1926 and she sang Liu in *Turandot* at the Rome Opera in the first performance of the work there in 1926. The role of Liu remained her particular starring part and she sang it in many places, including the Arena Festival in 1928. She was greatly admired at La Scala as Musetta in *La Bohème* in 1934. After her marriage in the early 1930's she made very few appearances.
Records: HMV (Including *La Bohème*).

TOUREL, JENNIE, soprano, b. June 26, 1910, Montreal, Canada. The daughter of Russian parents, she studied with Anna El-Tour in Paris and from her teacher's name drew her own stage name by a reversal of syllables. She made her debut (1931) at the Opéra Russe in

Paris and in 1933 sang Carmen as her debut role at the Opéra-Comique there. By 1939 she had acquired great fame at both the Opéra-Comique and the Opéra. Although she had already appeared at the Chicago Opera in 1936, she was not engaged at the Metropolitan Opera until 1939. She also had a successful career in the United States as a concert singer. After World War II she toured France, Italy, Belgium, Holland, and England and on Sept. 11, 1951, she sang in the world *première* of *The Rake's Progress* at the Teatro Fenice. She now teaches at the Juilliard School of Music in New York and gives concerts. On the stage she sang a repertory which included not only *Carmen*, but also coloratura parts for contralto; in the concert hall she was celebrated as a singer of art songs.

Records: American Columbia*, American Decca*, Haydn Society*, Odyssey*.

TOZZI, GIORGIO, bass, b. Jan. 8, 1923, Chicago. His family was of Italian extraction. Originally a concert singer, after further study in Italy and a guest appearance at La Scala he was invited to the Metropolitan Opera (1955). He had great success there as Figaro in *Le Nozze di Figaro*, as Don Basilio in *Il Barbiere di Siviglia*, and as Arkel in *Pelléas et Mélisande*. In 1958 he sang the part of the Doctor in the world *première* of *Vanessa* at the Metropolitan. He sang the same role when the work was presented at the Salzburg Festival in 1958. He has made guest appearances in Chicago and San Francisco, at the Vienna State Opera, and at the leading Italian opera houses. A large and very expressive bass voice.

Records: Cetra* (*Rigoletto* and *Guillaume Tell*), RCA Victor* (*Der Fliegende Holländer* and *Turandot*), and Decca (*Il Trovatore*). *U.S. re-issue:* London, Seraphim.

TRAUBEL, HELEN, soprano, b. 1899, St. Louis, Mo. She studied singing in St. Louis and New York City. In 1925 she gave her first concert, appearing with the St. Louis Symphony Orchestra. In 1926 she had great success in a concert at Lewisohn Stadium in New York. She was thereupon sent a contract by the Metropolitan Opera, but she declined it to continue her study and concert activity. In 1937 she finally made her debut at the Metropolitan in the world *première* of *The Man Without a Country*. She had a brilliant success there in 1939 as Sieglinde in *Die Walküre* with Kirsten Flagstad and Lauritz Melchior as her partners. In 1941, when Flagstad could no longer return to the Metropolitan from Norway, she became the leading Wagner soprano in the United States and had great success not only at the Metropolitan, but also in guest appearances and in concerts. After World War II she turned more and more to operettas, musicals, and musical films. She became so active as a night-club singer that in 1953 the Metropolitan Opera refused to renew her contract. A large and skillfully managed dramatic soprano voice; she was one of the best Wagner interpreters of her generation.

Records: American Columbia* and RCA Victor*. *U.S. re-issue:* Dot. *U.S. re-recording:* RCA Victor.

TRAXEL, JOSEF, tenor, b. 1918 (?), Mainz, Germany. He first studied at the Music High School in Darmstadt as a pupil of Noak. He was called into the army as a soldier in World War II and he made his debut (1942) while in the hospital at Mainz as Don Ottavio in *Don Giovanni*. Toward the end of the war he was held prisoner by the

English. In 1946 he began his real career in Nuremberg, which he left in 1952 for the Stuttgart State Opera. In 1952 he sang the role of Mercury in the world *première* of *Die Liebe der Danaë* at the Salzburg Festival. He first appeared at the Bayreuth Festival in 1953 as Walther in *Die Meistersinger*. He was engaged through guest-appearance contracts at the State Operas in Vienna and Munich and at the Düsseldorf Opera. He made highly successful guest appearances and concert tours in France, Austria, Holland, and Switzerland, and, in 1957, in the United States. He is an especially successful concert singer, particularly in the Evangelist roles in the *Passions* of J. S. Bach.

Records: HMV, Decca (*Der Fliegende Holländer*), DGG, and Eurodisc. *U.S. re-issue:* Electrola, Angel, London, Bruno.

TRENTINI, EMMA, soprano, b. 1878, Mantua, Italy; d. Mar. 23, 1959, Milan. She had her first important success at La Scala in 1904 in *Germania*. In 1905 she sang the role of Oscar in *Un Ballo in Maschera* and Musetta in *La Bohème* at Covent Garden. She had brilliant success at the Manhattan Opera House, particularly as Musetta (1906-09). She was toasted for her performance on Broadway in *Naughty Marietta* (1909-11). The acclaim she received encouraged her to appear almost exclusively in operettas and musicals. By 1914 she had given up her career and she lived later in Italy. An outstanding performer in soubrette roles.

Records: Nicole (London, 1904), G & T (Milan, 1904-05), and Columbia* (U.S., 1907). *U.S. re-issue:* Victor. *U.S. re-recording:* TAP.

TREPTOW, GÜNTHER, tenor, b. Oct. 22, 1907, Berlin. He studied at the Music High School in Berlin and made his debut at the German Opera House there (1936). Although he began in small roles, by 1942 he was having great success as Otello and as Max in *Der Freischütz*. In 1942 he became a member of the Munich State Opera, where he particularly specialized in Wagner roles. He joined the Vienna State Opera (1947-55). Guest appearances took him to La Scala, Covent Garden, and the most important houses in France, Spain, and Switzerland; he sang at the Zoppot Festival (1939), and at the Bayreuth Festival he sang Siegmund in *Die Walküre* (1951). He has been engaged at the Berlin State Opera since 1951.

Records: Imperial, DGG (*Tannhäuser*), and Decca (*Die Meistersinger*). *U.S. re-issue:* London.

TRÉVILLE, YVONNE DE, soprano, b. Aug. 25, 1881, Galveston, Tex.; d. Jan. 25, 1954, New York. Originally Edyth Le Gierse. She was brought up in Paris, studied violin and harp, and then studied singing with Mathilde Marchesi. In 1897 she made her debut with the Castle Square Opera Company in New York. With them she sang Mimi in an early American production of *La Bohème* in 1899; she returned in the same year to Paris and resumed her studies with Mme. Marchesi. In 1902 she made her debut at the Opéra-Comique as Lakmé. In the following decade she made guest appearances in Stockholm, St. Petersburg (1904-05), Bucharest, Budapest, Nice, Berlin, Vienna, and Prague. She was particularly admired at the Brussels Opera. In 1912 she returned to America, where she appeared briefly as a concert singer. In 1919 she made a few guest appearances in Brussels. She then lived and taught in New York. She had a brilliant coloratura voice trained according to the Marchesi method.

Records: Three Edison* discs and one unpublished Columbia record. *U.S. re-recording:* IRCC.

TRIGONA, ROSE DE ADER—(see Ader, Rose)

TRIANTI, ALEXANDRA, soprano, b. Jan. 9, 1901, Athens, Greece. She was a pupil of Philipp Forstén in Vienna, then of Maria Ivogün in Berlin. In 1929 she gave her first song recital, an activity to which she devoted her entire career. She caused great excitement in Berlin when she sang duet recitals with Maria Ivogün, with Michael Raucheisen at the piano. On her concert tours she was applauded in Amsterdam, Brussels, Paris, London, Budapest, and Vienna. After World War II she lived in Athens and taught singing there. She also gave singing courses at the Salzburg Mozarteum. Her career lasted a long time and she was giving concerts in Holland as late as 1951. She is a member of the directorate of the National Opera in Athens. One of the most famous song interpreters, not only of German lieder, but of French Impressionist songs.

Records: Very few records for HMV, including a volume for the Hugo Wolf Society.

TRÖTSCHEL, ELFRIEDE, soprano, b. July 16, 1913, Dresden; d. June 20, 1958, Berlin. She studied in Dresden with, among others, Paul Schöffler. In 1934 she was engaged at the Dresden State Opera through Karl Böhm, and she appeared there until 1944. Her first foreign guest appearances followed in London and Florence. In 1942 she sang at the Salzburg Festival. In 1947 she went to the Komische Oper in East Berlin and sang at the Berlin State Opera. After 1953 she was a member of the West Berlin City Opera. She died at the high point of her career. She was prized as a singer for the fineness of her interpretations and the lightness and beauty of her voice in a wide-ranging concert and operatic repertory.

Records: DGG* (*The Creation, The Seasons,* and *Carmina Burana*) and Urania (*Der Freischütz* and *The Taming of the Shrew*). U.S. re-issue: Urania, Fiesta, Vox, American Decca.

TUCCI, GABRIELLA, soprano, b. Aug. 4, 1932. She became known when she won an international singing competition in Spoleto. She made her debut there (1952) as Leonora in *La Forza del Destino*. She soon had a brilliant career on the largest Italian stages, particularly at La Scala and the Rome Opera as well as at the Arena Festivals. She sang at La Scala in the first performance there of *A Midsummer Night's Dream* (1961); she appeared at the San Francisco Opera (1959) and at Covent Garden and the Munich State Opera (1960). Guest appearances have taken her to the Far East as well as all over Europe. She made her Metropolitan Opera debut in the 1960-61 season. A lyric-dramatic voice of great expressive power, particularly as Tosca, Aïda, and Nedda.

Records: Decca (*I Pagliacci*) and Columbia (*Il Trovatore*). U.S. re-issue: London, Angel.

TUCKER, RICHARD, tenor, b. Aug. 20, 1913, Brooklyn. He sang in the choir of a New York synagogue at the age of six and later studied with Paul Althouse. He made his concert debut in New York (1944) and his stage debut at the Metropolitan Opera (1945) as Enzo in *La Gioconda*. Shortly thereafter he was highly successful as Radames in the broadcast version of *Aida* directed by Arturo Toscanini. He has been a member of the Metropolitan ever since his debut, and has had great success there. In 1947 at the Arena Festival he sang Enzo in *La Gioconda* opposite Maria Callas and both singers had a tremendous storm of applause for their performances. He then appeared at La Scala as guest and in 1958 completed a successful series of guest appearances at Covent Garden and the Vienna State Opera. He has also sung in opera in San Francisco, Los Angeles, and Chicago. Concert tours have taken him to Italy, Israel, and throughout North and South America. He has a sumptuous tenor voice, light in the higher register, yet of strong dramatic power, and he has been particularly successful in the Italian repertory.

Records: Columbia*, Philips (*Cavalleria Rusticana, La Bohème, Madama Butterfly, Norma* with Maria Callas, *Aida,* and *La Forza del Destino*) and RCA Victor* (*Aida* under Toscanini). *U.S. re-issue:* Angel.

TULDER, LOUIS VAN, tenor, b. 1892, Amsterdam. He first sang in a church choir and then became choir leader of a Catholic church in Amsterdam. After study with Aaltje Noordewier-Reddingius, he came in 1915 to the Netherlands Opera at Koopman, where he sang lyric roles especially. In 1921 he gave up his stage career and became the leading Dutch oratorio tenor of his time. He was especially esteemed as an interpreter of Bach's music and he very often sang the role of the Evangelist in the *St. Matthew Passion* in famous performances under Willem Mengelberg. He was also known as a lieder singer, particularly as an interpreter of the songs of Alphons Diepenbrock. Later he taught singing, first in Amsterdam, then in The Hague.

Records: Acoustic records for HMV, electrics for Odeon and Philips (*St. Matthew Passion* directed by Mengelberg).

TURNER, EVA, soprano, b. Mar. 10, 1892, Oldham, England. She began her study with Dan Rootham in London and then studied at the Royal Academy of Music there (1911-15). She began her career as a member of the chorus of the Carl Rosa Opera Company; later she took over small roles with this troupe. After further study with Albert Richards Broad she had great success after 1920 as a leading singer with the Carl Rosa Company. In 1920 she sang Santuzza in *Cavalleria Rusticana* at Covent Garden and in 1924 she made her debut at La Scala as Freia in *Das Rheingold*. She was highly successful thereafter at the leading Italian opera houses, being applauded in Turin, Naples, Trieste, Bologna, and Pisa, particularly when she appeared in her special starring role, *Turandot*. In 1925 she sang as guest at the opera houses in Berlin, Frankfurt, Dresden, Munich, and Vienna and in 1927 and 1931 she made guest appearances in South America, especially at the Teatro Colón. She was engaged at the Chicago Opera (1928-30; 1938); she also appeared at the Boston Opera and made concert tours in the United States. In 1928, after a highly successful appearance at Covent Garden as Turandot, she was thenceforth established there, as at La Scala, as an important dramatic soprano. In 1948 she accepted a professorship at the University of Oklahoma, but in 1959 she returned to London. She had a dark-toned, dramatic soprano voice, filled with exciting dramatic intensity and made more effective by her fine sense of singing style.

Records: Columbia*. *U.S. re-recording:* Angel.

TZVEYCH, BISERKA, contralto, b. 1926 (?), Yugoslavia. When she was a year old her parents moved to Liège in Belgium. In 1946 she returned to Yugoslavia, where she first worked as an interpreter. Her voice was discovered and trained by José Riavez. In 1950 during her studies she appeared for an indisposed colleague as Maddalena in *Rigoletto* at the Belgrade Opera.

Her official debut followed (1954) there as Charlotte in *Werther*. She also made guest appearances with the Belgrade company in Wiesbaden. In 1959 she sang as guest at the Vienna State Opera as Amneris in *Aïda* and in 1960 became a member of that company. Since 1961 she has been a member of the Metropolitan Opera, where she first appeared as Amneris. In 1962 she made guest appearances at Covent Garden and in 1963 at the Teatro Colón. She is married to a physician and teacher in Belgrade; he has also appeared as a singer and in 1958 sang with her at the World Youth Congress in Moscow. Her records have also appeared under the name Biserka Cvejič.

Records: Decca (including *Eugen Onégin, The Queen of Spades, Prince Igor,* and *The Snow Maiden*). U.S. re-issue: London.

U

UDOVICK, LUCILLE, soprano, b. 1920, Denver, Colo. She sang first in operetta and musical comedy and then studied in Italy. After her first successes on provincial Italian stages, she was applauded at the 1951 Glyndebourne Festival as Electra in *Idomeneo*. In 1953 at the Maggio Musicale Festival she sang the title role in *Agnes von Hohenstaufen*. Guest appearances followed at Covent Garden and in Brussels, Amsterdam, Chicago, and San Francisco. The wide-ranging repertory of this artist includes the difficult parts for a dramatic coloratura soprano, particularly Turandot.
Records: HMV (*Idomeneo*). *U.S. re-issue:* Angel.

UHDE, HERMANN, baritone, b. July 20, 1914, Bremen, Germany; d. Oct. 10, 1965, Copenhagen. His mother, an American, had been a voice pupil of Karl Scheidemantel. He studied with Philipp Kraus in Bremen and made his debut there (1936) as Titurel in *Parsifal*. He was engaged successively at Freiburg im Br. (1938-40), the Munich State Opera (1940-43), and the German Opera in The Hague (1943-44). Toward the end of World War II he was drafted into the Wehrmacht and was imprisoned by the United States army in France. He sang at the Hannover Opera (1947-48), the Hamburg State Opera (1948-50), the Vienna State Opera (1950-51), the Munich State Opera (1951-56), and the Stuttgart State Opera (1956-57). After 1957 he was again a member of the Vienna State Opera. At the Salzburg Festival in 1949 he sang Kreon in the world *première* of *Antigonae*. He appeared annually at the Bayreuth Festivals after 1951, being particularly admired there as Wotan in the *Ring* cycle. He made guest appearances at Covent Garden, the Paris Opéra, the Rome Opera, and on many other important stages—all of which brought him great success. In 1955 he became a member of the Metropolitan Opera and was especially admired there in *Wozzeck*. He died of a heart attack on the stage in Copenhagen. A heroic baritone, he was noted for his singing of the principal Wagner roles in his voice range.
Records: Decca (*Parsifal* from Bayreuth, *Der Fliegende Holländer* and *Lohengrin*); DGG*, Philips. *U.S. re-issue:* Columbia, London, Heliodor.

UHL, FRITZ, tenor, b. Apr. 2, 1928, Vienna. In 1947 he began his study of singing with Elisabeth Rado in Vienna. During his period of studies he undertook a tour of Holland with an operetta troupe and in 1950 he made his real debut in Graz. He came from there in 1952 to Lucerne and in 1953 to Oberhausen. There he began singing heroic tenor roles and he soon became known as a Wagner tenor. In 1957 he was engaged at the Munich State Opera and signed guest-appearance contracts with the Vienna and Stuttgart State Operas. He has proven himself as a Wagner singer since 1958 at the Bayreuth Festivals in such parts as Erik in *Der Fliegende Holländer* and Loge in the *Ring* cycle. He has also had notable success at the Salzburg Festivals and in his guest appearances on German and other stages.

Records: Decca (*Tristan und Isolde*), Philips (*Der Fliegende Holländer*), DGG* (*Elektra* and *Antigonae*). *U.S. re-issue:* Bach Guild, Mercury, London.

UNGER, GERHARD, tenor, b. Nov. 26, 1916, Bad Salzungen, Germany. He studied at the Music High School in Berlin, but his debut was delayed by World War II. After 1945 he was active as a concert and oratorio singer and he began his stage career in 1947 at the National Theater in Weimar, where he remained for two years. In 1949 he was engaged by the East Berlin State Opera. He was soon admired as one of the leading performers in *buffo* roles and was also successful as a lyric tenor. Guest appearances took him to the State Operas in Vienna and Dresden and other important houses. He was admired at the Bayreuth Festivals (1951-52) in one of his specialties, David in *Die Meistersinger*, and he also sang at the Salzburg Festival. He is an outstanding concert singer, especially as an interpreter of Bach. In 1961 he became a member of the Stuttgart State Opera.

Records: HMV, Columbia (*Die Entführung aus dem Serail* and *Die Meistersinger*) and DGG* (*Der Rosenkavalier* and *Madama Butterfly*). *U.S. re-issue:* Angel, Turnabout, Vox, Urania, Electrola.

UPPMAN, THEODOR, baritone, b. 1920, Palo Alto, Calif. He studied at Stanford University, where he made his debut as Sarastro in *Die Zauberflöte*, and at the Curtis Institute of Music. After World War II he sang in various opera productions in California, including a concert version of *Pelléas et Mélisande* with Maggie Teyte. In 1947 he received two grants which allowed him to concertize in the West. He made his New York debut in concert (1951) and his operatic debut there as Pelléas with the New York City Opera. In the same year he created the title role in *Billy Budd* at Covent Garden. He toured the United States (1952-53), appeared in various musicals, and sang in the American television *première* of *Billy Budd*. He made his Metropolitan debut in November, 1953, as Pelléas and has sung many roles there since. He created the role of Wade in the New York City Opera production of *The Passion of Jonathan Wade*. He has sung as soloist with orchestras and in motion pictures. He has appeared at the Central City and Santa Fe Opera Festivals.

Records: Internos, RCA Victor, Capitol.

URBANO, UMBERTO, baritone, b. Oct. 16, 1894, Livorno, Italy. Very little is known about the career of this artist. About 1920 he first appeared on Italian stages, including, among others, La Scala in Milan, where he sang the Herald in *Lohengrin*. In 1927 he sang as guest at the Vienna State Opera and also appeared at Covent Garden and on South American stages. In the

1930's he sang a great deal at the National Theater in Prague and made guest appearances in both Bratislava and Brno. One of the most beautiful baritone voices of his time, both in the rich dark timbre of his vocal material and in the deeply moving expressiveness of his art.

Records: Polydor and Parlophone. *U.S. re-recording:* Scala.

URLUS, JACQUES, tenor, b. Jan. 6, 1867, Hergenrath, Belgium; d. July 6, 1935, Noordwijk, Holland. The son of Dutch parents, he passed his youth in Tilburg and Utrecht and was first employed as a metal worker in Utrecht. After the discovery of his voice, he studied with Hugo Nolthenius, Anton Averkamp, and Cornélie van Zanten in Amsterdam. He made his debut at the Netherlands Opera in Amsterdam as Beppe in *I Pagliacci*. After five years there he was engaged as principal tenor at the Leipzig Opera (1900-14). At Leipzig he soon became famous and was particularly admired as a Wagner tenor. He sang annually at Covent Garden (1910-14), mostly in Wagner parts, and he was admired when (1911-12) he sang Siegmund in *Die Walküre* at the Bayreuth Festivals. In 1912 he was engaged by the Metropolitan Opera, where he stayed with great success until 1917. Thereafter he took no more long-term contracts, but lived in Holland and traveled world-wide, making guest appearances and giving concerts. Several of his United States tours were highly rewarding and guest appearances brought him to the leading opera houses in Germany, France, Austria, and the Scandinavian countries, but especially to Amsterdam, Antwerp, and Brussels. In the concert hall he was particularly admired as the soloist in Mahler's *Das Lied von der Erde*. The great beauty of his voice remained with him for many years; he sang Tristan at the age of sixty-five. In his voice dramatic skill and musical beauty were perfected to a degree rare in a Wagner tenor.

Records: Edison* cylinders and discs, Pathé*, Polydor, Odeon, and HMV; one electrical record for Odeon. *U.S. re-issue:* Victor, Odeon-Okeh. *U.S. re-recording:* TAP, Rococo.

URSULEAC, VIORICA, soprano, b. Mar. 23, 1899, Czernowitz, Rumania. The daughter of a Greek Orthodox priest, she studied at the Vienna Music Academy and with Lilli Lehmann in Berlin. She made her debut (1924) at the Opera in Frankfurt a. M. and there she met the conductor Clemens Krauss, whom she later married and who often accompanied her at the piano in her song recitals. By way of the Dresden State Opera, she came in 1929 to the Vienna State Opera. She sang at the Berlin State Opera (1933-37) and was then engaged with her husband at the Bavarian State Opera in Munich. She appeared regularly as guest at the State Operas in Berlin and Vienna and sang almost annually at the Salzburg Festivals. She made highly successful guest appearances at La Scala, Covent Garden, and the Operas in Rome and Brussels and was equally successful on her South American tours. The two artists Krauss and Ursuleac were close friends of Richard Strauss. Viorica Ursuleac sang in several world *premières* of his operas: she sang the title role in *Arabella* at the Dresden State Opera (1933); at the Munich State Opera (1938) she sang Maria in *Friedenstag*, and the score of this work was dedicated to the two artists; in Munich (1942) she sang the Countess in *Capriccio*. She remained at the Munich Opera until 1944. Later she lived in Vienna and was only heard in guest appearances and in concerts. After the death of her husband in 1954 she lived in retirement in Ehrwald in the Tyrol. A lyric-dramatic voice, particularly admired in Richard Strauss and Mozart.

Records: Polydor and Vox (including *Der Rosenkavalier* and *Der Fliegende Holländer*). *U.S. re-recording:* Vox, Belcanto.

UZINOV, DMITER, tenor, b. 1922, Starazagorra, Bulgaria. He studied singing at the Sofia Conservatory and made his debut at the National Opera there (1946). After he had first sung lyric roles, he became an internationally known heroic tenor and was especially applauded in the role of Otello. Since 1958 he has been a regular guest at the Vienna State Opera and has appeared frequently at La Scala. In 1960 he sang Canio in *I Pagliacci* at the Arena Festival. He was a member of the Metropolitan Opera (1951). In 1961 he made a brilliant tour of Germany with the ensemble of the Sofia Opera. In 1965 he sang at the Salzburg Festival. He is married to the Bulgarian soprano Ekaterina Georgiev.

Records: Supraphon. *U.S. re-recording:* Angel.

V

VAGUET, ALBERT, tenor, b. June 15, 1865, Elbeuf, France; d. 1943, Pau, France. He studied at the Paris Conservatory with Barbot, Obin, and Ponchard. In 1890 he made his debut in *Faust* at the Opéra there, and during his entire career he remained a member of that company. He sang a great number of roles; he created David in the first performance of *Die Meistersinger* and Hylas in *Briséis* (1899), as well as Marcomir in *Les Barbares* (1901). He married the soprano Alba Chrétien-Vaguet. After an accident in 1903 he gave up his singing career and lived in Pau as a teacher.

Records: A great many records for Pathé*, all made after he gave up his career. *U.S. re-recording:* IRCC.

VALDENGO, GIUSEPPE, baritone, b. 1914, Turin, Italy. He originally wanted to be an instrumental musician and he studied the cello, oboe, and English horn at the Conservatory in Turin; then he studied singing with Michele Accoriuti. He made his debut in Parma (1936) as Figaro in *Il Barbiere di Siviglia*. In 1939 he was engaged at La Scala, but the continuation of his career was hindered by the outbreak of the war. After being called into the army, he became an oboist in a military band. In 1945 he returned to La Scala and quickly became well known. In 1946 he undertook a tour of the United States and sang with the New York City Opera. In 1947 he made his debut at the Metropolitan Opera as Tonio in *I Pagliacci*. He was then heard principally in New York and at La Scala. Guest appearances took him to London, Paris, Vienna, Buenos Aires, Rio de Janeiro, and many other musical centers. He also appeared in films: in *The Great Caruso* he played the part of a great predecessor, Antonio Scotti.

Records: Cetra* (*Il Segreto di Susanna*), Philips (*Don Pasquale*), and RCA Victor* (*Falstaff* and *Otello* under Toscanini and *Aida*). *U.S. re-issue:* Columbia.

VALENTE, ALESSANDRO, tenor, b. 1890, Turin, Italy. As a child he sang in the opera chorus in Verona and later studied there. In 1912 he came to London and sang Turiddu at the Hippodrome in a production of *Cavalleria Rusticana* under the baton of the composer, but he was unsuccessful in that performance. He remained in England and under the name Alex Vallo sang in small theaters, vaudeville houses, and in musicals. During World War I he served in the Italian army. After the war he appeared in Italy in similar productions. In 1924 he accompanied Luisa Tetrazzini as supporting artist on her farewell tour. In 1927 by chance it happened that he recorded the two arias of Kalaf from *Turandot*. While these records were generally greatly admired and while he also left other and later records of operatic arias, he did not manage to develop a stage career. He lives in Italy where he is active as an inventor, including among other inventions, a drying apparatus for curtains.

Records: His records, much-sought-after by collectors, appeared first on HMV and then on Decca.

VALENTINO, FRANK, baritone, b. Jan. 6, 1907, Denver, Colo. Originally Francis Dinhaupt. He came of a German-American family. He began the study of singing in Denver, but then continued in Milan and made his debut in Italy (1930). He had his first successes at the largest Italian theaters, appearing early at La Scala and the Teatro Costanzi. In Italy he sang under the name Francesco Valentino. He was engaged at the Italian Opera in Holland (1935-37) and in 1939 he was much admired at the Arena Festival. After a decade-long career in Europe he was engaged at the Metropolitan Opera (1940), making his debut there as Enrico in *Lucia di Lammermoor* and remaining at that house for twenty years. Thereafter he was a well-known concert and operatic singer in the United States. He had a warm-timbred and expressive baritone voice and he was admired on the stage for his fine acting ability.

Records: Columbia*, RCA Victor (*La Bohème* under Toscanini), and Allegro Royale*. *U.S. re-issue:* ASCO.

VALERO, FERNANDO, tenor, b. 1854, Seville, Spain; d. 1914, St. Petersburg, Russia. After first studying law, he turned to singing and studied with Martin Salazar and Tamberlik. He made his debut (1878) at the Teatro Real as Lorenzo in *Fra Diavolo*. In 1880 he came to Italy, singing first in Bologna and then for three years in the provinces. He made his debut as Faust in Gounod's opera at La Scala in 1883 and was highly successful there; among other roles he sang Turiddu in *Cavalleria Rusticana* there in 1891. He was applauded in 1885 at the Imperial Opera in St. Petersburg, in Florence (1890), and at Covent Garden (1890; 1901). He sang at the Metropolitan Opera (1891-92), making his debut as Turiddu. In 1897 he was forced to interrupt his career for a time because of a lung illness. In 1902 he sang publicly for the last time, appearing at the Teatro Bellini. He then opened a singing studio in St. Petersburg. His voice, not wholly trained in the usual nineteenth-century tradition, was compared by the critics with that of the famous Julien Gayarré.

Records: He made four very rare records for G & T (London, 1902-03). *U.S. re-recording:* Herrold, Rococo.

VÄLKKI, ANITA, soprano, b. Oct. 25, 1926, Sääksmäki, Finland. At first an actress and operetta singer at the Kokkola Theater in Vaasa (1952-55), she then studied singing with Tyyne Haase, Jorma Huttunen, and Lea Piltti in Helsinki and made her concert debut there (1954). In 1955 she was engaged at the National Opera in Helsinki. In 1960 she appeared as guest with the ensemble of this theater in Stockholm and excited admiring comment for her singing of Santuzza. She also had great success in later guest appearances there as Brünnhilde in *Die Walküre*, and Aïda. She sang as guest in Prague (1960) and at Covent Garden

(1961; 1962; 1964). In 1962 she sang a single performance at the Metropolitan Opera, appearing as Brünnhilde in *Die Walkure*, and she sang the same role that year in Palermo. She made a guest appearance at the Mexico City Opera (1962) and at the Philadelphia Opera (1963). Again as Brünnhilde she was applauded at the Bayreuth Festivals (1963-64). She has had a guest-appearance contract with the Vienna State Opera since 1963.

Records: Only one recording of the beautiful-sounding dramatic soprano voice of this artist presently exists: for Decca she sang the Third Norn in *Götterdämmerung*. *U.S. re-issue:* London.

VALLANDRI, ALINE, soprano, b. 1878, Paris; d. May 30, 1952, Paris. She studied at the Conservatory in Paris with Isnardon and made her debut at the Opéra-Comique (1904) in the title role of *Mireille*. She had outstanding success there for almost thirty years. She created a great many roles there and was specially admired as Manon, Mélisande, Mireille, and Micaëla in *Carmen*. In 1906 she sang Mireille at the Festival in Arles. She made guest appearances in Lisbon, Ostend, and at the Théâtre Lyrique In 1911 she sang at the London Opera in *Quo Vadis*. In 1921 she sang in *Louise* at the Cologne Opera. She also had a brilliant career as a concert soprano. She was admired on the stage not only for her beautiful voice, but for her aristocratic manner and for her acting talent.

Records: Pathé* (including *Rigoletto* and *Carmen*), HMV (Paris, 1908), and Odeon (1913). *U.S. re-issue:* Victor.

VALLETTI, CESARE, tenor, b. Dec. 18, 1921, Rome. He was the son of a physician and after he had studied first in Rome, he became a pupil of Tito Schipa. He made his debut in 1946 and quickly developed a reputation at the largest Italian theaters through his fine singing of Mozart roles and parts from the classical *bel canto* literature of opera. After successful appearances at La Scala and the Rome Opera, he sang as guest at Covent Garden, the Vienna State Opera, the Teatro Colón, and in Paris, Amsterdam, San Francisco, Chicago, and Rio de Janeiro. In 1953 he was engaged at the Metropolitan Opera, where he first sang Don Ottavio in *Don Giovanni*. He was also highly successful at the Festivals at Glyndebourne, Aix-en-Provence, and Verona. At a song recital at the Salzburg Festival in 1960 he greatly excited the audience by the perfection of his singing of German lieder. Although he retired officially in 1967, he sang in *L'Incoronazione di Poppaea* at the 1968 Caramoor Festival.

Records: Cetra* (*Don Pasquale*, *L'Elisir d'Amore*, and *La Fille du Régiment*), RCA Victor* (*La Traviata* and *Madama Butterfly*), Columbia* (*L'Italiana in Algeri*), and HMV. *U.S. re-issue:* Angel.

VALLIN, NINON, soprano, b. Sept. 9, 1886, Mantalieu-Vercien, France; d. Nov. 22, 1961, on her estate, La Sauvagère, near Lyons, France. She studied first at the Lyons Conservatory, then with Meyriane Héglon in Paris, and she first appeared as a concert singer. In 1911 she sang in Paris in performances of *Le Martyre de Saint Sébastien* and *La Damoiselle Élue* by Claude Debussy, and in 1914 she gave song recitals accompanied by Debussy at the piano. In 1912 she made her stage debut at the Opéra-Comique as Micaëla in *Carmen*. She made her debut under the name Mme. Vallin-Pardo, since she had meanwhile married the Spanish violinist Pardo; she was soon separated from him. At the Opéra-Comique she was very successful and sang there in the world *premières* of *La Sorcière* (1912) and *Les Cadeaux de Noël* (1915). In 1916 she sang as guest at the Teatro Colón and she was so successful in South America that in the 1920's she sang there more often than she did in France. In 1917 she sang at La Scala in the local *première* of *Il Segreto di Susanna* and *Marouf*. In 1926 she was applauded at the Opéra-Comique in *La Vida Breve* and in 1934 in the *première* there of *Maria Egiziaca*. After 1930 she lived on her estate near Lyons, and traveled from there on her guest-appearance and concert tours. She appeared in public until after World War II. She was a professor at the Conservatory in Montevideo, Uruguay (1956-59). Ninon Vallin was the most famous French singer of her generation. Her complete mastery of singing technique and her mature and intelligent handling of characterizations were demonstrated in a wide repertory, of which the starring specialities were held to be Manon, Carmen, and Mignon.

Records: Pathé*, Odeou, Vega and Columbia* (including *Louise* and *Werther*). *U.S. re-issue:* American Decca. *U.S. re-recording:* Pathé-Marconi.

VAN DYCK, ERNEST, tenor, b. Apr. 2, 1861, Antwerp, Belgium; d. Aug. 31, 1923, Berlaer-les-Lierre. After originally studying law at the Universities of Louvain and Brussels, he became a journalist in Paris. There he studied singing with St. Yves Bax and with the composers Massenet and Chabrier. He made his concert debut in Paris (1883) in the cantata *Le Gladiateur*, by Vidal. After great successes at the Concerts Lamoureux there, he made his stage debut in Antwerp (1884). In 1887 he sang the role of Lohengrin at the Théâtre Eden in Paris in the French *première* of the work. He studied Wagner operas with Felix Mottl in Karlsruhe and had a huge success as Parsifal at the Bayreuth Festival in 1888. He sang this role regularly there until 1901; in 1894 he also sang Lohengrin there and in 1911-12 again sang Parsifal. In 1888 he joined the Vienna Imperial Opera and sang there with brilliant success until 1898. He sang the title role there in the world *première* of *Werther* in 1892. Guest appearances took him regularly to Paris and Antwerp. For Paris he created several Wagner heroes—for example, Siegmund in *Die Walküre* (1892), Siegfried in *Götterdämmerung* (1908). After 1891 he was a regular guest at Covent Garden and was a member of the Metropolitan Opera (1898-1902), appearing first as Tannhäuser. Later he made guest appearances in Brussels, Amsterdam, St. Petersburg, and Bucharest. After 1906 he was a professor in the Conservatories in Brussels and Antwerp. He sang Parsifal again in Antwerp in 1914. He founded the Nouveaux Concerts in Antwerp. He was one of the most important singer-personalities of his epoch, famous in both the French and Wagner repertories.

Records: A few records for Fonotipia (Paris, 1905) and also some on Pathé and Homophone. The poor technical quality of these records hardly permits one to know the true beauty of his voice. *U.S. re-issue:* IRCC. *U.S. re-recording:* FRP, Cantilena, Rococo.

VANELLI, GINO, baritone, b. Mar. 26, 1896. He made his debut in Lodi (1920) in *La Forza del Destino*. In 1924 he sang at the Cairo Opera and traveled to Brazil; in 1925 he visited Spain and in 1926 he was engaged at the Teatro Colón, where he had great success during the following years. In 1926 he came to La Scala, making his debut there as Ping in *Turandot*. At La

Scala and at the Teatro Costanzi, as well as on other important Italian stages, he had a very long and successful career. In 1935 and 1941 he sang as guest in Holland. As late as 1952 he sang Belcore in *L'Elisir d'Amore* at the Wexford Festival in Ireland.

Records: One for HMV; many for Columbia* (including *La Bohème, I Pagliacci,* and *Madama Butterfly* with Rosetta Pampanini).

VARNAY, ASTRID, soprano, b. Apr. 25, 1918, Stockholm. Her father, Alexander Varnay (1889-1924), was a Hungarian tenor and later *régisseur* at the Stockholm and Oslo Operas; her mother was the coloratura soprano Maria Yavor Varnay (b. 1889). When Astrid Varnay was two years old, the family came to the United States. She studied first with her mother, then with Hermann Weigert (1890-1955), whom she later married. In 1941 she made her debut at the Metropolitan Opera as Sieglinde in *Die Walküre*, appearing on short notice for Lotte Lehmann, who was indisposed. She soon became known as one of the important Wagner sopranos of her time. She had great success at the Metropolitan year after year. In 1948 she went to Europe for the first time; there she sang at Covent Garden and the Maggio Musicale Festival. Since 1951 she has been one of the mainstays of the Bayreuth Festivals, applauded especially as Brünnhilde in the *Ring* cycle, but also as Isolde and as Ortrud in *Lohengrin.* Important triumphs marked her guest appearances at La Scala, Covent Garden, the Vienna State Opera, the Düsseldorf Opera, and in Hamburg, Munich, Berlin, Buenos Aires, Rio de Janeiro, Mexico City, Chicago, San Francisco, and many other international centers of musical life. She has also sung at the Salzburg Festivals and now resides in Munich. A dramatic and dark-timbred soprano voice, especially admired in Wagner.

Records: Remington*, Decca (*Der Fliegende Holländer* and *Lohengrin*), Columbia* (Act III of *Die Walküre*, Bayreuth, 1951), and DGG*. *U.S. re-issue:* London.

VENTURA, ELVINO, tenor, b. 1875, Palermo, Sicily; d. 1951, Milan. He studied with Boni in Palermo and with Martin in Milan and made his debut (1896) in Pesaro as Turiddu in *Cavalleria Rusticana* under Mascagni. In 1897 he sang in Turin and in 1901 in Palermo. He also appeared on all the most famous Italian operatic stages, particularly the Teatro San Carlo and the Teatro Costanzi. Guest appearances followed in London, Paris, Buenos Aires, Madrid, St. Petersburg, and Warsaw. In 1909 he toured Holland and Belgium with the Castellano Opera Company. (The younger brother of this singer appeared as a *comprimario* under the name Lodovico Oliviero, singing first at the Chicago Opera and then at the Metropolitan Opera.)

Records: G & T (Milan, 1903-04, including duets with Giannina Russ), Zonophone* (New York, 1907), Odeon-Fonotipia (Milan, 1905-06), Pathé*, and one Edison* Amberola cylinder.

VENTURNINI, EMILIO, tenor, b. 1878, Brescia, Italy; d. November, 1952, Milan. He began his career in 1900 as a lyric tenor, but after a few years changed to *buffo* parts. He sang as *buffo* at the Sonzogno Stagione in Paris (1905) and at Covent Garden (1907). He was engaged at the Chicago Opera (1910-17). In 1911 in New York he replaced Angelo Bada, who was ill, as Cassio in *Otello* and as Spoletta in *Tosca.* In Chicago he occasionally sang leading roles, such as Turiddu in *Cavalleria Rusticana*, Edgardo in *Lucia di Lammermoor*, and Pinkerton in *Madama Butterfly*. He appeared as guest at the Teatro Massimo (1910; 1911; 1916). In 1921 he went to La Scala, where he sang *comprimario* roles until 1948, so that a performance without him at that house became unthinkable. At La Scala he appeared in an important series of world *premières:* Pong in *Turandot* (1926), Boito's *Nerone* (1924), *La Cena delle Beffe* (1924), *I Cavalieri di Ekebù* (1925), and *Sly* (1927). He was valued both for his knowledge of singing and for his acting talent.

Records: About 1903 he made a series of solo records for Columbia*; he later sang many small parts in electric recordings of operas for HMV and Columbia*. *U.S. re-recording:* Eterna.

VERBITSKAYA, EUGENIA, contralto, b. 1904, Kiev, Russia. She began her study of singing in 1923 in the voice classes at the Kiev Conservatory and made her debut (1926) at the Opera there as Pauline in *The Queen of Spades*. In 1931 she came to the Leningrad Opera, making her debut as the Princess in *Russalka*. In 1948 she was engaged by the Bolshoi Theater, where she was highly successful thereafter. She also gave concerts in the various musical centers of Russia. She had a well-handled and dark-timbred contralto voice.

Records: Russian State Record Trust (including *The Queen of Spades* and *May Night*). *U.S. reissue:* Bruno.

VERDIÈRE, RENÉ, tenor, b. July 26, 1899, Pas-de-Calais region, France. At the age of eighteen he volunteered for the French army during World War I. After the war's end he studied at the Paris National Conservatory and made his debut (1927) at the Opéra as Max in *Der Freischütz*. In 1930 he came to the Opéra-Comique and then had a starring career on both the great opera stages of Paris. He specialized in Wagner roles and in heroic parts from the French and Italian repertories and he was considered a worthy successor to the famous French heroic tenor Paul Franz. He appeared as guest at Covent Garden, in Monte Carlo, and in Amsterdam in 1952. He retired in 1956.

Records: Odeon.

VERGNES, PAUL-HENRI, tenor, b. May 11, 1905, Lagrasse, France. Helped by the patron of the arts Castellon de Beauxhoste, he was able to begin his singing studies at the Paris Conservatory at the age of nineteen. He made his debut at the Paris Opéra (1929) as Faust in Gounod's opera. Thereafter he was a prized lyric tenor at that house. After 1933 he also sang at the Opéra-Comique, where he first appeared as the title hero in *Les Contes d'Hoffmann*. He sang at the Opéra-Comique in the world *première* of *Ester de Carpentras* (1938). He made guest appearances in England, Italy, Switzerland, and Belgium. In 1956 he gave up his career and became a teacher in Paris. He is married to the soprano Lise Dalignan.

Records: Odeon.

VERLET, ALICE, soprano, b. 1873, Belgium; d. 1934, Paris. She made her debut (1892) at the Opéra-Comique and then sang in the French provinces. After she had been highly successful for several years at the Brussels Opera, she was engaged in 1904 at the Paris Opéra, singing there until 1914 and also appearing at the same time as guest at the Opéra-Comique. She sang as guest at Covent Garden (1910), taking the role of Konstanze in *Die Entführung aus dem Serail* under Sir Thomas Beecham and she gave concerts in Queen's Hall and Albert Hall. She was a member of the

Chicago Opera (1915-16); she remained in the United States until 1920 and had great success in concerts. She then taught in Paris. She had a brilliantly managed coloratura soprano voice.

Records: APGA (Paris, 1904-08), HMV (Paris, 1908; London, 1909), Pathé, many Edison* discs and clynders. *U.S. re-issue:* Victor.

VERONA, TULLIO, tenor, b. 1897 (?); d. May, 1939, Milan. He began his career in 1920 in the smaller Italian opera houses. In 1927 he sang Licinio in Spontini's *La Vestale* at the Arena Festival. He was engaged by the Italian Opera in Holland (1928; 1933-34). In 1928 he appeared for the first time at La Scala and in 1929 he was a guest at Covent Garden, where he sang Pollione opposite Rosa Ponselle in *Norma*. He had a large-dimensioned heroic tenor voice.

Records: A few Pathé records (1928-29).

VERRETT, SHIRLEY, contralto, b. 1938, New Orleans, La. She grew up in California; she began studying with Anna Fitziu in 1955 and later with Mme. Székély-Fresche at the Juilliard School of Music in New York. After she had won the Marian Anderson Prize, she made her debut at the Spoleto Festival (1963) as Carmen. In the same year she appeared as guest at the Bolshoi Theater and at the Kiev Opera, both with sensational success. Also in 1963 she began a starring career as a concert singer and recitalist in both the United States and Europe. She sang Carmen very successfully at the New York City Opera in 1964. Her full contralto voice is esteemed for her glowing and dramatic delivery.

Records: RCA Victor (Preziosilla in *La Forza del Destino* and *Luisa Miller*) and American Columbia*. Some records appeared under the name Shirley Verrett-Carter. *U.S. re-issue:* Everest.

VEZZANI, CÉSAR, tenor, b. Aug. 8, 1886, Bastia, Corsica; d. Nov. 11, 1951, Marseilles. He passed his childhood in Toulon and came to Paris in 1907, where his voice was discovered by the soprano Agnes Borgo, who financed his studies at the National Conservatory (1909-11). In 1911 he made his debut at the Opéra-Comique in *Richard Coeur de Lion* and in 1913 he married Agnes Borgo. In 1914 he sang at the Opéra-Comique in the world *première* of *Madame Roland*. In 1914 he and his wife signed contracts with the Boston Opera, but the outbreak of World War I prevented their leaving France. In the same year he quarreled with the directorate of the Opéra-Comique and thereafter sang no more in Paris. He did sing in the opera houses in Nice, Marseilles, Toulon, Toulouse, and Brussels and in Switzerland and North Africa. During World War II he sang at the opera house in Algiers, where he was very successful. During a rehearsal on the stage of the Toulon Opera in 1948 he suffered a stroke which left him completely paralyzed.

Records: A great many acoustic records for Odeon and HMV; electric for HMV (including a complete *Faust* with Marcel Journet). *U.S. re-issue:* Victor. *U.S. re-recording:* Rococo, Eterna, Scala, FRP, TAP.

VIALTZEVA, ANASTASIA, contralto, b. 1871; d. Feb. 4, 1913, St. Petersburg, Russia. She studied in St. Petersburg and made her debut (1887) on the stage of the S. S. Lencivskii Ballet Company in Kiev. In 1888 she joined the operetta theater of Setov and Blumenthal-Tamarin. In 1893 she came to the Aquarium Theater in Moscow, where she was a greatly admired operetta singer. She sang with the company of S. A. Palma, first in Moscow, then in St. Petersburg

(1893-97). After 1897 she sang in concerts consisting chiefly of Russian gypsy love songs, through which she acquired enormous success. She finally came to the operatic stage and sang in both St. Petersburg and Moscow in such roles as Carmen and Dalia. She was considered an outstanding actress. She had a dark-timbred and luxuriant voice.

Records: Zonophone (St. Petersburg, 1900-05), G & T (St. Petersburg, 1900-01), and HMV—all much-sought-after by collectors.

VICKERS, JON, tenor, b. Oct. 29, 1926, Prince Albert, Canada. He wanted to study medicine, but was unable to secure a place at the university. He then became a soloist in churches in Winnipeg and sang in the operetta *Naughty Marietta*. After formal study of singing with George Lambert at the Toronto Conservatory, he began singing in oratorios. In 1956 he made his operatic debut at Covent Garden as Aeneas in *Les Troyens*. In 1958 he was applauded as Siegmund in *Die Walküre* at the Bayreuth Festival and he has been a regular guest at the Vienna State Opera and at La Scala in Milan. At the Dallas Opera he was highly acclaimed as Jason in Cherubini's *Medea* with Maria Callas; he also sang the same role at Covent Garden (1959). In 1960 he was engaged by the Metropolitan Opera, where he had great success as Florestan in *Fidelio* and in *Peter Grimes*.

Records: His first records appeared on Canadian Victor (including *The Messiah*), then Decca (*Die Walküre*), and RCA Victor (*Otello* and *Aïda*). U.S. re-issue: Angel, Westminster, DGG.

VIEUILLE, FÉLIX, bass, b. 1872, Saugéon, France; d. 1946, Paris. He studied at the National Conservatory in Paris with Achard and Giraudet and made his debut (1898) at the Opéra-Comique there; he then appeared on this stage for almost fifty years as principal bass. He sang in a vast number of world *premières* and first performances there: a small role in *Louise* (1900), Arkel in *Pelléas et Mélisande* (1902), *La Fille de Roland* (1904), Bluebeard in *Ariane et Barbe-Bleue* (1907), MacDuff in Bloch's *Macbeth* (1910), and the Sultan in *Marouf* (1914). In a memorable production of *The Snow Maiden* (1908) he sang King Frost. He was engaged at the Metropolitan Opera (1908-09) and then returned to the Opéra-Comique, where he continued his career until 1940. In his last years he appeared only as Arkel in *Pelléas et Mélisande*.

Records: Odeon and Beka; unpublished records for Victor.

VIGLIONE-BORGHESE, DOMENICO, baritone, b. July 3, 1877, Mondivi, Italy; d. November, 1957, Milan. He made his debut (1899) in Lodi and sang for two years on various Italian stages, but then gave up his career and immigrated to the United States. In San Francisco he lived as a railroad and dock worker, but continued to study singing. On the recommendation of Enrico Caruso, the impresario Scognamillo engaged him for his opera troupe—a group to which Luisa Tetrazzini belonged—and he traveled with it to Mexico, the Caribbean islands, the Antilles, and Venezuela (1905-06). On this trip he had great success. On the strength of this triumph he returned to Italy. There he sang in 1907 at Parma as Amonasro in *Aïda* and was so successful that he went from one triumph to another and sang regularly at both La Scala and the Teatro Costanzi. In 1913 he was applauded at the Teatro Real. Until the 1930's he sang on the Italian radio and made guest appearances in the various Italian opera houses from Turin to Palermo. His special role was held to be that of Jack

Rance in *La Fanciulla del West*, which he had sung at its first performance in Italy in 1911 at the Teatro Costanzi. He did not give up his career until 1940, after which he lived and taught in Milan. He had a skillfully managed baritone voice, thought by connoisseurs to be one of the most voluminous ever put on records.

Records: Fonotipia and Polydor. *U.S. re-recording:* TAP.

VIGNAS, FRANCESO, tenor, b. 1863, Barcelona, Spain; d. July 13, 1933, Moya, Spain. After his studies at the Conservatory in Barcelona, he made his debut there (1888). He then sang in various Italian opera houses with great success and in 1893 came for the first time to London; there at the Shaftesbury Theater he sang Turiddu in the first performance in England of *Cavalleria Rusticana*. He was engaged at the Metropolitan Opera in 1893 and he created the same role for his first American performance there. Later he was admired at the Metropolitan as Don José in *Carmen* with Emma Calvé and as Edgardo in *Lucia di Lammermoor* with Nellie Melba. He also sang Wagner roles there, but in Italian-language productions. He stayed at the Metropolitan until 1897 and about the turn of the century made successful guest appearances in London, Paris, Madrid, and Barcelona; his success at La Scala was especially marked. In 1917 he sang his last stage performance in Madrid and thereafter lived and taught in Barcelona. A powerful heroic tenor voice; he was frequently spoken of as the successor to the great Spanish tenor Julien Gayarré (1844-90).

Records: G & T (Milan, 1903) and Fonotipia (Milan, 1905-07). *U.S. re-issue:* Columbia-Fonotipia, HRS. *U.S. re-recording:* TAP, Eterna, Belcanto, Cantilena, Rococo.

VILLABELLA, MIGUEL, tenor, b. Dec. 20, 1892, Bilbao, Spain; d. June 28, 1954, Paris. He wanted to pursue a commercial career and came to Paris to continue his study in this field. His voice was discovered by Lucien Fugère. He first sang publicly in a concert in San Sebastian in 1917. In the same year he began his studies with Jacques Isnardon in Paris and he made his stage debut (1918) in Poitiers as Cavaradossi in *Tosca*. In 1920 he was engaged at the Opéra-Comique in Paris, where, after first singing small roles, he soon became the celebrated principal tenor of the house. In 1928 he was made a concurrent member of the Paris Opéra. He was admired in his guest appearances in Monte Carlo and in Brussels, but the center of his career remained in the French capital. After he had ended his stage career in 1940, he lived and taught in Paris. A tenor of vocal brilliance and of great expressive power.

Records: Odeon and Pathé. *U.S. re-issue:* American Decca. *U.S. re-recording:* Eterna.

VILLANI, LUISA, soprano, b. 1885 (?), San Francisco. Her parents were Italian opera singers who in 1885 had embarked on a tour of the United States. She was taken to Italy as a child and there she studied with her father, Vincezo Villani, in Milan. She made her debut (1907) at La Scala, singing Eurydice in *Orphée et Eurydice*. She then sang at the Teatro Costanzi in Rome and toured the United States with small traveling companies. In 1913 she again sang at La Scala and there, on Apr. 10, 1913, she created the role of Fiora in *L'Amore dei Tre Re*. She sang with the Boston Opera Company (1913-17) and in December, 1915, at a guest performance at the Metropolitan Opera she sang *Madama Butterfly*. In 1918 she returned to Italy, where she lived as a teacher in Florence. The soprano Renata Villani is her niece.

Records: Three Columbia* records.

VINAY, RAMÓN, baritone-tenor, b. 1914, Chillan, Chile. His father was French and his mother Italian. He completed his education in France and then returned to his family, which had meanwhile moved to Mexico. He studied singing in Mexico City with Pierson. He made his debut there (1938) as a baritone, singing Count di Luna in *Il Trovatore*. For six years he confined himself to baritone roles, but after further study with René Maison in New York City, he sang his first tenor role, Otello, at the Mexico City Opera in 1944. In 1945 he came to the New York City Opera, and in 1947 he sang for the first time in Europe. His Otello brought him enormous success at La Scala. In 1948 he sang the same role, his real starring part, at the Arena Festival, and in 1951 he sang it at the Salzburg Festival under Wilhelm Furtwängler. After 1946 he was a member of the Metropolitan Opera and he sang as guest also at Covent Garden, the Paris Opéra, the Teatro Colón, and in Chicago and San Francisco. In San Francisco in 1950 he sang his first Wagner role, Tristan, and in 1952 he was greatly admired in this role at the Bayreuth Festival. In 1962 he returned to baritone roles when he sang Telramund in *Lohengrin* there. He has retained his heroic tenor parts along with his baritone repertory. A large, dark-toned, but highly expressive, heroic tenor voice, successful in both the Italian and French repertories as well as in Wagner parts.

Records: A few records for RCA Victor* (*Otello* under Toscanini) and Columbia.

VINCENT, JO, soprano, b. Mar. 8, 1898, Amsterdam. The daughter of the carillonneur of the Royal Palace in Amsterdam, Jacobus Vincent, she completed her study of singing there with Catherine von Rennes and Cornélie van Zanten. In 1921 she gave her first concert and thereafter had great success in the concert hall, both as an oratorio soprano and as an interpreter of songs. She frequently sang with the Concertgebouw Orchestra of Amsterdam and in concert halls in Germany, Belgium, France, and England. She never appeared on the operatic stage except in a single role, that of the Countess in *Le Nozze di Figaro*. In the oratorio field she was considered a worthy successor to the famous Aaltje Noordewier-Reddingius. In 1953 she gave up her active singing career and became a teacher at the Conservatory in Haarlem.

Records: Columbia* and Philips* (*St. Matthew Passion* and Brahms' *German Requiem* under Mengelberg).

VISHNEVSKAYA, GALINA, soprano, b. Oct. 25, 1926, Leningrad. She studied at the Conservatory in Leningrad with Mme. Garina. She sang in an operetta theater there at the age of eighteen and later gave concerts with the Leningrad Philharmonic Orchestra, but then decided on the career of an opera singer. In 1953 she was engaged at the Bolshoi Theater, where she was triumphantly successful. She also made guest appearances and sang in concerts in all the Russian music centers. She is married to the cellist Mstislav Rostropovich. She toured Czechoslovakia and Yugoslavia (1955), Finland and Italy (1957), gave concerts in Germany (1955; 1959), England (1959), and Australia (1960). She was greatly admired on a long tour of the United States in 1960 and she was engaged in 1961 by the Metropolitan Opera, where she was also very much liked. She has one of the most beautiful soprano voices of her generation on account of the great maturity of her conceptions and the special beauty of her tone production. She is admired in both French and Italian roles as well as in the Russian repertory, but she is also outstanding in the concert hall in both oratorio and song.

Records: Russian State Record Trust (including *Eugen Onégin*). She made one record for RCA Victor* and sang for Philips* (soprano soloist in the Verdi *Requiem* and Russian art songs). *U.S. reissue:* London, Artia, Period, Monitor.

VIX, GENEVIÈVE, soprano, b. 1879, Le Havre, France; d. Aug. 25, 1939, Paris. She came of a Dutch family and was originally Geneviève Brouwer. She studied at the Paris Conservatory and made her debut (1906) at the Opéra-Comique in the title role in *Aphrodite*. She immediately had great success in Paris and in 1908 she was engaged for a season at the Manhattan Opera House. She then returned to the Opéra-Comique and there, in 1911, she created the role of Concepcion in the world *première* of *L'Heure Espagnole*. Guest appearances took her to Nice, Monte Carlo, Brussels, and Bordeaux, all with brilliant success. In 1915 for the first performance of the work at the Teatro Colón she sang, in a transposition for soprano, the role of Jean in *Le Jongleur de Notre-Dame*. She was also uncommonly successful as a concert singer. Her career lasted until the 1930's. She was married to the Russian prince Nareshkin. She had an expressive soprano voice and her sovereign mastery of singing technique lifted her above the ordinary.

Records: Pathé, Odeon, and Ultraphone. *U.S. re-issue:* HRS.

VOGEL, ADOLF, bass, b. Aug. 18, 1897, Munich. He studied with Anna Bahr-Mildenburg in Munich and made his debut in Klagenfurt (1923) as Daland in *Der Fliegende Holländer*. Contracts with the theaters in Heilbronn and Karlsruhe followed. He sang at the Leipzig Opera (1928-30) and at the Munich State Opera (1930-37). In 1937 he was engaged by the Vienna State Opera, where he stayed for almost twenty years. He was especially admired as a singer of *buffo* roles. He made very successful guest appearances in London, Amsterdam, Milan, Rome, Buenos Aires, and many other music centers. He was a well-known singer at the Metropolitan Opera (1937-39). After 1940 he divided his time between singing and teaching at the Vienna Academy of Music.

Records: Very few records; he sang a small part in a complete *Salome* for Philips.

VOGELSTROM, FRITZ, tenor, b. Nov. 4, 1882, Herford, Germany; d. Dec. 25, 1963, Dresden. He was a pupil of Dora Erl in Dresden and made his debut (1903) in Mannheim, remaining there until 1912. During this time his guest appearances in German music centers made him well known. In 1909 he sang Parsifal, Lohengrin, and Frohe in *Das Rheingold* at the Bayreuth Festival; he received special recognition from Cosima Wagner for these performances. In 1912 he was engaged at the Dresden Royal Opera and he remained there as principal heroic tenor until his retirement from the stage in 1929. He also sang as guest at Covent Garden. After his retirement he first lived at Dresden as a teacher, but later moved to Köthen in Saxony.

Records: G & T (Mannheim, 1907), Parlophone, Odeon, Vox Pathé*, and one unpublished Edison record. *U.S. re-issue:* Odeon-Okeh.

VÖLKER, FRANZ, tenor, b. Mar.

31, 1899, Neu-Isenburg, Germany; d. Dec. 4, 1965, Darmstadt, Germany. At first he was a civil servant; his voice was discovered by Clemens Krauss and he studied very briefly in Frankfurt before he made his debut at the opera house there (1926); he was there until 1931. He first sang at the Salzburg Festivals (1931) and appeared there until the summer of 1939 in a large number of roles: Ferrando in *Così fan tutte*, Florestan in *Fidelio*, Max in *Der Freischütz*, and the Emperor in *Die Frau ohne Schatten*. But he had his greatest successes at the Bayreuth Festivals, where (1933-34) he was the chief attraction, being particularly admired for his incomparable Lohengrin. In 1935 he was engaged at the Berlin State Opera, where he had made regular guest appearances since 1933. He also was very successful at La Scala, Covent Garden, the Paris Opéra, and in Amsterdam, Brussels, Rome, Hamburg, and Munich. He remained in Berlin until 1945 and he then sang at the Munich State Opera (1945-52). In 1952 he gave up his career and lived as a teacher in Neu-Isenburg. After 1958 he was a professor at the Music High School in Stuttgart. In his voice both the vocal strength and dramatic qualities of a heroic tenor were joined to the flexibility and tonal beauty of a lyric tenor.

Records: A great many records for Polydor, Urania*, and Telefunken* (Bayreuth, 1936). *U.S. re-recording:* Scala, Eterna, TAP.

VOTIPKA, THELMA, soprano-contralto, b. 1906, Cleveland, Ohio. She made her debut (1928) at the Philadelphia Summer Opera and sang as a soprano at the Chicago Opera (1929-30). In a guest appearance with the Chicago company in San Francisco she sang the coloratura role of Sophie in *Der Rosenkavalier*. In 1935 she was engaged by the Metropolitan Opera and she made her debut as Flora Belvoir in *La Traviata*. She sang a great number of *comprimario* roles at the Metropolitan until 1962, both in the soprano and contralto ranges. In her particular starring part this artist was admired as the Witch in *Hänsel und Gretel*.

Records: Small roles in complete operas for Columbia* and RCA Victor* (including *Hänsel und Gretel, Carmen, Madama Butterfly, Faust, Cavalleria Rusticana,* and *Lucia di Lammermoor*). *U.S. re-recording:* IRCC.

VOYER, GIOVANNI, tenor, b. Oct. 28, 1901, in southern France. Originally Jean Boyer. He studied with Molajoli in Milan and began his career in Italy. In the 1930's he was particularly successful at La Scala in such heroic roles as Tristan, Lohengrin, Parsifal, and Herod in *Salome*. In 1933 he sang as guest at Covent Garden in *La Damnation de Faust*, and in 1936 he sang at the Italian Opera in Holland. He created the role of the Emperor in *Die Frau ohne Schatten* at its Italian *première* at the Rome Opera (1939) and again at its La Scala *première*, also in 1939. He sang at the Arena Festival (1938). In 1950 he accepted a professorship at the Conservatory in The Hague. In 1952 he sang again at the Holland Festival in a concert performance of *Les Troyens*. Since 1953 he has been a professor at the Conservatory in Lisbon.

Records: A few electric records for Columbia.

VULPIUS, JUTTA, soprano, b. Dec. 31, 1927, Weimar, Germany. She came from the same family as Christine Vulpius, the wife of Goethe. She studied with Franziska Martienssen-Lohmann in Weimar and made her debut at the Komische Oper in East Berlin as the Queen of the Night in *Die Zauberflöte* (1952). Since 1954 she has been a member of the East Berlin State Opera and later made guest appearances in Barcelona, Lisbon, Munich, Rome, Prague, and Hamburg. She sang at the Bayreuth Festivals (1954-56). Her coloratura soprano voice is outstanding because of the brilliance of her technique and the clarity of her tone production.

Records: Eterna (including *Die Entführung aus dem Serail*) and Philips. *U.S. re-issue:* Heliodor.

VYVYAN, JENNIFER, soprano, b. 1924 (?), Broadstairs, England. She studied at the Royal Academy of Music in London, first piano and then singing. After she had begun as a mezzo-soprano, her voice changed to that of a soprano under the direction of her teacher, Roy Henderson. After further study in Brussels, Geneva, and Milan, she won first prize in a singing contest in Geneva (1951). She was very successful in an appearance in 1951 at Sadler's Wells Opera in London as Konstanze in *Die Entführung aus dem Serail*. In 1953 she sang Lady Penelope Rich in the world *première* of *Gloriana* at Covent Garden. She sang in the world *première* of *The Turn of the Screw* at the Venice Festival (1954), creating the role of the Governess, a part which she then sang on many other European stages. In 1954 she also was highly applauded at the Edinburgh Festival as Elektra in *Idomeneo*. Guest appearances and concerts brought her to Milan, Rome, Munich, Vienna, Paris, and Amsterdam.

Records: Decca (including *The Turn of the Screw*, *The Fairy Queen*, *Semele*, and *The Messiah*). *U.S. re-issue:* Capitol, Everest, London, Richmond, RCA Victor, L'Oiseau Lyre, Caedmon.

W

WÄCHTER, EBERHARD, baritone, b. July 9, 1929, Vienna. After completing his university preparation in 1947, he studied piano and music theory at the Vienna High School of Music and after 1950 studied singing with Elisabeth Rado. In 1953 he made his debut at the Vienna Volksoper as Silvio in *I Pagliacci*. In 1955 he was engaged at the Vienna State Opera and he then began a highly successful international career. He sang as guest at Milan, Covent Garden, the State Operas in Munich and Stuttgart, and in Rome, Berlin, and Brussels. He appeared every year in productions at the Salzburg Festivals, where he was particularly admired as a Mozart singer. After 1958 he sang Amfortas in *Parsifal* and Wolfram in *Tannhäuser* at the Bayreuth Festivals. He later appeared at the Edinburgh and Glyndebourne Festivals and in 1960 he was engaged by the Metropolitan Opera. He has an expressive baritone voice, successful both in the concert hall and on the operatic stage.

Records: DGG*, Decca (*Salome, Arabella*, and *Das Rheingold*), Columbia (*Le Nozze di Figaro, Don Giovanni*, and *Capriccio*), Philips*, and RCA Victor (*Die Fledermaus*). *U.S. re-issue:* Angel, London, Amadeo, Epic.

WACHTER, ERNST, bass, b. May 19, 1872, Mulhouse, France; d. August, 1931, Leipzig. After first working in a commercial establishment, he studied singing with Albert Goldberg in Leipzig and made his debut at the Dresden Royal Opera (1894) as Ferrando in *Il Trovatore*. By 1896 he was singing both Fasolt and Hunding in the *Ring* cycle at the Bayreuth Festival; in 1897 he sang Hunding again and Gurnemanz in *Parsifal*; in 1899 he sang only Gurnemanz a few times. He appeared as guest at the Vienna Imperial Opera (1902). He remained a member of the Dresden company until 1912 and from 1915-19 he sang at the Leipzig Opera.

Records: A few rare records for G & T (Dresden, 1902).

WAGNER, SIEGLINDE, contralto, b. Apr. 21, 1921, Linz, Austria. She studied at the Conservatory in Linz, then with Luise Willer and Carl Hartmann in Munich, and made her debut at Linz as Erda in *Siegfried* (1943). She then resumed her study at the Munich Music High School and in 1947 was engaged at the Vienna Volksoper, where she remained until 1952.

After 1952 she was active at the Berlin City Opera. She made guest appearances, among others, at La Scala, the Rome Opera, and in Amsterdam, Madrid, and Barcelona. She sang at the Salzburg Festivals after 1956 and appeared at the Bayreuth Festival in 1962. She is also a very successful concert and oratorio contralto.

Records: DGG* and HMV. *U.S. re-issue:* Richmond, Westminster, Electrola, London, Angel, Haydn Society, Vox.

WALKER, EDYTH, contralto-soprano, b. Mar. 27, 1870, Hopewell, N.Y.; d. Feb. 9, 1950, New York. She studied with Aglaia von Orgeni in Dresden and made her debut (1894) at the Berlin Imperial Opera as Fidès in *Le Prophète*. She was engaged at the Vienna Imperial Opera (1895-1903). In 1896 she sang Magdalena in the Vienna *première* of *Der Evangelimann*. She sang Donna Elvira in *Don Giovanni* at the Salzburg Festival (1901). In 1903 she was engaged by the Metropolitan Opera, where she sang both contralto and dramatic soprano roles. She appeared at the Berlin Imperial Opera (1906-07) and was one of the celebrated artists at the Hamburg Opera (1907-12). She made highly successful guest appearances in Brussels, Amsterdam, Leipzig, Cologne, Prague, and London. She was especially admired as a Wagner interpreter and she sang Kundry in *Parsifal* and Ortrud in *Lohengrin* at the 1908 Bayreuth Festival. She was engaged by the Munich Royal Opera (1912-17). After 1917 she lived in Scheveningen in Holland. She taught at the American Conservatory in Fontainebleau, near Paris (1933-36) and then lived and taught in New York City.

Records: G & T (Vienna, 1902); also unpublished Edison discs. *U.S. re-issue:* IRCC.

WALLNÖFER, ADOLF, baritone-tenor, b. Apr. 26, 1854, Vienna; d. June 9, 1946, Munich. He studied composition and singing in Vienna with O. Dessoff and Krenn, then with Hans von Rokitansky. He made his debut in Olmütz (1878) as a baritone in the part of Count di Luna in *Il Trovatore*. He then lived for a time in Bayreuth, where Richard Wagner invited him to sing in the first Bayreuth Festivals. After 1880 he sang tenor parts and soon became the best-known German heroic tenor of his time. In 1882-83 he took part in a traveling company performing Wagner operas which Angelo Neumann organized. He then sang in Bremerhaven (1883-85), at the German Theater in Prague (1885-95), and at the Metropolitan Opera (1895-96). In 1896 he undertook a long tour of Russia, since he had already had great success at the Imperial Operas in Moscow and St. Petersburg in 1889. In 1896 he came to the Municipal Theater in Stettin and later to the opera house in Breslau. He sang in Nuremberg (1902-06) and at the Vienna Volksoper (1906-08). In addition to his career as a singer he composed more than four hundred songs and ballads, choir works and other vocal compositions, piano works, chamber music, and an opera, *Eddystone* (1899). After 1908 he lived in Munich as a composer and teacher. He wrote *Resonanztonlehre* (Berlin, 1911). He was prized for the strength and quality of his heroic tenor voice, both in Wagner roles and in the lieder repertory.

Records: Seven titles for Beka (Nuremberg, 1907) and five for Favorite (Vienna, 1908), all extremely rare.

WALTER, GEORG A., tenor, b. Nov. 13, 1875, Hoboken, N.J.; d. Sept. 13, 1952, Berlin. The son of German parents, he studied with

Melchiorre Vidal in Milan, Karl Scheidemantel in Dresden, Kurt von Zawilowski in Berlin, and Raimund von zur Mühlen in London. After 1905 he embarked from Berlin, where he lived, on a highly successful career as a concert singer. He was especially prized as a Bach and Handel interpreter of genius. The many cantatas of Johann Sebastian Bach first became known in wider musical circles particularly through his performances. He was also a master of the presentation of songs and he was able at his recitals to fascinate the public, both in Germany and abroad, by his intelligent interpretations. He was busy as a teacher in the Music High School at Stuttgart (1926-34), but after 1934 he lived and taught in Berlin. He himself composed songs and other vocal music and published editions of the solo cantatas of forgotten baroque masters. After 1945 he lived in retirement in Berlin.

Records: HMV and Die Cantorei.

WALTER, GUSTAV, tenor, b. Feb. 11, 1834, Bilin, Austria; d. Jan. 31, 1910, Vienna. He first studied violin at the Conservatory in Prague and then dedicated himself to technical studies at the Prague Polytechnicum. In 1853 he became an engineer in a sugar factory in Bilin. His voice was discovered through his singing in a male quartet. He thereupon studied singing with Vogl in Prague and made his stage debut (1855) at Brünn as Edgardo in *Lucia di Lammermoor*. Through the soprano Rosa Czillag he was engaged in 1856 at the Vienna Imperial Opera, making his debut there as Gomez in *Ein Nachtlager von Granada*. For over thirty years he was the celebrated first lyric tenor of the Vienna Imperial Opera, and was especially admired there in Mozart roles. In 1887 he bade farewell to the stage in a Vienna performance of *Mignon*. He then began a second, and even more successful, career as a concert and lieder singer. He was the first artist to give true song recitals. His presentations of the lieder of Franz Schubert were held to be incomparable. He was applauded in concert halls all over Europe, but especially in London. In 1891 he sang at the Mozart Festival in Salzburg. The beauty of his voice remained for a long time, so that even after the turn of the century he was still able to appear. His son, Roaul Walter (1865-1917), and his daughter, Minna Walter (1863-1901), both had successful careers as opera singers.

Records: In 1905 three records were made of his voice by G & T in Vienna; these are among the greatest rarities of the early days of recording and are of great documentary value. *U.S. re-recording:* Rococo.

WARFIELD, WILLIAM, bass, b. Jan. 22, 1920, West Helena, Ala. At the age of eighteen he won first prize in a singing contest and thereby won a scholarship to study at the Eastman School of Music in Rochester, New York. During World War II he was employed in the intelligence service of the American army. He gave his first concert in New York in 1950 and had a great success. In the same year he undertook a tour of Australia. In 1952 he went to Europe with a company of Negro singers who presented *Porgy and Bess* in London, Vienna, Berlin, and Russia and he was received with admiration. After returning to the United States, he turned more and more to concert and oratorio activity. In 1955 he traveled through Europe as a singer with the Philadelphia Symphony Orchestra; in 1956 he sang the bass solo in a performance of the Mozart *Requiem* in New York under Bruno Walter. He also became known through his singing on the radio and his work in films. He was married to the soprano Leontyne Price, but they were later divorced. A highly expressive voice of great tonal volume.

Records: American Columbia* and RCA Victor*. *U.S. re-issue:* Capitol.

WARREN, LEONARD, baritone, b. Apr. 21, 1911, New York; d. Mar. 4, 1960, New York. After singing in the chorus of the Radio City Music Hall in 1935, he studied with Sidney Dietch in New York and completed his study with Giuseppe Païs and Riccardo Picozzi in Milan. In 1939 he made his debut at the Metropolitan Opera as Paolo Albani in *Simone Boccanegra*. He remained an admired principal baritone of this opera house until the time of his death. He was especially well liked in the baritone roles from the Italian operatic literature. He made highly successful guest appearances in Chicago, San Francisco, Mexico City, at the Teatro Colón, and at the Rio de Janeiro Opera. In 1953 he sang as guest at La Scala, appearing as Iago in *Otello* and as Rigoletto. In 1958 he undertook a triumphal tour of Russia, singing as guest in Moscow and Kiev. He died suddenly on the stage of the Metropolitan Opera during a performance of *La Forza del Destino*. He had one of the most attractive baritone voices of his time and he was equally outstanding for his sumptuous voice and for the maturity of his characterizations.

Records: RCA Victor* (*I Pagliacci*, *Aïda*, *Un Ballo in Maschera*, *Rigoletto*, *Il Trovatore*, *La Traviata*, *Macbeth*, and *La Gioconda*). *U.S. re-issue:* Victrola.

WATSON, CLAIRE, soprano, b. 1927, New York. She began her study of singing with Elisabeth Schumann in New York City and then studied at the Conservatory in Amsterdam with Eduard Lichtenstein. She made her stage debut in Graz (1951) and remained there until 1956. She sang at the Frankfurt Opera (1956-58) and then was called to the Bavarian State Opera in Munich, where she was highly successful. Guest appearances have taken her to the Vienna Opera, Covent Garden, the Brussels Opera, and to the State Operas in Hamburg and Stuttgart. She is greatly admired in both the Mozart and Wagner repertoires. In 1964 she was engaged at the Metropolitan Opera. She has also been successful in concert appearances. She is married to the American tenor David Thaw.

Records: Decca (*Peter Grimes* and *Das Rheingold*). *U.S. re-issue:* RCA Victor, London.

WATTS, HELEN, contralto, b. 1927, Pembrokeshire, Wales. She studied piano and wanted to become a psychotherapist, but instead entered the Royal Academy of Music in London and studied singing with C. Hatchard and Fred Jackson. Deciding to become a concert singer, she joined the BBC chorus. She sang the title role in *Orphée et Eurydice* on the BBC radio in 1953 and was then engaged by its Third Programme to sing two cantatas by Bach. She completed recordings of two Handel operas in 1955, and she was much admired in her stage debut (1958) in the Handel Opera Society production of *Theodora* in London. She has had a brilliant stage career since then throughout Europe. She is especially noted for her singing of Bach and Handel.

Records: DGG*, Westminster*, L'Oiseau Lyre*, and Decca (Bach's *B Minor Mass*). *U.S. re-issues:* Angel, Somerset, London, Bach Guild.

WATZKE, RUDOLF, bass, b. Apr. 5, 1892, Niemes, Austria. He first studied singing in Reichenberg with Frau Kreisel-Hauptfeld, then with Karl Kittel in Bayreuth (1921-23), and finally with George Armin in Berlin. He made his debut in Karlsruhe (1923) and was a member of the Berlin State Opera (1924-28). In 1924-25 and 1927 he sang at the Bayreuth Festivals. After 1928 he sang in the concert hall and appeared only occasionally on the stage. He was especially admired as an oratorio soloist and as an outstanding lieder singer. He was also occupied as a teacher at the Conservatory in Dortmund. After World War II he lived in Wuppertal and continued to give concerts. He married the pianist Liliana Cristova, who often accompanied him during his song recitals.

Records: A few records for HMV and Polydor. *U.S. re-issue:* Brunswick.

WAYDA, GIANNINA (see Korolewicz-Wayda, Janina).

WEATHERS, FELICIA, soprano, b. 1939 (?), St. Louis, Mo. Her father was a Negro lawyer. In 1957 she won second prize in the Metropolitan Opera Auditions in New York. She then studied at Indiana University with Charles Kullman and Dorothea Manski. After appearances in Kansas City, Chicago, and Detroit she went to Europe in 1961. There she won a singing contest in Sofia and made guest appearances in Zürich. In the same year she joined the Kiel Opera. In 1965 she became a member of the Metropolitan Opera. She lives in Munich and has appeared as guest in Sweden, Yugoslavia, and on the most important German and American stages. While her stage repertory consists especially of dramatic roles, she is highly prized in the concert hall as a lieder singer.

Records: Decca. *U.S. re-issue:* London.

WEBER, LUDWIG, bass, b. July 27, 1899, Vienna. At first he planned to become an elementary school teacher, but then studied at the Vienna Technical Theater School with the stage designer Alfred Roller. His voice was discovered when he sang in the chorus of the Vienna Oratorio Society and he began to study singing with Alfred Boruttau. He made his debut (1920) at the Vienna Volksoper, where he remained for five years. He sang as principal bass at Wuppertal (1925-27) and at the Düsseldorf Opera (1927-32). In 1930 he made guest appearances at the Théâtre des Champs-Elysées in Wagner operas under Hoesslin. He sang at the Cologne Opera (1932-33) and then became a member of the State Opera in Munich, where he remained until 1945. In 1945 he was engaged at the Vienna State Opera, where his career reached its climax. He had great success at the Salzburg Festivals and he belonged to the Bayreuth Festival company (1951-56; 1958; 1960-61). He was particularly treasured there as a great Wagner bass. He made highly successful guest appearances at La Scala, Covent Garden, the Teatro Colón, and in Amsterdam and Brussels, as well as at the Maggio Musicale Festival. He was also a much-admired oratorio and lieder singer. After 1961 he was a professor at the Salzburg Mozarteum. He had a powerful but beautiful and musically well-trained voice.

Records: A great many records for Pathé, Philips, Columbia* (*Die Zauberflöte*), Vox* (*Der Fliegende Holländer*), and Decca (*Der Rosenkavalier, Salome, Der Fliegende Holländer,* and *Parsifal*). *U.S. re-issue:* London, Richmond, Epic.

WEDEKIND, ERIKA, soprano, b. Nov. 13, 1868, Hannover, Germany; d. Oct. 10, 1944, Zürich. She was the sister of the poet and playwright Frank Wedekind. At first she planned to become a teacher, but then studied singing with Gustav Scharfe and Aglaia von Orgeni in Dresden. She first sang in the concert hall and made her stage debut (1894) at the Dresden Royal Opera as Frau Fluth in *The Merry Wives of Windsor*. She was a sensational success at her debut and remained the celebrated principal coloratura soprano of the Dresden house until 1909. She sang as guest in Berlin, Hamburg, Wiesbaden, and Munich and in 1896 and 1897 she gave concerts in Moscow with brilliant success. In 1900 she toured Holland. At the Mozart Festival in Salzburg (1901) she sang Zerlina in *Don Giovanni* and Blondchen in *Die Entführung aus dem Serail*. She sang at the Vienna Imperial Opera as guest in 1904 and also appeared at the opera houses in Copenhagen, Oslo, and Ostend. After leaving the Dresden Royal Opera in 1909, she made guest appearances at the Royal Opera in Stockholm, the Komische Oper, and on the smaller German opera stages. She continued her concert activity until 1926. After 1930 she lived in retirement in Zurich. A virtuoso coloratura voice of astounding tonal range and a fine feeling for style in music.

Records: G & T (Dresden, 1906-08) and HMV.

WEEDE, ROBERT, baritone, b. 1903, Baltimore, Md. He began his stage career in 1927 with the De Feo Opera Company and then, after winning the Caruso Memorial Prize, he completed his vocal studies with Oscar Anselmi in Milan. After making guest appearances on various stages in the United States, he was engaged in 1933 by Roxy Rothafel for Radio City Music Hall in New York. He sang at the Metropolitan Opera (1936-42; 1944-45), making his debut as Tonio in *I Pagliacci*. He was greatly admired in San Francisco, where he appeared for over twenty years. He has also appeared in musicals and operettas.

Records: Capitol*, American Columbia*, and RCA Victor*.

WEGNER, WALBURGA, soprano, b. Aug. 25, 1913, Iserlohn, Germany. She studied at the Music High School in Cologne with Maria Philippi, made her concert debut in 1939, and her stage debut as a contralto in Düsseldorf in 1940, singing Suzuki in *Madama Butterfly*. She was engaged in Beuthen (1942-44). In 1944 she returned to Cologne for further study, this time with Klemens Glettenburg. In 1946 she made her debut as a soprano at the Cologne opera house in the title role of *Ariadne auf Naxos*. After guest appearances at the State Operas in Hamburg and Vienna, she sang at La Scala (1950). In 1951 she excited great comment at the Edinburgh Festival for her singing of Leonora in *La Forza del Destino*. She was highly successful at the Metropolitan Opera, particularly as Eva in *Die Meistersinger* and as Chrysothemis in *Elektra* (1951-53). In 1951 she traveled throughout South America; her concert appearances in Paris, London, Amsterdam, and Brussels were also very successful. She remained a member of the Cologne Opera until 1959, but later made only guest appearances on the stage and sang in concerts.

Records: She sang the title role in *Salome* for Philips. *U.S. re-issue:* Columbia.

WEIDEMANN, FRIEDRICH, baritone, b. Jan. 1, 1871, Ratzeburg, Germany; d. Jan. 30, 1919, Vienna. A pupil of Wilhelm Vilmar in Hamburg and Muschler in Berlin, he made his debut at Brieg in Silesia (1896). In 1897 he came to Essen and in 1898 to Hamburg, where he sang secondary roles. He sang at the Riga Opera (1901-03); then Gustav Mahler invited him to join the Imperial Opera in Vienna, where he remained until his death and where he was especially admired in Wagner and Mozart roles. He sang in several important first performances in Vienna: Orestes in *Elektra* (1909), Golaud in *Pelléas et Mélisande* (1910), and Faninal in *Der Rosenkavalier* (1911). At the Salzburg Festival (1906) he sang Count Almaviva in *Le Nozze di Figaro* and as guest at Covent Garden he sang Jochanaan in *Salome* and Kurwenal in *Tristan und Isolde* (1910).

Records: Many records for G & T (Vienna, 1905-08), Odeon (Vienna, 1905), Pathé, and HMV (Vienna, 1908). *U.S. re-issue:* Opera Disc. *U.S. re-recording:* Eterna.

WEIDT, LUCIE, soprano, b. 1879, Troppau, Germany; d. July 31, 1940, Vienna. A pupil of Rosa Papier-Paumgartner in Vienna, she made her debut (1900) at the Leipzig Opera, where she stayed for two years. In 1903 she was engaged at the Imperial Opera in Vienna, making her debut as Elisabeth in *Tannhäuser*; she soon had great success there. She also created several roles in their first Vienna performances: Lisa in *The Queen of Spades* (1906), the Marschallin in *Der Rosenkavalier* (1911), and Kundry in *Parsifal* (1914), a role which she also sang at the first La Scala performance in the same year. She sang the role of the Nurse in the world *première* of *Die Frau ohne Schatten* at the Vienna State Opera on Oct. 10, 1919. Guest appearances at the most important opera houses brought her great success; she sang at Covent Garden, the Paris Opéra, the Teatro Colón, and in Amsterdam and Brussels. She was a member of the Metropolitan Opera (1910-1911). In 1926 she gave up her stage career after having been a member of the Vienna State Opera for twenty-three years. She then taught in Vienna. A large dramatic soprano voice, especially admired in Wagner roles.

Records: G & T (Vienna, 1904-05) and Pathé. *U.S. re-recording:* Rococo.

WEIL, HERMANN, baritone, b. May 29, 1876, Mühlburg, Germany; d. July 6, 1949, of a heart attack while fishing in Blue Mountain Lake near New York City. He first planned to be an elementary school teacher, but then studied musicology with Felix Mottl in Karlsruhe. His voice was trained by Adolf Dippel in Frankfurt. In 1900 he became a *répétiteur* for the chorus in Karlsruhe and in 1901 he made his stage debut in Freiburg im Br. as Wolfram in *Tannhäuser*. From Freiburg he went to the Royal Opera in Stuttgart (1904), where he sang with great success until 1933. In the course of his career he appeared as guest at La Scala, Covent Garden, and in Madrid, Berlin, Amsterdam, and Brussels. At the Bayreuth Festivals he was counted as a great interpreter of Wagner; he sang Amfortas in *Parsifal* there and Gunther in *Götterdämmerung* (1911-12); in 1924-25 he sang Hans Sachs in *Die Meistersinger*. He had a very successful career at the Metropolitan Opera (1911-17), making his debut as Kurwenal in *Tristan und Isolde*. He sang at the Vienna State Opera (1920-23) and toured the United States with the German Opera Company (1923-24). In 1939, because he was Jewish, he was quired to leave Germany and he then lived and taught singing in New York.

Records: Odeon (*Tannhäuser*, Act II), American Columbia*, HMV, Pathé*. *U.S. re-issue:* Opera Disc.

WELITSCH, LJUBA, soprano, b. July 10, 1913, Borissovo, Bulgaria. Originally Ljuba Welitschkova. She studied at the Conservatory in Sofia and at the Vienna Music Academy. She made her debut in Graz (1933), where she remained for four years. She was engaged at the Hamburg State Opera (1940-44) and made guest appearances during this time at the State Operas in Berlin and Dresden. She was a member of the Munich State Opera (1943-45). In 1945 she was engaged by the Vienna State Opera and then began her brilliant international career. She created great excitement at the Salzburg and Edinburgh Festivals through her magnificent portrayals of dramatic soprano roles, particularly the title role in *Salome*, which remained her special starring part. She made guest appearances at Covent Garden, La Scala, in Paris, Rome, Hamburg, Stuttgart, and Munich. In 1948 she was engaged by the Metropolitan Opera and had sensational success there as Salome. She sang as guest at the Chicago and San Francisco Operas. After 1955 she was rarely heard on the operatic stage and later she developed a career in films. She had a skillfully managed, rich dramatic soprano voice, in which were joined powerful dramatic qualities and a high degree of musicality.

Records: Columbia* and Decca. *U.S. re-issue:* London, Angel, Mercury, RCA Victor.

WELTER, LUDWIG, bass, b. Nov. 14, 1917, Pirmasens, Germany; d. Feb. 21, 1965, Eppstein, Germany. He had his first successes at the opera house in Frankfurt. In 1958 he was engaged at the Vienna State Opera, where he was very well liked. He also sang as guest at several opera houses, including Berlin and Munich, and at the Salzburg Festival. His outstanding parts were comic roles, such as Kezal in *The Bartered Bride*, Osmin in *Die Entführung aus dem Serail*, and Baron Ochs in *Der Rosenkavalier*. He died of a heart attack.

Records: Eurodisc (including a small part in *I Vespri Siciliani*, 1951).

WERBER, MIA, soprano, b. Nov. 10, 1876, Vienna; d. 1943, Theresienstadt, Germany. Originally Maria Tachauer. She studied with Frau Dubois-Dollinger in Vienna and sang during this period at the English-French Conservation Club in Vienna. In 1897 she was engaged by Ferenczy for the Thalia Theater in Berlin; she made her debut there in what was to become her special starring role, Mimosa in *The Geisha*. With the Ferenczy ensemble she undertook highly successful guest tours in Germany and Russia. In 1899 she came to the Zentral Theater in Berlin and then went from one triumph to another on the various operetta stages in the German capital. She sang during the 1911-12 season at Königsberg, where she appeared in a few operatic roles, such as Gretel in *Hänsel und Gretel* and Rose Friquet in *Les Dragons des Villars*. Later she returned to the operetta stage, where she was especially applauded in revivals of *The Geisha*. She lived after her retirement in Berlin and in 1942, because she was Jewish, she was removed to Theresienstadt, where she died the following year.

Records: G & T (Berlin, 1902-03); in 1921 she sang for Parlophone (scenes from *The Geisha*). *U.S. re-issue:* American Columbia.

WERRENRATH, REINALD, baritone, b. Aug. 7, 1883, Brooklyn; d. Sept. 12, 1953, Plattsburgh, N.Y. His father, George Werrenrath, was a Danish tenor who taught singing in the United States. The son first studied with his father and then with Percy Rector Stephens in New York City. In 1907 he made his concert debut at the Worcester Festival and he then had a highly successful career as a concert and oratorio singer. After 1912 he was for many years the director of the

University Heights Choral Society. In 1919 he made his stage debut at the Metropolitan Opera as Silvio in *I Pagliacci*. He remained a member of the Metropolitan until 1921, but after that he sang no more on the stage. He visited England (1921-24; 1928), where he sang chiefly on the radio. In 1932 he was awarded an honorary doctorate by New York University. He composed several works for male chorus.

Records: Many Victor* records extending into the electrical period; one Edison* cylinder. *U.S. re-recording:* Rococo.

WETTERGREN, GERTRUD, contralto, b. Feb. 17, 1896, Eslöv, Sweden. Both her parents were singers. She began the study of singing at the age of fifteen with Kallie Sandberg and also studied at the Stockholm Conservatory. She then lost her voice, but after four years of rest she renewed her studies with Mme. Capiani and Gillis Bratt in Stockholm. She made her debut at the Royal Opera there (1924) as Cherubino in *Le Nozze di Figaro*; she was listed as a principal contralto of that house for twenty years. In 1933-34 she made highly successful guest appearances in Vienna and Prague and as a result she was engaged (1935) by the Metropolitan Opera; her debut role there was Amneris in *Aïda*. She remained until 1938 and was greatly admired as Carmen. She also sang at the Chicago Opera and was applauded at Covent Garden (1936; 1939). During World War II she sang only in Sweden, where she appeared under the name Gertrud Palsson Wettergren. In 1945 she gave up her career.

Records: One commercial record by this artist (arias from *Carmen* for HMV). A few private recordings of performances at the Metropolitan, including *Samson et Dalila*, have appeared.

WHITE, CAROLINA, soprano, b. Dec. 23, 1886, Dorchester, Mass.; d. Oct. 5, 1961, Rome. She studied with Weldon Hunt in Boston and made her debut as a concert singer there. In 1907 she went to Italy, where she continued her study with Sebastiani and with Paolo Longone in Naples; she married the latter (1910). In 1908 she made her stage debut at the Teatro San Carlo as Gutrune in *Götterdämmerung* and she soon had great success at other Italian theaters. She was a highly admired singer at the Boston and Chicago Operas (1910-14); she made her Chicago debut as Minnie in the first performance there of *La Fanciulla del West*. In 1912 she sang the role of Maliella in the first American production of *I Gioielli della Madonna*, also at Chicago. After 1914 she appeared mostly as a concert singer, and in 1918 she sang in operettas in New York City. In 1918 she appeared in a silent film, *My Cousin Caruso*, opposite Enrico Caruso. In 1922 she was separated from Paolo Longone and then dropped out of sight. She had a light and expressive soprano voice.

Records: American Columbia* and one Edison* cylinder.

WHITEHILL, CLARENCE, bass-baritone, b. May 5, 1871, Marengo, Iowa; d. Dec. 18, 1932, New York. He began the study of singing in Chicago (1894) and then became a pupil of Giovanni Sbriglia in Paris. In 1899 he made his debut at the Brussels Opera in *Roméo et Juliette*. In 1900 he was applauded at the Opéra-Comique as Nilakantha in *Lakmé*. In 1902 he resumed his studies, now with Julius Stockhausen in Frankfurt, and he sang at the Cologne Opera (1903-08). During this time he made guest appearances at the leading German opera houses. He was particularly admired as a Wagner singer; he sang Wolfram in *Tannhäuser* at the Bayreuth Festival (1904) and was applauded there as Amfortas in *Parsi-*

fal and as Gunther in *Götterdämmerung* (1908-09). In 1909 he was engaged by the Metropolitan Opera, making his debut as Amfortas. He remained there until 1911 and then sang at the Chicago Opera (1911-16). He was again a much-admired singer at the Metropolitan (1914-31). He was also well known as a concert singer. He later lived and taught in New York City.

Records: Zonophone* (New York City, 1903) and Victor*. *U.S. re-recording:* TAP.

WIDDOP, WALTER, tenor, b. Apr. 19, 1892, Norland, England; d. Sept. 9, 1949, London. He was first a wool dyer. After he had sung for Percy Pitt and Norman Allin in London in 1922, he studied for a short time with Dinh Gilly and made his debut (1923) with the British National Opera Company as Radames in *Aïda*. He traveled through the British Isles with this company until 1929. In 1938 he sang for the first time at Covent Garden, appearing as Rinaldo in *Armide*. He then developed quickly into the chief English Wagner tenor of his time. He sang the Wagner heroes in his voice range every year at Covent Garden. In 1927 he appeared as guest at the Teatro Liceo. He also had a successful career as an oratorio singer, particularly in Handel's works. In the United States he sang in the concert hall but never on the stage. His career lasted a long time; as late as 1948 he sang Aegisthus in *Elektra* in London opposite Erna Schlüter. During a London concert he suffered a fatal heart attack in the artists' room, while the audience still applauded in the hall.

Records: HMV. *U.S. re-issue:* RCA Victor. *U.S. re-recording:* Rococo.

WIEDEMANN, HERMANN, baritone, b. 1879; d. July 2, 1944, Berlin. He made his debut in Elberfeld (1905) and then sang successively at Brünn (1906-10), Hamburg (1910-14), and at the Berlin Imperial Opera (1914-16). In the latter year he was engaged at the Vienna Imperial Opera, where he remained until his death. He was very successful later at the Salzburg Festivals, where he first sang the role of Guglielmo in *Così fan tutte* in 1922; he returned there repeatedly until 1941, including a performance as Beckmesser in *Die Meistersinger* under Toscanini (1935). He made guest appearances at Covent Garden and at the Munich Festival, where he was especially admired as Alberich in the *Ring* cycle. He also sang at the Zoppot Festivals (1939-42).

Records: In spite of his very long singing career, there is only a single acoustic record of his voice, made for HMV in 1914. *U.S. re-issue:* Opera Disc.

WIEMANN, ERNST, bass, b. 1919, Stapelberg, Germany. He studied singing in Hamburg and Munich and made his debut (1938) in Kiel. He then sang in Stralsund and at the Berlin Volksoper. After World War II he resumed his career in 1946 at Gelsengirchen. From there he went to Nuremberg in 1950 and to the Hamburg State Opera in 1957. He sang as guest on the leading stages in Italy, Spain, and France. In 1961 he was engaged by the Metropolitan Opera. He was admired for his powerful and voluminous bass voice, particularly in Wagner roles.

Records: Electrola*. *U.S. re-issue:* Turnabout.

WIENER, OTTO, baritone, b. Feb. 13, 1913, Vienna. He sang as a boy with the Peterlini Children's Chorus in Vienna. He first studied at the Veterinary Institute in Vienna but then began the study of singing with Küper and Hans Duhan there. In 1939 he began his career as a concert singer and appeared as such on the radio. He was a soldier in World War II and was wounded in action in Greece. After the war he worked as a concert and oratorio singer. He first decided to appear on the stage in 1953 and made his debut in Graz in the title role in *Simone Boccanegra*. He sang at Düsseldorf (1956-59) and made guest appearances at the opera house in Frankfurt and the Berlin City Opera. He sang at the Bayreuth Festivals after 1957 and was admired there as Hans Sachs in *Die Meistersinger*, Gunther in *Götterdämmerung*, and as the Flying Dutchman. After 1957 he was a member of the Vienna State Opera and after 1960 simultaneously a member of the Munich State Opera. Guest appearances at La Scala, the Rome Opera, Covent Garden, and the Brussels Opera brought him great triumphs, particularly in Wagner parts. He was also a famous concert singer.

Records: MMS, Vox*, and DGG. *U.S. re-issue:* RCA Victor, (*Die Meistersinger*), Remington, Westminster, Columbia, SPA, Amadeo, Urania, Lyrichord, MGM.

WILDBRUNN, HELENE, soprano, b. Apr. 8, 1882, Vienna. She studied with Rosa Papier-Paumgartner in Vienna and made her debut as a contralto in Dortmund (1907). She remained there for seven years and then was engaged at the Royal Opera in Stuttgart (1914-18), where her voice changed to that of a dramatic soprano. She was especially noted as a Wagner interpreter. She sang at the Berlin State Opera (1918-25), the Berlin City Opera (1925-31), and was also concurrently a member of the Vienna State Opera after 1919. Guest appearances brought her great triumphs elsewhere; in 1922 she sang Kundry in *Parsifal* at La Scala and in the same year she completed a long guest season at the Teatro Colón in Buenos Aires. There she was especially admired as Isolde in *Tristan und Isolde*, as Brünnhilde in the *Ring* cycle, and as the Marschallin in *Der Rosenkavalier*. Later she sang at Covent Garden, the Paris Opéra, and in Zürich, Amsterdam, Budapest, and Brussels. She sang on the stage at the Vienna State Opera until 1932, but later appeared only in concerts. She was a professor at the Vienna Music Academy (1932-50). Her dark voice with its great volume, her dramatic skill, and her fine feeling for style made her a famous singer.

Records: Relatively few records for Odeon and Polydor. *U.S. re-issue:* Vocalion. *U.S. re-recording:* Rococo.

WILHELM, HORST, tenor, b. 1927, Berlin. He sang as a boy in Berlin church choirs and later in a youth chorus on the Berlin radio. He was a soldier in World War II and spent the last part of the war in an English prison camp. After 1947 he studied singing at the Berlin Music High School with Götte. He made his debut (1951) at the Berlin City Opera, where he remained as principal lyric tenor until 1956. Since that time he has been engaged at Kassel. He has made guest appearances in Berlin, Munich, Frankfurt, and Hannover, and he has also had a brilliant career as a concert and oratorio singer.

Records: for HMV, Vox, Orbis, and Bach Guild*. *U.S. re-issue:* Angel, Electrola.

WILLER, LUISE, contralto, b. 1888, Munich. Her voice was discovered by Rasbach, the chorus director of the Munich Royal Opera, and after 1906 she was a member of the chorus of this house. In 1910 she was brought forward in her first solo part—that of Annius in *La Clemenza di Tito*. She soon developed into one of the most noted singers at the Munich Opera. In 1917 she sang there in the world première of *Palestrina*. She sang as guest in London, Amsterdam, Berlin, Dresden, Stuttgart, and Vienna. At the Salzburg Festivals she sang Clytemnestra in *Iphigénie en Aulide* (1930) and Adelaide in *Arabella* (1942-43). In 1936 she went for a season to the Berlin State Opera, but in 1937 she returned to Munich, where she remained until 1947. She also sang there later as a guest. In 1955 she gave her farewell performance there, singing Erda in *Siegfried*. She lives in Icking, near Munich. A large, musically outstanding, and well-managed contralto voice.

Records: A few records for Polydor and Odeon. U.S. re-issue: Mercury.

WILLIAMS, CAMILLA, soprano, b. 1925, Danville, Va. She studied with Marianne Székély-Freschl in Philadelphia and in 1943 and 1944 won the Marian Anderson Prize. In 1945 she gave her first concert in Philadelphia and she made her stage debut (1946) at the New York City Opera, singing the title role in *Madama Butterfly*. Guest appearances in the United States followed, as well as a concert tour of the Caribbean Islands and Central America in 1950. In 1954 she went to Europe and sang as guest in Vienna, Berlin, and The Hague. She was the first Negro singer to appear at the Vienna State Opera. Her concert tours took her to both North and South America, the Scandinavian countries, Germany, Austria, Italy, France, and England. She is considered a song interpreter of the first rank.

Records: Columbia* (*Porgy and Bess*) and MGM*.

WILLIAMS, EVAN, tenor, b. 1867, Mineral Ridge, Ohio; d. May 24, 1918, Akron, Ohio. Originally Ffrangeon Davies. His parents immigrated to the United States from Wales. He first worked in a steel mill and his voice was discovered when he sang in an amateur ensemble. He studied singing with Louise von Feilitsch in Cleveland. In 1891 he gave his first concert in Galion, Ohio, but his official debut was made at the Worcester Festival (1896). After further study with Saubage, Ben Davies, and Frangon Davies in New York, he undertook a highly successful concert tour in England in 1903, followed by a second in 1906. He was considered one of the most famous American oratorio tenors of his time and was equally esteemed as an interpreter of songs. In the United States alone, during the course of his career he gave over one thousand recitals. In the years 1896-1911 he was highly applauded at the Worcester Festivals. In 1912 he undertook a more extended tour of England with the New Symphony Orchestra under Sir Landon Ronald and with the pianist Irene Scharrer.

Records: A great many records for G & T (London, 1906-07), HMV (London, 1908), and Victor*; some of these appeared under the name William T. Evans. U.S. re-recording: Cantilena.

WINDGASSEN, FRITZ, tenor, b. Feb. 9, 1883, Hamburg; d. Apr. 18, 1963, Murnau, Germany. At first a sailor, he began to study singing in 1907 at the Hamburg Conservatory. He made his stage debut (1909) at Hamburg as Manrico in *Il Trovatore*. His further engagements included Bremen (1910-11), the Hamburg Opera (1911-12), and Kassel (1912-23). He sang at the Stuttgart State Opera (1923-45), making his debut there as Walther in *Die Meistersinger* and becoming one of the best-liked singers in the company. After his retirement from the stage he was professor at the

Stuttgart Music High School. He was married to the coloratura soprano Vally van Osten, a sister of the famous soprano Eva von der Osten; his son, Wolfgang Windgassen, became a famous heroic tenor. His last years were passed on his estate in Uffing-am-Staffelsee.

Records: Acoustic records for Polyphone and Polydor.

WINDGASSEN, WOLFGANG, tenor, b. June 26, 1914, Annemasse, France. His father, Fritz Windgassen, was a tenor at the Stuttgart State Opera after 1923 and later a professor at the Stuttgart Music High School; his mother was the coloratura soprano Vally van Osten. He first became a technical apprentice at the Stuttgart Opera, then studied singing with his father and at the Music High School in Stuttgart. He made his debut at Pforzheim (1939), but soon thereafter he entered the army. In 1945 he was engaged by the Stuttgart State Opera, of which he has since remained a member. He quickly became known as a celebrated Wagner tenor. In 1951 he sang Parsifal at the first Bayreuth Festival after the war and he has since sung there annually in almost all the Wagner roles for his voice range. He is generally considered to be the most famous Wagner tenor of his generation. He sang regularly as guest at the Vienna State Opera, and has also been admired at Covent Garden, La Scala, the Teatro Liceo, the Paris Opéra, and at the State Operas in Berlin, Hamburg, and Munich. In 1957 he joined the Metropolitan Opera, where he was admired as a Wagner interpreter of genius. He is married to the soprano Lore Wissmann.

Records: A great many records, particularly for DGG* (*Die Meistersinger* and *Der Fliegende Holländer*), Decca (*Lohengrin, Siegfried,* and *Parsifal*) and HMV (*Fidelio*). *U.S. re-issue:* Electrola, London, Philips, Heliodor, Seraphim.

WINKELMANN, HERMANN, tenor, b. Mar. 8, 1849, Braunschweig, Germany; d. Jan. 18, 1912, Maur, near Vienna. He originally planned to become a pianomaker, but studied singing with Koch in Hannover and made his debut (1875) at Sondershausen in Thuringia as Manrico in *Il Trovatore*. In 1876 he went to Altenburg and in 1878 to the opera house in Hamburg, where in 1879 he sang the title roll in the world *première* of *Nero*. He soon became famous as a Wagner tenor. In 1882 he sang with the ensemble of the Hamburg Opera under Hans Richter at the Drury Lane Theater. Richard Wagner particularly admired the voice of this artist and he chose him for the title role in the world *première* of *Parsifal*, which he sang on July 26, 1882, at the Bayreuth Festival. He sang this role at the Bayreuth until 1891 and his acting as Parsifal was considered to be supreme. In 1884 he traveled to the United States and sang at Wagner festivals arranged by Theodore Thomas in New York, Boston, Chicago, Philadelphia, and Cincinnati. After 1883 he was a celebrated member of the Vienna Imperial Opera, where he was equally admired for his portrayals in Wagner roles. In 1907 he gave up his stage career and settled in Vienna as a teacher of singing.

Records: Rare records for G & T (Vienna, 1902-06) and Favorite (Vienna, 1905-06). *U.S. re-recording:* IRCC, Rococo, HRS.

WINTERNITZ-DORDA, MARTHA, soprano, b. 1885, Vienna. She began her career in Graz (1906) and then sang at the Raimund Theater in Vienna (1908-10). She was engaged as principal coloratura soprano at the Hamburg

Opera (1910-29) and was highly successful there. She sang as guest at the Vienna Imperial Opera in 1910 and was engaged at the Chicago Opera (1913-14). She gave guest performances until 1933 and then lived as a teacher in Hamburg. She had a technically admirable and thoroughly trained coloratura voice.

Records: Acoustics for Pathé and Parlophone.

WINTERS, LAWRENCE, baritone, b. Nov. 12, 1915, King's Creek, S. C.; d. Sept. 24, 1965, Hamburg. He came from a Negro family and sang as a child in a church choir. He began to study singing in Salisbury, North Carolina, and in 1941 entered Howard University; he was also a pupil of the baritone Robert Todd Duncan. After first being active in concerts, he was a soldier in World War II and resumed his career later. In 1948 he made his debut at the New York City Opera. Concert tours in Central America and the West Indian islands followed. In 1949 he went to Europe, where he greatly excited his auditors at a song recital in Berlin. In 1952 he was engaged by the Hamburg State Opera, where he had great success as a singer; he made his debut there as Amonasro in *Aïda*. He sang as guest at the Berlin City Opera, the New York City Opera, and the San Francisco Opera and was highly successful in concerts and recitals.

Records: Columbia* (*Porgy and Bess*) and DGG. *U.S. re-issue:* ASCO, Desto.

WIRL, ERIK, tenor, b. 1885, Ebensee, Austria; d. Feb. 15, 1954, Rottach-Egern, Germany. The son of a physician, he was successful as a boy soprano and studied singing in Munich with Schuegraf, who at first thought he would become a baritone; later in his studies he discovered that he really had a tenor voice. He made his debut (1906) at the Bayreuth Festival as the Steersman in *Tristan und Isolde* and as a Squire in *Parsifal*. He was the first lyric tenor of the Opera in Frankfurt (1906-22). There he sang Pelléas in the first German performance of *Pelléas et Mélisande* (1912), the Knight in the world *première* of *Der Ferne Klang* (1912), and the Fool in *Der Schatzgräber* (1920). In the 1920's he dedicated himself particularly to operetta in Berlin and Vienna. Thus he sang with Fritzi Massary in Berlin in *Die Geschiedene Frau* and created a role in *Die Strohwitwe* (1920). He sang at the Kroll Opera (1927-31) and then moved to the heroic repertory. In 1926 he sang as guest at the Vienna State Opera; in 1931 he appeared in The Hague in the role of Herod in *Salome*. In 1931 he sang at the Teatro Colón, where he undertook the part of Beckmesser in *Die Meistersinger*. He also appeared a few times in musical films, including *Zwei Herzen im Dreivierteltakt*. He sang at the Berlin State Opera (1928-33) and then appeared, partly in operetta and partly at the Berlin City Opera, until 1942. At the end of his life he lived in retirement in Upper Bavaria.

Records: HMV and Vox. *U.S. re-recording:* Rococo.

WISSMAN, LORE, soprano, b. June 22, 1922, Neckartailfingen, Germany. She began her study of singing in 1939 at the Music High School in Stuttgart and then became a pupil of Eduard Ewen. She made her debut at the State Opera in Stuttgart (1942) as Kordula in *Hans Sachs*. She remained at that theater more than twenty years; at first she sang only small parts but after 1946 she began to sing the principal roles in the lyric repertory. Guest appearances took her to the State Operas in Vienna, Munich, and Hamburg, to the Paris

Opéra, the Rome Opera, the Teatro São Carlos, and the opera houses in Geneva, Marseilles, and Bordeaux. She also sang at the Bayreuth Festivals and appeared very successfully as a concert soprano. She is married to the tenor Wolfgang Windgassen.

Records: DGG and Decca (*Parsifal*, Bayreuth). *U.S. re-issue*: American Decca.

WITHERSPOON, HERBERT, bass, b. July 21, 1873, Buffalo, N.Y.; d. May 10, 1935, New York. He was the son of an Episcopal minister. After his studies at Yale University, he began the study of singing with W. J. Hall and M. Treumann in New York and made his concert debut in New Haven (1895). In 1896 he sang in New York in a concert performance of *Parsifal* under Walter Damrosch. He made his stage debut (1898) with the Castle Square Opera Company in New York as Ramfis in *Aida*. He then went for further study with Bouhy and Victor Capoul in Paris, with Lamperti in Milan, and with Henry J. Wood in London. He had his first great success in England as an oratorio soloist. In 1908 he came to the Metropolitan Opera, making his debut there as Titurel in *Parsifal*. He remained with this company until 1916. Thereafter he worked as a singing teacher. He founded the American Academy of Teachers of Singing and in 1925 became the president of the Chicago Musical College. In 1930 he became director of the Chicago Opera and director of the Cincinnati Conservatory. In March of 1935 he was chosen to be director of the Metropolitan Opera in New York as successor to Giulio Gatti-Cazzaza, but he died suddenly of a heart attack before the opening of the new season.

Records: Victor* (1907-18). *U.S. re-recording*: Rococo.

WITT, JOSEF, tenor, b. May 17, 1901, Munich. He studied at the Munich Academy for Musical Art and made his debut there at the State Opera (1920). He then sang successively at Stettin, Breslau, Karlsruhe, Dortmund, Cologne, and Braunschweig. In 1937 he was engaged at the Vienna State Opera, where he was highly successful. At the Salzburg Festivals he sang Basilio in *Le Nozze di Figaro* (1942; 1948) and in 1947 he sang Robespierre in the world *première* of *Dantons Tod*, as well as in *Arabella*. After 1942 he became a *régisseur* at the Vienna State Opera and after 1955 the conductor of the opera studio there and a professor at the Vienna Academy of Music at the same time.

Records: Urania (*Macbeth*) and DGG* (a small part in *Ariadne auf Naxos*).

WITTE, ERICH, tenor, b. 1911, Graudenz, Germany. He made his debut in Bremen (1932) and sang there for five years. In 1937 he came to Wiesbaden, where he distinguished himself in *buffo* parts. As such he was engaged in the 1938-39 season at the Metropolitan Opera. He sang as guest at the Vienna State Oprea (1938; 1940). After 1940 he joined the ensemble of the Berlin State Opera. At the Bayreuth Festivals (1943-44) he sang David in *Die Meistersinger* and appeared later as Loge in the *Ring* cycle (1952-53). He remained at the Berlin State Opera until 1960, but later sang mostly heroic tenor roles. In 1961 he became chief stage director of the Frankfurt Opera.

Records: Urania* (*Abu Hassan*) and Eterna. *U.S. re-issue*: Vox.

WITTRISCH, MARCEL, tenor, b. Oct. 1, 1901, Antwerp, Belgium; d. June 2, 1955, Berlin. He came of a German family living in Antwerp but forced to leave Belgium in 1918. He studied at the Conservatories in Munich and Leipzig and completed his training in Milan. He made his debut in Halle (1925) as Konrad in *Hans Heiling*. He sang in Braunschweig (1926-29). In 1929 he was engaged at the Berlin State Opera and had a brilliant career there until 1944. He was especially admired in lyric parts from the French and Italian repertories and as a Mozart singer. In 1931 he was applauded at Covent Garden as Tamino in *Die Zauberflöte*. He also appeared as guest at the Vienna and Munich State Operas and at La Scala in Milan. In 1937 he sang Lohengrin at the Bayreuth Festival. He was also very successful as an operetta and film singer. After World War II he appeared only rarely in opera and occupied himself with concerts and operetta appearances. His expressive and brilliant tenor voice was frequently compared to that of the great Richard Tauber.

Records: HMV, Decca, and Telefunken. *U.S. re-issue:* RCA Victor. *U.S. re-recording:* Eterna, TAP, Electrola, Telefunken, Scala, Rococo.

WOLF, OTTO, tenor, b. Nov. 7, 1871, Bernburg, Germany; d. Mar. 28, 1946, Munich. He studied with Wilhelmine Niehr-Bingerheimer and Adolf Sondegg and made his debut (1897) at Sondershausen in Thuringia as Count Almaviva in *Il Barbiere di Siviglia*. He sang in Lübeck (1898-99), Mainz (1899-1900), and Darmstadt (1901-09). In the latter year he was engaged by the Munich Royal Opera and he remained there until 1928, a celebrated member of this company. He was chiefly famous as a Wagner tenor. He sang as guest at the Vienna State Opera (1921-24; 1926); in 1923 he sang Tristan in Amsterdam and later guest appearances took him to the opera houses in Brussels, Paris, Prague, and Berlin. He also toured the United States very successfully. After his active career as a singer had ended, he taught in Munich.

Records: Polydor, Pathé*, and Odeon.

WOLFF, FRITZ, tenor, b. Oct. 28, 1894, Munich; d. Jan. 18, 1957, Munich. He was first a military officer and took part in World War I. After the end of the war he studied with Heinrich König in Würzburg and made his debut at the Bayreuth Festival (1925) as Loge in the *Ring* cycle. He was considered unmatchable in this part and sang it every year at Bayreuth until 1941; he was later applauded there as Walther in *Die Meistersinger*, as Parsifal, and as Melot in *Tristan und Isolde*. In 1925 he was engaged at Hagen and by way of Chemnitz he came to the Berlin State Opera in 1928. In that year he sang in the world *première* of *Der Singende Teufel*. He sang as guest at the Vienna State Opera and in Budapest, Prague, and Paris; he appeared at Covent Garden (1928-35) and in the United States, particularly at the Chicago and Cleveland Operas. He sang at the Berlin State Opera until 1942. After World War II he became almost blind and had to give up his career. In 1950 he was named professor at the Music High School in Munich.

Records: He made a few records for Polydor (an abbreviated *Lohengrin*), Columbia* (Bayreuth, 1927), Muza, and Eterna. *U.S. re-issue:* Brunswick.

WOYTOWICZ, STEFANIA, soprano, b. 1926, Orynin, Poland. She passed her youth in Brest-Litovsk, but after 1943 lived in Warsaw. In 1945 she began her studies of Romanistic philology and musicology at the University of Cracow and studied singing at the same time with Stanislava Zawadska in Cracow. In 1950 she won a singing

Wunderlich

contest in Posnan, in 1951 the Bach Competition in Leipzig, and in 1954 the contest in connection with the Prague Spring Music Festival. After her first successes in Poland, she made a long tour through Austria, Russia, and China in 1955. Since then she has had brilliant success in concert halls all over the world—in London, Paris, Stockholm, Moscow, Holland, and Germany, as well as at the Edinburgh Festivals. In 1960 she undertook a long tour of the United States. She lives in Warsaw and has never appeared in staged opera, but only in television productions. She is especially recognized as a singer of contemporary music. A large, luxuriant soprano voice of uncommonly glowing timbre.

Records: Supraphon and DGG* (including the title role in *Tosca*). *U.S. re-issue:* Bruno.

WUNDERLICH, FRITZ, tenor, b. Sept. 26, 1930, Kusel, Germany; d. Oct. 8, 1966, Heidelberg, Germany, as a result of a fall. After the early death of his father, he had great difficulties to overcome before he could begin the study of singing. From 1950-55 he studied at the Music High School in Freiburg im Br. and after 1953 he was a student at the Municipal Theater there. In 1955 he was engaged by the State Opera in Stuttgart and he remained a member until his death. He was at the same time engaged after 1958 at the Opera in Frankfurt and after 1960 at the Munich State Opera. He was especially admired as a Mozart tenor. In 1958 he sang Tamino in *Die Zauberflöte* at the Aix-en-Provence Festival and after 1958 his art as a Mozart singer was admired at the Salzburg Festivals. In 1960 he sang the role of Tiresias in the world *première* of *Oedipus der Tyrann* in Stuttgart. He was a frequent guest at the Vienna State Opera, at the Berlin City Opera, and in Holland, France and Switzerland. He was to have made his debut at the Metropolitan Opera in November, 1966, but this was prevented by his accidental death.

Records: Opera, DGG* (*Orfeo*), Eurodisc and HMV (*Zar und Zimmermann, The Bartered Bride, Der Fliegende Holländer,* and *The Merry Wives of Windsor*). *U.S. re-issue:* Electrola, Vox, Bruno, Angel, London, Verve, Turnabout, Archive of Recorded Sound, Decca, Seraphim, Victrola, Heliodor.

Y

YAW, ELLEN BEACH, soprano, b. 1869, Boston, N.Y.; d. Sept. 9, 1947, Covina, Calif. At first the secretary to a New York lawyer, she studied singing with Mme. Bjorksten in New York and then with Mathilde Marchesi in Paris. In 1894 she made her concert debut in St. Paul, Minnesota, and in 1895 made a tour of Germany and Switzerland. In 1896 she sang at Carnegie Hall in New York and in 1899 at the Savoy Theater in London in the world première of *The Rose of Persia*. Her operatic debut was made (1905) at the Teatro Costanzi as Lucia di Lammermoor. She sang the same role in a single performance at the Metropolitan Opera in 1908 with Alessandro Bonci as her partner. In spite of encouraging success on the opera stage, she then dedicated herself entirely to concerts and until 1928 she undertook long tours in the United States and Europe. She resided in Covina, California, and gave concerts in the Lark Ellen Bowl, which she had erected. This artist, who was known under the name Lark Ellen, founded the Lark Ellen School for Boys in Los Angeles.

Records: A few titles for Victor* (1907-08) and Edison* Diamond Discs. In 1938 she made electric records, published by HMV, in which, however, her voice had completely aged. These records demonstrated a peculiar phenomenon in which her voice—schooled in the Marchesi method for coloratura soprano—could perform trills, not only in major and minor seconds, but also in fourths and fifths. One private record for Co-Art, published in California in 1941, contains the Mad Scene from Thomas' *Hamlet*. U.S. re-recording: Belcanto, IRCC.

YEEND, FRANCES, soprano, b. 1918, Vancouver, Wash. She began the study of the violin at the age of seven and vocal studies at the age of ten. After 1943 she sang in New York in operettas and on the radio. In 1944 she made a concert tour through the United States; in 1947 she made a long world tour with Mario Lanza and George London as the Bel Canto Trio. In 1946 she sang the role of Ellen Orford in the American *première* of *Peter Grimes* at the Tanglewood Festival. She sang with the New York City Opera (1948-65). In 1951 she appeared as guest at the Edinburgh Festival, in 1953 at Covent Garden, and in 1958 at the Arena Festival in the title role in *Turandot*. In 1961 she became a member of the Metropolitan Opera, making her debut as Chrysothemis in *Elektra*.

Records: Columbia*, ASCO* (*Carmen*), Da Vinci*, and Mercury*. *U.S. re-issue*: Odyssey.

Z

ZACCARIA, NICOLA, bass, b. Mar. 9, 1923, Athens. He studied at the Royal Conservatory in Athens and made his debut there at the Royal Opera as Raimundo in *Lucia di Lammermoor* in 1949. He became widely known through his guest appearances in Italy; in 1953 he had a brilliant success at La Scala in Milan as Sparafucile in *Rigoletto* and he appeared regularly thereafter at La Scala and at the Rome Opera. He was also admired at the Arena and Maggio Musicale Festivals. After 1956 he made annual guest appearances at the Vienna State Opera. He has also sung at the Salzburg Festivals, where, in addition to his operatic roles, he sang the bass part in Beethoven's *Missa Solemnis* in 1959. In the same year he was applauded at Covent Garden as Creon in Cherubini's *Medea*. His later guest appearances included Berlin, Cologne, Brussels, and the Edinburgh Festival. He is a famous concert bass.

Records: Columbia (*Aïda, Un Ballo in Maschera, La Sonnambula, Il Barbiere di Siviglia, Falstaff, Il Trovatore, Rigoletto*, et cetera). *U.S. re-issue:* Angel, London.

ZADEK, HILDE, soprano, b. Dec. 15, 1917, Bromberg, Germany. She passed her youth in Vienna and Stettin, but in 1934 she had to leave Germany because she was Jewish. She emigrated to Palestine and worked in Jerusalem as a nurse in a hospital clinic there. She studied singing with Rose Pauly in Jerusalem and in 1945 became a pupil of Ria Ginster in Zürich. She made her debut as Aïda (1947) at the Vienna State Opera and had a sensational success; since then she has been a member of this company. Guest appearances have brought her brilliant success all over the world: at the Festivals in Edinburgh, Salzburg, and Holland, at La Scala, the Teatro Colón, and in Paris, Brussels, Amsterdam, Rome, San Francisco, Düsseldorf, and Munich. Since 1952 she has been a member of the Metropolitan Opera. She has a highly expressive and deeply musical soprano voice; she has given her best performances in dramatic roles.

Records: Philips (*Don Giovanni*) and DGG. *U.S. re-issue:* London, Epic.

ZADOR, DESIDER, baritone, b. Mar. 8, 1873, Horna Krupa, Hungary; d. Apr. 24, 1931, Berlin. At first a teacher, he studied singing with Adele Passy-Cornet in Budapest and in Vienna; he made his debut (1898) at Czernowitz as

Count Almaviva in *Le Nozze di Figaro*. He sang at Elberfeld (1898-1901) and at the German Theater in Prague (1901-06). He made guest appearances at the Royal Operas in Dresden and Munich and in 1905 he was very successful at Covent Garden. He became famous chiefly for his incomparable performance as Alberich in the *Ring* cycle. He had a brilliant career at the Komische Oper (1906-11). He sang at the Dresden Royal Opera (1911-16) and was a singer and conductor at the Budapest National Opera (1916-19) and at the Berlin City Opera (1920-24). Later he sang as guest in Paris, Milan, Brussels, Vienna, Prague, and Chicago. Toward the end of his career he sang mostly bass roles. He was married to the Hungarian contralto Emma Zador-Bassth (b. Dec. 4, 1888). A dark-timbred bass-baritone of great flexibility and expressiveness.

Records: His first records appeared on G & T (Prague, 1904); later he recorded for Polydor and HMV (Valentin in *Faust*, Berlin 1908). *U.S. re-issue:* Opera Disc, RCA Victor. *U.S. re-recording:* Rococo.

ZAMBONI, MARIA, soprano, b. July 25, 1898, Peschiera, Italy. She was a pupil of M. Silva at the Conservatory in Parma and made her debut at Piacenza (1921) as Marguerite in *Faust*. She had great success on Italian operatic stages, particularly at La Scala, where she sang Liu in the memorable world *première* of *Turandot* in 1926 under Toscanini. She was also admired for her singing of Mimi in *La Bohème* at La Scala under his direction. She was particularly successful in South America, where she often sang at the Teatro Colón and at the opera houses in Rio de Janeiro, Montevideo, São Paulo, and Santiago de Chile. She lives in Milan.

Records: Columbia (*Manon Lescaut*) and HMV (duets with Beniamino Gigli). *U.S. re-recording:* TAP, Eterna, FRP, Rococo.

ZAMPIERI, GIUSEPPE, tenor, b. 1929 (?). He began his career by singing small *comprimario* roles at La Scala. In 1955, during a La Scala guest appearance in Berlin, he substituted for Giuseppe di Stefano as Edgardo in *Lucia di Lammermoor* and had an exciting success. His artistic career then developed very quickly. In 1955 he sang at the Arena Festival and after 1958 he sang regularly as guest at the Vienna State Opera, where he is greatly admired. Since 1958 he has also sung at the Salzburg Festivals. He has been highly successful at the Netherlands Opera in Amsterdam and at the Holland Festival. In the United States he was applauded for his appearances in San Francisco and Los Angeles. In 1959 he undertook a tour of Israel. A well-trained, intense voice, celebrated not only in the Italian repertory, but also in the German—as Florestan in *Fidelio*, for example.

Records: Up to the present he has made few records, and has sung mostly small roles for Decca. *U.S. re-issue:* London.

ZANELLI, RENATO, baritone-tenor, b. Apr. 1, 1892, Valparaiso, Chile; d. Mar. 25, 1935, Valparaiso. His father was Italian and his mother a *Chileno*. His younger brother later had a successful operatic career, also as a baritone, under the name Carlo Morelli. Since his parents were wealthy, he was brought up in boarding schools in Switzerland and Italy. In 1915 he began to study singing with Angelo Querze in Santiago de Chile and he made his debut there (1916) as a baritone, singing Valentin in *Faust*. After his first success there and at the Opera in Montevideo, he came to the United States in 1918, where he was discovered by Andres de Segurola. In 1919 he was engaged at the Metropolitan Opera in New York and made his debut as Amonasro in *Aida*; he remained there until 1923, making guest appearances at the Ravinia Summer Opera, near Chicago, and with the Scotti Opera Company. After renewed study with Lari and Yanara in Milan, he made his debut as a heroic tenor at the Teatro San Carlo in Naples (1924), singing Raoul in *Les Huguenots*. He then had a brilliant career and was famous above all for his singing of the title role in *Otello*. In 1928 he sang this part at Covent Garden and in 1927 he sang Lohengrin at the Teatro Regio in Parma. He made guest appearances at La Scala, the Teatro Costanzi, the Teatro Colón. He sang annually at the Opera in Santiago de Chile. In 1934, already very ill, he gave a few concerts in the United States. In 1935 he sang Otello again at the Opera in Santiago, but died a few weeks later. One of the most beautiful voices of his time. He joined both a complementary baritonal warmth and the brilliance of a heroic tenor to dramatic expressiveness.

Records: He sang as a baritone for Victor* and as a tenor for HMV.

ZARESKA, EUGENIA, mezzo-soprano, b. 1910, Lemberg, Germany. She studied with Adam Didur in Lvov, then in Vienna, where she won a singing competition in 1938. She was a pupil of Anna Bahr-Mildenburg and began her stage career in 1939. After 1940 she lived in Italy, where she appeared at the leading opera houses and had special success at La Scala. After the end of World War II she made a great many guest appearances in Paris; she was admired most there for her Marina in *Boris Godounov*. In 1952 she moved her residence to London; there she sang frequently at Covent Garden, while also appearing on opera stages in Italy, France, Belgium, and Holland. She was an internationally admired concert singer and was particularly outstanding in her interpretation of songs.

Records: Columbia, Decca, HMV (*Boris Godounov*), and Cetra*. *U.S. re-issue:* Capitol, Urania, RCA Victor.

ZBRUJEWA, EUGENIA, contralto, b. 1869, Moscow; d. 1936, Moscow. She was the daughter of the composer E.A. Lavrovski. She sang at the Imperial Opera in Moscow (1894-1905) and in the latter year was engaged at the Imperial Opera in St. Petersburg, where she remained until 1917. In 1913 she sang the role of Marfa in the *première* at that house of *Khovantchina* opposite Feodor Chaliapin. She appeared very successfully as guest in Germany and France (1907-12), and thus introduced contemporary Russian music to western Europe at a time when it was not very widely known. She was a professor at the St. Petersburg Conservatory (1915-17) and from 1921 until her death a professor at the Moscow Conservatory. A strong, dark contralto voice, outstanding for its wide range.

Records: G & T (St. Petersburg, 1906), Amour (St. Petersburg, 1909), and HMV, all very rare.

ZEANI, VIRGINIA, soprano, b. 1928, Rumania. Her father was Rumanian, her mother Italian. At the age of twenty she went to Milan and studied history, literature, and philosophy at the university there. At the same time she studied singing with Lydia Lipkowska. When the singer taking the part of Violetta in *La Traviata* at Bologna fell ill, she substituted on short notice and made her debut with brilliant success (1950). She then appeared on various opera stages in Italy and in 1956 came to La Scala, where she made her debut as Cleopatra in Handel's *Giulio Cesare*. She sang at the Arena Festivals (1956-63) and during these years she made guest appearances in Austria, Spain, France, England, Greece, Switzerland, Germany, South Africa, and Egypt. She sang the role of Blanche in the La Scala world *première* of *Les Dialogues des Carmélites* (1957). Also in 1957 she replaced Maria Callas at the Vienna Opera Festival. In 1958 she was engaged by the Metropolitan Opera and in the same year she married the bass Nicola Rossi-Lemeni. She has a coloratura voice, but has also mastered perfectly the roles in the lyric repertory.

Records: Decca. *U.S. re-issue:* Cetra, Vox, London.

ZENATELLO, GIOVANNI, tenor, b. Feb. 22, 1876, Verona, Italy; d. Feb. 11, 1949, New York. He studied in Verona, with Moretti in Milan, and made his debut as a baritone, singing Silvio in *I Pagliacci* (1899). Two years later he changed to tenor and made his debut in this range (1901) in Naples, this time singing Canio in the same opera. He immediately had great success on Italian stages, appearing at La Scala after 1903. He sang there in several important world *premières*: *Siberia* (1903), *La Figlia di Joro* (1906), and *Gloria* (1907). In 1904 he sang Pinkerton in the unlucky La Scala world *première* of *Madama Butterfly*. In 1905 he sang as guest at Covent Garden and in 1906 he sang for the first time the role of Otello. This remained the starring role in his repertory, and he sang it over five hundred times on the great stages of the world. He was considered the greatest interpreter of this part after Francesco Tamagno. Guest appearances in Paris, London, Berlin, Vienna, Madrid, and Barcelona validated his claim to be one of the greatest tenors of his time. He sang at the Manhattan Opera (1907-09) and at the Boston Opera (1909-14); he was also admired at the Chicago Opera. The first Arena Festival in 1913, at which he sang Radames in *Aida*, was started on his initiative. In 1913 he married the Spanish contralto Maria Gay. A world-wide concert and guest-appearance activity marked the later career of this artist, who finally gave up his stage career (1934). He then joined his wife in opening a singing studio in New York City. A magnificently handled and brilliant heroic tenor voice; one of the finest voices which Italy has produced in this century.

Records: A great many records for G & T (Milan, 1903-04), Fonotipia (Milan, 1905-07), Columbia*, and Edison* discs. Electric records for HMV. *U.S. re-issue:* Columbia-Fonotipia, Okeh, HRS, Victor. *U.S. re-recording:* Eterna, TAP, ASCO, Scala, Olympus, Rococo, Columbia, Belcanto, FRP.

ZEPILLI, ALICE, soprano, b. 1884 (?). She made her debut in Venice (1905) in *Cendrillon*. In 1907 she had her first successes at Parma and at Covent Garden. After guest appearances in Bucharest, Monte Carlo, and Buenos Aires, she became a celebrated member of the Manhattan Opera Company (1907-10), making her debut there as Olympia in *Les Contes d'Hoffmann*. She sang as guest at the Opéra-Comique and continued her voice studies there with Rose Caron (1908-10). She sang at the Chicago Opera (1910-14) and in the latter year she appeared at Covent Garden as Ann Ford in *Falstaff*, Susanna in *Le Nozze di Figaro*, Musetta in *La Bohème*, and Oscar in *Uno Ballo in Maschera*. She was greatly admired at Monte Carlo,

where she was a frequent guest and where, after she had given up her career, she lived as a teacher.
Records: One record for Columbia*.

ZEROLA, NICOLA, tenor, b. 1876, Naples; d. July 21, 1936, New York. He made his debut in 1898 and sang first in the Italian provinces. Guest appearances took him to Egypt, Spain, Holland, Belgium, and especially to South America. In 1908 he toured the United States with a small traveling company and was so successful that he was engaged at the Manhattan Opera in the same year. He sang with the Chicago - Philadelphia company (1915-16) and in 1920 was engaged at the Metropolitan Opera, but he sang there in only two concerts in the 1920-21 season. On the basis of this he brought suit against the directors of the Metropolitan for $250,000, but he lost the suit. In the following years he again sang with traveling companies in America and at the last lived as a singing teacher in New York. A powerful and brilliant heroic tenor voice, especially admired as Otello.
Records: G & T and Victor*. *U.S. re-issue:* HRS. *U.S. re-recording:* TAP.

ŽIDEK, IVO, tenor, b. June 4, 1926, Kravaře, Czechoslovakia. He studied at the schools in Hlučin and in Moravská Ostrava. He then studied singing with Rudolf Vasek in the latter city and in 1943 entered the local theater as an apprentice. His regular debut followed (1944) as the title hero in *Werther*. In 1948 he was engaged at the National Theater in Prague, to which he still belongs. Since 1956 he has appeared regularly as a guest at the Vienna State Opera, where he is greatly admired; he has also traveled through Spain with the Vienna ensemble. In 1960 he sang at the Holland Festival. He has also become a successful concert singer. He has an outstandingly well-trained lyric tenor voice.
Records: Supraphon. *U.S. re-issue:* DGG, Colosseum, Bruno, Crossroads.

ZIEGLER, BENNO, baritone, b. Jan. 8, 1887, Munich; d. Apr. 18, 1963, Munich. His father, Wilhelm Ziegler, was an opera singer. The son studied at the Munich Academy of Music and with Paul Bender there; he made his debut (1909) in Augsburg as Silvio in *I Pagliacci*. He sang at Dortmund (1911-13), at the Stuttgart Royal Opera (1913-16), at Karlsruhe (1917-20), and at the Berlin State Opera (1920-25). He appeared twice as guest in the United States. In 1925 he came to the Opera in Frankfurt, where his wife, the soprano Else Gentner-Fischer, also sang. He sang there until 1934, when he was forced to give up his career because he was Jewish. Thereafter he lived in Prien-am-Chiemsee. In 1939 he was forced to flee to England, where he worked first as a hatmaker and later as a locksmith. In 1947 he returned to Germany and lived in Munich.
Records: His baritone voice, especially admired in the Italian repertory, is to be heard on Odeon records, which include duets with both Richard Tauber and Vera Schwarz. *U.S. re-recording:* TAP.

ZILIANI, ALESSANDRO, tenor, b. June 3, 1906, Busseto, Italy. He studied with Alfredo Cecchi in Milan and made his debut (1929) at the Teatro dal Verme there as Pinkerton in *Madama Butterfly*. He sang at the Italian Opera in Holland (1930). In 1934 he came to La Scala, making his debut there as Enzo in *La Gioconda*. Thereafter he frequently appeared at La Scala and he sang there in the *première* of *Maria Egiziaca*. In 1938 he made successful guest appearances at the

San Francisco Opera. During World War II he sang a great deal on stages in Germany, including the State Operas in Vienna, Berlin, and Munich. After the war he appeared particularly in his Italian homeland, at the last chiefly as a concert singer. For a time he was married to the soprano Mafalda Favero.

Records: HMV (*La Traviata*). *U.S. re-issue:* RCA Victor. *U.S. re-recording:* Rococo.

ZIMMERMANN, ERICH, tenor, b. Nov. 29, 1892, Meissen, Germany; d. Feb. 24, 1968, Berlin. He was first a porcelain painter at the Meissen Porcelain Factory, but he then studied singing in Dresden and made his debut at the State Opera there (1918). After completing engagements in Dortmund, Braunschweig, and Leipzig, he sang at the Munich State Opera (1925-31), the Vienna State Opera (1931-34), and the Hamburg State Opera (1934-35). He accepted an engagement at the Berlin State Opera in 1935 and was highly successful there until 1944. He was also successful at the Bayreuth Festivals, particularly as Mime in the *Ring* cycle. He made guest appearances at the Paris Opéra, Covent Garden, in Brussels and Amsterdam, and at the Salzburg Festivals. As a *buffo* tenor he was considered a worthy successor to the great Julius Lieban. With guest appearances and concerts his career lasted until after World War II.

Records: Telefunken (Bayreuth, 1936), Vox, and HMV. *U.S. re-recording:* Telefunken, Electrola.

ZINETTI, GIUSEPPINA, contralto, b. 1890 (?), Milan. After studying in Milan, she made her debut (1913) at the Teatro Colón as Ursula in *Feuersnot*. She sang her first big role—that of Azucena in *Il Trovatore*—at the Teatro dal Verme (1917). Thereafter she had a highly successful career on the leading operatic stages in Italy. In 1923 she sang at the Italian Opera in Holland. In 1924 she first sang at La Scala, making her debut there as Carmen and she also had great success there in 1926 and in 1935. She sang as guest in Cairo, Madrid, Barcelona, and Rio de Janeiro and undertook a tour of Australia. At the Salzburg Festival (1931) she sang Fidalma in *Il Matrimonio Segreto*. Her daughter, Lina Zinetti, had a successful career as a contralto on the leading Italian stages.

Records: Acoustics and electrics for Columbia* (including Azucena in *Il Trovatore*, 1930).

ŽITEK, VILEM, bass, b. Sept. 9, 1890, Prague; d. Aug. 11, 1956, Prague. At first an optical mechanic, he then studied singing at the Conservatory in Prague. In 1917 he made his debut at the Czech National Theater there and remained at that house until the end of his career. He sang in a total of about three thousand performances there. Guest appearances brought him great success: Turin (1926), La Scala (1927), Paris (1928), Berlin (1929), Moscow and Leningrad (1933). In 1946 he was given the title of National Artist. He was considered the greatest Czech singer of his time. A magnificent bass voice, outstanding in the Czech but also in the Italian and Russian repertories.

Records: A few Parlophone records.